Rick Steves'®

VIENNA
SALZBURG
& TIROL

CONTENTS

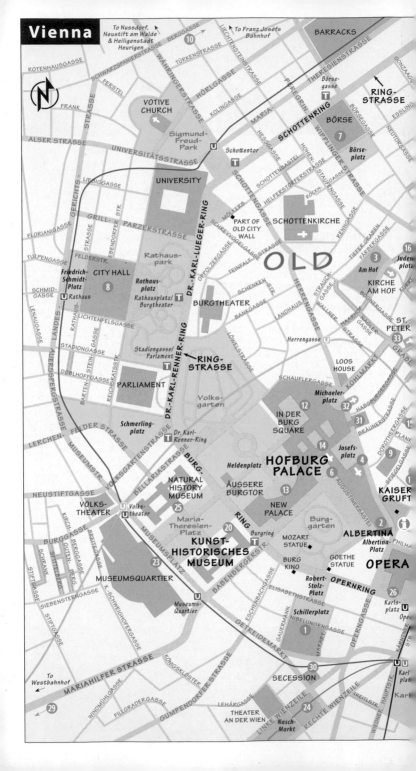

SIGHTS

1. Academy of Fine Arts
2. Albertina Museum
3. Am Hof Square
4. Augustinian Church & National Library
5. To Belvedere Palace & Mus. of Military History
6. Butterfly House
7. Börse (Stock Exchange)
8. City Hall
9. Dorotheum Auction House
10. To Freud Museum
11. Haus der Musik
12. Hofburg Imperial Apartments
13. Hofburg New Palace Museums
14. Hofburg Treasury & Boys' Choir Chapel
15. Jewish Museum Dorotheergasse
16. Judenplatz Memorial & Jewish Museum
17. Kaisergruft (Crypt)
18. To Karlskirche
19. To Kunst Haus Wien & Hundertwasser Haus
20. Kunsthistorisches Museum
21. Mozarthaus Vienna
22. Museum of Applied Art (MAK)
23. MuseumsQuartier
24. Naschmarkt
25. Natural History Museum
26. Opera
27. Plague Column
28. To Prater Park
29. To Schönbrunn Palace & Imperial Furniture Collection
30. Secession Building
31. Spanish Riding School
32. St. Michael's Church Crypt
33. St. Peter's Church
34. St. Stephen's Cathedral
35. Wien Museum Karlsplatz
36. Wien Ticket Pavilion

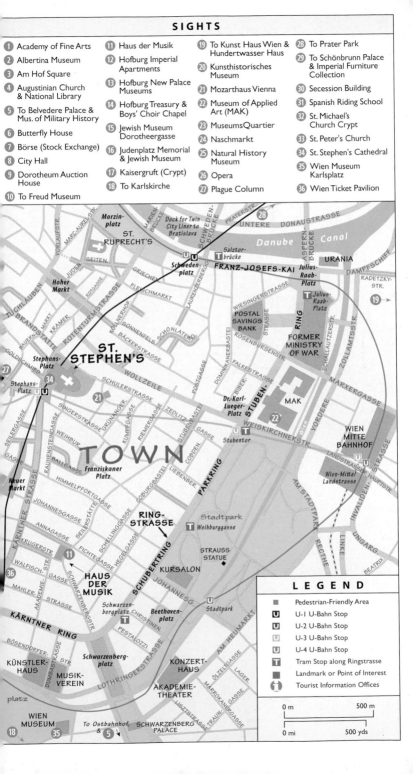

LEGEND

- Pedestrian-Friendly Area
- U-1 U-Bahn Stop
- U-2 U-Bahn Stop
- U-3 U-Bahn Stop
- U-4 U-Bahn Stop
- Tram Stop along Ringstrasse
- Landmark or Point of Interest
- Tourist Information Offices

0 m   500 m
0 mi   500 yds

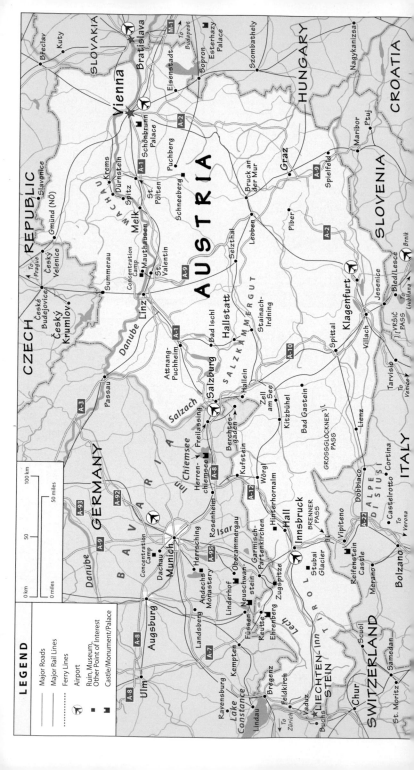

Schönbrunn Palace and Gardens in Vienna

Salzburg at sunset

Vienna's St. Stephen's Cathedral

Welcome to Austria!

Hallstatt in the Salzkammergut

Rick Steves'
VIENNA
SALZBURG
& TIROL

INTRODUCTION

Austria offers alpine scenery, world-class museums, cobbled quaintness, and Wiener schnitzel. Unlike Germany, its industrious neighbor to the northwest, Austria is content to bask in its good living and opulent past as the former head of one of Europe's grandest empires. Austrians are relaxed, gregarious people who love the outdoors as much as a good cup of coffee in a café.

This book focuses on Vienna and all of its cultural offerings, as well as the Danube Valley, Salzburg, Hallstatt (the gem of the Salzkammergut Lake District), and the mountainous Tirol region. Because some sights just across the border are so scenic and interesting, this book also ducks into Germany (Berchtesgaden and Bavarian sights) and Slovakia (Bratislava).

I'll give you all the information and opinions necessary to wring the maximum value out of your limited time and money. If you plan three weeks or less in Austria and have a normal appetite for information, this book is all you need. If you're a travel-info fiend, this book sorts through all the superlatives and provides a handy rack upon which to hang your supplemental information.

Experiencing Europe's culture, people, and natural wonders economically and hassle-free has been my goal for three decades of traveling, tour guiding, and travel writing. With this new edition, I pass on to you the lessons I've learned.

The destinations covered in this book are balanced to include a comfortable mix of cities and villages, mountaintop hikes and medieval castles, sleepy river cruises and sky-high gondola rides. While you'll find the predictable biggies (such as Mozart's house and the Vienna Opera), I've also mixed in a healthy dose of Back Door intimacy (thrilling mountain luges, a beer with monks, and a lakeside town reachable by boat). I've been selective, including only the most exciting sights. For example, there are dozens of quaint

INTRODUCTION

Map Legend

𝙡 Viewpoint	✈ Airport	)▨▨(Tunnel
↑ Entrance	Ⓣ Taxi Stand	Pedestrian Zone
✛ Tourist Info	Ⓣ Tram Stop	Railway
ⓌⒸ Restroom	Ⓑ Bus Stop	Ferry/Boat Route
▪ Castle	Ⓜ Metro Stop	⊢—⊢—⊣ Tram
⌂ Church	Ⓟ Parking	Stairs
▪ Statue/Point of Interest	)(Mtn. Pass	Walk/Tour Route
⊠ Elevator	Park	Trail

Use this legend to help you navigate the maps in this book.

villages in Austria's Salzkammergut Lake District. I take you to only the most charming: Hallstatt.

The best is, of course, only my opinion. But after spending a third of my adult life exploring and researching Europe, I've developed a sixth sense for what travelers enjoy. The places featured in this book will make anyone want to slap-dance and yodel.

About This Book

Rick Steves' Vienna, Salzburg & Tirol is a personal tour guide in your pocket. Each recommended destination is a mini-vacation on its own, filled with exciting sights, strollable neighborhoods, affordable places to stay, and memorable places to eat.

The first half of this book focuses on Vienna and contains the following chapters:

Austria offers an introduction to this delightful country.

Orientation to Vienna includes specifics on public transportation, helpful hints, local tour options, tourist information, and an easy-to-read map. The "Planning Your Time" section suggests a schedule for how best to use your limited time.

Sights in Vienna describes the top attractions and includes their cost and hours.

The **Self-Guided Walks** and **Tours** take you through interesting neighborhoods and must-see sights. In Vienna, these include a city walk, St. Stephen's Cathedral, the Hofburg Imperial Apartments and Treasury, and the Kunsthistorisches Museum. A breezy tram tour takes you around Vienna's Ringstrasse.

Sleeping in Vienna describes my favorite hotels, from good-value deals to cushy splurges.

Eating in Vienna serves up a range of options, from inexpensive cafés to fancy restaurants, clustered by neighborhood.

Key to This Book

Updates

This book is updated regularly, but things change. For the latest, visit www.ricksteves.com/update. For a valuable list of reports and experiences—good and bad—from fellow travelers, check www.ricksteves.com/feedback.

Abbreviations and Times

I use the following symbols and abbreviations in this book: Sights are rated:

▲▲▲	**Don't miss**
▲▲	**Try hard to see**
▲	**Worthwhile if you can make it**
No rating	**Worth knowing about**

Tourist information offices are abbreviated as TIs, and bathrooms are WCs. To categorize accommodations, I use a **Sleep Code** (described on page 19).

Like Austria, this book uses the **24-hour clock** for schedules. It's the same through 12:00 noon, then keep going: 13:00, 14:00, and so on. For anything over 12, subtract 12 and add p.m. (14:00 is 2:00 p.m.).

When giving **opening times,** I include both peak season and off-season hours if they differ. So, if a museum is listed as "May-Oct daily 9:00-16:00," it should be open from 9 a.m. until 4 p.m. from the first day of May until the last day of October (but expect exceptions).

If you see a ☉ symbol near a sight listing, it means that sight is described in far greater detail elsewhere—either with its own self-guided tour, or as part of a self-guided walk.

For **transit** or **tour departures,** I first list the frequency, then the duration. So, a train connection listed as "2/hour, 1.5 hours" departs twice each hour, and the journey lasts an hour and a half.

Entertainment in Vienna is your guide to evening fun, including classical concerts, opera, and things to do after dark.

Vienna Connections has information on Vienna's airport and how to get to nearby destinations by train, car, and boat.

The **Danube Valley,** just west of Vienna, covers tiny **Melk,** with its hulking riverside monastery, and the concentration-camp memorial in **Mauthausen.** Just east of Vienna is **Bratislava,** the Slovakian capital.

The **Salzburg** section covers this touristy but charming town, as well as nearby **Berchtesgaden** (home to Hitler's Eagle's Nest) and beautiful lakeside **Hallstatt.**

The **Tirol** section describes my favorite stops in this mountainous region: **Innsbruck** and its little sister just downriver, **Hall.**

INTRODUCTION

The section also covers the top sights in **Western Tirol** and southern **Bavaria,** including the famous castles of "Mad" King Ludwig.

The **Vienna: Past and Present** chapter introduces you to some of the key people and events in this city's complicated past, making your sightseeing more meaningful.

The **appendix** is a traveler's tool kit, with telephone tips, useful phone numbers, recommended books and films, information on driving and public transportation, a festival list, a climate chart, a handy packing checklist, a hotel reservation form, and German survival phrases.

Browse through this book, choose your favorite destinations, and link them up. Then have a *wunderbar* trip! Traveling like a temporary local, you'll get the absolute most out of every mile, minute, and dollar. As you visit places I know and love, I'm happy that you'll be meeting some of my favorite Austrians.

Planning

This section will help you get started on planning your trip—with advice on trip costs, when to go, and what you should know before you take off.

Travel Smart

Your trip to Austria is like a complex play—easier to follow and to really appreciate on a second viewing. While no one does the same trip twice to gain that advantage, reading this book before your trip accomplishes much the same thing.

Design an itinerary that enables you to visit the various sights at the best possible times. Note festivals, holidays, specifics on sights, and days when sights are closed. To get between destinations smoothly, read the tips in this book's appendix on taking trains and buses, and renting a car and driving. A smart trip is a puzzle—a fun, doable, and worthwhile challenge.

Be sure to mix intense and relaxed periods in your itinerary. To maximize rootedness, minimize one-night stands. It's worth taking a long drive after dinner (or a train ride with a dinner picnic) to get settled in a town for two nights. Hotels are also more likely to give a better price to someone staying more than one night. Every trip—and every traveler—needs slack time (laundry, picnics, people-watching, and so on). Pace yourself. Assume you will return.

Reread this book as you travel, and visit local TIs. Upon arrival in a new town, lay the groundwork for a smooth departure; write down the schedule for the train, bus, or boat you'll take when you depart. Drivers can study the best route to their next destination.

Get online at Internet cafés or your hotel, and carry a mobile phone (or use a phone card) to make travel plans: You can get tourist information, research transportation connections, learn the latest on sights (special events, English tour schedules, etc.), book tickets and tours, make reservations, reconfirm hotels, research transportation connections, and keep in touch with loved ones.

Enjoy the friendliness of the Austrian people. Connect with the culture. Set up your own quest for the best Baroque building, Sacher-Torte, wine garden, or whatever. Slow down and be open to unexpected experiences. Ask questions—most locals are eager to point you in their idea of the right direction. Keep a notepad in your pocket for confirming prices, noting directions, and organizing your thoughts. Wear your money belt, learn the currency, and figure out how to estimate prices in dollars. Those who expect to travel smart, do.

Trip Costs

Five components make up your trip costs: airfare, surface transportation, room and board, sightseeing and entertainment, and shopping and miscellany.

Airfare: A basic round-trip US-to-Vienna flight can cost, on average, about $1,000-1,800 total, depending on where you fly from and when (cheaper in winter). Consider saving time and money by flying into one city and out of another (for example, into Vienna and out of Munich).

Surface Transportation: For a two-week whirlwind trip of this book's destinations, allow $300 per person for public transportation (trains and buses) or $500 per person (based on two people sharing) for car rental, parking, tolls, gas, and insurance. Leasing is worth considering for trips of three weeks or more. Car rental and leases are cheapest if arranged from the US. Train passes are normally sold only outside of Europe, but aren't necessarily your best option—you may save money by simply buying tickets as you go. For more on public transportation and car rental, see "Transportation" in the appendix.

Room and Board: You can manage comfortably in Austria on an average of $110 a day per person for room and board (less in small towns, more in big cities such as Vienna and Salzburg). A $110-a-day budget allows $10 for lunch, $25 for dinner, $5 for beer and *Eis* (ice cream), and $70 for lodging (based on two people splitting the cost of a $140 double room that includes breakfast). That's doable. Students and tightwads can enjoy Austria for as little as $50 a day ($30 per hostel bed, $20 for meals and snacks).

Sightseeing and Entertainment: In big cities, figure about $15 per major sight (Vienna's Kunsthistorisches Museum-$16, Mozart's Residence in Salzburg-$13), $6 for minor ones, and $25-50 for bus tours and splurge experiences (such as concert tickets

INTRODUCTION

Vienna, Salzburg & Tirol: Best Two-Week Trip by Train

Day	Plan	Sleep in
1	Fly into Vienna	Vienna
2	Vienna	Vienna
3	Vienna	Vienna
4	Vienna	Vienna (or head to Melk in evening if biking or cruising Danube on Day 5)
5	Danube Valley (Melk to Krems and back)	Melk
6	To Salzburg via Mauthausen	Salzburg
7	Salzburg	Salzburg
8	Salzburg	Salzburg
9	To Hallstatt	Hallstatt
10	Hallstatt and surroundings	Hallstatt
11	To Innsbruck	Hall or Innsbruck
12	Innsbruck; to Bavaria	Füssen or Reutte
13	Bavaria and castles	Füssen or Reutte
14	Fly out of Innsbruck or Munich (or train back to Vienna)	

With more time: Depending on your interests, you could easily spend several more days in Vienna (for museums, the music scene, going to cafés and wine gardens, day-tripping to Bratislava) and a couple more days in Salzburg (for the music scene, nearby sights, day-tripping to Berchtesgaden). The coun-

and alpine lifts). An overall average of $30 a day works for most people. Don't skimp here. After all, this category is the driving force behind your trip—you came to sightsee, enjoy, and experience Austria.

Shopping and Miscellany: Figure $5 per stamped postcard, coffee, beer, and ice-cream cone. Shopping can vary in cost from nearly nothing to a small fortune. Good budget travelers find that this category has little to do with assembling a trip full of lifelong and wonderful memories.

Sightseeing Priorities

Depending on the length of your trip, and taking geographic proximity into account, these are my recommended priorities:

3 days:	Vienna
5 days, add:	Salzburg
7 days, add:	Hallstatt

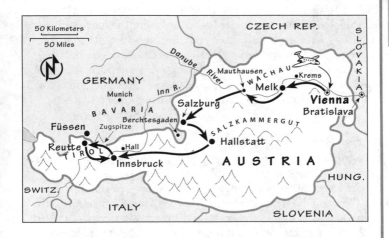

tryside of southern Bavaria and western Tirol are great places to linger and explore (consider a day or two of car rental).

With a car: Pick up your car when you leave Vienna. After Melk (in the Danube Valley), drive to Hallstatt, with a stop at Mauthausen en route. After Hallstatt, head to Salzburg. From Salzburg, you can drive (via Berchtesgaden, if you're interested) through southern Bavaria en route to Füssen or Reutte. Then drive eastward through Tirol's Inn Valley to Innsbruck to drop off your car.

10 days, add: Danube Valley, Tirol, and Bavaria
14 days, add: Innsbruck, Hall, and day trip to Bratislava
16 days, add: More time in Vienna

For a suggested itinerary, see sidebar above.

When to Go

The "tourist season" runs roughly from May through September. Summer has its advantages: best weather, snow-free alpine trails, very long days (light until after 21:00), and the busiest schedule of tourist fun.

Travel during "shoulder season" (late April-June and Sept-early Oct) is easier and a bit less expensive. Shoulder-season travelers get minimal crowds, decent weather, the full range of sights and tourist fun spots, and the ability to grab a room almost whenever and wherever they like—often at a flexible price. Also, in fall, fun harvest and wine festivals enliven many towns and villages, while forests and vineyards display beautiful colors.

Winter travelers find concert seasons in full swing, with absolutely no tourist crowds, but some accommodations and sights are either closed or run on a limited schedule. Confirm your sightseeing plans locally, especially when traveling off-season. The weather can be cold and dreary, and nightfall draws the shades on sightseeing well before dinnertime. But dustings of snow turn Austrian towns and landscapes into a wonderland, and December offers the chance to wander through traditional Christmas markets.

You may find the climate chart in the appendix helpful.

Know Before You Go

Your trip is more likely to go smoothly if you plan ahead. Check this list of things to arrange while you're still at home.

You need a **passport**—but no visa or shots—to travel in Austria. You may be denied entry into certain European countries if your passport is due to expire within three to six months of your ticketed date of return. Get it renewed if you'll be cutting it close. It can take up to six weeks to get or renew a passport (for more on passports, see www.travel.state.gov). Pack a photocopy of your passport in your luggage in case the original is lost or stolen.

Book rooms in advance if you'll be traveling during major holidays, festivals, or peak season (May-Sept).

Call your **debit- and credit-card companies** to let them know the countries you'll be visiting, to ask about fees, request your PIN (it will be mailed to you), and more. See page 13 for details.

Do your homework if you want to buy **travel insurance.** Compare the cost of the insurance to the likelihood of your using it and your potential loss if something goes wrong. Also, check whether your existing insurance (health, homeowners, or renters) covers you and your possessions overseas. For more tips, see www.ricksteves.com/insurance.

If you're planning on **renting a car** in Austria, bring your US driver's license. An International Driving Permit is required (see page 464).

I don't reserve ahead for events, but if you do, note that in Vienna and Salzburg (especially during its festival), major **musical events** can be sold out for weeks—though there are plenty of live music options available without advance booking. Planning ahead of time will guarantee you a seat to see the **Lipizzaner Stallions** (see page 62), **Vienna Boys' Choir** (page 207), and performances at the **Opera** (page 208); though again, I prefer cheap, on-the-spot experiences (such as same-day standing-room tickets for the Opera).

To get tickets to **Neuschwanstein Castle** (in Bavaria) during

Vienna, Salzburg & Tirol at a Glance

These attractions are listed (as in this book) roughly from east to west.

▲▲▲**Vienna** Austria's regal capital city, rich with swirling architecture and world-class museums; impressive Habsburg sights (Schönbrunn Palace, in-city royal apartments, treasury, crypt, and Lipizzaner stallions); massive St. Stephen's Cathedral; and a grand classical-music tradition, from its renowned Opera house to its famous Boys' Choir.

▲▲**Danube Valley** Romantic, bikeable valley west of Vienna, dotted with ruined castles, adorable villages and vineyards, and highlighted by the glorious Melk Abbey and somber Mauthausen concentration camp.

▲▲**Bratislava**, **Slovakia** Once-depressed communist town, now a thriving capital city, less than an hour from Vienna and bursting with colorfully restored buildings; a quirky traffic-free old town; and a people-friendly Danube riverfront area.

▲▲▲**Salzburg** Austrian musical mecca for fans of Mozart and *The Sound of Music,* offering a dramatic castle, Baroque churches, near-nightly concerts, and an old town full of winding lanes.

Berchtesgaden, **Germany** Alpine town across the border from Salzburg, famous for incredible views, a pristine lake—and as the site of Hitler's mountaintop retreat.

▲▲**Hallstatt and the Salzkammergut** Scenic lake district, home to the halcyon village of Hallstatt, with its medieval town center, fun salt mine, plentiful hiking opportunities, and placid swan-filled lake.

▲**Tirol** Austria's panhandle region and mountain-sports capital, centering around the distinctive city of Innsbruck and little neighboring Hall, with its quaint and colorful old town.

▲▲▲**Bavaria and Western Tirol** Pair of Alps-straddling regions boasting the fairy-tale castles of Neuschwanstein, Hohenschwangau, and Linderhof; inviting villages such as the Austrian retreat of Reutte and German towns of Füssen and Oberammergau; the towering Zugspitze and its high-altitude lifts; and hiking, luge, and other mountain activities.

peak season, you can email, go online, or phone ahead to avoid the long lines (see page 399 for tips).

If you plan to hire a **local guide,** reserve ahead by email. Popular guides can get booked up.

If you're bringing a **mobile device,** download any apps you might want to use on the road, such as translators, maps, and transit schedules. Check out **Rick Steves Audio Europe,** featuring audio tours of major sights, hours of travel interviews on Austria, and more (via www.ricksteves.com/audioeurope, iTunes, Google Play, or the Rick Steves Audio Europe smartphone app; for details, see page 471).

Because airline **carry-on restrictions** are always changing, visit the Transportation Security Administration's website (www.tsa.gov/travelers) for an up-to-date list of what you can bring on the plane with you...and what you have to check.

Practicalities

Emergency and Medical Help: Dial 112 for police or medical emergencies in Austria (and in Germany as well). If you get sick, do as the locals do and go to a pharmacy for advice (*Apotheke;* look for the stylized red *A*). If the pharmacy is closed, a sign near the door indicates the closest pharmacy that's open. Or ask at your hotel for help—they'll know the nearest medical and emergency services.

Theft or Loss: To replace a passport, you'll need to go in person to an embassy (see page 458). If your credit and debit cards disappear, cancel and replace them (see "Damage Control for Lost Cards" on page 14). File a police report either on the spot or within a day or two; it's required if you submit an insurance claim for lost or stolen railpasses or travel gear, and can help with replacing your passport or credit and debit cards. For more information, see www.ricksteves.com/help. Precautionary measures can minimize the effects of loss—back up your photos and other files frequently.

Time Zones: Austria, like most of continental Europe, is generally six/nine hours ahead of the East/West Coasts of the US. The exceptions are the beginning and end of Daylight Saving Time: Europe "springs forward" the last Sunday in March (two weeks after most of North America), and "falls back" the last Sunday in October (one week before North America). For a handy online time converter, try www.timeanddate.com/worldclock.

Business Hours: Most shops throughout Austria are open from about 9:00 until 18:00-20:00 on weekdays, but close earlier on Saturday (as early as 12:00 in towns and as late as 17:00 in cities), and are almost always closed on Sunday. Grocery stores in train stations are generally open daily until late. Banks in Vienna are open weekdays roughly from 8:00 until 15:00 (until 17:30 on Thu), but elsewhere in Austria, banks often close for lunch (open Mon-Fri 8:00-12:00 and 14:00-16:00). Many museums and sights are closed on Monday, and most regions, including Bavaria, shut down during religious holidays.

Sundays have the same pros and cons as they do for travelers in the US (special events pop up, sights may have limited hours, shops and banks are closed, public transportation options are fewer, and there's no rush hour). Popular destinations are even more crowded on weekends.

Watt's Up? Europe's electrical system is 220 volts, instead of North America's 110 volts. Most newer electronics (such as laptops, battery chargers, and hair dryers) convert automatically, so you won't need a converter, but you will need an adapter plug with two round prongs, sold inexpensively at travel stores in the US. Avoid bringing older appliances that don't automatically convert voltage; instead, buy a cheap replacement in Europe.

Discounts: Discounts aren't listed in this book. However, many sights offer discounts for seniors, groups of 10 or more, families, and students or teachers with proper identification cards (www.isic.org). Always ask. Some discounts are available only for EU citizens.

Money

This section offers advice on how to pay for purchases on your trip (including getting cash from ATMs and paying with plastic), dealing with lost or stolen cards, VAT (sales tax) refunds, and tipping.

What to Bring

Bring both a credit card and a debit card. You'll use the debit card at cash machines (ATMs) to withdraw euros for most purchases, and the credit card to pay for larger items. Some travelers carry a third card, in case one gets demagnetized or eaten by a temperamental machine.

For an emergency reserve, bring several hundred dollars in hard cash in easy-to-exchange $20 bills. Avoid using currency exchange booths (because of their lousy rates and/or outrageous fees).

Cash

Cash is just as desirable in Austria as it is at home. Small businesses (hotels, restaurants, and shops) prefer that you pay your bills with cash. Some vendors will charge you extra for using a credit card, and some won't take credit cards at all. Cash is the best—and sometimes only—way to pay for bus fare, taxis, and local guides.

Throughout Europe, ATMs are the standard way for travelers

INTRODUCTION

Exchange Rate

1 euro (€) = about $1.30

To convert prices in euros to dollars, add about 30 percent: €20 = about $26, €50 = about $65. (Check www.oanda.com for the latest exchange rates.) Just like the dollar, one euro (€) is broken down into 100 cents. Coins range from €0.01 to €2, and bills from €5 to €500.

So that €12 visit to the café is about $16, the €25 concert is about $33, and the €90 taxi ride through Vienna is...uh-oh.

to get cash. Stay away from "independent" ATMs such as Travelex, Euronet, and Forex, which charge huge commissions and have terrible exchange rates.

To withdraw money from an ATM (known as a *Bankomat* in Austria and a *Geldautomat* in Germany), you'll need a debit card (ideally with a Visa or MasterCard logo for maximum usability), plus a PIN code. Know your PIN code in numbers; there are only numbers—no letters—on European keypads. For security, it's best to shield the keypad when entering your PIN at an ATM. Although you can use a credit card for ATM transactions, it's generally more expensive (and only makes sense in an emergency), because it's considered a cash advance rather than a withdrawal. Try to withdraw large sums of money to reduce the number of per-transaction bank fees you'll pay.

Pickpockets target tourists. To safeguard your cash, wear a money belt—a pouch with a strap that you buckle around your waist like a belt and tuck under your clothes. Keep your cash, credit cards, and passport secure in your money belt, and carry only a day's spending money in your front pocket.

Credit and Debit Cards

For purchases, Visa and MasterCard are more commonly accepted than American Express. I typically use my debit card to withdraw cash to pay for most purchases. I use my credit card only in a few specific situations: to book hotel reservations by phone, to cover major expenses (such as car rentals, plane tickets, and hotel stays), and to pay for things near the end of my trip (to avoid another visit to the ATM). While you could use a debit card to make most large purchases, using a credit card offers a greater degree of fraud protection (because debit cards draw funds directly from your account).

Ask Your Credit- or Debit-Card Company: Before your trip, contact the company that issued your debit or credit cards.

• Confirm that your **card will work overseas,** and alert them that you'll be using it in Europe; otherwise, they may deny transactions if they perceive unusual spending patterns.

• Ask for the specifics on transaction **fees.** When you use your credit or debit card—either for purchases or ATM withdrawals—you'll often be charged additional "international transaction" fees of up to 3 percent (1 percent is normal) plus $5 per transaction. If your card's fees seem high, consider getting a different card just for your trip: Capital One (www.capitalone.com) and most credit unions have low-to-no international fees.

• If you plan to withdraw cash from ATMs, confirm your daily **withdrawal limit,** and if necessary, ask your bank to adjust it. Some travelers prefer a high limit that allows them to take out more cash at each ATM stop (saving on bank fees), while others prefer to set a lower limit in case their card is stolen. Note that foreign banks also set maximum withdrawal amounts for their ATMs.

• Get your bank's emergency **phone number** in the US (but not its 800 number, which isn't accessible from overseas) to call collect if you have a problem.

• Ask for your credit card's **PIN** in case you need to make an emergency cash withdrawal or encounter Europe's "chip-and-PIN" system; the bank won't tell you your PIN over the phone, so allow time for it to be mailed to you.

Chip and PIN: If your card is declined for a purchase in Europe, it may be because Europeans are increasingly using chip-and-PIN cards, which are embedded with an electronic chip (rather than the magnetic stripe used on our American-style cards). Much of Europe is adopting this system, and some merchants rely on it exclusively. You're most likely to encounter chip-and-PIN problems at automated payment machines, such as those at train and subway stations, toll roads, parking garages, luggage lockers, and self-serve gas pumps. If a machine won't take your card, find a cashier who can make your card work (they can print a receipt for you to sign), or find a machine that takes cash.

But don't panic. Most travelers who are carrying only magnetic-stripe cards never encounter any problems. Still, it pays to carry plenty of euros (you can always use an ATM with your magnetic-stripe debit card). Memorizing the PIN lets you use it at some chip-and-PIN machines—just enter your PIN when prompted.

If you're still concerned, you can apply for a chip card in the US (though I think it's overkill). While big US banks offer these cards with high annual fees, a better option is the no-annual-fee GlobeTrek Visa, offered by Andrews Federal Credit Union in Maryland (open to all US residents; see www.andrewsfcu.org).

Dynamic Currency Conversion: If merchants offer to convert your purchase price into dollars (called dynamic currency conversion, or DCC), refuse this "service." You'll pay even more in fees for the expensive convenience of seeing your charge in dollars.

Damage Control for Lost Cards

If you lose your credit, debit, or ATM card, you can stop people from using it by reporting the loss immediately to the respective global customer-assistance centers. Call these 24-hour US numbers collect: Visa (tel. 303/967-1096), MasterCard (tel. 636/722-7111), and American Express (tel. 336/393-1111). In Austria, to make a collect call to the US, dial 0800-200-288; then press zero or stay on the line to talk to an English-speaking operator. In Germany, dial 0800-225-5288. European toll-free numbers (listed by country) can be found at the websites for Visa and MasterCard.

At a minimum, you'll need to know the name of the financial institution that issued you the card, along with the type of card (classic, platinum, or whatever). Providing the following information will allow for a quicker cancellation of your missing card: full card number, whether you are the primary or secondary cardholder, the name exactly as printed on the card, billing address, home phone number, circumstances of the loss or theft, and identification verification (your birth date, your mother's maiden name, or your Social Security number—memorize this, don't carry a copy). If you are the secondary cardholder, you'll also need to provide the primary cardholder's identification-verification details. You can generally receive a temporary card within two or three business days.

If you report your loss within two days, you typically won't be responsible for any unauthorized transactions on your account, although many banks charge a liability fee of $50.

Tipping

Tipping in Austria isn't as automatic and generous as it is in the US, but for special service, tips are appreciated, if not expected. As in the US, the proper amount depends on your resources, tipping philosophy, and the circumstances, but some general guidelines apply.

Restaurants: Tipping is an issue only at restaurants that have table service. If you order your food at a counter, don't tip.

At Austrian restaurants that have a waitstaff, a service charge is generally included in the bill, although it's common to round up after a good meal (usually 5-10 percent; so, for an €18.50 meal, pay €20). Give the tip directly to your server. Rather than leaving coins, Austrians usually pay with paper, saying how much they'd like the bill to be (for example, for an €8.10 meal, give a €20 bill and say *"Neun Euro"*—"Nine euros"—to get €11 change).

Taxis: To tip the cabbie, round up. For a typical ride, round up about 5-10 percent (to pay a €4.50 fare, give €5; for a €28 fare, give €30). If the cabbie hauls your bags and zips you to the airport to help you catch your flight, you might want to toss in a little more. But if you feel like you're being driven in circles or otherwise ripped off, skip the tip.

Services: In general, if someone in the service industry does a super job for you, a small tip of a euro or two is appropriate...but not required. If you're not sure whether (or how much) to tip for a service, ask your hotelier or the TI.

Getting a VAT Refund

Wrapped into the purchase price of your Austrian souvenirs is a Value-Added Tax (VAT) of 20 percent. You're entitled to get most of that tax back if you purchase more than €75.01 (about $100) at a store that participates in the VAT-refund scheme. Typically, you must ring up the minimum at a single retailer—you can't add up your purchases from various shops to reach the required amount.

Getting your refund is usually straightforward and, if you buy a substantial amount of souvenirs, well worth the hassle. If you're lucky, the merchant will subtract the tax when you make your purchase. (This is more likely to occur if the store ships the goods to your home.) Otherwise, you'll need to:

Get the paperwork. Have the merchant completely fill out the necessary refund document. You'll have to present your passport. Get the paperwork done before you leave the store to ensure you'll have everything you need (including your original sales receipt).

Get your stamp at the border or airport. Process your VAT document at your last stop in the EU (such as at the airport) with the customs agent who deals with VAT refunds. Before checking in for your flight, find the local customs office, and be prepared to stand in line. Keep your purchases readily available for viewing by the customs agent (ideally in your carry-on bag—don't make the mistake of checking the bag with your purchases before you've seen the agent). You're not supposed to use your purchased goods before you leave. If you show up at customs wearing your new lederhosen, officials might look the other way—or deny you a refund.

Collect your refund. You'll need to return your stamped document to the retailer or its representative. Many merchants work with a service, such as Global Blue or Premier Tax Free, that has offices at major airports, ports, or border crossings (either before or after security, probably strategically located near a duty-free shop). These services, which extract a 4 percent fee, can refund your money immediately in your currency of choice or credit your card (within two billing cycles). If the retailer handles VAT refunds directly, it's up to you to contact the merchant for your refund. You can also mail the documents from your point of departure (using an envelope you've prepared in advance or one that's been provided by the merchant). You'll have to wait—it can take months.

Customs for American Shoppers

You are allowed to take home $800 worth of items per person duty-free, once every 30 days. You can also bring in duty-free a liter of alcohol. As for food, you can take home many processed and packaged foods: vacuum-packed cheeses, dried herbs, jams, baked goods, candy, chocolate, oil, vinegar, mustard, and honey. Fresh fruits and vegetables and most meats are not allowed. Any liquid-containing foods must be packed in checked luggage, a potential recipe for disaster. To check customs rules and duty rates, visit www.cbp.gov.

Sightseeing

Sightseeing can be hard work. Use these tips to make your visits to Austria's finest sights meaningful, fun, efficient, and painless.

Plan Ahead

Set up an itinerary that allows you to fit in all your must-see sights. For a one-stop look at opening hours in Vienna and Salzburg, see the "At a Glance" sidebars on page 58 and page 278. Most sights keep stable hours, but you can easily confirm the latest by checking with the local TI or visiting museum websites.

Don't put off visiting a must-see sight—you never know when a place will close unexpectedly for a holiday, strike, or restoration. On holidays (see list on page 475), expect shorter hours or closures.

When possible, visit major sights first thing (when your energy is best) and save other activities for the afternoon. Hit the highlights first, then go back to other things if you have the stamina and time.

Going at the right time can also help you avoid crowds. This book offers tips on the best times to see specific sights, such as Schönbrunn Palace in Vienna and Neuschwanstein Castle in Bavaria. Try visiting very early, at lunch, or very late. Evening visits are usually peaceful, with fewer crowds.

Study up. To get the most out of the self-guided tours and sight descriptions in this book, reread them the night before your visit. Schönbrunn Palace is much more fascinating if you've polished your knowledge of the Habsburg dynasty in advance.

At Sights

Here's what you can typically expect:

Some important sights require you to check daypacks and

coats. To avoid checking a small backpack, carry it under your arm like a purse as you enter. From a guard's point of view, a backpack is generally a problem while a purse is not.

At churches—which often offer interesting art (usually free) and a cool, welcome seat—a modest dress code (no bare shoulders or shorts) is encouraged.

Flash photography is often banned, but taking photos without a flash is usually allowed. Flashes damage oil paintings and distract others in the room. Even without a flash, a handheld camera will take a decent picture (or buy postcards or posters at the museum bookstore).

Museums may have special exhibits in addition to their permanent collection. Some exhibits are included in the entry price; others come at an extra cost (which you may have to pay even if you don't want to see the exhibit).

Expect changes—artwork can be on tour, on loan, out sick, or shifted at the whim of the curator. To adapt, pick up any available free floor plans as you enter. Ask museum staff if you can't find a particular piece.

Many sights rent audioguides, which usually offer excellent recorded descriptions in English (generally included in admission, otherwise about $4). If you bring along your earbuds, you can enjoy better sound and avoid holding the device to your ear. To save money, bring a Y-jack and share one audioguide with your travel partner. I've produced free downloadable audio tours of the major sights in Vienna and Salzburg; see page 471.

Important sights have an on-site café or cafeteria (usually a handy place to rejuvenate during a long visit). The WCs are generally free and clean.

Many places sell postcards that highlight their attractions. Before you leave, scan the postcards and thumb through the biggest guidebook (or skim its index) to be sure you haven't overlooked something that you'd like to see.

Most sights stop admitting people 30-60 minutes before closing time, and some rooms may close early (often 45 minutes before the actual closing time). Guards usher people out, so don't save the best for last.

Every sight or museum offers more than what is covered in this book. Use the information in this book as an introduction—not the final word.

Sleeping

I favor hotels and restaurants that are handy to your sightseeing activities. Rather than list hotels scattered throughout a city, I choose two or three favorite neighborhoods and recommend the best accommodations values in each, from dorm beds to fancy doubles with all of the comforts.

While accommodations in Austria are fairly expensive, they are normally very comfortable and usually come with breakfast. A triple is much cheaper than a double and a single. Single travelers get the best value at B&B-type lodgings, where the single price is often little more than half the double-room price. Hotels, in contrast, charge almost as much for a single room as for a double. Hostels and dorms always charge per person.

A major feature of this book is its extensive listing of good-value rooms. I like places that are clean, central, relatively quiet at night, reasonably priced, friendly, small enough to have a hands-on owner and stable staff, run with a respect for Austrian traditions, and not listed in other guidebooks. (In Austria, for me, six out of these eight criteria means it's a keeper.) I'm more impressed by a convenient location and a fun-loving philosophy than flat-screen TVs and shoeshine machines.

Book your accommodations well in advance if you'll be traveling during busy times. See page 475 for a list of major holidays and festivals in Austria; for tips on making reservations, see page 22.

Rates and Deals

I've described my recommended accommodations using a Sleep Code (see sidebar). Prices listed are for one-night stays in peak season, breakfast is generally included (sometimes continental, but often buffet) and assume you're booking directly (not through a TI or online hotel-booking engine). Using an online booking service costs the hotel about 20 percent and logically closes the door on special deals. Book direct.

These days, many hotels change prices from day to day according to demand. Given the economic downturn, hoteliers are often willing and eager to make a deal. I'd suggest emailing several hotels to ask for their best price. Comparison-shop and make your choice.

As you look over the listings, you'll notice that some accommodations promise special prices to my readers who book direct (without using a room-finding service or hotel-booking website,

Sleep Code

(€1 = about $1.30, country code: 43)

Price Rankings

To help you sort easily through these listings, I've divided the rooms into three categories based on the price for a standard double room with bath:

$$$	**Higher Priced**
$$	**Moderately Priced**
$	**Lower Priced**

I always rate hostels as $, whether or not they have double rooms, because they have the cheapest beds in town.

Prices can change without notice; verify the hotel's current rates online or by email.

Abbreviations

To give maximum information in a minimum of space, I use the following code to describe the accommodations. Prices listed are per room, not per person. When a price range is given for a type of room (such as double rooms listing for €100-150), it means the price fluctuates with the season, size of room, or length of stay; expect to pay the upper end for peak-season stays.

S = Single room (or price for one person in a double).

D = Double or twin. "Double beds" can be two twins sheeted together and are usually big enough for non-romantic couples.

T = Triple (a double bed with a single, or three twin beds).

Q = Quad (usually two double beds; adding an extra child's bed to a T is usually cheaper).

b = Private bathroom with toilet and shower or tub.

s = Private shower or tub only (the toilet is down the hall).

According to this code, a couple staying at a "Db-€90" hotel would pay a total of €90 (about $120) for a double room with a private bathroom. Unless otherwise noted, breakfast is included, hotel staff speak basic English, and credit cards are accepted.

There's almost always Wi-Fi and/or Internet access available, either free or for a fee.

which take a commission). To get these rates, you must mention this book when you reserve, and then show the book upon arrival. Rick Steves discounts apply to readers with ebooks as well as printed books. Discounts may not apply to promotional rates.

In general, prices can soften if you do any of the following: offer to pay cash, stay at least three nights, or mention this book. You can also try asking for a cheaper room or a discount, or offer to skip breakfast.

Types of Accommodations

Hotels

In this book, the price for a double room in a hotel ranges from €45 (very simple, toilet and shower down the hall) to €200-plus (maximum plumbing and the works). In small towns such as Hallstatt or Innsbruck, you can find a good double with a private bath for under €70; in more expensive cities like Vienna or Salzburg, you'll usually pay at least €90.

Room prices depend on the season and the day of the week, but peak times vary from one town to the next. High season in Füssen is June-September. In Vienna, business hotels have their highest rates in September and October, and rates are also high around New Year's Eve. In Salzburg, rates always rise significantly during the music festival, during the four weeks leading up to Christmas, and usually around Easter.

Hotel lobbies, halls, and breakfast rooms are off-limits to smokers, though they can light up in their rooms. Most hotels have non-smoking rooms or floors—let them know your preference when you book. Some hotels have gone completely non-smoking.

Bigger hotels commonly have elevators. When you're inside an elevator, press "E" if you want to descend to the "ground floor" *(Erdgeschoss)*. Hotel elevators can be very small, forcing you to send your bags up separately—pack light.

If you're arriving early in the morning, your room probably won't be ready. You can drop your bag safely at the hotel and dive right into sightseeing.

Hoteliers can be a great help and source of advice. Most know their city well, and can assist you with everything from public transit and airport connections to finding a good restaurant, the nearest launderette, or an Internet café.

Even at the best places, mechanical breakdowns occur: Air-conditioning malfunctions, sinks leak, hot water turns cold, and toilets gurgle and smell. Report your concerns clearly and calmly at the front desk. For more complicated problems, don't expect instant results.

If you suspect night noise will be a problem (if, for instance, your room is over a café), ask for a quieter room in the back or on

INTRODUCTION

an upper floor. To guard against theft in your room, keep valuables out of sight. Some rooms come with a safe, and other hotels have safes at the front desk. I've never bothered using one.

Checkout can pose problems if surprise charges pop up on your bill. If you settle your bill the afternoon before you leave, you'll have time to discuss and address any points of contention (before 19:00, when the night shift usually arrives).

Above all, keep a positive attitude. Remember, you're on vacation. If your hotel is a disappointment, spend more time out enjoying the city you came to see.

B&Bs *(Pensions)* and Private Rooms

Compared to hotels, a *Pension* gives you double the cultural intimacy for half the price (and usually includes a hearty continental breakfast). While you may lose some of the conveniences of a hotel—such as in-room phones, frequent bed-sheet changes, and the ease of paying with a credit card—I happily make the trade-off for the lower rates and personal touches. Similarly priced, a *Gasthof* is a small, family-run hotel.

Private rooms *(Zimmer)* are simply rooms rented out to travelers in private homes. These are inexpensive—as little as €25 per person with a hearty breakfast—and very common in areas popular with travelers (such as the Salzkammergut Lake District and Germany's Bavaria). Look for *Zimmer Frei* or *Privatzimmer* signs (green signs indicate that rooms are available; orange means they're booked/*belegt*). TIs often have a list of private rooms; use the list to book rooms yourself to avoid having the TI take a cut from you and your host. Especially in private homes, where the boss changes the sheets, people staying several nights are most desirable. One-night stays are quite often charged extra.

You'll get your own key to a private room that's clean, comfortable, and simple, though usually homey. Some private rooms are like mini-guesthouses, with a separate entrance and several rooms, each with a private bath. Others are family homes with spare bedrooms (the rooms sometimes lack sinks, but you have free access to the bathroom and shower in the home). Be considerate: Avoid excessively long showers and turn off lights when you leave.

Hostels

For about $30 a night, you can stay at a youth hostel. Follow signs marked *Jugendherberge* (with triangles) or with the logo showing a tree next to a house. Travelers of any age are welcome, if they don't mind dorm-style accommodations and meeting other travelers. Most hostels offer kitchen facilities, Internet access, Wi-Fi, and a self-service laundry. Nowadays, concerned about bedbugs, hostels are likely to provide all bedding, including sheets. Family

INTRODUCTION

Making Hotel Reservations

Given the good value of the accommodations I've found for this book, reserve your rooms several weeks in advance—or as soon as you've pinned down your travel dates—particularly if you'll be traveling during peak times. Note that some national holidays jam things up and merit your making reservations far in advance (see "Holidays and Festivals" on page 475).

Requesting a Reservation: It's usually easiest to book your room through the hotel's website; many have a reservation-request form built right in. (For the best rates, be sure to use the hotel's official site and not a booking agency's site.) Just type in your preferred dates and the website will automatically display a list of available rooms and prices. Simpler websites will generate an email to the hotelier with your request. If there's no reservation form, or for complicated requests, send an email from your personal address. Other options include calling (see "Phoning" later, and be mindful of time zones) or faxing. Most recommended hotels are accustomed to guests who speak only English.

The hotelier wants to know these key pieces of information (also included in the sample request form in the appendix):

- number and type of rooms
- number of nights
- date of arrival
- date of departure
- any special needs (such as bathroom in the room or down the hall, twin beds vs. double bed, air-conditioning, quiet, view, ground floor, etc.)

When you request a room, use the European style for writing dates: day/month/year. For example, for a two-night stay in July of 2013, I would request "1 double room for 2 nights, arrive 16/07/2013, depart 18/07/13." Consider carefully how long you'll stay; don't just assume you can tack on extra days once you arrive. Make sure you mention any discounts—for Rick Steves readers or otherwise—when you make the reservation.

If you don't get a response to your email, it usually means the hotel is already fully booked—but try sending the message again or call to follow up.

Confirming a Reservation: Most places will request your credit-card number to hold the room. To confirm a room using a hotel's secure online reservation form, enter your contact information and credit-card number; the hotel will email a confirmation.

If you sent an email to request a reservation, the hotel will reply with its room availability and rates. This is not a confirmation. You must email back to say that you want the room at the given rate. While you can email your credit-card information (I do), it's safer to share that confidential info via phone call, two emails (splitting your number between them), or the hotel's secure online reservation form.

Canceling a Reservation: If you must cancel your reservation, it's courteous to do so with as much notice as possible. Simply make a quick phone call or send an email. Family-run places lose money if they turn away customers while holding a room for someone who doesn't show up. Understandably, many hoteliers bill no-shows for one night.

Cancellation policies can be strict: For example, you might lose a deposit if you cancel within two weeks of your reserved stay, or you might be billed for the entire visit if you leave early. Internet deals may require prepayment, with no refunds for cancellations. Ask about cancellation policies before you book.

If canceling via email, request confirmation that your cancellation was received to avoid being accidentally billed.

Reconfirming a Reservation: Always call to reconfirm your room reservation a few days in advance. Smaller hotels and pensions appreciate knowing your estimated time of arrival. If you'll be arriving late (after 17:00), let them know. On the small chance that a hotel loses track of your reservation, bring along a hard copy of their confirmation.

Reserving Rooms as You Travel: You can make reservations as you travel, calling hotels and pensions a few days to a week before your arrival. If everything's full, don't despair. Call a day or two in advance and fill in a cancellation. If you'd rather travel without any reservations at all, you'll have greater success snaring rooms if you arrive at your destination early in the day. When you anticipate crowds (weekends are worst), call hotels at about 9:00 or 10:00 on the day you plan to arrive, when the receptionist knows who'll be checking out and which rooms will be available. If you encounter a language barrier, ask the fluent receptionist at your current hotel to call for you.

Phoning: To call Austria from the US or Canada, dial 011-43 and then the local number (drop the local number's initial 0). The 011 is our international access code, and 43 is Austria's country code. If you're calling Austria from another European country, dial 00-43-local number (drop the local number's initial 0). The 00 is Europe's international access code. To make calls within Austria, if you're dialing within an area code, you just dial the local number; but if you're calling outside your area code, you have to dial both the area code (which starts with 0) and the local number. For more tips on calling, see page 451.

and private rooms may be available on request.

Independent hostels tend to be easygoing, colorful, and informal (no membership required); see www.hostelz.com, www.hostelseurope.com, www.hostels.com, and www.hostelbookers.com. **Official hostels** are part of Hostelling International (HI) and share an online booking site (www.hihostels.com). HI hostels typically require that you either have a membership card or pay extra per night.

Eating

Traditional Austrian cuisine is heavy, hearty, and—by European standards—inexpensive. Though it's tasty, it can get monotonous if you fall into a schnitzel-filled rut. Be adventurous. Each region has its specialties, and all but the smallest towns have a restaurant serving non-Austrian cuisine.

For breakfast, expect fresh-baked bread and jam, plus cereal, cold cuts, and cheese. Austrians eat lunch and dinner about when we do, though they tend to eat a bigger lunch and smaller dinner.

Austrians are health-conscious, but many starchy, high-fat, high-calorie traditional foods remain staples on restaurant menus. As a new generation takes over their grandparents' restaurants and inns, however, it's becoming easier to find lighter versions of the meaty standards—and organic ingredients are getting more popular. Order house specials whenever possible.

The classic dish, a stand-by on menus across Austria, is Wiener schnitzel (veal cutlet that's been pounded flat with a mallet, breaded, and fried; many restaurants offer only cheaper pork cutlets). Variations include Cordon bleu (filled with ham and cheese), and *Naturschnitzel* (not breaded, and served with rice and sauce). Chicken *(Huhn)* is usually served grilled or breaded and baked. Pork *(Schwein)* comes in all forms, including *Schweinsbraten* (roasted and served with dumplings and sauerkraut). Beef appears in goulash, as schnitzel, and in the Viennese *Tafelspitz* (boiled and served with vegetables). Fish dishes are generally very good. The Austrian version of *Gulasch*—a thick, meaty stew inspired by the similar Hungarian dish—is a traditional favorite.

Vegetarians will want to try *Eiernockerl* (egg gnocchi) and *Geröstete Knödel* (roasted dumplings). Noodles, potatoes, lettuce, and rice are standard side dishes. *Spargel* (giant white asparagus) is a must in early summer. For a meal-sized salad, order the *Salatteller.*

Treats include *Apfelstrudel, Topfenstrudel* (pastry filled with sweet cheese and raisins), and *Palatschinken* (filled crepes). The very Austrian *Kaiserschmarr'n* ("Emperor's crumbs") consists of fluffy, caramelized pancake strips, usually served with jam or raisins and nuts. Delectable, fancy specialty desserts, like Sacher-Torte, Vienna's famous chocolate cake, are plentiful in city cafés.

Ethnic restaurants provide a welcome break from Austrian fare. Foreign cuisine is either the legacy of a crumbled empire (Hungarian and Bohemian, from which Austrian cuisine gets its goulash and dumplings) or a new arrival to feed recent immigrants. Italian, Turkish, Greek, and Asian food are good values.

Hotels often serve fine food. A *Gaststätte* is a simple, less-expensive restaurant. For smaller portions, order from the *kleine Hunger* (small hunger) section of the menu.

When restaurant-hunting, choose a spot filled with locals, not the place with the big neon signs boasting, "We Speak English and Accept Credit Cards." Venturing even a block or two off the main drag leads to higher-quality food for less than half the price of the tourist-oriented places. Locals eat better at lower-rent locales.

Most restaurants tack a menu onto their door for browsers and have an English menu inside. Only a rude waiter will rush you. Good service is relaxed (slow to an American). You might be charged for bread you've eaten from the basket on the table; have the waiter take it away if you don't want it. To wish others "Happy eating!" offer a cheery *"Guten Appetit!"* When you want the bill, say, *"Rechnung* (REKH-nung), *bitte."* For tips on tipping, see page 14.

Cheap Meals

In Austria, you're never far from a *Würstelstand* (sausage stand)—for details, see the sidebar. Most bakeries sell small, cheap sandwiches; look for *Leberkäsesemmel* (roll filled with Austrian meatloaf) as well as *Schnitzelsemmel* (schnitzel sandwich). *Stehcafés* (food counters) usually offer open-face finger sandwiches *(belegte Brote)* with a wide array of toppings. Other cheap eateries include department-store cafeterias, *Schnell-Imbiss* (fast-food) stands, university cafeterias *(Mensas)*, hostels, and—especially in big cities—*Döner Kebab* kiosks (serving either sliced meat and vegetables, or falafel, in pita bread, as well as other Middle Eastern fast-food options). For a quick, cheap bite, have a deli make you a *Wurstsemmel*—a basic sausage sandwich.

Best of the Wurst

Sausage (wurst) is a staple of the Germanic diet. Most restaurants offer it (often as the cheapest thing on the menu), but it's more commonly eaten at take-out fast-food stands and counters. Sausage is fast, tasty, very local—and even a chance for culinary adventure, as your options go far beyond the hometown hot dog. Some sausages are boiled *(gekocht)*, and some are grilled *(gegrillt)*. Most are pork-based. Generally, the darker the weenie, the spicier it is.

The generic term Bratwurst simply means "grilled sausage," as opposed to boiled *Brühwurst*. Regional variations of both abound. While some types of wurst can be found all over, others are unique to a particular area. Here are some key words:

Blutwurst, Blunzn: Made from congealed blood.

Bosna: With onions and sometimes curry.

Burenwurst: Pork sausage similar to what we'd call "kielbasa."

Debreziner: Boiled, thin, and spicy, with paprika.

Frankfurter: A boiled sausage, like our hot dog (also called *Wiener Würstchen*).

Käsekrainer: Boiled, with melted cheese inside.

Thüringer: Long, skinny, peppery, and wedged into a much shorter roll.

Waldviertler: Smoked sausage.

Weisswurst: Boiled white sausage (typically Bavarian; peel off the casing before you eat it), served with sweet mustard and a pretzel.

Sauces and sides include *Senf* (mustard; ask for *süss*—sweet; or *scharf*—sharp), *Ketchup*, *Curry-Ketchup* (a tasty curry-infused ketchup), Kraut (sauerkraut), and sometimes horseradish (called *Kren* in Austria and southern Germany).

At sausage stands, you'll most commonly get a roll with your wurst (which won't resemble an American hot-dog bun). Sometimes the sausage is inside the roll; sometimes you get it on a plate with a fork and the roll to the side. You might be given the choice of a slice of bread *(Brot)*, a pretzel *(Breze)*, or (in restaurants) potato salad instead of a roll. Traditionally, if the wurst is *frisch* (fresh), you're supposed to "eat it before the noon bell tolls."

Beverages

For most visitors, it's not only the rich pastries that provide the fondest memories of Austrian cuisine, but the wine and the beer as well.

Wine: The wine (85 percent white) from the Danube River Valley and eastern Austria is particularly good.

The Austrian wine industry specializes in fine boutique wines (generally not exported, and therefore not well-known) rather than

Smoke Free? We'll See.

While many of its neighbors (including Italy, France, and many German states) have passed strict, extensive bans on smoking in public places, Austria has remained a haven for cigarette smokers. Austrian restaurants and cafés are only required to set aside at least half their space for non-smokers. Smaller establishments (under 50 square meters, or 540 square feet) that physically can't accommodate two viable zones can go all-smoking or entirely non-smoking. Restaurant and café owners who ignore the law can be fined up to €10,000 (and the smokers themselves can be fined up to €1,000).

But a host of exemptions and exceptions means that many establishments have escaped making any real changes. The law was toughened a bit in 2010, but it remains to be seen whether it will have much effect. In general, you should expect the possibility of some smoke in any restaurant (unless I've noted that it's "non-smoking"). Even "non-smoking" sections can be inundated with secondhand smoke. Fortunately for non-smokers, many eateries offer plenty of outdoor seating.

focusing on mass production. Locals order white or red Austrian wines expecting quality equal to French and Italian wines. When in Austria, I go for the better local wines when dining—well worth the cost (generally about €4 per small glass).

Some menus list wine prices by the tenth of a liter, or deciliter (dl); keep in mind that a normal-sized glass of wine (2 deciliters, often listed as "0,2 l") will cost twice what's listed. You can also order your wine by the *Viertel* (quarter-liter, 8 oz) or *Achtel* (eighth-liter, 4 oz).

When sampling Austrian wine, some vocabulary helps. You can say, "*Ein Viertel Weisswein* (white wine), *bitte* (please)." Order it *süss* (sweet), *halb trocken* (medium), or *trocken* (dry). *Rotwein* is red wine and *Sekt* is sparkling wine.

Try *Grüner Veltliner* if you like a dry white wine. *Traubenmost* is a heavenly grape juice—alcohol-free but on the verge of wine. *Most* is the same thing, but lightly alcoholic. *Sturm* is "new wine," stronger than *Most*, available only in autumn and part of the *Heuriger* phenomenon (described on page 202). Many locals claim it takes several years of practice to distinguish between *Sturm* wine and vinegar. The local red wine, called *Portugieser*, is pretty good. In fall, try the red "new" wine, *roter Sturm;* it's so fruity that locals say "Eat up!" when toasting with it. If you ask for a *gespritzter Wein* (or *gespritzte Weisse*), you'll get a spritzer—white wine pepped up with a little sparkling water. Locals find this refreshing in the summer.

INTRODUCTION

How Was Your Trip?

Were your travels fun, smooth, and meaningful? If you'd like to share your tips, concerns, and discoveries, please fill out the survey at www.ricksteves.com/feedback. I value your feedback. Thanks in advance—it helps a lot.

Beer: While better known for its wine than its beer, Austria offers plenty of fun for beer drinkers. Each region is proud of its local breweries—in Vienna, try Ottakringer; in Salzburg, look for Stiegl and Augustiner Bräu; and in Tirol, check out Frastanzer and Fohrenburger. Lager (called *Märzen* here) is popular, as are *Pils* (barley-based), *Weissbier* (yeasty and wheat-based), and *Bock* (hoppy seasonal ale). A few more terms: *Flaschenbier* is bottled, *vom Fass* is on tap, and *Malzbier* is the malted soft drink that children learn on. *Radler* is half beer and half lemon soda. Dark beer *(Dunkles)* is uncommon in Austria, but easy to find if you make a foray into Bavaria. Designated drivers can try Ottakringer's delicious non-alcoholic beer, called "Null Komma Josef." When you order beer, ask for *ein Pfiff* (a fifth-liter, about 7 oz), *ein Seidel* (third-liter, 10 oz), *ein Krügerl* (half-liter, 17 oz), or *eine Mass* (a whole liter—about a quart).

Water, Juice, and Soda: Tap water *(Leitungswasser)* is standard with a glass of wine, but otherwise an unusual request. Waiters would prefer that you buy *Mineralwasser* (*mit/ohne Gas*, with/without carbonation). Popular soft drinks include *Apfelsaft gespritzt* (half apple juice, half sparkling water), *Spezi* (Coke and orange soda), and the *über*-Austrian Almdudler (a thirst-quenching ginger-ale-like soda). In cafés, look for *Himbeersoda* (raspberry soda) and the refreshing *Holunder gespritzt* (sparkling water flavored with elderberry blossoms).

Hang on to the half-liter mineral-water bottles (sold everywhere for about €1). Buy juice in cheap liter boxes, then drink some and store the extra in your water bottle.

Traveling as a Temporary Local

We travel all the way to Europe to enjoy differences—to become temporary locals. You'll experience frustrations. Certain truths that we find "God-given" or "self-evident," such as cold beer, ice in drinks, bottomless cups of coffee, hot showers, and bigger being better, are suddenly not so true. One of the benefits of travel is the eye-opening realization that there are logical, civil, and even better alternatives. A willingness to go local ensures that you'll enjoy a full dose of Austrian hospitality.

The Austrian people (and most Europeans in general) like Americans. But if there is a negative aspect to the image Austrians have of Americans, it's that we are loud, wasteful, ethnocentric, too informal (which can seem disrespectful), and a bit naive.

While Austrians look bemusedly at some of our Yankee excesses—and worriedly at others—they nearly always afford us individual travelers all the warmth we deserve.

Judging from all the happy feedback I receive from travelers who have used this book, it's safe to assume you'll enjoy a great, affordable vacation—with the finesse of an independent, experienced traveler.

Thanks, and *gute Reise!*

Back Door Travel Philosophy

From *Rick Steves' Europe Through the Back Door*

Travel is intensified living—maximum thrills per minute and one of the last great sources of legal adventure. Travel is freedom. It's recess, and we need it.

Experiencing the real Europe requires catching it by surprise, going casual..."through the Back Door."

Affording travel is a matter of priorities. (Make do with the old car.) You can eat and sleep—simply, safely, and enjoyably—anywhere in Europe for $120 a day plus transportation costs. In many ways, spending more money only builds a thicker wall between you and what you traveled so far to see. Europe is a cultural carnival, and time after time, you'll find that its best acts are free and the best seats are the cheap ones.

A tight budget forces you to travel close to the ground, meeting and communicating with the people. Never sacrifice sleep, nutrition, safety, or cleanliness to save money. Simply enjoy the local-style alternatives to expensive hotels and restaurants.

Connecting with people carbonates your experience. Extroverts have more fun. If your trip is low on magic moments, kick yourself and make things happen. If you don't enjoy a place, maybe you don't know enough about it. Seek the truth. Recognize tourist traps. Give a culture the benefit of your open mind. See things as different, but not better or worse. Any culture has plenty to share.

Of course, travel, like the world, is a series of hills and valleys. Be fanatically positive and militantly optimistic. If something's not to your liking, change your liking.

Travel can make you a happier American, as well as a citizen of the world. Our Earth is home to seven billion equally precious people. It's humbling to travel and find that other people don't have the "American Dream"—they have their own dreams. Europeans like us, but with all due respect, they wouldn't trade passports.

Thoughtful travel engages us with the world. In tough economic times, it reminds us what is truly important. By broadening perspectives, travel teaches new ways to measure quality of life.

Globetrotting destroys ethnocentricity, helping us understand and appreciate other cultures. Rather than fear the diversity on this planet, celebrate it. Among your most prized souvenirs will be the strands of different cultures you choose to knit into your own character. The world is a cultural yarn shop, and Back Door travelers are weaving the ultimate tapestry. Join in!

AUSTRIA

Österreich

During the grand old Habsburg days, Austria was Europe's most powerful empire. Its royalty built a giant kingdom (*Österreich* means "Eastern Empire") of more than 60 million people by making love, not war—having lots of children and marrying them into the other royal houses of Europe.

Today, this small, landlocked country clings to its elegant past more than any other nation in Europe. The waltz is still the rage. Music has long been a key part of Austria's heritage. The giants of classical music—Haydn, Mozart, Beethoven—were born here or moved here to write and perform their masterpieces. Music lovers flock to Salzburg every summer to attend its famous festival. But traditional folk music is also part of the Austrian soul. The world's best-loved Christmas carol, "Silent Night," was written by Austrians with just a guitar for accompaniment. Don't be surprised if you hear yodeling for someone's birthday—try joining in.

Austrians are very sociable—it's important to greet people in the breakfast room and those you pass on the streets or meet in shops. The Austrian version of "Hi" is a cheerful *"Grüss Gott"* (for more on the language, see "Hurdling the Language Barrier" on page 450 and "German Survival Phrases for Austria" on page 481).

While Austria has gained recent notoriety for electing racist right-wingers, that attitude does not prevail everywhere. Large parts of the country may be conservative, but its capital city, Vienna, is extremely liberal. Vienna has enjoyed many progressive people-oriented programs that locals attribute to its socialistic city government. In fact, for 80 years (except for the Nazi occupation), Vienna has had a socialist government. Since the fall of the Soviet Union, the party changed its name to "Social Democrat"...but its people-oriented agenda is still the same.

AUSTRIA

Austria Almanac

Official Name: Republik Österreich ("Eastern Empire"), or simply Österreich.

Population: Austria's 8.3 million people (similar population to the state of Georgia) are 91 percent ethnic Austrian, plus 4 percent from the former Yugoslavia. Three out of four Austrians are Catholic; about one in 20 is Muslim. German is the dominant language (though there are a few Slovene- and Hungarian-speaking villages in border areas).

Latitude and Longitude: 47°N and 13°E. The latitude is the same as Minnesota or Washington state.

Area: With 32,400 square miles, Austria is similar in size to South Carolina or Maine.

Geography: The northeast is flat and well-populated; the less-populated southwest is mountainous, with the Alps rising up to the 12,450-foot Grossglockner. The 1,770-mile-long Danube River meanders west-to-east through the upper part of the country, passing through Vienna.

Biggest Cities: One in five Austrians lives in the capital of Vienna (1.7 million in the city; 2.4 million in the greater metropolitan area). Graz has 255,000, and Linz has 191,000.

Economy: Austria borders eight other European countries and is well-integrated into the EU economy. The Gross Domestic Product is $350 billion (similar to Massachusetts'). It has a GDP per capita of $40,000—among Europe's highest. One of its biggest moneymakers is tourism. Austria produces wood, paper products (nearly half the land is forested)...and Red Bull Energy Drink. The country faces an aging population that increasingly collects social security—a situation that will strain the national budget in years to come.

Government: Austria has been officially neutral since 1955, and its citizens take a dim view of European unity. Although right-leaning parties made substantial gains in recent elections, the government continues to be a center-left coalition, currently headed by Federal President Heinz Fischer and Chancellor Werner Faymann (both Social Democrats). The resurgent right—buoyed by anti-immigrant and anti-EU sentiment—was dealt a blow in October 2008 when its "yuppie fascist" leader Jörg Haider died in a car accident. Austria is the only EU nation that lets 16- and 17-year-olds vote.

Flag: Three horizontal bands of red, white, and red.

The Average Austrian: A typical Austrian is 43 years old, has 1.41 children, and will live to be 79. He or she inhabits a 900-square-foot home, and spends leisure time with a circle of a few close friends. Chances are high that someone in that closely knit circle is a smoker—Austrians smoke more cigarettes per day than any other Europeans.

AUSTRIA

While Vienna sits in the flat Danube valley, much of Austria's character is found in its mountains. Austrians excel in mountain climbing and winter sports such as alpine skiing. Innsbruck was twice the site of the Winter Olympics, and Salzburg was a finalist for the 2014 games. When watching ski races, you'll often see fans celebrating with red-and-white flags at the finish line—Austria has won more Olympic medals in alpine skiing than any other country.

Austria lost a piece of its mountains after World War I, when the Tirol was divided between Austria and Italy. Many residents of Italy's South Tirol still speak German, and it's the first language in some of their schools. Though there was bitterness at the time of the division, today, with no border guards and a shared currency, you can hardly tell you're in a different country.

While Austrians speak German and talked about unity with Germany long before Hitler ever said *"Anschluss,"* they cherish their distinct cultural and historical traditions. They are not Germans. Austria is mellow and relaxed compared to Deutschland. *Gemüt-lichkeit* is the word most often used to describe this special Austrian cozy-and-easy approach to life. It's good living—whether engulfed in mountain beauty or bathed in lavish high culture. People stroll as if every day were Sunday, topping things off with a cheerful visit to a coffee or pastry shop.

It must be nice to be past your prime—no longer troubled by being powerful, able to kick back and celebrate life in the clean, peaceful mountain air.

VIENNA
Wien

ORIENTATION TO VIENNA

Vienna is the capital of Austria, the cradle of classical music, the home of the rich Habsburg heritage, and one of Europe's most livable cities. The city center is skyscraper-free, pedestrian-friendly, dotted with quiet parks, and traversed by electric trams. Many buildings still reflect 18th- and 19th-century elegance, when the city was at the forefront of the arts and sciences. Compared with most modern European urban centers, the pace of life is slow.

For much of its 2,500-year history, Vienna (*Wien* in German—pronounced "veen") was on the frontier of civilized Europe. Located on the south bank of the Danube, it was threatened by Germanic barbarians (in Roman times), marauding Magyars (today's Hungarians, 10th century), Mongol hordes (13th century), Ottoman Turks (the sieges of 1529 and 1683), and encroachment by the Soviet Empire after World War II.

Vienna reached its peak in the 19th century. Politically, it hosted European diplomats at the 1814 Congress of Vienna, which reaffirmed Europe's conservative monarchy after the French Revolution and Napoleon. Vienna became one of Europe's cultural capitals, home to groundbreaking composers (Beethoven, Mozart, Brahms, Strauss), scientists (Doppler, Boltzmann), philosophers (Freud, Husserl, Schlick, Gödel, Steiner), architects (Wagner, Loos), and painters (Klimt, Schiele, Kokoschka). By the turn of the 20th century, Vienna sat on the cusp between stuffy Old World monarchism and subversive modern trends.

After the turmoil of the two world wars, Vienna has settled down into a somewhat sleepy, pleasant place where culture is still king. Classical music is everywhere. People nurse a pastry and coffee over the daily paper at small cafés. It's a city of world-class museums, big and small. Anyone with an interest in painting, music,

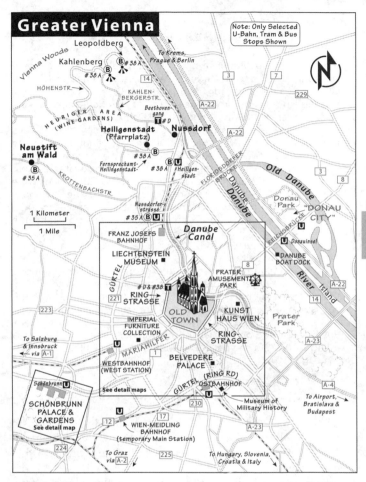

Greater Vienna

Note: Only Selected U-Bahn, Tram & Bus Stops Shown

Leopoldberg

Vienna Woods

Kahlenberg · B · #38A

#38A

HÖHENSTR·

To Krems, Prague & Berlin

KAHLEN-BERGERSTR·

14

HEURIGER AREA (WINE GARDENS)

Beethoven-gang · T · #D

Heiligenstadt (Pfarrplatz) · Nussdorf

A-22

A-22

3

7

229

Old Danube

3

8

Neustift am Wald · B ·

#35A

KROTTENBACHSTR·

Fernsprechamt-Heiligenstadt-

#38A

B · U ·

#38A · #Heiligen-stadt

Nussdorfer-strasse

#35A · B · U ·

Danube

Danube

FLORIDSDORFER BRÜCKE

Donau Park

"DONAU CITY"

REICHSBRÜCKE

River

Island

A-22

FRANZ JOSEFS BAHNHOF

LIECHTENSTEIN MUSEUM

Danube Canal

U · Donauinsel

DANUBE BOAT DOCK

GÜRTEL

221

223

#D & #38 · T ·

RING-STRASSE

OLD TOWN

PRATER AMUSEMENT PARK

8

KUNST HAUS WIEN

Prater Park

A-22

14

IMPERIAL FURNITURE COLLECTION

U · MARIAHILFER

1

RING-STRASSE

A-23

To Salzburg & Innsbruck ← via A-1

WESTBAHNHOF (WEST STATION)

BELVEDERE PALACE

GÜRTEL (RING RD) · OSTBAHNHOF

U

To Airport, Bratislava & Budapest

A-4

See detail maps

Museum of Military History

Schönbrunn · U ·

SCHÖNBRUNN PALACE & GARDENS See detail map

224

U

12

17

230

WIEN-MEIDLING BAHNHOF (temporary Main Station)

A-23

To Graz via A-2

225

To Hungary, Slovenia, Croatia & Italy

1 Kilometer

1 Mile

architecture, beautiful objects, or Sacher-Torte with whipped cream will feel right at home.

Vienna: A Verbal Map

Vienna sits between the Vienna Woods (Wienerwald) and the Danube (Donau). To the southeast is industrial sprawl. The Alps, which arc across Europe from Marseille, end at Vienna's wooded hills, providing a popular playground for walking and sipping new wine. This greenery's momentum carries on into the city. More than half of Vienna is parkland, filled with ponds, gardens, trees, and statue-maker memories of Austria's glory days.

Think of the city map as a target with concentric sections: The bull's-eye is St. Stephen's Cathedral, the towering cathedral south of the Danube. Surrounding that is the old town, bound tightly by

ORIENTATION

Vienna Past and Present

Vienna is a head without a body. The capital of the once-grand Habsburg Empire for 640 years, Vienna started and lost World War I and, with it, its far-flung holdings. Culturally, historically, and touristically, this city is the sum of its illustrious past, ranking right up there with Paris, London, and Rome.

Vienna has always been the easternmost city of the West. In Roman times, it was Vindobona, on the Danube facing the Germanic barbarians. In the Middle Ages, Vienna was Europe's bastion against the Ottomans—a Christian breakwater against the rising tide of Islam (hordes of up to 200,000 Ottomans were repelled in 1529 and 1683). During this period, as the Ottomans dreamed of conquering what they called "the big apple" for their sultan, Vienna lived with a constant fear of invasion (and the Habsburg court ruled from safer Prague). You'll notice none of Vienna's great palaces were built until after 1683, when the Turkish threat was finally over.

The Habsburgs, who ruled the enormous Austrian Empire from 1273 to 1918, shaped Vienna. Some ad agency has convinced Vienna to make Elisabeth, wife of Emperor Franz Josef—with her narcissism and struggles with royal life—the darling of the local tourist scene. You'll see images of "Sisi" (SEE-see) all over town. But stay focused on the Habsburgs who mattered: Maria Theresa (ruled 1740-1780, see page 67) and Franz Josef (ruled 1848-1916, see page 150).

the circular road known as the Ringstrasse, marking what used to be the city wall. The Gürtel, a broader ring road, contains the rest of downtown. Outside the Gürtel lies the uninteresting sprawl of modern Vienna.

Addresses start with the *Bezirk* (district), followed by the street and building number. The Ringstrasse (a.k.a. the Ring) circles the first *Bezirk*. Any address higher than the ninth *Bezirk* is beyond the Gürtel, far from the center. The middle two digits of Vienna's postal codes show the *Bezirk*. The address "7, Lindengasse 4" is in the seventh district, #4 on Linden street. Its postal code would be 1070.

Much of Vienna's sightseeing—and most of my recommended restaurants—are located in the old town (inside the Ringstrasse). Walking across this circular district takes about 30 minutes. St. Stephen's Cathedral sits in the center, at the intersection of the two main (pedestrian-only) streets: Kärntner Strasse runs north-south and Graben runs east-west.

Several sights sit along, or just beyond, the Ringstrasse: To the southwest are the Hofburg and related Habsburg sights, and

After Napoleon's defeat and the Congress of Vienna in 1815 (which shaped the political landscape of 19th-century Europe), Vienna enjoyed its violin-filled belle époque, giving us our romantic image of the city: fine wine, chocolates, cafés, waltzes, and the good life.

In 1900, Vienna's 2.2 million inhabitants made it the world's fifth-largest city—after New York, London, Paris, and Berlin.

While Vienna's old walls had held out would-be invaders (including the Ottomans), they were no match for WWII bombs, which destroyed nearly a quarter of the city's buildings. In modern times, neutral Austria took a big bite out of the USSR's Warsaw Pact buffer zone. Today, Vienna is a springboard for many popular destinations in Eastern Europe.

Vienna's population has dropped to 1.7 million, with dogs being the preferred "child" and the average Viennese mother having only 1.3 children. Even with fewer residents, Vienna is still a grand and elegant capital containing one-fifth of Austria's population.

The truly Viennese person is not Austrian, but rather a second-generation Habsburg cocktail, with grandparents from the distant corners of the old empire: Hungary, the Czech Republic, Slovakia, Poland, Slovenia, Croatia, Bosnia, Serbia, Romania, and Italy. Vienna is the melting-pot capital of a now-collapsed empire that, in its heyday, consisted of more than 60 million people—only 8 million of whom were Austrian.

the Kunsthistorisches Museum; to the south is a cluster of intriguing sights near Karlsplatz; to the southeast is Belvedere Palace. A branch of the Danube River (*Donau* in German, DOH-now) borders the Ring to the north.

As a tourist, concern yourself only with this compact old center. When you do, sprawling Vienna suddenly becomes manageable.

Planning Your Time

For a big city, Vienna is pleasant and laid-back. Packed with sights, it's worth two days and two nights on even the speediest trip. If you have more time, Vienna can easily fill it; art and music lovers in particular won't regret adding a third or fourth day.

If you're visiting Vienna as part of a longer European trip, you could sleep on the train on your way in and out—Berlin, Prague, Kraków, the Swiss Alps (via Zürich), Venice, Rome, Paris, and the Rhine Valley are each handy night trains away.

Palace Choices: The Hofburg and Schönbrunn are both world-class **palaces,** but seeing both is redundant—with limited

ORIENTATION

Daily Reminder

Sunday: All sights (except the Postal Savings Bank) and most tourist shops are open, but department stores and other shops are closed, including the Naschmarkt open-air market and the Dorotheum auction house. Most churches have restricted hours for sightseers, and there are no tours of the crypt at St. Michael's Church. In spring and fall, the Spanish Riding School's Lipizzaner stallions perform at 11:00.

Monday: Most of the major sights are open (such as St. Stephen's Cathedral, Opera, Hofburg Imperial Apartments and Treasury, Schönbrunn Palace, and Belvedere Palace), but many sights are closed, including the Kunsthistorisches Museum, New Palace museums, Wien Museum, Secession, Academy of Fine Arts, Imperial Furniture Collection, Military Museum, Museum of Applied Art (MAK), Otto Wagner exhibit, Opera Museum, and Austrian National Library. The Kunst Haus Wien is half-price.

Tuesday: All sights are open, except the Hofburg Treasury, New Palace museums, and Natural History Museum. The Leopold Museum (at the MuseumsQuartier) is closed except in summer. The Museum of Applied Art (MAK) is free after 18:00 and stays open until 22:00. The Haus der Musik is half-price after 20:00.

Wednesday: All sights are open. The Albertina, Natural History Museum, and Belvedere Lower Palace stay open until 21:00.

Thursday: All sights are open. The Kunsthistorisches and MuseumsQuartier museums (Leopold and Modern Art) stay open until 21:00.

Friday: All sights are open. The Spanish Riding School's Lipizzaner stallions often perform at 19:00 in spring and fall.

Saturday: All sights are open, except the Jewish Museum Vienna (both locations). The Spanish Riding School's Lipizzaner stallions often perform at 11:00 in spring and fall. The Third Man Museum is open only today (14:00-18:00).

time or money, I'd choose just one. The Hofburg comes with the popular Sisi Museum and is right in the town center, making for an easy visit. With more time, a visit to Schönbrunn—set outside town amid a grand and regal garden—is also a great experience. (For efficient sightseeing, drivers should note that Schönbrunn Palace is conveniently on the way out of town toward Salzburg.)

Vienna in One to Four Days

Below is a suggested itinerary for how to spend your time. I've left the **evenings** open for your choice of activities. The best options are taking in a concert, opera, or other musical event; enjoying leisurely dinner (and people-watching) in the stately old town or atmospheric Spittelberg Quarter; heading out to the *Heuriger* wine pubs in the foothills of the Vienna Woods; or touring the Haus der Musik interactive music museum (open nightly until 22:00). Plan your evenings based on the schedule of musical events while you're in town. If you've downloaded my audio tours (see "Rick Steves Audio Europe" sidebar, later), both the Vienna City Walk and Ringstrasse Tram Tour work wonderfully in the evening. Whenever you need a break, linger in a classic Viennese café.

Day 1

9:00	Circle the Ringstrasse by tram (following my self-guided tram tour).
10:30	Drop by the TI for planning and ticket needs.
11:00	Take the Opera tour.
14:00	Follow my Vienna City Walk, including Kaisergruft visit and St. Stephen's Cathedral Tour (nave closes at 16:30, or 17:30 June-Aug).
18:00	Take the 1.5-hour Red Bus City Tour for a look at greater Vienna.

Day 2

9:00	Browse the colorful Naschmarkt.
11:00	Tour the Kunsthistorisches Museum.
14:00	Tour the Hofburg Palace Imperial Apartments and Treasury.

Day 3

10:00	Visit Belvedere Palace, with its fine collection of Viennese art and great city views.
15:00	Tour Schönbrunn Palace to enjoy the royal apartments and grounds.

Day 4

10:00	Enjoy (depending on your interest) the engaging Karlsplatz sights (Karlskirche, Wien Museum, Academy of Fine Arts, and The Secession).
12:00	Tour the Albertina Museum.
15:00	Shoppers can stroll Mariahilfer Strasse. Non-shoppers can rent a bike and head out to the modern Donau City "downtown" sector, Danube Island (for fun people-watching), and the Prater amusement park.

With More Time...

Vienna itself can easily fill a longer visit. But a day trip can be more rewarding than spending extra time in town. For rustic pastoral

ORIENTATION

Rick Steves Audio Europe

If you're bringing a mobile device, be sure to check out **Rick Steves Audio Europe,** where you can download free audio tours and hours of travel interviews (via the Rick Steves Audio Europe smartphone app, www.ricksteves.com/audioeurope, iTunes, or Google Play).

My self-guided **audio tours** are user-friendly, easy to follow, fun, and informative, covering Vienna's Ringstrasse, historic city center, and St. Stephen's Cathedral, as well as Salzburg's old town. Although you have the basic script of these tours in this book, it's curiously relaxing to wander through the city, listening to the narration rather than reading it. Compared to live tours, my audio tours are hard to beat: Nobody will stand you up, the quality is reliable, you can take the tour exactly when you like, and they're free.

Rick Steves Audio Europe also offers a far-reaching library of intriguing **travel interviews** with experts from around the globe.

ORIENTATION

beauty, head for Melk and the Danube Valley; for an exciting detour into the Slavic world, hit the up-and-coming Slovak capital of Bratislava.

Overview

Tourist Information

Vienna's main TI is a block behind the Opera at Albertinaplatz (daily 9:00-19:00, tel. 01/211-140, www.vienna.info). There's also an airport TI (daily 6:00-23:00). At either TI, confirm your sightseeing plans, and pick up two copies of the free and essential city map with a list of museums and hours (also available at most hotels). Rip up one copy of the Vienna map—reducing it down to just the city-center inset—and keep it in your pocket for ready reference. (Stuff the other copy in your backpack in case you need it.) Also look for the monthly program of concerts (called *Wien-Programm*) and the *Vienna from A to Z* booklet (both described below), and the annual city guide (called *Vienna Journal*). Ask about their program of guided walks (€14 each). While hotel and ticket-booking agencies at the train station and airport can answer questions and give out maps and brochures, I'd rely on the official TI.

Wien-Programm: This monthly entertainment guide is particularly important, listing all sorts of events, including music, theater, walks, expositions, and museum exhibits. It's organized this way: First you see the current month's festivals and live music (jazz, rock, and more). Next come the schedules for the Spanish Riding

School and the Vienna Boys' Choir, followed by listings for museums and exhibitions, theater options, and the opera (noting which performances are projected on the big screen outside the Opera house). The next section lists classical concerts (also organized by date, with phone numbers to call direct to check seat availability and to save the 20 percent booking fees that you pay if you buy tickets through an agency). Last is a list of guided walks offered (*E* means "in English"). Note the key for abbreviations on the inside cover, which helps make this dense booklet useful even for non-German speakers.

Vienna from A to Z: Consider this handy booklet, sold by the TI for €3.60. Every major building in Vienna sports a numbered flag banner that keys into this booklet and into the TI's city map. If you get lost, find one of the "famous-building flags" and match its number to your map. If you're at a famous building, check the map to see what other key numbers are nearby, then check the *A to Z* book description to see if you want to go in. This system is especially helpful for those just wandering aimlessly among Vienna's historic charms.

Vienna Card: The much-promoted €20 Vienna Card is not worth the mental overhead for most travelers. It gives you a 72-hour transit pass (worth €13.60) and discounts of 10-40 percent at the city's museums. It might save the busy sightseer a few euros (though seniors and students will do better with their own discounts).

Arrival in Vienna

For a comprehensive rundown on Vienna's various train stations and its airport, as well as tips on arriving or departing by car or boat, see the Vienna Connections chapter.

Helpful Hints

Sisi Ticket: This €23.50 ticket covers the Royal Imperial Apartments at the Hofburg (including the Sisi Museum and Imperial Porcelain and Silver Collection—but *not* the Hofburg Treasury), Schönbrunn Palace's Grand Tour, and the Imperial Furniture Collection; the ticket saves €0.50 off the combined cost of the Hofburg apartments and Schönbrunn, making the good Furniture Collection effectively free (sold at any participating sight).

Teens Sightsee Free: Those under 19 get in free to state-run museums and sights.

Music Sightseeing Priorities: Be wary of Vienna's various music sights. Many "homes of composers" are pretty disappointing. My advice to music lovers is to concentrate on these activities: Take in a concert, tour the Opera house, snare cheap standing-room tickets to see an opera there (even just part of a performance), enjoy the Haus der Musik, and scour the wonderful Collection of Ancient Musical Instruments in the Hofburg's New Palace. If in town on a Sunday, don't miss the glorious music at the Augustinian Church Mass (see page 63).

Skip This: The highly advertised experience called Time Travel Vienna (just off the Graben on Habsburgergasse) promises "history, fun, and action." In reality, it's €18 and 45 minutes wasted in a tacky succession of amusement-park history vignettes with much of the information in German only.

Internet Access: The TI has a list of Internet cafés. **Netcafe** is near the Danube Canal (€4/hour with drink, daily 9:00-22:00, Schwedenplatz 3); **Surfland Internet Café** is near the Opera (€6/hour, daily 10:00-23:00, Krugerstrasse 10, tel. 01/512-7701); and **Netcafe-Refill** is close to many of my recommended hotels (€4.50/hour, daily 9:00-22:00, Mariahilfer Strasse 103, tel. 01/595-5558). See map on page 55 for first two locations and page 183 for last location.

Post Offices: The main post office is near Schwedenplatz at Fleischmarkt 19 (Mon-Fri 7:00-22:00, Sat-Sun 9:00-22:00). Branch offices are at the Westbahnhof (Mon-Fri 7:00-22:00, Sat-Sun 9:00-20:00), near the Opera (Mon-Fri 7:00-19:00, closed Sat-Sun, Krugerstrasse 13), and scattered throughout town.

English Bookstore: Stop by the woody and cool **Shakespeare & Co.,** in the historic and atmospheric Ruprechtsviertel district near the Danube Canal (Mon-Sat 9:00-21:00, closed Sun, north of Hoher Markt at Sterngasse 2, tel. 01/535-5053, www.shakespeare.co.at). **Freytag & Berndt** travel bookstore (Mon-Sat 9:30-18:30, Kohlmarkt 9, tel. 01/533-8685, www.freytag-berndt.at) is a great place if you need a map or book in English or one of my guidebooks for the next leg of your journey. See map on page 55 for locations.

Keeping Up with the News: Don't buy newspapers. Read them for free in Vienna's marvelous coffeehouses. It's much classier.

Travel Agency: Conveniently located just off the Graben, **Ruefa** sells tickets for flights, trains, and boats to Bratislava. They'll waive the service charge for train tickets for my readers (Mon-Fri 9:00-18:00, Sat 10:00-13:00, closed Sun, Spiegelgasse 15—see map on page 55, tel. 01/513-4000, Gertrude speaks English).

Drinking Water: Vienna, in response to—and anticipation of—global warming, is creating shady spots with benches and installing shiny public water fountains with signs reminding people to stay hydrated. These are especially useful for older travelers and elderly locals, who'll suffer the most as scorching summers become the norm.

The Viennese are proud of their perfectly drinkable tap water from Alpine springs. "Leitungswasser" is happily served in any restaurant. You'll spot locals refilling their little bottles at fountains all over town.

Updates to This Book: For news about changes to this book's coverage since it was published, see www.ricksteves.com/update.

Getting Around Vienna
By Public Transportation

Take full advantage of Vienna's simple, cheap, and super-efficient transit system, which includes trams (a.k.a. streetcars), buses, U-Bahn (subway), and S-Bahn (faster suburban trains). The smooth, modern trams are Porsche-designed, with "backpack technology" that locates the engines and mechanical hardware on the roofs for a lower ride and easier entry. I generally stick to the tram to zip around the Ring and take the U-Bahn to outlying sights or hotels. Trams #1, #2, and #D all travel partway around the Ring. (See the Ringstrasse Tram Tour chapter.)

The free Vienna map, available at TIs and hotels, includes a smaller schematic map of the major public transit lines, making the too-big €2.50 transit map unnecessary. (Transit maps are also posted conveniently on U-Bahn station walls.) As you study the map, note that tram lines are marked with numbers or letters (such as #38 or #D). Buses have numbers followed by an *A* or *B* (such as #38A); three-digit numbers are for buses into the outskirts.

Night buses, which start with *N* (such as #N38), operate after other public transit stops running. U-Bahn lines begin with U (e.g., U-1), and the directions are designated by the end-of-the-line stops. Blue lines are the speedier S-Bahns. Transit info: tel. 01/790-9100, www.wiener-linien.at.

Trams, buses, the U-Bahn, and the S-Bahn all use the same tickets. Buy tickets from *Tabak-Trafik* shops, station machines, marked *Vorverkauf* offices in the station, or—for trams or buses only—on board (tickets only, more expensive). You have lots of choices:

- Single tickets (€2, €2.40 if bought on tram or bus, good for one journey with necessary transfers)
- 24-hour transit pass (€6.70)
- 48-hour transit pass (€11.70)

- 72-hour transit pass (€14.50)
- 7-day transit pass (*Wochenkarte*, €15—the catch is that the pass runs from Monday to Monday, so you may get less than seven days of use)
- 8-day "Climate Ticket" *(Acht-Tage-Klimakarte,* €34, can be shared—for example, four people for two days each). With a per-person cost of €4.24/day (compared to €6.70/day for a 24-hour pass), this can be a real saver for groups.

Kids under 15 travel free on Sundays and holidays; kids under 6 always travel free.

Stamp a time on your ticket as you enter the Metro system, tram, or bus (stamp it only the first time for a multiple-use pass). Cheaters pay a stiff €70 fine, plus the cost of the ticket.

Rookies miss stops because they fail to open the door. Push buttons, pull latches—do whatever it takes. Before you exit a U-Bahn station, study the wall-mounted street map. Choosing the right exit—signposted from the moment you step off the train—saves lots of walking.

Cute little electric buses wind through the tangled old center (from Schottentor to Stubentor). Bus #1A is best for a joyride—hop on and see where it takes you.

By Taxi

Vienna's comfortable, civilized, and easy-to-flag-down **taxis** start at €2.50. You'll pay about €10 to go from the Opera to the Westbahnhof. Pay only what's on the meter—any surcharges (other than the €2 fee for calling a cab or €11 fee for the airport) are just crude cabbie rip-offs. Rates are legitimately higher at night.

Consider the luxury of having your own **car and driver.** Johann (a.k.a. John) Lichtl is a kind, honest, English-speaking cabbie who can take up to four passengers in his car (€27/1 hour, €22/hour for 2 hours or more, €27 to or from airport, mobile 0676-670-6750). Consider hiring gentle Johann for a day trip to the Danube Valley (€160, up to 8 hours; see Danube Valley chapter) or to drive you to Salzburg with Danube sightseeing en route (€350, up to 14 hours; other trips can be arranged). These special prices are valid with this book in 2013 and 2014.

By Bike

With more than 600 miles of bike lanes, Vienna is a great city on two wheels. With the inability of any single party to get a clear majority, Vienna's government is ruled by a coalition—that gives the Green Party more clout than it might otherwise have. Consequently, life is good for the city's bikers; for one thing, bikes ride the U-Bahn for free (but they aren't allowed during weekday rush hours).

The bike path along the Ring is wonderfully entertaining (in fact, my Ringstrasse Tram Tour works even better by bike than by tram)—you'll enjoy the shady park-like ambience of the boulevard while rolling by many of the city's top sights. Besides the Ring, your best sightseeing by bike is through Stadtpark (City Park), across Danube Island, and out to the modern Donau City business district (for more on biking on Danube Island and to Donau City, see page 98). These routes are easy to follow on the free tourist city map available from the TI.

Borrowing a Free/Cheap Bike: Citybike Wien lets you borrow bikes from public racks all over town (toll tel. 0810-500-500, www.citybikewien.at). The three-speed bikes are heavy and clunky—and come with a basket, built-in lock, and ads on the side—but they're perfect for a short, practical joyride in the center (such as around the Ringstrasse).

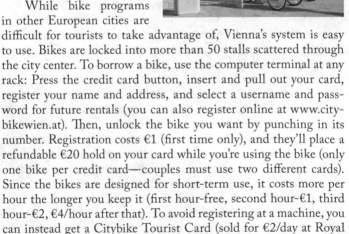

While bike programs in other European cities are difficult for tourists to take advantage of, Vienna's system is easy to use. Bikes are locked into more than 50 stalls scattered through the city center. To borrow a bike, use the computer terminal at any rack: Press the credit card button, insert and pull out your card, register your name and address, and select a username and password for future rentals (you can also register online at www.citybikewien.at). Then, unlock the bike you want by punching in its number. Registration costs €1 (first time only), and they'll place a refundable €20 hold on your card while you're using the bike (only one bike per credit card—couples must use two different cards). Since the bikes are designed for short-term use, it costs more per hour the longer you keep it (first hour-free, second hour-€1, third hour-€2, €4/hour after that). To avoid registering at a machine, you can instead get a Citybike Tourist Card (sold for €2/day at Royal Tours, near the Hofburg at Herrengasse 1-3—see map on page 55), but this extra step isn't worth the trouble. When you're done, drop off your bike at any stall, and make sure it's fully locked into the rack to avoid being charged for more time.

Renting a Higher-Quality Bike: If you want to ride beyond the town center—or you simply want a better set of wheels—check out **Pedal Power,** with a handy central location near the Opera house. The local authority on bike touring in town and to points along the Danube, Pedal Power rents bikes and provides good biking info (€5/hour, €17/4 hours, €27/24 hours, daily May-Sept 8:30-18:00, Elisabethstrasse 13 at the corner of Eschenbachgasse—see map on page 55, tel. 01/729-7234, www.pedalpower.at). For a better selection and better gear, it's smart to use their main office by Prater Park. While less central, it's very easy to get to (U-1 or U-2: Praterstern, then walk 100 yards to Ausstellungssttr 3). They can also deliver a bike to your hotel and pick it up when you're done (€32/day including delivery, service available year-round), and they organize bike tours (described later). Pedal Power offers a 10 percent discount to anyone with this book.

Tours in Vienna

ORIENTATION

To sightsee on your own, download my series of free audio tours that illuminate some of Vienna's top sights and neighborhoods (see sidebar, earlier).

Walking Tours—The *Walks in Vienna* brochure (available at the TI) describes the city's many guided walks. The basic 1.5-hour "Vienna at First Glance" introductory walk is offered daily throughout the summer (€14, leaves at 14:00 from the main TI just behind the Opera, in both English and German, just show up, tel. 01/774-8901, mobile 0664-260-4388, www.wienguide.at). Various specialized tours go once a week and are listed on the website.

Bike Tours—**Pedal Power** runs two different three-hour tours daily from May to September. The morning tour covers the central district, while the afternoon tour crosses the Danube (€29/tour includes bike, €49 for both tours, €14 extra to keep the bike for the day, departs at 10:00 and 14:30 from the statue in Schillerplatz in front of the Academy of Fine Arts, across the Ring from the Opera, tel. 01/729-7234, www.pedalpower.at). They also rent bikes and offer Segway tours daily in summer (www.segway-vienna.at).

For a private bike tour, contact guide **Wolfgang Höfler** (€140/3 hours, mobile 0676-304-4940, www.vienna-aktivtours.com, office@vienna-aktivtours.com; also leads walking tours—see listing, later, under "Local Guides").

Bus Tours—**Red Bus City Tours'** convertible buses do a 1.5-hour loop, hitting the highlights of the city with a 20-minute shopping break in the middle. They cover the main first-district attractions as well as a big bus can, along with the entire Ringstrasse. But the most interesting part of the tour is outside the center—zipping through Prater Park, over the Danube for a glimpse of the city's Danube Island playground, and into the "Donau City" skyscraper zone. If the weather's good, the bus goes topless and offers great opportunities for photos. Tours start one block behind the Opera at the main TI—see the map on page 55 for the location (€14 ticket from driver, €2 discount with this book if purchased from office at Lobkowitzplatz 1—100 yards from where the tour begins; departs hourly April-Oct 10:00-18:00, less frequently off-season, pretty good recorded narration in any language, your own earbuds are better than the beat-up headphones they provide, tel. 01/512-4030, www.redbuscitytours.at, Gabriel).

Vienna Sightseeing offers a three-hour city tour, including a tour of Schönbrunn Palace (€39, 3/day April-Oct, 2/day Nov-March). They also run hop-on, hop-off bus tours with recorded commentary. The schedule is posted curbside (three different one-hour routes, €13/1 route, €16/2 routes, €20/all day, departs from the Opera 4/hour July-Aug 10:00-20:00, runs less frequently and stops earlier off-season, tel. 01/7124-6830, www.viennasightseeing.at). Given the city's excellent public transportation and mostly walkable sights, I'd skip this tour; if you just want a quick guided city tour, take the Red Bus tours recommended earlier.

Ring Tram Tour—The **Vienna Ring Tram,** a yellow made-for-tourists streetcar, runs clockwise along the entire Ringstrasse (€7 for 30-minute loop, €9 for 24-hour hop-on, hop-off privileges, 2/hour 10:00-18:00, July-Aug until 19:00, recorded narration, includes a good set of earbuds you can keep and reuse). The tour starts at the top and bottom of each hour on the Opera side of the Ring at Kärntner Ring. At each stop, you'll see an ad for this tram tour (look for *VRT Ring-Rund Sightseeing*). The schedule clearly notes the next departure time.

To save money, follow my self-guided tram tour using city trams that circle the Ring. You'll need to make one transfer, but the trams run frequently and you'll sit alongside real *Wieners* (see Ringstrasse Tram Tour chapter).

Horse-and-Buggy Tour—These traditional horse-and-buggies, called *Fiakers,* take rich romantics on clip-clop tours lasting 20 minutes (€55-old town), 40 minutes (€80-old town and the Ring), or one hour (€110-all the above, but more thorough). You can share the ride and cost with up to five people. Because it's a kind of guided tour, talk to a few drivers before choosing a carriage, and pick someone who's fun and speaks English (tel. 01/401-060).

Local Guides—You'll pay about €140 for two hours. Get a group of six or more together and call it a party. The tourist board's website (www.vienna.info) has a long list of local guides with their specialties and contact information. My favorite private Vienna guides are: **Lisa Zeiler** (mobile 0699-120-37550, lisa.zeiler@gmx.at); **Wolfgang Höfler** (a generalist with a knack for having psychoanalytical fun with history, enjoys the big changes of the 19th and 20th centuries, €150/2 hours, mobile

ORIENTATION

0676-304-4940, www.vienna-aktivtours.com, office@vienna-aktivtours.com, also leads bike tours—described earlier); **Adrienn Bartek-Rhomberg** (€140/half-day, see website for tour topics, mobile 0650-826-6965, www.experience-vienna.at, bartek-rhomberg@chello.at); and **Gerhard Strassgschwandtner** (who runs the Third Man Museum and is passionate about history in all its marvelous complexity, €65/hour, mobile 0676-475-7818, www.special-vienna.com, gerhard@special-vienna.com). If these folks are booked, any of them can set you up with another good guide.

SIGHTS IN VIENNA

The sights listed in this chapter are arranged by neighborhood for handy sightseeing. When you see a ✪ in a listing, it means the sight is covered in much more depth in my Vienna City Walk or one of my self-guided tours. This is why Vienna's most important attractions get the least coverage in this chapter—we'll explore them later in the book.

For tips on sightseeing, see page 16.

In the Old Town, Within the Ring

These sights are listed roughly from south to north. For a self-guided walk connecting many of central Vienna's top sights—including some of the ones below—✪ see the Vienna City Walk chapter.

▲▲▲**Opera (Wiener Staatsoper)**—The Opera house, facing the Ring and near the TI, is a central point for any visitor. Vienna remains one of the world's great cities for classical music, and this building still belts out some of the finest opera, both classic and cutting-edge. While the critical reception of the building 130 years ago led the architect to commit suicide, and though it's been rebuilt since its destruction by WWII bombs, it's still a sumptuous place. The interior has a chandeliered lobby and carpeted staircases perfect for making the scene. The theater itself features five wraparound balconies, gold-and-red decor, and a bracelet-like chandelier.

Depending on your level of tolerance for opera, you can simply admire the Neo-Renaissance building from the outside, take a guided tour of the lavish interior, visit the Opera Museum, or attend a performance of Vienna's opera company.

Tours: You can only enter the Opera if you're attending a performance or joining a guided 45-minute tour in English (€6.50, ticket covers modest Opera Museum, described next; tours run

July-Aug generally daily at the top of each hour 10:00-16:00; Sept-June fewer tours, afternoons only, none on Sun; buy tickets 20 minutes before tour departs—ticket office is around the left side, as you face the main entrance; tel. 01/514-442-606, www.wiener-staatsoper.at). Tour times are often changed or canceled due to rehearsals and performances. Schedules with daily listings for each month (including tour times) are posted all around the building. A list of today's tours in each language is posted to the right of the entry door; you can also pick up the monthly *Prolog* program, which includes the schedule. The entry door opens 30 minutes before each tour and closes when it starts.

Opera Museum (Staatsopernmuseum): This permanent exhibit chronologically traces the illustrious history of the Vienna State Opera, highlighting the most famous singers, directors (including Gustav Mahler and Herbert von Karajan), and performances. It also features old posters, costumes, and lots of photographs (€3, included in Opera tour ticket; Tue-Sun 10:00-18:00, closed Mon; across the street and a block away from the Opera toward the Hofburg, tucked down a courtyard at Hanuschgasse 3, near Albertina Museum, tel. 01/514-442-100).

Performances: For information on buying tickets and attending a performance, see page 208.

▲▲Haus der Musik—Vienna's "House of Music" is a high-tech experience that celebrates this hometown specialty. The museum, spread over five floors and well-described in English, is unique for its effective use of interactive touch-screen computers and headphones to explore the physics of sound. Really experiencing the place takes time. It's open late and makes a good evening activity.

Cost and Hours: €11, includes audioguide for third floor only, half-price after 20:00, €17 combo-ticket with Mozarthaus, daily 10:00-22:00, last entry one hour before closing, two blocks from the Opera at Seilerstätte 30, tel. 01/513-4850, www.hdm.at.

Visiting the Museum: The first floor features a small exhibit on the Vienna Philharmonic Orchestra, including the batons of prominent conductors and Leonard Bernstein's tux. Throw the dice to randomly "compose" a piece of music.

On the second floor, wander through the "sonosphere" and marvel at the amazing acoustics. Spend some time at the well-presented, interactive headphone stations to learn about the nature of sound and music; I could actually hear what I thought only a piano tuner could discern. You can twist, dissect, and bend sounds to make your own musical language, merging your voice with a duck's quack or a city's traffic roar. A tube filled with pebbles demonstrates the power of sound waves...watch them bounce. The "instrumentarium" presents various tools of the trade, new and old.

The third floor features fine audiovisual exhibits on each of the famous hometown boys (Haydn, Mozart, Beethoven, Schubert, Strauss, and Mahler). Before leaving, pick up a virtual baton to conduct the Vienna Philharmonic. Each time you screw up, the musicians put their instruments down and ridicule you; make it through the piece, and you'll get a rousing round of applause.

▲**Dorotheum Auction House (Palais Dorotheum)**—For an aristocrat's flea market, drop by Austria's answer to Sotheby's. The ground floor has shops, an info desk with a schedule of upcoming auctions, and a few auction items. Some pieces are available for immediate sale (marked *VKP,* for *Verkaufpreis*—"sales price"), while others are up for auction (marked *DIFF. RUF*). Labels on each item predict the auction value.

The upstairs floors have antique furniture and fancy knickknacks (some for immediate sale, others for auction), many brought in by people who've inherited old things and don't have room for them. The top floor has a fancy antique gallery with fixed prices. Wandering through here, you feel like you're touring a museum with exhibits you can buy. Afterward, you can continue your hunt for the perfect curio on the streets around the Dorotheum, which are lined with many fine antique shops.

Cost and Hours: Free, Mon-Fri 10:00-18:00, Sat 9:00-17:00, closed Sun, classy little café on second floor, between the Graben pedestrian street and Hofburg at Dorotheergasse 17, tel. 01/51560, www.dorotheum.com.

▲**St. Peter's Church (Peterskirche)**—Baroque Vienna is at its best in this gem, tucked away a few steps from the Graben.

Cost and Hours: Free, Mon-Fri 7:00-20:00, Sat-Sun 9:00-21:00; free organ concerts Mon-Fri at 15:00, Sat-Sun at 20:00; just off the Graben between the Plague Monument and Kohlmarkt, tel. 01/533-6433.

Visiting the Church: Admire the rose-and-gold, oval-shaped Baroque interior, topped with a ceiling fresco of Mary kneeling to be crowned by Jesus and the Father, while the dove of the Holy Spirit floats way up in the lantern. Taken together, the church's

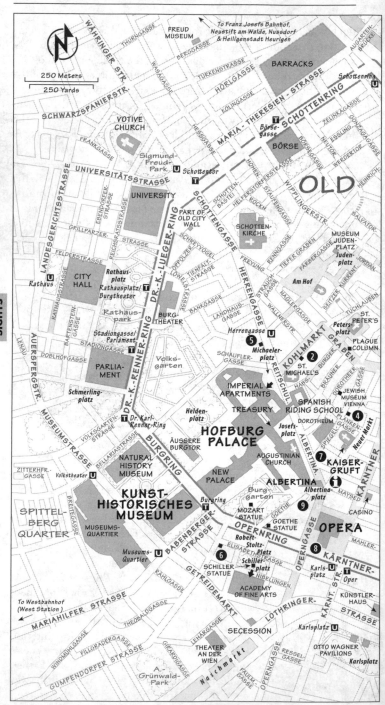

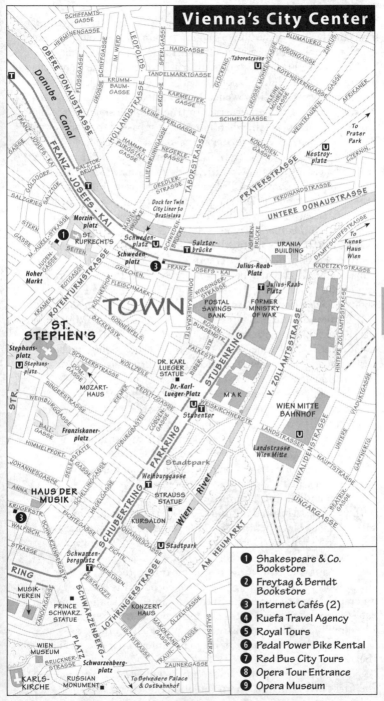

Vienna's City Center

SIGHTS

1. Shakespeare & Co. Bookstore
2. Freytag & Berndt Bookstore
3. Internet Cafés (2)
4. Ruefa Travel Agency
5. Royal Tours
6. Pedal Power Bike Rental
7. Red Bus City Tours
8. Opera Tour Entrance
9. Opera Museum

elements—especially the organ, altar painting, pulpit, and coat of arms (in the base of the dome) of church founder Leopold I—make St. Peter's one of the city's most beautiful and ornate churches.

To the right of the altar, a dramatic golden statue shows the martyrdom of St. John Nepomuk (c. 1340-1393). The Czech saint defied the heretical King Wenceslas, so he was tossed to his death off the Charles Bridge in Prague. In true Baroque style, we see the dramatic peak of his fall, when John has just passed the point of no return. The Virgin Mary floats overhead in a silver cloud.

The present church (from 1733) stands atop earlier churches dating back 1,600 years. On either side of the nave are glass cases containing skeletons of Christian martyrs from Roman times. Above the relic on the left is a painting of the modern saint Jose-maría Escrivá, founder of the conservative Catholic organization Opus Dei, of *Da Vinci Code* notoriety.

▲▲▲**St. Stephen's Cathedral (Stephansdom)**—This massive Gothic church with the skyscraping spire sits at the center of Vienna. Its highlights are the impressive exterior, the view from the top of the south tower, a carved pulpit, and a handful of quirky sights associated with Mozart and the Habsburg rulers.

Cost and Hours: Church foyer—free, daily 6:00-22:00; main nave—€3.50, Mon-Sat 9:00-11:30 & 13:30-16:30, Sun 13:00-16:30, until 17:30 June-Aug; cathedral's other sights, including the south and north towers, catacombs, and treasury, have varying costs and hours.

○ See the St. Stephen's Cathedral Tour chapter.

Mozarthaus Vienna—Exhibits fill the only surviving Mozart residence in Vienna, where he lived from 1784 to 1787, when he had lots of money (and produced some of his most famous works, including *The Marriage of Figaro* and *Don Giovanni*). Opened in 2006 to commemorate Wolfgang's 250th birthday, this museum is easy to get excited about, but it disappoints.

Cost and Hours: €10, includes audioguide, €17 combo-ticket with Haus der Musik, daily 10:00-19:00, last entry 30 minutes before closing, a block behind the cathedral, go through arcade at #5a and walk 50 yards to Domgasse 5, tel. 01/512-1791, www.mozart hausvienna.at.

Visiting the Museum: Begin by riding the elevator to the third floor, then work your way down through his life story, with an emphasis on the years he lived here. Included is a rundown on the Vienna music scene during the Mozart years, a quirky look at his gambling habits and his interest in crudely erotic peep shows, and a four-minute montage of his most famous arias in a miniature theater.

Your visit ends in his actual apartment *(Mozartwohnung)* on the first floor, which has been intentionally left vacant (since they have no record of how it would have been furnished). The management, which admits they know next to nothing about how Wolfie really lived, has made the whole experience maddeningly wishy-washy.

Sadly, visiting this promising museum is like reading a book standing up—rather than turning pages, you walk from room to room. There are almost no real artifacts (except for a few period instruments). Wolfie would have found the audioguide dreadfully dull; the whole place manages to make his notoriously outsized personality seem like a bore. While the museum might be worth the time and money for enthusiasts, both Mozart sights in Salzburg (the Birthplace and the Residence—see Salzburg chapter) are more gratifying. And in Vienna, I much prefer the Haus der Musik (described earlier).

Judenplatz Memorial—The classy square called Judenplatz marks the location of Vienna's 15th-century Jewish community, one of Europe's largest at the time. Once filled with a long-gone synagogue, the square is now dominated by a blocky **memorial** to the 65,000 Viennese Jews killed by the Nazis. The memorial—a library turned inside out—invokes Jewish identity as a "people of the book" and asks viewers to ponder the huge loss of culture, knowledge, and humanity that took place between 1938 and 1945.

Jewish Museum Vienna (Jüdisches Museum Wien)—The museum operates two buildings, one on Judenplatz and another on Dorotheergasse, a block south of the Graben.

Cost and Hours: €10 ticket includes both museums; Judenplatz location, at #8—Sun-Thu 10:00-18:00, Fri 10:00-14:00, closed Sat; Dorotheergasse location, at #11—Sun-Fri 10:00-18:00, closed Sat; tel. 01/535-0431, www.jmw.at.

Visiting the Museums: The **Museum Judenplatz,** while sparse, has displays on medieval Jewish life and a well-done video re-creating the ghetto as it looked five centuries ago. Wander the scant remains of the medieval synagogue below street level—discovered during the construction of the Holocaust memorial. This was the scene of a medieval massacre. Since Christians weren't allowed to lend money, Jews were Europe's moneylenders. As so often happened in Europe, when Viennese Christians fell too deeply into debt, they found a convenient excuse to wipe out the local ghetto—and their debts at the same time. In 1421, the synagogue was destroyed, and Jews who refused a forced conversion were expelled from the city or murdered.

The **Jewish Museum Dorotheergasse** is small and modern.

Vienna at a Glance

▲▲▲**Opera** Dazzling, world-famous opera house. **Hours:** By guided tour only, July-Aug generally daily at the top of each hour 10:00-16:00; Sept-June fewer tours, afternoon only, none on Sun. See page 51.

▲▲▲**St. Stephen's Cathedral** Enormous, historic Gothic cathedral in the center of Vienna. **Hours:** Church—daily 6:00-22:00; main nave—Mon-Sat 9:00-11:30 & 13:30-16:30, Sun 13:00-16:30, until 17:30 June-Aug. See page 56.

▲▲▲**Hofburg Imperial Apartments** Lavish main residence of the Habsburgs. **Hours:** Daily July-Aug 9:00-18:00, Sept-June 9:00-17:30. See page 60.

▲▲▲**Hofburg Treasury** The Habsburgs' collection of jewels, crowns, and other valuables—the best on the Continent. **Hours:** Wed-Mon 9:00-17:30, closed Tue. See page 61.

▲▲▲**Kunsthistorisches Museum** World-class exhibit of the Habsburgs' art collection, including works by Raphael, Titian, Caravaggio, Bosch, and Bruegel. **Hours:** Tue-Sun 10:00-18:00, Thu until 21:00, closed Mon. See page 69.

▲▲▲**Schönbrunn Palace** Spectacular summer residence of the Habsburgs, rivaling the grandeur of Versailles. **Hours:** Daily July-Aug 8:30-18:30, April-June and Sept-Oct 8:30-17:30, Nov-March 8:30-17:00. See page 92.

▲▲**Haus der Musik** Modern museum with interactive exhibits on Vienna's favorite pastime. **Hours:** Daily 10:00-22:00. See page 52.

▲▲**Hofburg New Palace Museums** Uncrowded collection of armor, musical instruments, and ancient Greek statues, in the elegant halls of a Habsburg palace. **Hours:** Wed-Sun 10:00-18:00, closed Mon-Tue. See page 61.

▲▲**Albertina Museum** Habsburg residence with decent apartments and world-class temporary exhibits. **Hours:** Daily 10:00-18:00, Wed until 21:00. See page 65.

▲▲**Kaisergruft** Crypt for the Habsburg royalty. **Hours:** Daily 10:00-18:00. See page 66.

▲▲**Belvedere Palace** Elegant palace of Prince Eugene of Savoy, with a collection of 19th- and 20th-century Austrian art (including

Klimt). **Hours:** Daily 10:00-18:00, Lower Palace only until 21:00 on Wed. See page 79.

▲**St. Peter's Church** Beautiful Baroque church in the old center. **Hours:** Mon-Fri 7:00-20:00, Sat-Sun 9:00-21:00. See page 53.

▲**Spanish Riding School** Prancing white Lipizzaner stallions. **Hours:** Spring (Feb-June) and fall (Sept-Dec) only, performances Sun at 11:00 and either Sat at 11:00 or Fri at 19:00, plus less-impressive training sessions generally Tue-Fri and many Sat 10:00-12:00. See page 62.

▲**St. Michael's Church Crypt** Final resting place of about 100 wealthy 18th-century Viennese. **Hours:** By tour Mon-Sat at 11:00 and 13:30. See page 68.

▲**Natural History Museum** Big building facing the Kunsthistorisches, featuring the ancient *Venus of Willendorf*. **Hours:** Wed-Mon 9:00-18:30, Wed until 21:00, closed Tue. See page 69.

▲**Karlskirche** Baroque church offering the unique (and temporary) chance to ride an elevator up into the dome. **Hours:** Mon-Sat 9:00-18:00, Sun 13:00-18:00. See page 71.

▲**Academy of Fine Arts** Small but exciting collection by 15th- to 18th-century masters. **Hours:** Tue-Sun 10:00-18:00, closed Mon. See page 73.

▲**The Secession** Art Nouveau exterior and Klimt paintings *in situ*. **Hours:** Tue-Sun 10:00-18:00, closed Mon. See page 75.

▲**Naschmarkt** Sprawling, lively outdoor market. **Hours:** Mon-Fri 6:00-18:30, Sat 6:00-17:00, closed Sun, closes earlier in winter. See page 78.

▲**Museum of Military History** Huge collection of artifacts tracing the military history of the Habsburg Empire. **Hours:** Tues-Sun, 10:00-17:00, closed Mon. See page 88.

▲**Kunst Haus Wien Museum** Modern art museum dedicated to zany local artist/environmentalist Hundertwasser. **Hours:** Daily 10:00-19:00. See page 89.

▲**Imperial Furniture Collection** Eclectic collection of Habsburg furniture. **Hours:** Tue-Sun 10:00-18:00, closed Mon. See page 91.

Its exhibits document the Viennese Jewish community before 1938 and in recent decades. Its evocative third floor is a "visible storage" archive with stacks of Judaica and works of art that once ornamented synagogues. The collection is well described in English and by the €2 audioguide.

The Hofburg Palace

The complex, confusing, and imposing Imperial Palace, with 640 years of architecture, demands your attention. This first Habsburg residence grew with the family empire from the 13th century until 1913, when the last "new wing" opened. The winter residence of the Habsburg rulers until 1918, it's still home to the Austrian president's office, 5,000 government workers, and several important museums. For an overview of the palace layout, see page 143.

Planning Your Time: Don't get confused by the Hofburg's myriad courtyards and many museums. Focus on three sights: the Imperial Apartments, Treasury, and the museums at the New Palace (Neue Burg). With more time, consider the Hofburg's many other sights, covering virtually all facets of the imperial lifestyle: Watch the famous Lipizzaner stallions prance at the Spanish Riding School; visit the Augustinian Church, which holds the Habsburgs' hearts—in more ways than one (as the site of royal weddings, and the crypt with the actual Habsburg hearts); peruse the Habsburgs' book collection at the Austrian National Library; stroll through the inviting imperial-turned-public Burggarten park; ogle some of the great Habsburg art collection at the Albertina Museum (or, better yet, the Kunsthistorisches Museum—described later); or see the Vienna Boys' Choir at the Imperial Music Chapel (described on page 207).

Eating at the Hofburg: Down the tunnel to Heldenplatz is a tiny but handy sandwich bar called **Hofburg Stüberl.** It's ideal for a cool, quiet sit and a drink or snack (same €3 sandwich price whether you sit or go, Mon-Fri 7:00-18:00, Sat-Sun 10:00-16:00). The recommended **Soho Kantine,** in the basement of the National Library, is a cheap-but-not-cheery option.

▲▲▲**Hofburg Imperial Apartments (Kaiserapartements)**—These lavish, Versailles-type, "wish-I-were-God" royal rooms are the downtown version of the grander Schönbrunn Palace. If you're rushed and have time for only one palace, make it this one. Palace visits are a one-way romp through three sections: a porcelain and silver collection, a museum dedicated to the enigmatic and troubled Empress Sisi, and the luxurious apartments themselves.

The Imperial Apartments are a mix of Old World luxury and modern 19th-century conveniences. Here, Emperor Franz Josef I lived and worked along with his wife Elisabeth, known as Sisi. The

Sisi Museum traces the development of her legend, analyzing how her fabulous but tragic life created a 19th-century Princess Diana. You'll read bits of her poetic writing, see exact copies of her now-lost jewelry, and learn about her escapes, dieting mania, and chocolate bills.

Cost and Hours: €10.50, includes well-done audioguide, covered by Sisi Ticket (see page 43), daily July-Aug 9:00-18:00, Sept-June 9:00-17:30, last entry one hour before closing; enter from under the rotunda just off Michaelerplatz, through the Michaelertor gate; tel. 01/533-7570, www.hofburg-wien.at.

○ See the Hofburg Imperial Apartments Tour chapter.

▲▲▲**Hofburg Treasury (Weltliche und Geistliche Schatzkammer)**—One of the world's most stunning collections of royal regalia, the Hofburg Treasury shows off sparkling crowns, jewels, gowns, and assorted Habsburg bling in 21 darkened rooms. The treasures, well-explained by an audioguide, include the crown of the Holy Roman Emperor, Charlemagne's saber, a unicorn horn, and more precious gems than you can shake a scepter at.

Cost and Hours: €12, €18 combo-ticket with Kunsthistorisches Museum and New Palace museums, Wed-Mon 9:00-17:30, closed Tue; from the Hofburg's central courtyard pass through the black, red, and gold gate, then follow *Schatzkammer* signs to the Schweizerhof; tel. 01/525-240, www.khm.at.

○ See the Hofburg Treasury Tour chapter.

▲▲**Hofburg New Palace Museums: Armor, Music, and Ancient Greek Statues**—The New Palace (Neue Burg) houses three separate collections—an armory (with a killer collection of medieval weapons), historical musical instruments, and classical statuary from ancient Ephesus. The included audioguide brings the exhibits to life and lets you hear the collection's fascinating old instruments being played. An added bonus is the chance to wander alone among the royal Habsburg halls, stairways, and painted ceilings.

Cost and Hours: €12, ticket covers all three collections and the Kunsthistorisches Museum across the Ring, €18 combo-ticket with the Hofburg Treasury, Wed-Sun 10:00-18:00, closed Mon-Tue, last entry 30 minutes before closing, almost no tourists, tel. 01/525-240, www.khm.at.

Visiting the Museums: The **Arms and Armor Collection** displays weaponry and body armor from all over the vast Habsburg Empire, including exotic Turkish suits of armor. Long after gunpowder had rendered medieval weaponry obsolete, the Habsburgs staunchly maintained the knightly code of chivalry and celebrated family events with tournaments and jousts.

The **Ancient Musical Instruments Collection** shows instruments through the ages, especially the rapid evolution from harpsichord to piano. In the 19th century, Vienna was the world's musical capital. Admire Beethoven's (supposed) clarinet, Leopold Mozart's violin, a keyboard perhaps played by Wolfgang Mozart, and Brahms' piano.

The **Ephesus Museum** has artifacts from that bustling ancient Roman city of 300,000 people (located in modern-day Turkey, near Kuşadası on the southwestern coast). The *Bronze Statue of an Athlete* is a jigsaw of 234 shattered pieces meticulously put back together. Look at the scale model of the city of Ephesus; you can make out the theater, the stadium, and—in the middle of an open plain—the Temple of Artemis that is now in the museum's collection (down the stairs). The *Statue of Artemis* from the temple, representing a fertility goddess, is draped with sexy round objects—which may have symbolized breasts, eggs, or bulls' testicles.

▲**Spanish Riding School (Spanische Hofreitschule)**—This stately 300-year-old Baroque hall at the Hofburg Palace is the home of the renowned Lipizzaner stallions. The magnificent building was an impressive expanse in its day. Built without central pillars, it offers clear views of the prancing horses under lavish chandeliers, with a grand statue of Emperor Charles VI on horseback at the head of the hall.

Lipizzaner stallions were a creation of horse-loving Habsburg Archduke Charles, who wanted to breed the perfect animal. He imported Andalusian horses from his homeland of Spain, then mated them with a local line to produce an extremely intelligent and easily trainable breed. Italian and Arabian bloodlines were later added to tweak various characteristics. Lipizzaner stallions are known for their noble gait and Baroque profile. These regal horses have changed shape with the tenor of the times: They were bred strong and stout during wars, and frilly and slender in more cultured eras. But they're always born black, fade to gray, and turn a distinctive white in adulthood.

Visiting the Riding School: The school offers three options for seeing the horses (tel. 01/533-9031, www.srs.at).

Performances: The Lipizzaner stallions put on great 80-minute shows in spring and fall. Each performance is packed, but with just a few rows of seats and standing-room spots that are right there, there's not a bad view in the house. The formal emcee thoughtfully introduces each number in German and English as horses do their choreographed moves to jaunty recorded Viennese classical music (in 4:4 meter rather than 3:4—I guess the horses don't waltz). The pricey seats book up months in advance, but standing room is usually available the same day (seats-€47-173, standing room-€23-31, prices vary depending on the show; Feb-June and Sept-Dec Sun at 11:00 and either Sat at 11:00 or Fri at 19:00, no shows in Jan or July-Aug; box office opens at 9:00 and is located inside the Hofburg—go through the main Hofburg entryway from Michaelerplatz, then turn left into the first passage).

Training Sessions: Luckily for the masses, training sessions with music take place in the same hall and are open to the public. Don't have high expectations, as the horses often do little more than trot and warm up. Tourists line up early at Josefsplatz (the large courtyard between Michaelerplatz and Albertinaplatz), at the door marked *Spanische Hofreitschule*. But there's no need to show up when the doors open at 10:00, since tickets never really "sell out." Only the horses stay for the full two hours. As people leave, new tickets are printed, so you can just prance in with no wait at all. You can also buy tickets for the training sessions at the box office, described above (€14 at the door, roughly March-June and mid-Aug-Dec Tue-Fri and many Sat 10:00-12:00—but only when the horses are in town; check schedule at www.srs.at).

Stables: Any time of day, you can see the horses in their stalls and view videos of them prancing in the Reitschulgasse corridor. Guided one-hour tours of stalls are given daily (€16; tours at 14:00, 15:00, and 16:00; in English and German, reserve by calling 01/533-9031).

▲Augustinian Church (Augustinerkirche)—This is the Gothic and Neo-Gothic church where the Habsburgs got latched (weddings took place here), then dispatched.

Cost and Hours: Free, open long hours daily, Augustinerstrasse 3—facing Josefsplatz, with its statue of the great reform emperor Josef II and the imperial library next door.

Visiting the Church: In the front, notice the windows above on the right, from which royals witnessed the Mass in private. Don't miss the exquisite, tomb-like Canova memorial (Neoclassical, 1805) to Maria Theresa's favorite daughter, Maria Christina, with its incredibly sad white-marble procession. Left of that is the chapel to Charles I, the last Habsburg emperor (r. 1916-1918).

SIGHTS

SIGHTS

Sunday-Morning Culture in Vienna

Sunday morning in Vienna can provide a cultural thrill for visitors. Three wonderful events take place within 200 yards of each other on most Sunday mornings. The Vienna Boys' Choir sings at the 9:15 Mass in the Hofburg's Imperial Music Chapel (Sept-June, see page 207). Without reservations, you'll stand in the lobby craning your neck to see the church service, though you can easily watch the boys on the video monitor while you listen to them live. At 11:00, choose between two other Viennese high-culture experiences. At the Hofburg's Spanish Riding School, nab a standing-room spot for the performance of the Lipizzaner stallions (spring and fall only, see page 62). Or, easiest of all, sit down in the Augustinian Church for the 11:00 Mass, with a glorious orchestra and choir leading the music (page 63).

Pushed by Habsburg royalists who worship here, Charles is on a dubious road to sainthood. (The Catholic Church requires that you perform a miracle before they'll make you a saint. Charles I's miracle: He healed the varicose veins of a nun.)

The church's 11:00 Sunday Mass is a hit with music lovers—both a Mass and a concert, often with an orchestra accompanying the choir (acoustics are best in front). Pay by contributing to the offering plate and buying a CD afterwards. Programs are posted by the entry. The royal hearts are in the vault (usually open to the public for €2.50 immediately after Mass on Sun morning only).

Austrian National Library (Österreichische Nationalbibliothek)—Next to the Augustinian Church, this Baroque building was once the library of the Habsburgs. Wandering through this impressive temple of learning—with a statue of Charles VI in the center—you find yourself whispering. The setting takes you back to 1730 and gives you the sense that, in imperial times, knowledge of the world was for the elite—and with that knowledge, the elite had power. There are four specialized museums within the library: the State Hall (Baroque heart of the library), the Papyrus Museum (all things papyrus), the Globe Museum (250 terrestrial and celestial globes), and the Esperanto Museum (who knew?). The recommended Soho Kantine in the basement is good for a cheap lunch.

Cost and Hours: Library—free, main reading room open

daily 9:00-21:00; museums—€3-7, open Tue-Sun 10:00-18:00, Thu until 21:00, closed Mon; www.onb.ac.at.

Burggarten (Palace Garden) and Butterfly House—This greenbelt, once the backyard of the Hofburg and now a people's park, welcomes visitors to loi-ter on the grass. On nice days, it's lively with office workers enjoying a break. The statue of Mozart facing the Ringstrasse is popular. The iron-and-glass pavilion (c. 1910 with play-ful Art Nouveau touches) now houses the recommended Café Restaurant Palmenhaus and a small but fluttery butterfly

exhibit (€5.50; April-Oct Mon-Fri 10:00-16:45, Sat-Sun 10:00-18:15; Nov-March daily 10:00-15:45). The butterfly zone is de-lightfully muggy on a brisk off-season day, and trippy any time of year. If you tour it, notice the butterflies hanging out on the trays with rotting slices of banana. They lick the fermented banana juice as it beads, and then just hang out there in a stupor...or fly giddy loop-de-loops.

▲▲Albertina Museum—This building, at the southern tip of the Hofburg complex (near the Opera), was the residence of Maria Theresa's favorite daughter, Maria Christina, who was the only one allowed to marry for love rather than political strategy. Her many sisters were jealous. (Marie-Antoinette had to marry the French king...and lost her head over it.) Maria Christina's husband, Albert of Saxony, was a great collector of original drawings and amassed an enormous assortment of works by Dürer, Rembrandt, Rubens, Schiele, and others. As it's Albert and Christina's gallery, it's clev-erly called the "Albertina."

Cost and Hours: €11, generally meaningless without €4 au-dioguide, daily 10:00-18:00, Wed until 21:00, overlooking Alber-tinaplatz across from the TI and Opera, tel. 01/534-830, www.albertina.at.

Visiting the Museum: To understand both the imperial apart-ments and the wonderful Batliner works, invest in the audioguide, which makes this collection a luxurious lesson in modern art ap-preciation—from Monet to today.

Head first to the Albertina's elegant French-Classicist-style **state rooms** *(Prunkräume)* for a great opportunity to wander freely under the chandeliers of a Habsburg palace, with its pure 19th-century imperial splendor unconstrained by velvet ropes. Because the original artworks are so light-sensitive, you'll see only repro-ductions of some works. Then follow signs for *Meisterwerke der*

SIGHTS

Moderne (*Die Sammlung Batliner*, on the top floor). These modern galleries hold a wonderful rotating exhibit from the museum's **Batliner collection** of modern art (from Impressionism to Abstract Expressionism, with minor works by major artists—Monet, Picasso, Chagall, Matisse), along with temporary exhibits.

Church Crypts near the Hofburg

Two churches near the Hofburg offer starkly different looks at dearly departed Viennese: the Habsburg coffins in the Kaisergruft, and the commoners' graves in St. Michael's Church.

▲▲Kaisergruft (Imperial Crypt)—Visiting the imperial remains is not as easy as you might imagine. These original organ donors left their bodies—about 150 in all—in the unassuming Kaisergruft, their hearts in the Augustinian Church (vaults open to public Sun after mass), and their entrails in the crypt below St. Stephen's Cathedral (described on page 56). Don't tripe.

Cost and Hours: €5, daily 10:00-18:00, last entry at 17:40; crypt is in the Capuchin Church at Tegetthoffstrasse 2 at Neuer Markt; tel. 01/512-6853, www.kaisergruft.at.

Visiting the Kaisergruft: As you enter, buy the €0.50 map with a Habsburg family tree and a chart locating each coffin.

Find the pewter double-coffin under the dome. This tomb of **Maria Theresa** (1717-1780) and her husband, **Franz I** (1708-1765), is worth a close look for its artwork. Maria Theresa outlived her husband by 15 years—which she spent in mourning. Old and fat, she installed a special lift enabling her to get down into the crypt to be with her dear, departed Franz (even though he had been far from faithful). The couple recline—Etruscan-style—atop their fancy lead coffin. At each corner are the crowns of the Habsburgs—the Holy Roman Empire, Hungary, Bohemia, and Jerusalem. Notice the contrast between the Rococo splendor of Maria Theresa's tomb and the simple box holding her more modest son, **Josef II** (at his parents' feet). This understated tomb is in keeping with his enlightened politics.

Nearby, find the appropriately austere military tomb of **Franz Josef** (1830-1916; see sidebar on page 150) in the more brightly lit modern section. Flanking Franz Josef are the tombs of his son, the archduke **Rudolf,** and Empress Elisabeth. Rudolf and his teenage mistress supposedly committed suicide together in 1889 at Mayerling hunting lodge and—since the Church figured he forced her to take her own life and was therefore a murderer—it took considerable legal

Empress Maria Theresa (1717-1780) and Her Son, Emperor Josef II (1741-1790)

Maria Theresa was the only woman to officially rule the Habsburg Empire in that family's 640-year reign. She was a strong and effective empress (r. 1740-1780). People are quick to remember Maria Theresa as the mother of 16 children (10 survived into adulthood). Imagine that the most powerful woman in Europe either was pregnant or had a newborn for most of her reign. Maria Theresa ruled after the Austrian defeat of the Ottomans, when Europe recognized Austria as a great power. (Her rival, the Prussian emperor, said, "When at last the Habsburgs get a great man, it's a woman.") For an abridged Habsburg family tree, see page 438.

The last of the Baroque imperial rulers, and the first of the modern rulers of the Age of Enlightenment, Maria Theresa marked the end of the feudal system and the beginning of the era of the grand state. She was a great social reformer. During her reign, she avoided wars and expanded her empire by skillfully marrying her children into the right families. For instance, after daughter Marie-Antoinette's marriage into the French Bourbon family (to Louis XVI), a country that had been an enemy became an ally. (Unfortunately for Marie-Antoinette, Maria Theresa's timing was off.)

To stay in power during the era of revolution, Maria Theresa had to be in tune with her age. She taxed the Church and the nobility, provided six years of obligatory education to all children, and granted free health care to all in her realm. Maria Theresa also welcomed the boy genius Mozart into her court.

The empress' legacy lived on in her son, Josef II, who ruled as emperor himself for a decade (1780-1790). He was an even more avid reformer, building on his mother's accomplishments. An enlightened monarch, Josef mothballed the too-extravagant Schönbrunn Palace, secularized the monasteries, established religious tolerance within his realm, freed the serfs, made possible the founding of Austria's first general hospital, and promoted relatively enlightened treatment of the mentally ill. Josef was a model of practicality (for example, reusable coffins à la *Amadeus*, and no more than six candles at funerals)—and very unpopular with other royals. But his policies succeeded in preempting the revolutionary anger of the age, enabling Austria to largely avoid the turmoil that shook so much of the rest of Europe.

SIGHTS

hair-splitting to win Rudolf this spot (after examining his brain, it was determined that he was mentally disabled and therefore incapable of knowingly killing himself and his girl). *Kaiserin* Elisabeth (1837-1898), a.k.a. **Sisi,** always gets the "Most Flowers" award (see sidebar on page 145).

In front of those three are the two most recent Habsburg

tombs. **Empress Zita** was laid to rest here in 1989, followed by her son, **Karl Ludwig,** in 2007. The funeral procession for Karl, the fourth son of the last Austrian emperor, was probably the last such Old Regime event in European history. The monarchy died hard in Austria. Today there are about 700 living Habsburg royals, mostly living in exile. When they die, they get buried in their countries of exile.

Body parts and ornate tombs aside, the real legacy of the Habsburgs is the magnificence of this city. Step outside. Pan up. Watch the clouds glide by the ornate gables of Vienna.

▲**St. Michael's Church Crypt (Michaelerkirche)**—St. Michael's Church, which faces the Hofburg on Michaelerplatz, offers a striking contrast to the imperial crypt. Regular tours take visitors underground to see a typical church crypt—filled with the rotting wooden coffins of well-to-do commoners.

Cost and Hours: €5 for 45-minute tour, Mon-Sat at 11:00 and 13:30, mostly in German but with enough English, wait at the sign that advertises the tour at the church entrance and pay the guide directly.

Visiting the Crypt: Climbing below the church, you'll see about a hundred 18th-century coffins and stand on three feet of debris, surrounded by niches filled with stacked lumber from decayed coffins and countless bones. You'll meet a 1769 mummy in lederhosen and a wig, along with a woman who is clutching a cross and has flowers painted on her high heels. You'll learn about death in those times—from how the wealthy didn't want to end up in standard shallow graves, instead paying to be laid to rest below the church, to how, in 1780, the enlightened emperor Josef II ended the practice of cemetery burials in cities but allowed the rich to become the stinking rich in crypts under churches. You'll also discover why many were buried with their chin strapped shut (because when the muscles rot, your jaw falls open and you get that ghostly skeleton look that nobody wants).

St. Michael's Church itself has an interesting history. In 1791, a few days after Mozart's death, his *Requiem* was performed here for the first time. (See the small monument just inside the door on the right.) In the rear of the nave, to the right as you enter, is a small memorial to Austrian victims of the concentration camp at Dachau. The cross was made in 1945 at Dachau by newly freed inmates and is dedicated to Austrian martyrs.

Kunsthistorisches Museum and Nearby

In the 19th century, the Habsburgs planned to create a series of triumphal arches spanning the Ringstrasse to connect their museum buildings and the Hofburg Palace in an awe-inspiring ensemble. The vision died with the empire, but today their great museums face off across Maria Theresienplatz, where a huge monument to perhaps the greatest of the Habsburgs, Maria Theresa, sits above it all (for more on this monument, see page 115 of the Vienna City Walk chapter).

▲▲▲**Kunsthistorisches Museum**—This exciting museum, across the Ring from the Hofburg Palace, showcases the grandeur and opulence of the Habsburgs' collected artwork in a grand building (built in 1888 to display these works). While there's little Viennese art here, you will find world-class European masterpieces galore (including canvases by Raphael, Caravaggio, Velázquez, Dürer, Rubens, Vermeer, Rembrandt, and a particularly exquisite roomful of Bruegels), all well-displayed on one glorious floor, plus a

fine display of Egyptian, classical, and applied arts. Another highlight, filling a wing of the ground floor, is the Habsburg "Chamber of Wonders" *(Kunstkammer)*, showing off the imperial collection of exquisite fine-art objects and exotic curios.

Cost and Hours: €12 (free for kids under 18), ticket also covers New Palace museums across the Ring, €18 combo-ticket also includes the Hofburg Treasury, Tue-Sun 10:00-18:00, Thu until 21:00, closed Mon, on the Ringstrasse at Maria-Theresien-Platz, U-2 or U-3: Volkstheater/Museumsplatz, tel. 01/525-240, www. khm.at.

✪ See the Kunsthistorisches Museum Tour chapter.

▲**Natural History Museum (Naturhistorisches Museum)**— In the twin building facing the Kunsthistorisches Museum, you'll find moon rocks, dinosaur stuff, and the fist-sized *Venus of Willendorf*—at 25,000 years old, the world's oldest sex symbol. Even

though the museum is not glitzy or high-tech, it's a hit with children and scientifically curious grown-ups. Of the museum's 20 million objects, you're sure to find something interesting. The collection's presentation is almost charming in its old school-ness.

Cost and Hours: €10, Wed-Mon 9:00-18:30, Wed until 21:00, closed Tue, on the Ringstrasse at Maria-Theresien-Platz, U-2 or U-3: Volkstheater/Museumsplatz, tel. 01/521-770, www.nhm-wien.ac.at.

Visiting the Museum: For a quick visit, head first to the *Venus of Willendorf*—she's on the mezzanine level, in Room 11 (from the entrance lobby, climb the first 12 steps, then swing around to the left at the first landing to reach the mezzanine level). The four-inch-tall, chubby stone statuette, found in the Danube Valley, is a generic female (no face or feet) resting her hands on her ample breasts. The statue's purpose is unknown, but she may have been a symbol of fertility for our mammoth-hunting ancestors. In Room 10 nearby are big dinosaur skeletons. Also on this floor is an impressive exhibit of rocks, including one of the largest collections of meteorites in the world (mezzanine, Rooms 1-5, to the right of the entrance lobby).

For a more chronological visit, start upstairs on the first floor (in Room 21), and follow hundreds of millions of years of evolution—from single cells to sea creatures, reptiles, birds, mammals, and primates. If hall after hall of stuffed animals gets you down, seek out the "vivarium" downstairs, with live animals. Finish with the hairless primate—man—also downstairs, in Rooms 11-14.

MuseumsQuartier—The vast grounds of the former imperial stables now corral a cutting-edge cultural center for contemporary arts and design, including several impressive museums; the best are the Leopold Museum and the Museum of Modern Art. For many, the MuseumsQuartier is most enjoyable not for its galleries but as a youthful gathering spot in the evening for light, fun meals and cocktails.

Visiting the MuseumsQuartier: Walk into the complex from the Hofburg side, where the main entrance (with visitors center, shop, and ticket office) leads to a big courtyard with cafés, fountains, and ever-changing "installation lounge furniture," all surrounded by the quarter's various museums. At the visitors center, various **combo-tickets** are available for those interested in more than just the Leopold and Modern Art museums. You can also  rent a €4 **audioguide** that explains the complex (behind Kunsthistorisches Museum, U-2 or U-3: Volkstheater/Museumsplatz, tel. 01/525-5881, www.mqw.at).

The **Leopold Museum** features several temporary exhibits of modern Austrian art. The top floor holds the largest collection of works by Egon Schiele (1890-1918; these works make some people uncomfortable—Schiele's nudes are *really* nude) and a few paintings by Gustav Klimt, Kolo Moser, and Oskar Kokoschka. While this is a great collection, you can see even better works from these artists in the Belvedere Palace, described later (€12, €3 audioguide—worth it only for enthusiasts; June-Aug daily 10:00-18:00,

Thu until 21:00; Sept-May Wed-Mon 10:00-18:00, Thu until 21:00, closed Tue; tel. 01/525-700, www.leopoldmuseum.org).

The **Museum of Modern Art** (Museum Moderner Kunst Stiftung Ludwig, a.k.a. "MUMOK") is Austria's leading gallery for international modern and contemporary art. It's the striking lava-paneled building—three stories tall and four stories deep, offering seven floors of far-out art that's hard for most visitors to appreciate. This state-of-the-art museum shows off its huge and rotating collection of works by "classical" modernists (Paul Klee, Pablo Picasso, Pop artists) and more contemporary art (€9, good €3 audioguide, Mon 14:00-19:00, Tue-Sun 10:00-19:00, Thu until 21:00, tel. 01/52500, www.mumok.at).

Rounding out the sprawling MuseumsQuartier are an architecture center, Electronic Avenue, design forum, children's museum, "Quartier 21" (with gallery space and shops), and the **Kunsthalle Wien**—an exhibition center for contemporary art (two halls with different exhibitions, €8.50 for one, €7 for the other, €11.50 for both; daily 10:00-19:00, Thu until 21:00, tel. 01/521-8933, www.kunsthallewien.at).

Karlsplatz and Nearby

These sights cluster around Karlsplatz, just southeast of the Ringstrasse (U-1, U-2, or U-4: Karlsplatz). From the U-Bahn station's passageway, it's a 30-minute walk around the sights on Karlsplatz: the Karlskirche, Secession, and Naschmarkt.

Karlsplatz—This picnic-friendly square, with its Henry Moore sculpture in the pond, is ringed with sights. The massive, domed Karlskirche and its twin spiral columns dominates the square. The small green, white, and gold pavilions that line the street across the square from the church are from the late 19th-century municipal train system *(Stadtbahn)*. One of Europe's first subway systems, this precursor to today's U-Bahn was built with a military purpose in mind: to move troops quickly in time of civil unrest—specifically, out to Schönbrunn Palace. With curvy iron frames, decorative marble slabs, and painted gold trim, these are pioneering works in the *Jugendstil* style, designed by Otto Wagner, who influenced Klimt and the Secessionists. One of the pavilions has a sweet little exhibit on **Otto Wagner** that illustrates the Art Nouveau lifestyle around 1900. It also shows models for his never-built dreams and the grand expansion of Vienna (€4, described in English, April-Oct Tue-Sun 10:00-18:00, closed Mon and Nov-March, near the Ringstrasse, tel. 01/5058-7478-5177, www.wienmuseum.at).

▲**Karlskirche (St. Charles' Church)**—Charles Borromeo, a 16th-century bishop from Milan, inspired his parishioners during plague times. This "votive church" was dedicated to him in 1713, when an epidemic spared Vienna. The church offers the best

Baroque in the city, with a unique combination of columns (show-ing scenes from the life of Charles Borromeo, à la Trajan's Column in Rome), a classic pediment, and an elliptical dome.

Cost and Hours: €6, ticket covers church interior, elevator ride, and skippable one-room museum; audioguide-€2; Mon-Sat 9:00-18:00, Sun 13:00-18:00, last entry 30 minutes before closing; elevator runs until 17:30, last ascent at 17:00. The entry fee may seem steep, but remember that it helps to fund the restora-tion.

Visiting the Church: The dome's color-ful 13,500-square-foot fresco—painted in the 1730s by Johann Michael Rottmayr—shows Signor Borromeo (in red-and-white bishops' robes) gazing up into heaven, spreading his arms wide, and pleading with Christ to spare Vienna from the plague.

The church is especially worthwhile for the chance to ride an **elevator** (installed for renovation work) up into the cupola. The industrial lift takes you to a platform at the base of the 235-foot dome (if you're even slightly afraid of heights, skip this trip). Consider that the church was built and deco-rated with a scaffolding system essentially the same as this one. Once up top, you'll climb stairs to the steamy lantern at the ex-treme top of the church.

At that dizzying height, you're in the clouds with cupids and angels. Many details that appear smooth and beautiful from ground level—such as gold leaf, paintings, and fake marble—look rough and sloppy up close. It's surreal to observe the 3-D figures from an unintended angle—check out Christ's leg, which looks dwarf-sized up close. Give yourself a minute to take it in: Faith, Hope, and Charity triumph and inspire. Borromeo lobbies heaven for relief from the plague. Meanwhile, a Protestant's Lutheran Bible is put to the torch by angels. At the very top, you'll see the tiny dove representing the Holy Ghost, surrounded by a cheering squad of nipple-lipped cupids.

Wien Museum Karlsplatz—This underappreciated city history museum, worth ▲ for those intrigued by Vienna's illustrious past, walks you through the story of Vienna with well-presented arti-facts.

Cost and Hours: €10, free first Sun of the month, open Tue-

Sun 10:00-18:00, closed Mon, Karlsplatz 8, tel. 01/505-8747, www.wienmuseum.at.

Visiting the Museum: Work your way up chronologically. The ground floor exhibits prehistoric and Roman fragments, along with a fine digital reconstruction of the Roman city of Vindobona. Compare that to the model of medieval Vienna (c. 1420), looking much as it does today (but notice the castle at the location of today's Hofburg and the city wall tracing the Ringstrasse). Also dating from this period are some original statues from St. Stephen's Cathedral (c. 1350), with various Habsburgs showing off the slinky hip-hugging fashion of the day. You'll also enjoy a rare close-up look at original stained class (circa 1500) from the cathedral.

The first floor focuses on the Renaissance and Baroque eras, including suits of armor, old city maps, booty from an Ottoman siege, and an 1850 city model showing the town just before the wall was replaced by the Ring. Finally, the second floor picks up after 1815. Look for architect Adolf Loos' minimalist living room (while you might imagine this less-is-more pioneer—described on page 108—lived in an empty cardboard box, his cozy home has more decoration than you might expect). The city model from 1898 shows off the new Ringstrasse. There's also a modest, eclectic art collection, including sentimental Biedermeier paintings and objets d'art, and early 20th-century paintings (including four by Klimt, as well as works by Schiele, Kokoschka, and other Secessionists). Look for the model of a never-built new home for the Academy of Fine Arts—an Art Nouveau design by Otto Wagner.

▲**Academy of Fine Arts (Akademie der Bildenden Künste)**— This museum—in a grand Neo-Renaissance building—features a small but impressive collection of works by Bosch, Botticelli, Guardi, Rubens, Van Dyck, and other great masters. It's housed upstairs in a working art academy, giving it a certain sense of realness.

Cost and Hours: €8 includes permanent collection and special exhibits, audioguide-€2; Tue-Sun 10:00-18:00, closed Mon, 3 blocks from the Opera at Schillerplatz 3, tel. 01/588-162-222, www.akademiegalerie.at.

➋ **Self-Guided Tour:** Head into the academy building and go up two floors to the museum (follow signs for *Gemäldegalerie*). Upon entering, the contemporary art collection is on your right and the painting gallery

(Gemäldegalerie) is on your left. Between them are statues celebrating the body, whose exposed musculature is a reminder that to realistically portray the human form you must first study it.

Walk into the painting gallery, which (confusingly) runs in reverse chronological order. Bear left into the first, smaller room, dedicated to the Academy of Fine Arts itself. At the end of this room is a portrait of the school's founder, Empress Maria Theresa (see photo on previous page). This portrait, from 1750, is considered one of the best. It's by the Swedish painter Martin Meytens, whose self-portrait looks on approvingly from the right. Also nearby you'll see (pictured in the fine gold frame) one of the major donors of the collection, and early professors painting, drawing, and sculpting a nude model.

Go through the door to the right of Maria Theresa, and work your way counterclockwise through the exhibit. The section of 18th-century Italian works includes a Venice series by **Francesco Guardi.** In the long hall are typically Dutch and Flemish 17th-century still lifes and landscapes, as well as one **Rembrandt** (*Portrait of a Young Woman,* c. 1632). A group of paintings by **Peter Paul Rubens** includes his typical fleshy nudes, as well as quick, sketchy cartoons used to create giant canvases that once decorated a Jesuit church in Antwerp, Belgium (it later burned down, leaving only these rough plans). Don't miss his voluptuous *Three Graces.* Nearby, in an oversized frame, Rubens' talented protégé, **Anthony van Dyck,** shows his prowess in a famous self-portrait painted at the age of 15 (pictured).

The Italian and Spanish Renaissance are well-represented by the likes of Titian and Murillo. At the end of the hall is one of the museum's prize pieces, a round **Botticelli** canvas (recently cleaned to show off its vivid colors) depicting the Madonna tenderly embracing the Baby Jesus while angels look on.

At the end of the hall is the collection's grand finale, the captivating, harrowing *Last Judgment* triptych by **Hieronymus Bosch** (c. 1482, with some details added by Lucas Cranach). This is the polar opposite of Bosch's other most famous work, *The Garden of Earthly Delights* (in Madrid's El Prado). Read the altarpiece from left to right, following the pessimistically medieval narrative about

humankind's fall from God's graces: In the left panel, at the bottom, God pulls Eve from Adam's rib in the Garden of Eden. Just above that, we see a female (representing the serpent) hold out the forbidden fruit to tempt Eve. Above that, Adam and Eve are being shooed away by an angel. At the top of this panel, God sits on his cloud, evicting the fallen angels (who turn into insect-like monsters). In the middle panel, Christ holds court over the living and the dead. Notice the jarring contrast between Christ's serene expression and the grotesque scene playing out beneath him. These disturbing images crescendo in the final (right) panel, showing an unspeakably horrific vision of hell that few artists have managed to top in the more than half-millennium since Bosch.

On your way out of the academy, ponder how history might have been different if Adolf Hitler—who applied to study architecture here six years in a row but was rejected each time—had been accepted as a student. Before leaving, peek into the ground floor's Neo-Renaissance central hall: It's textbook Historicism, the Ringstrasse style of the late 1800s.

▲**The Secession**—This little building, strategically located behind the Academy of Fine Arts, was created by the Vienna Secession movement, a group of nonconformist artists led by Gustav Klimt, Otto Wagner, and friends. (For more on the art movement, see the sidebar on page 76.)

The young trees carved into the walls and the building's bushy "golden cabbage" rooftop are symbolic of a renewal cycle. Today, the Secession continues to showcase cutting-edge art, as well as one of Gustav Klimt's most famous works, the *Beethoven Frieze*.

Cost and Hours: €8.50 includes special exhibits, Tue-Sun 10:00-18:00, closed Mon, Friedrichstrasse 12, tel. 01/587-5307, www.secession.at.

◆ **Self-Guided Tour:** The staff hopes you take a look at the temporary exhibits here, designed to illustrate how the spirit of the Secession survives a century after its founding. An association of 350 members chooses a dozen or so special exhibits each year to highlight local art happenings (and they're included in the ticket price whether you like it or not).

Art Nouveau (a.k.a. *Jugendstil* or the Vienna Secession), c. 1896-1914

As Europe approached the dawn of a new *(nouveau)* century, it embraced a new art: Art Nouveau. Though the movement began in Paris and Belgium, each country gave it its own spin. In German-speaking lands (including Austria), Art Nouveau was called *Jugendstil* (meaning "youth style").

Background

Art Nouveau was forward-looking and modern, embracing the new technology of iron and glass. But it was also a reaction against the sheer ugliness of the mass-produced, boxy, rigidly geometrical art of the Industrial Age. Art Nouveau artists returned to nature (which abhors a straight line) and were inspired by the curves of plants. Art Nouveau street lamps twist and bend like flower stems. Ironwork fountains sprout buds that squirt water. Dining rooms are paneled with leafy garlands of carved wood. Advertising posters feature flowery typefaces and beautiful young women rendered in pure, curving lines. Art Nouveau was a total "look" that could be applied to furniture, jewelry, paintings, and the building itself.

Imagine being a cutting-edge artist in late-19th-century Vienna, surrounded not by creativity, but by conformity. Take, for example, the Ringstrasse, with its Neo-Greek, Neo-Gothic, Neo-Baroque architecture. There was nothing daring or new—it was simply redoing what had already been done (Historicism). This drove Vienna's impatient young generation of artists (Gustav Klimt, Otto Wagner, Egon Schiele, Oskar Kokoschka, and company) to escape, or "secede," from all this conventionalism. They established "The Secession" (Vienna's own *Jugendstil* movement) and transcended into a world of pure beauty, hedonism, eroticism, and aesthetics.

The Secession preferred buildings that were simple and geometrically pure, decorated with a few unadulterated Art Nouveau touches. Architects, painters, and poets had no single unifying style, except a commitment to what was new. The Secessionist motto was: "To each age its art, and to art its liberty."

Understandably—but unfortunately—most tourists head directly for the basement, home to the museum's highlight: Gustav Klimt's classic *Beethoven Frieze*. One of the masterpieces of Viennese Art Nouveau, this 105-foot-long fresco was the multimedia centerpiece of a 1902 exhibition honoring Ludwig van Beethoven. Read the free flier, which explains Klimt's still-powerful work, inspired by Beethoven's *Ninth Symphony*. Klimt embellished the work

Secession Sights

The TI has a free brochure *(Architecture from Art Nouveau to the Present)* that lays out Vienna's 20th-century architecture. Here are some of the best *Jugendstil* sights:

The Secession: This clean-lined building was the headquarters of The Secession and where young artists first exhibited their "youth-style" art in 1897. It's nicknamed the "golden cabbage" for its bushy gilded rooftop (actually, those are the laurel leaves of Apollo, the God of Poetry) designed by Klimt.

Belvedere Palace: This museum's collection includes work by Klimt, who gained fame painting slender young women entwined together in florid embraces, exploring the highly charged erotic terrain of his contemporary, Sigmund Freud. Klimt took the decorative element of Art Nouveau to extremes (for more about the palace, see page 79).

The Anchor Clock on Hoher Markt: This mosaic-decorated clock (1911-1917) was actually an advertisement for a life insurance company. Spanning two buildings, it's full of symbolism, stretching from the butterfly on the left to the Grim Reaper on the right. The clock honors 12 great figures from Vienna's history, from Marcus Aurelius to Joseph Haydn. While each gets his own top-of-the-hour moment, all parade by at high noon in a musical act. A plaque on the left names each figure. Notice the novel way to mark the time.

Karlsplatz: Wagner, Vienna's premier *Jugendstil* architect, designed several structures for Vienna's subway system, including these original arched entrances (see page 71).

Austrian Postal Savings Bank: This early-20th-century building is a key example of Wagner's modern work (see page 88).

---

with painted-on gold (his brother, and colleague, was a goldsmith) and by gluing on reflective glass and mother-of-pearl for the ladies' dresses and jewelry. Working clockwise around the room, follow Klimt's story:

Left Wall: Floating female figures drift and weave and search—like we all do—for happiness. Unfortunately, their aspirations are dashed and brought to earth, leaving them kneeling and humble. They plead for help from heroes stronger than themselves—represented by the firm knight in gold, who revives their hopes and helps them carry on.

Center Wall: The women encounter many obstacles in their pursuit of happiness—the three dangerous Gorgons (naked ladies with snake hair), the gorilla-faced monster of fear, and the three seductive women of temptation. These obstacles can leave us bent over with grief (like the woman on the right) while our hopes pass by overhead.

Right Wall: But we can still find happiness through art, thanks to Lady Poetry (with the lyre) and the great hero of the arts: Beethoven. In the original 1902 exhibition, a statue of Beethoven appeared at this crucial turning point in the narrative, where the blank space is today.

Beethoven's presence inspires the yearning souls to carry on, and they finally reach true happiness. At the climax of the frieze, a naked couple embraces in ecstasy as a heavenly choir sings the "Ode to Joy" from the Ninth Symphony: "Joy, you beautiful spark of the gods...under thy gentle wings, all men shall become brothers."

▲**Naschmarkt**—In 1898, the city decided to cover up its Vienna River. The long, wide square they created was filled with a lively produce market that still bustles most days (closed Sun). It's long been known as *the* place to get exotic faraway foods. In fact, locals say, "From here start the Balkans."

Hours and Location: Mon-Fri 6:00-18:30, Sat 6:00-17:00, closed Sun, closes earlier in winter; between Linke Wienzeile and Rechte Wienzeile, U-1, U-2, or U-4: Karlsplatz.

Visiting the Naschmarkt: From near the Opera, the Naschmarkt (roughly, "Munchies Market") stretches along Wienzeile street. This "Belly of Vienna" comes with two parallel lanes—one lined with fun and reasonable eateries, and the other featuring the town's top-end produce and gourmet goodies. This is where top chefs like to get their ingredients. At the gourmet vinegar stall, you can sample the vinegar—like perfume—with a drop on your wrist (see photo). Farther from the center, the Naschmarkt becomes likably seedy and surrounded by sausage stands, Turkish *Döner Kebab* stalls, cafés, and theaters. At the market's far end is a line of buildings with fine Art Nouveau facades. Each Saturday, the Naschmarkt is infested by a huge flea market where, in olden days, locals would come to hire a monkey to pick little critters out of their hair (flea market sets up west of the Kettenbrückengasse U-Bahn station).

Picnickers can pick up their grub in the market and head over to Karlsplatz (described earlier) or the Burggarten. In recent years, some stalls have been taken over by hip new eateries and bars, bringing a youthful vibe and fun new tastes to the market scene.

Mariahilfer Strasse—While there are more stately and elegant streets in the central district, the best opportunity to simply feel the pulse of workaday Viennese life is a little farther out, along Mariahilfer Strasse. An easy plan is to ride the U-3 to the Zieglergasse stop, then stroll and browse your way downhill to the MuseumsQuartier U-Bahn station. If you're interested in how Austria handles its people's appetite for marijuana, search out two interesting stores along the way: Bushplanet Headshop (at Esterhazygasse 32, near the Neubaugasse U-Bahn stop) and Bushplanet Growshop (set back in a courtyard off Mariahilfer Strasse at #115, both locations Mon-Sat 10:00-19:00, closed Sun, www.bushplanet.at).

More Sights Beyond the Ring

The following museums are located outside the Ringstrasse but inside the Gürtel, or outer ring road.

South of the Ring

▲▲**Belvedere Palace (Schloss Belvedere)**—This is the elegant palace of Prince Eugene of Savoy (1663-1736), the still-much-appreciated conqueror of the Ottomans. Eugene, a Frenchman considered too short and too ugly to be in the service of Louis XIV, offered his services to the Habsburgs. While he was indeed short and ugly, he became the greatest military genius of his age, the savior of Austria, and the toast of Viennese society. When you conquer cities,

as Eugene did, you get really rich. With his wealth he built this palace complex. Only Eugene had the cash to compete with the Habsburgs, and from his new palace he looked down on the Hofburg—both literally and figuratively. He lived in the lower palace and entertained in the upper one, which he built to rival Schönbrunn with its similar layout and feel.

Prince Eugene had no heirs, so the state got his property, and Emperor Josef II established the Belvedere as Austria's first great

The Third Man:
Movie, Museum, and Fans

Released in 1949 and voted one of the greatest films of all time by the British Film Institute, The Third Man is still screened several times a week at Vienna's Burg Kino cinema, and has inspired one of the city's most fascinating museums.

With a screenplay by British novelist Graham Greene, the European *noir* thriller *The Third Man* takes place in post-World War II Vienna—a time when the city was divided, like Berlin, among the four victorious Allies. Rife with intrigue, with a dramatic cemetery scene, coffeehouse culture surviving amid the rubble, and Orson Welles being chased through the sewers, this tale of a divided city about to fall under Soviet rule is an enjoyable two-hour experience.

You can catch *The Third Man* in Vienna at the Burg Kino cinema (€8, in English; 3-4 showings weekly—usually Fri evening, Sun afternoon, and Tue early evening; a block from the Opera at Opernring 19, tel. 01/587-8406, www.burgkino.at).

The Third Man Museum (Dritte Mann Museum) is the life's work of Karin Höfler and Gerhard Strassgschwandtner. They have lovingly collected a vast collection of artifacts about the film, postwar Vienna, and the movie's popularity around the world. *Third Man* fans will love the quirky movie artifacts, but even if you're just interested in Vienna in the pre- and postwar years, the museum is worthwhile. Displays cover the 1930s, when Austria was ripe for the *Anschluss* (annexation with Germany); the plight of 1.7 million displaced people in Austria after the war; the challenges of de-Nazification after 1945; and candid interviews with soldiers. As a bonus, the museum takes a fascinating look at moviemaking and marketing around 1950.

Don't be shy about asking for a personal tour from Gerhard or Karin (€7.50, Sat only 14:00-18:00, or by appointment for *Third Man* nuts, private showings for groups, U4: Kettenbrückengasse, a long block south of the Naschmarkt at Pressgasse 25, tel. 01/586-4872, www.3mpc.net).

public art gallery. Today you can tour Eugene's lavish palace, see sweeping views of the gardens and the Vienna skyline, and enjoy world-class art starring Gustav Klimt, French Impressionism, and a grab bag of other 19th- and early-20th-century artists. While Vienna's other art collections show off works by masters from around Europe, this has the city's best collection of homegrown artists.

Cost and Hours: €11 for Upper Belvedere Palace only, €16 for Upper and Lower palaces (generally not worth it), gardens free except for the Orangerie (included in big ticket), audioguide-€4 or €6/2 people, daily 10:00-18:00, Lower Palace only until 21:00 on Wed, grounds open until dusk, no photos allowed inside, entrance at Prinz-Eugen-Strasse 27, tel. 01/7955-7134, www.belvedere.at.

Eating at the Belvedere: There's a charming little café on the ground floor of the Upper Palace, where you can dine with portraits of the emperor and empress looking down upon you; in summer you can sit outdoors in the garden.

Getting There: The palace is a 15-minute walk south of the Ring. To get there from the center, catch tram #D at the Opera (direction: Südbahnhof). Get off at the Schloss Belvedere stop (just below the Upper Palace gate), cross the street, walk uphill one block, go through the gate (on left), and look immediately to the right for the small building with the ticket office.

◑ Self-Guided Tour: The Belvedere Palace is actually two grand buildings—the Upper Palace and Lower Palace—separated by a fine garden. For our purposes, the **Upper Palace** is what matters. Buy your ticket at the office behind the palace, then go around to the front to enter. Once inside, the palace's eclectic collection is tailor-made for browsing. There are two grand floors, set around impressive middle halls.

Ground Floor: The main floor displays a collection of Austrian Baroque (on the left) and medieval art (on the right). The Baroque section includes a fascinating room of grotesquely grimacing heads by **Franz Xaver Messerschmidt** (1736-1783), a quirky 18th-century

Habsburg court sculptor who left the imperial life to follow his own, somewhat deranged muse. After his promising career was cut short by mental illness, Messerschmidt relocated to Bratislava and spent the rest of his days sculpting a series of eerily lifelike "character heads" *(Kopfstücke)*. Their most unusual faces are contorted by extreme emotions. They're not just smiling but guffawing; not just frightened but terrified; not just in pain but in agony; not just angry but furious. Strolling through this collection made my cheeks hurt. Messerschmidt served as his own model for these works, pinching himself to create a pain reaction he could replicate in stone. Stroll around the circle.

• *From the entrance, climb the staircase to the **first floor** and enter the grand red-and-gold, chandeliered...*

Marble Hall: This was Prince Eugene's party room. The ceiling fresco shows Eugene (in the center, wearing blue and pink) about to be crowned with a laurel wreath for his military victories and contributions to Vienna. While it's easy to think of the palace as a museum, see it also as a monument to a military hero. It's strewn with images of war in which the adversaries wear lots of turbans, as some of Austria's enemies were Muslims. Look for

SIGHTS

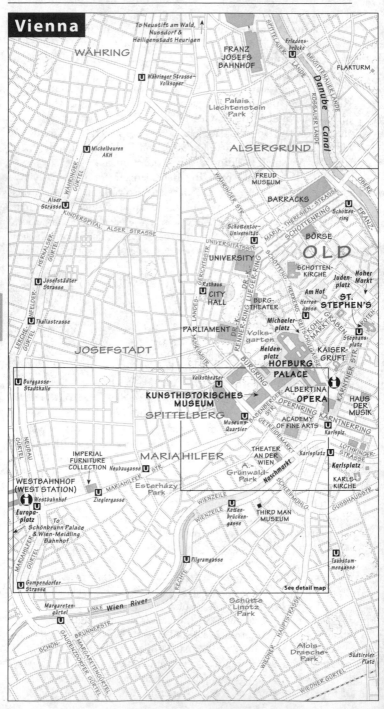

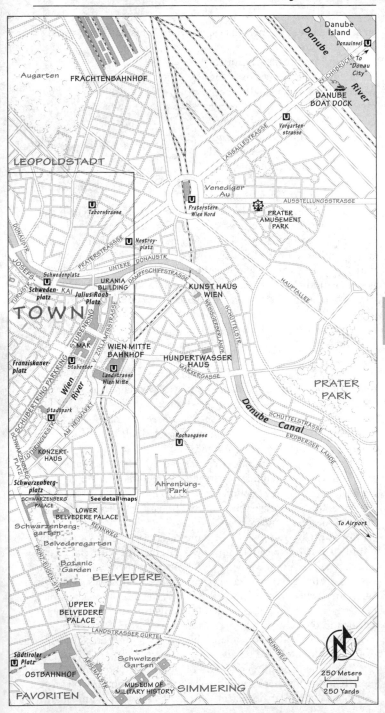

SIGHTS

small copper engravings that show the rooms as they looked in Eugene's day.

Belvedere means "beautiful view," and the **view from the Marble Hall** is especially spectacular. Look over the Baroque gardens, the mysterious sphinxes (which symbolized solving riddles and the finely educated mind of your host, Eugene), the Lower Palace, and the city. Left to right, find the green dome of

St. Peter's Church, the spire of St. Stephen's (where Eugene is buried, see page 123), and much nearer, the black dome of the Silesian Church. St. Stephen's spire is 400 feet tall, and no other tall buildings are allowed inside the Ringstrasse. The hills beyond—covered with vineyards—are where the Viennese love to go to sample new wine. Behind the spire you can see Kahlenberg, from where you can walk down to several recommended *Heurigen* (wine gardens— see page 200). These hills are the beginnings of the Alps, which stretch from here all the way to Marseille, France.

The square you're overlooking was filled with people on May 15, 1955, as city leaders stood on the balcony just in front of you and proclaimed the famous words "Austria is free"—heralding Austrian independence after the decade-long Allied occupation following World War II. The Allied powers—France, Great Britain, the US, and the Soviet Union—signed the treaty reestablishing Austria as a sovereign country right here in the Marble Hall.

• *Facing the garden, to the right is the...*

East Wing: Alongside Renoir's ladies, Monet's landscapes, and Van Gogh's rough brushstrokes are similar works by their lesser-known Austrian counterparts. Around 1900, Austrian artists come to the fore, soaking up Symbolism, Expressionism, and other Modernist trends.

In the two rooms full of sumptuous paintings by **Gustav Klimt,** you can get caught up in his fascination with the beauty and danger he saw in women. To Klimt, all art was erotic art. He painted during the turn of the century, when Vienna was a splendid laboratory of hedonism. For him, Eve was the prototypical woman; her body, not the apple, provided the seduction. Frustrated by the censorship of his age, Klimt refused every form of state support. Even fully clothed, his women have a bewitching eroticism in a world full of pollen and pistils.

The famous painting of *Judith I* (1901) shows no biblical heroine—Klimt paints her as a high-society Vienna woman with an ostentatious dog-collar necklace. With half-closed eyes and slightly

Gustav Klimt
(1862-1918)

Klimt, a noted womanizer, made a career painting the female form as beautiful, seductive, and dangerous. His erotic paint-

ings scandalized official Vienna, and he was a founder of the Secessionist art group, whose members "seceded" from bourgeois constraints. He dedicated his later years to works commissioned by the liberal elite.

Klimt explored multimedia. Besides oil paints, he painted with gold leaf or applied bright objects to the canvas/panel for decorative effect. He often worked in a square-frame format. (Occasionally he and his brother, a gold engraver, made the frames as well.) There's no strong perspective in his paintings; the background and foreground are merged together into a flat decorative pattern. His women are clearly drawn, emerging from the complex design. With their come-hither looks and erotic poses, they capture the overripe beauty and edgy decadence of turn-of-the-century Vienna.

parted lips, she's dismissive...yet mysterious and bewitching. Holding the head of her biblical victim, she's the modern femme fatale.

In what is perhaps Klimt's best-known painting, *The Kiss*, two lovers are wrapped up in the colorful gold-and-jeweled cloak of bliss. Klimt's woman is no longer dominating, but submissive, abandoning herself to her man in a fertile field and a vast universe. In a glow emanating from a radiance of desire, the body she presses against is a self-portrait of the artist himself. Look at it with your partner and search for meaning. Don't miss the later but also hauntingly beautiful Klimt paintings that hang nearby.

Klimt nurtured the next generation of artists, especially **Egon Schiele.** While Klimt's works are mystical and otherworldly, Schiele's tend to be darker and more introspective. One of Schiele's most recognizable works, *The Embrace*, shows a couple engaged in an erotically charged, rippling moment of passion. Striking a darker tone is *The Family*, which depicts a crouching couple. This family portrait from 1918 is especially poignant because his wife died while he was still working on it. (Schiele and his child were soon taken by the influenza epidemic that swept through Europe after World War I.) There's also a room of Schiele portraits, including *Mother with Two Children*.

The Rest of the Upper Palace: The Belvedere's collection goes through the whole range of 19th- and 20th-century art:

Historicism, Romanticism, Impressionism, Realism, tired tourism, Expressionism, Art Nouveau, and early Modernism. In the west wing of the first floor are some **Max Oppenheimer** portraits, famous for the way they almost comically exaggerate the subjects' features to demonstrate their personality traits.

The **second floor** shows off early 19th-century paintings in the Biedermeier style. This was the period (1815-1848) when conservative elements in Central Europe clamped down on Napoleon's revolutionary ideas. The paintings here are realistic portraits, landscapes, and scenes from everyday life and from history, as well as Romanticism. The style is soft-focus, hypersensitive, super-sweet, and sentimentally Romantic—the poor are happy, things are lit impossibly well, and folk life is idealized. (Then came the democratic revolutions of 1848, the invention of the camera, Realism and Impressionism...and all hell broke loose.)

Grounds and Gardens: The delightfully manicured grounds are free and fun to explore. The only area with an entry fee is the **Orangerie garden,** along the west side of the Lower Palace (and accessed through that palace).

Lower Palace: Covered by a separate ticket, this is the home where Prince Eugene actually hung his helmet. Today it contains a small stretch of three of his private apartments (relatively uninteresting compared to the sumptuous Habsburg apartments elsewhere in town). The Lower Palace also houses some generally good special exhibits, as well as the entrance to the Orangerie, privy garden, and stables (until 12:00). If

the special exhibits intrigue you, it's worth buying the combo-ticket to get in here; otherwise, I wouldn't bother to visit.

East of the Ring
Museum of Applied Art (Österreichisches Museum für Angewandte Kunst)—Facing the old town from across the Ring, the MAK, as it's called, is Vienna's answer to London's Victoria and Albert Museum.

Cost and Hours: €8, €10 includes a hefty English guidebook, free Tue after 18:00; open Wed-Sun 10:00-18:00, Tue 10:00-22:00, closed Mon, Stubenring 5, tel. 01/711-360, www.mak.at.

Visiting the Museum: The MAK is more than just another grand building on the Ringstrasse. It was built to provide models of historic design for Ringstrasse architects and is a delightful space in itself (many locals stop in to enjoy a coffee on the plush couches in the main lobby). The collection of furniture, ceramics, textiles,

Restitution of Art Stolen by Nazis

The Austrian government has worked diligently to fairly reimburse victims of the Nazis, whose buildings, businesses, personal belongings, and art were taken after the 1938 *Anschluss* (when Germany annexed Austria).

A fund of more than $200 million was established by the Austrian government and corporations that profited through collaboration with the Nazis. Surviving locals (mostly Jews) who paid a *Reichsfluchtsteuer* ("tax for fleeing the country") were located and given some money. Former slave laborers were also tracked down and given €5,000 each. (Imagine what a difference that could make for an 80-year-old Romanian peasant woman.)

Most significantly for sightseers, great art was restored to its rightful owners. The big news for the Vienna art world was the return of several Gustav Klimt paintings to their former owners, most notably Klimt's portrait of Adele Bloch-Bauer, which for years was part of Vienna's Belvedere Palace collection. The painting was restored to Adele's heirs living in America, who in 2006 sold the portrait for $135 million—one of the highest prices ever paid for a painting. While the Austrian government had an opportunity to buy back the portrait, it found the price too high. Fortunately for art viewers visiting Vienna, the most famous Klimt (*The Kiss*) remains in the Belvedere Palace. And the Adele portrait? It is now in the collection of the Neue Galerie, a New York City museum devoted to early-20th-century German and Austrian art and design.

SIGHTS

metalwork, and more shows off the fancies of local aristocratic society, including fine Biedermeier and *Jugendstil* pieces (among them, Klimt designs for a palace in Brussels).

Each wing is dedicated to a different era. Exhibits, well-described in English (borrow the captions in each room), come with a playful modern flair—notable modern designers were assigned various spaces. An interesting section covers the Vienna Workshop project (Wiener Werkstätte). Inspired by England's Arts and Crafts movement, it was born about 1903 to keep craftspeople (cabinetmakers, bookbinders, metalworkers, and so on) competitive in the Industrial Age. While the workshop lasted a decade, it had more idealism than business savvy. Mass production eventually won out, and its products faded into oblivion.

The unique gift shop also makes for a fun diversion.

Eating at the MAK: The beautiful lobby hosts an inviting **café.** The **Restaurant Österreicher im MAK,** in the same building, is named for Chef Helmut Österreicher, who's renowned for his classic and modern Viennese cuisine. Classy and mod, it's trendy for locals (€9-23 plates, daily 10:00-1:00 in the morning, reserve for evening, tel. 01/714-0121).

Austrian Postal Savings Bank (Die Österreichische Postsparkasse)—Built between 1904 and 1912, Vienna's Postal Savings Bank offers a fascinating look into the society, as well as the architecture, of that age. The main part of the building, which still functions as a bank, is open to the public.

Cost and Hours: Bank foyer—free, museum—€6, Mon-Sat 9:00-17:00, closed Sun, just off the Ringstrasse at Georg-Coch-Platz 2, www.ottowagner.com.

Visiting the Postal Savings Bank: The postal savings system was intended for working-class people, who did not have access to the palatial banks of the 19th century. Secessionist architect Otto Wagner believed "necessity is the master of art," and he declared that "what is impractical can never be beautiful." Everything about his design—so gray, white, and efficient—is practical. It's so clean that the service provided here feels almost sacred. This is a textbook example of form following function, and the form is beautiful (for more on the Secession movement, see page 76).

The product of an age giddy with advancement, the building dignifies the technological and celebrates it as cultural. Study the sleek, yet elegantly modern exterior: Angles high above—made of an exciting new material, aluminum—seem to proclaim the modern age. The facade and its unadorned marble siding panels, secured by aluminum bolts, give the impression that the entire building is a safe-deposit box. The interior is similarly functionalist. The glass roof lets in light; the glass floor helps illuminate the basement. Fixtures, vents, and even the furniture fit right in—all bold, geometrical, and modern. In the back, the fine little **Museum Postsparkasse** is dedicated to Wagner and provides a visual review of his work.

▲ **Museum of Military History (Heeresgeschichtliches Museum)**—While much of the Habsburg Empire was built on strategic marriages rather than the spoils of war, a big part of Habsburg history is military. And this huge place, built about 1860 as an arsenal by Franz Josef, tells the story well with a thoughtful motto (apparently learned from the school of hard knocks): "War belongs to museums."

Cost and Hours: €5 includes good audioguide, daily 9:00-17:00, on Arsenalstrasse near the Ostbahnhof (a.k.a. Südbahnhof), tel. 01/795-610, www.hgm.or.at. It's a 10-minute walk behind the Belevedere Palace.

Visiting the Museum: Located inconveniently outside the Ring, you'll wander the wings of this vast museum nearly all alone. Its two floors hold a rich collection of artifacts and historic treasures from the times of Maria Theresa to Prince Eugene to Franz

Joseph. The particularly interesting 20th-century section includes exhibits devoted to Sarajevo in 1914 (with the car Franz Ferdinand rode in and the uniform he wore when he was assassinated), Chancellor Dolfuss and the pre-Hitler Austrian Fascist party, the *Anschluss*, and World War II.

▲**Kunst Haus Wien Museum and Hundertwasser Haus**—This "make yourself at home" museum and nearby apartment complex are a hit with lovers of modern art, mixing the work and philosophy of local painter/environmentalist Friedensreich Hundertwasser (1928-2000).

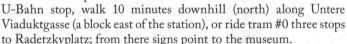

Cost and Hours: €10 for Hundertwasser Museum, €12 combo-ticket includes special exhibitions, half-price on Mon, open daily 10:00-19:00, extremely fragrant and colorful garden café, tel. 01/712-0491, www.kunsthauswien.com.

Getting There: It's located at Untere Weissgerberstrasse 13 (tram #1: Radetzkyplatz or U-3: Landstrasse). Note that the tram stop is much closer than the U-Bahn stop. From the Landstrasse U-Bahn stop, walk 10 minutes downhill (north) along Untere Viaduktgasse (a block east of the station), or ride tram #0 three stops to Radetzkyplatz; from there signs point to the museum.

Visiting the Museum and Apartments: Stand in front of the colorful checkerboard building that houses the **Kunst Haus Wien Museum.** Consider Hundertwasser's style. He was against "window racism": Neighboring houses allow only one kind of window, but $100H_2O$'s windows are each different—and he encouraged residents in the Hundertwasserhaus (a 5-10 minute walk away, described later) to personalize them. He recognized "tree tenants" as well as human tenants. His buildings are spritzed with a forest and topped with dirt and grassy little parks—close to nature and good for the soul.

Floors and sidewalks are irregular—to "stimulate the brain" (although current residents complain it just causes wobbly furniture and sprained ankles). Thus $100H_2O$ waged a one-man fight—during the 1950s and 1960s, when concrete and glass ruled—to save the human soul from the city. (Hundertwasser claimed that "straight lines are godless.")

Inside the museum, start with his interesting biography. His fun paintings are half psychedelic *Jugendstil* and half just kids' stuff. Notice the photographs from his 1950s days as part of Vienna's bohemian scene. Throughout the museum, keep an eye out for the fun philosophical quotes from an artist who believed, "If man is creative, he comes nearer to his creator."

The Kunst Haus Wien provides by far the best look at Hundertwasser, but for an actual lived-in apartment complex by the green master, walk 5-10 minutes to the one-with-nature **Hundertwasserhaus Haus** (at Löwengasse and Kegelgasse). This complex of 50 apartments, subsidized by the government to provide affordable housing, was built in the 1980s as a breath of architectural fresh air in a city of boring, blocky apartment complexes. While not open to visitors, it's worth visiting for its fun and colorful patchwork exterior and the Hundertwasser festival of shops across the street. Don't miss the view from Kegelgasse to see the "tree tenants" and the internal winter garden that residents enjoy.

Hundertwasser detractors—of which there are many—remind visitors that 100H$_2$O was a painter, not an architect. They describe the Hundertwasserhaus as a "1950s house built in the 1980s" that was colorfully painted with no real concern for the environment, communal living, or even practical comfort. Almost all of the original inhabitants got fed up with the novelty and moved out.

North of the Ring

Sigmund Freud Museum—Freud enthusiasts enjoy seeing the humble apartment and workplace of the man who fundamentally changed our understanding of the human psyche. Dr. Sigmund Freud (1856-1939), a graduate of Vienna University, established his practice here in 1891. For the next 47 years, he received troubled patients who hoped to find peace by telling him their dreams, life traumas, and secret urges. It was here that he wrote his influential works, including the landmark *Interpretation of Dreams* (1899).

Cost and Hours: €8 includes audioguide, daily 9:00-18:00, cool shop, half a block downhill from the Schlickgasse tram #D stop, Berggasse 19, tel. 01/319-1596, www.freud-museum.at.

Visiting the Museum: Today, you can walk through his three-room office (but not the apartments next door, where Freud lived with his large family). The rooms are tiny and disappointingly bare. Freud, who was Jewish, fled Vienna when the Nazis came to power. He took most of his furniture with him, including the famous couch that patients reclined on (now in a London museum).

In the entryway, you can see Freud's cane, hat, pocket flask,

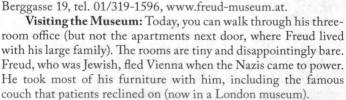

and a few other objects. The waiting room is the most furnished, with original furniture, his books, and his collection of primitive fertility figurines. The consulting room and study are lined with old photos and documents that trace Freud's fascinating (if Vienna-centric)

life: a happy childhood; medical school in the then-pioneering field of psychology; research into the effects of cocaine; a happy marriage, large family, and wholesome middle-class lifestyle; use of hypnosis as therapy; years of self-analysis and first patients in analysis; publication of controversial works on dreams and sexuality; association with other budding psychologists such as the Swiss Carl Jung; and, finally, his hard-earned recognition and worldwide fame.

Other rooms contain plenty of papers, photos, videos, and temporary exhibits about Freud and cutting-edge psychotherapy. All in all, the museum is quite old-fashioned—tediously described in a three-ring binder loaned to visitors, which complements the more general audioguide.

West of the Ring, on Mariahilfer Strasse

▲**Imperial Furniture Collection (Hofmobiliendepot)**—Bizarre, sensuous, eccentric, or precious, this collection (on four fascinating floors) is your peek at the Habsburgs' furniture—from the empress's wheelchair ("to increase her fertility she was put on a rich diet and became corpulent") to the emperor's spittoon—all thoughtfully described in English. Evocative paintings help bring the furniture to life. The Habsburgs had many palaces, but only the Hofburg was permanently furnished. The rest were done on the fly—set up and taken down by a gang of royal roadies called the "Depot of Court Movables" (Hofmobiliendepot). When the monarchy was dissolved in 1918, the state of Austria took possession of the Hofmobiliendepot's inventory—165,000 items. Now this royal storehouse is open to the public in a fine and sprawling museum. Don't go here for the *Jugendstil* furnishings. The older Baroque, Rococo, and Biedermeier pieces are the most impressive and tied most intimately to the royals. Combine a visit to this museum with a stroll down the lively shopping boulevard, Mariahilfer Strasse.

Cost and Hours: €8, covered by Sisi Ticket (see page 43), Tue-Sun 10:00-18:00, closed Mon, Mariahilfer Strasse 88, main entrance around the corner at Andreasgasse 7, U-3: Zieglergasse, tel. 01/5243-3570, www.hofmobiliendepot.at.

▲▲▲Schönbrunn Palace (Schloss Schönbrunn)

Among Europe's palaces, only Schönbrunn rivals Versailles. This former summer residence of the Habsburgs is big, with 1,441 rooms. But don't worry—only 40 rooms are shown to the public. Of the plethora of sights at the palace, the highlight is a tour of the Royal Apartments—the chandeliered rooms where the Habsburg nobles lived. You can also stroll the gardens, tour the coach museum, and visit a handful of lesser sights nearby.

Getting There: While on the outskirts of Vienna, Schönbrunn is an easy 10-minute subway ride from downtown. Take U-4 to Schönbrunn and follow signs for *Schloss Schönbrunn*. Exit bearing right, then cross the busy road and continue to the right along the yellow building to the main entry courtyard, which will be on your left. Tickets are sold at the visitors center, just left of the main entrance to the palace grounds (well before you get to the actual palace).

▲▲▲Royal Apartments—Although the palace's exterior is Baroque, the interior was finished under Maria Theresa in let-them-eat-cake Rococo. As with the similar apartments at the Hofburg (the Habsburgs' winter home), these apartments give you a sense of the quirky, larger-than-life personalities who lived here—especially Franz Josef (r. 1848-1916) and Sisi. Your tour of the apartments, accompanied by an audioguide, covers one small section of the palace's grand interior on a clearly signed route. You have two tour options: Imperial (shorter and cheaper) or Grand (longer and more expensive). Both follow the same route at first, but after a certain point the Imperial group is politely excused while the Grand gang continues on to see a few more rooms.

Cost: The 22-room **Imperial Tour** is €10.50 (35 minutes, includes audioguide, Grand Palace rooms plus apartments of Franz Josef and Sisi—mostly 19th-century and therefore least interesting). The much better 40-room **Grand Tour** costs €13.50 (50 minutes, includes audioguide, everything on Imperial Tour plus Maria Theresa's apartments—18th-century Rococo). If venturing beyond the apartments, consider one of two combo-tickets: The **Classic Pass** includes the Grand Tour, as well as other sights on the grounds—the Gloriette viewing terrace, maze, and privy garden (€16.50, available April-Oct only). The **Classic Pass Plus** includes all of the above, plus the court bakery (complete with *Apfelstrudel* demo and tasting; €19.50, available April-Oct only). However, none of the extra sights covered by either pass is really worth the

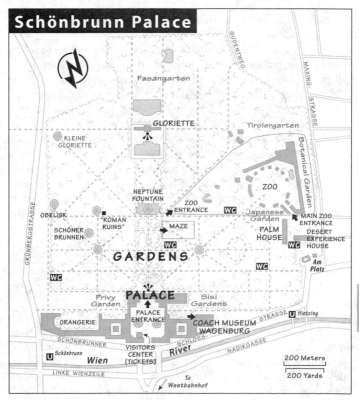

cost of entry, so I'd skip them and just do the Grand Tour, followed by a mosey through the impressive grounds (which are free).

Hours: Daily July-Aug 8:30-18:30, April-June and Sept-Oct 8:30-17:30, Nov-March 8:30-17:00.

Information: Tel. 01/8111-3239, www.schoenbrunn.at.

Reservations: To avoid getting stuck in the ticket-buying line, book advance tickets online at the palace website. You'll reserve an entry time and date, then print your tickets before you come (ask at your hotel if you need access to a printer). Tickets can also be reserved by phone and picked up at the visitors center (tel. 01/8111-3239).

Crowd-Beating Tips: Schönbrunn suffers from crowds. It can be a jam-packed sauna in the summer. It's busiest from 9:30 to 11:30, especially on weekends and in July and August; it's least crowded after 14:00, when there are no groups. To avoid the long delays in summer, make a reservation online or by phone (see above). If you show up in peak season without an advance ticket, you deserve the frustration. You'll have to wait in line at the ticket desk, and then wait until the listed time to enter—which could be the end of the day. If you have time to kill, spend it exploring the gardens or Coach Museum.

Visiting the Royal Apartments: Moving from room to room, you're immersed in imperial splendor. The chandeliers are made either of Bohemian crystal or hand-carved wood with gold-leaf gilding. Thick walls hid the servants as they ran around stoking the ceramic stoves from the back and attending to other behind-the-scenes matters.

Franz Josef's study includes the desk where he conducted state business and ate lunch (the workaholic FJ always took a "working lunch"). Franz Josef's bedroom features his praying chair, a spartan little toilet, and the bed he actually died in. Sisi slept in a separate bedroom—while Franz Josef adored her, the feeling was not necessarily mutual. The Mirrored Room was where six-year-old Wolfie Mozart performed his first concert. The opulent, chandeliered Great Gallery—with its mirrored walls and dramatically frescoed ceilings—was the site of a famous 1961 summit between John F. Kennedy and Nikita Khrushchev. The "Chinese Cabinets," with porcelain decorations and inlaid wood floors, exemplify how Asian style was in vogue back then.

As the Imperial Tour ends, the Grand Tour continues on for several more rooms. The Lacquer Room contains a memorial from Maria Theresa to her late husband (like an Austrian Queen Vic, she mourned her departed spouse for the last several decades of her life). The Napoleon Room is where the diminutive dictator resided both times he took Vienna (in 1805 and 1809). The so-called "Millions Room" features exceedingly rare, priceless rosewood paneling inlaid with miniatures.

Fortunately, the palace managed to escape destruction when WWII bombs rained on the city and the palace grounds. The palace itself took only one direct hit. Thankfully, that bomb, which crashed through three floors—including the sumptuous central ballroom—was a dud. Most of the public rooms are decorated in Neo-Baroque, as they were under Franz Josef and Sisi. The rest of the palace was converted to simple apartments and rented to the families of 260 civil servants, who enjoy rent control and governmental protections so they can't be evicted.

▲▲**Palace Gardens**—Unlike the gardens of Versailles, meant to shut out the real world, Schönbrunn's park was opened to the public in 1779 while the monarchy was in full swing. It was part of Maria Theresa's reform policy, making the garden a celebration of the evolution of civilization from autocracy into real democracy.

Today it's a delightful, sprawling place to wander—especially on a sunny day. You can spend hours here, enjoying the views and the people-watching. And most of the park is free, as it has been for

more than two centuries (open daily sunrise to dusk, entrance on either side of the palace).

Getting Around the Gardens: A **tourist train** makes the rounds all day, connecting Schönbrunn's many attractions (€6, 2/hour in peak season, none Nov-mid-March, one-hour circuit). Unfortunately, there's no bike rental nearby.

Visiting the Gardens: The large, manicured grounds are laid out on angled, tree-lined axes that gradually incline, offering dramatic views back to the palace. The small side gardens flanking the palace are the most elaborate. As you face the back of the palace, to the right is the **privy garden** (*Kronprinzengarten*, €2.50); to the left are the free **Sisi Gardens.** Better yet, just explore, using a map (such as the one in this book, or pick one up at the palace) to locate several whimsical **fountains,** such as the faux "Roman ruins," the obelisk, and the Neptune Fountain (straight back from the palace). Next to the Neptune Fountain is a kid-friendly **maze** (*Irrgarten*) and playground area (€3.50).

If the weather is good, huff up the zigzag path above the Neptune Fountain to the **Gloriette,** a purely decorative monument celebrating an obscure Austrian military victory. You can pay for a pricey drink in the café, shell out €2.50 to hike up to the viewing terrace, or skip the whole thing, as views are about as good from the lawn in front (included in Schönbrunn passes described earlier, daily April-Sept 9:00-18:00, July-Aug until 19:00, Oct 9:00-17:00, closed Nov-March).

To the left as you face the back of the palace is a large zoo complex and several affiliated sights. Europe's oldest **zoo** (*Tiergarten*)

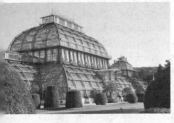

was built by Maria Theresa's husband for the entertainment and education of the court in 1752 (€15, €20 combo-ticket with palm and desert houses, daily April-Sept 9:00-18:30, closes earlier off-season, tel. 01/877-9294, www.zoovienna.at). Nearby are two skippable sights. The **palm house** (*Palmenhaus*), with its stately green ribcage on the outside, is disappointing inside (€4, €6 combo-ticket with desert house, €20 combo-ticket also includes zoo, daily May-Sept 9:30-18:00, Oct-April 9:30-17:00, last entry 30 minutes before closing). Likewise, the **Desert Experience House** *(Wüstenhaus),* featuring desert flora and fauna in an arid climate, is nothing special (€4, same combo-tickets and hours as palm house).

▲**Coach Museum Wagenburg**—The Schönbrunn coach museum is a 19th-century traffic jam of 50 impressive royal carriages and sleighs. Highlights include silly sedan chairs, the death-black hearse carriage (used for Franz Josef in 1916, and most recently for Empress Zita in 1989), and an extravagantly gilded imperial carriage pulled by eight Cinderella horses. This was rarely used other than for the coronation of Holy Roman Emperors, when it was disassembled and taken to Frankfurt for the big event. You'll also get a look at one of Sisi's impossibly narrow-waisted gowns, and (upstairs) Sisi's "Riding Chapel," with portraits of her 25 favorite horses.

Cost and Hours: €6, audioguide-€2, daily April-Oct 9:00-18:00, Nov-March 10:00-16:00, 200 yards from palace, walk through right arch as you face palace, tel. 01/525-24-3470.

Activities in Vienna

These activities allow you to take it easy and enjoy the Viennese good life.

▲▲**Cafés**—A break for *Kaffee und Kuchen* (coffee and cake) in one of the city's historical cafés is a must on any Viennese visit (see my recommended cafés in the Eating in Vienna chapter).

▲*Heuriger* **Wine Gardens**—Locals and tourists alike enjoy lingering in these rustic wine gardens in rural neighborhoods, easily accessible by public transportation from downtown Vienna (see listings in the Eating in Vienna chapter).

▲**Stadtpark (City Park)**—Vienna's major park, along the eastern edge of the Ring, is a waltzing world of gardens, memorials to local musicians, ponds, peacocks, music in bandstands, and Viennese escaping the city. Notice the *Jugendstil* entrance at the Stadtpark U-Bahn station. The faux-Renaissance Kursalon hall, where Johann Strauss was the violin-toting master of waltzing ceremonies, hosts daily touristy concerts in three-quarter time (for details, see page 210). Find the famous golden statue of Strauss with his violin (next to the Kursalon, straight in from the Weihburggasse tram stop).

▲**Prater Park (Wiener Prater)**—Since the 1780s, when the reformist Emperor Josef II gave his hunting grounds to the people of Vienna as a public park, this place has been Vienna's playground. For the tourist, the "Prater" is the sugary-smelling, tired, and sprawling amusement park (Wurstelprater). For locals, the "Prater" is the vast, adjacent green park with its three-mile-long, tree-lined main boulevard (Hauptallee). The park still tempts visitors with

Shopping in Vienna

Traditional Austrian Clothing

If you're interested in picking up a classy felt suit or dirndl, you'll find shops all over town. Most central is the fancy **Loden-Plankl** shop, with a vast world of traditional Austrian formal-wear upstairs (across from the Hofburg, at Michaelerplatz 6). The **Tostmann Trachten** shop is the ultimate for serious shopping. Frau Tostmann powered the resurgence of this style. Her place is like a shrine to traditional Austrian and folk clothing (called Tracht)—handmade and very expensive (Schottengasse 3A, 3-minute walk from Am Hof, tel. 01/533-5331).

Artsy Gifts

Vienna's museum shops are some of Europe's best. The design store in the Museum of Applied Art (MAK) is a delight; the shops of the Albertina Museum, Kunsthistorisches Museum, Belvedere Palace, Kunst Haus Wien, Sigmund Freud Museum, and the MuseumsQuartier museums are also particularly good.

Window Shopping

The narrow streets north and west of the cathedral are sprinkled with old-fashioned shops that seem to belong to another era, carrying a curiously narrow range of items for sale (old clocks, men's ties, gloves, and so on). Dedicated window-shoppers will enjoy the Dorotheum auction house (see page 53).

SIGHTS

its huge 220-foot-tall, famous, and lazy Ferris wheel *(Riesenrad)*, roller coaster, bumper cars, Lilliputian railroad, and endless eateries. Especially if you're traveling with kids, this is a fun, goofy place to share the evening with thousands of Viennese.

Cost and Hours: Rides run May-Sept 9:00-24:00—but quiet after 22:00, March-April and Oct 10:00-22:00, Nov-Dec 10:00-20:00, grounds always open, U-1: Praterstern, www.prater.at. For a local-style family dinner, eat at Schweizerhaus (good food, great Czech Budvar—the original "Budweiser"—beer, classic conviviality).

Danube Island (Donauinsel)—In the 1970s, as part of a flood protection program, the city dug a channel (the so-called Neue Donau—New Danube) parallel to the Danube River. With the dredged-out dirt, the engineers formed 12-mile-long Danube Island. Originally just an industrial site, it's evolved into a much-loved idyllic escape from the city (easy U-Bahn access on U-1: Donauinsel).

The skinny island provides a natural wonderland. All along the pedestrianized, grassy park, you'll find locals—especially immigrants and those who can't afford their own cabin or fancy vacation—at play. The swimming comes tough, though, with rocky entries rather than sand. The best activity here is a bike ride. If you venture far from the crowds, you're likely to encounter nudists on inline skates.

Biking Danube Island: For a simple, breezy joyride, bike up and down the traffic-free and people-filled island. Weather permitting, you can rent a bike from the shop at the **Reichsbrücke,** the bridge spanning the island (€6/hour, €25/day, March-Oct daily 9:00-21:00, closed off-season, 70 yards from U-1: Donauinsel, tel. 01/263-5242, www.fahrradverleih.at).

Donau City (Danaustadt)—This modern part of town, just beyond Danube Island, is the skyscraping "Manhattan" of Austria. It was laid out as a potential Vienna-Budapest expo site in the 1990s. But Austrians voted down the fair idea, and eventually the real estate became today's modern planned city: It's quiet and traffic-free, with inviting plazas and a small church dwarfed by towering places of business. The high-rise DC Towers are the tallest office buildings in Austria. With business, residential, and shopping zones surrounded by inviting parkland, this corner of the city is likely to grow as Vienna expands. Its centerpiece is the futuristic UNO City, one of four United Nations headquarters worldwide. While it lacks the Old World character, charm, and elegance of the rest of Vienna, Donau City may interest travelers who are into contemporary glass-and-steel architecture (U-1: Kaisermühlen VIC).

Biking to Donau City and Beyond: Sightseers on bikes can cross the Danube to Donau City. From the Opera, it's pretty much a straight pedal around the center via the Ringstrasse, past Prater Park, and across the river. The way is easy enough to find with the help of the basic tourist map from the TI. (Recommended local guide Wolfgang Höfler leads tours along this route, which he shared with me; see page 49).

The route will take you over four stretches of water: the Danube Canal, the actual Danube, the New Danube, and the Old Danube. Along the way, you'll gain a better understanding of the massive engineering done over the years to contain and tame the river.

As you leave the city center, you'll first pedal over the Danube Canal, an arm of the river that brings river traffic into the city; then you hit the main part of the river and the man-made Danube Island (itself a part of the city's flood barriers). From the Reichsbrücke bridge over the island, survey the river's traffic. The cruise industry is booming, and Vienna's river cruise port is hosting more boats than ever. Many of them sail from here all the way to Romania and the Black Sea coast. You may also be inspired by the entire Austrian navy: Look for the two tiny camouflaged gunboats moored in the shade of the bridge.

In the distance, across the river, are the skyscrapers of Donau City. To reach it, continue across the bridge over Danube Island and cross the New Danube. From Donau City, the bike path leads across the Old Danube (Alte Donau), an old arm of the river but now a lake, which hosts a frolicking park with all the water fun a hot-and-tired city could hope for, including lakeside cafés and boat rentals. From here you can simply retrace your route, or you can make a big circle by following the delightful bike path southeast along the Old Danube to the next bridge (Praterbrücke). This leads to the vast Prater Park, where you'll follow the breezy main boulevard (Hauptallee) back to the big Ferris wheel and ultimately to downtown.

A Walk in the Vienna Woods (Wienerwald)—For a quick side-trip into the woods and out of the city, catch the U-4 subway line to Heiligenstadt, then bus #38A to Kahlenberg, where you'll enjoy great views and a café overlooking the city. From there, it's a peaceful 45-minute downhill hike to the *Heurigen* of Nussdorf or to enjoy some new wine (see page 200). Your free TI-produced city map can be helpful...just go downhill.

For the very best views, stay on bus #38A to Leopoldsberg (if your #38A bus goes only to Kahlenberg—see the destination marked on the front of the bus or ask the driver—hop off in Kahlenberg and wait for the next bus to Leopoldsberg, 2/hour). There you'll find a lovely Baroque church, a breezy *Weinstube* (wine pub), and shady tables with expansive panoramas of the city and the Danube. While it seems like a long way to go for a big view, buses are cheap (or free with a transit pass) and run frequently (2/hour to Leopoldsberg, last bus around 17:30; buses that end at Kahlenberg run 4-8/hour, last bus around midnight). For an overview of this area, see the map on page 37.

Naschmarkt—Vienna's busy produce market is a great place for people-watching (see page 78).

VIENNA CITY WALK

Vienna, one of Europe's grandest cities of the past, is also a vibrant city of today. Here in Vienna's urban core, where old meets new, you'll get the lay of the land as you stroll between the city's three most important landmarks: the Opera, St. Stephen's Cathedral, and the Hofburg Palace. Along the way, we'll drop into some of the smaller sights that help make this city so intriguing (many of which are covered in greater detail elsewhere in the book): the poignant monuments that subtly cobble together this proud nation's often-illustrious, sometimes-tragic history; the genteel stores, cafés, and pastry shops where the Viennese continually perfect their knack for fine living; the unassuming churches where the remains of the Habsburg monarchs are entombed; and the defiantly stern architectural styles that emerged to counteract all that frilly Habsburg excess. Use this walk as a springboard for exploring this fine city—and, along the way, get an overview of Vienna's past and present.

Orientation

Length of This Walk: Allow one hour and more time if you plan to stop at any of the major sights along the way.

Opera House: A visit is possible only with a 45-minute guided tour—€6.50, July-Aug generally daily at the top of each hour 10:00-16:00; Sept-June fewer tours, afternoons only, and none on Sun; tel. 01/514-442-606. For information on attending a performance, see page 208.

Café Sacher: Daily 8:00-24:00, Philharmoniker Strasse 4, tel. 01/51456.

Albertina Museum: €11, audioguide-€4, daily 10:00-18:00, Wed until 21:00, overlooking Albertinaplatz across from the TI and the Opera, tel. 01/534-830, www.albertina.at.

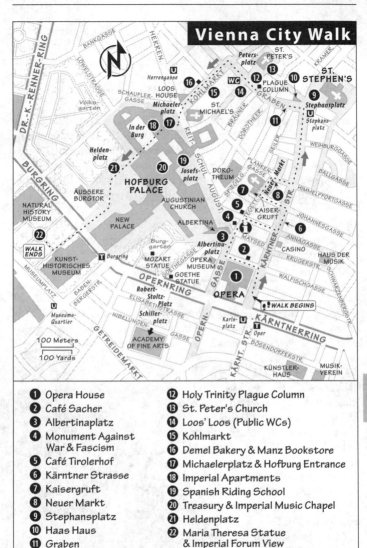

1. Opera House
2. Café Sacher
3. Albertinaplatz
4. Monument Against War & Fascism
5. Café Tirolerhof
6. Kärntner Strasse
7. Kaisergruft
8. Neuer Markt
9. Stephansplatz
10. Haas Haus
11. Graben
12. Holy Trinity Plague Column
13. St. Peter's Church
14. Loos' Loos (Public WCs)
15. Kohlmarkt
16. Demel Bakery & Manz Bookstore
17. Michaelerplatz & Hofburg Entrance
18. Imperial Apartments
19. Spanish Riding School
20. Treasury & Imperial Music Chapel
21. Heldenplatz
22. Maria Theresa Statue & Imperial Forum View

VIENNA CITY WALK

Kaisergruft: €5, daily 10:00-18:00, last entry at 17:40, Tegetthoff-strasse 2, off Neuer Markt, tel. 01/512-6853, www.kaisergruft.at.

St. Stephen's Cathedral: Church foyer—free, daily 6:00-22:00; main nave—€3.50, Mon-Sat 9:00-11:30 & 13:30-16:30, Sun 13:30-16:30, until 17:30 June-Aug. The cathedral's other sights, including the south and north towers, catacombs, and treasury, have varying costs and hours—for details, see page 117.

St. Peter's Church: Free; Mon-Fri 7:00-20:00, Sat-Sun 9:00-21:00; free organ concerts Mon-Fri at 15:00, Sat-Sun at 20:00; just off the Graben between the Plague Monument and Kohlmarkt, tel. 01/533-6433.

St. Michael's Church Crypt: €5 for 45-minute tour, Mon-Sat at 11:00 and 13:30.

Hofburg Imperial Apartments: €10.50, covered by €23.50 Sisi Ticket (see page 43); daily July-Aug 9:00-18:00, Sept-June 9:00-17:30, last entry one hour before closing; tel. 01/533-7570, www.hofburg-wien.at.

Hofburg Treasury: €12, €18 combo-ticket with Kunsthistorisches Museum, Wed-Mon 9:00-17:30, closed Tue, tel. 01/525-240, www.khm.at.

Starring: Vienna's "big three" (Opera house, cathedral, palace), plus an array of sights, squares, and shops tucked between them.

The Walk Begins

• *Begin at the square outside Vienna's landmark Opera house. (The entrance faces the Ringstrasse; we're starting at the busy pedestrian square that's to the right of the entrance as you're facing it.)*

❶ Opera House

If Vienna is the world capital of classical music, this building is its throne room, one of the planet's premier houses of music. It's typical of Vienna's 19th-century buildings in that it features a revival style—Neo-Renaissance—with arched windows, half-columns, and the sloping, copper mansard roof typical of French Renaissance *châteaux* (see sidebar on page 139).

Since the structure was built in 1869, almost all of the opera world's luminaries have passed through here. Its former musical directors include Gustav Mahler, Herbert von Karajan, and Richard Strauss. Luciano Pavarotti, Maria Callas, Placido Domingo, and many other greats have sung from its stage.

In the pavement along the side of the Opera (and all along Kärntner Strasse, the bustling shopping street we'll visit shortly), you'll find star plaques forming a Hollywood-style walk of fame. These represent the stars of classical music—famous composers, singers, musicians, and conductors.

Looking up at the Opera, notice the giant outdoor screen onto which some live performances are projected (as noted in the posted schedules).

If you're a fan, take a guided tour of the Opera (see page 51). If you're not, you still might consider springing for an evening performance (standing-room tickets are surprisingly cheap; see page 208). Regular opera tickets are sold at various points near here: The closest ticket office is the small one just below the screen, while the main one is on the other side of the building, across the street on Operngasse. For information about other entertainment options during your visit, check in at the Wien Ticket kiosk in the booth on this square.

The Opera house marks a busy intersection in Vienna, where Kärntner Strasse meets the Ring. The Karlsplatz U-Bahn station in front of the Opera is an underground shopping mall with fast food, newsstands, and lots of pickpockets.

• *Walk behind the Opera and across the street toward the dark-red awning to find the famous...*

❷ Café Sacher

This is the home of the world's classiest chocolate cake, the Sacher-Torte: two layers of cake separated by apricot jam and covered in dark-chocolate icing, usually served with whipped cream. It was

invented in a fit of improvisation in 1832 by Franz Sacher, dessert chef to Prince Metternich (the mastermind diplomat who redrew the map of post-Napoleonic Europe). The cake became world famous when the inventor's son served it next door at his hotel (you may have noticed the fancy doormen). Many locals complain that the cakes here have gone downhill, and many tourists are surprised by how dry they are—you really need that dollop of *Schlagobers*. Still, coffee and a slice of cake here can be €8 well invested for the historic ambience alone. While the café itself is grotesquely touristy, the adjacent Sacher Stube has ambience and natives to spare (same prices). For maximum elegance, sit inside.

• *Continue past Hotel Sacher. At the end of the street is a small, triangular, cobbled square adorned with modern sculptures.*

❸ Albertinaplatz

As you enter the square, to the right you'll find the **TI** (see page 42).

On your left, the tan-and-white Neoclassical building with the statue alcoves marks the tip of the Hofburg Palace—the sprawling complex of buildings that was long the seat of Habsburg power (we'll end this walk at the palace's center). The balustraded terrace up top was originally part of Vienna's defensive rampart. Later, it was the balcony of Empress Maria Theresa's daughter Maria Christina, who lived at this end of the palace. Today, her home houses the **Albertina Museum,** topped by a sleek, controversial titanium canopy (called the "diving board" by critics). The museum's plush, 19th-century staterooms are hung with facsimiles from its choice collection of prints, watercolors, and drawings (the originals are too light-sensitive to be displayed continuously). An entire floor is dedicated to the Batliner collection of classical modern art, covering each artistic stage from Impressionism to the present day (see page 65).

Albertinaplatz itself is filled with statues that make up the powerful, thought-provoking ❹ **Monument Against War and Fascism,** which commemorates the dark years when Austria came under Nazi rule (1938-1945).

The statue group has four parts. The split white monument, *The Gates of Violence*, remembers victims of all wars and violence. Standing directly in front of it, you're at the gates of a concentration camp. Then, as you explore the statues, you step into a montage of wartime images: clubs and WWI gas masks, a dying woman birthing a future soldier, and chained slave laborers sitting on a pedestal of granite cut from the infamous quarry at Mauthausen concentration camp (see page 235). The hunched-over figure on the ground behind is a Jew forced to scrub anti-Nazi graffiti off a street with a toothbrush. Of Vienna's 200,000 Jews, more than 65,000 died in Nazi concentration camps. The statue with its head buried in the stone is Orpheus entering the underworld, meant to remind Austrians (and the rest of us) of the victims of Nazism...and the consequences of not keeping our governments on track. Behind that, the 1945 declaration that established Austria's second republic—and enshrined human rights—is cut into the stone.

Viewing this monument gains even more emotional impact when you realize what happened on this spot: During a WWII bombing attack, several hundred people were buried alive when the cellar they were using as shelter was demolished.

Austria was led into World War II by Germany, which annexed the country in 1938, saying Austrians were wannabe Germans anyway. But Austrians are not Germans—never were, never will be. They're quick to proudly tell you that Austria was founded in the 10th century, whereas Germany wasn't born until 1870. For seven years just before and during World War II (1938-1945), there was no Austria. In 1955, after 10 years of joint occupation by the victorious Allies, Austria regained total independence on the condition that it would be forever neutral (and never join NATO or the Warsaw Pact). To this day, Austria is outside of NATO (and Germany).

Behind the monument is ❺ **Café Tirolerhof,** a classic Viennese café full of things that time has passed by: chandeliers, marble tables, upholstered booths, waiters in tuxes, and newspapers. For more on Vienna's cafés, see page 197.

Often parked nearby are the Red Bus City Tour buses, offering a handy way to get a quick overview of the city (see page 48).

• *From the café, turn right on Führichsgasse, passing the cafeteria-style Rosenberger Markt Restaurant. Walk one block until you hit...*

❻ Kärntner Strasse

This grand, traffic-free street is the people-watching delight of this in-love-with-life city. Today's Kärntner Strasse (KAYRNT-ner SHTRAH-seh) is mostly a crass commercial pedestrian mall—its famed elegant shops long gone. But locals know it's the same road Crusaders marched down as they headed off from St. Stephen's Cathedral for the Holy Land in the 12th century. Its name indicates that it leads south, toward the region of Kärnten (Carinthia, a province divided between Austria and Slovenia). Today it's full of shoppers and street musicians.

Where Führichsgasse meets Kärntner Strasse, note the city **Casino** (across the street and a half-block to your right, at #41)—once venerable, now tacky, it exemplifies the worst of the street's evolution. Turn left to head up Kärntner Strasse, going away from the Opera. As you walk along, be sure to look up, above the modern storefronts, for glimpses of the street's former glory. Near the end of the block, on the left at #26, **J & L Lobmeyr Crystal** ("Founded in 1823") still has its impressive brown storefront with gold trim, statues, and the Habsburg double-eagle. In the market for some $400 napkin rings? Lobmeyr's your place. Inside, breathe in the classic Old

World ambience as you climb up to the glass museum (free entry, Mon-Fri 10:00-19:00, Sat 10:00-18:00, closed Sun).

• *At the end of the block, turn left on Marco d'Aviano Gasse (passing the fragrant flower stall) to make a short detour to the square called Neuer Markt. Straight ahead is an orange-ish church with a triangular roof and cross, the Capuchin Church. In its basement is the...*

❼ Kaisergruft

Under the church sits the Imperial Crypt, filled with what's left of Austria's emperors, empresses, and other Habsburg royalty. For centuries, Vienna was the heart of a vast empire ruled by the Habsburg family, and here is where they lie buried in their fancy pewter coffins. You'll find all the Habsburg greats, including Maria Theresa, her son Josef II (Mozart's patron), Franz Josef, and Empress Sisi. Before moving on, consider paying your respects here (see page 66).

• *Stretching north from the Kaisergruft is the square called...*

❽ Neuer Markt

A block farther down, in the center of Neuer Markt, is the **four rivers fountain** showing Lady Providence surrounded by figures symbolizing the rivers that flow into the Danube. The sexy statues offended Empress Maria Theresa, who actually organized "Chastity Commissions" to defend her capital city's moral standards. The modern buildings around you were rebuilt after World War II. Half of the city's inner center was intentionally destroyed by Churchill to demoralize the Viennese, who were disconcertingly enthusiastic about the Nazis.

• *Lady Providence's one bare breast points back*

to Kärntner Strasse (50 yards away). Before you head back to the busy shopping street, you could stop for a sweet treat at the heavenly, recommended Kurkonditorei Oberlaa (to get there, disobey the McDonald's arrows—it's at the far-left corner of the square).

Leave the square and return to Kärntner Strasse. Turn left and continue down Kärntner Strasse. As you approach the cathedral, you're likely to first see it as a reflection in the round-glass windows of the post-modern Haas Haus. Pass the U-Bahn station (which has WCs) where the street spills into Vienna's main square...

❾ Stephansplatz

The cathedral's frilly spire looms overhead, worshippers and tourists pour inside the church, and shoppers and top-notch street entertainers buzz around the outside. You're at the center of Vienna.

The Gothic **St. Stephen's Cathedral** (c. 1300-1450) is known for its 450-foot south tower, its colorful roof, and its place in Viennese history. When it was built, it was a huge church for what was then a tiny town, and it helped put the fledgling city on the map. At this point, you may want to take a break from the walk to tour the church (❂ see the St. Stephen's Cathedral Tour chapter). Even if you don't go inside, check out the old facade and World War II-era photos that show the destruction during the war (across the square to the right of the church, next to the door marked *3a Stephansplatz*).

Where Kärntner Strasse hits Stephansplatz, the grand, soot-covered building with red columns is the **Equitable Building** (filled with lawyers, bankers, and insurance brokers). It's a fine example of Neoclassicism from the turn of the 20th century—look up and imagine how slick Vienna must have felt in 1900.

Facing St. Stephen's is the sleek concrete-and-glass ❿ **Haas Haus,** a postmodern building by noted Austrian architect Hans Hollein (finished in 1990). The curved facade is supposed to echo the Roman fortress of Vindobona (its ruins were found near here).

VIENNA CITY WALK

Adolf Loos
(1870-1933)

"Decoration is a crime," wrote Adolf Loos, the turn-of-the-20th-century architect who was Vienna's answer to Frank Lloyd Wright. Foreshadowing the Modernist style of "less is more" and "form follows function," Loos stripped buildings down to their structural skeleton.

In his day, most buildings were plastered with fake Greek columns, frosted with Baroque balustrades, and studded with statues. Even the newer buildings featured flowery Art Nouveau additions. Loos' sparse, geometrical style stood out at the time—and it still does more than a century later. Loos was convinced that unnecessary ornamentation was a waste of workers' valuable time and energy, and was a symbol of an unevolved society. (He even went so far as to compare decoration on a facade with a lavatory wall smeared with excrement.) On this walk, you'll pass four examples of his work:

American Bar (a half-block off Kärntner Strasse, on the left just before Stephansplatz at Kärntner Durchgang 10): Built in 1908, the same year that Loos published his famous essay *Ornament and Crime*, this tiny bar features Loos' specialties—and fine cocktails. The facade is cubical, with square columns and crossbeams (and no flowery capitals). The interior is elegant and understated, with rich marble and mirrors that appear to expand the small space. As they have little patience with gawkers, the best way to admire the interior is to sit down and order a drink.

Public WCs on Graben: These are some of the classiest bathrooms in town (see page 110).

Manz Bookstore: The facade is a perfect cube, divided into other simple, rectangular shapes.

Loos House on Michaelerplatz: This boldly stripped-down facade (pictured above) peers defiantly across the square at the over-the-top Hofburg. Compare it with the Hofburg's ornate, Neo-Rococo look (done only a few decades earlier) to see how revolutionary Loos was (see page 112).

Although the Viennese initially protested having this stark modern tower right next to their beloved cathedral, since then, it's become a fixture of Vienna's main square. Notice how the smooth, rounded glass reflects St. Stephen's pointy architecture, providing a great photo opportunity—especially at twilight. The café and pricey restaurant on the rooftop offer a nice perch, complete with a view of Stephansplatz below—though not necessarily of the cathedral (take the elevator up to the sixth floor, which has a glassed-in lounge; walk up one flight to reach the terrace and restaurant).

· *Exit the square with your back to the cathedral. Walk past the Haas Haus, and bear right down the street called...*

⓫ Graben

This was once a *Graben,* or ditch—originally the moat for the Roman military camp. Back during Vienna's 19th-century heyday, there were nearly 200,000 people packed into the city's inner center (inside the Ringstrasse), walking through dirt streets. Today this area houses 20,000. Graben was a busy street with three lanes of traffic until the 1970s, when it was turned into one of Europe's first pedestrian-only zones. Take a moment to absorb the scene—you're standing in an area surrounded by history, postwar rebuilding, grand architecture, fine cafés, and people enjoying life...for me, quintessential Europe.

As you stroll down the Graben from Stephansplatz, after about 50 yards, you'll reach a modern water dispenser. Vienna has suffered fiercely hot summers lately, leading the city government to install watering stations and shady benches for its citizens and visitors.

In another fifty yards, you reach Dorotheergasse, on your left, which leads (after two more long blocks) to the **Dorotheum** auction house. Consider poking your nose in here later for some fancy window-shopping (see page 53). Also along this street are two recommended eateries: the sandwich shop Buffet Trześniewski—one of my favorite places for lunch—and the classic Café Hawelka.

In the middle of the Graben pedestrian zone is the extravagantly blobby ⓬ **Holy Trinity plague column** *(Pestsäule).* The 60-foot pillar of clouds sprouts angels and cherubs, with the wonderfully gilded Father, Son, and Holy Ghost at the top (all protected by an anti-pigeon net).

In 1679, Vienna was hit by a massive epidemic of bubonic plague. Around 75,000 Viennese died—about a third of the city. Emperor Leopold I dropped to his knees (something emperors never did in public) and begged God to save the city. (Find Leopold about a quarter of the way up the monument, just above the brown banner. Hint: The typical inbreeding of royal families left him with a gaping underbite.) His prayer was heard by Lady Faith (the statue below Leopold, carrying a cross). With the help of a heartless little cupid, she tosses an old naked woman—symbolizing the plague—into the abyss and saves the city. In gratitude, Leopold vowed to erect this monument, which became a model for other cities ravaged by the same plague.

• *Thirty yards past the plague monument, look down the short street to the right, which frames a Baroque church with a stately green dome.*

⑬ St. Peter's Church

Leopold I ordered this church to be built as a thank-you for surviving the 1679 plague. The church stands on the site of a much older church that may have been Vienna's first (or second) Christian church. Inside, St. Peter's shows Vienna at its Baroque best (see page 53). Note that the church offers free organ concerts (Mon-Fri at 15:00, Sat-Sun at 20:00).

• *Continue west on Graben, where you'll immediately find some stairs leading underground to...*

⑭ Loos' Loos

In about 1900, a local chemical-maker needed a publicity stunt to prove that his chemicals really got things clean. He purchased two wine cellars under Graben and had them turned into classy WCs in the Modernist style (designed by Adolf Loos—see sidebar on page 108), complete with chandeliers and finely crafted mahogany. While the chandeliers are gone, the restrooms remain a relatively appealing place to do your business—in fact, they're so inviting that they're used for poetry readings. Locals and tourists happily pay €0.50 for a quick visit.

• *Graben dead-ends at the aristocratic supermarket Julius Meinl am Graben (see listing on page 195). From here, turn left. In the distance is the big green-and-gold dome of the Hofburg, where we'll head soon. The street leading up to the Hofburg is...*

⓯ Kohlmarkt

This is Vienna's most elegant and unaffordable shopping street, lined with Cartier, Armani, Gucci, Tiffany, and the emperor's palace at the end. Strolling Kohlmarkt, daydream about the edible window displays at ⓰ **Demel,** the ultimate Viennese chocolate shop (#14, daily 10:00-19:00). The room is filled with Art Nouveau

boxes of Empress Sisi's choco-dreams come true: *Kandierte Veilchen* (candied violet petals), *Katzenzungen* (cats' tongues), and so on. The cakes here are moist (compared to the dry Sacher-Tortes). The enticing window displays change monthly, reflecting current happenings in Vienna. Wander inside. There's an impressive cancan of Vienna's most beloved cakes—displayed to tempt visitors into springing for the €10 cake-and-coffee deal (point to the cake you want). Farther in, you can see the bakery in action. Sit inside, with a view of the cake-making, or outside, with the street action (upstairs is less crowded). Shops like this boast "K.u.K."—signifying that during the Habsburgs' heyday, it was patronized by the *König und Kaiser* (king and emperor—same guy). If you happen to be looking through Demel's window at exactly 19:01, just after closing, you can witness one of the great tragedies of modern Europe: the daily dumping of its unsold cakes.

Next to Demel, the **Manz Bookstore** has a Loos-designed facade (see sidebar on page 108). By the way, across the street (and back a few steps) is a fine travel book and map shop (Freytag & Berndt, which carries most of my guidebooks).

• *Kohlmarkt ends at the square called...*

⓱ Michaelerplatz

This square is dominated by the **Hofburg Palace.** Study the grand Neo-Baroque facade, dating from about 1900. The four heroic giants illustrate Hercules wrestling with his great challenges (Emperor Franz Josef, who commissioned the gate, felt he could relate).

In the center of this square, a scant bit of **Roman Vienna** lies exposed just beneath street level.

Spin Tour: Do a slow, clockwise pan to get your bearings, starting (over your left shoulder as you face the Hofburg) with **St. Michael's Church,** which offers fascinating tours of its crypt (see

Michaelerplatz:
Where New Faces Down Old

It's fascinating to think of Michaelerplatz as the architectural embodiment of a fundamental showdown that took place at the dawn of the 20th century, between the old and the new.

Emperor Franz Josef came to power during the popular revolution year of 1848 (as an 18-year-old, he was locked in his palace for safety). Once in power, he saw that the real threat to him was not from without, but from within. He dismantled the city wall and moved his army's barracks to the center of the city. But near the end of his reign, the modern world was clearly closing in.

Franz Josef's Neo-Rococo design for the Hofburg, featuring huge statues of Hercules in action at the gate, represents a desperate last stand of the absolutism of the emperor. Hercules was a favorite of emperors—a prototype of the modern ruler. The only mythical figure that was half-god, Hercules earned this half-divinity with hard labors. Like Hercules, the emperor's position was a combination of privileged birth and achievement—legitimized both by God and by his own hard work.

A few decades after Franz Josef erected his celebration of divine right, Loos responded with his starkly different house across the street. Although the Loos House might seem boring today, in its time, this anti-Historicist, anti-Art Nouveau statement was shocking. Inspired by Frank Lloyd Wright, it was considered to be Vienna's first "modern" building, with a trapezoidal footprint that makes no attempt to hide the awkwardly shaped street corner it stands on. Windows lack the customary cornice framing the top—a "house without eyebrows."

And so, from his front door, the emperor had to look at the modern world staring him rudely in the face, sneering, "Divine power is B.S. and your time is past." The emperor was angered by the bank building's lack of decor. Loos relented only slightly by putting up the 10 flower boxes (or "moustaches") beneath the windows.

But a few flowers couldn't disguise the notion that the divine monarchy was beginning to share Vienna with new ideas. As Loos worked, Stalin, Hitler, Trotsky, and Freud were all rattling about Vienna. Women were smoking and riding bikes. It was a scary time...a time ripe with change. And, of course, by 1918, after a Great War, the Habsburgs and the rest of Europe's imperial families were history.

page 68). To the right of that is the fancy **Loden-Plankl shop,** with traditional Austrian formalwear, including dirndls. Farther to the right, across Augustinerstrasse, is the wing of the palace that houses the **Spanish Riding School** and its famous white Lipizzaner stallions (see page 62). Farther down this street lies **Josefsplatz,** with the Augustinian Church (see page 63), and the Dorotheum auction house. At the end of the street are Albertinaplatz and the Opera (where we started this walk).

Continue your spin: Two buildings over from the Hofburg (to the right), the modern **Loos House** (now a bank; see Loos sidebar on page 108) has a facade featuring a perfectly geometrical grid of square columns and windows. Compared to the Neo-Rococo facade of the Hofburg, the stern Modernism of the Loos House appears to be from an entirely different age. And yet, both of these—as well as the Eiffel Tower and Mad Ludwig's fairytale Neuschwanstein Castle—were built in the same generation, roughly around 1900. In many ways, this jarring juxtaposition exemplifies the architectural turmoil of the turn of the 20th century, and represents the passing of the torch from Europe's age of divine monarchs to the modern era (see sidebar).

• *Let's take a look at where Austria's glorious history began—at the...*

Hofburg

This is the complex of palaces where the Habsburg emperors lived (except in summer, when they lived out at Schönbrunn Palace).

Enter the Hofburg through the gate, where you immediately find yourself beneath a big rotunda (the netting is there to keep birds from perching). The doorway on the right is the entrance to the ⓲ **Imperial Apartments,** where the Habsburg emperors once lived in chandeliered elegance. Today you can tour its lavish rooms, as well as a museum about Empress Sisi, and a porcelain and silver collection (✪ see the Hofburg Imperial Apartments Tour chapter). To the left is the ticket office for the ⓳ **Spanish Riding School** (see page 62).

Continuing on, you emerge from the rotunda into the main courtyard of the Hofburg, called **In der Burg.** The Caesar-like

statue is of Habsburg Emperor Franz II (1768-1835), grandson of Maria Theresa, grandfather of Franz Josef, and father-in-law of Napoleon. Behind him is a tower with three kinds of clocks (the yellow disc shows the phase of the moon tonight). To the right of Franz are the Imperial Apartments, and to the left are the offices of Austria's mostly ceremonial president (the more powerful chancellor lives in a building just behind this courtyard).

Franz Josef faces the oldest part of the palace. The colorful red, black, and gold gateway (behind you), which used to have a draw-bridge, leads over the moat and into the 13th-century Swiss Court (Schweizerhof), named for the Swiss mercenary guards once sta-tioned there. Study the gate. Imagine the drawbridge and the chain. Notice the Habsburg coat of arms with the imperial eagle above and the Renaissance painting on the ceiling of the passageway.

As you enter the Gothic courtyard, you're passing into the historic core of the palace, the site of the first fortress, and, his-torically, the place of last refuge. Here you'll find the ⑳ **Treasury** (Schatzkammer; ✪ see the Hofburg Treasury Tour chapter) and the **Imperial Music Chapel** (Hofmusikkapelle, see page 207), where the Boys' Choir sings Mass. Ever since Joseph Hayden and Franz Schubert were choirboys here, visitors have gathered like groupies on Sundays to hear the famed choir sing.

Returning to the bigger In der Burg courtyard, face Franz and turn left, passing through the **tunnel,** with a few tourist shops and restaurants, to spill out into spacious ㉑ **Heldenplatz** (Heroes' Square). On the left is the impressive curved facade of the **New Palace** (Neue Burg). This vast wing was built in the early 1900s to be the new Habsburg living quarters (and was meant to have a matching building facing it). But in 1914, the heir to the throne, Archduke Franz Ferdinand—while waiting politely for his long-lived uncle, Emperor Franz Josef, to die—was assassinated in Sara-jevo. The archduke's death sparked World War I and the eventual end of eight centuries of Habsburg rule.

Today the building houses the **New Palace museums,** an eclectic collection of weaponry, suits of armor, musical instru-ments, and ancient Greek statues (see page 61). The two equestrian statues depict Prince Eugene of Savoy (1663-1736), who battled the Ottoman Turks, and Archduke Charles (1771-1847), who battled Napoleon. Eugene gazes toward the far distance at the prickly spires of Vienna's City Hall.

Spin Tour: Make a slow 360-degree turn, and imagine this huge square filled with people.

In 1938, over 200,000 Viennese gathered here on Helden-platz, entirely filling vast Heroes' Square, to welcome Adolf Hitler and celebrate their annexation with Germany—the *"Anschluss."* The Nazi tyrant stood on the balcony of the New Palace and declared, "Before the face of German history, I declare my former homeland now a part of the Third Reich. One of the pearls of the Third Reich will be Vienna." He never mentioned "Austria," and from that moment on, it was forbidden to say the word.

Many wonder how Austria could so eagerly embrace Hitler and the *Anschluss* (although the notion of annexation with Germany had been batted around even before Hitler's rise). Let me hazard an explanation: Imagine post-WWI Austria. One of the mightiest empires on earth had started—and lost—a great war. In a few bloody years, it went from being a grand empire of 55 million people to a relatively insignificant landlocked state of six million. Treaty stipulations required the republic to remain unaligned with any other power. The capital, Vienna, was left with little to rule. The city alone comprised a third of the entire country's population. In the global economic crisis we know as the Great Depression (which swept the Nazis to power in Germany in 1933), Austria found itself ruled by a fascist government, complete with a dictator named Engelbert Dollfuss. He was as right-wing and anti-Semitic as Hitler, but also anti-Nazi (he was pro-Roman Catholic Church and pro-Habsburg). Under Dollfuss, the Austrian fascists eliminated any leftist opposition. When an Austrian Nazi assassinated Dollfuss in 1934, it created a power vacuum, paving the way for the German Nazis to easily take over four years later. The German Nazis just took over their Austrian counterparts' file cabinets. And, Hitler promised greatness again, and jobs—something that has driven voters to support crazy political notions to this day.

• *Walk on through the Greek-columned passageway (the Äussere Burgtor, an old castle gate), cross the Ringstrasse, and stand in the square between the twin museums, near the...*

㉒ Maria Theresa Monument

Vienna's biggest monument shows the empress holding a scroll

from her father granting the right of a woman to inherit his throne. The statues and reliefs surrounding her speak volumes about her reign: Her four top generals sit on horseback while her four top advisors stand. Behind them, reliefs celebrate cultural leaders of her day,

including little Wolfie Mozart with mentor "Papa" Joseph Haydn (with his hand on Mozart's shoulder, facing the Natural History Museum). The moral of this propaganda: a strong military and a wise ruler are prerequisites for a thriving culture—attributes that characterized the 40-year rule of the woman who was perhaps Austria's greatest monarch.

Standing here, it's fascinating to consider Austrian aspirations for greatness through the ages. Had World War I not messed things up for them, the Habsburgs would have created a vast cultural forum stretching from here across the Ringstrasse. While they never fully realized their vision, the ensemble that was completed is impressive. Two awe-inspiring buildings, purpose-built in the 1880s, house the private art and history collections of the empire, and celebrate its culture and power. The giant Kunsthistorisches and Natural History Museums face each other across a square, with a towering monument to Maria Theresa in the center of it all.

• *Our walk is finished. You're in the heart of Viennese sightseeing. Surrounding this square are some of the city's top museums. And the Hofburg Palace itself contains many of Vienna's best sights and museums. From the Opera to the Hofburg, from chocolate to churches, from St. Stephen's to Sacher-Tortes—Vienna waits for you.*

ST. STEPHEN'S CATHEDRAL TOUR

Stephansdom

This massive church is the Gothic needle around which Vienna spins. According to the medieval vision of its creators, it stands like a giant jeweled reliquary, offering praise to God from the center of the city. The church and its towers, especially the 450-foot south tower, give the city its most iconic image. (Check your pockets for €0.10 coins; those minted in Austria feature the south tower on the back.) The cathedral has survived Vienna's many wars and today symbolizes the city's spirit and love of freedom.

Orientation

Cost: It's free to enter the foyer and north aisle of the church, but it costs €3.50 to get into the main nave, where most of the interesting items are located (more for special exhibits). The towers, catacombs, treasury, and audioguide cost extra (all described later). The €16 combo-ticket—covering entry, both towers, catacombs, treasury, and audioguide—is overkill for most visitors.

Hours: The church doors are open daily 6:00-22:00, but the main nave is open for tourists Mon-Sat 9:00-11:30 & 13:30-16:30, Sun 13:00-16:30, until 17:30 June-Aug. During services, you can't enter the main nave (unless you're attending Mass) or access the north tower elevator or catacombs, but you can go into the back of the church.

Information: Tel. 01/515-523-526, www.stephanskirche.at.

Tours: The €4.50 tours in English are entertaining (daily at 15:45, check information board inside entry to confirm schedule; price includes main nave entry). The €1 audioguide is helpful.

Treasury: Consider riding the elevator (just inside the cathedral's entry) to the treasury. Tucked away in a loft in the oldest part

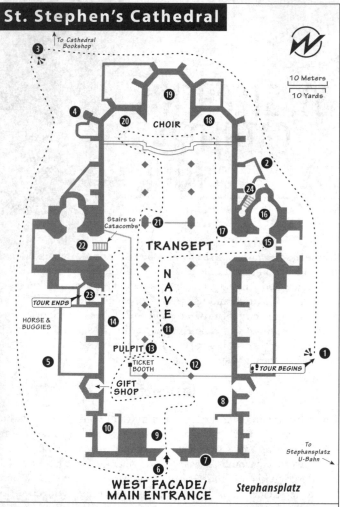

St. Stephen's Cathedral

- **1** South Side View & Old Photos
- **2** Reliefs, Memorials & Former Tombstones
- **3** North Tower View
- **4** Pulpit with Vanquished Turk
- **5** Stonemason's Hut
- **6** West Facade & Main Entrance
- **7** 05 Sign
- **8** Maria Pócs Icon
- **9** Organ & Treasury
- **10** Chapel of Prince Eugene of Savoy
- **11** Main Nave
- **12** Pillar Statues (Madonna with the Protective Mantle)
- **13** Pulpit with Self-Portrait
- **14** Similar Self-Portrait
- **15** Mozart Plaque
- **16** Mozart Baptistery
- **17** Madonna of the Servants
- **18** Tomb of Frederick III
- **19** High Altar
- **20** Wiener Neustädter Altar
- **21** Plaque of Rebuilding
- **22** Catacombs Entry
- **23** North Tower (Elevator)
- **24** South Tower (Stairs)

of the church, it offers precious relics, dazzling church art, a portrait of Rudolf IV (considered the earliest German portrait), and wonderful views down on the nave (€4 admission includes audioguide, daily 10:00-18:00).

Catacombs: The catacombs are open to the public only by guided tour (€4.50, daily 10:00-11:30 & 13:30-16:30, tours depart on the half-hour and are in German and English). Just be at the stairs in the left/north transept to meet the guide—you'll pay at the end. You'll see a crypt for bishops and archbishops, and crock-pots of Habsburg guts filling dusty shelves.

Towers: The iconic **south tower** rewards a tough climb up a claustrophobic, 343-step staircase with dizzying views. You can reach it via the entrance outside the church, around the right as you face the west facade (€3.50, daily 9:00-17:30).

The shorter **north tower** holds the famous "Pummerin" bell and is easier to ascend (no stairs, elevator), but it's much lower and not as exciting, with lesser views (€4.50, daily 9:00-11:30 & 13:00-16:30, until 17:30 in June-Aug, entrance inside the church on the left/north side of the nave; you can access this elevator without buying a ticket for the main nave).

English Service: There's a Mass in English each Saturday at 19:00.

Theft Alert: All the commotion in and around the church makes it a favorite for pickpockets. Be on guard.

Starring: The cathedral's mighty exterior and evocative interior, including an ornately carved pulpit and various bits and pieces of Austrian history.

The Tour Begins

Cathedral Exterior

Before we go inside, let's circle around the cathedral for a look at its impressive exterior. We'll stop at several points along the way to take it all in.

❶ South Side

• *As you face the church's main entry, go to the right across the little square, and find the old-time photos next to the door marked* 3a Stephansplatz *(see map). From here, you can take in the sheer magnitude of this massive church, with its skyscraping spire.*

The church we see today is the third one on this spot. It dates mainly from 1300 to 1450, when builders expanded on an earlier structure and added two huge towers at the end of each transept. When it was built, St. Stephen's—covering almost an acre of land—was a huge church for what was then just a modest town of 10,000. The ruler who built the church was competing with St. Vitus Cathedral, which was being built at the same time in Prague; he made sure that Vienna's grand church was bigger than Prague's. This helped convince the region's religious authorities that Vienna deserved a bishop, thus making St. Stephen's a "cathedral." Politically, this helped Vienna become a city to be reckoned with, and it soon replaced Prague as the seat of the Holy Roman Empire.

The impressive 450-foot **south tower**—capped with a golden orb and cross—took two generations to build (65 years) and was finished in 1433. The tower is a rarity among medieval churches in that it was completed before the Gothic style—and the age of faith—petered out.

Find the Turkish **cannonball** stuck in a buttress (above the low, green roof on the middle buttress, marked with the date *1683*)—a remnant of one of several Ottoman sieges of the city.

The half-size **north tower** (223 feet), around the other side of the church, was meant to be a matching steeple. But around 1500, it was abandoned in mid-construction, when the money was needed to defend the country against the Ottomans rather than to build church towers.

The nave's sharply pitched **roof** stands 200 feet tall and is covered in 230,000 colorful ceramic tiles. The zigzag pattern on the south side is purely decorative, with no special symbolism.

The cathedral was heavily damaged at the end of World War II. Near where you are standing are **old photos** showing the destruction. In 1945, Vienna was caught in the chaos between the occupying Nazis and the approaching Soviets. Allied bombs sparked fires in nearby buildings, and the embers leapt to the cathedral rooftop. The original timbered Gothic roof burned, the cathedral's huge bell crashed to the ground, and the fire raged for two days. Civic pride prompted a financial outpouring, and the roof was rebuilt to its original splendor by 1952—doubly impressive considering the bombed-out state of the country at that time. Locals who contributed to the postwar reconstruction each had a chance to "own" one tile for their donation. Inside, we'll see a plaque honoring the rebuilding of the cathedral.

The little buildings lining the church exterior are **sacristies** (utility buildings used for running the church).

• *Circle the church exterior counterclockwise, passing the **entrance to the*** *south tower. If you're up for climbing the 343 stairs to the top, you could do it now, but it's better to wait until the end of this tour (tower climb described at the end of this chapter).*

Near the tower entrance, look for the carved ❷ **reliefs and memorials** and former **tombstones** now decorating the church wall. These are a reminder that the area around the church was a graveyard until 1780.

Look high above at the colorful **roof tiles,** with the double-headed Habsburg eagle, the date 1831, and the initials FI (for Emperor Franz I, who ruled when the roof was installed).

• *As you hook around behind the church, look for the cathedral bookshop (Dombuchhandlung) at the end of the block. Pause in front of that shop.*

❸ North Tower View

This spot provides a fine, wide-angle view of the stubby north tower and the apse of the church. From this vantage point, you can see the exoskeletal fundamentals of **Gothic architecture:** buttresses shoring up a very heavy roof, allowing for large windows that could be filled with stained glass to bathe the interior in colorful light. A battalion of storm-drain gargoyles stands ready to vomit water during downpours. Colored tiles on the roof show not the two-headed eagle of Habsburg times (as on the other side), but two distinct eagles of modern times (1950): the state of Austria on the left and the city of Vienna on the right.

Just above street level, notice the marble ❹ **pulpit** under the golden starburst. The priest would stand here, stoking public opinion against the Ottomans, in front of crowds far bigger than could fit into the church. Above the pulpit (in a scene from around 1700), a saint stands victoriously atop a vanquished Turk.

• *Continue circling the church, passing a line of horse carriages waiting to take tourists for a ride. Watch for the blocky, modern-looking building huddled next to the side of the cathedral. This is the...*

❺ Stonemason's Hut

There's always been a stonemason's hut here, as workers must keep the church in good repair. Even today, the masonry is maintained in the traditional way—a never-ending task. Unfortunately, the local limestone used in the Middle Ages is quite porous and absorbs modern pollution. Until the 1960s, this was a very busy traffic circle, and today's acidic air still takes its toll. Each winter, when rainwater soaks into the surface and then freezes, the stone corrodes—and must be repaired. Your church entry ticket helps fund this ongoing work.

Across the street (past the horse carriages) is the **archbishop's palace,** where the head of this church still lives today (enjoying a very short commute).

• *Around the corner is the cathedral's front door. Stand at the back of the square, across from the main entrance, to take in the entire...*

❻ West Facade

The Romanesque-style main entrance is the oldest part of the church (c. 1240—part of a church that stood here before). Right behind you is the site of Vindobona, a Roman garrison town. Before the Romans converted to Christianity, there was a pagan temple here, and this entrance pays homage to that ancient heritage. Roman-era statues are embedded in the facade, and the two **octagonal towers** flanking the main doorway are dubbed the "heathen towers" because they're built with a few recycled Roman stones (flipped over to hide the pagan inscriptions and expose the smooth sides).

To the right of the main doorway is a reminder of the time the city was under Nazi rule. Anti-Nazi rebels carved **"O5"** into the wall, about chest high (❼ behind the Plexiglas, under the first plaque). The story goes that Hitler—who'd actually grown up in Austria—spurned his roots. When he attained power, he refused to call the country "Österreich," its native name, insisting on the Nazi term "Ostmark." Austrian patriots wrote the code "O5" to keep the true name alive: The "5" stands for the fifth letter of the alphabet (E), which often stands in for an umlaut, giving the "O" its correct pronunciation for "Österreich."

Before entering, study the details of the **main doorway.** Christ—looking down from the tympanum over the door—is triumphant over death. Flanked by angels with dramatic wings, he welcomes all. Ornate, tree-like pillars support a canopy of foliage and creatures, all full of meaning to the faithful medieval worshipper. The fine circa-1240 carvings above the door were once brightly painted. The paint was scrubbed off in the 19th century, when pure stone was more in vogue.

• *Enter the church.*

Cathedral Interior

Find a spot to peer through the gate down the immense nave—more than a football field long and nine stories tall. It's lined with clusters of slender pillars that soar upward to support the ribbed crisscross arches of the ceiling. Stylistically, the nave is Gothic with a Baroque overlay. It's a spacious, glorious venue that's often used for high-profile concerts (there's a ticket office outside the church, to the right as you face the main doorway).

• *We'll venture down the nave soon, but first take some time to explore the area at the...*

Cathedral Foyer

To the right as you enter, in a gold-and-silver sunburst frame, is a crude Byzantine-style ❽ **Maria Pócs Icon** (Pötscher Madonna), brought here from a humble Hungar-

ian village church. The picture of Mary and Child is said to have wept real tears in 1697, as Central Europe was once again being threatened by the Turks. Prince Eugene of Savoy (described below) saved the day at the stunning Battle of Zenta in modern-day Serbia—a victory that broke the back of the Ottoman army. If you see crowds of pilgrims leaving flowers or lighting candles around the icon, they're most likely Hungarians thanking the Virgin for helping Prince Eugene drive the Ottomans out of their homeland.

Over the main doorway is the choir loft, with the 10,000-pipe ❾ **organ,** a 1960 replacement for the famous one destroyed during World War II. This organ is also one of Europe's biggest, but it's currently broken and sits unused...too large to remove. Architects aren't sure whether it serves a structural purpose and adds support to the actual building.

Along the left wall is the **gift shop.** Step in to marvel at the 14th-century statuary decorating its wall—some of the finest carvings in the church.

To the left of the gift shop is the gated entrance to the ❿ **Chapel of Prince Eugene of Savoy.** Prince Eugene (1663-1736), a teenage seminary student from France, arrived in Vienna in 1683 as the city was about to be overrun by the Ottoman Turks. He volunteered for the army and helped save the city, launching a brilliant career as a military man for the Habsburgs. His specialty was conquering the Ottomans. When he died, the grateful Austrians buried him here, under this chapel, marked by a tomb hatch in the floor.

• *Nearby is the entrance to the main nave. Buy a ticket and walk to the center of the...*

❶ Main Nave

• *Looking down the nave, note the statues on the columns (about 30-40 feet above the ground).*

❷ Pillar Statues

The nave's columns are richly populated with 77 life-size stone statues, making a saintly parade to the high altar.

Check out the first pillar on the right. Facing the side wall is the **Madonna with the Protective Mantle,** shown giving refuge to people of all walks of life (notice all the happy people of faith tucked under her cape). Also on that same pillar, find Moses with the Ten Commandments. On other columns, Bible students can find their favorite characters and saints—more Madonnas, St. George (killing the dragon), St. Francis of Assisi, arrow-pierced St. Sebastian, and so on.

• *Start down the nave toward the altar. At the second pillar on the left is the...*

❸ Pulpit

The Gothic sandstone pulpit (c. 1500) is a masterpiece carved from three separate blocks (see if you can find the seams). A spi-

ral stairway winds up to the lectern, surrounded and supported by the four church "fathers," whose writings influenced early Catholic dogma. Each has a very different and very human facial expression (from back to front): Ambrose (daydreamer), Jerome (skeptic), Gregory (explainer), and Augustine (listener).

The pulpit is as crammed with religious meaning as it is with beautifully realistic carvings. The top of the stairway's railing swarms with lizards (animals of light) and toads (animals of darkness). The "Dog of the Lord" stands at the top, making sure none of those toads pollutes the sermon. Below the toads, wheels with three parts (the Trinity) roll up, while wheels with four spokes (the four seasons and four cardinal directions, symbolizing mortal life on earth) roll down.

Find the guy peeking out from under the stairs. This may be a **self-portrait** of the sculptor. In medieval times, art was done for the glory of God, and artists worked anonymously. But this pulpit was carved as humanist Renaissance ideals were creeping in from

ST. STEPHEN'S CATHEDRAL

Italy—and individual artists were becoming famous. So the artist included what may be a rare self-portrait bust in his work. He leans out from a window, sculptor's compass in hand, to observe the world and his work. The artist's identity, however, is disputed. Long thought to be Hungarian mason Anton Pilgram, many scholars now believe it's Dutch sculptor Nicolaes Gerhaert van Leyden; both worked extensively on the cathedral.

A few steps past the next column, look through the fence and find on the left wall a ❶ **similar self-portrait** of Pilgram (or is it Gerhaert?) in color, taken from the original organ case. He holds a compass and L-square and symbolically shoulders the heavy burden of being a master builder of this huge place.

• *Continue up the nave. We'll visit several sights at the front of the church, moving in a roughly counterclockwise direction.*

When you reach the gate that cuts off the front of the nave, turn right and enter the south transept. Go all the way to the doors, then look left to find the...

❶ Mozart Plaque

Wolfgang Amadeus Mozart (1756-1791) was married in St. Stephen's, attended Mass here, and had two of his children baptized here.

Mozart spent most of his adult life in Vienna. Born in Salzburg, Mozart was a child prodigy who toured Europe. He performed for Empress Maria Theresa's family in Vienna when he was eight. At age 25, he left Salzburg in a huff (freeing himself from his domineering father) and settled in Vienna. Here he found instant fame as a concert pianist and freelance composer, writing *The Marriage of Figaro, Don Giovanni,* and *The Magic Flute.* He married Constanze Weber in St. Stephen's, and they set up house in a lavish apartment a block east of the church (this house is now the lackluster Mozarthaus museum—see page 56). Mozart lived at the epicenter of Viennese society—among musicians, actors, and aristocrats. He played in a string quartet with Joseph Haydn. At church, he would have heard Beethoven's teacher playing the organ. (Mozart may have met the star-struck young Beethoven in Vienna—or maybe not; accounts vary.)

After his early success, Mozart fell on hard times, and the couple had to move to the suburbs. When Mozart died at age 35 (in 1791), he was not buried at St. Stephen's, because the cemetery that once surrounded the church had been cleared out a decade earlier as an anti-plague measure. Instead, his remains (along with most

Viennese of his day) were dumped into a mass grave outside of town. But he was honored with a funeral service in St. Stephen's—held in the Prince Eugene of Savoy Chapel, where they played his famous (unfinished) *Requiem*.

Look into the adjacent chapel at the fine ❶ **baptistery** (stone bottom, matching carved-wood top, from around 1500). This is where Mozart's children were baptized.

On the right-hand column near the entrance to the south transept, notice the fine carved statue of the ❶ **Madonna of the Servants** (from 1330). This remains a favorite of working people, such as the housekeepers who clean your hotel room.

• *Now walk down the right aisle to the front. Dominating the chapel at the front-right corner of the church is the...*

❶ Tomb of Frederick III

This imposing, red-marble tomb is like a big king-size-bed coffin with an effigy of Frederick lying on top (not visible—but there's

a photo of the effigy on the left). The top of the tomb is decorated with his coats of arms, representing the many territories he ruled over. It's likely by the same Nicolaes Gerhaert van Leyden who may have done the pulpit.

Frederick III (1415-1493) is considered the "father" of Vienna for turning the small village into a royal town with a cosmopolitan feel. Frederick secured a bishopric, turning the newly completed St. Stephen's church into a cathedral. The emperor's major contribution to Austria, however, was in fathering Maximilian I and marrying him off to Mary of Burgundy, instantly making the Habsburg Empire a major player in European politics. The lavish tomb (made of marble from Salzburg) is as long-lasting as Frederick's legacy. To make sure it stayed that way, locals saved his tomb from damage during World War II by encasing it, like the pulpit, in a shell of brick.

• *Walk to the middle of the church and face the...*

❶ High Altar

The tall, ornate, black marble altarpiece (1641, by Tobias and Johann Pock) is topped with a statue of Mary that barely fits under the towering vaults of the ceiling. It frames a large painting of the stoning of

St. Stephen, painted on copper. Stephen (at the bottom), having refused to stop professing his faith, is pelted with rocks by angry pagans. As he kneels, ready to die, he gazes up to see a vision of Christ, the cross, and the angels of heaven. The stained glass behind the painting—some of the oldest in the church—creates a kaleidoscopic jeweled backdrop.

• *To the left of the main altar is the...*

❷⓿ Wiener Neustädter Altar

The triptych altarpiece—the symmetrical counterpart of Frederick III's tomb—was commissioned by Frederick in 1447. Its gilded wooden statues are especially impressive.

• *Walk back up the middle of the nave, toward the gate. When you reach the gate, look immediately to the right (on the third column—with the gate attached). About 10 feet above the ground is the...*

❷❶ Plaque of Rebuilding

St. Stephen's is proud to be Austria's national church. The plaque explains in German how each region contributed to the rebuilding after World War II: *Die Glocke* (the bell) was financed by the state of Upper Austria. *Das Tor* (the entrance portal) was from Steiermark, the windows from Tirol, the pews from Vorarlberg, the floor from Lower Austria, and so on.

During World War II, many of the city's top art treasures were stowed safely in cellars and salt mines—hidden by both the Nazi occupiers (to protect against war damage) and by citizens (to protect against Nazi looters). The stained-glass windows behind the high altar were meticulously dismantled and packed away. The pulpit was encased in a shell of brick. As the war was drawing to a close, it appeared St. Stephen's would escape major damage. But as the Nazis were fleeing, the bitter Nazi commander in charge of the city ordered that the church be destroyed. Fortunately, his underlings disobeyed. Unfortunately, the church accidentally caught fire during Allied bombing shortly thereafter, and the wooden roof collapsed onto the stone vaults of the ceiling. The Tupperware-colored glass on either side of the nave dates from the 1950s. Before the fire, the church was lit mostly with clear Baroque-era windows.

• *Head back toward the main entrance. Along the north side of the nave, you have two options: Tour the catacombs or ascend the north tower. Or you can head outside for the pulse-raising climb up the south tower.*

Other Cathedral Sights

• *Near the middle of the church, at the left/north transept, is the entrance to the...*

㉒ Catacombs *(Katakomben)*

The catacombs (viewable by guided tour only) hold the bodies—or at least the innards—of 72 Habsburgs, including that of Rudolf IV, the man who began building the south tower. This is where Austria's rulers were buried before the Kaisergruft was built (see page 66), and where later Habsburgs' entrails were entombed. The copper urns preserve the imperial organs in alcohol. I touched Maria Theresa's urn and it wobbled.

• *Also in the north nave, but closer to the cathedral's main door (look for the Aufzug zur Pummerin sign), is the entrance for the...*

㉓ North Tower

The cramped north tower elevator takes you to a mediocre view and a big bell. Nicknamed "the Boomer" (Pummerin), it's old (first cast in 1711), big (nearly 10 feet across), and very heavy (21 tons). By comparison, the Liberty Bell is four feet across and weighs one ton. It's supposedly the second-biggest bell in the world that rings by swinging. A physical symbol of victory over the Ottomans in 1683, the Pummerin was cast from cannons (and cannonballs) captured from the Ottomans when the siege of Vienna was lifted. During the WWII fire that damaged the church, the Pummerin fell to the ground and cracked. It had to be melted down and recast. These days, locals know the Pummerin as the bell that rings in the Austrian New Year. You'll see its original 1,700-pound clapper in the catacombs if you take that tour.

• *Exit the church. Make a U-turn to the left if you're up for a climb up the...*

㉔ South Tower

The 450-foot-high south tower, once key to the city's defense as a lookout point, is still dear to Viennese hearts. (It's long been affectionately nicknamed "Steffl," Viennese for "Stevie.") No church spire in (what was) the Austro-Hungarian Empire is taller—by Habsburg decree. It offers a far better view than the north tower, but you'll earn it by hiking 343 tightly wound steps up the spiral staircase (this hike burns about one Sacher-Torte worth of calories). From the top, use your city map to locate the famous sights. There are great views of the colorful church roof, the low-level Viennese skyline (major skyscrapers are regulated in the city center), and—in the distance—the Vienna Woods.

• *Your tour is over. You're at the very center of Vienna. Explore.*

RINGSTRASSE
TRAM TOUR

In the 1860s, Emperor Franz Josef had the city's ingrown medieval wall torn down and replaced with a grand boulevard 190 feet wide. The road, arcing nearly three miles around the city's core, predates all the buildings that line it—so what you'll see is very "Neo": Neoclassical, Neo-Gothic, and Neo-Renaissance. It's textbook Historicism (see sidebar on page 139). One of Europe's great streets, the Ringstrasse is lined with many of the city's top sights.

This self-guided tram tour gives you a fun orientation and a ridiculously quick glimpse of some major sights as you glide by. Vienna's red trams (a.k.a. streetcars) circle the Ring. Most of them are sleek and modern, with a few lovably clickety-clackety older ones still running. Neither tram #1 nor #2 makes the entire loop around the Ring, but you can see it all by making one transfer between them (at the Schwedenplatz stop). It's a no-stress way to sit shoulder-to-shoulder with ordinary *Wiener*s and see their city. In fact, my hope is that you'll feel like a *Wiener* yourself as you make this big loop.

If you have a transit pass (instead of a ticket), you can—and should—jump on and off as you go, seeing sights that interest you. Some of the best stops are: Weihburggasse (Stadtpark), Stubentor (Museum of Applied Art, a.k.a. MAK), Rathausplatz (City Hall and its summertime food circus), and Burgring (Kunsthistorisches Museum and Hofburg Palace).

You'll find that the tram goes faster than you can read. It's best to look through this chapter ahead of time, then ride with an eye out for the various sights described here. As you go, use time spent waiting at red lights and tram stops to catch up or read the next segment to better anticipate what's coming up.

Or, to do this tour at your own pace, consider renting a **bike**. Frankly, this tour is better by bike than by tram, allowing you to

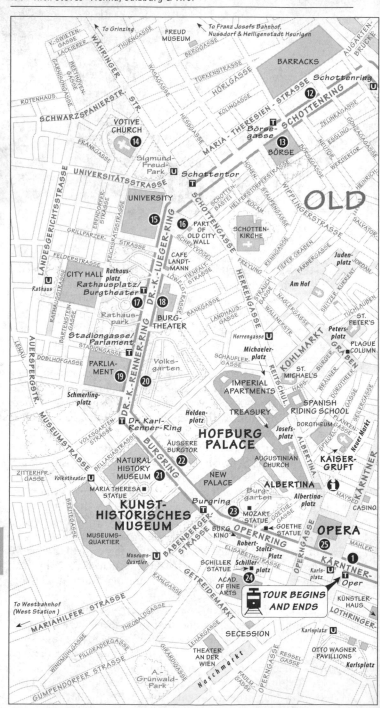

To Grinzing

FREUD MUSEUM

To Franz Josefs Bahnhof, Nussdorf & Heiligenstadt Heurigen

V.-SWIETEN-GASSE

LACKIERER-GASSE

WÄHRINGER STR.

THURYGASSE

BERGGASSE

AUGARTEN-BRÜCKE

BARRACKS

Schottenring

BEETHOVENG.

GARNISONGASSE

ROTENHAUS

WASAGASSE

TÜRKENSTRASSE

HÖRLGASSE

KOLINGASSE

MARIA THERESIEN-STRASSE

SCHOTTENRING

12

SCHWARZSPANIERSTR. STR.

HESSGASSE

Börse-gasse

ZELINKAGASSE

GONZAGAG.

ESSLINGG.

U

VOTIVE CHURCH

14

BÖRSE

13

WERDERTOR-G.

NESTOR-G.

FRANKGASSE

Sigmund-Freud-Park

U

Schottentor

SCHOTTEN-BASTEI

HOHENSTAUFENGASSE

HELFERSTÖRFERSTRASSE

WIPPLINGERSTRASSE

HEINRICH-

SALVATOR-G.

UNIVERSITÄTSSTRASSE

SCHOTTENGASSE

OLD

EBENDORFER-STRASSE

UNIVERSITY

15

16

PART OF OLD CITY WALL

SCHOTTEN-KIRCHE

GRILLPARZER-

LANDESGERICHTSSTRASSE

STRASSE

FELDERSTRASSE

CAFE LANDT-MANN

SCHREYVOGEL-

TIEFER GRABEN

FARBERGASSE

Juden-platz

JORDAN-

SEITZER-KURRENT-

FELDERSTRASSE

FRIEDRICHSTRASSE

DR.-K.-LUEGER-RING

LÖWELSTRASSE

FREYUNG

STRAUCH-G.

Am Hof

TUCHLAUBEN

CITY HALL

Rathaus-platz

Rathausplatz/ Burgtheater

Rathaus

17

18

HERRENGASSE

ST. PETER'S

RATHAUSSTRASSE

BARTENSTEIN-GASSE

Rathaus-park

BURG THEATER

BANGGASSE

LANDHAUS-GASSE

NAGLERGASSE

Peters-platz

PLAGUE COLUMN

DOROTHEER-

Stadiongasse/ Parlament

Herrengasse

U

STADIONGASSE

MICHAELER-platz

ST. MICHAEL'S

REITSCHUL-

GRABEN

BURGERG.

LEHARG.

DOBLHOFGASSE

PARLIA-MENT

19

Volks-garten

20

SCHAUFLER-GASSE

IMPERIAL APARTMENTS

BRÄUNER-

SPANISH RIDING SCHOOL

DOROTHEUM

SPIEGEL-

STRASSE

Schmerling-platz

AUERSPERGSTR.

Helden-platz

TREASURY

Josefs-platz

DOROTHEERG.

PLANKEN-G.

Neuer Markt

MUSEUMSTRASSE

VOLKSGARTEN-STRASSE

Dr. Karl-Renner-Ring

T

DR.-K.-RENNER-RING

BURGRING

ÄUSSERE BURGTOR

22

HOFBURG PALACE

AUGUSTINIAN CHURCH

KAISER-GRUFT

BELLARIASTRASSE

NATURAL HISTORY MUSEUM

21

NEW PALACE

ALBERTINA

ZITTERHPR.-GASSE

Volkstheater

U

MARIA THERESA STATUE

Burg-garten

Albertina-platz

CASINO

MAYSED-

KÄRNTNER

BREITEGASSE

KUNST-HISTORISCHES MUSEUM

Burgring

T

Mozart STATUE

23

GOETHE-GASSE

GOETHE STATUE

MUSEUMS-QUARTIER

BABENBERGER-STRASSE

Burg KINO

OPERNRING

OPERNGASSE

OPERA

Museums-Quartier

U

Robert-Stoltz-Platz

25

To Westbahnhof (West Station)

MARIAHILFER STRASSE

RAHLGASSE

GETREIDEMARKT

SCHILLER STATUE

24

Schiller platz

ACAD. OF FINE ARTS

Karls-platz

U

1

T

Oper

KÄRNTNER-

MAHLER-

THEOBALDGASSE

TOUR BEGINS AND ENDS

KÜNSTLER-HAUS

LOTHRINGER-

FILLGRADERGASSE

WINDMÜHLGASSE

GUMPENDORFER STRASSE

A.-Grünwald-Park

THEATER AN DER WIEN

SECESSION

LEHARGASSE

GIRARDIGASSE

Naschmarkt

FAULM-GASSE

Karlsplatz

RESSEL-GASSE

OPERNGASSE

OTTO WAGNER PAVILLIONS

Karlsplatz

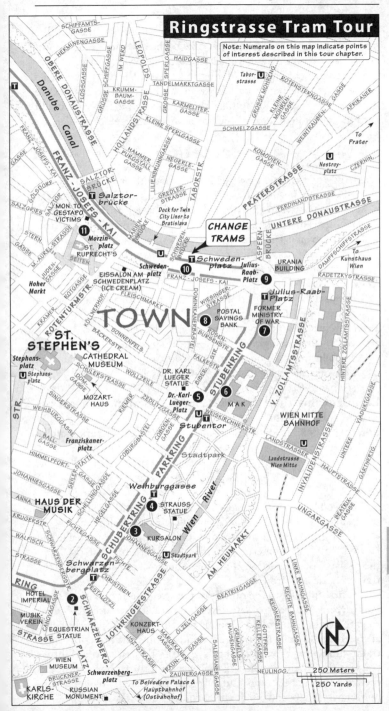

Ringstrasse Tram Tour

Note: Numerals on this map indicate points of interest described in this tour chapter.

SCHIFFAMTS-GASSE

HERMINENGASSE

HAIDGASSE

Tabor-strasse 🚇

To Prater

OBERE DONAUSTRASSE

FLOSSGASSE

GROSSE SCHIFFGASSE

IM WERD

LEOPOLDS

SPERLGASSE

TANDELMARKTGASSE

ROTENSTERNGASSE

AFRIKANER-

Danube Canal

KRUMM-BAUM-GASSE

GROSSE MOHREN-

KLEINE MOHREN-

KOMÖDIEN-GASSE

WEINTRAUBEN-

CZERNIN-

🚋 T

FRANZ-JOSEFS-KAI

HOLLANDSTRASSE

KARMELITER-GASSE

KLEINE SPERLGASSE

SCHMELZGASSE

Nestroy-platz 🚇

FRANZ-JOSEFS-KAI

SALZTOR-BRÜCKE

HAMMER-PURGSTALL-GASSE

NEGERLE-GASSE

LILIENBRUNNGASSE

PRÄTERSTRASSE

FERDINANDSTRASSE

UNTERE DONAUSTRASSE

GOLDSCHMI...

SALZTORGASSE

T **Salztor-brücke**

MAREN...

GREDLER-STRASSE

TABORSTR.

Dock for Twin City Liner to Bratislava

ASPERN-BRÜCKE

DAMPFSCHIFFSTRASSE

To Kunsthaus Wien

SALZGRIES

MON. TO GESTAPO VICTIMS ⑪

Morzin-platz

CHANGE TRAMS

RADETZKYSTRASSE

STERN-GASSE

M.-AUREL-STRASSE

JUDEN-GASSE

ST. RUPRECHT'S

SEITEN...

🚇

SCHWEDEN-BRÜCKE

Schweden-⑩ **platz**

T ⑩ **Schweden-platz**

Julius-Raab-Platz

URANIA BUILDING

Hoher Markt

KRAMER

ROTGASSE

Schweden-platz

FRANZ-JOSEFS-KAI

WIESINGER-STRASSE

Julius-Raab-Platz T

ROTENTURMSTR.

EISSALON AM SCHWEDENPLATZ (ICE CREAM)

FLEISCHMARKT

DOMINIKANERBASTEI

⑨

KÖLLNERHOF...

SONNENFELS...

POSTAL SAVINGS BANK ⑧

ROSEN-BURGENSTR.

FORMER MINISTRY OF WAR ⑦

TOWN

V. ZOLLAMTSSTRASSE

HINTERE ZOLLAMTSSTRASSE

BÄCKERSTR.

ST. STEPHEN'S

CATHEDRAL MUSEUM

WOLLZEILE

DR. KARL LUEGER STATUE

DIBER-STR.

FALKESTR.

STUBENRING

🚋

WIEN MITTE BAHNHOF

Stephans-platz

🚇 Stephans-platz

SCHULERSTRASSE

DOM-GASSE

ZEDLITZ...

NIEMER...

Dr.-Karl-Lueger-Platz ⑤

⑥

M A K

LANDSTRASSE

SINGERSTRASSE

MOZART-HAUS

WEISKIRCHNERSTR.

Landstrasse Wien Mitte

WEIHBURGGASSE

COBDEN...

COBURGBASTEI

🚇 T

UNTERE...

HAUPTSTRASSE

BALL-GASSE

Franziskaner-platz

Stubentor

VIADUKTGASSE

HIMMELPFORT...

COBURGBASTEI

Stadtpark

GÄRTNERG.

JOHANNESGASSE

SCHELLING...

PARKRING

Wien River

ANNA-GASSE

Weihburggasse

🚋 T

UNGARGASSE

HAUS DER MUSIK

HEGELGASSE

④ **STRAUSS STATUE**

KRUGERSTR.

FICHTEGASSE

SCHWARZENBERGSTR.

③

KURSALON

BEATRIX-GASSE

WALFISCH...

JOHANNESGASSE

🚇 **Stadtpark**

LINKE BAHNGASSE

RECHTE BAHNGASSE

STRASSE

SCHUBERTRING

Schwarzen-bergplatz

PESTALOZZI...

CHRISTINEN...

AM HEUMARKT

REISNERSTRASSE

GOTTFRIED KELLER-GASSE

RING

HOTEL IMPERIAL

②

SCHWARZENBERG-

GLUCK-GASSE

CHRISTINEN.

BEATRIXGASSE

AM HEUMARKT

SALESIANERGASSE

MUSIK-VEREIN

③ EQUESTRIAN STATUE

PLATZ

SCHWARZENBERG-PLATZ

LOTHRINGERSTRASSE

KONZERT-HAUS

MAROKKANER-GASSE

TRAUN...

NEULINGG...

STRASSE

WIEN MUSEUM

BRÜCKNER-STRASSE

Schwarzenberg-platz

LISZT-STRASSE

AMBRAN...

ZAUNERGASSE

N

KARLS-KIRCHE

RUSSIAN MONUMENT ■

To Belvedere Palace & Hauptbahnhof (Ostbahnhof)

250 Meters

250 Yards

easily stop at sights or to detour to nearby points of interest. The grassy median strip has excellent bike paths that run along almost the entire circuit of the Ring (except for a few blocks after the votive church, near the end of this tour). And the Citybike Wien program lets you rent a basic bike for an hour or two for next to nothing (simply find a Citybike Wien rack, and insert your credit card in the automated machine; for more details, see page 47).

Orientation

Cost: €2 (one transit ticket), €2.40 if bought on tram. A single ticket can be used to cover the whole route, including the transfer between trams (you're not allowed to interrupt your trip, except to transfer). A transit pass works better for this ride, as you're free to hop off whenever you like, then hop back on another tram (they come along every few minutes). For more on riding Vienna's trams, see page 45.

When to Go: While this tour works fine in the daylight, the tram ride is also pleasant after dark, when nearly every sight on the route is well-lit.

Pricier Option: A yellow just-for-tourists streetcar circles the Ring without requiring a transfer—but it costs more and runs less frequently (€7 for one 30-minute loop, €9 for 24-hour hop-on, hop-off privileges, 2/hour 10:00-18:00, July-Aug until 19:00, see page 49).

Length of This Tour: About 30 minutes; allow more time if you hop off along the way.

Starring: Vienna's grandest boulevard, major landmarks, and a dizzyingly quick, once-over-lightly look at the city.

The Tour Begins

To help you keep your bearings, this tour includes the name of each tram stop you'll pass, and tells you which way to look along the way. Stop names are announced in German as you approach and labeled (in small, sometimes hard-to-read lettering) at the stops themselves. Be aware that if no one requests a particular stop, the tram may zip on through.

Catch tram #2 in the middle of the street in front of the Opera house (from the underpass next to the Opera, follow signs to *Opernring*; the tram stop, called **Oper,** is to your right when you emerge at street level). You want the tram going against the direction of car traffic (direction Friedrich-Engels-Platz)—that is, to the right, as you face the Opera. If you can, grab a seat on the right-hand side of the tram. On many trams, annoying advertisements blur the window views; try to find a seat with a view clear of these.

The Birth of Modern Vienna

This tour quickly passes a statue of Dr. Karl Lueger (1844-1910), the influential mayor of Vienna during the pivotal period around the turn of the 20th century. Although controversial for his anti-Semitism, Lueger worked together with architect Otto Wagner (1841-1918) to shape the modern Vienna you see today. Read this information during any down time (or before you board the tram), so you can recognize Lueger when you see him (at stop #5).

When Lueger was mayor (1897-1910), Vienna was in the midst of an incredible growth spurt: In 1850, the city had 500,000 residents; at its peak, around 1900, the population was 2.2 million—about 20 percent more than the city's current population of 1.7 million.

Emperor Franz Josef put Lueger and Wagner (the "Father of Modern Vienna") to work with a staff of 60 architects to turn the city into a capital befitting the grandiose Habsburg Empire. Consider the dramatic changes this team oversaw in a relatively short time: In the previous generation, Roman-style aqueducts still brought fresh spring water into the city from the Alps. By the 20th century, the city had modern plumbing. Thomas Edison supervised the electrical lighting of Schönbrunn Palace, and shortly after that, gas lighting brightened the entire Ringstrasse. The Danube was tamed by building solid banks, along with other flood-control projects. In the 1870s, engineers even began an artificial island that took a century to complete.

As Vienna grew and sprawled, it became decentralized, as with "city centers" all over the place. To tie it all together, the new Vienna needed a fine tram and subway system. Consequently, much of the city's subway infrastructure also dates from this era. Around town, you'll notice that some of the older U-Bahn stops are still Art Nouveau in design. Also during this time (in 1898), the horse-drawn tram line around the Ringstrasse was converted to electric power.

In so many ways, the Vienna of today was created during this brief spurt of architectural and engineering energy a century ago.

Again, this commentary is ridiculously fast. With a transit pass, feel free to hop off to get a closer look at anything that intrigues you, or just to catch your breath—trams come by every few minutes.

• *Let's go. Before you leave the* **Oper stop***...*

❶ Look Left

Just next to the Opera house, the city's main pedestrian drag, Kärntner Strasse, leads to the zigzag-mosaic roof of **St. Stephen's**

Cathedral. This tram tour makes a 360-degree circle around the cathedral, staying about this same distance from the great church that marks the center of Vienna.

• *As the tram sets off...*

❷ Look Right

Along this stretch, you'll pass a string of Vienna's finest five-star hotels, including **Hotel Imperial**—the choice of nearly every visiting big shot, from the Rolling Stones to Queen Elizabeth.

Just after the hotel, at Schwarzenbergplatz, an **equestrian statue** honors Prince Charles Schwarzenberg, who fought Napoleon. From the end of World War II until 1955, Austria and its capital were occupied by foreign troops, including Russian forces; during that time the square was named Stalinplatz after the Soviet dictator.

In the distance beyond the prince, at the far end of the long square, look for a fountain with a big colonnade just behind it. This **Russian monument** was built in 1945 as a forced thank-you to the Soviets for liberating Austria from the Nazis. Formerly a sore point, now the monument is just ignored.

• *Coming up soon is the* **Schwarzenbergplatz stop.** *When you pass it...*

❸ Look Right

Three blocks beyond the Schwarzenbergplatz stop is the huge **Stadtpark** (City Park). This inviting green space honors many great Viennese musicians and composers with statues. At the beginning of the park, the gold-and-cream concert hall behind the trees is the **Kursalon,** opened in 1867 by the Strauss brothers, who directed

many waltzes here. Touristy Strauss concerts are held in this building (for details, see page 210). If the weather's nice, hop off at the next stop (Weihburggasse) for a stroll in the park.

• *Right at the* **Weihburggasse stop***...*

❹ Look Right

In the park but barely visible from the tram (squint through the park gate near the stop), the gilded statue of "Waltz King" **Johann Strauss** holds a violin as

RINGSTRASSE TRAM

he did when he conducted his orchestra, whipping his fans into a three-quarter-time frenzy.

• *The next several sights pass quickly, so read about them while you're waiting at the next stop (**Stubentor**). Just after the tram sets off again...*

❺ Look Left
Centered in a public square, a bronze statue (now turned green) of **Dr. Karl Lueger** honors the popular mayor who shaped Vienna into a modern city (see sidebar on page 133).

• *Immediately after the Lueger statue...*

❻ Look Right
The big, red-brick building across the street is the **Museum of Applied Art** (MAK), showing furniture and design through the ages (also has good café and gift shop; see page 86).

• *A block after the museum...*

❼ Look Right
The long, white building used to be the **Austrian Ministry of War**—back when that was a major operation. Above its oval windows, you can see busts of soldiers wearing Stratego-style military helmets. The equestrian statue at the entrance is Field Marshal Radetzky, a military big shot in the 19th century under Franz Josef.

• *Now...*

❽ Look Left
Radetzky is pointing across the street toward the **Postal Savings Bank** (set back on a little square; see page 88). Designed by Otto Wagner, it's one of the rare Secessionist buildings facing the Ring. (For more on The Secession, see the sidebar on page 76.)

• *Immediately after the **Julius-Raab-Platz stop**, the tram makes a sharp left turn, when you should...*

❾ Look Right
The white-domed building on your right is the **Urania**, Franz Josef's 1910 observatory. On the horizon behind the Urania, visually trace the canal and squint to get a glimpse of the huge red cars of the giant hundred-year-old Ferris wheel in Vienna's **Prater**

amusement park (fun and characteristically Viennese, described on page 96).

• *At the next stop,* **Schwedenplatz***...*

⓾ Prepare to Get Off and Transfer

Hop off tram #2 at the Schwedenplatz stop and wait for tram #1 (heading in the same direction you've been going; trams come along every 5-10 minutes). Gelato fans may want to prolong the wait a little with a break at Eissalon am Schwedenplatz (daily 10:00-23:00). Before venturing away, check the electronic board at the stop to see how many minutes until the next tram arrives.

While You Wait...

Notice the waterway next to you, and how blue it isn't: It's the **Danube Canal** (a.k.a. the "Baby Danube"), one of the many small arms of the river that once made up the Danube at this location. The rest have been gathered together in a mightier modern-day Danube, farther away. This area

was once the center of the original Roman town, Vindobona, located on the banks of the Danube—beyond which lay the barbarian Germanic lands. The modern boat station is for the fast boat to Bratislava, Slovakia, about an hour downstream.

If some of the buildings across the canal seem a bit drab, that's because this neighborhood was thoroughly bombed in World War II. These postwar buildings were constructed on the cheap and are now being replaced by sleek, futuristic buildings.

By the way, this is called Schwedenplatz ("Sweden Square") because after World War I, Vienna was overwhelmed with hungry orphans. The Swedes took several thousand in, raised them, and finally sent them home healthy and well-fed.

• *Get ready—here comes tram #1. This time, grab a seat on the left if you can. Keep an eye toward the old city center. After three blocks, opposite the gas station (be ready—it passes fast)...*

⓫ Look Left

You'll see the ivy-covered walls and round Romanesque arches of **St. Ruprecht's** (Ruprechtskirche), the oldest church in Vienna. It was built in the 11th century on a bit of Roman ruins.

The low-profile, modern-looking, concrete **monument** in the corner of the park (close to the tram, on the left) commemorates the victims of the Gestapo, whose headquarters were here.

• *Take a breather for a bit—there's not much to see until after the next two stops (*Salztorbrücke *and* Schottenring*).*

In the Meantime...

It's interesting to remember that the Ringstrasse replaced the mighty walls that once protected Vienna from external enemies.

Imagine the great imperial capital contained within its three-mile-long wall, most of which dated from the 16th to 18th century. As was typical of city walls, it was lined with cannons (2,200, in Vienna's case) and surrounded by a "shooting field" or "cannonball zone." This swath of land, as wide as a cannonball could fly (about 400 yards), was clear-cut so no one could approach without being targeted.

After the popular unrest and uprisings of 1848, the emperor realized the real threat against him was from within. He rid the city of its walls in about 1860, built this boulevard and transportation infrastructure (good for moving both citizens in good times and soldiers in bad), and, as you'll see in a moment, moved his army closer at hand. Napoleon III's remodel of Paris demonstrated that wide boulevards make it impossible for revolutionaries to erect barricades to block the movement of people and supplies. That encouraged Franz Josef to implement a similarly broad street plan for his Ring. A straight stretch of boulevard may seem just stately, but for an embattled emperor, it's an easy-to-defend corridor.

When the emperor had the walls taken down, the shooting field was wide open and ripe for development. Hence, the wonderful architecture that lines the outer edge of the Ringstrasse is all from the same era (post 1860).

• *The tram leaves the canal after the* **Schottenring stop**, *and turns left. But you should...*

⓲ Look Right

Through a gap in the buildings, on the right, you'll get a glimpse of

a huge, red-brick castle—actually high-profile **barracks** built here at the command of a nervous Emperor Franz Josef (who found himself on the throne as an 18-year-old in 1848, the same year people's revolts against autocracy were sweeping across Europe).

• *When you pull into the* **Börsegasse stop**...

⑬ Look Left

The orange-and-white, Neo-Renaissance temple of money—the **Börse**—is Vienna's stock exchange. The next block is lined with banks and insurance companies—the financial district of Austria.
• *At the next stop (**Schottentor**)...*

⑭ Look Right

The huge, frilly, Neo-Gothic church across the small park is a **"votive church,"** a type of church built to fulfill a vow in thanks for God's help—in this case, when an 1853 assassination attempt on Emperor Franz Josef failed.

If you have an extra moment at the Schottentor stop, look ahead and left down the long, straight stretch of boulevard and imagine the city's impressive wall and that vast swath of no-man's land that extended as far as a cannonball could fly.
• *Just after the **Schottentor stop**...*

⑮ Look Right

You're looking at the main building of the **University of Vienna** (Universität Wien). Established in 1365, the university has no real campus, as its buildings are scattered around town. It's considered the oldest continuously operating university in the German-speaking world.
• *Immediately opposite the university...*

⑯ Look Left

A chunk of the old **city wall** is visible (behind a gilded angel). Beethoven lived and composed in the building just above the piece of wall.
• *As you pull into the **Rathausplatz/Burgtheater stop**, first...*

⑰ Look Right

The Neo-Gothic **City Hall** (Rathaus) flies both the flag of Austria and the flag of Europe. The square in front (Rathausplatz) is a festive site in summer, with a thriving food circus and a huge screen showing outdoor movies, operas, and concerts (mid-July-mid-Sept 11:00-late; see pages 195 and 212). In December, the City Hall becomes a huge Advent calendar, with 24 windows opening—one each day—as Christmas approaches.
• *And then...*

RINGSTRASSE TRAM

Historicism

Most of the architecture along the Ring is known as "Historicism" because it's all Neo-this and Neo-that. It takes design elements from the past—Greek columns, Renaissance arches, Baroque frills—and plasters them on the facade to simulate a building from the past.

Generally, the style fits the purpose of the particular building. For example, the Neoclassical parliament building celebrates ancient Greek notions of democracy. The Neo-Gothic City Hall recalls when medieval burghers ran the city government in Gothic days. Neo-Renaissance museums, such as the Kunsthistorisches and Natural History Museums, celebrate learning. And the Neo-Baroque National Theater recalls the age when opera and theater flourished.

⑱ Look Left

Immediately across the street from City Hall is the **Burgtheater,** Austria's national theater. Locals brag it's the "leading theater in the German-speaking world." Next door (on the left) is the recommended **Café Landtmann** (the only café built with the Ringstrasse buildings, and one of the city's finest).

• *Just after the **Stadiongasse/Parlament stop**...*

⑲ Look Right

The Neo-Greek temple of democracy houses the **Austrian Parliament.** The lady with the golden helmet is Athena, goddess of wisdom.

• *And then swivel to...*

⑳ Look Left

Across the street from the Parliament is the imperial park called the **Volksgarten,** with a fine public rose garden.

• *The next stop is **Dr. Karl-Renner-Ring.** When the tram pulls away...*

㉑ Look Right

The vast building is the **Natural History Museum** (Naturhistorisches Museum), which faces its twin, the **Kunsthistorisches Museum,** containing the city's greatest collection of paintings. The **MuseumsQuartier** behind them completes the ensemble with a collection of mostly modern art museums. A hefty statue of Empress Maria Theresa squats between the museums, facing the grand gate to the Hofburg Palace.

• *Now...*

㉒ Look Left

Opposite Maria Theresa, the arched gate (the Äussere Burgtor, the only surviving castle gate of the old town wall) leads to the **Hofburg,** the emperor's palace. Of the five arches, the center one was used only by the emperor.

Your tour is nearly finished, so consider hopping off here to visit the Hofburg, the Kunsthistorisches Museum, or one of the museums in the MuseumsQuartier.

• *Fifty yards after the* **Burgring stop***...*

㉓ Look Left

Until 1918, the appealing **Burggarten** was the private garden of the emperor. Today locals enjoy relaxing here, and it's also home to a famous statue of **Mozart** (pictured here; hard to see from the tram).

A hundred yards farther (also on the left, just out of the park, but also difficult to see), the German philosopher **Goethe** sits in a big, thought-provoking chair.

• *Now it's time to...*

㉔ Look Right

Goethe seems to be playing trivia with German poet **Schiller** across the street (in the little park set back from the street). Behind the statue of Schiller is the **Academy of Fine Arts** (described on page 73); next to it (on the right, facing the Ring) is the Burg Kino, which plays the movie *The Third Man* three times a week in English (see page 213).

• *Get ready to...*

㉕ Look Left...and Get Off

Hey, there's the **Opera** again. Jump off the tram and see the rest of the city. (To join me on a walking tour of Vienna's center, which starts here at the Opera, see the Vienna City Walk chapter.)

HOFBURG IMPERIAL APARTMENTS TOUR

Silberkammer • Sisi Museum • Kaiserappartements

In this tour of the Hofburg Imperial Apartments, see the lavish, Versailles-like rooms that were home to the hardworking Emperor Franz Josef I and his reclusive, eccentric empress, known as "Sisi." From here, the Habsburgs ruled their vast empire.

Franz Josef was (for all intents and purposes) the last of the Habsburg monarchs, and these apartments straddle the transition from old to new. You'll see chandeliered luxury alongside office furniture and electric lights.

Franz Josef and Sisi were also a study in contrasts. Where Franz was earnest, practical, and spartan, Sisi was poetic, high-strung, and luxury-loving. Together, they lived their lives in the cocoon of the Imperial Apartments, seemingly oblivious to how the world was changing around them.

Orientation

Cost: €10.50, includes well-done audioguide; also covered by €23.50 "Sisi Ticket" (see page 43), which includes the Schönbrunn Palace Grand Tour and the Imperial Furniture Collection.

Hours: Daily July-Aug 9:00-18:00, Sept-June 9:00-17:30, last entry one hour before closing.

Getting There: Enter from under the rotunda just off Michaelerplatz, through the Michaelertor gate.

Information: You'll find some helpful posted information in English, and the included audioguide brings the exhibit to life. With those tools and this chapter, you won't need the €8 *Imperial Apartments/Sisi Museum/Silver Collection* guidebook. Tel. 01/533-7570, www.hofburg-wien.at.

Length of This Tour: If you listen to the entire audioguide, allow 40 minutes for the silver collection, 30 minutes for the Sisi Museum, and 40 minutes for the apartments.

The Tour Begins

Your ticket grants you admission to three separate exhibits, which you'll visit on a pretty straightforward one-way route. The first floor holds a collection of precious porcelain and silver knickknacks *(Silberkammer)*. You then go upstairs to the Sisi Museum, which has displays about her life. This leads into the 20-odd rooms of Imperial Apartments *(Kaiserappartements)*, starting in Franz Josef's rooms, then heading into the dozen rooms where his wife Sisi lived.

Imperial Porcelain and Silver Collection

Your visit (and the excellent audioguide) starts on the ground floor, with the Habsburg court's vast tableware collection, which the audioguide actually manages to make fairly interesting. Browse the collection to gawk at the opulence and to take in some colorful Habsburg trivia. (Who'd have thunk that the court had an official way to fold a napkin—and that the technique remains a closely guarded secret?)

• *Once you're through all those rooms of dishes, climb the stairs—the same staircase used by the emperors and empresses who lived here. At the top is a timeline of Sisi's life. Swipe your ticket to pass through the turnstile, consider the WC, and enter the room with the...*

Model of the Hofburg

Circle to the far side to find where you're standing right now, near the smallest of the Hofburg's three domes.

The Hofburg was the epicenter of one of Europe's great political powers—600 years of Habsburgs lived here. The Hofburg started as a 13th-century medieval castle (near where you are right now) and expanded over the centuries to today's 240,000-square-meter (60-acre) complex, now owned by the state.

To the left of the dome (as you face the facade) is the steeple of the Augustinian Church. It was there, in 1854, that Franz Josef married 16-year-old Elisabeth of Bavaria, and their story began.

• *Now enter a darkened room at the beginning of the...*

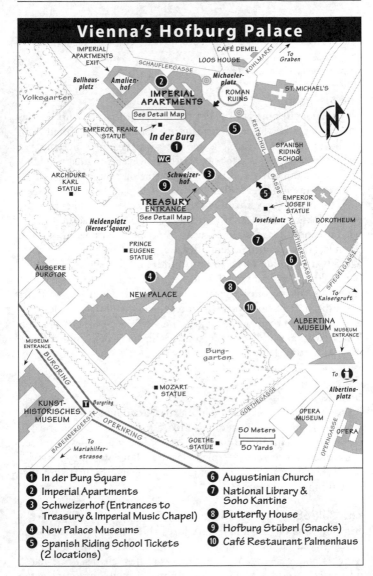

Vienna's Hofburg Palace

1. In der Burg Square
2. Imperial Apartments
3. Schweizerhof (Entrances to Treasury & Imperial Music Chapel)
4. New Palace Museums
5. Spanish Riding School Tickets (2 locations)
6. Augustinian Church
7. National Library & Soho Kantine
8. Butterfly House
9. Hofburg Stüberl (Snacks)
10. Café Restaurant Palmenhaus

Sisi Museum

Empress Elisabeth (1837-1898)—a.k.a. "Sisi" (SEE-see)—was Franz Josef's mysterious, beautiful, and narcissistic wife. This museum traces her fabulous but tragic life.

Sisi's Death

The exhibit starts with Sisi's sad end, showing her **death mask,** photos of her **funeral procession** (by the Hercules statues facing

Michaelerplatz), and an **engraving** of a grieving Franz Josef. It was at her death that the obscure, private empress' legend began to grow.

• *Continue into the corridor.*

The Sisi Myth

Newspaper clippings of the day make it clear that the empress was not a major public figure in her lifetime. She was often absent from public functions, and the censored press was gagged from reporting on her eccentricities. After her death, however, her image quickly became a commodity and began appearing on everyday items such as **candy tins** and **beer steins.**

The plaster-cast **statue** captures the one element of her persona everyone knew: her beauty. Sisi was nearly 5'8" (a head taller than her husband), had a 20-inch waist, and weighed only about 100 pounds. (Her waistline eventually grew...to 21 inches. That was at age 50, after giving birth to four children.) This statue, a copy of one of 30 statues that were erected in her honor in European cities, shows her holding one of her trademark fans. It doesn't show off her magnificent hair, however, which reached down to her ankles.

Sisi-mania really got going in the 1950s with a series of **movies** based on her life (starring Romy Schneider), depicting the empress as beautiful and innocent.

• *Round the corner into the next room.*

Sisi's Childhood

Sisi grew up on a noble estate in Bavaria, amid horses and country-side, far from sophisticated city life. (See her **baby shoes** and the picture of her **childhood palace.**) At 15, Franz Josef—who'd been engaged to someone else—spied Sisi and fell in love. They married. At the wedding reception, Sisi burst into tears, the first sign that something was not right.

The Ballroom: Sisi at Court

Big portraits of Sisi and Franz Josef show them dressed to the nines. **Jewels** (actually, replicas) reproduce some of the finery she wore as empress—but to her, they were her "chains." She hated official court duties and the constraints of public life, and hated being the center of attention. Sisi's mother-in-law dominated her child-rearing, her first-born died, and she complained that she couldn't sleep or eat. However, she did participate in one political cause—championing rights for Habsburg-controlled Hungary (see her **bust** and **portrait as Queen of Hungary**).

• *Head into the next, darkened room.*

Sisi
(1837-1898)

Empress Elisabeth—Franz Josef's beautiful wife—was the 19th-century equivalent of Princess Diana. Known as "Sisi" since childhood, she became an instant celebrity when she married Franz Josef at the age of 16.

Sisi's main goals in life seem to have been preserving her reputation as a beautiful empress, maintaining her Barbie-doll figure, and tending to her fairy-tale, ankle-length hair. In the 1860s, she was considered one of the most beautiful women in the world. But, in spite of severe dieting and fanatical exercise, age took its toll. After turning 30, she refused to allow photographs or portraits, and was generally seen in public with a delicate fan covering her face (and bad teeth).

Complex and influential, Sisi was adored by Franz Josef, whom she respected. Although Franz Josef was supposed to have married her sister Helene (in an arranged diplomatic marriage), he fell in love with Sisi instead. It was one of the Habsburgs' few marriages for love.

Sisi's personal mission and political cause was promoting Hungary's bid for autonomy within the empire. Her personal tragedy was the death of her son Rudolf, the crown prince, in an apparent suicide (an incident often dramatized as the "Mayerling Affair," named after the royal hunting lodge where it happened). Disliking Vienna and the confines of the court, Sisi traveled more and more frequently. (She spent so much time in Budapest, and with Hungarian statesman Count Andrássy, that many believe her third daughter to be the count's.) As the years passed, the restless Sisi and her hardworking husband became estranged. In 1898, while visiting Geneva, Switzerland, she was murdered by an Italian anarchist.

Sisi's beauty, bittersweet life, and tragic death helped create her larger-than-life legacy. However, her importance is often inflated by melodramatic accounts of her life. The Sisi Museum seeks to tell a more accurate story.

Sisi's Beauty

Sisi longed for the carefree days of her youth. She began to withdraw from public life, passing time riding horses (see **horse** statuettes and pictures) and tending obsessively to maintaining her physical beauty. Her **recipes for beauty preparations** included creams and lotions as well as wearing a raw-meat face mask while she slept. Sisi weighed herself obsessively on her gold-trimmed **scale** and tried all types of diets, including bouillon made with a **duck press.** (She never gave up pastries and ice cream, however.) After she turned 30, Sisi refused to appear in any portraits or photographs, preferring that only her more youthful depictions be preserved. Appreciate the **white nightgown, white gloves,** and **ivory fan,** because her life was about to turn even more dark.

• *Then enter the darkest room.*

Death of Sisi's Son

A mannequin wears a replica of Sisi's **black dress.** In 1889, Sisi's and Franz Josef's son, Prince Rudolf—whose life had veered into sex, drugs, and liberal politics—apparently killed his lover and himself in a suicide pact. Sisi was shattered and retreated further from public life.

• *Stroll through several more rooms.*

Escape

Sisi consoled herself with **poetry** (the museum has quotes on the walls) that expresses a longing to escape into an ideal world. She also consoled herself with travel. (See a reconstruction of her **rail car**—a step above a *couchette*.) The **map** shows her visits to Britain, Eastern Europe, and her favorite spot, Greece.

Final Room: Assassination

Sisi met her fate while traveling. While walking along a street in Geneva, Sisi was stalked and attacked by an Italian anarchist who despised royal oppressors and wanted notoriety for his cause. (He'd planned on assassinating a less-famous French prince that day—whom he'd been unable to track down—but quickly changed plans when word got out that Sisi was in town.) The **murder weapon** was this small, crude, knife-like file. It made only a small wound, but it proved fatal.

• *After the Sisi Museum, a one-way route takes you through a series of royal rooms. The first room—as if to make clear that there was more to the Habsburgs than Sisi—shows a family tree tracing the Habsburgs from 1273 to their messy WWI demise. From here, enter the private apartments of the royal family (Franz Josef's first, then Sisi's). Much of the following commentary complements the information you'll hear listening to the audioguide.*

Imperial Apartments

These were the private apartments and public meeting rooms for the emperor and empress. Franz Josef I lived here from 1857 until his death in 1916. (He had hoped to move to new digs in the New Palace, but that was not finished until after his death.)

Franz Josef was the last great Habsburg ruler. (For an abridged

Habsburg family tree, see page 438.) In these rooms, he presided over defeats and liberal inroads as the world was changing and the monarchy becoming obsolete. Here he met with advisors and welcomed foreign dignitaries, hosted lavish, white-gloved balls and stuffy formal dinners, and raised three children. He slept (alone) on his austere bed while his beloved wife Sisi retreated to her own rooms. He suffered through the assassination of his brother, the suicide of his son and heir, the murder of his wife, and the assassination of his nephew, Archduke Ferdinand, which sparked World War I and spelled the end of the Habsburg monarchy.

The Emperor's Rooms
Waiting Room for the Audience Room
Mannequins from the many corners of the Habsburg realm illustrate the multiethnic nature of the vast empire. (Also see the **map** of the empire, by the window.) Every citizen had the right to meet privately with the emperor, and people traveled fairly far to do so. While they waited nervously, they had these **three huge paintings** to stare at—propaganda showing crowds of commoners enthusiastic about their Habsburg rulers.

The painting on the right shows an 1809 scene of Emperor Franz II (Franz Josef's grandfather) returning to Vienna, celebrating the news that Napoleon had begun his retreat.

In the central painting, Franz II makes his first public appearance to adoring crowds after recovering from a life-threatening illness (1826).

In the painting on the left, Franz II returns to Vienna (see the Karlskirche in the background) to celebrate the defeat of Napoleon. The 1815 Congress of Vienna that followed was the greatest assembly of diplomats in European history. Its goal: to establish peace by shoring up Europe's monarchies against the rise of democracy and nationalism. It worked for about a century, until a colossal war—World War I—wiped out the Habsburgs and other European royal families.

This room's **chandelier**—considered the best in the palace—is Baroque, made of Bohemian crystal. It lit things until 1891, when the palace installed electric lights.

Audience Room
This is the room where Franz Josef received commoners from around the empire. They came from far and wide to show gratitude or to make a request. Imagine you've traveled for days to have your say before the emperor. You're wearing your new fancy suit—Franz Josef required that men coming before him wear a tailcoat, women a black gown with a train. You've rehearsed what you want to say. You hope your hair looks good.

Hofburg Imperial Apartments Tour

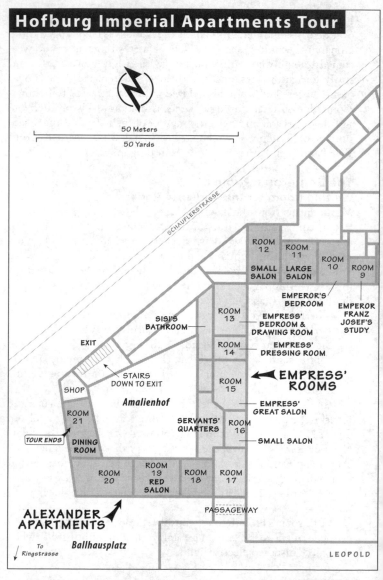

50 Meters
50 Yards

SCHAUFLERSTRASSE

ROOM 12
ROOM 11
ROOM 10
ROOM 9

SMALL SALON
LARGE SALON

EMPEROR'S BEDROOM

EMPEROR FRANZ JOSEF'S STUDY

ROOM 13

SISI'S BATHROOM

EMPRESS' BEDROOM & DRAWING ROOM

EXIT

ROOM 14

EMPRESS' DRESSING ROOM

STAIRS DOWN TO EXIT

ROOM 15

►EMPRESS' ROOMS

SHOP

Amalienhof

EMPRESS' GREAT SALON

ROOM 21

SERVANTS' QUARTERS

ROOM 16

SMALL SALON

TOUR ENDS

DINING ROOM

ROOM 20

ROOM 19 RED SALON

ROOM 18

ROOM 17

ALEXANDER APARTMENTS

PASSAGEWAY

Ballhausplatz

To Ringstrasse

LEOPOLD

Suddenly, you're face-to-face with the emp himself. (The **portrait** on the easel shows Franz Josef in 1915, when he was more than 80 years old.) Despite your efforts, you probably weren't in this room long. He'd stand at the **high table** (far left) as the visiting commoners had their say. (Standing kept things moving.) You'd hear a brief response from him (quite likely the same he'd given all day), and then you'd back out of the room while bowing (also re-

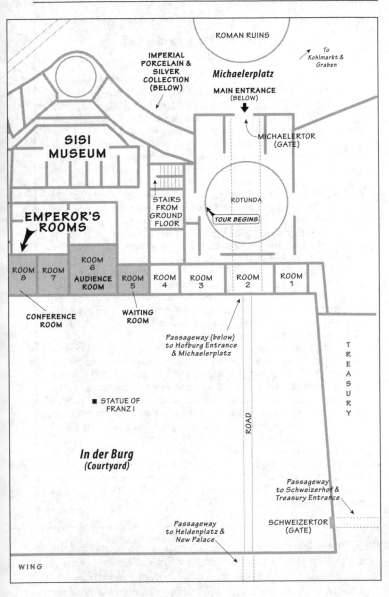

quired). On the table is a partial **list** of 56 appointments he had on January 3, 1910 (three columns: family name, meeting topic, and *Anmerkung*—the emperor's "action log").

Conference Room

The emperor presided here over the equivalent of cabinet meetings. An ongoing topic was what to do with unruly Hungary. After

Emperor Franz Josef
(1830-1916)

Franz Josef I—who ruled for 68 years (1848-1916)—was the embodiment of the Habsburg Empire as it finished its six-century-long ride. Born in 1830, Franz Josef had a stern upbringing that instilled in him a powerful sense of duty and—like so many men of power—a love of all things military.

His uncle, Ferdinand I, suffered from profound epilepsy, which prevented him from being an effective ruler. As the revolutions of 1848 rattled royal families throughout Europe, the Habsburgs forced Ferdinand to abdicate and put 18-year old Franz Josef on the throne. Ironically, as one of his first acts as emperor, Franz Josef—whose wife would later become closely identified with Hungarian independence—put down the 1848 revolt in Hungary with bloody harshness. He spent the first part of his long reign understandably paranoid, as social discontent continued to simmer.

Franz Josef was very conservative. But worse, he wrongly believed that he was a talented military tactician, leading Austria into catastrophic battles against Italy (which was fighting for its unification and independence) in the 1860s. As his army endured severe, avoidable casualties, it became clear: Franz Josef was a disaster as a general.

Wearing his uniform to the end, Franz Josef never saw what a dinosaur his monarchy was becoming, and never thought it strange that the majority of his subjects didn't even speak German. Franz Josef had no interest in democracy and pointedly never set foot in Austria's parliament building. But, like his contemporary Queen Victoria, he was a microcosm of his empire—old-fashioned but sacrosanct. His passion for low-grade paperwork earned him the nickname "Joe Bureaucrat." Mired in these petty details, he missed the big picture. In 1914, he helped start a Great War that ultimately ended the age of monarchs. The year 1918 marked the end of Europe's big royal families: Hohenzollerns (Prussia), Romanovs (Russia), and Habsburgs (Austria).

1867, Franz Josef granted Hungary a measure of independence (thus creating the "Austro-Hungarian Empire"). Hungarian diplomats attended meetings here, watched over by **paintings** on the wall showing Austria's army suppressing the popular Hungarian uprising...subtle.

Emperor Franz Josef's Study

This room evokes how seriously the emperor took his responsibilities as the top official of a vast empire. Famously energetic, Franz Josef lived a spartan life dedicated to duty. The **desk** was originally between the windows. Franz Josef could look up from his work and see his lovely, long-haired, tiny-waisted Empress Elisabeth's reflection in the mirror. Notice the **trompe l'oeil paintings** above each door, giving the believable illusion of marble relief. Notice also all the **family photos**—the perfect gift for the dad/uncle/hubby who has it all.

The walls between the rooms are wide enough to hide servants' corridors (the hidden door to his valet's room is in the back-left corner). The emperor lived with a personal staff of 14: "three valets, four lackeys, two doormen, two manservants, and three chambermaids."

Emperor's Bedroom

Franz Josef famously slept on this no-frills **iron bed** and used the **portable washstand** until 1880 (when the palace got running water). He typically rose at 3:30 and started his day in prayer, kneeling at the **prayer stool** against the far wall. After all, he was a "Divine Right" ruler. While he had a typical emperor's share of mistresses, his dresser was always well-stocked with **photos** of Sisi. Franz Josef lived here after his estrangement from Sisi. An **etching** shows the empress—a fine rider and avid hunter—sitting side-saddle while jumping a hedge.

Large Salon

This room was for royal family gatherings and went unused after Sisi's death. The big, ornate **stove** in the corner was fed from behind (this remained a standard form of heating through the 19th century).

Small Salon

This room is dedicated to the memory of Franz Josef's brother (see the **bearded portrait**), the Emperor Maximilian I of Mexico, who was overthrown and executed in 1867. It was also a smoking room. This was a necessity in the early 19th century, when smoking was newly fashionable for men, and was never done in the presence of women.

After the birth of their last child in 1868, Franz Josef and Sisi began to drift further apart. Left of the door is a small **button** the emperor had to buzz before entering his estranged wife's quarters. You, however, can go right in.

• *Climb a few steps and enter Sisi's wing.*

Empress' Rooms
Empress' Bedroom and Drawing Room

This was Sisi's room, refurbished in the Neo-Rococo style in 1854. There's the red **carpet,** covered with oriental rugs. There were always lots of fresh flowers. She not only slept here, but also lived here—the bed was rolled in and out daily—until her death in 1898. The **desk** is where she sat and wrote her letters and poems.

Empress' Dressing/Exercise Room

Servants worked three hours a day on Sisi's famous hair, while she passed the time reading. She'd exercise on the **wooden structure** and on the **rings** suspended from the doorway to the left. Afterward, she'd get a massage on the red-covered **bed.** You can psychoanalyze Sisi from the **portraits and photos** she chose to hang on her walls. They're mostly her favorite dogs, her Bavarian family, and several portraits of the romantic and anti-monarchist poet Heinrich Heine. Her infatuation with the liberal Heine, whose family was Jewish, caused a stir in royal circles.

Empress' Bathroom

Detour into the behind-the-scenes palace. In the narrow passageway, you'll walk by Sisi's hand-painted porcelain, dolphin-head **WC** (on the right). In the main bathroom, you'll see her huge copper tub (with the original wall coverings behind it), where servants washed her hair—an all-day affair. Sisi was the first Habsburg to have running water in her bathroom (notice the hot and cold faucets). You're walking on the first linoleum ever used in Vienna (c. 1880).

Servants' Quarters

Next, enter the servants' quarters, with hand-painted **tropical scenes.** Take time to enjoy the playful details. As you leave these rooms and re-enter the imperial world, look back to the room on the left.

Empress' Great Salon

The room is **painted** with Mediterranean escapes, the 19th-century equivalent of travel posters. The **statue of Polyhymnia** (the mythical Muse of poetry) is by the great Neoclassical master Antonio Canova. It has the features of Elisa, Napoleon's oldest sister, who hobnobbed with the Habsburgs. A **print** shows how Franz Josef and Sisi would—on their good days—share breakfast in this room.

Small Salon

The portrait is of **Crown Prince Rudolf,** Franz Josef's and Sisi's only son. On the morning of January 30, 1889, the 30-year-old Rudolf and a beautiful baroness were found shot dead in his hunting lodge in Mayerling. An investigation never came up with a complete explanation, but Rudolf had obviously been cheating on his wife, and the affair ended in an apparent murder-suicide. The scandal shocked the empire and tainted the Habsburgs; Sisi retreated further into her fantasy world, and Franz Josef carried on stoically with a broken heart. The mysterious "Mayerling Affair" has been dramatized in numerous movies, plays, an opera, and even a ballet.

• *Leaving Sisi's wing, turn the corner into the white-and-gold rooms occupied by the czar of Russia during the 1814–1815 Congress of Vienna. Sisi and Franz Josef used the rooms for formal occasions and public functions.*

Alexander Apartments
Red Salon
The Gobelin wall hangings were a 1776 gift from Marie-Antoinette and Louis XVI in Paris to their Viennese counterparts.

Dining Room
It's dinnertime, and Franz Josef has called his extended family

together. The settings are modest…just silver. Gold was saved for formal state dinners. Next to each name card was a menu listing the chef responsible for each dish. (Talk about pressure.) While the Hofburg had tableware for 4,000, feeding 3,000 was a typical day. The cellar was stocked with 60,000 bottles of wine. The kitchen was huge—50 birds could be roasted at once on the hand-driven spits.

The emperor sat in the center of the long table. "Ladies and gentlemen" alternated in the seating. The green glasses were for Rhenish wine. Franz Josef enforced strict protocol at mealtime: No one could speak without being spoken to by the emperor, and no one could eat after he was done. While the rest of Europe was growing democracy and expanding personal freedoms, the Habsburgs preserved their ossified worldview to the bitter end.

In 1918, World War I ended, Austria was created as a modern nation-state, the Habsburgs were tossed out…and Hofburg Palace was destined to become a museum.

• *Drop off your audioguide, zip through the shop, go down the stairs, and you're back on the street. Two quick lefts take you back to the palace square (In der Burg), where the Treasury awaits just past the black, red, and gold gate on the far side (see the next chapter).*

HOFBURG TREASURY TOUR

Weltliche und Geistliche Schatzkammer

The Hofburg Palace's "Treasure Room" contains the best jewels on the Continent. Slip through the vault doors and reflect on the glitter of 21 rooms filled with secular and religious ornaments: scepters, swords, crowns, orbs, weighty robes, double-headed eagles, gowns, gem-studded bangles, and a unicorn horn.

There are plenty of beautiful objects here—I've highlighted those that have the most history behind them. But you could spend days in here marveling at the riches of the bygone empire.

Use this chapter to get the lay of the land, but rent the excellent audioguide to really delve into the Treasury (and to make up for the lack of written English descriptions).

Orientation

Cost: €12, €18 combo-ticket with Kunsthistorisches Museum and New Palace museums.

Hours: Wed-Mon 9:00-17:30, closed Tue.

Getting There: The Treasury is tucked away in the Hofburg Palace complex. From the Hofburg's central courtyard (In der Burg), salute the Caesar-esque statue and turn about-face. Pass through the black, red, and gold gate (Schweizertor), following *Schatzkammer* signs, which lead into the Schweizerhof courtyard; the Treasury entrance is in the far-right corner. Follow signs to a stairway that climbs up to the Treasury (see map on page 143).

Information: Tel. 01/525-240, www.khm.at.

Audioguides: A basic audioguide covering the top 11 jewels is included with your ticket. Or, for €2, you can rent an audioguide programmed to describe the top 100 stops—well worth it to get the most out of this dazzling collection.

Starring: The Imperial Crown and other accessories of the Holy Roman Emperors, plus many other crowns, jewels, robes, and priceless knickknacks.

The Tour Begins

The Habsburgs saw themselves as the successors to the ancient Roman emperors, and they wanted crowns and royal regalia to match the pomp of the ancients. They used these precious objects for coronation ceremonies, official ribbon-cutting events, and their own personal pleasure. You'll see the prestigious crowns and accoutrements of the rulers of the Holy Roman Empire (a medieval alliance of Germanic kingdoms so named because it wanted to be considered the continuation of the Roman Empire). Other crowns belonged to Austrian dukes and kings, and some robes and paraphernalia were used by Austria's religious elite. And many costly things were created simply for the enjoyment of the wealthy (but not necessarily royal) Habsburgs.

• *Skip through Room 1 to where we'll begin, in Room 2.*

From the First Habsburg to Napoleon
Room 2

The personal **crown of Rudolf II** (1602) occupies the center of the room along with its accompanying scepter and orb; a bust of Rudolf

II (1552-1612) sits nearby. The crown's design symbolically merges a bishop's miter ("Holy"), the arch across the top of a Roman emperor's helmet ("Roman"), and the typical medieval king's crown ("Emperor"). Accompanying the crown are the matching **scepter** (made from the ivory tusk of a narwhal) and **orb** (holding four diamonds to symbolize the four corners of the world, which the emperor ruled). Orbs have been royal symbols of the world since ancient Roman times. They seem to indicate that, even in pre-Columbus days, Europe's intelligentsia assumed the world was round.

This crown was Rudolf's personal one. He wore a different crown (which we'll see later) in his official role as Holy Roman Emperor. In many dynasties, a personal crown like this was dismantled by the next ruler to custom-make his own. But Rudolf's crown was so well-crafted that it was passed down through the generations, even inspiring crown-shaped church steeples as far away as Amsterdam (when that city was under Habsburg control).

Two centuries later (1806), this crown and scepter became the official regalia of Austria's rulers, as seen in the large **portrait of Franz I** (the one behind you). Napoleon Bonaparte had just conquered Austria and dissolved the Holy Roman Empire. Franz (ruled 1792-1835) was allowed to remain in power, but he had to downgrade his title from "Franz II, Holy Roman Emperor" to "Franz I, Emperor of Austria."

Rooms 3 and 4

These rooms contain some of the **coronation vestments and regalia** needed for the new Austrian (not Holy Roman) Emperor. There was a different one for each of the emperor's subsidiary titles, e.g., King of Hungary or King of Lombardy. So many crowns and kingdoms in the Habsburgs' vast empire! Those with ermine collars are modeled after Napoleon's coronation robes.

• *For more on how Napoleon had an impact on Habsburg Austria, pass through Room 9 and into...*

Room 5

Ponder the **Cradle of the King of Rome,** once occupied by Napoleon's son, who was born in 1811 and made King of Rome. The little eagle at the foot is symbolically not yet able to fly, but glory-bound. Glory is symbolized by the star, with dad's big *N* raised high. While it's fun to think of Napoleon's baby snoozing in here, this was a ceremonial "throne bed" that was rarely used.

Napoleon Bonaparte (1769-1821) was a French commoner who rose to power as a charismatic general in the Revolution. While pledging allegiance to democracy, he in fact crowned himself Emperor of France and hobnobbed with Europe's royalty. When his wife Josephine could not bear him a male heir, Napoleon divorced her and married into the Habsburg family.

Portraits show Napoleon and his new bride, Marie Louise, Franz I/II's daughter (and Marie-Antoinette's great-niece). Napoleon gave her a **jewel chest** decorated with the bees of industriousness, his personal emblem. With the birth of the baby King of Rome, Napoleon and Marie Louise were poised to start a new dynasty of European rulers...but then Napoleon met his Waterloo, and the Habsburgs remained in power.

Miscellaneous Wonders
Room 6

For Divine Right kings, even child-rearing was a sacred ritual that needed elaborate regalia for public ceremonies. The 23-pound **gold basin and pitcher** were used to baptize noble children, who were dressed in the **hooded baptismal dresses** displayed nearby.

Room 7

These jewels are the true "treasures," a cabinet of wonders used by Habsburgs to impress their relatives (or to hock when funds got low). The irregularly shaped, 2,680-karat **emerald** is rough-cut, as the cutter wanted to do only the minimum to avoid making a mistake and shattering the giant gem. Check out the milky

opal, the **"hair amethyst,"** and a 492-karat **aquamarine.** The helmet-like, jewel-studded **crown** was a gift from Muslim Turks supporting a Hungarian king who, as a Protestant, was a thorn in the side of the Catholic Habsburgs (who eventually toppled him).

Room 8

The eight-foot-tall, 500-year-old **"unicorn horn"** (actually a narwhal tusk), was considered to have magical healing powers bestowed from on high. This one was owned by the Holy Roman Emperor—clearly a divine monarch. The huge **agate bowl,** cut

from a single piece, may have been made in ancient Roman times and eventually found its way into the collection of their successors, the Habsburgs.

Religious Rooms

After Room 8, you enter several rooms of **religious objects**—crucifixes, chalices, mini-altarpieces, reliquaries, and bishops' vestments. Habsburg rulers mixed the institutions of church and state, so these precious religious accoutrements were also part of their display of secular power.

• *Browse these rooms, then backtrack, passing by the Cradle of the King of Rome, and eventually reaching...*

Regalia of the Holy Roman Empire
Room 10

The next few rooms contain some of the oldest and most venerated objects in the Treasury—the robes, crowns, and sacred objects of the Holy Roman Emperor.

The big red-silk and gold-thread **mantle,** nearly 900 years old,

was worn by Holy Roman Emperors at their coronations. Notice the oriental imagery: a palm tree in the center, flanked by lions subduing camels. The hem is written in Arabic (wishing its wearer "great wealth, gifts, and pleasure"). This robe, brought back from the East by Crusaders, gave the Germanic emperors an exotic look that recalled great biblical kings such as Solomon. Many Holy Roman Emperors were

Charlemagne (Karl der Grosse) and the Holy Roman Empire

The title Holy Roman Emperor conveyed three important concepts:

Holy = The emperor ruled by divine authority (and not as a pagan Roman).
Roman = He was a successor to the empire that fell in A.D. 476.
Emperor = He was a ruler over many different nationalities.

Charlemagne (747-814) briefly united much of Western Europe—that is, the former Roman Empire. On Christmas Eve in the year 800, he was crowned "Roman Emperor" by the pope in St. Peter's Basilica in Rome. After Charlemagne's death, the empire split apart. His successors (who ruled only a portion of Charlemagne's empire) still wanted to envision themselves as inheritors of Charlemagne's greatness. They took to calling themselves Roman Emperors, adding the "Holy" part in the 11th century to emphasize that they ruled by divine authority.

The Holy Roman Emperorship was an elected, not necessarily hereditary, office. Traditionally, the rulers of four important provinces would gather with three powerful archbishops to pick the new ruler; these seven "kingmakers" each held the prestigious title of Elector. The practice lasted through medieval and Renaissance times to the Napoleonic Wars, with most of the emperors hailing from the Habsburg family.

At the empire's peak around 1520, it truly was great. Emperor Charles V ruled Spain in addition to the HRE, so his realm stretched from Vienna to Spain, from Holland to Sicily, and from Bohemia to Bolivia in the New World. But throughout much of its existence, the HRE consisted of little more than petty dukes, ruling a loose coalition of independent nobles. It was Voltaire who quipped that the HRE was "neither holy, nor Roman, nor an empire."

Napoleon ended the title in 1806. The last Habsburg emperors (including Franz Josef) were merely Emperors of Austria.

crowned by the pope himself. That fact, plus this Eastern-looking mantle, helped put the "Holy" in Holy Roman Emperor.

Room 11

The collection's highlight is the 10th-century **crown of the Holy Roman Emperor.** It was probably made for Otto I (c. 960), the first king to call himself Holy Roman Emperor.

The Imperial Crown swirls with symbolism "proving" that the emperor was both holy and Roman: The cross on top says the HRE ruled as Christ's representative on earth, and the jeweled arch over the top is reminiscent of the parade helmet of ancient Romans. The jewels themselves allude to the wearer's king-hood in the here and now. Imagine the impres-sion this priceless, glittering crown must have made on the emperor's medieval subjects.

King Solomon's portrait on the crown (to the right of the cross) is Old Testament proof that kings can be wise and good. King David (next panel) is similar proof that they can be just. The crown's eight sides represent the celestial city of Jerusa-lem's eight gates. The jewels on the front panel symbolize the 12 apostles.

On the forehead of the crown, notice that beneath the cross there's a pale-blue, heart-shaped sapphire. Look a little small for the prime spot? That's because this is a replacement for a long-lost opal said to have had almost mythical, magical powers.

Nearby is the 11th-century **Imperial Cross** that preceded the emperor in ceremonies. Encrusted with jewels, it had a hol-low compartment (its core is wood) that carried substantial chunks thought to be from *the* **cross** on which Jesus was crucified and *the* **Holy Lance** used to pierce his side (both pieces are displayed in the same glass case). Holy Roman Emperors actually carried the lance into battle in the 10th century. Look behind the cross to see how it was a box that could be clipped open and shut, used for holding holy relics. You can see bits of the "true cross" anywhere, but this is a prime piece—with the actual nail hole.

The other case has additional objects used in the coronation ceremony: The **orb** (orbs were modeled on late-Roman ceremonial objects, then topped with the cross) and **scepter** (the one with the oak leaves), along with the sword, were carried ahead of the em-peror in the procession. In earlier times, these objects were thought to have belonged to Charlemagne himself, the greatest ruler of me-dieval Europe, but in fact they're mostly from 300 to 400 years later (c. 1200).

Yet another glass case contains more objects said to belong to Charlemagne. Some of these may be authentic, since they're closer to his era. You'll see the jeweled, purse-like **reliquary of St. Ste-phen** and the **saber of Charlemagne.** The gold-covered **Book of the Gospels** was the Bible that emperors placed their hands on to swear the oath of office. On the wall nearby, the **tall painting** de-

picts Charlemagne modeling the Imperial Crown—although the crown wasn't made until a hundred years after he died.

Room 12

Now picture all this regalia used together. The **painting** shows the coronation of Maria Theresa's son Josef II as Holy Roman Emperor in 1764. Set in a church in Frankfurt (filled with the bigwigs—literally—of the day), Josef is wearing the same crown and royal garb that you've just seen.

Emperors followed the same coronation ritual that originated in the 10th century. The new emperor would don the mantle. The entourage paraded into a church for Mass, led by the religious authorities carrying the Imperial Cross. The emperor placed his hand on the Book of the Gospels and swore his oath. Then he knelt before the three archbishop Electors, who placed the Imperial Crown on his head (sometimes he even traveled to Rome to be crowned by the pope himself). The new emperor rose, accepted the orb and scepter, and—dut dutta dah!—you had a new ruler.

The Rest of the Treasury

Room 12 also displays the **leather cases** used to store and transport the crowns, crosses, and other objects. Another glass case contains **relics**—such as a fragment of Jesus' manger, a piece of Christ's loincloth, and a shred of the Last Supper tablecloth.

Rooms 13-15 have (among other things) **portraits of important Habsburgs,** such as Maximilian I and Mary of Burgundy. Room 16 contains the **royal vestments** (15th century), which display perhaps the most exquisite workmanship in the entire Treasury. Look closely—they're "painted" with gold and silver threads. But after seeing so much bling, by the time you view these vestments, they can seem downright understated—just another example of the pomp and circumstance of the majestic Habsburgs.

KUNSTHISTORISCHES MUSEUM TOUR

The Kunsthistorwhateveritis Museum—let's just say "Koonst"—houses the family collection of Austria's luxury-loving Habsburg rulers. Their joie de vivre is reflected in this collection—some of the most beautiful, sexy, and fun art from two centuries (c. 1450-1650). At their peak of power in the 1500s, the Habsburgs ruled Austria, Germany, northern Italy, the Netherlands, and Spain—and you'll see a wide variety of art from all these places and beyond.

The building itself is worth notice—a lavish textbook example of Historicism. Despite its palatial feel, it was originally designed for the same purpose it serves today: to showcase its treasures in an inviting space while impressing visitors with the grandeur of the empire.

Orientation

Cost: €12, also includes New Palace museums across the Ring; free for kids under 18, €18 combo-ticket also includes the Hofburg Treasury.

Hours: Tue-Sun 10:00-18:00, Thu until 21:00, closed Mon.

Getting There: It's on the Ringstrasse at Maria-Theresien-Platz, U-2 or U-3: Volkstheater/Museumsplatz (exit toward *Burg-ring*).

Information: Tel. 01/525-240, www.khm.at.

Audioguide: An excellent €4 audioguide is available at the desk in the atrium, just before the main staircase. Covering nearly 600 items, the audioguide is worthwhile if you want an in-depth tour beyond the items covered in this chapter.

Services: There's a free cloakroom. The restaurant is on the first floor.

Starring: The world's best collection of Bruegel, plus Titian, Caravaggio, a Vermeer gem, and Rembrandt self-portraits.

The Tour Begins

Of the museum's many exhibits, we'll tour only the Painting Gallery (Gemäldegalerie) on the first floor. Climb the main staircase, featuring Antonio Canova's statue of *Theseus Clubbing the Centaur*. Italian, Spanish, and French art is in the right half of the building (as you face Theseus), and Northern European art is to the left. Notice that the museum labels the largest rooms with Roman numerals (Saal I, II, III) and the smaller rooms around the perimeter with Arabic (Rooms 1, 2, 3). The museum is reorganizing its paintings, and the locations of some works (especially from the Italian Renaissance) may have shifted by the time you visit.

• *Bear right up the stairs at Theseus; at the top of the staircase, make a U-turn to the left. Saal I is ahead of you and on your right. Enter Saal I and walk right into the High Renaissance.*

Venetian Renaissance

About the year 1500, Italy embarked on a 100-year renaissance, or "rebirth," of interest in the art and learning of ancient Greece and Rome. In painting, that meant that ordinary humans and Greek gods joined saints and angels as popular subjects.

Saal I spans the long career of **Titian** the Venetian (it rhymes). He painted portraits, Christian Madonnas, and sexy Venuses with equal ease. He seemed particularly intimate with the pre-Christian gods and their antics. In *Mars, Venus, and Amor,* a busy cupid oversees the goddess of love, making her case that war is not the answer. Mars—his weapons blissfully discarded—sees her point.

Danae features more pre-Christian mythology. Zeus, the king of the gods, was always zooming to earth in the form of some creature or other to fool around with mortal women. Here, he descends as a shower of gold to consort with the willing Danae. You can almost see the human form of Zeus within the cloud. Danae is

KUNSTHISTORISCHES

Kunsthistorisches Museum—First Floor

ROOM 17 VERMEER

ROOM 16

ROOM 15 BOSCH & VAN DER WEYDEN

ROOM 14 VAN EYCK

SAAL TEMPORARY

WC

STAIRS TO SECOND FLOOR

SAAL XI

SAAL X

SAAL IX

ROOM 18

THESEUS STATUE

BRUEGEL

ROOM 19

SAAL XII

NORTHERN EUROPEAN ART

STAIRS FROM GROUND FLOOR

SNYDERS

SAAL XIII RUBENS

SAAL XIV RUBENS

SAAL XV DÜRER & HOLBEIN

SHOP

ROOM 20

ROOM 21 REMBRANDT

ROOM 22 BRUEGHEL

ROOM 23

ROOM 24 CRANACH & ALTDORFER

TOUR ENDS

MAIN

Maria-Theresien-

helpless with rapture, opening her legs to receive him, while her servant tries to catch the heavenly spurt with a golden dish. Danae's rich, luminous flesh is set off by the dark servant at right and the threatening sky above. The white sheets beneath her make her glow even more. This is not just a classic nude—it's a Renaissance Miss August. How could ultra-conservative Catholic emperors have tolerated such a downright pagan and erotic painting? Apparently, without a problem.

In the large *Ecce Homo*, Titian tackles a Christian theme. A crowd mills about, when suddenly there's a commotion. They nudge each other and start to point. Follow their gaze diagonally up the stairs

to a battered figure entering way up in the corner. "Ecce Homo!" says Pilate. "Behold the man." And he presents Jesus to the mob. For us, as for the unsympathetic crowd, the humiliated Son of God is not the center of the scene, but almost an afterthought.

In **Saal II,** colorful works by **Paolo Veronese** reflect the wealth of Venice, the funnel through which luxury goods from the exotic East flowed into northern Europe. In Veronese's *Adoration of the Magi (Anbetung der Könige),* these-Three-Kings-from-Orient-are dressed not in biblical costume, but in the imported silks of Venetian businessmen.

In **Saal III**, **Tintoretto**'s many portraits give us a peek at the movers and shakers of the Venetian Empire.

• *The following paintings are generally found in the smaller rooms that adjoin Saals I, II, and III.*

Italian Renaissance and Mannerism

In **Room 1**, *St. Sebastian (Der Hl. Sebastian)*, by **Andrea Mantegna,** is shot through with arrows. Sebastian was an early Christian martyr, but he stands like a Renaissance statue—on a pedestal, his weight on one foot, displaying his Greek-god anatomy. Mantegna places the three-dimensional "statue" in a three-dimensional setting, using floor tiles and roads that recede into the distance to create the illusion of depth.

In **Correggio**'s *Jupiter and Io* (**Room 2,** see photo), the king of the gods appears in a cloud—see his foggy face and hands?—to get a date with a beautiful nymph named Io. ("Io, Io, it's off to earth I go.") Correggio tips Renaissance "balance"—the enraptured Io may be perched vertically in the center of the canvas right now, but she won't be for long.

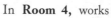

Find the little round painting nearby (**Room 2**). In this *Self-Portrait in a Convex Mirror (Selbstbildnis im Konvexspiegel)*, 21-year-old **Parmigianino** (like the cheese) gazes into a convex mirror and perfectly reproduces the curved reflection on a convex piece of wood. Amazing.

In **Room 4,** works by the young **Raphael** capture the spirit of the High Renaissance, combining symmetry, grace, beauty, and emotion. His *Madonna of the Meadow (Die Madonna im Grünen)* is a mountain of motherly love—Mary's head is the summit and her flowing robe is the base—enfolding Baby Jesus and John the Baptist. The geometric perfection, serene landscape, and Mary's adoring face make this a masterpiece of sheer grace—but then you get smacked by an ironic fist: The cross the little tykes play with foreshadows their gruesome deaths.

Farther along, through the small rooms along the far end of this wing (likely **Room 7**), find the cleverly deceptive portraits by **Giuseppe Arcimboldo.** His *Summer (Sommer)*—a.k.a. "Fruit Face"—is one of four paintings the Habsburg court painter did showing the seasons (and elements) as people. Its grotesque weird-

ness is what makes it typical of Mannerist art. With a pickle nose, pear chin, and corn-husk ears, this guy literally is what he eats.
• *Find Caravaggio in Saal V.*

Caravaggio

Caravaggio shocked the art world with brutally honest reality. Compared with Raphael's super-sweet *Madonna of the Meadow*, Caravaggio's *Madonna of the Rosary (Die Rosenkranzmadonna*, the biggest canvas in the room) looks perfectly ordinary, and the saints kneeling around her have dirty feet.

In *David with the Head of Goliath (David mit dem Haupt des Goliath)*—in the corner near the window—Caravaggio turns a third-degree-interrogation light on a familiar Bible story. David shoves the dripping head of the slain giant right in our noses. The painting, bled of color, is virtually a black-and-white crime-scene photo—slightly overexposed. Out of the deep darkness shine only a few crucial details. This David is not a heroic Renaissance man like Michelangelo's famous statue, but a homeless teen that Caravaggio paid to portray God's servant. And the severed head of Goliath is none other than Caravaggio himself, an in-your-face self-portrait.
• *Move into Room 10, in the corner of the museum.*

Velázquez

When the Habsburgs ruled both Austria and Spain, cousins kept in touch through portraits of themselves and their kids. Diego Velázquez was the greatest of Spain's "photojournalist" painters — heavily influenced by Caravaggio's realism, capturing his subjects without passing judgment, flattering, or glorifying them.

Watch little Margarita Habsburg grow up in three different *Portraits of Margarita Theresa (Infantin Margarita Teresa)*, from age two to age nine. Margarita was destined from birth to marry her Austrian cousin, the future Emperor Leopold I. Pictures like these, sent from Spain every few years, let her pen pal/fiancé get to know her. The kids' oh-so-serious faces, regal poses, and royal trappings are contradicted by their natural precociousness. No wonder Velázquez was so popular.

Also see a portrait of Margarita's little brother, *Philip Prosper,* wearing a dress. Sadly, Philip was a sickly boy who would only live two years longer. The amulets he's wearing were intended to fend off illness. His hand rests limply on the back of the chair—above an adorable puppy who seems to be asking, "But who will play with me?"

Velázquez had a talent for capturing the essence of a subject—showing even the warts so perfectly that the subject could not be offended. In this case, Velázquez even seems to foreshadow the tyke's untimely death.

Also notice that all of these kids are quite, ahem, homely. To understand why, look to the wall on your right—their dad, Philip V, shows the defects of royal inbreeding: weepy eyes and a pointed chin (sorry, that pointy moustache doesn't do enough to distract from these features).

• *Return to the main Saals and continue on, past glimpses of Baroque art, featuring large, colorful canvases showcasing over-the-top emotions and pudgy, winged babies (the surefire mark of Baroque art). If you don't have time to get out to Schönbrunn Palace on this visit, you can get a good look at it here—find two versions of* **Canaletto's** *Schloss Schönbrunn in* **Saal VII,** *one of which also shows the Viennese skyline in the distance.*

Exit Saal VII, go past the top of the stairs, and then turn right. Enter Saal IX (opposite the Titian Room), then turn right to enter Room 14.

Early Northern Art

The "Northern Renaissance," brought on by the economic boom of Dutch and Flemish trading, was more secular and Protestant than Catholic-funded Italian art. We'll see fewer Madonnas, saints, and Greek gods and more peasants, landscapes, and food. Paintings are smaller and darker, full of down-to-earth objects. Northern artists sweated the details, encouraging the patient viewer to appreciate the beauty in everyday things.

This section features three early northern painters. In the painstakingly detailed *Portrait of Cardinal Niccolò Albergati* (**Room 14**), **Jan van Eyck** refuses to airbrush out the jowls and wrinkles, showcasing the quiet dignity of an ordinary man.

In **Room 15**, Rogier van

der Weyden's *Crucifixion Triptych (Kreuzigungsaltar)* strips the Crucifixion down to the essential characters, set in a sparse landscape. The agony seems understated, seen in just a few solemn faces and dramatically creased robes. And yet, compared to the very restrained art of its era, this piece is extremely emotive—Mary clutches the cross and presses her face against the trickle of blood.

In the same room (in a freestanding case), **Hieronymus Bosch**'s *Christ Carrying the Cross (Kreuztragung Christi)* is crammed with puny humans, not supermen. Originally one wing of a hinged altarpiece, the piece depicts two groups: the soldiers above prodding Jesus, and the commoners and sympathizers below. The fat frog on the shield (in front of Jesus) represents evil. Below Christ are the two thieves about to be crucified next to him: The good thief confesses to a monk, while the bad thief stands defiant. Circle around to the back side of the altarpiece, with a naked child—perhaps an innocent Baby Jesus at play?

• *The adjoining Saal X contains the largest collection of Bruegels in captivity. Linger. If you like it, linger longer.*

Pieter Bruegel

The undisputed master of the slice-of-life village scene was Pieter Bruegel the Elder (c. 1525-1569)—think of him as the Norman Rockwell of the 16th century. His name (pronounced "BROY-gull") is sometimes spelled *Brueghel*. Don't confuse Pieter Bruegel the Elder with his sons, Pieter Brueghel the Younger and Jan Brueghel, who added luster and an "h" to the family name (and whose works are also displayed in this room). Despite his many rural paintings, Bruegel was actually a cultivated urbanite who liked to wear peasants' clothing to observe country folk at play (a trans-fest-ite?). He celebrated their simple life, but he also skewered their weaknesses—not to single them out as hicks, but as universal examples of human folly.

The Peasant Wedding (Bauernhochzeit), Bruegel's most famous work, is less about the wedding than the food. It's a farmers' feeding frenzy, as the barnful of wedding guests scrambles to get their share of free eats. Two men bring in the next course, a tray of fresh pudding. The bagpiper pauses to check it out. A guy grabs bowls and passes them down the table, taking our attention with them. Everyone's going at it, including a kid in an oversized red cap who licks the bowl with his fingers. In the middle of it all, look who's been completely forgotten—the demure bride sitting in front of the blue-green cloth. According to Flemish tradition, the bride was not allowed to speak or eat at the party, and the groom was not in attendance at all. (One thing: The guy carrying the front end of the food tray—is he stepping forward with his right leg, or with his left, or with...all three?)

Speaking of two left feet, Bruegel's *Peasant Dance (Bauerntanz)* shows a celebration at the consecration of a village church. Peasants happily clog to the tune of a lone bagpiper, who wails away while his pit crew keeps him lubed with wine. Notice the overexuberant guy in the green hat on the left, who accidentally smacks his buddy in the face. As with his other peasant paintings, Bruegel captures the warts-and-all scene accurately—it's neither romanticized nor patronizing.

The three Bruegel landscape paintings are part of an original series of six "calendar" paintings, depicting the seasons of the year. *Gloomy Day (Der düstere Tag)* opens the cycle, as winter turns to spring...slowly. The snow has melted, flooding the distant river, the trees are still leafless, and the

villagers stir, cutting wood and mending fences. We skip ahead to autumn in *The Return of the Herd (Heimkehr der Herde)*—still sunny, but winter's storms are fast approaching. We see the scene from above, emphasizing the landscape as much as the people. Finally,

in *Hunters in Snow (Jäger im Schnee)* it's the dead of winter, and three dog-tired hunters with their tired dogs trudge along with only a single fox to show for their efforts. As they crest the hill, the grove of bare trees opens up to a breathtaking view—they're almost home, where they can join their mates playing hockey. Birds soar like the hunters' rising spirits—emerging from winter's work and looking ahead to a new year.

The Tower of Babel (Trumbach zu Babel), modeled after Rome's Colosseum, stretches into the clouds, towering over the village. Impressive as it looks, on closer inspection the tower is crooked—destined eventually to tumble onto the village. Even so, the king (in the foreground) demands further work.

• *Linger among the Bruegels, then find your way to the corner and little* **Room 17.**

Jan Vermeer

In his small canvases, the Dutch painter Jan Vermeer quiets the world down to where we can hear our own heartbeat, letting us appreciate the beauty in common things.

The curtain opens and we see *The Art of Painting (Die Mal-kunst),* a behind-the-scenes look at Vermeer at work. He's paint-

ing a model dressed in blue, starting with her laurel-leaf headdress. The studio is its own little dollhouse world framed by a chair in the foreground and the wall in back. Then Vermeer fills this space with the few gems he wants us to focus on—the chandelier, the map, the painter's costume. Everything is lit by a crystal-clear light, letting us see these everyday items with fresh eyes.

The painting is also called *The Allegory of Painting.* The model has the laurel leaves, trumpet, and book that symbolize the muse of history and fame. The artist—his back to the public—earnestly tries to capture fleeting fame with a small sheet of canvas.

• *Hook left into the long hallway. About halfway down, turn left into* **Saal XII.**

Frans Snyders

In *Fish Market (Fischmarkt),* we see a dramatic still life of a merchant's stand piled high with still-wriggling fish. Under the table, notice the cute seal cub and, behind that, the gleaming eyes of a cat. Aside from its impressive array of marine life, this canvas shows off the collaborative nature of artistic endeavor: Notice the expressive faces of the customers on the right. While Snyders specialized in fish, he knew that portraits weren't his strong suit—so he enlisted his friend Anthony van Dyck to paint these faces for him. (A student of Rubens, Van Dyck went on to great acclaim as a court painter for England's Charles I.)

More Northern Art

If you like fine details and straightforward realism, seek out these fine works.

In *Flowers in a Wooden Vessel* (*Grosser Blumenstrauss*, in Room 22), **Jan Brueghel,** son of the famous Pieter Bruegel, puts meticulously painted flowers from different seasons together in one artfully arranged vase. It's like a botany textbook on canvas.

Lucas Cranach's *Crucifixion* (*Kreuzigung Christi,* in Room 24) is all too human—Christ is twisted, bleeding, scarred, and vomiting blood, as the storm clouds roll in (contrast Cranach's representation with Dürer's powerful Renaissance Christ in Saal XV).

Albrecht Altdorfer's garish *The Resurrection* (*Auferstehung Christi,* in Room 24—see photo on right) looks like a poster for a bad horror film: "Easter Sunday III. He's back from the dead...and he's ticked!" Christ's glowing halo ignites the dark cave, illuminating the faces of the dazed guards.

Hans Holbein painted *Jane Seymour* (in Saal XV), wife number III of the VI wives of England's Henry VIII. The former lady in waiting—timid and modest—poses stiffly (see photo on left), trying very hard to look the part of Henry's queen. Next.

• Now enter the big-canvas, bright-colored world of Baroque in **Saal XIII.**

Peter Paul Rubens

Stand in front of Rubens' *Self-Portrait (Selbstbildnis)* and admire the darling of Catholic-dominated Flanders (northern Belgium) in his prime: famous, wealthy, well-traveled, the friend of kings and princes, an artist, diplomat, man about town, and—obviously—confident. Rubens' work runs the gamut, from realistic portraits to lounging nudes, Greek myths to altarpieces, from pious devotion to violent sex.

But, can we be sure it's Baroque? Ah yes, I'm sure you'll find a pudgy, winged baby somewhere.

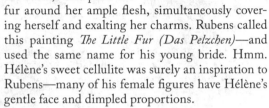

In the large *Ildefonso Altarpiece (Il-defonso-Altar)*, a glorious Mary appears (with her entourage of p.w.b.'s) to reward the grateful Spanish St. Ildefonso with a chasuble (priest's smock).

The 53-year-old Rubens married Hélène Fourment, a dimpled girl of 16

(find her portrait across the room). She pulls the fur around her ample flesh, simultaneously covering herself and exalting her charms. Rubens called this painting *The Little Fur (Das Pelzchen)*—and used the same name for his young bride. Hmm. Hélène's sweet cellulite was surely an inspiration to Rubens—many of his female figures have Hélène's gentle face and dimpled proportions.

How could Rubens paint all these enormous canvases in one lifetime? He didn't. He kept a workshop of assistants busy painting backgrounds and minor figures, working from his own small sketches. Then the master stepped in to add the finishing touches. In **Saal XIV,** see the giant canvas *The Miracles of St. Ignatius of Loyola (Wunder des hl. Ignatius von Loyola)*, with the sketches displayed nearby.

• *Head into Saal XV.*

Albrecht Dürer

As the son of a goldsmith and having traveled to Italy, Dürer combined meticulous Northern detail with Renaissance symmetry. So

his *All Saints' Picture (Allerheiligen-bild)*, a.k.a. *Landauer Altarpiece*, may initially look like a complex hog pile of saints and angels, but it's perfectly geometrical. The crucified Christ forms a triangle in the center, framed by triangular clouds and flanked by three-sided crowds of people—appropriate for a painting about the Trinity. Dürer practically invented the self-portrait as an art form, and he included himself, the lone earthling in this heavenly vision (bottom right), with a plaque announcing that he, Albrecht Dürer, painted this in 1511.

The Case of the Missing Salt Cellar

In the middle of the night of May 11, 2003, someone broke into the Kunsthistorisches Museum, smashed the glass case containing Benvenuto Cellini's delightful salt cellar (*saliera*), and set off the alarm. The thief grabbed the $60 million, gold-plated salt bowl and ran, scrambling through a second-story window and down some construction scaffolding. The security guard, assuming it was a false alarm, simply turned it off and went back to sleep.

For two years, the salt cellar vanished from sight. Police looked everywhere—including a foray into Italy, chasing a tip from a prankster—but came up empty. Meanwhile, the 10-inch-high masterpiece lay hidden right nearby, tucked under a bed in a Vienna apartment.

In October 2005, a ransom note arrived at the insurance company: Pay $12 million and the statue will be returned. The thief even sent proof he really had it, enclosing the tiny pickle-fork trident held by Neptune. An exchange was arranged, but on the appointed day, the thief suddenly got suspicious. He called it off by sending a text message from his mobile phone. Crafty police traced the call and located the Vienna store where the phone had been purchased. They pored over the store's security camera footage until they found who had bought it. When they published the images in the media, the thief turned himself in. He was an otherwise ordinary security-alarm salesman who'd almost pulled off the art crime of the century.

Police found the salt bowl carefully wrapped, boxed, and buried in the woods near Vienna, with only a few scratches on it. The 1,000-day ordeal was over, and Cellini's one-of-a-kind masterpiece returned home, displayed for all in Vienna to marvel at and enjoy.

• *From here, pass through Rooms 22–24 (where you'll see paintings by Cranach, Altdorfer, and Brueghel, among others) to find corner* **Room 21,** *where you'll finish your tour.*

Rembrandt van Rijn

Rembrandt became wealthy by painting portraits of Holland's upwardly mobile businessmen, but his greatest subject was himself. In the *Large Self-Portrait (Grosses Selbstbildnis)* we see the hands-on-hips, defiant, open-stance determination of a man who will do what he wants, and if people don't like it, tough.

In typical Rembrandt style, most of the canvas is a dark, smudgy brown, with only the

side of his face glowing from the darkness. (Remember Caravaggio? Rembrandt did.) Unfortunately, the year this was painted, Rembrandt's fortunes changed. Looking at the *Small Self-Portrait (Kleines Selbstbildnis)* from 1657, consider Rembrandt's last years. His wife died, his children died young, and commissions for paintings dried up as his style veered from the common path. He had to auction off paintings to pay his debts, and he died a poor man. Rembrandt's numerous self-portraits painted from youth until old age show a man always changing—from wide-eyed youth to successful portraitist to this disillusioned, but still defiant, old man.

The Rest of the Kunst

We've seen only the *Kunst* (art) half of the Kunsthistorisches ("art history") Museum. The museum's ground floor has several world-class collections of Greek, Roman, Egyptian, and Near Eastern antiquities. You can see a statue of the Egyptian pharaoh Thutmosis III and the Gemma Augustea, a Roman cameo thought to be kept by Augustus on his private desk. Or view the *Kunstkammer*—the personal collections of the House of Habsburg. Amassed by 17 emperors over the centuries, the *Kunstkammer* ("art cabinet") is a dazzling display of 2,000 ancient treasures, medieval curios, and *objets d'art* from 800 B.C. to 1891. The highlight is Cellini's famous salt cellar (see sidebar).

SLEEPING IN VIENNA

As you move out from the middle of the city, hotel prices drop. My listings are in the old center (figure at least €100 for a decent double), along the likeable Mariahilfer Strasse (about €90), and near the Westbahnhof (about €70).

Book ahead for Vienna if you can, particularly for holidays (see page 475; for tips on making reservations, see page 22). Business hotels have their highest rates in September and October, when it's peak convention time. Prices are also high right around New Year's Eve.

While few accommodations in Vienna are air-conditioned, you can generally get fans on request. Places with elevators often have a few stairs to climb, too. Viennese elevators can be confusing: In most of Europe, 0 is the ground floor, and 1 is the first floor up (our "second floor"). But in Vienna, elevators can also have floors P, U, M, and A before getting to 1—so floor 1 can actually be what we'd call the fifth floor.

For more tips on accommodations, see the "Sleeping" section in the Introduction. And for guidance on reaching your hotel upon arrival in Vienna, see the Vienna Connections chapter.

Within the Ring, in the Old City Center

You'll pay extra to sleep in the atmospheric old center, but if you can afford it, staying here gives you the best classy Vienna experience.

$$$ Hotel am Stephansplatz is a four-star business hotel with 56 rooms. It's plush but not over-the-top, and reasonably priced for its sleek comfort and incredible location facing the cathedral. Every detail is modern and quality; breakfast is superb, with a view of the city waking up around the cathedral; and the staff is always ready with a friendly welcome (Sb-€180, Db-€210-250, prices vary with

Sleep Code

(€1 = about $1.30, country code: 43, area code: 01)
S = Single, **D** = Double/Twin, **T** = Triple, **Q** = Quad, **b** = bathroom, **s** = shower only, **t** = toilet only. English is spoken at each place. Unless otherwise noted, credit cards are accepted, rooms have no air conditioning, and breakfast is included.

To help you easily sort through these listings, I've divided the accommodations into three categories, based on the price for a double room with bath:

$$$ **Higher Priced**—Most rooms €130 or more.
  $$ **Moderately Priced**—Most rooms between €75-130.
    $ **Lower Priced**—Most rooms €75 or less.

Prices can change without notice; verify the hotel's current rates online or by email.

season and room size, prices shoot up during conventions—most often in Sept-Oct; generally less Fri-Sun, July-Aug, and in winter; extra bed-€50, children stay for free or very cheap, air-con, elevator, free Internet access and Wi-Fi, gym and sauna, Stephansplatz 9, U-1 or U-3: Stephansplatz, tel. 01/534-050, fax 01/5340-5710, www.hotelamstephansplatz.at, office@hotelamstephansplatz.at).

$$$ Hotel Pertschy, circling an old courtyard, is big and hotelesque. Its 56 huge rooms are elegantly creaky, with chandeliers and Baroque touches. Those on the courtyard are quietest (Sb-€95-114, Db-€140-170 depending on size, €20-30 cheaper off-season, extra bed-€36, non-smoking rooms, elevator, free Internet access and Wi-Fi, Habsburgergasse 5, U-1 or U-3: Stephansplatz, tel. 01/534-490, fax 01/534-4949, www.pertschy.com, pertschy@pertschy.com).

$$$ Pension Aviano is a peaceful, family-run place. It has 17 comfortable rooms with flowery carpet and other Baroque frills, all on the fourth floor above lots of old-center action (Sb-€104, Db-€148-169 depending on size, roughly €20-30 cheaper per room in July-Aug and Nov-March, 5 percent discount if you book direct and mention Rick Steves, extra bed-€25-33, non-smoking, fans, elevator, free Internet access and Wi-Fi, between Neuer Markt and Kärntner Strasse at Marco d'Avianogasse 1, tel. 01/512-8330, fax 01/5128-3306, www.secrethomes.at, aviano@secrethomes.at).

$$$ Hotel Schweizerhof is classy, with 55 big rooms, all the comforts, shiny public spaces, and a formal ambience. It's centrally located midway between St. Stephen's Cathedral and the Danube Canal (Sb-€85-100, Db-€120-160, low prices are for July-Aug and slow times, with cash and this book get your best price and then

SLEEPING

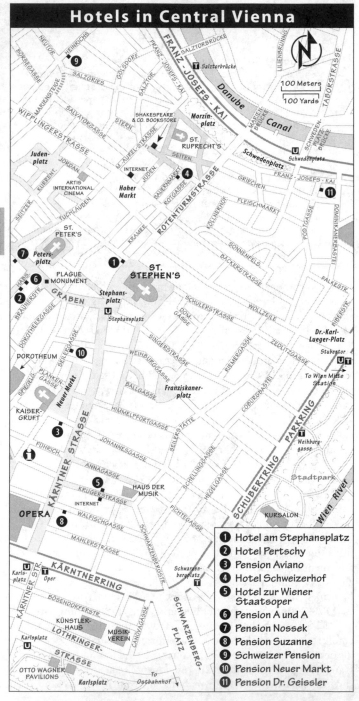

Hotels in Central Vienna

100 Meters
100 Yards

1 Hotel am Stephansplatz
2 Hotel Pertschy
3 Pension Aviano
4 Hotel Schweizerhof
5 Hotel zur Wiener Staatsoper
6 Pension A und A
7 Pension Nossek
8 Pension Suzanne
9 Schweizer Pension
10 Pension Neuer Markt
11 Pension Dr. Geissler

claim a 10 percent discount, extra bed-€35, grand breakfast, elevator, free Wi-Fi, Bauernmarkt 22, U-1 or U-3: Stephansplatz, tel. 01/533-1931, fax 01/533-0214, www.schweizerhof.at, office@schweizerhof.at). It can be noisy on weekends (Thu-Sat). If you'll be here then, ask for a quiet room when you reserve.

$$$ **Hotel zur Wiener Staatsoper,** the Schweizerhof's sister hotel, is quiet, with a more traditional elegance. Its 22 tidy rooms come with high ceilings, chandeliers, and fancy carpets on parquet floors (tiny Sb-€85-100, Db-€120-150, Tb-€135-175, rates depend on demand, extra bed-€25, fans on request, elevator, free Wi-Fi, a block from the Opera at Krugerstrasse 11; U-1, U-2, or U-4: Karlsplatz; tel. 01/513-1274, fax 01/513-127-415, www.zurwiener-staatsoper.at, office@zurwienerstaatsoper.at, manager Claudia).

$$ **Pension A und A,** a friendly nine-room B&B run by Andreas and Andrea, offers a sleek, mod break from crusty old Vienna. This place, wonderfully located just off the Graben, replaces Baroque doilies with contemporary style and blinding-white minimalist public spaces (Db-€100-150, air-con, free Wi-Fi, Habsburgergasse 3, floor M, tel. 01/890-5128, www.aunda.at, office@aunda.at).

$$ At **Pension Nossek,** an elevator takes you above any street noise into Frau Bernad and Frau Gundolf's world, where the children seem to be placed among the lace and flowers by an interior designer. With 32 rooms right on the wonderful Graben, this is a particularly good value (S-€52-60, Ss-€65, Sb-€85, Db-€125, €30 extra for sprawling suites, extra bed-€35, cash only, air-con, elevator, pay Internet access and Wi-Fi, Graben 17, U-1 or U-3: Stephansplatz, tel. 01/5337-0410, fax 01/535-3646, www.pension-nossek.at, reservation@pension-nossek.at).

$$ **Pension Suzanne,** as Baroque and doily as you'll find in this price range, is wonderfully located a few yards from the Opera. It's small, but run with the class of a bigger hotel. The 25 rooms are packed with properly Viennese antique furnishings and paintings (Sb-€88, Db-€106-136 depending on size, 4 percent discount with this book and cash, extra bed-€25, spacious apartment for up to 6 also available, discounts in winter, fans on request, elevator, free Internet access and Wi-Fi, Walfischgasse 4; U-1, U-2, or U-4: Karlsplatz and follow signs for Opera exit; tel. 01/513-2507, fax 01/513-2500, www.pension-suzanne.at, info@pension-suzanne.at, delightfully run by manager Michael).

$$ **Schweizer Pension** has been family-owned for four generations. Anita and her son Gerald offer lots of tourist info and 11 homey rooms for a great price, with parquet floors. True to its name, it feels very Swiss—tidy and well-run (S-€46-55, big Sb-€68-81, D-€68-79, Db-€89-98, Tb-€109-125, prices depend on season and room size, cash only, entirely non-smoking, elevator,

free Wi-Fi, laundry-€18/load, Heinrichsgasse 2, U-2 or U-4: Schottenring, tel. 01/533-8156, fax 01/535-6469, www.schweizer pension.com, schweizer.pension@chello.at). They also rent a quad with bath (€129-139—too small for 4 adults but great for a family of 2 adults/2 kids under age 15).

$$ Pension Neuer Markt is family-run, with 37 comfy but faded rooms in a perfectly central locale. Its hallways have the ambience of a cheap cruise ship (Ss-€70-80, Sb-€90-100, smaller Ds-€80-90, Db-€90-135, prices vary with season and room size, extra bed-€20, request a quiet room when you reserve, fans, elevator, free Internet access and Wi-Fi, Seilergasse 9, tel. 01/512-2316, fax 01/513-9105, www.hotelpension.at/neuermarkt, neuermarkt@ hotelpension.at, Wolfgang).

$$ Pension Dr. Geissler has 23 plain-but-comfortable rooms in a modern, nondescript apartment building about 10 blocks northeast of St. Stephen's, near the canal (S-€48, Ss-€68, Sb-€76, D-€65, Ds-€77, Db-€95, 20 percent less in winter, elevator, Postgasse 14, U-1 or U-4: Schwedenplatz—Postgasse is to the left as you face Hotel Capricorno, tel. 01/533-2803, fax 01/533-2635, www.hotelpension.at/dr-geissler, dr.geissler@hotelpension.at).

On or near Mariahilfer Strasse

Lively Mariahilfer Strasse connects the Westbahnhof (West Station) and the city center. The U-3 line, starting at the Westbahnhof, goes down Mariahilfer Strasse to the cathedral. This tourist-friendly, vibrant area is filled with shopping malls, simpler storefronts, and cafés. Its smaller hotels and private rooms are generally run by people from the non-German-speaking part of the former Habsburg Empire (i.e., Eastern Europe). Most hotels are within a few steps of a U-Bahn stop, just one or two stops from the Westbahnhof (direction from the station: Simmering). The nearest place to do laundry is **Schnell & Sauber Waschcenter** (€4.50 to wash a small load or €9 for a large load, plus a few euros to dry, daily 6:00-23:00, a few blocks north of Westbahnhof on the east side of Urban-Loritz-Platz).

$$$ NH Atterseehaus Suites, part of a Spanish chain, is a stern, stylish-but-passionless business hotel on Mariahilfer Strasse. It rents ideal-for-families suites, each with a living room, two TVs, bathroom, desk, and kitchenette (rack rate: Db suite-€99-200, going rate usually closer to €110-125, €17/person for optional breakfast, apartments for 2-3 adults, 1 kid under 12 free, non-smoking rooms, elevator, free Wi-Fi, Mariahilfer Strasse 78, U-3: Zieglergasse, tel. 01/524-5600, fax 01/524-560-015, www. nh-hotels.com, nhatterseehaus@nh-hotels.com).

$$ Hotel Pension Corvinus is bright, modern, and proudly and warmly run by a Hungarian family: Miklós, Judit, Anthony, and Zoltan. Its 12 comfortable rooms are spacious, and some are downright sumptuous (Sb-€69-79, Db-€99-109, Tb-€119-129, breakfast included for Rick Steves readers who book direct, extra bed-€26, also has apartments with kitchens, air-con, elevator, free Internet access and Wi-Fi, parking garage-€17/day, on the third floor at Mariahilfer Strasse 57-59, U-3: Neubaugasse, tel. 01/587-7239, fax 01/587-723-920, www.corvinus.at, hotel@corvinus.at).

$$ Hotel Pension Mariahilf's 12 rooms are clean, well-priced, and good-sized (if outmoded), with a slight Art Deco flair (Sb-€60-75, twin Db-€78-98, Db-€88-109, Tb-€99-139, 5-6-person apartment with kitchen-€129-169, lower prices are for Nov-Feb or longer stays, book direct and ask about Rick Steves discount, elevator, free Wi-Fi, parking-€18/day, Mariahilfer Strasse 49, U-3: Neubaugasse, tel. 01/586-1781, fax 01/586-178-122, www.maria hilf-hotel.at, info@mariahilf-hotel.at).

$$ K&T Boardinghouse rents spacious, comfortable, good-value rooms in two locations. The first has three bright and airy rooms three flights above lively Mariahilfer Strasse (no elevator). The second location, just across the street, is a bit more modern and spacious, with five units on the first floor (Db-€79, Tb-€99, Qb-€119, 2-night minimum, no breakfast, air-con-€10/day, cash only but reserve with credit card, coffee in rooms, free Internet access and Wi-Fi; first location: Mariahilfer Strasse 72, second location: Chwallagasse 2; for either, get off at U-3: Neubaugasse; tel. 01/523-2989, mobile 0676-553-6063, fax 01/522-0345, www.ktboardinghouse.at, k.t@chello.at, Tina). To reach the Chwallagasse location from Mariahilfer Strasse, turn left at Café Ritter and walk down Schadekgasse one short block; tiny Chwallagasse is the first right.

$$ Haydn Hotel is big and formal, with masculine public spaces and 50 spacious rooms (Sb-€90, Db-€120, suites and family apartments, ask about 10 percent Rick Steves discount, extra bed-€30, all rooms non-smoking, air-con, elevator, free Internet access, Wi-Fi, parking-€15/day, Mariahilfer Strasse 57-59, U-3: Neubaugasse, tel. 01/5874-4140, fax 01/586-1950, www.haydn-hotel.at, info@haydn-hotel.at, Nouri).

$$ Hotel Kugel is run with pride and attitude. "Simple quality and good value" is the motto of the hands-on owner, Johannes Roller. It's a big 32-room hotel with simple Old World charm, offering a fine value (Db-€90, supreme Db with canopy beds-€100,

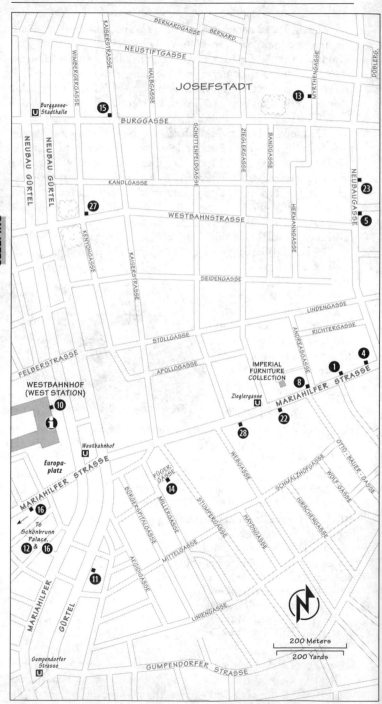

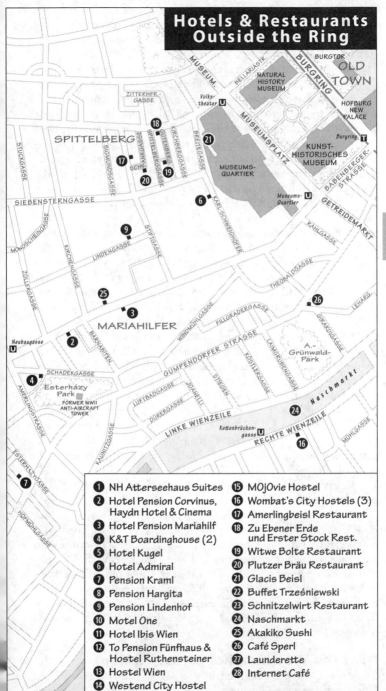

Hotels & Restaurants Outside the Ring

1. NH Atterseehaus Suites
2. Hotel Pension Corvinus, Haydn Hotel & Cinema
3. Hotel Pension Mariahilf
4. K&T Boardinghouse (2)
5. Hotel Kugel
6. Hotel Admiral
7. Pension Kraml
8. Pension Hargita
9. Pension Lindenhof
10. Motel One
11. Hotel Ibis Wien
12. To Pension Fünfhaus & Hostel Ruthensteiner
13. Hostel Wien
14. Westend City Hostel
15. MOjOvie Hostel
16. Wombat's City Hostels (3)
17. Amerlingbeisl Restaurant
18. Zu Ebener Erde und Erster Stock Rest.
19. Witwe Bolte Restaurant
20. Plutzer Bräu Restaurant
21. Glacis Beisl
22. Buffet Trześniewski
23. Schnitzelwirt Restaurant
24. Naschmarkt
25. Akakiko Sushi
26. Café Sperl
27. Launderette
28. Internet Café

SLEEPING

free Internet access and Wi-Fi, some tram noise, Siebensterngasse 43, at corner with Neubaugasse, U-3: Neubaugasse, tel. 01/523-3355, fax 01/5233-3555, www.hotelkugel.at, office@hotelkugel.at). Herr Roller also offers several cheaper basic rooms for backpackers.

$$ Hotel Admiral is huge and practical, with 80 large, workable rooms. This last resort is on a dreary street across from a rowdy nightclub (request a quiet room), and lacks the charm and personality of my other listings (Sb-€70, Db-€94, mention this book for these special prices, cheaper in winter, extra bed-€25, breakfast-€6/person, free Internet access and Wi-Fi; limited free parking is first-come, first-served—otherwise €12/day; a block off Mariahilfer Strasse at Karl-Schweighofer-Gasse 7, U-2 or U-3: Volkstheater, tel. 01/521-410, fax 01/521-4116, www.admiral.co.at, hotel@admiral.co.at).

$ Pension Kraml is a charming, 17-room place tucked away on a small street between Mariahilfer Strasse and the Naschmarkt. It's family-run and old school, with a typical 1950s-style Viennese breakfast room, no elevator, lots of stairs, big quiet homey rooms, and an Old-World elegance (D-€56, Ds or Dt-€66, Db-€76, extra bed-€23, family apartment available, free Wi-Fi, midway between U-3: Zieglergasse and U-4: Pilgramgasse at Brauergasse 5, tel. 01/587-8588, www.pensionkraml.at, pension.kraml@chello.at).

$ Pension Hargita rents 19 generally small, bright, and tidy rooms (mostly twins) with Hungarian woody-village decor. While the pension is directly on bustling Mariahilfer Strasse, its windows block noise well. This spick-and-span, well-located place is a great value (S-€40, Ss-€47, Sb-€57, D-€54, Ds-€60, tiny Db-€65, Db-€68, Ts-€75, Tb-€82, Qb-€114, reserve with credit card but pay with cash to get these rates, extra bed-€12, breakfast-€5, completely non-smoking, lots of stairs and no elevator, free Internet access, Wi-Fi, corner of Mariahilfer Strasse at Andreasgasse 1, U-3: Zieglergasse, tel. 01/526-1928, fax 01/526-0492, www.hargita.at, pension@hargita.at, Erika and Tibor).

$ Pension Lindenhof rents 19 very basic, very worn but clean rooms. It's a dark and mysteriously dated time warp filled with plants (and a fun guest-generated postcard wall); the stark rooms have outrageously high ceilings and teeny bathrooms (S-€30, Sb-€35, D-€54, Db-€72, T-€81, Tb-€100, Q-€108, Qb-€144, cheaper during slow times, hall shower-€3, cash only, elevator, next door to a harmless strip bar at Lindengasse 4, U-3: Neubaugasse, tel. 01/523-0498, fax 01/523-7362, www.pensionlindenhof.at, pension lindenhof@yahoo.com, run by Gebrael family).

Near the Westbahnhof (West Station)

$$ Motel One, a German chain that seems ready to take on the hotel world, surveyed business customers and offers only what they want to pay for. The result is what the chain calls a "low-budget design hotel": 440 sleek and modern rooms, built cruise-ship tight with quality materials but no frills, 24-hour reception but minimal service, and refreshingly straightforward pricing (Sb-€72, Db-€87, no triples but you can slip in a child up to age 15 for free, breakfast-€7.50, free Wi-Fi in lounge and in room if you buy breakfast, air-con, attached to the Westbahnhof at Europaplatz 3, tel. 01/359-350, www.motel-one.com, wein-westbahnhof@motel-one.com).

$$ Hotel Ibis Wien, a modern high-rise hotel with American charm, is ideal for anyone tired of quaint old Europe. Its 340 cookie-cutter rooms are bright, comfortable, and modern, with all the conveniences (Sb-€69-75, Db-€87-93, Tb-€106, breakfast-€11, air-con, elevator, free Internet access and Wi-Fi, parking garage-€13/day; exit Westbahnhof to the right and walk 400 yards, Mariahilfer Gürtel 22-24, U-3: Westbahnhof; tel. 01/59998, fax 01/597-9090, www.ibishotel.com, h0796@accor.com).

$ Pension Fünfhaus is big, plain, clean, and bare-bones—almost institutional—with tile floors. The neighborhood is run-down (with a few ladies loitering late at night), but this 47-room pension offers the best doubles you'll find for the price (S-€34, Sb-€43, D-€49, Db-€60, Tb-€84-92, 4-person apartment-€104, cash only, closed mid-Nov-Feb, includes basic breakfast, Sperrgasse 12, U-3: Westbahnhof, tel. 01/892-3545 or 01/892-0286, fax 01/892-0460, www.pension5haus.at, vienna@pension5haus.at, Frau Susi Tersch). Half the rooms are in the main building and half are in the annex, which has good rooms but is near the train tracks and a bit scary on the street at night. From the station, ride tram #52 or #58 two stops down Mariahilfer Strasse away from center, and ask for Sperrgasse.

Cheap Dorms and Hostels near Mariahilfer Strasse

$ Hostel Wien is your classic huge and well-run youth hostel, with 260 beds (€17-21/person in 2- to 6-bed rooms, price depends on season, includes sheets and breakfast, nonmembers pay €3.50 extra, pay Internet access, free Wi-Fi in lobby, always open, no curfew, lockers and lots of facilities, coin-op laundry, Myrthengasse 7, tel. 01/523-6316, fax 01/523-5849, hostel@chello.at).

$ Westend City Hostel, just a block from the Westbahnhof and Mariahilfer Strasse, is well-run and well-located in a residential neighborhood, so it's quiet after 20:00. It has a small lounge and 180 beds in 4- to 12-bed dorms (€22-29/person depending on season and how many in the room, Db-€66-92, cheaper Nov-mid-March—except around New Year's; includes sheets and locker, breakfast included when you book direct, cash only, pay Internet

SLEEPING

access, free Wi-Fi, laundry-€7, Fügergasse 3, tel. 01/597-6729, fax 01/597-672-927, www.westendhostel.at, info@westendhostel.at).

$ MOjOvie is a creative "little neighbourette," combining a residential apartment feel with a hostel vibe. This network of apartments offers dorm beds as well as private units sleeping two to four (dorm bed-€20, €23-26/person in a private room with shared bathroom, €35-45/person for apartment with private bathroom, includes sheets and towels, cash only for charges under €100, free Wi-Fi, laundry service, shared kitchen, reception open 8:00-23:00, Kaiserstrasse 77, tram #5 or a 10-minute walk from Westbahnhof, mobile 0676-551-1155, www.mymojovie.at, accommodation@mymojovie.at).

$ *More Hostels:* Other hostels with €18-22 beds and €60-70 doubles near Mariahilfer Strasse are **Wombat's City Hostel** (3 well-run locations—each with about 250 beds, 4-6 beds/room, lockers, bar, free Wi-Fi, and generous public spaces: one near tracks behind the station at Grangasse 6, another even closer to station at Mariahilfer Strasse 137, and one near the Naschmarkt at Rechte Wienzeile 35; tel. 01/897-2336, www.wombats-hostels.com, office@wombats-vienna.at) and **Hostel Ruthensteiner** (smoke-free; leave the Westbahnhof to the right and follow Mariahilfer Strasse behind the station, then left on Haidmannsgasse for a block, then turn right and find Robert-Hamerling-Gasse 24; tel. 01/893-4202, www.hostelruthensteiner.com, info@hostelruthensteiner.com).

EATING IN VIENNA

The Viennese appreciate the fine points of life, and right up there with waltzing is eating. The city has many atmospheric restaurants. As you ponder the Eastern European specialties on menus, remember that Vienna's diverse empire may be no more, but its flavors linger. In addition to restaurants, this chapter covers two uniquely Viennese institutions: the city's classic café culture, and its unique *Heuriger* wine pubs nestled in the foothills of the Vienna Woods.

While cuisines are routinely named for countries, Vienna claims to be the only *city* with a cuisine of its own: Viennese soups come with fillings (semolina dumpling, liver dumpling, or pancake slices). *Gulasch* is a beef ragout based on a traditional Hungarian shepherd's soup (spiced with onion and paprika). Of course, Wiener schnitzel is traditionally a breaded and fried veal cutlet (though pork is more common these days). Another meat specialty is boiled beef *(Tafelspitz)*. While you're sure to have *Apfelstrudel*, try *Topfenstrudel*, too (wafer-thin strudel pastry filled with sweet cheese and raisins). The *dag* you see in some prices stands for "decigram" (10 grams). Therefore, *10 dag* is 100 grams, or about a quarter-pound. For some background on Austria's excellent wines, see page 26.

On nearly every corner, you can find a colorful *Beisl* (BYE-zul). These uniquely Viennese taverns are a characteristic cross between an English pub and a French brasserie—filled with poetry teachers and their students, couples loving without touching, housewives on their way home from cello lessons, and waiters who enjoy serving hearty food and drinks at an affordable price. Ask at your hotel for a good *Beisl*. (Beware: Despite non-smoking laws, *Beisls* may still be quite smoky; fortunately, most have outdoor seating. For more on smoking sections in restaurants, see page 27.)

Many restaurants offer a "*menu*," a fixed-price bargain meal, at lunchtime. Besides price, the season impacts my choice of restaurant in Vienna. In winter, beer cellars have great appeal, but they're empty in summer. That's when balmy evenings drive people into the hills to enjoy wine gardens *(Heurigen)* surrounded by fields of grapevines. Consider the weather and then review this list of recommended restaurants with indoor or outdoor dining in mind.

Restaurants in Vienna

Near St. Stephen's Cathedral

Each of these eateries is within about a five-minute walk of the cathedral (U-1 or U-3: Stephansplatz).

Gigerl Stadtheuriger offers a fun, near-*Heuriger* wine cellar experience without leaving the city center. Just point to what looks good. Food is sold by the piece or weight; 100 grams *(10 dag)* is about a quarter-pound (cheese and cold meats cost about €3 per 100 grams, salads are about €2 per 100 grams; price sheet posted on wall to right of buffet line). The *Karree* pork with herbs is particularly tasty and tender. They also have entrées, spinach strudel, quiche, *Apfelstrudel,* and, of course, casks of new and local wines (sold by the *Achtel,* about 4 oz). Meals run €7-12 (daily 15:00-24:00, indoor/outdoor seating, behind cathedral, a block off Kärntner Strasse, a few cobbles off Rauhensteingasse on Blumenstock, tel. 01/513-4431).

Zu den Drei Hacken, another fun and typical *Weinstube*, is famous for its local specialties (€10 plates, Mon-Sat 11:00-23:00, closed Sun, indoor/outdoor seating, Singerstrasse 28, tel. 01/512-5895).

Buffet Trześniewski is an institution—justly famous for its elegant and cheap finger sandwiches and small beers (€1 each). Three different sandwiches and a *kleines Bier (Pfiff)* make a fun, light lunch. Point to whichever delights look tasty (or grab the English translation sheet and take time to study your 22 sandwich options). The classic favorites are *Geflügelleber* (chicken liver), *Matjes mit Zwiebel* (herring with onions), and *Speck mit Ei* (bacon and eggs). Pay for your sandwiches and a drink. Take your drink tokens to the lady on the right. Sit on the bench and scoot over to a tiny table when a spot opens up. Trześniewski has been a Vienna favorite for more than a century...and many of its regulars seem to have been here for the grand opening. You can grab an early, quick dinner here, but the selection can get paltry by the end of the day (Mon-Fri 8:30-19:30, Sat 9:00-17:00, closed Sun; 50 yards off the Graben, nearly across from brooding Café Hawelka, Dorotheergasse 2; tel. 01/512-3291). In the fall, this is a good opportunity to try the fancy grape juices—*Most* or *Traubenmost* (described on page 27). Their other locations—at Mariahilfer Strasse 95 (near many recommended hotels, Mon-Fri 8:30-19:00, Sat 9:00-18:00, closed

Sun, U-3: Zieglergasse, tel. 01/596-4291) and in the Westbahn-hof train station (near the tracks, Mon-Fri 7:00-23:00, Sat-Sun 8:00-23:00, U-3: Westbahnhof, tel. 01/982-2975)—serve the same sandwiches with the same menu but without the historic ambience.

Reinthaler's Beisl is a time warp that serves simple, tradi-tional *Beisl* fare all day. It's handy for its location (a block off the Graben, across the street from Buffet Trześniewski) and because it's a rare restaurant in the center that's open on Sunday. Its fun, classic interior winds way back, and it also has a few tables on the quiet street outside (use the handwritten daily menu rather than the printed English one, €6-12 plates, daily 11:00-22:30, at Doro-theergasse 4, tel. 01/513-1249).

Cantinetta La Norma, a short walk from the cathedral, serves fresh, excellent Italian dishes amid a cozy, yet energetic ambience. Even on weeknights the small dining area is abuzz with friendly chatter among its multinational, loyal regulars (€8 pizzas and pas-tas, €7-18 entrées, lunch specials, daily 11:00-24:00, outdoor seat-ing, Franziskaner Platz 3, tel. 01/512-8665, run by friendly Paco and Hany).

Gyros is a humble little Greek/Turkish joint run by Yilmaz, a fun-loving Turk from Izmir. He simply loves to feed people—the food is great, the prices are decent, and you almost feel like you took a quick trip to Istanbul (€8-12 plates, Mon-Sat 10:00-23:00, closed Sun, a long block off Kärntner Strasse at corner of Fichte-gasse and Seilerstätte, mobile 0699-1016-3726).

Akakiko Sushi is a small chain of Japanese restaurants with an easy pan-Asian menu that's worth considering if you're just schnitzeled out. They serve sushi, of course, but also noodles, stir-fry, and other meals. The €11 bento box meals are a decent value. There are several convenient locations: Singerstrasse 4 (a block off Kärntner Strasse near the cathedral), Rotenturmgasse 6 (also near the cathedral), Heidenschuss 3 (near other recommended eateries just off Am Hof, U-3: Herrengasse), and Mariahilfer Strasse 42-48 (fifth floor of Kaufhaus Gerngross, near many recommended ho-tels, U-3: Neubaugasse). Though they lack charm, these are fast, modern, air-conditioned, and reasonable (€8-14 meals, all open daily 10:30-23:30).

Motto am Fluss Café and Restaurant is good for a bite or drink overlooking the Danube Canal. The modern, shipshape café and restaurant share space on a barge moored canalside at Schwe-denplatz just at the Schwedenbrücke (bridge). The café is upstairs (classy on the deck and inside, moderately priced simple meals from same fine kitchen as the restaurant, daily 8:00-24:00); the pricier restaurant is one floor down (indoor seating only but with great canal-perch tables, elegant with modern cuisine—€3 cover, €15-20 plates, extensive wine-by-the-glass list, €21-three-course specials

EATING

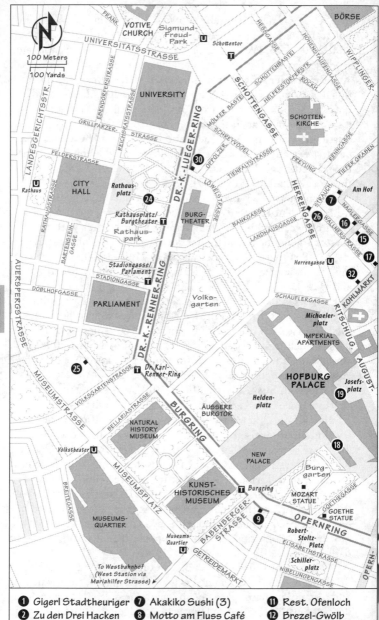

1. Gigerl Stadtheuriger
2. Zu den Drei Hacken
3. Buffet Trześniewski
4. Reinthaler's Beisl & Café Hawelka
5. Cantinetta La Norma
6. Gyros
7. Akakiko Sushi (3)
8. Motto am Fluss Café & Restaurant
9. Zanoni & Zanoni Gelateria (2)
10. Zum Schwarzen Kameel Rest. & Wine Bar
11. Rest. Ofenloch
12. Brezel-Gwölb
13. Beisl zum Scherer
14. Biobar von Antun Vegetarian Rest.
15. Esterhazykeller
16. Hopferl Bierhof

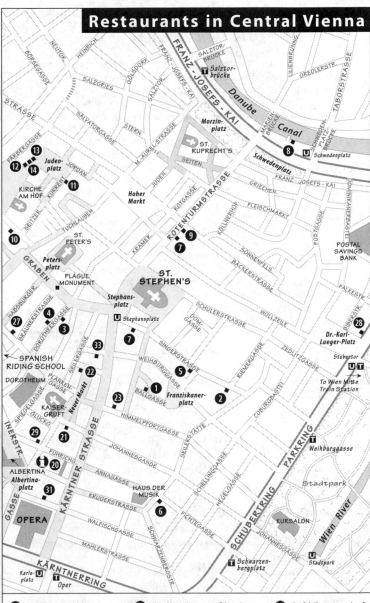

Restaurants in Central Vienna

EATING

17 Julius Meinl am Graben Deli

18 Café Rest. Palmenhaus

19 Soho Kantine

20 Rosenberger Markt Rest.

21 Lucky Chinese Rest.

22 Kurkonditorei Oberlaa, Le Bol Patisserie Bistro, Billa Corso & Henry

23 Danieli Ristorante

24 City Hall Food Circus

25 Justizcafe

26 Café Central

27 Café Bräunerhof

28 Café Pruckel

29 Café Tirolerhof

30 Café Landtmann

31 Café Sacher

32 Demel

33 American Bar

Wieners in Wien

For hard-core Viennese cuisine, drop by a *Würstelstand*. The local hot-dog stand is a fixture on city squares throughout the old center, serving a variety of hot dogs and pickled side dishes with a warm corner-meeting-place atmosphere. The *Wiener* we know is named for Vienna, but the guy who invented the weenie studied in Frankfurt. Out of nostalgia for his school years, he named his fun fast food for that city...a Frankfurter. Only in Vienna are *Wieners* called *Frankfurters*. (Got that?) When it comes to wieners, there's no pretense of being healthy. When Viennese eat at a *Würstelstand*, their friends will know it for the rest of the day by their burps.

Explore the fun menus. Be adventurous. The many varieties of hot dogs cost €3-4 each. Check out the sausage terms on page 26. Convenient stands are on Hoher Markt, the Graben, and in front of the Albertina Museum—a fun place to hang out after an opera performance as musicians and local opera buffs drop by. (By the way, the sleek modern design of the Albertina Museum stand is by famous local architect Hans Hollein (who also did the "diving board" entrance of the museum—look up).

always offer a vegetarian entrée, daily 11:30-14:30 & 18:00-24:00, tel. 01/252-5510).

Ice Cream!: **Zanoni & Zanoni** is a very Italian *gelateria* run by an Italian family. They're mobbed by happy Viennese hungry for their huge €2 cones to go. Or, to relax and watch the thriving people scene, lick your gelato in their fun outdoor area (daily 7:00-24:00, 2 blocks up Rotenturmstrasse from cathedral at Lugeck 7, tel. 01/512-7979). There's another location behind the Kunsthistorisches Museum, facing the Ring (at Burgring 1, U-2 or U-3: Volkstheater/Museumsplatz).

Near Am Hof Square

The square called Am Hof (U-3: Herrengasse) is surrounded by a maze of atmospheric medieval lanes; the following eateries are all within a block of the square.

Zum Schwarzen Kameel Wine Bar ("The Black Camel") is filled with a professional local crowd enjoying small plates from the same kitchen as their fancy restaurant, but at a better price. This is *the* place for horseradish and thin-sliced ham (*Beinschinken mit Kren*, €10/plate, *Achtung*—the horseradish is *hot*). Stand, grab a stool, find a table on the street, or sit anywhere you can—it's customary to share tables in the wine-bar section. Fine Austrian wines are sold by the *Achtel* (eighth-liter glass) and listed on the board. They also have a buffet of tiny €1-2 sandwiches. Prices are the same inside or at their street-side outdoor tables (Mon-Sat 8:30-24:00, closed Sun, Bognergasse 5, tel. 01/533-8125).

For a splurge, the adjacent **Zum Schwarzen Kameel Restaurant** (same hours, phone, and address as the wine bar) is a tiny, elegant alternative. The dark-wood, 12-table, Art Nouveau restaurant serves fine gourmet Viennese cuisine (€36 three-course lunch, €80 four-course dinner, plus pricey wine.

Restaurant Ofenloch serves good, old-fashioned Viennese cuisine with formal service, both indoors and out. This 300-year-old eatery, with great traditional ambience, is dressy (with white tablecloths) but intimate and woodsy (€14 lunch specials; €15-19 main courses—meat, fish, and vegetarian; Mon-Sat 11:00-22:30, closed Sun, Kurrentgasse 8, tel. 01/533-8844).

Brezel-Gwölb, a Tolkienesque wine cellar with outdoor dining on a quiet square, serves forgettable food in an unforgettable atmosphere. It's ideal for a romantic late-night glass of wine (daily 11:30-23:30; leave Am Hof on Drahtgasse, then take first left to Ledererhof 9; tel. 01/533-8811).

Beisl zum Scherer, around the corner, is untouristy and serves traditional plates for €8-20. Sitting outside, you'll face a stern Holocaust memorial. Inside comes with a soothing woody atmosphere and intriguing decor. It's named for a pre-World War I satirical newspaper that was published here. Let friendly Sakis explain the daily specials—which don't show up on the English menu (Mon-Sat 11:30-22:00, closed Sun, Judenplatz 7, tel. 01/533-5164).

Biobar von Antun Vegetarian Restaurant is a cheery and earthy little place with an €8 or €11 lunch special and hearty €10 salads, plenty of vegan options, and the fancy juices you'd expect (daily 12:00-23:00, on Judenplatz at Drahtgasse 3, tel. 01/968-9351).

Esterhazykeller, both ancient and popular, has traditional fare deep underground. For a cheap and sloppy buffet, climb down to the lowest level. This wine cellar, which dates back to 1683, comes with a hearty deli counter. While the food is self-serve (a meal-sized plate costs around €10), you'll order drinks at your table. For table service from a pricier menu on a pleasant square, sit outside (Mon-Sat 11:00-23:00, Sun 16:00-23:00, may close for lunch in Aug-Sept and/or in bad weather, just below Am Hof at Haarhof 1, tel. 01/533-3482).

The outdoor seating at **Hopferl Bierhof** on the same square might be a better option if it's hot and you're in the mood for a beer. It can offer a heartier value and nicer ambience (daily 11:30-24:00, Naglergasse 13, tel. 01/533-2641).

Julius Meinl am Graben, a posh supermarket with two floors of temptations right on the Graben, has been famous since 1862 as a top-end delicatessen with all the gourmet fancies. Assemble a meal from the picnic fixings on the shelves. There's also a café, with light meals and great outdoor seating; a stuffy and pricey restaurant upstairs; and a take-out counter with good benches for people-watching while you munch (shop open Mon-Fri 8:00-19:30, Sat 9:00-18:00, closed Sun; restaurant open Mon-Sat until 24:00, closed Sun; Am Graben 19, tel. 01/532-3334).

Near the Opera

These eateries are within easy walking distance of the Opera (U-1, U-2, or U-4: Karlsplatz).

Café Restaurant Palmenhaus overlooks the Palace Garden (Burggarten—see page 65). Tucked away in a green and peaceful corner two blocks behind the Opera in the Hofburg's backyard, this is a world apart. If you want to eat modern Austrian cuisine surrounded by palm trees rather than tourists, this is the place. And, since it's at the edge of a huge park, it's great for families. Their fresh fish with generous vegetables specials are on the board (€9 lunch plates available Mon-Fri, €15-18 entrées, open daily 10:00-24:00, serious vegetarian dishes, fish, extensive fine-wine list, indoors in greenhouse or outdoors, Burggarten 1, tel. 01/533-1033).

Soho Kantine is a grim, government-subsidized cantina serving the National Library and offering the best cheap, sit-down lunches in the Hofburg. Pay for your meal—your choice of bland meat or bland vegetarian—and a drink at the bar, take your token to the kitchen, and then sit down and eat with the locals (€6 two-course lunch, Mon-Fri 11:30-15:00, closed Sat-Sun and Aug, hard to find on ground floor of library—opposite the butterflies in a forlorn little square with no sign, Burggarten, Josefsplatz 1, tel. 01/532-8566, mobile 0676-309-5161).

Rosenberger Markt Restaurant is mobbed with tour groups. Still, if you don't mind a freeway-cafeteria ambience in the center of the German-speaking world's classiest city, this self-service eatery is fast and easy. It's just a block toward the cathedral from the Opera. The best cheap meal here is a small salad or veggie plate stacked high (daily 10:30-23:00, lots of fruits, veggies, fresh-squeezed juices, addictive banana milk, ride the glass elevator downstairs, Maysedergasse 2, tel. 01/512-3458).

Lucky Chinese Restaurant is a good option for Chinese food, but may close in 2013 to make way for a pizza place. The inside is fresh and air-conditioned, the outside seating is on a great square, and the service is friendly (€10-15 plates, daily 11:30-23:00, Neuer Markt 8, tel. 01/512-3428). You'll enjoy better Chinese and Asian food at the Naschmarkt (described later).

Kurkonditorei Oberlaa may not have the royal and plush fame of Demel (see page 111), but this is where Viennese con-

---

City Hall Food Circus

During the summer, scores of outdoor food stands and hundreds of picnic tables are set up in the park in front of the City Hall (Rathausplatz). Local mobs enjoy mostly ethnic meals for decent-but-not-cheap prices and classical entertainment on a big screen (see page 212). The fun thing here is the energy of the crowd and a feeling that you're truly eating as the Viennese do...not schnitzel and quaint traditions, but trendy "world food" with young people out having fun in a fine Vienna park setting (July-Aug daily from 11:00 until late, in front of City Hall on the Ringstrasse, U-2: Rathaus).

---

noisseurs serious about the quality of their pastries go to get fat. With outdoor seating on Neuer Markt, it's particularly nice on a hot summer day. Upstairs has more temptations and good seating (€10 daily three-course lunches, great selection of cakes, daily 8:00-20:00, Neuer Markt 16, other locations about town, including the Naschmarkt, tel. 01/5132-9360).

Le Bol Patisserie Bistro (next to Oberlaa) satisfies your need for something French. The staff speaks to you in French, serving fine €8 salads, baguette sandwiches, and fresh croissants (Mon-Sat 8:00-22:00, Sun 10:00-20:00, Neuer Markt 14).

Billa Corso is a top-end member of the Billa supermarket chain. This location sells hot, gourmet, ready-made foods (by weight) with its restaurant partner called **Henry.** You're welcome to sit and enjoy whatever you've purchased in either eating area: inside (air-conditioned) and out on the square. They also have a great deli selection of salads, soups, and picnic items (warm food €1.80/100 grams, WC on ground floor, Mon-Sat 8:00-20:00, closed Sun, Neuer Markt 17, on the corner where Seilergasse hits Neuer Markt, tel. 01/961-2133).

Danieli Ristorante is your best classy Italian bet in the old town. White-tablecloth dressy, but not stuffy, it has reasonable prices. Dine in their elegant back room or on the street (€13-18 pizzas and pastas, €18-25 main courses, fresh fish specialties, daily 10:00-24:00, 30 yards off Kärntner Strasse opposite Neuer Markt at Himmelpfortgasse 3, tel. 01/513-7913).

Just West of the Ring

Justizcafe, the cafeteria serving Austria's Supreme Court of Justice, offers a fine view, great prices, and a memorable lunchtime experience—even if the food is somewhat bland. Enter the Palace of Justice through its grand front door, pass through tight security (no guns), say "wow" to the Historicist architecture in the courtyard, and ride the elevator to the rooftop. You can sit behind the windows inside or dine outside on the roof, enjoying one of the best views of Vienna while surrounded by legal beagles—go early or late to miss the crush (€8-12 main dishes, Mon-Fri 11:00-14:30, closed Sat-Sun, Schmerlingplatz 10, U-2 or U-3: Volkstheater/Museums-splatz, mobile 0676-755-6100).

Spittelberg Quarter

Spittelberg has a Prague-like ambiance that is rare in Vienna. Most of the city's architecture dates from 1880 to 1910, when the population exploded. But the Spittelberg quarter dates from before 1880. This charming cobbled grid of traffic-free lanes and Biedermeier apartments has become a favorite neighborhood for Viennese wanting a little dining charm between the Museums-Quartier and Mariahilfer Strasse (handy to many recommended hotels; take Stiftgasse from Mariahilfer Strasse, or wander over here after you close down the Kunsthistorisches Museum; U-2 or U-3: Volkstheater/Museumsplatz). Tables tumble down sidewalks and into breezy courtyards filled with appreciative natives enjoying dinner or a relaxing drink. It's only worth the trip on a balmy summer evening, as it's dead in bad weather. Stroll Spittelberggasse, Schrankgasse, and Gutenberggasse, then pick your favorite. Don't miss the vine-strewn wine garden at Schrankgasse 1. To locate these restaurants, see the map on page 183.

Amerlingbeisl, with a charming, casual atmosphere both on the cobbled street and in its vine-covered courtyard, is a great value, serving a mix of traditional Austrian and international dishes (always a €7 vegetarian daily special, other specials for €6-10, €9-14 dinners, daily 9:00-2:00 in the morning, Stiftgasse 8, tel. 01/526-1660).

Zu Ebener Erde und Erster Stock ("Downstairs, Upstairs") is a charming little restaurant with a near-gourmet menu. True to its name, it has two distinct eating zones (with the same menu): a casual, woody bistro downstairs (traditionally the quarters of the poor); and a fancy Biedermeier-style dining room with red-velvet chairs and violet tablecloths upstairs (where the wealthy convened). There are also a few al fresco tables out front. Reservations are smart (€10-19 main dishes, €25 traditional three-course fixed-price meal, seasonal specials, Mon-Fri 7:30-21:30, last seating at 20:00, closed Sat-Sun, Burggasse 13, tel. 01/523-6254).

Witwe Bolte is classy and a good choice for uninspired Viennese cuisine with tablecloths. The interior is tight, but its tiny square has a wonderful leafy ambience (€11-17 main dishes, daily 11:30-23:30 except closed 15:00-17:30 mid-Jan-mid-March, Gutenberggasse 13, tel. 01/523-1450).

Plutzer Bräu, next door to Amerlingbeisl, feels a bit more touristy. It's a big, sprawling, impersonal brewpub serving stick-to-your-ribs pub grub (€7-9 vegetarian dishes, €9-20 meals, ribs, burgers, traditional dishes, Tirolean beer from the keg, also brew their own, daily 11:00-2:00 in the morning, food until 24:00, Schrankgasse 4, tel. 01/526-1215).

Glacis Beisl, located at the top edge of the MuseumsQuartier just before Spittelberg, is popular with locals. Tucked away in a gravelly wine garden atop a city fortification, it's particularly appealing on a balmy evening, when locals fill the rickety outdoor tables to enjoy good €15 plates and the breezy ambience (daily 11:00-24:00, Breitegasse 4, tel. 01/526-5660).

Mariahilfer Strasse and the Naschmarkt

Mariahilfer Strasse (see map on page 183) is filled with reasonable cafés serving all types of cuisine. For a quick yet traditional bite, consider the venerable **Buffet Trześniewski** sandwich bar at Mariahilfer Strasse 95 (see page 188).

Schnitzelwirt is an old classic with a 1950s patina and a clientele to match. In this smoky, working-class place, no one finishes their schnitzel ("to-go" for the dog is wrapped in newspaper, "to-go" for you is wrapped in foil). You'll find no tourists, just cheap €6-11 schnitzel meals (Mon-Sat 10:00-23:00, closed Sun, Neubaugasse 52, U-3: Neubaugasse, tel. 01/523-3771).

For a picnic or a trendy dinner, try the **Naschmarkt,** Vienna's sprawling produce market. This thriving Old World scene comes with plenty of fresh produce, cheap local-style eateries, cafés, kebab and sausage stands, and the best-value sushi in town (Mon-Fri 6:00-18:30, Sat 6:00-17:00, closed Sun, closes earlier in winter; U-1, U-2, or U-4: Karlsplatz, follow *Karlsplatz* signs out of the station). Picnickers can buy supplies at the market and eat on nearby Karlsplatz (plenty of chairs facing the Karlskirche) or pop into the Burggarten behind the famous Mozart statue.

In recent years, the Naschmarkt has become fashionable for dinner (or cocktails), with an amazing variety of local and ethnic eateries to choose from. Prices are great, the produce is certainly fresh, and the dinners are as local as can be. The best plan: Stroll through the entire market to survey the many options, and then pick the place that appeals. For more on the Naschmarkt, see page 78.

Vienna's Café Culture

In Vienna, the living room is down the street at the neighborhood coffeehouse. This tradition is just another example of the Viennese expertise in good living. Each of Vienna's many long-established (and sometimes even legendary) coffeehouses has its individual

Viennese Coffee:
From Ottomans to Starbucks

The story of coffee in Vienna is steeped in legend. In the 17th century, the Ottomans (invaders from the Turkish Empire) were laying siege to Vienna. A spy working for the Austrians who infiltrated the Ottoman ranks got to know the Turkish lifestyle...including their passion for a drug called coffee. After the Austrians persevered, the ecstatic Habsburg emperor offered the spy anything he wanted. The spy asked for the Ottomans' spilled coffee beans, which he gathered up to start the first coffee shop in town. (It's a nice story. But actually, there was already an Armenian in town running a coffeehouse.)

In the 18th century, coffee boomed as an aristocratic drink. In the 19th-century Industrial Age, people were expected to work 12-hour shifts, and coffee became a hit with the working class, too. By the 20th century, the Vienna coffee scene became so refined that old-timers remember when waiters brought a sheet with various shades of brown (like paint samples) so customers could make clear exactly how milky they wanted their coffee.

In 2003, Vienna's first Starbucks boldly opened next to the Opera—across the street from the ultimate Old World coffeehouse, the Café Sacher. (Their goal was 27 branches. They managed nine before stalling out.) The locals like the easy-chair ambience and quality of Starbucks coffee, but think it's overpriced. Viennese coffee connoisseurs aren't impressed by quantity, can't relate to flavored coffee, and think drinking out of a paper cup is really trashy. The consensus: For the same price, you can have an elegant and traditional experience in an independent, Vienna-style coffee shop instead. While the "coffee-to-go" trend has been picked up by many bakeries and other joints, the Starbucks invasion has stalled, with nowhere near as many outlets as the Seattle-based coffee empire had planned.

character (and characters). These classic cafés can be a bit tired, with a shabby patina and famously grumpy waiters who treat you like an uninvited guest invading their living room. Yet these spaces somehow also feel welcoming, offering newspapers, pastries, sofas, quick and light workers' lunches, elegant ambience, and "take all the time you want" charm for the price of a cup of coffee. Rather than buy the *International Herald Tribune* ahead of time, spend the money on a cup of coffee and read the paper for free, Vienna-style, in a café.

Viennese Coffee Terms

As in Italy and France, Viennese coffee drinks are espresso-based. Obviously, *Kaffee* means coffee and *Milch* is milk; *Obers* is cream, while *Schlagobers* is whipped cream. Beyond those basics, here are some uniquely Viennese coffee terms (use them elsewhere, and you'll probably get a funny look):

- *Schwarzer, Mokka:* straight, black espresso; order it *kleiner* (small) or *grosser* (big)
- *Verlängeter* ("lengthened"): espresso with water, like an Americano
- *Brauner:* with a little milk
- *Schale Gold* ("golden cup"): with a little cream
- *Melange:* like a cappuccino
- *Franziskaner:* a *Melange* with whipped cream rather than foamed milk, often topped with chocolate flakes
- *Kapuziner:* strong coffee with a dollop of sweetened cream (oddly, not a cappuccino, which derives its name from the same word)
- *Verkehrt* ("incorrect"), *Milchkaffee:* with lots and lots of milk—similar to a *caffè latte*
- *Einspänner* ("buggy"): with lots and lots of whipped cream, served in a glass with a handle (as it was the drink of horse-and-buggy drivers, who only had one hand free)
- *Fiaker* ("horse-and-buggy driver"): black, with kirsch liqueur or rum, served with a cherry
- *(Wiener) Eiskaffee:* coffee with ice cream
- *Maria Theresia:* coffee with orange liqueur

Americans who ask for a "latte" are mistaken for Italians and given a cup of hot milk.

Cafés

These are some of my favorite Viennese cafés. All of them, except for Café Sperl, are located inside the Ring (see map on page 191).

Café Hawelka has a dark, "brooding Trotsky" atmosphere, paintings by struggling artists who couldn't pay for coffee, a saloon-wood flavor, chalkboard menu, smoked velvet couches, an international selection of newspapers, and a phone that rings for regulars. Frau Hawelka died just a couple weeks after Pope John Paul II did. Locals suspect the pontiff wanted her much-loved *Buchteln* (marmalade-filled doughnuts) in heaven. The café remains family-run (Wed-Mon 8:00-21:00, closed Tue, just off the Graben, Dorotheergasse 6, U-1 or U-3: Stephansplatz, tel. 01/512-8230).

Café Central, while a bit touristy, remains a classic place, lavish under Neo-Gothic columns. They serve fancy coffees (€4-6) and two-course daily specials (€10), and entertain guests with live piano—schmaltzy tunes on a fine, Vienna-made Bösendorfer each evening from 17:00-22:00 (daily 7:30-22:00, corner of Herrengasse and Strauchgasse, U-3: Herrengasse, tel. 01/533-3764).

Café Sperl dates from 1880 and is still furnished identically to the day it opened—from the coat tree to the chairs (Mon-Sat 7:00-23:00, Sun 11:00-20:00 except closed Sun July-Aug, just off Naschmarkt near Mariahilfer Strasse, Gumpendorfer 11, U-2: MuseumsQuartier, tel. 01/586-4158; see map on page 183).

Café Bräunerhof, between the Hofburg and the Graben, offers classic ambience with no tourists and live music on weekends (light classics, no cover, Sat-Sun 15:00-18:00), along with a practical menu with daily lunch specials (daily 8:00-20:00, Stallburggasse 2, U-1 or U-3: Stephansplatz, tel. 01/512-3893).

Other Classics in the Old Center: All of these places are open long hours daily: **Café Pruckel** (at Dr.-Karl-Lueger-Platz, across from Stadtpark at Stubenring 24); **Café Tirolerhof** (2 blocks from the Opera, behind the TI on Tegetthoffstrasse, at Führichgasse 8); and **Café Landtmann** (directly across from the City Hall on the Ringstrasse at Dr.-Karl-Lueger-Ring 4). The Landtmann is unique, as it's the only grand café built along the Ring with all the other grand buildings. **Café Sacher** (see page 103) and **Demel** (see page 111) are famous for their cakes, but they also serve good coffee drinks.

Wein in Wien: Vienna's Wine Gardens

The *Heuriger* (HOY-rih-gur) is a uniquely Viennese institution. When the Habsburgs let Vienna's vintners sell their own new wine (called *Sturm*) tax-free, several hundred families opened *Heurigen* (HOY-rih-gehn)—wine-garden restaurants clustered around the edge of town. A tradition was born. Today, they do their best to maintain the old-village atmosphere, serving their homemade wine (the most recent vintage, until November 11, when a new vintage year begins) with small meals and strolling musicians. Most *Heurigen* are decorated with enormous antique presses from their vineyards. (For a near-*Heuriger* experience in downtown Vienna, drop by Gigerl Stadtheuriger—see page 188.)

Many places close one day a week and in winter, so call first. Several employ gypsy-type strolling musicians (accordionists and violinists who add ambience for tips). Most *Heurigen* have play zones for kids. And, depending on the weather, it's either all outside or all inside.

I've listed three good *Heuriger* neighborhoods, all on the outskirts of Vienna (see the map on page 37). To reach the neighborhoods from downtown Vienna, it's best to use public transportation (cheap, 30 minutes, runs late in the evening, directions given per listing below), or you can take a 15-minute taxi ride from the Ring (about €15-20).

While there are some "destination" *Heurigen*, it can be disappointing to seek out a particular place, because the ambience can change depending on that evening's clientele (locals vs. tour groups). Each neighborhood I've described is a square or hub with two or three recommended spots and many other wine gardens worth considering. Wander around, then choose the *Heuriger* with the best atmosphere.

Neustift am Walde

This district is farthest from the city but is still easy to reach by public transit. It feels a little less touristy than other places.

Fuhrgassl Huber, which brags it's the biggest *Heuriger* in Vienna, can accommodate 1,000 people inside and just as many outside. You can lose yourself in its sprawling backyard, with vineyards streaking up the hill from terraced tables. Musicians stroll most nights (Tue-Sat after 19:00; open daily 14:00-24:00, Neustift am Walde 68, tel. 01/440-1405, www.fuhrgassl-huber.at, family Huber).

Das Schreiberhaus Heurigen-Restaurant is another popular, family-owned place with creaky old-time dining rooms papered with celebrity photos, with 600 spaces inside and another 600 outside, music nightly after 19:00, and a backyard reaching deep into its vineyards (open daily 11:00-24:00, Rathstrasse 54, tel. 01/440-3844, www.dasschreiberhaus.at).

Weinhof Zimmermann, while a bit of a walk from the bus stop, is my favorite. It's a sprawling farmhouse where the green tables on patios echo the terraced fields all around. While dining, you'll feel like you're actually right in the vineyard. The idyllic setting comes with rabbits in petting cages, great food, no city views but fine hillside vistas, and wonderful peace (Mon-Sat 15:00-24:00, closed Sun, tel. 01/440-1207, www.weinhof-zimmermann.at). Ride bus #35A to the Agnesgasse stop (at the corner of Rathstrasse and Agnesgasse, just before the Neustift am Walde stop), then hike uphill on Agnesgasse to the farm at Mitterwurzergasse 20.

***Getting to the Neustift am Walde* Heurigen:** Simply ride bus #35A to the stop in Neustift am Walde (catch the bus from the Nussdorfer Strasse stop on the U-6).

Nussdorf

An untouristy district, characteristic and popular with the Viennese, Nussdorf has plenty of *Heuriger* ambience. This area feels very real, with a working-class vibe, streets lined with local shops,

The *Heuriger* Experience

There are more than 1,700 acres of vineyards within Vienna's city limits and countless *Heuriger* taverns. Here's what you can expect when you visit a *Heuriger*:

First go to the buffet to get your food—simply tell them what you want, and they'll fill your plate. Many *Heuriger* staff speak English, but pointing also works.

Food is generally sold by weight, often in *"10 dag"* units (that's 100 grams, or about a quarter-pound). The buffet has several sections: The core of your meal is a warm dish, generally meat (such as ham, roast beef, roast chicken, roulade, or meat loaf) carved off a big hunk. There are also warm sides *(Beilagen),* such as casseroles and sauerkraut, and a wide variety of cold sides—various salads and spreads. Rounding out the menu are bread and cheese (they'll slice it off for you).

Here's a menu decoder of items to look for...or to avoid:

Aufstrich	spread
Backhühner	roasted chicken
Blunzen	black pudding (sausage made from blood)
Bohnen	big white beans
Bratlfett	gelatinous jelly made from fat drippings
Fleckerl	noodles
Fleischlaberln	fried ground-meat patties
Kartoffel	potato
Kernöl	vegetable oil

and characteristic *Heurigen* that feel a little bit rougher around the edges.

Schübel-Auer Heuriger is my favorite here—with a big and user-friendly buffet (many dishes are labeled and the patient staff speaks English). Its rustic ambience can be enjoyed indoors or out (Tue-Sat 16:00-24:00, closed Sun-Mon, Kahlenberger Strasse 22, tel. 01/370-2222, www.schuebel-auer.at).

Heuriger Kierlinger, next door, is also good, with a particularly rollicking, woody room around its buffet (daily 15:30-24:00, Kahlenberger Strasse 20, tel. 01/370-2264, www.kierlinger.at).

Bamkraxler ("Tree-Climber") is the only *Biergarten* amid all these vineyards. It's a fun-loving, youthful place with fine keg beer

Knoblauch	garlic
Knödl	dumpling
Kornspitz	whole-meal bread roll
Krapfen	donut
Kräuter	herbs
Kren	horseradish
Kummelbraten	*crispy* roast pork with caraway
Lauch	leek
Leberkäse	meat loaf
Liptauer	spicy cheese spread
Presskopf	jellied brains and innards
Roastbeef	roast beef
Schinken	ham
Schinkenfleckerln	pasta with cheese and ham
Schmalz	a spread made with pig fat
Spanferkel	suckling pig
Speck	fatty bacon
Specklinsen	lentils with bacon
Stelze	grilled knuckle of pork
Sulz	gelatinous brick of meaty goo
Waldbauernflade	rustic bread
Zwiebel	onion

Pay for your food at the buffet, then find a table. Once seated, order your wine (or other drinks) from a server. A quarter-liter (*Viertel*, FEER-tehl, 8 oz) glass of new wine costs about €2-3. *Most* (mohst) is lightly alcoholic grape juice—wine in its earliest stages. Once it gets a little more oomph, it's called *Sturm* (shtoorm). Teetotalers can order *Traubenmost* (TROW-behn-mohst), grape juice. For more on Austrian wines, see page 27.

EATING

and a regular menu—traditional, ribs, veggie, kids' menu—rather than the *Heuriger* cafeteria line (€7-13 meals, kids' playground, Tue-Sat 16:00-24:00, Sun 11:00-24:00, closed Mon, Kahlenberger Strasse 17, tel. 01/318-8800, www.bamkraxler.at). To get here, walk all the way through the others, pop out on Kahlenberger Strasse, and walk 20 yards uphill.

Getting to the Nussdorf Heurigen: Take tram #D from the Ringstrasse (stops include the Opera, Hofburg/Kunsthistorisches Museum, and City Hall) to its endpoint (the stop labeled *Nussdorf* isn't the end—stay on for one more stop to Beethovengang). Exit the tram, cross the tracks, go uphill 40 yards, and look for the *Heurigen* on your left.

Heiligenstadt (Pfarrplatz)

Not far from Nussdorf, hiding just above the unappealing main road, is Pfarrplatz, which feels like a charming village square watched over by a church. Beethoven lived—and began work on his Ninth Symphony—here in 1817; he'd previously written his Sixth Symphony *(Pastorale)* while staying in this then-rural district. He hoped the local spa would cure his worsening deafness. (Confusingly, the name "Heiligenstadt" is used for two different locations: this little neighborhood, and the big train and U-Bahn station near the river.)

Mayer am Pfarrplatz (a.k.a. Beethovenhaus), right next to the church, is famous, touristy, and feels more polished—almost trendy—compared to the other *Heurigen* I list. This place has a charming inner courtyard under cozy vines with an accordion player, along with a sprawling backyard with a big children's play zone (Mon-Fri 16:00-24:00, Sat-Sun 12:00-24:00, Pfarrplatz 2, tel. 01/370-1287, www.pfarrplatz.at).

Weingut and Heuriger Werner Welser is a block uphill (go up Probusgasse). It's big (serving large tour groups) and traditional, with dirndled waitresses and lederhosened waiters. It feels a bit crank-'em-out, but it's still lots of fun, with music nightly from 19:00 (open daily 15:30-24:00, Probusgasse 12, tel. 01/318-9797, www.werner-welser.at).

***Getting to the Heiligenstadt* Heurigen:** Take the U-4 line to its last station, Heiligenstadt, then transfer to bus #38A. Get off at Fernsprechamt/Heiligenstadt, walk uphill, and take the first right onto Nestelbachgasse, which leads to Pfarrplatz and the Beethovenhaus. Bus #38A also runs uphill from here to the Kahlenberg and Leopoldsberg viewpoints (see page 99).

ENTERTAINMENT IN VIENNA

Vienna—the birthplace of what we call classical music—still thrives as Europe's music capital. On any given evening, you'll have your choice of opera, Strauss waltzes, Mozart chamber concerts, and lighthearted musicals. The Vienna Boys' Choir lives up to its worldwide reputation.

Besides music, you can spend an evening enjoying art, watching a classic film, or sipping Viennese wine in a village wine garden. Save some energy for Vienna after dark.

Music

As far back as the 12th century, Vienna was a mecca for musicians—both sacred and secular (troubadours). The Habsburg emperors of the 17th and 18th centuries were not only generous supporters of music, but fine musicians and composers themselves. (Maria Theresa played a mean double bass.) Composers such as Haydn, Mozart, Beethoven, Schubert, Brahms, and Mahler gravitated to this music-friendly environment. They taught each other, jammed together, and spent a lot of time in Habsburg palaces. Beethoven was a famous figure, walking—lost in musical thought—through the Vienna Woods. In the city's 19th-century belle époque, "Waltz King" Johann Strauss and his brothers kept Vienna's 300 ballrooms spinning.

This musical tradition continues into modern times, leaving many prestigious Viennese institutions for today's tourists to enjoy: the Opera, the Boys' Choir, and the great Baroque halls and churches, all busy with classical and waltz concerts. As you poke into churches and palaces, you may hear groups practicing. You're welcome to sit and listen.

For music lovers, Vienna is also an opportunity to make

ENTERTAINMENT

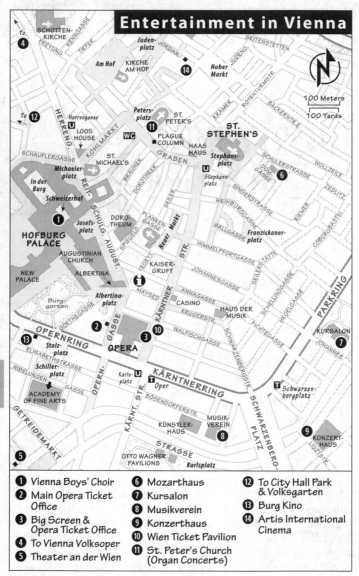

Entertainment in Vienna

100 Meters
100 Yards

1. Vienna Boys' Choir
2. Main Opera Ticket Office
3. Big Screen & Opera Ticket Office
4. To Vienna Volksoper
5. Theater an der Wien
6. Mozarthaus
7. Kursalon
8. Musikverein
9. Konzerthaus
10. Wien Ticket Pavilion
11. St. Peter's Church (Organ Concerts)
12. To City Hall Park & Volksgarten
13. Burg Kino
14. Artis International Cinema

pilgrimages to the homes (now mostly small museums) of favorite composers. If you're a fan of Schubert, Brahms, Haydn, Beethoven, or Mozart, there's a sight for you. But I find these homes inconveniently located and generally underwhelming. The centrally located Haus der Musik (see page 52) is my favorite setting for celebrating the great musicians and composers who called Vienna home.

Vienna remains the music capital of Europe, with 10,000 seats in various venues around town mostly booked with classical performances. The best-known entertainment venues are the Staatsoper (a.k.a., "the Opera"), the Volksoper (for musicals and operettas), the Theater an der Wien (opera and other performances), the Wiener Musikverein (home of the Vienna Philharmonic Orchestra), and the Wiener Konzerthaus (various events). The events held in these places are listed in the monthly *Wien-Programm* (available at TI, described on page 42).

In Vienna, it's music *con brio* from October through June, reaching a symphonic climax during the Vienna Festival each May and June. Sadly, in summer (generally July and August), the Boys' Choir, Opera, and many other serious music companies are—like you—on vacation. But Vienna hums year-round with live classical music; touristy, crowd-pleasing shows are always available.

Buying Tickets: Most tickets run from €40 to €55 (plus a stiff booking fee when purchased in advance or through a box office like the one at the TI). A few venues charge as little as €25; look around if you're not set on any particular concert. While it's easy to book tickets online long in advance, spontaneity is also workable, as there are invariably people selling their extra tickets at face value or less outside the door before concert time. If you call a concert hall directly, they can advise you on the availability of (cheaper) tickets at the door. Vienna takes care of its starving artists (and tourists) by offering cheap standing-room tickets to top-notch music and opera (generally an hour before each performance).

Vienna Boys' Choir (Wiener Sängerknaben)

The boys sing (from a high balcony, heard but not seen) at the 9:15 Sunday Mass from September through June in the Hofburg's Imperial Music Chapel (Hofmusikkapelle). The entrance is at Schweizerhof; you can get there from In der Burg square or go through the tunnel from Josefsplatz.

Reserved seats must be booked two months in advance (€5-29; reserve by fax, email, or mail: fax from the US 011-431-533-992-775, send email to office@hofburgkapelle.at, or write Wiener Hofmusikkapelle, Hofburg-Schweizerhof, 1010 Wien; call 01/533-9927 for information only—they can't book tickets at this number; www.hofburgkapelle.at).

Much easier, standing room inside is free and open to the first 60 who line up. Even better, rather than line up early, you can simply swing by and stand in the narthex just outside, where you can hear the boys and see the Mass on a TV monitor.

Boys' Choir concerts are also given Fridays at 16:00 in late April, May, June, September, and October on stage at the Musikverein, near the Opera and Karlsplatz (€36-56, around 30 standing-room tickets go on sale at 15:30 for €15, Karlsplatz 6; U-1, U-2, or U-4: Karlsplatz; tel. 01/5880-4173).

They're talented kids, but, for my taste, not worth all the commotion. Remember, many churches have great music during Sunday Mass. Just 200 yards from the Boys' Choir chapel, the Augustinian Church has a glorious 11:00 service each Sunday (see page 63).

Opera

The Opera—The Vienna State Opera (Staatsoper) puts on 300 performances a year, featuring the "Orchestra of the Opera" in the pit. (Any musician aspiring to join the Vienna Philharmonic Orchestra must put in three years here before even being considered.) In July and August the singers rest their voices (or go on tour). Since there are dif-

ferent operas nearly nightly, you'll see big trucks out back and constant action backstage—all the sets need to be switched each day. Even though the expensive seats normally sell out long in advance, the opera is perpetually in the red and subsidized by the state. The excellent "electronic libretto" translation screens help make the experience worthwhile for opera newbies. (Press the button to turn yours on; press again for English.)

Opera Tickets: Seats range from €8 to €168. You can book tickets in advance by phone (tel. 01/513-1513, phone answered daily 10:00-21:00) or online (www.wiener-staatsoper.at); you'll give them your credit-card number, then pick up your tickets at the box office just before show time. If you want to inquire about tickets in person, head to the theater's box office, which is open from 9:00 until one hour before each performance. The Opera has two ticket offices. The main one is on the west side of the building, across Operngasse and facing the Opera. A smaller one is just under the big screen on the east side of the Opera (facing Kärntner Strasse).

Unless Placido Domingo is in town, it's easy to get one of 567 **standing-room tickets** (*Stehplätze*, €3 up top or €4 downstairs). While the front doors open one hour before the show starts, a side door (middle of building, on the Operngasse side) opens 80 minutes before curtain time, giving those in the know an early grab at standing-room tickets (tickets sold until 20 minutes after curtain time). Just walk straight in, then head right until you see the ticket booth marked *Stehplätze*. If fewer than 567 people are in line, there's no need to line up early. If you're one of the first 160 in line, try for the "Parterre" section and you'll end up dead-center at stage level, directly under the Emperor's Box (otherwise, you can choose between the third floor—*Balkon,* or the fourth floor—*Galerie*). Dress is casual (but do your best) at the standing-room bar. Locals save their spot along the rail by tying a scarf to it.

Rick's Crude Tips: For me, three hours is a lot of opera. But just to see and hear the Opera in action for half an hour is a treat. You can buy a standing-room spot and just drop in for part of the show. Ending time is posted in the lobby—you could stop by for just the finale. If you go at the start or finish, you'll get the added entertainment of seeing Vienna all dressed up. Of the 567 people with cheap standing-room tickets, invariably many will not stand through the entire performance. If you drop by after showtime, you can wait for people to leave and bum their tickets off them—be sure to ask them for clear directions to your spot. (While it's perfectly legal to swap standing-room spots, be discreet if finding your spot mid-performance—try to look like you know where you're going.) Even those with standing-room tickets are considered "ticket holders," and are welcome to explore the building. As you leave, wander around the first floor (fun if skipping out early, when halls are empty) to enjoy the sumptuous halls (with prints of famous stage sets and performers) and the grand entry staircase. The last resort (and worst option) is to drop into the Café Oper Vienna and watch the performance live on TV screens (inside the Opera, reasonable menu and drinks).

"Live Opera on the Square": Demonstrating its commitment to bringing opera to the masses, each spring and fall the Vienna Opera projects several performances live on a huge screen on its building, puts out chairs for the public to enjoy...and it's all free. (These projected performances are noted as *Oper live am Platz* in the official Opera schedule—posted all around the Opera building; they are also listed in the *Wien-Programm* brochure.)

Vienna Volksoper—For less-serious operettas and musicals, try Vienna's other opera house, located along the Gürtel, west of the city center (see *Wien-Programm* brochure or ask at TI for schedule, Währinger Strasse 78, tel. 01/5144-43670, www.volksoper.at).

Theater an der Wien—Considered the oldest theater in Vienna, this venue was designed in 1801 for Mozart operas—intimate, with just a thousand seats. It treats Vienna's music lovers to a different opera every month—generally Mozart with a contemporary setting and modern interpretation. Although Vienna now supports three opera companies, this is the only company playing through the summer (facing the Naschmarkt at Linke Wienzeile 6, tel. 01/5883-0200 for information, tickets available at www.theater-wien.at).

Touristy Mozart and Strauss Concerts

If the music comes to you, it's touristy—designed for flash-in-the-pan Mozart fans. Powdered-wig orchestra performances are given almost nightly in grand traditional settings (€25-50). Pesky wigged-and-powdered Mozarts peddle tickets in the streets. They rave about the quality of the musicians, but you'll get second-rate chamber orchestras, clad in historic costumes, performing the greatest hits of Mozart and Strauss. These are casual, easygoing concerts with lots of tour groups. While there's not a Viennese person in the audience, the tourists generally enjoy the evening.

To sort through your options, check with the ticket office in the TI (same price as on the street, but with all venues to choose from). Savvy locals suggest getting the cheapest tickets, as no one seems to care if cheapskates move up to fill unsold pricier seats. Critics explain that the musicians are actually very good (often Hungarians, Poles, and Russians working a season here to fund an entire year of music studies back home), but that they haven't performed much together so aren't "tight."

Mozarthaus—Of the many fine venues, the Mozarthaus might be my favorite. Intimate chamber-music concerts take place in a small room richly decorated in Venetian Renaissance style (€35-42, Thu-Fri at 19:30, Sat at 18:00, near St. Stephen's Cathedral at Singerstrasse 7, tel. 01/911-9077, www.mozarthaus.at).

Strauss Concerts in the Kursalon—For years, Strauss concerts have been held in the Kursalon, the hall where the "Waltz King" himself directed wildly popular concerts 100 years ago (€40-60, concerts generally nightly at 20:15, tel. 01/512-5790 to check on availability—generally no problem to reserve—or buy on-line at www.soundofvienna.at). Shows last two hours and are a mix of ballet, waltzes, and a 15-piece orchestra. It's touristy—tour guides holding up banners

with group numbers wait out front after the show. Even so, the performance is playful, visually fun, fine quality for most, and with a tried-and-tested, crowd-pleasing format. The conductor welcomes the crowd in German (with a wink) and English; after that...it's English only.

Sightseeing After Dark

Every night in Vienna some sights stay open late. Here's the scoop from Monday through Sunday:

St. Stephen's Cathedral: Nightly until 22:00 (but main nave closes earlier). See page 56.

Kunst Haus Wien: Nightly until 19:00. See page 89.

Haus der Musik: Nightly until 22:00. See page 52.

Museum of Applied Art (MAK): Tuesday until 22:00. See page 86.

Albertina Museum: Wednesday until 21:00. See page 65.

Natural History Museum: Wednesday until 21:00. See page 69.

Kunsthistorisches Museum: Thursday until 21:00. See page 69.

Leopold Museum: Thursday until 21:00. See page 70.

Museum of Modern Art (MUMOK): Thursday until 21:00. See page 71.

Other late-night activities include: going to an opera or concert (see "Music," earlier in this chapter); a free, open-air cultural event outside City Hall (see next page); or a fun outing at the Prater amusement park (see page 96). Also remember that Vienna's coffee shops (see page 197) and wine gardens (see page 200) are generally open late.

Other Music

Musicals—The Wien Ticket pavilion next to the Opera (near Kärntner Strasse) sells tickets to contemporary American and British musicals performed in German (€10-109). Same-day tickets are available at a 24 percent discount from 14:00 until 18:00 (ticket pavilion open daily 10:00-19:00). Or you can reserve (full-price) tickets for the musicals by phone (call Wien Ticket at tel. 01/58885).

Films of Concerts—To see free films of great concerts in a lively, outdoor setting near City Hall, see "Nightlife," next.

Ballroom Dancing—If you like to dance (waltz and ballroom), or watch people who are really good at it, consider the Dance Evening at the Tanz Café in the Volksgarten (€5-6, May-Aug Sun from 18:00, www.volksgarten.at).

Organ Concerts—St. Peter's Church puts on free organ concerts weekdays at 15:00 and weekends at 20:00 (see page 53).

Classical Music to Go—To bring home Beethoven, Strauss, or the Wiener Philharmonic on a top-quality CD, shop at Gramola on the Graben or EMI on Kärntner Strasse. The Arcadia shop at the Opera is also good.

Nightlife

If powdered wigs and opera singers in Viking helmets aren't your thing, Vienna has plenty of alternatives. For an up-to-date run-down on fun after dark, check www.viennahype.at.

The Evening Scene—More than ever, Vienna has become a great place to just be out and about on a balmy evening. While tourists are attracted to the historic central district and its charming, flood-lit corners, locals go elsewhere. Depending on your mood and taste, you can join them. Survey and then enjoy lively scenes with bars, cafés, trendy restaurants, and theaters in these areas: **Donaukanal** (the Danube Canal, especially popular in the summer for its imported beaches); **Naschmarkt** (after the produce stalls close up, the bars and eateries bring new life to the place through the evening; see page 78); **MuseumsQuartier** (surrounded by far-out museums, a young scene of bars with local students filling the courtyard; see page 70); and **City Hall** (on the park-like Rathausplatz, where in summer free concerts and a food circus of eateries attract huge local crowds—described next).

City Hall Open-Air Classical-Music Cinema and Food Circus—A thriving people scene erupts each evening in summer (July-Aug) at the park in front of City Hall (Rathaus, on the Ringstrasse). Thousands of people keep a food circus of 24 simple stalls busy. There's not a plastic cup anywhere, just real plates and glasses—Vienna wants the quality of eating to be as high as the music that's about to begin. About 2,000 folding chairs face a 60-foot-wide screen up against the City Hall's Neo-Gothic facade.  When darkness falls, an announcer explains the program, and then the music starts. The program is different every night—mostly movies of opera and classical concerts, with some films. The TI has the schedule (programs generally last about 2 hours, starting when it's dark—between 21:30 in July and 20:30 in Aug).

Since 1991, the city has paid for 60 of these summer event nights each year. Why? To promote culture. Officials know that the City Hall Music Festival is mostly a "meat market" where young people come to hook up. But they believe many of these people will develop a little appreciation of classical music and high culture on the side.

Heurigen—Viennese wine gardens, called *Heurigen,* are a great way to enjoy new wine, a light meal, and a festive local atmosphere.

Eat and drink in intimate taverns or leafy courtyards, surrounded by antique wine presses, friendly *Wieners,* strolling musicians, and fellow tourists. Most gardens are located on the outskirts of town—in the legendary Vienna Woods—but they're easy to reach by tram, bus, or taxi. For more on the *Heurigen,* including recommendations and transportation information, see page 200.

English Cinema—Several great theaters offer three or four screens of English movies nightly (€6-9): **Burg Kino,** a block from the Opera, facing the Ring (see below), tapes its weekly schedule to the door—box office opens 30 minutes before each showing; **English Cinema Haydn,** near my recommended hotels on Mariahilfer Strasse (Mariahilfer Strasse 57, tel. 01/587-2262, www.haydnkino. at); and **Artis International Cinema,** right in the town center a few minutes from the cathedral (Schultergasse 5, tel. 01/535-6570).

***The Third Man* at Burg Kino**—This movie is set in 1949 Vienna—when it was divided, like Berlin, between the four victorious Allies. Reliving the cinematic tale of a divided city about to fall under Soviet rule and rife with smuggling is an enjoyable two-hour experience while in Vienna (€8, in English; 3-4 showings weekly—usually Friday evening, Sunday afternoon, and Tuesday early evening; Opernring 19, tel. 01/587-8406, www.burgkino.at). For more on *The Third Man* (and the museum of the same name), see page 80.

VIENNA CONNECTIONS

This chapter covers Vienna's major train stations and its airport, and includes tips for connections to/from Vienna by car and boat.

By Train

Vienna's train stations will be in disarray for the next few years, as the city builds a central train station in the former Südbahnhof location to handle most traffic. Until this is done (likely in 2014), trains to different destinations depart from various stations scattered around the city. As these departure points are prone to change, confirm carefully which station your train uses, and, as the stations themselves are also in flux (the main ones are all being renovated), the details I've listed below for each one are also subject to change. From most stations, the handiest connection to the center is usually the U-Bahn (subway) system; line numbers and stop names are noted below. For some stations, there's also a handy tram connection. (See "Getting Around Vienna" on page 45.)

For schedules, the first place to check is Germany's excellent all-Europe timetable at www.bahn.com. You can also check Austria's own timetable website at www.oebb.at, which may have prices for more Austrian trains, but is not as easy to navigate as the German site. For general train information in Austria, call 051-717 (to get an operator, dial 2, then 2). For information on types of trains, schedules, passes, and tickets, see "Transportation" on page 459 in the appendix.

Westbahnhof (West Station)

This wonderful station (at the west end of Mariahilfer Strasse, on the U-3 and U-6 U-Bahn lines) has been beautifully renovated. The old 1950s shell is now filled with a modern, user-friendly mall of services, shops, and eateries (including the recommended Buf-fet Trześniewski— near the tracks—with €1.10 finger sandwiches). From here trains run to/from many points in **Austria** (including **Melk, Hallstatt, Salzburg,** and **Innsbruck**), as well as **Germany (Munich)** and **Switzerland.** You'll find travel agencies, grocery stores, ATMs, change offices, a post office, luggage lockers, and a left-luggage desk (€3, daily 10:00-22:00, near track 1). To reach airport buses and taxis, from the platforms, head outside and to the left.

Getting into Vienna: For the city center, just follow orange *U-3* signs to the subway (direction: Simmering; buy your ticket or transit pass from a machine). If your hotel is along Mariahilfer Strasse, your stop is on this line. If you're sleeping in the center—or just can't wait to start sightseeing—ride five stops to Stephansplatz, at the very center of town.

Wien-Meidling Bahnhof

This temporary "main station" (a mile and a half southeast of Schönbrunn Palace, at the Philadelphiabrücke stop on the U-6 sub-way line and tram #62) serves many international trains, including southbound trains to/from **Italy, Slovenia,** and **Croatia,** as well as northbound trains to/from the **Czech Republic** and **Poland.** The once-small suburban station has been souped up to accommodate the traffic that formerly passed through the Südbahnhof. It has a train info desk (near track 1 and underground, near track 4), ATMs (near tracks 1 and 6), luggage lockers (underground, near track 7), and airport bus services.

Getting into Vienna: To reach the hotels on Mariahilfer Strasse, or to head to Stephansplatz, take the U-Bahn on the U-6 line (direction: Floridsdorf) to the Westbahnhof, then change to the U-3 line (see "Westbahnhof," earlier). If you're staying near the Opera, catch the direct tram #62 (direction: Karlsplatz). For Schwedenplatz, take the U-6 (direction: Floridsdorf) two stops to Längenfeldgasse, then change to the U-4 (direction: Heiligen-stadt).

Ostbahnhof (East Station), a.k.a. Südbahnhof (South Station)

The temporary Ostbahnhof (just south of Belvedere Palace) is near the former Südbahnhof, and is in the midst of the massive construc-tion zone for the brand-new Hauptbahnhof (Main Station), which is slated to be operational in 2014. Confusingly, during this period of construction, this station goes by any of these three names. For now, this station serves trains to/from **Bratislava,** Slovakia.

Getting into Vienna: To reach the city center, take tram #D to the Ring; to reach Mariahilfer Strasse, hop on bus #13A (U-1: Südtiroler Platz is also nearby).

Franz Josefs Bahnhof

This small station in the northern part of the city serves **Krems** and other points on the **north bank of the Danube** (as well as **Český Krumlov,** Czech Republic).

Getting into Vienna: Although the station doesn't have an U-Bahn stop, convenient tram #D connects it to the city center. Also note that trains coming into town from this direction stop at the Spittelau station (on the U-4 and U-6 lines), one stop before they end at the Franz Josefs station; consider hopping off your train at Spittelau for a handy connection to other points in Vienna. (Similarly, if you're headed out of town and you're not near the tram #D route, take the U-Bahn to Spittelau and catch your train there.)

Suburban Stations

In addition to the long-distance train stations noted above, Vienna has other stations for suburban and regional trains (such as the **Wien-Mitte Bahnhof,** with trains to the airport).

Train Connections

Again, confirm which station your train leaves from.

From Vienna by Train to: Melk (2/hour, 1.25 hours, some with change in St. Pölten), **Krems** (at least hourly, 1 hour), **Mauthausen** (about hourly until 17:30, 2 hours, change in St. Valentin or Linz), **Bratislava** (2/hour, 1 hour, alternating between Bratislava's main station and less-convenient Petržalka station; or try going by bus or boat, described on page 265), **Salzburg** (3/hour, 2.5-3 hours), **Hallstatt** (hourly, 4 hours, change in Attnang-Puchheim), **Innsbruck** (almost hourly, 5 hours), **Budapest** (every 2 hours direct, 3 hours, more with transfers; may be cheaper by Orange Ways bus: 3-4/day, 3 hours, www.orangeways.com), **Prague** (6/day direct, 4.75 hours; more with 1 change, 5-6 hours; 1 night train, 6 hours), **Český Krumlov** (7/day with at least one change, 5-6 hours), **Munich** (6/day direct, 4.25 hours; otherwise about hourly, 5-5.75 hours, transfer in Salzburg or Plattling), **Berlin** (9/day, most with 1 change, 9.5 hours, some via Czech Republic; longer on night train), **Dresden** (2/day direct, 7 hours; plus 1 night train/day, 8.75 hours), **Zürich** (nearly hourly, 9-10 hours, 1 with changes in Innsbruck and Feldkirch, night train), **Ljubljana** (1 convenient early-morning train, 6 hours; otherwise 7/day with change in Villach, Maribor, or Graz, 6-7 hours), **Zagreb** (5/day, 6-9 hours, 2 direct, others with 1 change), **Kraków** (5/day, 8—10.5 hours with 1-3 changes, plus a night train), **Warsaw** (2/day direct including 1 night train, 7.75-8.5 hours), **Rome** (3/day, 12-13 hours, plus several overnight options), **Venice** (3/day, 8-9.5 hours with changes—some may involve bus connection; plus 1 direct night train, 12 hours), **Frankfurt** (6/day direct, 7 hours; plus 1 direct night train, 10 hours), **Paris** (7/day, 12-13 hours, 1-3 changes), **Strasbourg** (5/day, 9-11 hours, 1-2 changes), **Amsterdam** (2/day, 11-12 hours, 1-2 changes).

To Prague and Budapest: Vienna is the springboard for a quick trip to these two magnificent cities—it's three hours by train to Budapest and about five hours to Prague (including a Prague night train, leaves Westbahnhof around 22:00). Americans and Canadians do not need visas to enter the Czech Republic or Hungary. Purchase tickets at the station or at most travel agencies.

By Plane

Vienna International Airport

The airport, 12 miles from the center, has easy connections to Vienna's various train stations (airport code: VIE, airport tel. 01/700-722-233, www.viennaairport.com).

Airlines use three different terminals, which merge into one efficient "check-in zone." As you exit baggage claim, all the terminals lead into a single arrivals hall with an array of services: shops, ATMs, and restaurants. This is also where you'll find the various connections into town (described next).

Connecting the Airport and Central Vienna

By Train: Two different trains transport airport passengers into Vienna. Both go to the same point in the city center: the Wien-Mitte Bahnhof, on the east side of the Ring (adjacent to the Landstrasse U-Bahn stop, with a handy connection to Mariahilfer Strasse hotels and other accommodations neighborhoods). The main differences between them are time and cost. The **S-Bahn** commuter train (S-7 yellow line) works just fine and is plenty fast (€4, 2/hour, 24 minutes, buy 2-zone ticket from machines on the platform, price includes any bus or S- or U-Bahn transfers). The fast **CAT** (City Airport Train) takes a third less time but costs triple (€12, €13.50 includes a ride to your final destination on Vienna's transit system, 2/hour, usually departs at :05 and :35, 16 minutes, www.cityairporttrain.com). I'd take the S-Bahn, unless the CAT is departing first and you're in a hurry. You can see when the next trains are leaving by looking on the overhead screens in the arrivals hall (with a red strip along the top—note that the green screens show only the premium CAT train, not the cheaper S-Bahn alternative).

Both trains leave from underground tracks just outside the arrivals hall: Exit straight ahead, go through the green entrance (marked *CAT*), and go down the stairs. The CAT train is to the left. The S-Bahn is to the right, then left down the dull hallway (poorly marked—look for train logo).

By Bus: Convenient express airport buses go to various points in Vienna: Morzinplatz/Schwedenplatz U-Bahn station (for city-center hotels), Westbahnhof (for Mariahilfer Strasse hotels), and Wien-Meidling Bahnhof. To reach these buses from the arrivals hall, go outside and to your left (note destination and times on curbside TV monitors; €8, 2/hour, generally 30 minutes, buy ticket from driver, tel. 0810-222-333 for timetable info, www.postbus.at).

By Taxi: The 30-minute ride into town costs about €35-40 (including the €11 airport surcharge). From the arrivals hall, the taxi stand is out the door to the right; taxis also wait at the downtown terminus of each airport transit service (especially considering the big airport surcharge, you can save substantially by riding the cheap train/bus downtown, then taking a taxi to your destination). Hotels arrange for a €30 fixed-rate car service to the airport; you'll also see several desks for this in the arrivals hall.

Connecting the Airport and Other Cities
There are direct bus connections (from stalls 7, 8, and 9) to **Bratislava** and its airport (hourly, two different companies: Blaguss and Slovak Lines/Post Bus; see page 265); **Budapest** (6-7/day, 3-3.5 hours, operated by Blaguss/Volánbusz); and **Prague** (4/day, 5.5 hours, operated by Student Agency Express, Czech tel. 841-101-101, www.studentagency.cz, also stops in Brno).

Bratislava Airport
The airport in nearby Bratislava, Slovakia—a hub for some low-cost flights—is just an hour away from Vienna (see page 266 in the Bratislava chapter).

By Car
Route Tips for Drivers
Approaching Vienna: Navigating your way into Vienna is straightforward, but study your map first. Approaching Vienna on the A-1 expressway from **Melk** or **Salzburg**, it's simple: You'll pass Schönbrunn Palace before hitting the Gürtel (the city's outer ring road); turn left onto the Gürtel to reach Mariahilfer Strasse hotels, or continue on to reach hotels inside the Ringstrasse (the city's inner ring; clockwise traffic only).

If you're approaching from **Krems,** stay on A-22 as it follows the Danube, and cross the river at the fourth bridge (Reichsbrücke). At the big roundabout, take the second right onto Praterstrasse, which leads directly to the Ringstrasse. Circle around until you reach the "spoke" street you need.

From **Budapest,** get on A-4 at Nickelsdorf; from there it's a straight shot into Vienna along the Danube Canal. From the canal, turn left at the Aspernbrücke bridge and cross the canal, which puts you directly on the Ringstrasse.

In Vienna: The city has deliberately created an expensive hell for cars in the center. Don't even try to drive here. If you must bring a car into Vienna, leave it at an expensive garage.

Leaving Vienna: To leave Vienna for points west (such as the Danube Valley and Salzburg), circle the Ringstrasse clockwise until just past the Opera. Then follow the blue signs past the Westbahnhof to *Schloss Schönbrunn* (Schönbrunn Palace), which is directly on the way to the West A-1 autobahn to Linz. If you stop at the palace for a visit, leave the palace by 15:00 and you should beat rush hour.

By Boat

High-speed boats connect Vienna to the nearby capitals of Bratislava (Slovakia) and Budapest (Hungary). While it's generally cheaper and faster to take the train—and the boat is less scenic and romantic than you might imagine—some travelers enjoy the Danube riverboat experience.

To Bratislava: For details on this connection, see page 266 in the Bratislava chapter.

To Budapest: In the summer, the Budapest-based Mahart line runs daily high-speed hydrofoils down the Danube to Budapest (€109 one-way, Tue and Thu May-Sept only). The boat leaves Vienna at 9:00 and arrives in Budapest at 14:30 (Budapest to Vienna: 9:00-15:30). On any of these boats, you can also stop in Bratislava (explained on page 266). In Vienna, you board at the DDSG Blue Danube dock at the Reichsbrücke (Handelskai 265, U-1: Vorgartenstrasse). To confirm times and prices, and to buy tickets, contact DDSG Blue Danube in Vienna (Austrian tel. 01/58880, www.ddsg-blue-danube.at) or Mahart in Budapest (Hungarian tel. 1/484-4013 or 1/484-4010, www.mahartpassnave.hu).

CONNECTIONS

NEAR
VIENNA

DANUBE VALLEY

Melk • The Wachau Valley
• Mauthausen

From the Black Forest in Germany to the Black Sea in Romania, the Danube flows 1,770 miles through 10 countries. Western Europe's longest river (the Rhine is only half as long), it's also the only major river flowing west to east, making it invaluable for commercial transportation.

The Danube is at its romantic best just west of Vienna. Mix a cruise with a bike ride through the Danube's Wachau Valley, lined with ruined castles, beautiful abbeys, small towns, and vineyard upon vineyard. After touring the glorious Melk Abbey, douse your warm, fairy-tale glow with a bucket of Hitler at the Mauthausen concentration camp memorial.

Planning Your Time

Allow one day to visit Melk's abbey and to cruise the Wachau Valley by boat or bike; a second day gives you time to get to Mauthausen. Visiting this concentration camp, though a little difficult to get to for non-drivers, is unforgettable and worthwhile, even if you've already seen other camps. Mauthausen should be seen en route to or from Salzburg or Hallstatt.

For tips on enjoying Melk and the nearby riverside sights by boat, bike, bus, and train, see "Getting Around the Wachau Valley" on page 232.

Day Trip from Vienna: If you want to day-trip to the Danube, catch the early train to Melk, tour its abbey, eat lunch, and take an afternoon trip along the river from Melk to Krems (it's easier in this direction, as you're going downstream). From Krems, catch the train back to Vienna. The Austrian railway sells a convenient Kombi-ticket, which includes the train trip from Vienna to Melk, entry to the Melk Abbey, a boat cruise to Krems, and the return train trip to Vienna, for a total of €47 (a decent savings off indiv al tickets; buy at any Vienna train station). Or, for groups of at least two adults, save yet a few more euros by buying an Einfach-Raus train ticket (see page 464) and taking a regional train (after 9:00 on weekdays) to Melk, then pay for the boat and the abbey separately.

Trains to Melk leave from Vienna's Westbahnhof. Trains from Krems arrive in Vienna at the small Franz Josefs Bahnhof; consider getting off at the previous stop, Spittelau, for better connections (on the U-4 and U-6 subway lines) to other points in Vienna.

From Vienna by Car and Driver: Johann Lichtl, based in Vienna, can take you on a day tour of the Danube Valley (see page 46).

To Hallstatt: Those heading to Hallstatt by train need to avoid arriving there in the evening, when the boat stops running (see "Arrival in Hallstatt" on page 338). Plan a morning or afternoon arrival, even if that means going first to Salzburg and then doubling back to Hallstatt.

Melk

Sleepy and elegant under its huge abbey, which seems to police the Danube, the town of Melk offers a pleasant stop and is a handy springboard for the beautiful Wachau Valley.

Orientation to Melk

Tourist Information

The TI is a block off the main square, close to the river, and has info on nearby castles, the latest on bike rental, specifics on bike rides along the river, a free WC, a free town map with a self-guided walking tour, and a list of Melk hotels and *Zimmer* in private homes (May-Aug Mon-Sat 9:30-18:00, Sun 9:30-16:00, limited hours off-season, Kremser Strasse 5, tel. 02752/51160, www.donau.com).

DANUBE VALLEY

Arrival in Melk

Melk is just off the A-1 autobahn that runs between Salzburg and Vienna. The town is also on the main Salzburg-Vienna train line, but only slower trains stop here; faster trains bypass the town (so you'll have to transfer in Amstetten or St. Pölten).

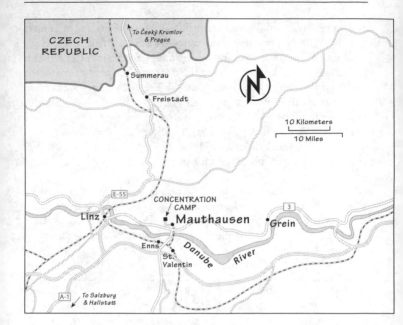

By Train: Walk straight out of Melk's train station (lockers–€2-3.50) and continue ahead for several blocks; at the curve, keep straight and go down the stairs, following the cobbled alley that dumps you into the center of the village. Access to Melk Abbey is up on your right (follow signs to *Zum Stift* or *Fussweg Stift Melk*), and the TI is to your left, a block past the square, near the river.

By Boat: Turn right as you leave the boat dock and follow the canalside bike path toward the big yellow abbey (the village is beneath its far side). In about five minutes, you'll come to a flashing light (at intersection with bridge); turn left and you're steps from downtown.

To reach the boat dock from Melk, leave the town toward the river, with the abbey on your right. Turn right when you get to the busy road and follow the canal (at the fork just before the gas station, it's quicker to jog left onto the bike path than to follow the main road). Follow signs for *Linienschifffahrt-Scheduled Trips-Wachau*.

Sights in Melk

▲▲▲Melk Abbey (Benediktinerstift Melk)

Melk's restored abbey, beaming proudly over the Danube Valley, is one of Europe's great sights. Established as a fortified Benedictine abbey in the 11th century, it was later destroyed by fire (what you see today is 18th-century Baroque). Architect Jakob Prandtau

Danube River Valley

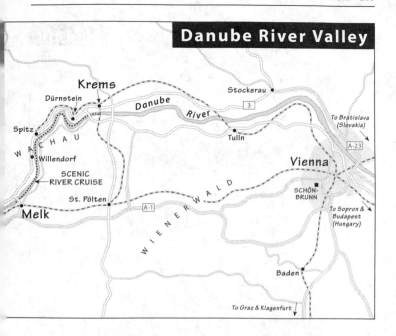

made the building one with nature. The abbey church, with its 200-foot-tall dome and symmetrical towers, dominates the complex—emphasizing its sacred purpose.

Freshly painted and gilded throughout, it's a Baroque dream, a lily alone. The grand restoration project was completed by 1996 to celebrate the 1,000th anniversary of the first reference to a country named Österreich (Austria).

Cost and Hours: €10, includes entrance to the abbey's park and its bastions; **abbey**—daily May-Sept 9:00-17:30, April and Oct 9:00-16:30, last entry 30 minutes before closing, Nov-March by guided tour only (see below); **park**—May-Oct daily 9:00-18:00, closed Nov-April; tel. 02752/555-232, www.stiftmelk.at.

Tours: English tours of the abbey are offered daily (April-Oct at 10:55 and 14:55, €12 ticket includes tour and admission). A private guide can be reserved at least one day in advance (€55 plus the 0-per-person entrance fee). From Nov-March, the abbey is open y for tours in German with a little English at 11:00 and 14:00.

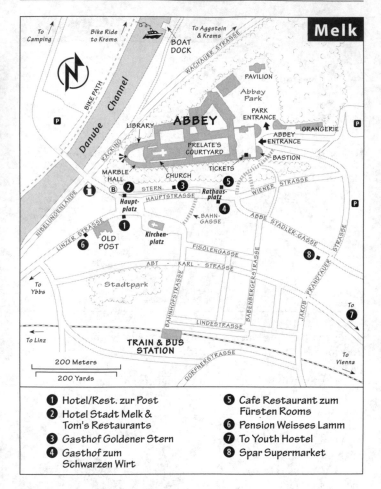

Melk

To Camping
Bike Ride to Krems
BOAT DOCK
To Aggstein & Krems
WACHAUER STRASSE
PAVILION
Abbey Park
PARK ENTRANCE
BIKE PATH
Danube Channel
LIBRARY
ABBEY
ORANGERIE
ABBEY ENTRANCE
RACKING
PRELATE'S COURTYARD
BASTION
MARBLE HALL
CHURCH
TICKETS
STERN.
Hauptplatz
HAUPTSTRASSE
Rathaus-platz
WIENER STRASSE
NIBELUNGENLÄNDE
BAHN-GASSE
LINZER STRASSE
OLD POST
Kirchen-platz
ABBE STADLER-GASSE
FISOLENGASSE
To Ybbs
ABT - KARL - STRASSE
Stadtpark
BAHNHOFSTRASSE
BABENBERGERSTRASSE
JAKOB - PRANDTAUER - STRASSE
STRASSE
To Linz
LINDESTRASSE
TRAIN & BUS STATION
200 Meters
200 Yards
DORFNERSTRASSE
To Vienna
To Youth Hostel ❼

❶ Hotel/Rest. zur Post
❷ Hotel Stadt Melk & Tom's Restaurants
❸ Gasthof Goldener Stern
❹ Gasthof zum Schwarzen Wirt
❺ Cafe Restaurant zum Fürsten Rooms
❻ Pension Weisses Lamm
❼ To Youth Hostel
❽ Spar Supermarket

DANUBE VALLEY

Book guided tours in advance by calling 02752/555-232 or emailing tours@stiftmelk.at.

○ **Self-Guided Tour:** Although you can take a guided tour, it's easiest just to wander through on your own. Each room is described in English.

• *Go through the first passageway and approach the grand entry to the...*

East Facade: Imagine the abbot on the balcony greeting you as he used to greet important guests. Flanking him are statues of Peter and Paul (leaders of the apostles and patron saints of the abbey church) and the monastery's coat of arms (crossed keys). High above are the Latin words "Glory only in the cross" and a huge copy of the Melk Cross (one of the abbey's greatest treasures—the original hiding in the treasury and viewable only with special permission

• *Pass into the main courtyard.*

Prelate's Courtyard: This is more than a museum. For 900 years, monks of St. Benedict have lived and worked here. Their task: bringing and maintaining Christianity and culture to the region. (Many of the monks live outside the abbey in the community.) They run a high school with about 800 students, a small boarding school, and a busy retreat center.

There have been low points. During the Reformation (1500s), only eight monks held down the theological fort. Napoleon made his headquarters here in 1805 and 1809. And in 1938, when Hitler annexed Austria, the monastery was squeezed into one end of the complex and nearly dissolved. But today, the institution survives—that's the point of the four modern frescoes gracing the courtyard—funded by agriculture (historically, monasteries are big landowners) and your visit.

• *In the far left-hand corner, climb the stairs to the...*

Imperial Corridor and Abbey Museum: This 640-foot-long corridor, lined with paintings of Austrian royalty, is the spine of the Abbey Museum. Duck into the first room of the museum (on the left, near beginning of hall). Art treasures and a recently updated exhibit (with creepy sound-and-light effects and some English explanations) fill several rooms.

• *Continue through the museum—walking parallel to the corridor, passing through the trippy mirrored room and around a beautifully preserved Northern Renaissance altarpiece—and go through the room at the end, with the big rotating model of the abbey.*

Marble Hall: While the door frames are real marble, most of this large dining room/ballroom is stucco. The treasure here is the ceiling fresco (by Tirolean Paul Troger, 1731), best appreciated from the center of the room. Notice three themes: 1) The Habsburgs liked to be portrayed as Hercules; 2) Athena, the goddess of wisdom, is in-

cluded, because the Habsburgs were smart as well as strong; and 3) The Habsburgs were into art and culture. This is symbolized by angels figuratively reining in the forces of evil, darkness, and brutality. Through this wise moderation, goodness, beauty, art, and science can rule. Look up again as you leave the room to see how the columns were painted at an angle to give the illusion of a curved ceiling.

Balcony: Here you'll enjoy dramatic views of the Danube Valley, the town of Melk, and the facade of the monastery church. The huge statue above everything shows the risen Christ, cross in hand and victorious over death—the central message of the entire place.

Library: For the Benedictine monks, the library was—except for the church itself—the most important room in the abbey. Consider how much money they must have invested in its elaborate decor.

In the Middle Ages, monasteries controlled information and hoarded it in their libraries. At a time when most everyone else was illiterate, monks were Europe's educated elite, and had the power to dictate what was true...and what wasn't.

The inlaid bookshelves, matching bindings, and another fine Troger fresco combine harmoniously to create a thematic counterpart to the Marble Hall. This room celebrates not wise politics, but faith. The ceiling shows a woman surrounded by the four cardinal virtues (wisdom, justice, fortitude, and recycling)—natural traits that lead to a supernatural faith. The statues flanking the doors represent the four traditional university faculties (law, medicine, philosophy, and theology).

There would be a Gutenberg Bible in this room...but the abbey sold it in 1925 (it was later donated to Yale University).

Church: The finale is the church, with its architecture, ceiling frescoes, stucco marble, grand pipe organ, and sumptuous chapels adorned with chubby cherubs (how many can you count?). All these elements combine in full Baroque style to make the theological point: A just battle leads to victory. The ceiling shows St. Benedict's triumphant entry into heaven (on a fancy carpet). In the front, below the huge papal crown, the saints Peter and Paul shake hands before departing for their final battles, martyrdom, and ultimate victory. And, high  above, the painting in the dome shows that victory: the Holy Trinity, surrounded by saints of particular importance to Melk, happily in heaven.

Other Abbey Sights: Near the entrance (and exit) to the abbey, you'll find the abbey's park and bastions (included in your abbey ticket, otherwise €4 for both). The park is home to a picturesque Baroque pavilion housing some fine frescoes by Johann Wenzel Bergel and a café. The bastions offer some decent views from the top terrace, and exhibits by students at the abbey's school are displayed on the second floor. Nearby, in the former orangerie, is the abbey's expensive restaurant.

Sleeping in Melk

Melk makes a fine and inexpensive overnight stop and has plentiful, usually free parking. Except during August, you shouldn't have any trouble finding a good room at a reasonable rate. The TI has a long list of people renting rooms to travelers for about €20 per person. Most of these are a few miles from the center.

$$$ Hotel zur Post is Melk's most modern-feeling hotel—professional and well-run by the Ebner family, with 27 comfy and tidy rooms over a good restaurant (Sb-€64-74, Db-€102-120 depending on size, Db suite-€155, has bigger suites that sleep 3-5 people; 8 percent discount when you book direct, pay with cash, and show this book; closed Jan-mid-Feb, elevator, free Wi-Fi, sauna, Linzer Strasse 1, tel. 02752/52345, fax 02752/523-4550, www.hotelpost-melk.at, info@hotelpost-melk.at). The hotel has free loaner bikes for guests and also rents them to non-guests.

$$$ Hotel Stadt Melk, a block below the main square, has pink halls and drab, outmoded rooms. Melk's moderately priced options (listed next) offer better rooms for less, but this will do in a pinch (Sb-€58-65, Db-€75-93, Hauptplatz 1, tel. 02752/524-750, fax 02752/524-7519, www.hotelstadtmelk.com, hotel.stadtmelk@netway.at).

$$ Gasthof Goldener Stern's 11 rooms have barn-themed elegance and flowers on every pillow. The pricier canopy-bed rooms are very romantic. This lively place buzzes with locals eating in the atmospheric old restaurant—and with Regina and Kurt Schmidt's five children. It's on the small alley that veers off the main square above the twin turrets (D-€42-56, Db-€58-80, Db suite-€104, prices depend on room size, rooms for up to 6 also available, cash only, all rooms non-smoking, free Wi-Fi, free boat ticket to Spitz with 3-night booking, Sterngasse 17, tel. 02752/52214, fax 02752/522-144, www.sternmelk.at, goldenerstern.melk@aon.at).

$$ Gasthof zum Schwarzen Wirt offers seven rooms with nice floors and decor with a modern African touch, right in the middle of town (Db-€63, cash only, free Wi-Fi for guests in the restaurant, Rathausplatz 13, tel. & fax 02752/52257, www.schwarzerwirt.at, addo@schwarzerwirt.at, Addo family). They also run a recommended restaurant (described later).

$$ Cafe Restaurant zum Fürsten rents 10 clean rooms over its self-consciously classic café. Run by the Madar family, it's right on the traffic-free main square, with a fountain outside the door and the Melk Abbey hovering overhead (Sb-€39-47, small Db-

Sleep Code

(€1 = about $1.30, country code: 43, area code: 02752)
S = Single, **D** = Double/Twin, **T** = Triple, **Q** = Quad, **b** = bathroom, **s** = shower only. Breakfast is included and everyone speaks at least some English. Credit cards are accepted unless otherwise noted.

To help you sort easily through these listings, I've divided the accommodations into three categories, based on the price for a standard double room with bath:

$$$ Higher Priced—Most rooms €75 or more.
  $$ Moderately Priced—Most rooms between €50-75.
    $ Lower Priced—Most rooms €50 or less.

Prices can change without notice; verify the hotel's current rates online or by email.

€62, big Db with bathtub-€74, cash only, Rathausplatz 3-5, tel. 02752/52343, fax 02752/523-434, www.kaffeehaustradition.at, madar@kaffeehaustradition.at).

$ Pension Weisses Lamm is a bit dark and low on atmosphere, but has the cheapest beds in the center. Its 14 rooms, above a lackluster restaurant, are basic but newly renovated (Sb-€35, Db-€50, Tb-€75, cash only, Linzer Strasse 7, look for namesake white lamb on sign, tel. 0664/231-5297, fax 02752/51224, www.pension-weisses-lamm-melk.at, pension.weisses.lamm@hotmail.com).

$ *Hostel:* The modern, institutional **youth hostel** is a 10-minute walk from the station. Go straight out from the station down Bahnhofstrasse, then turn right at the next corner onto Abt-Karl-Strasse; the hostel is past the soccer field (20 4-bed rooms, four 2-bed rooms, one 8-bed room, all with sink and shower; beds-€23, Sb-€33, Db-€55, €2 less if staying 3 or more nights, €3 extra for nonmembers, includes sheets and breakfast, free Wi-Fi, no curfew, reception open daily 16:00-21:00, call ahead before arriving in Nov-March, Abt-Karl-Strasse 42, tel. 02752/52681, fax 02752/526-815, http://melk.noejhw.at, melk@noejhw.at).

DANUBE VALLEY

Eating in Melk

All of my recommended lodgings have restaurants, and you'll also find cheap Italian and Asian options in the town center. **Cafe Restaurant zum Fürsten** (open daily) and **Gasthof Goldener Stern** (closed Mon or Tue and on Sun evenings) also have fine, inexpensive local cuisine.

Gasthof zum Schwarzen Wirt is popular with locals, who swear by the good Austrian food here (€8-11 main dishes, lunch specials, May-Oct usually daily 10:00-22:00; Nov-April Mon-Wed and Fri-Sat 10:00-14:30 & 16:30-22:00, Sun 10:00-14:30 only, closed Thu; Rathausplatz 13, tel. 02752/52257, run by the Ghanaian-Austrian Addo family).

Hotel Restaurant zur Post, classier and pricier, is worth the few extra euros. Downstairs is a fun and atmospheric wine cellar, with both local and international wines (€9-19 main dishes, €34 four-course fixed-price meal, daily 11:30-21:30, closed Jan-mid-Feb, courtyard and fine streetside seating with an abbey view, Linzer Strasse 1, tel. 02752/52345).

Tom's Gourmet, located in Hotel Stadt Melk, serves the city's most elegant cuisine, with delicate nouvelle cuisine-type fixed-price meals (€85 for seven-course blowout). A second restaurant in the same place, **Tom's Leger,** offers typical Austrian specialties for much less (€12-20 main dishes; both restaurants open Thu-Tue 12:00-14:00 & 18:00-21:00, closed Wed, terrace seating, reservations smart, Hauptplatz 1, tel. 02752/524-750). **Tom's Café,** right at the hotel entrance, has homemade goodies and a rare-in-Austria treat: coffee to go.

Supermarket: Pick up picnic supplies at the easy-to-reach **Spar** (Mon-Fri 7:00-18:30, Sat 7:00-18:00, closed Sun, on Jakob-Prandtauer-Strasse near Abbe Stadler-Gasse).

Melk Connections

From Melk by Train to: Vienna's Westbahnhof (2/hour, 1.25 hours, some with transfer in St. Pölten), **Salzburg** (at least hourly, 2.5-3 hours, transfer in Amstetten or St. Pölten), **Mauthausen** (hourly, 1.5 hours, transfer in Amstetten and St. Valentin). Train info: tel. 051-717 (to get an operator, dial 2, then 2), www.oebb.at.

By Car to/from the Danube Valley: See "Route Tips for Drivers," page 235.

The Wachau Valley

The 24-mile stretch of the Danube between Melk and Krems is as
pretty as they come—worth ▲▲.
This region, called the Wachau, is
blanketed with vineyards and ornamented with cute villages. Keep
an eye out for wreaths of straw or
greenery, hung out as an invitation
to come in and taste. (Why do they

call it the Blue Danube? Maybe because in local slang, someone
who's feeling his wine is "blue.") Note that in German, Danube is
Donau (DOH-now), as you'll see by the signs.

Getting Around the Wachau Valley

Biking and boating are the most enjoyable ways to experience the
stretch from Melk to Krems. Your transportation options for the
return trip, however, require some advance thought. You can ride
the boat in both directions, but because of the river current, it takes
twice as long coming upstream (from Krems to Melk). You can ride
a bike in both directions, but given that it's 48 miles round-trip and
slightly uphill all the way back, returning via bus or train may be
the better option. Also, keep in mind that you can bring bikes on
boats and trains—but not on buses.

The following assumes that you're starting in Melk, biking or
boating to Krems, and returning by bus or train. You can mix and
match options, or stop off at villages in between (such as Spitz).
A half-and-half option is cruising by boat from Melk to Spitz—a
good midway point—and then biking from Spitz on to Krems (or
vice versa).

From Melk to Krems

By Boat: Five boats per day sail
from Melk to Krems (May-
Sept; 2/day late April and Oct,
no boats off-season). They're
run by two different companies:
Brandner (tel. 07433/259-021,
www.brandner.at) and **DDSG**
(tel.   01/58880,   www.ddsg-
blue-danube.at), but both have
similar timings and use adjacent boat docks. Both charge the same
amount (€22 one-way, €26 round-trip, round-trip allows stop-

overs, bikes ride for €2; railpass-holders get a 20 percent discount on DDSG and 10 percent on Brandner).

In peak season (May-Sept), boats leave from Melk daily at 8:25 (Brandner), 11:00 (DDSG), 13:50 (both companies), and 16:15 (DDSG, requires change in Spitz). The trip to Krems takes 1.75 hours; because of the six-knot flow of the Danube, the same ride back upstream takes three hours. Both companies also offer longer cruises that start or end in Vienna (check their websites for details).

By Bike: It's a three- to four-hour, gently downhill pedal from Melk to Krems. Bicyclists rule here, and you'll find all the amenities that make this valley so popular with Austrians on two wheels. Bike routes are clearly marked with green *Donau-Radweg* signs. (Note: The bike-in-a-red-border signs mean "no biking.") The local TIs give out a *Donauradweg* brochure with a helpful if basic route map.

You can bike either the south or the north side of the river. The advantage of the south side is that there's a dedicated, paved bike path the whole way; at worst you ride next to—but never on—the road (which has less traffic than the north side). The south side is much quieter and more rural, but there are still plenty of vineyards and small *Gasthöfe* in the villages along the way. The north side has more attractions (Willendorf, Spitz, and Dürnstein), but also heavier traffic and arguably poorer views. Little ferries shuttle bikers and vacation-goers regularly across the river at three points (Spitz, Weissenkirchen, and Dürnstein), so you can also change sides midstream.

In Melk, ask your hotel or the TI for the latest on **bike-rental** options. Some hotels rent or loan bikes; try Hotel zur Post (€12/day, €9/half-day, free for guests). You may see stands for **Nextbike** along the Danube, near train stations, or at TIs (€1/hour, €8/24 hours). Their rental system works best for locals, but if you have a mobile phone, you can give it a try (register online first; when you want to borrow a bike, go to one of the stands, call Nextbike, enter the number of the bike you want, and receive a code to unlock it; you'll call again to check in the bike; call center open 24 hours, tel. 02742/229-901, www.nextbike.at).

From Krems Back to Melk

At the Krems train station, ask at the ticket office for help sorting through your return options (or visit www.oebb.at). If you have a bike or if it's after about 18:00, your only option is the **train** back to Melk with a change in St. Pölten (€11.90, about 1.5 hours, last train leaves about 20:45, no river views).

Otherwise, the **train-bus combination** back along the north side of the river is cheaper and more scenic: First you take a train to Spitz, and then a bus the rest of the way to Melk (€8, about 1 hour, runs hourly Mon-Fri, fewer on weekends, buy through ticket in Krems).

There are also **direct buses** from Krems to Melk, which drive on the south side of the river (€8, buy ticket from driver, 1 hour); these leave from the platforms on the side of the Krems station.

When you **arrive in Melk,** ask the bus driver to let you off at Hauptplatz, which is more convenient to my recommended hotels than the station.

Sights in the Wachau Valley

Krems—This town is much bigger than Melk, and home to a small university. Boats from Melk stop about a mile from Krems town center. It's a 20-minute walk in, or you can pay €7 to ride a little hop-on, hop-off choo-choo shuttle that connects the dock with the old town and the station.

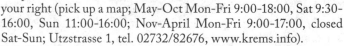

To walk, go inland from the boat dock to the second roundabout, turn right on Steiner Donaulände, go under the railroad bridge, walk three blocks farther to a park, then (after the park) turn left on Utzstrasse. The **TI** is on your right (pick up a map; May-Oct Mon-Fri 9:00-18:00, Sat 9:30-16:00, Sun 11:00-16:00; Nov-April Mon-Fri 9:00-17:00, closed Sat-Sun; Utzstrasse 1, tel. 02732/82676, www.krems.info).

The old Krems city gate is a few doors up Utzstrasse from the TI. Stroll the large, traffic-free old town, a shopper's wonderland with a lively restaurant scene. When you're done, find Krems' rail and bus station between the old town and the river. In addition to its hourly train and bus connections to Melk (described earlier), Krems is connected to Vienna's Franz Josefs station by frequent trains (1-1.5 hours).

Dürnstein—This touristic flypaper of a town lures hordes of tour-bus and cruise-ship visitors with its traffic-free quaintness and its one claim to fame (and fortune): Richard the Lionhearted was imprisoned here in 1193. You can probably sleep in his bedroom. Still, the town is a delight, and the ruined castle above can be reached by a good hike with great river views.

Willendorf—This is known among prehistorians as the town where the oldest piece of European art was found. There's a tiny museum in the village center (free, limited hours). A block farther uphill (follow the signs to *Venus,* just under tracks, follow stairs to right), you can see the monument where the well-endowed, 25,000-year-old fertility symbol, the *Venus of Willendorf,* was discovered. (The fist-sized original is now in Vienna's Natural History Museum—see page 69.)

Wachau Valley Connections

By Train
For train connections from **Melk,** see page 231.

Route Tips for Drivers
Vienna to Hallstatt, via the Wachau Valley, Melk, and Mauthausen (210 miles): Leave Vienna by crossing the Danube to reach the A-22 autobahn. Head north (following *Praha/Prague* signs) to Stockerau, then take exit #30 to the S-5 highway, which leads to Krems. After Krems, take Route 3 along the river until just after Schallemmersdorf (and just before Emmersdorf), where a bridge leads across the river to Melk. In Melk, signs to *Stift Melk* lead to the Benediktinerstift (Benedictine Abbey).

From Melk, it's a speedy hour to Mauthausen via the autobahn, but the curvy and scenic Route 3 along the river is worth the nausea. At Mauthausen, follow *Ehemaliges KZ-Gedenkstätte Lager* signs to the concentration camp memorial. Leaving Mauthausen, cross the Danube and follow signs to *Enns* (five minutes from Mauthausen town), and join the autobahn there (heading west). Leave the autobahn at exit #224 and follow scenic Route 145 past Gmunden to Stambach, then to road 166, which leads to Hallstatt.

For tips on going from Hallstatt to Vienna with a stop in the Wachau, see "Hallstatt Connections" on page 357.

Mauthausen Concentration Camp

On top of one of the rolling hills flanking the Danube River, halfway between Vienna and Salzburg, stands the notorious former concentration camp at Mauthausen (MOWT-how-zehn), worth ▲▲▲.

This slave-labor and death camp is the most powerful concentration-camp experience that a traveler can have in Western Europe. The camp functioned from 1938 to 1945, initially to detain and exploit Hitler's domestic political opponents, and

DANUBE VALLEY

then (after 1943) primarily to house Jews and prisoners of war from Eastern Europe. Mauthausen also spawned a network of satellite camps (the nearby one at Gusen has also been turned into a memorial).

Although some of the Nazis' camps, such as Auschwitz-Birkenau in Poland, were designed to exterminate people en masse in gas chambers, at others, such as Mauthausen, inmates were essentially worked to death (Mauthausen is located above a granite quarry—the region has long supplied building stone to Vienna and Budapest). In these camps, your ability to endure forced labor amounted to a stay of execution. Among Mauthausen's most famous prisoners was Simon Wiesenthal, who dedicated himself after the war to hunting down Nazis and making sure they paid for their crimes. He was one of the lucky survivors—about half of Mauthausen's 200,000 prisoners died, mostly from starvation or exhaustion. Mauthausen was the last concentration camp to be liberated—on May 5, 1945, a week after Hitler's death.

Today enough of Mauthausen's buildings survive to give a gripping sense of the camp's history. Allow at least two hours to visit the camp itself, or three if you watch the film at the visitors center.

Getting to Mauthausen

You can visit Mauthausen on the way between Salzburg (or Hallstatt) and Vienna (or Melk). It's also an easy day trip from Melk (1.5 hours by train). If you come by train, budget in time for the taxi trip between the station and the camp (taxis may take a few minutes to arrive).

By Train: Let the railway schedule computer work out the best connection for you; this may mean a change in either Linz or St. Valentin, or two changes in St. Valentin and Ennsdorf. Train info: tel. 051-717 (to get an operator, dial 2, then 2), www.oebb.at.

The Mauthausen train station is three miles from the camp, on the other side of town (no lockers; you can store luggage at the camp's visitors center).

There's no bus from the station to the camp. Taxis run about €10-13 (share cost with other tourists, minibus taxis available). Call either **Taxi Brixner** (tel. 07238/2439, mobile 0664-562-3699) or **Taxi Knoll** (mobile 0664-200-0080). Confirm these numbers on signs in the station; the station attendant may call for you, if you ask politely. Arrange a return pickup with your driver, or ask the camp ticket office to call a taxi for you when you are ready.

By Car: As you arrive at the camp, bear right to reach the visitors center and parking lot. The entrance to the actual camp is all the way around to the left (as is the path to the quarry and "Stairway of Death"). If you want to see the quarry—but avoid the steep hike down to it from the camp grounds (and back up again)—leave the main parking lot, head down the hill to the main road, turn right, and park next to the quarry.

Orientation to Mauthausen

Cost: €2.

Hours: Daily 9:00-17:30, last entry at 16:45.

Information: Pick up a free map at the visitors center. Although not essential, a free, 45-minute **audioguide** is also available at the visitors center (leave ID as deposit), or consider the excellent €2.60 English **guidebook.** Tel. 07238/2269, www.mauthausen-memorial.at.

Services: The visitors center has a bookstore and a café serving drinks, snacks, and sandwiches (but no hot meals; open daily 9:00-17:30, tel. 07238/29184).

Visiting the Camp

The visitors center has good exhibits and an informative film. Begin in the **exhibition hall,** where you can peruse the well-done display about the camp's history (with English captions), including a ring of benches and monitors where you can watch video interviews with 20 Mauthausen survivors. A graphic 45-minute **film** is shown at the top of each hour (last showing starts at 16:00). There are several screening rooms—ask the staff which room has the English version.

Exit the visitors center and circle all the way around to the camp entrance at the left side of the complex. You can either walk along the road, or go through the gateway, across the aptly named Garagenhof courtyard and up the stairs.

In the park-like area outside the camp entrance are gripping **memorials** to those who perished here, erected by each home country of the camp's victims. Many yellowed photos have fresh flowers to honor loved ones who are still not forgotten.

Entering the camp brings you onto a long, open area, which was used for roll call several times a day. To either side are some original **barracks** (the others have been torn down) with exhibits. The barracks on the left show inmates' housing quarters. On the right, at the end of the third barracks, is the small **gas chamber,** where about 3,500 inmates were killed, and the **crematoriums** (go downstairs). In the fourth barracks is an older exhibition about the history of Mauthausen and about Austrians in other concentration camps (this exhibit dates from before the visitors center was built).

Back outside the camp (right in front of you as you exit the entrance), find the huge, black **menorah-like sculpture** overlooking the quarry. To your right, a rough cobbled path leads a couple of hundred yards down to the **"Stairway of Death"** (inmates had a much rougher ascent before it was rebuilt in 1942). Connecting the quarry with the camp and its stone depot, the long stairway earned its name for good reason. Inmates were fed the bare minimum to continue working. If they couldn't carry slabs of rocks on their back up the stairway all day long—under the harshest of conditions and on this starvation diet—they were shot on the spot. Most died within a year of their arrival. (Towards the end of the war, the work shifted to making aircraft parts in a factory.) Hike down to the ground level of the vast quarry and ponder the scene; you'll be left with a lasting and poignant impression.

By visiting a concentration camp and putting ourselves through this emotional wringer, we heed and respect the fervent wish of the victims of this fascism—that we never forget.

Sleeping and Eating near Mauthausen

I'd try to overnight in Vienna, Melk, or Salzburg instead of around Mauthausen. But if you're driving and have a special reason to stay near the camp, **$$$ Hotel zum Goldenen Schiff,** in the town of Enns across the river (just off the autobahn, less than four miles southwest of Mauthausen), is a decent value. It has 19 comfy rooms and a quaint location facing Enns' delightful main square (Sb-€50, Db-€76-100, family rooms, Internet access, free Wi-Fi, free parking, Hauptplatz 23, tel. 07223/86086, fax 07223/860-8615, www. hotel-brunner.at, office@hotel-brunner.at).

Moststube Frellerhof, a farmhouse 50 yards below the Mauthausen parking lot, offers a refreshing, peaceful lunch or dinner break after your visit. Their specialty is apple and pear wine (called *Most* in this part of Austria—not the same as the Viennese *Most* made from grapes) and homemade schnapps, and they serve light, farm-fresh meals (May-mid-Sept Mon-Fri 15:00-22:00, Sat-Sun 13:00-22:00; April and mid-Sept-Oct Sat-Sun 13:00-22:00 only; closed Nov-March; playground, tel. 07238/2789).

Mauthausen Connections

From Mauthausen by Train: Trains leave Mauthausen station hourly with connections to **Melk** (1.5 hours, change in St. Valentin and sometimes also Ennsdorf), **Vienna** (every 2 hours, 2.25 hours, change in Linz), **Salzburg** (2 hours, change in Linz or St. Valentin), **Hallstatt** (3 hours, tight transfer at St. Valentin or Linz and another at Attnang-Puchheim—you'll need to leave Mauthausen surprisingly early to be sure to arrive in Hallstatt in time for the last boat, explained on page 338).

BRATISLAVA, SLOVAKIA

Pressburg/Pozsony

Bratislava's priceless location—on the Danube (and the tourist circuit) smack-dab between Vienna and Budapest—makes it a very worthwhile "on the way" destination.

Long a drab lesson in the failings of the communist system, the city is turning things around. A decade ago, Bratislava's city center was grim, deserted, and dangerous—a place where only thieves and fools dared to tread. Today it's downright charming, bursting with colorfully restored facades, lively outdoor cafés, swanky boutiques, in-love-with-life locals, and (on sunny days) an almost Mediterranean ambience.

The rejuvenation doesn't end in the old town. The ramshackle quarter to the east is gradually being flattened and redeveloped into a new forest of skyscrapers. Bratislava is working together with its neighbor Vienna to forge a new twin-city relationship for trade and commerce, bridging the former Eastern Europe and the former Western Europe. The hilltop castle is getting a facelift. And even the glum commie suburb of Petržalka is undergoing a Technicolor makeover. Before our eyes, Bratislava is becoming the quintessential post-communist Central European city—showing what can happen when government and business leaders make a concerted effort to jump-start a failing city.

And yet, it's still a city in transition, with sometimes striking contrasts. Tucked between the quaint old town and super-modern Euro-commerce zones, large pockets of post-communist decrepitude remain. (There's a reason why movie makers wanting to show the stereotypically gloomy "communist Eastern Europe" decide to film here.)

You get the feeling that workaday Bratislavans—who strike some visitors as gruff—are being pulled to the cutting edge of the 21st century kicking and screaming. But many Slovaks embrace the changes and fancy themselves as the yang to Vienna's yin: If Vienna is a staid, elderly aristocrat sipping coffee, then Bratislava is a vivacious young professional jet-setting around Europe. Bratislava at night is a lively place; its very youthful center thrives. While it has tens of thousands of university students, there are no campuses as such—so the old town is the place where students go to play.

Frankly, Bratislava used to leave me cold. But all the changes are positively inspiring. While they still have a long way to go, the Slovaks have made the city well worth a quick visit to get a glimpse of a country in transition.

Planning Your Time

A few hours are plenty to get the gist of Bratislava. Head straight to the old town and follow my self-guided walk, finishing with a stroll along the Danube riverbank to the thriving, modern Eurovea development. With more time, take advantage of one or more of the city's fine viewpoints: Ascend to the "UFO" observation deck atop the funky bridge, ride the elevator up to the Sky Bar for a peek (and maybe a drink), or hike up to the castle for the views (but skip the ho-hum museum inside). There's little reason to spend the night here, but if you do, you'll find Bratislava lively with students, busy cafés, and nightlife.

Note that all museums and galleries are closed on Monday. That said, it's not a big deal if you're here on a Monday, since none of them is worth planning a trip around anyway (the Primate's Palace is the best, but even that is skippable). Bratislava is more about wandering and catching the town's vibe than seeing specific sights.

Day-Tripping Tip: Bratislava is perfect for a side-trip from Vienna, or as a stopover on the way from Vienna to Budapest. But pay careful attention to train schedules, as the Vienna connection alternates between Bratislava's two train stations (Hlavná Stanica and Petržalka). If checking your bag at the station, be sure that your return or onward connection will depart from there.

Orientation to Bratislava

Bratislava, with nearly a half-million residents, is Slovakia's capital and biggest city. It has a small, colorful old town *(staré mesto)*, with the castle on the hill above. This small area is surrounded by a vast construction zone of new buildings, rotting residential districts desperately in need of beautification, and some colorized communist suburbs (including Petržalka, across the river). The northern and western parts of the city are hilly and cool (these "Little Carpathians" are draped with vineyards), while the southern and eastern areas are flat and warmer.

You've dropped in to visit Bratislava just as the city is trying

Bratislava

1. Hotel Marrol's
2. Hotel Michalská Brána
3. Hotel Ibis
4. Penzión Virgo
5. Penzión Gremium
6. Downtown Backpackers Hostel
7. Prazdroj Beer Hall
8. "1. Slovak" Pub
9. Bratislavský Meštiansky Pivovar
10. Lemon Tree/Sky Bar/Rum Club
11. Shtoor (3)
12. Coffee & Bagel Story;
    Café Roland; Kaffee Mayer

ULICA PALISÁDY

ŠTETINOVÁ

PANENSKÁ

KOZIA ULICA

PODJAVOR...

LYCEJNÁ

KONVENTNÁ

STAROMESTSKÁ

ZOCHOVA

DANKOVSKÉHO

KORENIČOVA

ULICA PALISÁDY

ŠKARNICLOVA ULICA

SVORADOVA

ZÁMOCKA ULICA

Župné Nám.

TVARÓŽKOVA

KRÁTKA

STRELECKÁ

VODNY

ŽIDOVSKÁ

B Zochova

BAŠTOVÁ

Fashion Courtyard

KLARISKÁ

KAPITULSKÁ

PREPOŠTSKÁ

CASTLE

SUMMER RIDING SCHOOL

ENTRY

KNIGHTS HALL

TREASURE ROOM

TICKETS

STAROMESTSKÁ

OLD

VENTÚRSKA

PARLIAMENT

ZÁM. SCHODY

SCHODY PRI STAREJ VODÁRNI

WALK ENDS

ST. MARTIN'S CATHEDRAL

HOLOCAUST MEMORIAL

NÁBR. ARMÁDNEHO GENERÁLA L. SVOBODU

B Nový Most

RÁZUSOVO NÁBR.

N

100 Meters
100 Yards

NEW BRIDGE

To Petržalka

"UFO" OBSERVATION DECK

BRATISLAVA

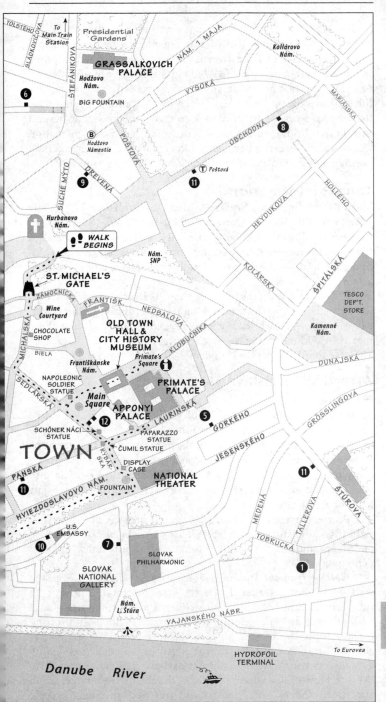

to undo the brutally ugly infrastructure inflicted upon it by the communists. Eventually, the highway that barrels between the old town and the castle will be diverted underground (through a tunnel beneath the Danube); the TGV bullet train from Paris will swoosh to a stop at a slick new train station; and a new six-station subway line will lace the city together. The entire riverfront is being transformed into a people-friendly park (to match the new zone beyond the old iron bridge, in Eurovea). But Europe's economic situation has substantially slowed progress. Expect lots of construction (and possible public-transit and traffic headaches) during your visit.

Tourist Information

The TI is on **Primate's Square** behind the Old Town Hall (daily May-Sept 9:00-19:00, Oct-April 9:00-18:00, tel. 02/16186 or 02/5935-6661, www.bratislava.sk). Pick up the free *Bratislava Guide* (with map) and browse their brochures; they can help you find a room in town for a small fee. They also have a branch at the airport.

Discount Card: The TI sells the €10 **Bratislava City Card,** which includes free transit and sightseeing discounts for a full day—but it's worthwhile only if you're doing the old town walking tour (€14 without the card—see "Tours in Bratislava," later; also available for €12/2 days, €15/3 days).

Arrival in Bratislava

By Train

Main Train Station (Hlavná Stanica): This glum and depressing station is about a half-mile north of the old town. It was still standing on my last visit—but barely. In the next few years the city plans to tear it down and start from scratch (to accommodate, among other things, a new high-speed rail line connecting Bratislava to Paris). Therefore, these arrival instructions are likely to change; just look for signs.

As you emerge from the tracks, the left-luggage desk is to your right (€1-2, depending on size; look for *úschovňa batožín;* there are no lockers, and the check desk closes for 30-minute lunch and dinner breaks).

Getting from the Station to Downtown: It's an easy 15-minute **walk** to the town center. Leave the station straight ahead, take the overpass across the busy cross street, and continue straight on Štefánikova. This once-elegant old boulevard is lined with rotting facades from Bratislava's high-on-the-hog Habsburg era. After about 10 minutes, you'll pass the nicely manicured presidential gardens on your left, then the Grassalkovich Palace, Slovakia's "White House." Continue straight through the busy intersection onto Súche Mýto, and head for the green onion-domed steeple (take the narrow street next to the mod, green, white-capped building). This is St. Michael's Gate, at the start of the old town (and the beginning of my self-guided walk, described later).

If you want to shave a few minutes off the trip, go part of the way by tram or bus. The **tram** is a bit easier (but may be closed for reconstruction): From the train station's main hall, with the tracks at your back, look left for signs to *električky*; take the escalator down, buy a ticket from the machine, hop on tram #13, and ride it to the Poštová stop, then walk straight down Obchodná street toward St. Michael's Gate. If the tram isn't running, you can take **bus** #X13 or #93: Walk out the front station door and find the bus stops lining the road to the right. Ride two stops to Hodžovo Námestie, across the street from Grassalkovich Palace. Facing the palace, turn left and curve with the busy street past the pink-and-white church and toward the onion-topped tower. Both the tram and bus are covered by a €0.70/15-minute ticket (buy from a kiosk or one of many machines, select *základný lístok—latí 15 minút*, then insert coins—change given).

ŽST Petržalka: About half the trains from Vienna arrive at Bratislava's other train station, in the Petržalka suburb. From this station, walk out front and ride bus #80, #93, or #94 to the Zochova stop (near St. Michael's Gate), or bus #91 or #191 to the Nový Most stop (at the old town end of the New Bridge). Buses #93 (by day) and #N93 (by night) also connect the two stations. Any of these rides is covered by the same €0.70/15-minute ticket described earlier.

By Boat or Plane

For information on Bratislava's riverboats and airport, see "Bratislava Connections," at the end of this chapter.

Helpful Hints

Money: Slovakia uses the same currency as Austria (€1=about $1.30).

Language: While many people in Bratislava speak English, the official language is Slovak (closely related to Czech and Polish). The local "ciao"—used informally for both "hi" and "bye"—is easy to remember: *ahoj* (pronounced "AH-hoy," like a pirate). "Please" is *prosím* (PROH-seem), "thank you" is *ďakujem* (DYAH-koo-yehm), "good" is *dobrý* (DOH-bree), and "Cheers!" is *Na zdravie!* (nah ZDRAH-vyeh).

Phone Tips: Slovakia's phone system works similarly to Austria's. When calling locally (such as within Bratislava), dial the number without the area code. To make a long-distance call within Slovakia, start with the area code (which begins with 0). Slovakia's country code is 421. To call from Austria to Slovakia,

BRATISLAVA

Welcome to Slovakia

In many ways, Slovakia is the "West Virginia of Europe"—relatively poor and undeveloped, but spectacularly beautiful in its own rustic way. Sitting quietly in the very center of Central Europe, wedged between bigger and stronger nations (Hungary, Austria, the Czech Republic, and Poland), Slovakia was brutally disfigured by the communists, then overshadowed by the Czechs. But in recent years, this fledgling republic has found its wings.

With about 5.5 million people in a country of 19,000 square miles (similar to Massachusetts and New Hampshire combined), Slovakia is one of Europe's smallest nations. Recent economic reforms have caused two very different Slovakias to emerge: the modern, industrialized, flat, affluent west, centered on the capital of Bratislava; and the remote, poorer, mountainous, "backward" east, with high unemployment and traditional lifestyles. Slovakia is ethnically diverse: In addition to the Slavic Slovaks, there are Hungarians (about 10 percent of the population, "stranded" here when Hungary lost this land after World War I) and Roma (Gypsies, also about 10 percent). Slovakia has struggled to incorporate both of these large and often-mistreated minority groups.

Slovakia has spent most of its history as someone else's backyard. For centuries, Slovakia was ruled from Budapest and known as "Upper Hungary." At other times, it was an important chunk of the Habsburg Empire, ruled from neighboring Vienna. But most people think first of another era: the 75 years that Slovakia was joined with the Czech Republic as the country of "Czechoslovakia." From its start in the aftermath of World War I, this union of the Czechs and Slovaks was troubled; some Slovaks chafed at being ruled from Prague, while many Czechs resented the financial burden of their poorer neighbors to the east.

After they gained their freedom from the communists during 1989's peaceful "Velvet Revolution," the Czechs and Slovaks

dial 00-421, then the area code minus the initial zero, then the number (from the US, dial 011-421-area code minus zero, then the number). To call from Slovakia to Austria, you'd dial 00-43, then the area code (minus the initial zero) and number.

Internet Access: You'll see signs advertising Internet cafés around the old town. If you have a laptop or other Wi-Fi-enabled device, you can get online for free at the three major old town began to think of the future. The Slovaks wanted to rename the country Czecho-Slovakia, and to redistribute power to give themselves more autonomy within the union. The Czechs balked, relations gradually deteriorated, and the Slovak nationalist candidate Vladimír Mečiar fared surprisingly well in the 1992 elections. Taking it as a sign that the two peoples wanted to part ways, politicians pushed through (in just three months) the peaceful separation of the now-independent Czech and Slovak Republics. (The people in both countries never actually voted on the change, and most opposed it.) The "Velvet Divorce" became official on January 1, 1993.

At first the Slovaks struggled. Communist rule had been particularly unkind to them, and their economy was in a shambles. Visionary leaders set forth bold solutions, including the 2003 implementation of a flat tax (19 percent), followed by EU membership in 2004. Before long, major international corporations began to notice the same thing the communists had: This is a great place to build stuff, thanks to a strategic location (300 million consumers live within a day's truck drive), low labor costs, and a well-trained workforce. Not surprisingly, multiple foreign automakers have plants here. Today Slovakia produces one million cars a year, making Slovakia the world's biggest car producer (per capita) and leading the *New York Times* to dub Slovakia "the European Detroit."

The flat tax and other aggressively pro-business policies have not been without their critics—especially in the very impoverished eastern half of the country, where poor people feel they're becoming even poorer. With the rollback of social services and the proverbial cracks widening, many seem to have been left behind by Slovakia's bold new economy.

Even so, particularly if you zoom in on its success story around Bratislava, the evidence is impressive. Bratislava has only 3 percent unemployment. The standard of living (as it relates to local costs) puts Bratislava in 10th place among European cities. Slovakia joined the EU in 2004; in 2009, it adopted the euro currency. While most of Europe is struggling through difficult economic times, much of Slovakia seems poised for its brightest future yet.

squares (Main Square, Primate's Square, and Hviezdoslav Square).

Local Guidebook: For in-depth suggestions on Bratislava sightseeing, dining, and more, look for the excellent and eye-pleasing *Bratislava Active* guidebook by Martin Sloboda (see "Tours in Bratislava," next; around €10, sold at every postcard rack).

Updates to This Book: For news about changes to this book's coverage since it was published, see www.ricksteves.com/update.

Tours in Bratislava

Walking Tour—The **TI** offers a one-hour old town walking tour in English every day in the summer at 14:00 (€14, or free with €10 Bratislava City Card; you must book and pay at least two hours in advance). Those arriving by boat will be accosted by guides selling their own 1.5-hour tours (half on foot and half in a little tourist train, €10, in German and English).

Local Guide—MS Agency, run by **Martin Sloboda** (can-do entrepreneur and tireless Bratislava booster, and author of the great local guidebook described earlier), can set you up with a good guide (€130/3 hours, €150/4 hours); he can also help you track down your Slovak roots. Martin, whose expertise has made much of this chapter possible, is a fine example of the youthful energy and leadership responsible for

Bratislava's success story (mobile 0905-627-265, tel. 02/5464-1467, www.msagency.sk, info@msagency.sk).

Self-Guided Walk

Bratislava's Old Town

This orientation walk passes through the heart of delightfully traffic-free old Bratislava and then down to its riverside commercial zone (figure 1.5 hours, not including stops, for this walk). If you're coming from the station, make your way toward the green onion-domed steeple of St. Michael's Gate (explained in "Arrival in Bratislava," earlier). Before going through the passage into the old town, peek over the railing on your left to the inviting garden below—once part of the city moat.

• *Step through the first gate, walk along the passageway, and pause as you come through the onion-domed...*

St. Michael's Gate (Michalská Brána)

This is the last surviving tower of the city wall. Just below the gate, notice the "kilometer zero" plaque in the ground, marking the point from which distances in Slovakia are measured.

• *You're at the head of...*

Michalská Street

Pretty as it is now, the old town was a decrepit ghost town during the communist era.

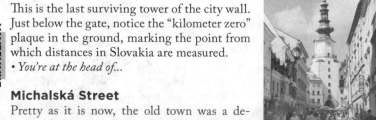

Bratislava was a damaged husk after World War II. The communist regime cared only for the future—they had no respect for the town's heritage. In the 1950s, they actually sold Bratislava's original medieval cobbles to cute German towns that were rebuilding themselves with elegant Old World character. Locals avoided this desolate corner of the city, preferring to spend time in the Petržalka suburb across the river.

With the fall of communism in 1989, the new government began a nearly decade-long process of restitution—sorting out who had the rights to the buildings, and returning them to their original owners. During this time, little repair or development took place (since there was no point investing in a property until ownership was clearly established). By 1998, most of these property issues had been sorted out, and the old town was made traffic-free. The city replaced all the street cobbles, spruced up the public buildings, and encouraged private owners to restore their buildings. (If you see any remaining decrepit buildings, it's likely that their ownership is still in dispute.)

The cafés and restaurants that line this street are inviting, especially in summer. But if you don't look beyond the facades and outdoor tables, you'll miss much of Bratislava's charm. Poke around. Courtyards and galleries—most of them open to the public—burrow through the city's buildings. For example, a half-block down Michalská street on the left, the gallery at #12 was once home to vintners who lived within the walls for safety; their former cellars are now coffee shops, massage parlors, crafts boutiques, and cigar shops. Across the street, on the right, the gallery at #7 is home to several fashion designers.

Speaking of fashion...are you noticing a lot of skin? Tight jeans? Low-cut tops? Slovak women are known for their provocative dress. When pressed for a reason for this, one male resident of "Leg-islava" smirked and told me, "Women like to show what they have. Why should they hide it?"

On the left (at #6), the **Čokoládovňa pod Michalom** chocolate shop is highly regarded among locals for its delicious hot chocolate and creamy truffles (Mon-Thu 9:00-21:00, Fri-Sat 9:00-22:00, Sun 10:00-21:00, tel. 02/5443-3945).

Above the shop's entrance, the **cannonball** embedded in the wall commemorates Napoleon's two sieges of Bratislava, which together caused massive devastation—even worse than the city suffered during World War II. Keep an eye out for these cannonballs all over town...somber reminders of one of Bratislava's darkest times.

• *Two blocks down from St. Michael's Gate, the street jogs slightly right and its name changes to Ventúrska. At the jog, detour left (along Sedlárska) and head for the...*

BRATISLAVA

Main Square (Hlavné Námestie)

This is the bustling centerpiece of Old World Bratislava. Cute little kiosks, with old-time cityscape engravings on their roofs, sell local handicrafts and knickknacks (Easter through October). Similar stalls fill the square from mid-November until December 23, when the Christmas market here is a big draw (www.vianocnetrhy.sk).

Virtually every building around this square dates from a different architectural period, from Gothic (the yellow tower) to Art Nouveau (the fancy facade facing it from across the square). When these buildings were restored a few years ago, great pains were taken to achieve authenticity—each one matches the color most likely used when it was originally built.

Extremely atmospheric cafés line the bottom of the square. You can't go wrong here. Choose the ambience you like best (indoors or out) and sip a drink with arguably Slovakia's best urban view. **Café Roland** is known for its 1904 Klimt-style mosaics and historic photos of Pressburg/Pozsony. The barista stands where a different kind of bean counter once did, guarding a vault that now holds coffee (€2-3 coffee drinks and beer, full menu, daily 8:30-23:00, Hlavné Námestie 5, tel. 02/5443-1372). The classic choice is the kitty-corner **Kaffee Mayer.** This venerable café, an institution here, has been selling coffee and cakes to a genteel clientele since 1873. You can enjoy your pick-me-up in the swanky old interior or out on the square (€2-3 cakes, Mon-Fri 9:30-22:00, Sat-Sun 9:30-23:00, Hlavné Námestie 4, tel. 02/5441-1741).

Peering over one of the benches on the square is a cartoonish statue of a **Napoleonic officer** (notice the French flag marking the embassy right behind him). With bare feet and a hat pulled over his eyes, it's hardly a flattering portrait—you could call it the Slovaks' revenge for the difficulties they faced at Napoleon's hands. Across the square, another soldier from that period stands at attention.

At the top of the Main Square is the impressive **Old Town Hall** (Stará Radnica), marked by a bold yellow tower. Near the bottom of the tower (to the left of the window), notice the cannonball embedded in the facade—yet another reminder of Napoleon's impact on Bratislava. Over time, the Old Town Hall gradually grew, annexing the buildings next to it and creating a mishmash of architectural styles along this side of the square. (A few steps down the street to the right are the historic apartments and wine museum at the **Apponyi House**—described later, under "Sights in Bratislava.")

Step through the passageway into the Old Town Hall's gorgeously restored **courtyard,** with its Renaissance arcades. (The **City History Museum**'s entrance is here—described later.)

Then, to see another fine old square, continue through the other end of the courtyard into **Primate's Square** (Primaciálne Námestie). The pink mansion on the right is the **Primate's Palace,** with a fine interior decorated with six English tapestries (described later). Do you see a lot of people using laptops? In a progressive move befitting its status as an emerging European business center, Bratislava provides free Wi-Fi on three squares in the old town. The huge student population (not to mention tourists) happily surfs in this beautiful setting. At the far end of this square is the **TI.**

• *Backtrack to the Main Square. With your back to the Old Town Hall, go to the end of the square and follow the street to the left (Rybárska Brána). Soon you'll pass a pair of...*

Whimsical Statues

Playful statues (such as the Napoleonic officer we met earlier) dot Bratislava's old town. Most date from the late 1990s, when city leaders wanted to entice locals back into the newly prettied-up center.

A half-block down this street (on the left), you'll come to a jovial chap doffing his top hat. This is a statue of **Schöner Náci,** who lived in Bratislava until the 1960s. This eccentric old man, a poor carpet cleaner, would dress up in his one black suit and top hat, and go strolling through the city, offering gifts to the women he fancied. (He'd often whisper *"schön"*—German for "pretty"—to the women, which is how he got his nickname.) Schöner Náci now gets to spend eternity greeting visitors outside his favorite café, Kaffee Mayer. Schöner is missing an arm: A bunch of drunks broke it off. As Prague gets more expensive, Bratislava is becoming the cheaper alternative for weekend "stag parties," popular with Brits lured here by cheap flights and cheap beer. Locals hope this is a short-lived trend, and that those rowdy louts will move farther east before long.

• *Continue down Rybárska.*

At the end of this block, at the intersection with Panská, watch out on the right for **Čumil** ("the Peeper"), grinning at passersby from a manhole. This was the first and is still the favorite of Bratislava's statues.

There's no story behind this one—the artist simply wanted to create a fun icon and let the townspeople make up their own tales. Čumil has survived being driven over by a truck—twice—and he's still grinning.

For a peek at a third statue—a nosy **Paparazzo**—you can take a side-trip left up Panská and go one block, watching the corner on the left.

• *Back at Čumil, continue along Rybárska to reach the long, skinny square called...*

Hviezdoslav Square (Hviezdoslavovo Námestie)

The landscaped park in the center of this square is particularly inviting. At this end is the impressive, silver-topped Slovak National Theater (Slovenské Národné Divadlo). Beyond that, the opulent yellow Neo-Baroque building is the Slovak Philharmonic (Slovenská Filharmónia). The prominence of these two venues is evidence of Bratislava's strong performing arts tradition.

Right in front of the theater (by the McDonald's), look down into the glass **display case** to see the foundation of the one-time Fishermen's Gate into the city. Surrounding the base of the gate is water. This entire square was once a tributary of the Danube, and the Carlton Hotel across the way was a series of inns on different islands. The buildings along the old town side of the square mark where the city wall once stood.

Stroll down the long art-and-people-filled park, nicknamed **"The Promenade."** Each summer, as part of an arts festival, the park is ornamented with entertaining modern art. After passing a statue of the square's namesake (Pavol Országh Hviezdoslav, a beloved Slovak poet), you'll come upon an ugly fence and barriers on the left, which mark the fortified US Embassy. Just past the embassy is the entrance to the Sky Bar, offering excellent views over this square, the cathedral, and the castle (ride elevator to seventh floor; see "Eating in Bratislava," later). Farther along, after the giant chessboard, the glass pavilion is a popular venue for summer concerts. On the right near the end of the park, a statue of Hans Christian Andersen is a reminder that the Danish storyteller enjoyed his visit to Bratislava, too.

• *Reaching the end of the square, you run into the barrier for a busy highway. Turn right and walk one block to find the big, black marble slab facing a modern monument—and, likely, a colorful wooden reconstruction of a synagogue.*

Holocaust Memorial

This was the site of Bratislava's original synagogue. To echo ages past, a replica of the building was recently erected here (with painted plywood). If the reconstruction is gone, you should still be able to see an etching of the building in the big slab.

Turn your attention to the memorial. The word "Remember" carved into the base in Hebrew and Slovak commemorates the 90,000 Slovaks who were deported to Nazi death camps. Nearly all were killed. The fact that the town's main synagogue and main church (to the right) were located side by side illustrates the tolerance that characterized Bratislava before Hitler. Ponder the modern statue: The two pages of an open book, faces, hands in the sky, and bullets—all under the Star of David—evoke the fate of 90 percent of the Slovak Jews.

• *Now head toward the adjacent church, up the stairs.*

St. Martin's Cathedral (Dóm Sv. Martina)

This historic church isn't looking too sharp these days—and the highway thundering a few feet in front of its door doesn't help matters. If it were any closer, the off-ramp would go through the nave. Sad as it is now, the cathedral has been party to some pretty important history. While Buda and Pest were occupied by Ottomans for a century and a half, Bratislava was the capital of Hungary. Nineteen Hungarian kings and queens were crowned in this church—more than have been crowned anywhere in Hungary. In fact, the last Hungarian coronation (not counting the Austrian Franz Josef) was

not in Budapest, but in Bratislava. A replica of the Hungarian crown still tops the steeple.

It's worth walking up to the cathedral's entrance to observe

City of Three Cultures:
Pressburg, Pozsony, Bratislava

Historically a Hungarian and Austrian city as much as a Slovak one, Bratislava has always been a Central European melting pot. The Hungarians used Pozsony (as they called it) as their capital during the century and a half that Buda and Pest were occupied by Ottoman invaders. Later, the city was a retreat of Habsburg Empress Maria Theresa (who used its German name, Pressburg). Everyone from Hans Christian Andersen to Casanova sang the wonders of this bustling burg on the Danube.

By its late-19th-century glory days, the city was a rich intersection of cultures. Shop clerks had to be able to greet customers in German, Hungarian, and Slovak. It was said that the mornings belonged to the Slovaks (farmers who came into the city to sell their wares at market), the afternoons to the Hungarians (diplomats and office workers filling the cafés), and the evenings to the Austrians (wine producers who ran convivial neighborhood wine pubs where all three groups would gather). In those wine pubs, the vintner would listen to which language his customers used, then automatically bring them the correct size glass: 0.3 liters for Hungarians, 0.25 liters for Austrians, and 0.2 liters for Slovaks (a distinction that still exists today). Jews (one-tenth of the population), Romanians, and Roma (Gypsies) rounded out the city's ethnic brew.

When the new nation of Czechoslovakia was formed from the rubble of World War I, the city shed its German and Hungarian names, proudly taking the new Slavic name Bratislava. The Slovak population—which had been at only about 10 percent—was on the rise, but the city remained tri-cultural.

World War II changed all of that. With the dissolution of Czechoslovakia, Slovakia became an "independent" country under the thumb of the Nazis—who all but wiped out the Jewish

some fragments of times past (circle around the building, along the busy road, to the opposite, uphill side). Directly across from the church door is a broken bit of the 15th-century town wall. The church was actually built into the wall, which explains its unusual north-side entry. In fact, notice the fortified watchtower (with a WC drop on its left) built into the corner of the church just above you.

There's relatively little to see inside the cathedral—I'd skip it (€2, Mon-Sat 9:00-11:30 & 13:00-18:00, Thu until 17:00, Sun 13:30-16:00). If you do duck in, you'll find a fairly gloomy interior, some fine carved-wood altarpieces (a Slovak specialty), a dank crypt, a replica of the Hungarian crown, and a treasury in the back with a whimsical wood carving of Jesus blessing Habsburg Emperor Franz Josef.

population. Then, at the end of the war, in retribution for Hitler's misdeeds, a reunited Czechoslovakia expelled people of Germanic descent (including all of those Austrians). And finally, a "mutual exchange of populations" sent the city's ethnic Hungarians back to Hungary.

Bratislava suffered terribly under the communists. The historic city's multilayered charm and delicate cultural fabric were ripped apart, then shrouded in gray. For example, the communists were more proud of their ultramodern New Bridge than of the historic Jewish quarter they razed to make way for it. Now the bridge and its highway slice through the center of the old town, and the heavy traffic rattles the stained-glass windows of St. Martin's Cathedral.

But Bratislava's most recent chapter is one of great success. Over the last few decades, the city has gone from gloomy victim of communism to thriving economic center and social hub. Its population of 450,000 includes some 70,000 students (at the city's six universities), creating an atmosphere of youthful energy and optimism. Its remarkable position on the Danube, a short commute from Vienna, is prompting its redevelopment as one of Europe's up-and-coming cities.

Bratislava and Vienna have realized that it's mutually beneficial to work together to bring the Slovak capital up to snuff. They're cooperating as a new "twin city" commerce super-zone. In the coming years, foreign investors plan to erect a skyline of 600-foot-tall skyscrapers and a clutch of glittering new megamalls. You'd never have guessed it a few years ago, but today calling Bratislava "the next Berlin on a smaller scale" is only a bit of a stretch.

Head back around the church for a good view (looking toward the river) of the **New Bridge** (Nový Most, a.k.a. Most SNP), the communists' pride and joy. As with most Soviet-era landmarks in former communist countries, locals aren't crazy about this structure—not only for the questionable starship *Enterprise* design,  but also because of the oppressive regime it represented. However, the restaurant and observation deck up top has been renovated into a posh eatery called (appropriately enough) "UFO." You can visit it for the views, a drink, or a full meal.

• *You could end the walk here. Two sights (both described later, under "Sights in Bratislava") are nearby. You could hike up to the **castle** (take the underpass beneath the highway, go up the stairs on the right marked by the* Hrad/Castle *sign, then turn left up the stepped lane marked Zámocké Schody). Or hike over the New Bridge (pedestrian walkway on lower level) to ride the elevator up to the **UFO** viewing platform.*

*But to really round out your Bratislava visit, head for the river and stroll downstream (left) to a place where you get a dose of modern development in Bratislava—**Eurovea**. Walk about 10 minutes downstream, past the old town, boat terminals, and iron bridge, until you come to a big, slick complex with a grassy park leading down to the riverbank.*

Eurovea

Just downstream from the old town is the futuristic Eurovea, with four vibrant layers, each a quarter-mile long: a riverside park, luxury condos, a thriving modern shopping mall, and an office park. Walking out onto the view piers jutting into the Danube and surveying the scene, it looks like a computer-generated  urban dreamscape come true. Exploring the old town gave you a taste of where this country has been. But wandering this riverside park, enjoying a drink in one of its chic outdoor lounges, and then browsing through the thriving mall, you'll enjoy a glimpse of where Slovakia is heading.

• *Our walk is finished. If you haven't already visited them, consider circling back to some of the sights described below.*

Sights in Bratislava

If Europe had a prize for "city with the most underwhelming museums," I'd cast my vote for Bratislava. You can easily have a great day here without setting foot in a museum, instead focusing on Bratislava's charming, fun-to-stroll streets and grand views from the castle and UFO restaurant. But if you're feeling particularly driven to visit a museum, the Primate's Palace (with its cheap admission and fine tapestries) ranks slightly above the rest.

On or near the Old Town's Main Square

All three of these museums are within a few minutes' walk of one another, on or very near the Main Square.

City History Museum (Mestské Múzeum)—Delving into the bric-a-brac of Bratislava's past, this museum includes ecclesiastical art on the ground floor and a sprawling, chronological look at local history upstairs. The displays occupy rooms once used by the town council—courthouse, council hall, chapel, and so on. Everything is described in English, and the included audioguide tries hard, but nothing quite succeeds in bringing meaning to the place. On your way upstairs, you'll have a chance to climb up into the Old Town Hall's tower, offering so-so views over the square, cathedral, and castle.

Cost and Hours: €5 includes dry audioguide, covered by Apponyi House ticket, Tue-Fri 10:00-17:00, Sat-Sun 11:00-18:00, closed Mon, in the Old Town Hall—enter through courtyard, tel. 02/5920-5130, www.muzeum.bratislava.sk.

Apponyi House (Apponyiho Palác)—This nicely restored mansion of a Hungarian aristocrat is meaningless without the included audioguide (dull but informative). The museum has two parts. The cellar and ground floor feature an interesting exhibit on the vineyards of the nearby "Little Carpathian" hills, with historic presses and barrels, and a replica of an old-time wine-pub table.

Upstairs are two floors of urban apartments from old Bratislava, called the Period Rooms Museum. The first floor up shows off the 18th-century Rococo-style rooms of the nobility—fine but not ostentatious, with ceramic stoves. The second floor up (with lower ceilings and simpler wall decorations) illustrates 19th-century bourgeois/middle-class lifestyles, including period clothing and some Empire-style furniture.

Cost and Hours: €6, includes City History Museum admission, Tue-Fri 10:00-17:00, Sat-Sun 11:00-18:00, closed Mon, last entry 30 minutes before closing, Radničná 1, tel. 02/5920-5135, www.muzeum.bratislava.sk.

▲Primate's Palace (Primaciálny Palác)—Bratislava's most interesting museum, this tastefully restored French-Neoclassical mansion (formerly the residence of the archbishop, or "primate") dates from 1781. The religious

counterpart of the castle, it filled in for Esztergom when that religious capital of the Hungarians was taken by the Ottomans. Throughout the Ottoman occupation, from 1543 to the late 1800s, this was the winter residence of Hungary's archbishops.

Cost and Hours: €2, Tue-Fri 10:00-17:00, Sat-Sun 11:00-18:00, closed Mon, Primaciálne Námestie 3, tel. 02/5935-6394.

BRATISLAVA

Visiting the Museum: The palace features one fine floor of exhibits. Walk up the grand staircase, then turn left into the Mirror Hall, used for concerts, city council meetings, and other important events.

From here, do a U-turn and progress through the large public rooms—designed to impress. Displayed in several of these rooms is the museum's collective highlight: a series of six English **tapestries,** illustrating the ancient Greek myth of the tragic love between Hero and Leander. The tapestries—the only complete cycle of royal English tapestries in existence—were woven in England by Flemish weavers for the court of King Charles I (in the 1630s). They were kept in London's Hampton Court Palace until Charles was deposed and beheaded in 1649. Cromwell sold them to France to help fund his civil war, but after 1650, they disappeared. Centuries later, in 1903, restorers broke through a false wall in this mansion and discovered the six tapestries, neatly folded and perfectly preserved. Nobody knows how they got there (perhaps they were squirreled away during the Napoleonic invasion, and whoever hid them didn't survive). The archbishop—who had just sold the palace to the city, but emptied it of furniture before he left—cried foul and tried to get the tapestries back...but the city said, "A deal's a deal."

After traipsing through the grand rooms, find the hallway that leads through the smaller rooms of the archbishop's private quarters, now decorated with Dutch, Flemish, German, and Italian paintings. At the end of this hall, a bay window looks down into the archbishop's own private marble chapel. When the archbishop became too ill to walk down to Mass, this window was built for him to take part in the service.

Bratislava Castle (Bratislavský Hrad)

This imposing fortress, nicknamed the "upside-down table," is the city's most prominent landmark. There surely has been a castle on this spot for centuries. The oldest surviving chunk is the 13th-century Romanesque watchtower (the one slightly taller than the other three). When Habsburg Empress Maria Theresa took a liking to Bratislava in the 18th century, she transformed the castle from a military fortress to a royal residence suitable for holding court. She added a summer riding school (the U-shaped complex next to the castle), an enclosed winter riding school out back, and lots more. Maria Theresa's favorite daughter, Maria Christina, lived here with her husband, Albert, when they were newlyweds. Locals nicknamed the

place "little Schönbrunn," in reference to the Habsburgs' summer palace on the outskirts of Vienna.

But M.T.'s castle burned to the ground in an 1811 fire, and it was left as a ruin for 150 years before being reconstructed in 1953. Unfortunately, the communist rebuild was drab and uninviting; the inner courtyard feels like a prison exercise yard.

A more recent renovation has done little to improve things, and the museum exhibits inside aren't really worth the cost of admission (described next). The best visit is to simply hike up (it's free to enter the grounds), enjoy the views over town, and take a close-up look at the stately old building (the big, blocky, modern building next door is the Slovak Parliament).

For details on the best walking route to the castle, see page 256.

Castle Museum—The castle displays include the misnamed Treasure Room, a sparse collection of items found at the castle site, including coins and fragments of Roman jugs, and the Knights Hall, offering a brief history lesson in the castle's construction and reconstruction.

You can also enter the palace itself. A blinding-white staircase with gold trim leads to the Music Hall, with a prized 18th-century *Assumption* altarpiece by Anton Schmidt (first floor); a collection of historical prints depicting Bratislava and its castle (second floor); and temporary exhibits (third/top floor). From the top floor, a series of very steep, modern staircases take you up to the Crown Tower (the castle's oldest and tallest) for views over town—though the vista from the terrace in front of the castle is much easier to reach and nearly as good.

Cost and Hours: €4 for all-inclusive "Road A" ticket, €2 for pointless "Road B" (covers Treasure Room, Knights Hall, and less interesting parts of palace); April-Oct Tue-Sun 10:00-18:00, Nov-March Tue-Sun 9:00-17:00, closed Mon year-round; ticket office is right of main riverfront entrance—enter exhibits from central courtyard, tel. 02/2048-3110, www.snm.sk.

▲▲The UFO at New Bridge (Nový Most)

The bizarre, flying-saucer-capped bridge near the old town—completed in 1972 in heavy-handed communist style—has been reclaimed by capitalists. It's now a spruced-up, overpriced café/restaurant, with an observation deck allowing sweeping 360-degree views of Bratislava from about 300 feet above the Danube. Think of it as the "Slovak Space Needle."

Cost and Hours: €6.50, daily 10:00-23:00, elevator free if you have a meal reservation or order food at the restaurant—main courses steeply priced at €22-30, tel. 02/6252-0300, www.u-f-o.sk.

Getting There: Walk across the New Bridge from the old town (there's a pedestrian walkway on the lower level)—the elevator entrance is underneath the tower on the Petržalka side.

⊘ Self-Guided Tour: The "**elevator**" that takes you up is actually a funicular—you'll notice you're moving at an angle. At the top, walk up the stairs to the observation deck.

Begin by viewing the **castle** and **old town.** The area to the right of the old town, between and beyond the skyscrapers, is a

massive construction zone. A time-lapse camera set up here over the next few years would catch skyscrapers popping up like dandelions. International investors are throwing lots of money at Bratislava. (Imagine having so much prime, undeveloped real estate available downtown in the capital of an emerging European economic power...just an hour down the road from Vienna, no less.) Most of the development is taking place along the banks of the Danube. In a decade, this will be a commercial center.

The huge TV tower caps a forested hill beyond the old town. Below and to the left of it, the pointy monument is **Slavín,** where more than 6,800 Soviet soldiers who fought to liberate Bratislava from the Nazis are buried. A nearby church had to take down its steeple so as not to draw attention away from the huge Soviet soldier on top of the monument.

Now turn 180 degrees and cross the platform to face **Petržalka,** a planned communist suburb that sprouted here in the 1970s. The site was once occupied by a village, and the various districts of modern Petržalka still carry their original names (which now seem ironic): "Meadows" *(Háje),* "Woods" *(Lúky),* and "Courtyards" *(Dvory).* The ambitious communist planners envisioned a city laced with Venetian-style canals to help drain the marshy land, but the plans were abandoned after the harsh crackdown on the 1968 Prague Spring uprising. Today, one in four Bratislavans lives in Petržalka. A few years ago, this was a grim and decaying sea of

miserable concrete apartment *panelák* ("panel buildings," so called because they're made of huge prefab panels). But things are changing fast. Many of the *panelák* are being retrofitted with new layers of insulation, and the apartments inside are being updated. And, like Dorothy opening the door to Oz, the formerly drab buildings are being splashed with bright new colors. Far from being a slum, Petržalka is a popular neighborhood for Bratislavan yuppies who can't yet afford to build their dream house. Locals read the Czech-language home-improvement magazine *Panel Plus* for ideas on how to give their *panelák* apartments some style (www.panelplus.cz).

Still facing Petržalka, notice that construction is also happening along this riverbank (such as the supermall down below). But there's still history here. The **park** called Sad Janka Kráľa, a.k.a. "Aupark"—just downriver from the bridge—was technically the first public park in Europe and is still a popular place for locals to relax and court.

Scanning the **horizon** beyond Petržalka, two things stick out: on the left, the old communist oil refinery (which has been fully updated and is now state-of-the-art); and on the right, a sea of modern windmills. These are just over the border, in Austria...and Bratislava is sure to grow in that direction quickly. Austria is about three miles that way, and Hungary is about six miles farther to the left.

Before you leave, consider a drink at the café (€3-4 coffee or beer, €7-20 cocktails). If nothing else, be sure to use the memorable WCs (guys can enjoy a classic urinal photo).

Sleeping in Bratislava

I'd rather sleep in Vienna or Budapest—particularly since good-value options in central Bratislava are slim, and service tends to be surly. But if Bratislava entices you to stay longer than a day trip, these options are all inside or within a short walk of the old town. Business-oriented places charge more on weekdays than on weekends. Hotel Michalská Brána is right in the heart of the old town,

BRATISLAVA

Sleep Code

(€1 = about $1.30, country code: 421, area code: 02)
S = Single, **D** = Double/Twin, **T** = Triple, **Q** = Quad, **b** = bathroom. English is spoken at each place. Unless otherwise noted, breakfast is included and you can pay by credit card.

To help you sort easily through these listings, I've divided the accommodations into three categories, based on the price for a standard double room with bath:

$$$ **Higher Priced**—Most rooms €100 or more.
$$ **Moderately Priced**—Most rooms between €50-100.
$ **Lower Priced**—Most rooms €50 or less.

Prices can change without notice; verify the hotel's current rates online or by email.

while the others are just outside of it—but still within a 5-10-minute walk.

$$$ Hotel Marrol's is the town's most enticing splurge. Although it's in a drab urban neighborhood, it's a five-minute walk from the old town, and its 54 rooms are luxurious and tastefully appointed Old World country-style. While pricey, the rates drop on weekends (prices flex, but generally Mon-Thu: Db-€160, Fri-Sun: Db-€120, Sb-€10 less, non-smoking rooms, elevator, air-con, free Internet access and Wi-Fi, loaner laptops, free minibar, gorgeous lounge, Tobrucká 4, tel. 02/5778-4600, www.hotelmarrols. sk, rec@hotelmarrols.sk).

$$$ Hotel Michalská Brána is a charming boutique hotel just inside St. Michael's Gate in the old town. The 14 rooms are sleek, mod, and classy, and the location is ideal—right in the heart of town, but on a relatively sleepy lane just away from the hubbub (Mon-Thu: Db-€105, Fri-Sun: Db-€90, pricier suites also available, €5 less in July-Aug, non-smoking, air-con, elevator, free Wi-Fi in lobby, free cable Internet in rooms, Baštová 4, tel. 02/5930-7200, www.michalskabrana.com, reception@michalskabrana.com).

$$ Hotel Ibis, part of the Europe-wide chain, offers 120 nicely appointed rooms just outside the old town, overlooking a busy tram junction—request a quieter room (Mon-Thu: Sb/Db-€85, Fri-Sun: Sb/Db-€69, rates flex with demand, you'll likely save €20 or more with advance booking on their website, breakfast-€10, elevator, air-con, free Wi-Fi, Zámocká 38, tel. 02/5929-2000, fax 02/5929-2111, www.ibishotel.com, h3566@accor.com).

$$ Penzión Virgo sits on a quiet residential street, an eight-minute walk from the old town. The 11 boutiqueish rooms are classy and well-appointed (Sb-€61, Db-€74, breakfast-€6, free Wi-

Fi, Panenská 14, tel. 02/2092-1400, www.penzionvirgo.sk, recep tion@penzionvirgo.sk).

$$ Penzión Gremium has eight nondescript rooms and two apartments in a very central location, just a block behind the National Theater and a few steps from the old town. It's on a busy street with good windows but no air-conditioning, so it can be noisy on rowdy weekends (Sb-€60, Db-€70, Db apartment-€90, prices soft—cheaper in slow times, breakfast-€5, free Wi-Fi, Gorkého 11, tel. 02/070-4874, www.penziongremium.sk, recepcia@penzion gremium.sk).

$ Downtown Backpackers Hostel is a funky but well-run place located in an old-fashioned townhouse. Rooms are named for famous artists and decorated with reinterpretations of their paintings (61 beds in 12 rooms, D-€54, bunk in 7-8-bed dorm-€20, bunk in 10-bed dorm-€18, breakfast-€3-5, free Wi-Fi, laundry facilities, kitchen, bike rental nearby, Panenská 31—across busy boulevard from Grassalkovich Palace, five-minute walk from old town, tel. 02/5464-1191, www.backpackers.sk, info@backpackers.sk).

Eating in Bratislava

Slovak cuisine shows some Austrian and Hungarian influences, but it's closer to Czech—lots of starches and gravy, and plenty of pork, cabbage, potatoes, and dumplings. Keep an eye out for Slovakia's national dish, *bryndzové halušky* (small potato dumplings with sheep's cheese and bits of bacon). Like the Czechs, the Slovaks produce excellent beer (*pivo*, PEE-voh). One of the top brands is Zlatý Bažant ("Golden Pheasant"). For a fun drink and snack that locals love, try a Vinea grape soda and a sweet *Pressburger* bagel in any bar or café.

Long a wine-producing area, the Bratislava region makes the same wines that Vienna is famous for. But, as nearly all is consumed locally, most people don't think of Slovakia as wine country.

Bratislava is packed with inviting new eateries. In addition to the heavy Slovak staples, you'll find trendy new bars and bistros, and a smattering of ethnic offerings. The best plan may be to stroll the old town and keep your eyes open for the setting and cuisine that appeals to you most. Or consider one of these options.

Beer Halls

While not quite as famous as their Czech cousins, Slovak beers are well regarded by connoisseurs. Bratislava's beer halls are good places to sample Slovak and Czech beers, and to get a hearty, affordable meal of stick-to-your-ribs pub grub. Here are several options around town.

Prazdroj ("Urquell") is a Czech-style, copper-vats-and-pipes beer hall with lively ambience and good, hearty traditional food. It sprawls through several rooms of a building just off Hviezdoslav Square at the edge of the old town, with outdoor seating facing the Philharmonic. Pilsner Urquell is on tap (€7-15 main courses, Mon-Fri 10:00-24:00, Sat-Sun 11:00-24:00, Mostová 8, tel. 02/5441-1108).

1. Slovak Pub (as in "the first") is the Slovak equivalent of Prazdroj, attracting a younger crowd. Enter from a bustling modern shopping street just outside the old town, and climb the stairs into a vast warren of rustic, old countryside-style pub rooms with uneven floors. While enjoying the lively, loud, almost chaotic ambience, you'll dine on affordable and truly authentic Slovak fare, made with products from the pub's own farm. This is a good place to try the Slovak specialty, *bryndzové halušky*. It feels like a tourist trap, but it's filled with locals—go figure (€5-12 main courses, Mon-Sat 10:00-24:00, Sun 12:00-24:00, Obchodná 62, tel. 02/5292-6367).

Bratislavský Meštiansky Pivovar ("Bratislava Town Brew-pub"), in a modern zone just outside the old town, brews its own beer and also sells a variety of others. Seating stretches over several levels in the new-meets-old interior (€6-10 meals, daily 11:00-24:00, Drevená 8, mobile 0944-512-265).

Upscale Dining Neighborhoods

As this scene is changing fast, I've suggested two neighborhoods worth exploring for good-quality eateries. These zones feel jammed with visiting European businessmen looking for good-quality, expense-account meals of international fare.

Hviezdoslav Square (Hviezdoslavovo Námestie): This long square, running along the bottom of the old town, is a delightful people zone with several fine restaurants offering al fresco tables. The highest concentration, including some splurgy steakhouses, is near the silver-roofed National Theater building. But for one of the best views in town, walk just past the US Embassy to find the low-profile door for **Lemon Tree/Sky Bar/Rum Club.** This three-in-one place features the same Thai-meets-Mediterranean menu throughout (€8-11 pasta and noodle dishes, €14-16 main courses). But the real reason to come here is for the seventh-floor Sky Bar, which has fantastic views. It's smart to reserve a view table in advance if you want to dine here—or just drop by for a pricey vodka cocktail on the small terrace (daily 11:00-late, Sun from 12:00, Hviezdoslavovo Námestie 7, mobile 0948-109-400).

Eurovea: Huge outdoor terraces rollicking with happy eaters line this swanky riverfront residential and shopping-mall complex, about a 10-minute walk downstream from the old town. You'll pay high prices for the great atmosphere and views at international eateries—French, Italian, Brazilian—and a branch of the Czech beer-hall chain Kolkovna.

Fast and Cheap

Two local chains, with branches throughout the old town and beyond, offer a good, quick bite. The hip, rustic-chic **Shtoor** (named for a beloved 19th-century champion of Slovak culture, Ľudovít Štúr) is a "homemade café" with coffee drinks and €3-5 sandwiches and quiches (takeaway or table service, open long hours daily). They have three locations: in the heart of the old town at Panská 23; just east of the old town (near Eurovea) at Štúrova 8; and inside a Barnes & Noble-type bookstore, Martinus.sk, at Obchodná 26. Also in the old town, the **Coffee & Bagel Story** chain sells...coffee and €3-5 bagel sandwiches (handiest location on Main Square at Hlavné Námestie 8).

Bratislava Connections

By Train

Bratislava has two major train stations. The main train station (Hlavná Stanica, abbreviated "Bratislava hl. st." on schedules) is closer to the old town, while the Petržalka station (ŽST Petržalka) is in the suburb across the river. When checking schedules (www. bahn.com is helpful), pay attention to which station your train uses. Bus #93 connects these two Bratislava stations (5-12/hour, 10 minutes; take bus #N93 at night).

From Bratislava by Train to: Vienna (2/hour, 1 hour, round-trip ticket is cheaper than one-way fare—simply buy it moments before and hop on; departures alternate between the two stations—half from main station, half from Petržalka), **Budapest** (5/day direct, 2.5 hours to Keleti Station, more with transfers; may be cheaper by Orange Ways bus: 1-4/day, 2.5 hours, www. orangeways.com), **Sopron** (at least hourly, 2.5-3 hours, generally 2 transfers—often at stations in downtown and/or suburban Vienna), **Prague** (5/day direct, 4.25 hours). For more Austrian destinations (such as **Salzburg** or **Innsbruck**), you'll connect through Vienna.

By Bus

Two different companies run handy buses that connect Bratislava, **Vienna,** and the **airports** in each city: Blaguss (www.eurolines.at)

and Slovak Lines/Post Bus (tel. 0810-222-3336, www.slovaklines.sk). You can prebook online, or just take whichever connection is leaving first. The bus schedules are handily posted at www.airportbratislava.sk (find the "Navigation—From the Airport" tab).

The buses run about hourly from Bratislava's airport to Bratislava (15 minutes, stops either at the main bus station east of the old town or at the New Bridge), continue on to Vienna's airport (1 hour), and end in Vienna (1.25 hours, Erdberg stop on the U-3 subway line). They then turn around and make the reverse journey (€7.50-10, depending on route).

By Boat

Riverboats connect Bratislava to Budapest and Vienna. Conveniently, these boats dock right along the Danube in front of Bratislava's old town. While they are more expensive, less frequent, and slower than the train, some travelers enjoy getting out on the Danube. Passports are not required.

To Vienna: The **Twin City Liner** offers several daily boat trips between downtown Bratislava and Vienna's Schwedenplatz (where Vienna's town center hits the canal; €29 each way, 1.25-hour trip; daily April-Oct only, Austrian tel. 01/58880, www.twincityliner.com).

Two competing lines, the Slovak **LOD** (www.lod.sk) and the Hungarian **Mahart** (www.mahartpassnave.hu) connect the cities a little more cheaply, but only once a day. These boats are slower (1.5-1.75 hours), as they use Vienna's Reichsbrücke dock on the main river, and therefore need to go through the locks.

To Budapest: Mahart links Bratislava and Budapest once daily (€79 one-way, 4-4.5 hours, daily late April-early Oct only, www.mahartpassnave.hu).

By Plane

Bratislava Airport (Letisko Bratislava, airport code: BTS, www.letiskobratislava.sk) is six miles northeast of downtown Bratislava. The airport offers budget flights on low-cost carriers Ryanair (www.ryanair.com) and Danube Wings (www.danubewings.eu). Some airlines market it as "Vienna-Bratislava," thanks to its proximity to both capitals. The airport is officially named for Milan Rastislav Štefánik, who worked toward the creation of Czechoslovakia at the end of World War I. It's compact and manageable, with all the usual amenities (including ATMs).

From the Airport to Downtown Bratislava: The airport has easy **public bus** connections to Bratislava's main train station (€1.30, bus #61, 4-5/hour, 30 minutes). To reach the bus stop, exit straight out of the arrivals hall, cross the street, buy a ticket at the kiosk, and look for the bus stop on your right. For directions from the train station into the old town, see "Arrival in Bratislava," earlier. A **taxi** from the airport into central Bratislava should cost less than €20.

To Vienna: A slow option is to connect through Bratislava's train station (described earlier). More direct and still affordable, you can take a Eurolines bus from Bratislava Airport to the Erdberg stop on Vienna's U-3 subway line (described earlier, under "By Bus"). A taxi from Bratislava Airport directly to Vienna costs €60-90 (depending on whether you use a cheaper Slovak or more expensive Austrian cab).

To Budapest: Take the bus or taxi to Bratislava's train station (described earlier), then hop a train to Budapest.

SALZBURG
and the
Salzkammergut

SALZBURG

Salzburg and its residents—or at least its tourism industry—are forever smiling to the tunes of Mozart and *The Sound of Music*. Thanks to its charmingly preserved old town, splendid gardens, Baroque churches, and Europe's largest intact medieval fortress, Salzburg feels made for visitors. As a musical mecca, the city puts on a huge annual festival, as well as constant concerts. It's a city with class. Vagabonds wish they had nicer clothes.

Even without Mozart and the Von Trapps, Salzburg is steeped in history. In about A.D. 700, Bavaria gave Salzburg to Bishop Rupert in return for his promise to Christianize the area. Salzburg remained an independent city (belonging to no state) until Napoleon came in the early 1800s. Thanks in part to its formidable fortress, Salzburg managed to avoid the ravages of war for 1,200 years... until World War II. Much of the city was destroyed by WWII bombs (mostly around the train station), but the historic old town survived.

Eight million tourists crawl its cobbles each year. That's a lot of Mozart balls—and all that popularity has led to a glut of businesses hoping to catch the tourist dollar. Still, Salzburg is both a must and a joy.

Planning Your Time

While Salzburg's sights are, frankly, mediocre, the town itself is a Baroque museum of cobbled streets and elegant buildings—simply a touristy stroller's delight. Even if your time is short, consider allowing half a day for the *Sound of Music* tour. The *S.O.M.* bus tour kills a nest of sightseeing birds with one ticket (city overview, *S.O.M.* sights, and a fine drive by the lakes).

You'd probably enjoy at least two nights in Salzburg—nights are important for swilling beer in atmospheric gardens and attending concerts in Baroque halls and chapels. Seriously consider one of Salzburg's many evening musical events (a few are free, some are as cheap as €12, and most average €40).

To get away from it all, bike down the river or hike across the Mönchsberg cliffs that rise directly from the middle of town. Or consider swinging by Berchtesgaden, just 15 miles away in Germany. A direct bus gets you there from Salzburg in 45 minutes (see next chapter).

A day trip from Salzburg to Hallstatt (the small-town high-light of the Salzkammergut Lake District—see page 337) is do-able, but involves about five hours for the round-trip transportation alone and makes for a very long day. An overnight in Hallstatt is better.

Orientation to Salzburg

Salzburg, a city of 150,000 (Austria's fourth-largest), is divided into old and new. The old town, sitting between the Salzach River and its mini-mountain (Mönchsberg), holds nearly all the charm and most of the tourists. The new town, across the river, has the train station, a few sights and museums, and some good accommodations.

Tourist Information

Salzburg has three helpful TIs (main tel. 0662/889-870, www.salzburg.info): at the **train station** (daily June-Aug 8:30-19:00, Sept-May 9:00-18:00, tel. 0662/8898-7340); on **Mozartplatz** in the old center (daily 9:00-18:00, July-Aug until 19:00,

closed Sun mid-Jan-Easter and Oct-mid-Nov, tel. 0662/889-870); and at the **Salzburg Süd park-and-ride** (April-Sept generally Tue-Sat 10:00-16:30 but sometimes longer hours, closed Sun-Mon and all of Oct-March, tel. 0662/8898-7360).

At any TI, you can pick up a free city-center map (the €0.70 map has a broader coverage and more information on sights, and is particularly worthwhile if biking out of town), the Salzburg Card brochure (listing sights with current hours and prices), and a bi-monthly events guide. The TIs also book rooms (€2.20 fee and 10

SALZBURG

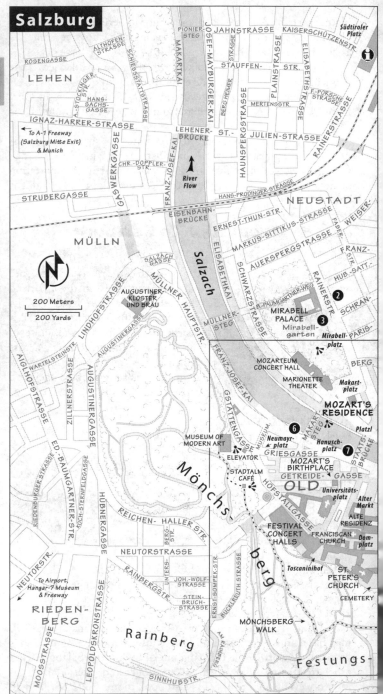

Salzburg

RÖSENGASSE

LEHEN

ALTHOFENSTRASSE

A.-STOCKINGER-STR.

SCHIESSSTÄTTSTRASSE

HANS-SACHS-GASSE

IGNAZ-HARRER-STRASSE

To A-1 Freeway
(Salzburg Mitte Exit)
& Munich

CHR.-DOPPLER-STR.

GASWERKGASSE

FRANZ-JOSEF-KAI

STRUBERGASSE

MÜLLN

N

200 Meters
200 Yards

SALZACH-GASSE

MÜLLNER HAUPTSTR.

AUGUSTINER-KLOSTER UND BRÄU

LINDHOFSTRASSE

AUGUSTINERGASSE

AIGLHOFSTRASSE

WARTELSTEINSTR.

ZILLNERSTRASSE

ED.-BAUMGARTNER-STR.

RIEDENBURGER STRASSE

KOCH-STERNFELDGASSE

HÜBNERGASSE

REICHEN-HALLER STR.

NEUTORSTRASSE

NEUTORSTR.

To Airport,
Hangar-7 Museum
& Freeway

RIEDEN-BERG

MOOSSTRASSE

LEOPOLDSKRONSTRASSE

RAINBERGSTR.

UNTERS.

JOH.-WOLF-STRASSE

STEIN-BRUCH-STRASSE

SINNHUBSTR.

Rainberg

BERG-STR.

ERNST-SOMPEK-STR.

BUCKLREUTH STRASSE

W. RAINER

PIONIER-STEG

JOSEF-MAYBURGER-KAI

MAKARTKAI

JAHNSTRASSE

KAISERSCHÜTZENSTR.

Südtiroler Platz

i

BERGHEIMER STRASSE

STAUFFEN-STR.

PLAINSTRASSE

ELISABETHSTRASSE

F.-PORSCHE-STRASSE

RAINERSTRASSE

LEHENER-BRÜCKE

ST.-

HAUNSPERGSTRASSE

MERTENSSTR.

JULIEN-STRASSE

River
Flow

HANS-PRODINGER-STRASSE

NEUSTADT

EISENBAHN-BRÜCKE

Salzach

ERNEST-THUN-STR.

ELISABETHKAI

MARKUS-SITTIKUS-STRASSE

FABER-WEISER-STR.

AUERSPERGSTRASSE

RAINERSTR.

FRANZ-JOS.-STR.

HUB.-SATT.-

SCHWARZSTRASSE

B.-PAUMGARTNER-WEG

MÜLLNER STEG

2

MIRABELL PALACE

3

Mirabell-garten

SCHRAN-

Mirabell-platz

PARIS-

FRANZ-JOSEF-KAI

BERG

MOZARTEUM CONCERT HALL

Makart-platz

MARIONETTE THEATER

MOZART'S RESIDENCE

MAKART-STEG

Platzl

6

Neumayr-platz

MUSEUM

Hanusch-platz

7

STAATS-BRÜCKE

MUSEUM OF MODERN ART

GSTÄTTENGASSE

ELEVATOR

GRIESGASSE

GETREIDE-GASSE

MOZART'S BIRTHPLACE

STADTALM CAFÉ

HOFSTALLGASSE

OLD

Universitäts-platz

Alter Markt

ALTE RESIDENZ

Mönchs-

FESTIVAL CONCERT HALLS

FRANCISCAN CHURCH

Dom-platz

Toscaninihof

ST. PETER'S CHURCH

berg

CEMETERY

MÖNCHSBERG WALK

Festungs-

SALZBURG

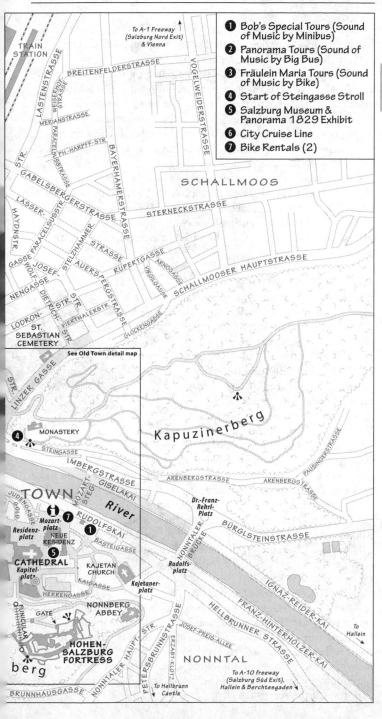

1 Bob's Special Tours (Sound of Music by Minibus)
2 Panorama Tours (Sound of Music by Big Bus)
3 Fräulein Maria Tours (Sound of Music by Bike)
4 Start of Steingasse Stroll
5 Salzburg Museum & Panorama 1829 Exhibit
6 City Cruise Line
7 Bike Rentals (2)

percent deposit). Inside the Mozartplatz TI is the privately run Salzburg Ticket Service counter, where you can book concert tickets (see "Music in Salzburg," page 307).

Salzburg Card: The TIs sell the Salzburg Card, which covers all your public transportation (including the Mönchsberg elevator and funicular to the fortress) and admission to all the city sights (including Hellbrunn Castle and a river cruise). The card is pricey, but if you'd like to pop into all the sights, it can save money and enhance your experience (€25/24 hours, €34/48 hours, €40/72 hours). To analyze your potential savings, here are the major sights and what you'd pay without the card: Hohensalzburg Fortress and funicular-€11; Mozart's Birthplace and Residence-€17; Hellbrunn Castle-€9.50; Salzburg Panorama 1829-€3; Salzach River cruise-€14; 24-hour transit pass-€4.20. Busy sightseers can save plenty. Get this card, feel the financial pain once, and the city will be all yours.

Arrival in Salzburg

By Train: The Salzburg station is a gleaming commercial center with all the services you need: train information, tourist information, luggage lockers, and a handy SPAR supermarket (daily 6:00-23:00)—plus a popular shopping mall that's open on weekends. The transit info desk down the stairs from bus platform C has information on local buses.

Getting downtown from the station is a snap. Simply step outside, find **bus platform C** (labeled *Zentrum-Altstadt*), and hop on the next bus. Buses #1, #3, #5, #6, and #25 all do the same route into the city center before diverging at the far end of town. For most sights and city-center hotels, get off just after the bridge, at the fifth stop. For my recommended new town hotels, get off at Makartplatz (the fourth stop), just before the bridge.

Taxis don't make much sense to get from the train station into town, as they're expensive for short rides (€2.50 drop charge, about €8 for most rides in town).

To **walk** downtown (15 minutes), turn left as you leave the station, and walk straight down Rainerstrasse, which leads under the tracks past Mirabellplatz, turning into Dreifaltigkeitsgasse. From here, you can turn left onto Linzergasse for many of my recommended hotels, or cross the river to the old town. For a slightly longer but more dramatic approach, leave the station the same way but follow the tracks to the river, turn left, and walk the riverside path toward the fortress.

By Car: Mozart never drove in the old town, and neither should you. The best place to park is the **Salzburg Süd park-and-ride** lot. Coming on A-1 from Vienna or Munich, take A-10 toward Hallein, and then take the next exit (Salzburg Süd) in the direction of Anif. First, you'll pass Hellbrunn Castle (and zoo), then the Salzburg Süd TI, before arriving at the parking lot. Park your car (€5/24 hours), get sightseeing information and transit tickets from the TI, and catch bus #3 or #8 into town (€1.90 single-ride ticket or €4.20 *Tageskarte* 24-hour pass, more expensive if you buy tickets on board, every 5 minutes). If traveling with more than one other person, take advantage of a park-and-ride combo-ticket: For €13 (€10 July-Aug), you get 24 hours of parking and a 24-hour bus pass for up to five people.

If you don't believe in park-and-rides, head to the easiest, cheapest, most central parking lot—the 1,500-car Altstadtgarage, in the tunnel under the Mönchsberg (€14/day, note your slot number and which of the twin lots you're in, tel. 0662/846-434). Your hotel may provide discounted parking passes. If staying in the new town, the Mirabell-Congress garage makes more sense than the Altstadtgarage (see page 311 for directions).

Helpful Hints

Recommendations Skewed by Kickbacks: Salzburg is addicted to the tourist dollar, and it can never get enough. Virtually all hotels are on the take when it comes to concert and tour recommendations, influenced more by their potential kickback than by what's best for you. Take any tour or concert advice with a grain of salt.

Music Festival: The Salzburg Festival (Salzburger Festspiele) runs each year from late July to the end of August (see page 307).

Internet Access: A small Internet café is next to the base of the Mönchsberg elevator (€2/hour, daily 10:00-22:00, Gstättengasse 11). The city has several free Wi-Fi hotspots (one is in the Mirabell Gardens; info at www.salzburg-surft.at). Travelers with this book can get free Wi-Fi or use a computer for a few minutes (long enough to check email) at the Panorama Tours terminal on Mirabellplatz (daily 8:00-18:00).

Post Office: A full-service post office is located in the heart of town, in the New Residenz (Mon-Fri 8:00-18:00, Sat 9:00-12:00, closed Sun).

Laundry: A handy launderette is at Paris-Lodron-Strasse 16, at the corner of Wolf-Dietrich-Strasse, near my recommended Linzergasse hotels (€10 self-service, €15 same-day full-service, Mon-Fri 7:30-18:00, Sat 8:00-12:00, closed Sun, tel. 0662/876-381).

Cinema: Das Kino is an art-house movie theater that plays films in their original language (a block off the river and Linzergasse on Steingasse, tel. 0662/873-100, www.daskino.at).

Smoking Policies: Conservative Austria has been slow to embrace the smoke-free movement. By law, big restaurants must offer smoke-free zones (and smoking zones, if they choose). Smaller places choose to be either smoking or non-smoking, indicated by red or green stickers on the door.

Market Days: Popular farmer's markets pop up in the old town on Saturdays and in the new town on Thursdays. On summer weekends, a string of craft booths with fun goodies for sale stretches along the river.

Morning Joggers: Salzburg is a great place for running. Within minutes you can be huffing and puffing "The hills are alive..." in green meadows outside of town. The obvious best bets in town are through the Mirabell Gardens, along the riverbank's pedestrian lanes.

Updates to This Book: For news about changes to this book's coverage since it was published, see www.ricksteves.com/update.

Getting Around Salzburg

By Bus: At machines and *Tabak/Trafik* shops, you can buy €1.90 single-ride tickets or a €4.20 day pass *(Tageskarte)* good for 24 hours (€2.30 and €5.20 from the driver, respectively). To get from the old town to the train station, catch bus #1 from the inland side of Hanuschplatz. From the other side of the river, find the Makartplatz/Theatergasse stop and catch bus #1, #3, #5, or #6. Bus info: www.svv-info.at, tel. 800-660-660.

By Bike: Salzburg is great fun for cyclists. The following two bike-rental shops offer 20 percent off to anyone with this book—ask for it: **Top Bike** rents bikes on the river next to the Staatsbrücke (€6/2 hours, €10/4 hours, €15/24 hours, usually daily April-June and Sept-Oct 10:00-17:00, July-Aug 9:00-19:00, closed Nov-March, easy return available 24/7, free helmets with this book, mobile 0676-476-7259, www.topbike.at, Sabine). **A'Velo Radladen** rents bikes in the old town, just outside the TI on Mozartplatz (€4.50/1 hour, €10/4 hours, €16/24 hours, more for electric or mountain bikes; daily 9:00-18:00, until 19:00 July-Aug, but hours unreliable, shorter hours off-season and in bad weather; passport number for security deposit, mobile 0676-435-5950, www.a-velo. at). Some of my recommended hotels and pensions also rent bikes, and several of the B&Bs on Moosstrasse have free loaner bikes for guests.

By Funicular and Elevator: The old town is connected to the top of the Mönchsberg mountain (and great views) via funicular and elevator. The **funicular** *(Festungsbahn)* whisks you up into the imposing Hohensalzburg Fortress (included in castle admission, goes every few minutes—for details, see page 295). The **elevator** (Mönchsberg Aufzug) on the west side of the old town lifts you to the recommended Gasthaus Stadtalm café and hostel, the Museum of Modern Art and its chic café, wooded paths, and more great views (€2 one-way, €3.20 round-trip, normally Mon 8:00-19:00, Tue-Sun 8:00-24:00).

By Buggy: The horse buggies *(Fiaker)* that congregate at Residenzplatz charge €36 for a 25-minute trot around the old town (www.fiaker-salzburg.at).

Tours in Salzburg

Walking Tours—Any day of the week, you can take a one-hour guided walk of the old town without a reservation—just show up at the TI on Mozartplatz and pay the guide. The tours are informative. While generally in English only, on slow days you may be listening to everything in both German and English (€9, daily at 12:15, Mon-Sat also at 14:00, tel. 0662/8898-7330). To save money, you can easily do it on your own using this chapter's self-guided walk (or download a free Rick Steves **audio tour** of my walk to your mobile device—see page 471).

Local Guides—Salzburg is home to over a hundred licensed guides. I have worked with three who are art historians and well worth recommending: **Christiana Schneeweiss** ("Snow White") has been instrumental in both my guidebook research and my TV production in Salzburg, and has her own minibus for private tours outside of town (on foot: €135/2 hours, €160/3 hours; with minibus: €220/4 hours, €350-400/day, up to 6 people; mobile 0664-340-1757, other options explained at www.kultur-tourismus. com, info@kultur-tourismus.com). Both **Sabine Rath** (mobile 0664-201-6492, www.tourguide-salzburg.com, info@tourguide-salzburg.com) and **Anna Stellnberger** (mobile 0664-787-5177, anna.stellnberger@aon.at) are excellent guides and a joy to learn from; they charge similar rates (€145/2 hours, €185/4 hours, €275/8 hours). Salzburg has many other good guides (to book, call 0662/840-406).

Boat Tours—**City Cruise Line** (a.k.a. Stadt Schiff-Fahrt) runs a basic 40-minute round-trip river cruise with recorded commentary (€14, 9/day July-Aug, 7/day May-June, fewer Sept-Oct and March-April, no boats Nov-Feb). For a longer cruise, ride to Hellbrunn and return by bus (€17, 1-2/day April-Oct). Boats leave from the old town side of the river just downstream of the Makartsteg bridge (tel. 0662/825-858, www.salzburghighlights.at). While views can be cramped, passengers are treated to a fun finale just before docking, when the captain twirls a fun "waltz."

Salzburg at a Glance

▲▲▲**Salzburg's Old Town Walk** Old town's best sights in handy orientation walk. **Hours:** Always open. See page 281.

▲▲**Salzburg Cathedral** Glorious, harmonious Baroque main church of Salzburg. **Hours:** May-Sept Mon-Sat 9:00-19:00, Sun 13:00-19:00; March-April, Oct, and Dec closes at 18:00; Jan-Feb and Nov closes at 17:00. See page 285.

▲▲**Getreidegasse** Picturesque old shopping lane with characteristic wrought-iron signs. **Hours:** Always open. See page 290.

▲▲**Hohensalzburg Fortress** Imposing castle capping the mountain overlooking town, with tourable grounds, several mini-museums, commanding views, and good evening concerts. **Hours:** Fortress museums open daily May-Sept 9:00-19:00, Oct-April 9:30-17:00. Concerts nearly nightly. See page 295.

▲▲**Salzburg Museum** Best place to learn more about the city's history. **Hours:** Tue-Sun 9:00-17:00, closed Mon. See page 293.

▲▲**The Sound of Music Tour** Cheesy but fun tour through the *S.O.M.* sights of Salzburg and the surrounding Salzkammergut Lake District, by minibus, big bus, or bike. **Hours:** Various options daily at 9:00, 9:30, 14:00, and 16:30. See page 278.

▲▲**Mozart's Birthplace** House where Mozart was born in 1756, featuring his instruments and other exhibits. **Hours:** Daily 9:00-17:30, July-Aug until 20:00. See page 294.

▲▲**Hellbrunn Castle** Palace on the outskirts of town featuring gardens with trick fountains. **Hours:** Daily May-Sept 9:00-17:30, July-Aug until 21:00, April and Oct-Nov 9:00-16:30, closed Dec-March. See page 304.

▲**Old Residenz** Prince Archbishop Wolf Dietrich's palace, with

▲▲***The Sound of Music* Tours**—I took one of these tours skeptically (as part of my research)—and had a great time. The bus tour version includes a quick but good general city tour, hits the *S.O.M.* spots (including the stately home used in the movie, flirtatious gazebo, and grand wedding church), and shows you a lovely stretch of the Salzkammergut Lake District. This is worthwhile for *S.O.M.* fans and those who won't otherwise be going into the Salzkammergut. Warning: Many think rolling through the Austrian countryside with 30 Americans singing "Doe, a deer..." is pretty schmaltzy.

ornate rooms and good included audioguide. **Hours:** Daily 10:00-17:00. See page 284.

▲**Salzburg Panorama 1829** A vivid peek at the city in 1829. **Hours:** Daily 9:00-17:00. See page 294.

▲**Mozart's Residence** Restored house where the composer lived. **Hours:** Daily 9:00-17:30, July-Aug until 20:00. See page 301.

▲**Mönchsberg Walk** "The hills are alive" stroll you can enjoy right in downtown Salzburg. **Hours:** Doable anytime during daylight hours. See page 299.

▲**Mirabell Gardens and Palace** Beautiful palace complex with fine views, Salzburg's best concert venue, and *Sound of Music* memories. **Hours:** Gardens—always open; concerts—free in the park May-Aug Sun at 10:30, in the palace nearly nightly. See page 300.

▲**Steingasse** Historic cobbled lane with trendy pubs—a tranquil, tourist-free section of old Salzburg. **Hours:** Always open. See page 302.

▲**St. Sebastian Cemetery** Baroque cemetery with graves of Mozart's wife and father, and other Salzburg VIPs. **Hours:** Daily April-Oct 9:00-18:30, Nov-March 9:00-16:00. See page 303.

St. Peter's Cemetery Atmospheric old cemetery with mini-gardens overlooked by cliff face with monks' caves. **Hours:** Cemetery—daily April-Sept 6:30-19:00, Oct-March 6:30-18:00. See page 288.

St. Peter's Church Romanesque church with Rococo decor. **Hours:** Daily April-Oct 8:00-21:00, Nov-March 8:00-19:00. See page 288.

Local Austrians don't understand all the commotion. For more on *S.O.M.*, see the sidebar on page 308.

You have plenty of *S.O.M.* options: big buses (heavy on the countryside around Salzburg, cannot go into old town), minibuses (a mix of town and countryside), and bike (best for the town and meadows nearby but doesn't get you into the foothills of the Alps). Guides are generally native English-speakers—young, fun-loving, and entertaining.

Of the many companies doing the tour by bus, consider Bob's

Special Tours (usually uses a mini-bus) and Panorama Tours (big 50-seat bus). Each one provides essentially the same tour (in English with a live guide, 4 hours); with Bob's you pay a little more for being in a smaller group, while Panorama offers a more predictable, professional experience. You'll get a €5 discount from either if you book direct, mention Rick Steves, pay cash, and bring this book along (you'll need to show them this book to get the deal). Getting a spot is simple—just call and make a reservation. Note: Your hotel will be eager to call to reserve for you—to get their commission—but if you let them do it, you won't get the discount I've negotiated.

Minibus Option: Most of **Bob's Special Tours** use an eight-seat minibus (and occasionally a 20-seat bus) and therefore have good access to old town sights, promote a more casual feel, and spend less time waiting to load and unload. As it's a smaller operation, the quality of guides can be mixed (my readers have found some of their guides gruff or rude), and they may cancel with short notice if the tour doesn't fill up. Conversely, during busy times it can fill up early—calling in advance increases your chances of getting a seat (€45 for adults, €5 discount with this book if you pay cash and book direct, €40 for kids over age 6 and students with ID, €35 for kids ages 0-6—includes required car seat but must reserve in advance, daily at 9:00 and 14:00 year-round, they'll pick you up at your hotel for the morning tour, afternoon tours leave from Bob's office along the river just east of Mozartplatz at Rudolfskai 38, tel. 0662/849-511, mobile 0664-541-7492, www.bobstours.com). Nearly all of Bob's tours stop for a fun luge ride when the weather is dry (mountain bobsled-€4.50 extra, generally April-Oct, confirm beforehand). While the afternoon tour leaves promptly, you'll waste up to 30 minutes on the morning tour doing the hotel pick-ups.

For a private minibus tour consider **Christina Schneeweiss,** who does an *S.O.M.* tour with more history and fewer jokes (€220, up to 6 people, see "Local Guides," earlier).

Big-Bus Option: Panorama Tours depart from their smart kiosk at Mirabellplatz daily at 9:30 and 14:00 year-round (€37, €5 discount for *S.O.M.* tours with this book if you book direct by phone and pay cash, tel. 0662/874-029 or 0662/883-2110, www.panoramatours.com). Many travelers appreciate their more businesslike feel, roomier buses, and higher vantage point. As they do not pick up at hotels, you won't waste any time making the rounds before starting the tour.

Bike Tours by "Fräulein Maria": For some exercise with your *S.O.M.* tour, you can meet your guide (likely a man) at the Mirabell Gardens (at Mirabellplatz 4, 50 yards to the left of palace entry). The main attractions that you'll pass during the eight-mile pedal include the Mirabell Gardens, the horse pond, St. Peter's Cemetery, Nonnberg Abbey, Leopoldskron Palace, and, of course, the gazebo. The tour is very family-friendly, and you'll get lots of stops for goofy photo ops (€26 includes bike, €18 for kids ages 11-16, €12 for kids under age 11, €2 discount for adults and kids with this book, daily May-Sept at 9:30, June-Aug also at 16:30, allow 3.5 hours, reservations required only for afternoon tours, tel. 0650/342-6297, www.mariasbicycletours.com). For €8 extra (€20 per family), you're welcome to keep the bike all day.

Beyond Salzburg

Both Bob's and Panorama Tours also offer an extensive array of other day trips from Salzburg (e.g., Berchtesgaden/Eagle's Nest, salt mines, Hallstatt, and Salzkammergut lakes and mountains).

Bob's Special Tours offers two particularly well-designed day tours (both depart daily at 9:00; either one costs €90 with a €10 discount if you show this book and book direct, does not include entrance fees). Their *Sound of Music*/**Hallstatt Tour** first covers everything in the standard four-hour *Sound of Music* tour, then continues for a four-hour look at the scenic, lake-speckled Salzkammergut (with free time to explore charming Hallstatt). Bob's **Bavarian Mountain Tour** covers the main things you'd want to do in and around Berchtesgaden (Königssee, Hitler's mountaintop Eagle's Nest, Obersalzberg Documentation Center, salt mine tour). Although you can do all the top Berchtesgaden sights on your own with the information I've provided in that chapter, Bob's makes it easy for those without a car to see these sights in one busy day.

Self-Guided Walk

▲▲▲Salzburg's Old Town

I've linked the best sights in the old town into this handy self-guided orientation walk. You can download a free Rick Steves **audio tour** of this walk to your mobile device; see page 471.

• *Begin in the heart of town, just up from the river, near the TI on...*

❶ Mozartplatz

All the happy tourists around you probably wouldn't be here if not for the man honored by this statue—Wolfgang Amadeus Mozart. (Many consider this to be a terrible likeness.) The statue was erected in 1842 on the 50th anniversary of Mozart's death, during a

music festival that included his two sons (making this event, in a sense, the first Salzburg Festival). Mozart spent much of his first 25 years (1756-1777) in Salzburg, the greatest Baroque city north of the Alps. But the city itself is much older: The Mozart statue sits on bits of Roman Salzburg, and the pink Church of St. Michael that overlooks the square dates from A.D. 800. The first Salzburgers settled right around here. Near you is the TI (with a concert box office), and just around the downhill corner is a pedestrian bridge leading over the Salzach River to the quiet and most medieval street in town, Steingasse (described on page 302).

You may see lots of conservative Muslim families vacationing in Salzburg. While there are plenty of Muslims in Austria, most of the conservatively dressed women you'll see here are generally from the United Arab Emirates. Lots of wealthy families from the Middle East come here in the summer to escape the heat back home, to enjoy a break from their very controlled societies, or for medical treatment. Nearby Munich is a popular destination for hospital visits, and the entire family usually joins in for sightseeing and shopping.

• *Walk toward the cathedral and into the big square with the huge fountain.*

❷ Residenzplatz

Important buildings have long ringed this square. Salzburg's energetic Prince Archbishop Wolf Dietrich von Raitenau (who ruled 1587-1612) was raised in Rome, was a cousin of the influential Florentine Medici family, and had grandiose Italian ambitions for Salzburg. After a convenient fire destroyed the town's cathedral, Wolf Dietrich set about building the "Rome of the North." This square, with his new cathedral and palace, was the centerpiece of his Baroque dream city. A series of interconnecting squares—like you'll see nowhere else—make a grand processional way, leading from here through the old town. As we stroll through this heart and soul of historic Salzburg, notice how easily we slip from noisy commercial streets to peaceful, reflective courtyards. Also notice the two dominant kinds of stone around town: a creamy red marble and a chunky conglomerate (see the cathedral's exterior wall). The conglomerate was cheap—actually cut right out of the town's little mountain. As you wander, enjoy the pedestrian-friendly peace and quiet. After 11:00 each morning, barrier stumps go up around the perimeter of the old town, keeping traffic out.

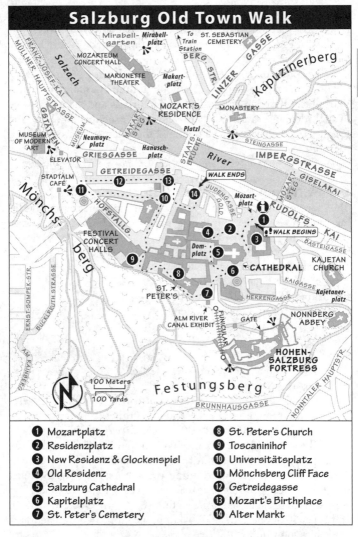

Salzburg Old Town Walk

1 Mozartplatz
2 Residenzplatz
3 New Residenz & Glockenspiel
4 Old Residenz
5 Salzburg Cathedral
6 Kapitelplatz
7 St. Peter's Cemetery

8 St. Peter's Church
9 Toscaninihof
10 Universitätsplatz
11 Mönchsberg Cliff Face
12 Getreidegasse
13 Mozart's Birthplace
14 Alter Markt

For centuries, Salzburg's leaders were both important church officials *and* princes of the Holy Roman Empire, hence the title "prince archbishop"—mixing sacred and secular authority. But Wolf Dietrich misplayed his hand, losing power and spending his last five years imprisoned in the Hohensalzburg Fortress. (It's a complicated story—basically, the pope counted on Salzburg to hold the line against the Protestants for several generations following the Reformation. Wolf Dietrich was a good Catholic, as were most Salzburgers. But the town's important businessmen and the region's salt miners were Protestant, and for Salzburg's financial good, Wolf Dietrich dealt with them in a tolerant and pragmatic way. So the pope—who allowed zero tolerance for Protestants in those heady Counter-Reformation days—had Wolf Dietrich locked up and replaced.)

The fountain (completed in 1661) is as Italian as can be, with a Triton matching Bernini's famous Triton Fountain in Rome. During the Baroque era, skilled Italian artists and architects were in high demand in central European cities such as Salzburg and Prague. Local artists even Italianized their names in order to raise their rates.

• *Along the left side of Residenzplatz (as you face the cathedral) is the...*

❸ New (Neue) Residenz and Glockenspiel

This former palace, long a government administration building, now houses the central post office, the **Heimatwerk** (a fine shop showing off all the best local handicrafts, Mon-Sat 9:00-18:00, closed Sun), and two worthwhile sights: the fascinating **Salzburg Panorama 1829** exhibit; and the **Salzburg Museum,** which offers the best peek at the history of this one-of-a-kind city (described on pages 294 and 293).

The famous **glockenspiel** rings atop the New Residenz. This bell tower has a carillon of 35 17th-century bells (cast in Antwerp) that chimes throughout the day and plays tunes (appropriate to the month) at 7:00, 11:00, and 18:00. A big barrel with adjustable tabs turns like a giant music-box mechanism, pulling the right bells in the appropriate rhythm. Notice the ornamental top: an upside-down heart in flames surrounding the solar system (symbolizing that God loves all of creation). Twice-weekly tours let you get up close to watch the glockenspiel action (€3, April-Oct Thu at 17:30 and Fri at 10:30, no tours Nov-March, meet in Salzburg Panorama 1829, just show up).

Look back, past Mozart's statue, to the 4,220-foot-high **Gaisberg**—the forested hill with the television tower. A road leads to the top for a commanding view. Its summit is a favorite destination for local nature-lovers and strong bikers.

• *Head to the opposite end of the square. This building is the...*

❹ Old (Alte) Residenz

Across from the New Residenz is Wolf Dietrich's palace, the Old Residenz, which is connected to the cathedral by an arched bridge. Its series of ornately decorated "stately rooms" *(Prunkräume)* is well-described in an included audioguide, which gives you a good feel for the wealth and power of the prince archbishop. Walking through 15 fancy rooms (all on one floor), you'll see Renaissance, Baroque, and Classicist styles—200 years of let-them-eat-cake splendor.

Cost and Hours: €9, daily 10:00-17:00, tel. 0662/8042-2690, www.residenz-salzburg.at.

• *Walk under the prince archbishop's skyway and step into Domplatz (Cathedral Square), where you'll find...*

❺ Salzburg Cathedral (Salzburger Dom)

This cathedral, rated ▲▲, was one of the first Baroque buildings north of the Alps. It was consecrated in 1628, during the Thirty Years' War. (Pitting Roman Catholics against Protestants, this war devastated much of Europe and brought most grand construction projects to a halt.) Experts differ on what motivated the determined builders: emphasizing Salzburg's commitment to the Roman Catholic cause and the power of the Church here, or showing that there could be a peaceful alternative to the religious strife that was racking Europe at the time. Salzburg's  archbishop was technically the top papal official north of the Alps, but the city managed to steer clear of the war. With its rich salt production, it had enough money to stay out of the conflict and carefully maintain its independence from the warring sides, earning it the nickname "Fortified Island of Peace."

Domplatz, the square in front of the cathedral, is surrounded by the prince archbishop's secular administration buildings. The **statue of Mary** (from 1771) is looking away from the church, welcoming visitors. If you stand in the rear of the square, immediately under the middle arch, you'll see that she's positioned to be crowned by the two angels on the church facade.

The dates on the cathedral's iron gates refer to milestones in the church's history: In 774, the previous church (long since destroyed) was founded by St. Virgil, to be replaced in 1628 by the church you see today. In 1959, a partial reconstruction was completed, made necessary by a WWII bomb that had blown through the dome.

Cost and Hours: Free, but donation prominently requested; May-Sept Mon-Sat 9:00-19:00, Sun 13:00-19:00; March-April, Oct, and Dec closes at 18:00; Jan-Feb and Nov closes at 17:00; www.salzburger-dom.at.

Visiting the Cathedral: Enter the cathedral as if part of a festival procession—drawn toward the resurrected Christ by the brightly lit area under the dome, and cheered on by ceiling paintings of the Passion.

Built in just 14 years (1614-1628), the church boasts harmonious architecture. When Pope John Paul II visited in 1998, some 5,000 people filled the cathedral (330 feet long and 230 feet tall). The baptismal font (dark bronze, left of the entry) is from the previous cathedral (basin from about 1320, although the lid is modern). Mozart was baptized here (Amadeus means "beloved by God"). Concert and Mass schedules are posted at the entrance; the Sunday Mass at 10:00 is famous for its music (usually choral; more info at www.kirchen.net/dommusik).

The **paintings** lining the nave, showing events leading up to Christ's death, are relatively dark. But the Old Testament themes that foreshadow Jesus' resurrection, and the Resurrection scene painted at the altar, are well-lit. The church has never had stained glass—just clear windows to let light power the message.

The stucco, by a Milanese artist, is exceptional. Sit under the **dome**—surrounded by the tombs of 10 archbishops from the 17th century—and imagine all four organs playing, each balcony filled with musicians...glorious surround-sound. Mozart, who was the organist here for two years, would advise you that the acoustics are best in pews immediately under the dome. Study the symbolism of the decor all around you—intellectual, complex, and cohesive. Think of the altar in Baroque terms, as the center of a stage, with sunrays as spotlights in this dramatic and sacred theater.

In the left transept, stairs lead down into the **crypt** *(Krypta),* where you can see foundations of the earlier church, more tombs, and a tourist-free chapel (reserved for prayer) directly under the dome.

Other Cathedral Sights: The **Cathedral Excavations Museum** (Domgrabungsmuseum, outside the church on Residenzplatz and down the stairs) offers a chance to see the foundations of the medieval church, some Roman engineering, and a few Roman mosaics from (Roman) street level. It has the charm of an old basement garage; unless you've never seen anything Roman, I'd skip it (€2.50, July-Aug daily 9:00-17:00, closed Sept-June, www.salzburgmuseum.at).

The **Cathedral Museum** (Dom Museum) has a rich collection of church art (entry at portico, €6, mid-May-Oct and Dec Mon-Sat 10:00-17:00, Sun 11:00-18:00, closed Nov and Jan-mid-May, tel. 0662/8047-1870), www.kirchen.net/dommuseum.

• *From the cathedral, exit left and walk toward the fortress into the next square.*

❻ Kapitelplatz

Head past the underground public WCs (€0.50) to the giant **chessboard.** It's just under the golden orb topped by a man gazing up at the castle, trying to decide whether to walk up or shell out €11 for the funicular. Every year since 2002, a foundation has commissioned a different artist to create a new work of public art somewhere in the city; this is the piece from 2007.

Detour across the square to the fountain. This was a **horse bath,** the 18th-century equivalent of a car wash. Notice the puzzle above it—the artist wove the date of the structure into a phrase. It says, "Leopold the Prince Built Me," using the letters LLDVICMX-VXI, which total 1732 (add it up...it works)—the year it was built. Return to the chessboard and face away from the cathedral. Look for the arrow pointing to the *Stieglkeller;* here a small road leads uphill to the fortress (and fortress funicular). To the right is a gate with a sign that reads *zum Peterskeller.* Walk through this gate, which leads to a waterwheel and St. Peter's Cemetery.

It's fair to say that Salzburg is glorious in great part because of its clever use of its water. The **waterwheel** is part of a canal system that has brought water into Salzburg from Berchtesgaden, 15 miles away, since the 13th century. Climb up the steps to watch the in-flow and imagine the thrill felt by medieval engineers harnessing this raw power. The stream was divided into smaller canals and channeled through town to provide fire protection, to flush out the streets (Thursday morning was flood-the-streets day), and to power factories. As late as the 19th century there were still more than 100 watermill-powered firms in Salzburg. Because of its water-powered hygiene (relatively good for the standards of the time), Salzburg never suffered from a plague—it's probably the only Austrian town you'll see with no plague monument. For more on the canal system, check out the **Alm River Canal exhibit** (at the exit of the funicular, described on page 298).

Before leaving, drop into the fragrant and traditional **bakery** at the waterfall, which sells various fresh rolls—both sweet and not, explained on the wall—for less than €1 (Mon-Tue 8:00-17:30, Thu-Fri 7:00-17:30, Sat 7:00-13:00, closed Wed and Sun). From here there's a good view of the funicular climbing up to the castle.

• *Now find the* Katakomben *sign and step into...*

❼ St. Peter's Cemetery

This collection of lovingly tended mini-gardens abuts the Mönchberg's rock wall.

Cost and Hours: Cemetery—free, silence is requested, daily April-Sept 6:30-19:00, Oct-March 6:30-18:00; www.stift-stpeter.at.

Visiting the Cemetery: Walk in about 50 yards to the intersection of lanes at the base of the cliff marked by a stone ball. You're surrounded by three churches, each founded in the early Middle Ages atop a pagan Celtic holy site. St. Peter's Church is closest to the stone ball. Notice the fine Romanesque stonework on the apse of the chapel nearest you, and the rich guys' fancy Renaissance-style tombs decorating its walls. Wealthy as those guys were, they ran out of caring relatives. The graves surrounding you are tended by descendants of the deceased. In Austria, gravesites are rented, not owned. Rent bills are sent out every 10 years. If no one cares enough to make the payment, your tombstone is removed.

While the cemetery where the Von Trapp family hid out in *The Sound of Music* was a Hollywood set, it was inspired by this one. Look up the cliff. Legendary medieval hermit monks are said to have lived in the hillside—but "catacombs" they're not. You can climb lots of steps to see a few old caves, a chapel, and some fine views (€1.50, entrance at far end of cemetery, visit takes 10 minutes).

Stroll past the stark Gothic funeral chapel (c. 1491) to the up-hill corner of the cemetery, and follow the high lane back to see the finer tombs in the arcade. Tomb #XXXI belongs to the cathedral's architect—forever facing his creation. Tomb #LIV, at the catacomb entry, is a chapel carved into the hillside, holding the tombs of Mozart's sister and Joseph Haydn's younger brother Michael, also a composer of note.

• *Continue downhill through the cemetery and out the opposite end. Just outside, hook right and drop into...*

❽ St. Peter's Church (Stiftskirche St. Peter)

Just inside, enjoy a carved Romanesque welcome. Over the inner doorway, a fine tympanum shows Jesus on a rainbow flanked by Peter and Paul over a stylized Tree of Life and under a Latin inscription reading, "I am the door to life, and only through me can you find eternal life." Enter the nave and notice how the once purely Romanesque vaulting has since been iced with a sugary Rococo finish. Salzburg's only Rococo interior feels Bavarian (because it is—the fancy stucco work was done by Bavarian artists). Up the right side aisle is the tomb of St. Rupert, with a painting showing Salzburg in 1750 (one bridge, salt ships sailing the river, and angels hoisting barrels of salt to heaven as St. Rupert prays for his city). Salt was Salzburg's white gold, granting the city enough wealth to maintain its independence as a prince-archbishopric for an entire millennium (798-1803). On pillars farther up the aisle are faded bits of 13th-century Romanesque frescoes. Similar frescoes hide under Rococo whitewash throughout the church.

Cost and Hours: Free, daily April-Oct 8:00-21:00, Nov-March 8:00-19:00, www.stift-stpeter.at.

• *Leaving the church, notice on the left the **Stiftskeller St. Peter** restaurant—known for its Mozart Dinner Concert. Charlemagne ate here in the year 803, allowing locals to claim that it's the oldest restaurant in Europe. Opposite where you entered the square (look through the arch), you'll see St. Rupert holding his staff and waving you into the next square. Once there, you're surrounded by early 20th-century Bauhaus-style dorms for student monks. Notice the modern crucifix (1926) painted on the far wall. Here's a good place to see the two locally quarried stones (marble and conglomerate) so prevalent in all the town's buildings.*

Walk through the archway under the crucifix into...

❾ Toscaninihof

This small courtyard is wedged behind the 1925 **Festival Hall**. The hall's three theaters seat 5,000 (see a photo of the main theater ahead on the wall, at the base of the stairs). This is where, in *The Sound of Music,* Captain von Trapp nervously waits before walking onstage to sing "Edelweiss," just before he escapes with his family. On the left is an entrance to the city's 1,500-space, inside-the-mountain parking lot; ahead, behind the *Felsenkeller* sign, is a tunnel (generally closed) leading to the actual concert hall; and to the right is the backstage of a smaller hall where carpenters are often building stage sets (door open on hot days). The stairway leads a few flights up to a picnic perch with a fine view, and then up to the top of the cliff and the recommended Gasthaus Stadtalm café and hostel.

Walk downhill through the archway onto **Max-Reinhardt-Platz.** Pause here to survey the line of Salzburg Festival concert halls to your left. As the festival was started in the austere 1920s, the city remodeled existing buildings (e.g., the prince archbishop's stables and riding school) for venues.

• *Continue straight—passing the big church on your left, along with popular wurst stands and a public WC—into...*

❿ Universitätsplatz

This square hosts an **open-air produce market**—Salzburg's liveliest, though it's pricey (mornings Mon-Sat, best on Sat). The market really bustles on Saturday mornings, when the farmers are in town.

Public marketplaces have fountains for washing fruit and vegetables. Bear left around the church and you'll find the one here—a part of the medieval water system. The sundial (over the fountain's drain) is accurate (except for the daylight savings hour) and two-dimensional, showing both the time (obvious) and the date (less obvious). The fanciest facade overlooking the square (the yellow one) is the backside of Mozart's Birthplace (we'll see the front soon).

• *Continue past the fountain to the far end of the square. Most of the houses on your right have nicely arcaded medieval passages that connect the square to Getreidegasse, which runs parallel to Universitätsplatz. Just for fun, you could weave between this street and Getreidegasse several times, following these "through houses" as you work your way toward the cliff face ahead.*

⓫ Mönchsberg Cliff Face

Look up—200 feet above you is the Mönchsberg, Salzburg's mountain. Today you see the remains of an aborted attempt in the 1600s to cut through the Mönchsberg. It proved too big a job, and when new tunneling technology arrived, the project was abandoned. The stones cut did serve as a quarry for the city's 17th-century growth spurt—the bulk of the cathedral, for example, is built of this economic and local conglomerate stone.

Early one morning in 1669, a huge landslide killed more than 200 townspeople who lived close to where the elevator is now (to the right). Since then the cliffs have been carefully checked each spring and fall. Even today, you might see crews on the cliff, monitoring its stability.

Across the busy road are giant horse troughs. Cross the street (looking left at the string of Salzburg Festival halls again) for a closer look. Paintings show the various breeds and temperaments of horses in the prince's stable. Like Vienna, Salzburg had a passion for the equestrian arts.

• *Turn right (passing a courtyard on your left that once housed a hospital for the poor, and now houses a toy museum and a museum of historic musical instruments), and then right again, which brings you to the start of a long and colorful pedestrian street. (At this point you could take a short side-trip up the mountain via the elevator—Mönchsberg Aufzug— described on page 299.)*

⓬ Getreidegasse

This street, rated ▲▲, was old Salzburg's busy, colorful main drag. It's been a center of trade since Roman times (third century). It's lined with *Schmuck* (jewelry) shops and other businesses. This is the burgher's (secular) Salzburg. The buildings, most of which date from the 15th century, are tall for that age, and narrow, and densely packed. Space was tight here because such little land was available between the natural fortifications provided by the mountain and the river, and so much of what was available was used up by the

Church. Famous for its old wrought-iron signs, the architecture on the street still looks much as it did in Mozart's day—though much of its former elegance is now gone, replaced by chain outlets. Some doorways might be marked with the message "20 + C + M + B + 13"; to find out why, see page 416.

As you walk away from the cliffs, look up and enjoy the traditional signs indicating what each shop made or sold: Watch for spirits, bookmakers, a horn (indicating a place for the postal coach), brewery (the star for the name of the beer, Sternbräu—"Star Brew"), glazier (window-maker), locksmith, hamburgers, pastries, tailor, baker (the pretzel), pharmacy, and a hatter.

On the right at #39, **Sporer** serves up homemade spirits (€1.60/ shot, Mon-Sat 9:30-17:00, closed Sun). This has been a family-run show for a century—fun-loving, proud, and English-speaking. *Nuss* is nut, *Marille* is apricot (typical of this region), the *Kletzen* cocktail is like a super-thick Baileys with pear, and *Edle Brande* are the stronger schnapps. The many homemade firewaters are in jugs at the end of the bar.

After noticing the building's old doorbells—one per floor— continue down Getreidegasse. At #40, **Eisgrotte** serves good ice cream (€1/scoop). Across from Eisgrotte, a tunnel leads to the recommended **Balkan Grill** (signed as *Bosna Grill*), the local choice for the very best wurst in town. At #28, Herr Wieber, the iron- and locksmith, welcomes the curious. Farther along, you'll pass McDonald's (required to keep its arches Baroque and low-key).

The knot of excited tourists and salesmen hawking goofy gimmicks by #9 marks the home of Salzburg's most famous resident: **⓭ Mozart's Birthplace** *(Geburtshaus)*—the house where Mozart was born, and where he composed many of his early works (described on page 294).

At #3, dip into the passage and walk under a whalebone, likely once used to advertise the wares of an exotic import shop. Look up at the arcaded interior. On the right, at the venerable **Schatz Konditorei,** you can enjoy coffee under the vaults with your choice of top-end cakes and pastries.

With your back to the pastry shop, go straight ahead through the passage to Sigmund-Haffner-Gasse. Before heading right, look left to see the tower of the old City Hall at the end. The blue-and-white ball halfway up is an 18th-century moon clock. It still tells the phase of the moon.

Battlefield Salzburg: Popes vs. Emperors

Salzburg is so architecturally impressive today to a great degree because of the Roman Catholic Church. This town was on the frontline of a centuries-long power struggle between Church and emperor. The town's mighty Hohensalzburg Fortress—a symbol of the Church's determination to assert its power here—was built around 1100, just as the conflict was heating up.

The medieval church-state argument, called the "Lay Investiture Controversy," was a classic tug-of-war between a series of popes and Holy Roman Emperors. The prize: the right to appoint (or "invest") church officials in the Holy Roman Emperor's domain. (Although called "Holy," the empire was headed not by priests, but by secular—or "lay"—rulers.)

The Church impinged on the power of secular leaders in several ways: Their subjects' generous tithes went to Rome, leaving less for the emperor to tax. In many areas, the Church was the biggest landowner (people willed their land to the Church in return for prayers for their salvation). And the pope's appointees weren't subject to secular local laws. Holy Roman Emperors were plenty powerful, but not as powerful as the Church.

In 1075, Emperor Henry IV bucked the system, appointing his own set of church officials and boldly renouncing Gregory VII as pope. In retaliation, Gregory excommunicated both Henry and the bishops he'd appointed. One of Henry's chief detractors was

• *Go right, then take your first left to....*

⓮ Alter Markt

Here in Salzburg's old marketplace, you'll find the recommended **Café Tomaselli.** On the other side of the fountain, look for the fun **Josef Holzermayr candy shop,** and, next door, the beautifully old-fashioned **Alte F.E. Hofapotheke** pharmacy—duck in discreetly to peek at the Baroque shelves and containers (be polite—the people in line are here for medicine; no photography). Even in our fast-changing, modern age, the traditional soul of Salzburg—embraced by its citizens—lives on.

• *Our walk is finished. From here, you can circle back to some of the old town sights (such as those in the New Residenz, described next); head up to the Hohensalzburg Fortress on the cliffs over the old town (see page 295); or continue to some of the sights across the river. To reach those new town sights, head for the river, jog left (past the fast-food fish restaurant and free WCs), climb to the top of the Makartsteg pedestrian bridge, and follow my walking directions (see page 299).*

Salzburg's pope-appointed archbishop, Gebhard, who started construction of Hohensalzburg Fortress in a face-off with the defiant emperor.

The German nobility seized on the conflict as an opportunity to rebel, seizing royal property and threatening to elect a new emperor. To placate the nobles, Henry sought to regain the Church's favor. In January of 1077, Henry traveled south to Italy—supposedly crossing the Alps barefoot and in a monk's hairshirt—to Canossa, where the pope was holed up. The emperor knelt in the snow outside the castle gate for three days, begging the pope's forgiveness. (To this day, the phrase "go to Canossa" is used to refer to any act of humility.)

But the German princes continued their revolt, electing their own king (Henry's brother-in-law, Rudolf of Rheinfelden). Henry's reconciliation with the Church was brief: In short order he named an antipope (Clement III), killed Rudolf in battle, and invaded Rome. Archbishop Gebhard was forced out of Salzburg and spent a decade in exile, raising forces against Henry in an attempt to reclaim the Salzburg archdiocese.

The back-and-forth continued until 1122, when a power-sharing accord was finally reached between Henry's son, Emperor Henry V, and Pope Calistus II.

Sights in Salzburg

In the Old Town
In the New (Neue) Residenz
▲▲**Salzburg Museum**—This two-floor exhibit is the best in town for history. The included audioguide wonderfully describes the great artifacts in the lavish prince archbishop's residence.

Cost and Hours: €7, €8.50 combo-ticket with Salzburg Panorama, includes audioguide, Tue-Sun 9:00-17:00, closed Mon, tel. 0662/620-8080, www.salzburgmuseum.at.

Visiting the Museum: The Salzburg Personalities exhibit fills the first floor with a charming look at Salzburg's greatest historic characters—mostly artists, scientists, musicians, and writers who would otherwise be forgotten. The *Kunsthalle* in the basement shows off special exhibits.

But upstairs is the real reason to come. Here you'll see lavish ceremonial rooms filled with an exhibit called The Salzburg Myth, which traces the city's proud history, art, and culture since early modern times. The focus is on its quirky absolutist prince archbishop and its long-standing reputation as a fairy-tale "Alpine Arcadia."

From the Salzburg Museum, the Panorama Passage (clearly marked from the entry) leads underground to the Salzburg Panorama (described next). This passage is lined with archaeological finds (Roman and early medieval), helping you trace the development of Salzburg from its Roman roots until today.

▲**Salzburg Panorama 1829**—In the early 19th century, before the advent of photography, 360-degree "panorama" paintings of great cities or events were popular. These creations were even taken on extended road trips. When this one was created, the 1815 Treaty of Vienna had just divvied up post-Napoleonic Europe, and Salzburg had become part of the Habsburg realm. This photo-realistic painting served as a town portrait done at the emperor's request. The circular view, painted by Johann Michael Sattler, shows the city as seen from the top of its castle. When complete, it spent 10 years touring the great cities of Europe, showing off Salzburg's breathtaking setting.

Today, the exquisitely restored painting, hung in a circular room, offers a fascinating look at the city in 1829. The river was slower and had beaches. The old town looks essentially as it does today, and Moosstrasse still leads into idyllic farm country. Your ticket also lets you see the temporary exhibitions in the room that surrounds the Panorama, which is part of the Salzburg Museum, but with a separate entrance and ticket counter.

Cost and Hours: €3, €8.50 combo-ticket with Salzburg Museum, open daily 9:00-17:00, Residenzplatz 9, tel. 0662/620-808-730, www.salzburgmuseum.at.

▲▲Mozart's Birthplace (Geburtshaus)

The Mozart family lived here for 26 years. Of the seven Mozart children born here, two survived. Wolfgang was born here in 1756. It was in this building that he composed most of his boy-genius works. Today it's the most popular Mozart sight in town—for fans, it's almost a pilgrimage. Shuffling through with all the crowds, you'll peruse three floors of  rooms with exhibits displaying paintings, letters, personal items, and lots of facsimiles, all attempting to bring life to the Mozart story. There's no audioguide, but everything's described in English.

Cost and Hours: €10, €17 combo-ticket includes Mozart's Residence in the new town—see page 301, daily 9:00-17:30, July-

Aug until 20:00, Getreidegasse 9, tel. 0662/844-313, www.mo-zarteum.at.

SALZBURG

Visiting Mozart's Birthplace: Start by walking to the top floor, where you enter the Mozart family apartment—furnished only with the violin given to him at age six. This section introduces Mozart's family, shows you the room where he was born, tells of his wife's and children's fates after his death, and tries to explain his enduring fame. Next is an exhibition on his life in Vienna, and a room of computer terminals with a wonderful program allowing you to see his handwritten scores and hear them performed at the same time (Mozart's Residence, across town, has the same terminals). The middle floor includes a room of dioramas showing stage sets for Mozart's operas and an old clavichord he supposedly composed on. (A predecessor of the more complicated piano, the clavichord's keys hit the strings with a simple teeter-totter motion that allows you to play very softly—ideal for composers living in tight apartment quarters.) The lower-floor exhibit takes you on the road with the child prodigy, and gives a slice-of-life portrait of Salzburg during Mozart's time, including a bourgeois living room furnished much as the Mozart family's would have been.

If I had to choose between Mozart's birthplace (*Geburtshaus*) and his residence (*Wohnhaus*), I'd go with the birthplace, since its exhibits are more extensive and educational. If you're truly interested in Mozart and his times, take advantage of the combi-ticket and see both. If Mozart isn't important to you, skip both museums and concentrate on the city's other sights and glorious natural surroundings.

Atop the Cliffs Above the Old Town

Atop the Mönchsberg—the mini-mountain that rises behind the old town—is a tangle of paved walking paths with great views, a hostel with a pleasant café/restaurant, a modern art museum, a neighborhood of very fancy homes, and one major sight (the Hohensalzburg Fortress, perched on the Festungsberg, the Mönchsberg's southern arm). You can walk up from several points in town, including Festungsgasse (behind the cathedral), Toscaninihof, and the Augustiner Bräustübl beer garden. At the west end of the old town, the Mönchsberg elevator whisks you up to the top for a couple euros. The funicular directly up to the fortress is expensive, and worthwhile only if you plan to visit the fortress, which is included in the funicular ticket.

▲▲Hohensalzburg Fortress (Festung)

Construction of Hohensalzburg Fortress was begun by Archbishop Gebhard of Salzburg as a show of the Catholic Church's power (see sidebar). Built on a rock (called Festungsberg) 400 feet above the

Salzach River, this fortress was never really used. That's the idea. It was a good investment—so foreboding, nobody attacked the town for nearly a thousand years. The city was never taken by force, but when Napoleon stopped by, Salzburg wisely surrendered. After a stint as a military barracks, the fortress was opened to the public in the 1860s by Habsburg Emperor Franz Josef. Today, it remains one of Europe's mightiest castles, dominating Salzburg's skyline and offering incredible views, as well as a couple mediocre museums.

Cost: You'll pay to enter the castle, whether you reach the castle on foot (the walk is easier than it looks), or, for a couple euros more, by funicular.

On Foot: If you walk up to the fortress (or walk over from the Mönchsberg, reachable either by stairs from Toscaninihof or the elevator from the west end of Griesgasse/southern end of Gstättengasse), you'll pay €7.80 to enter (at the fortress gate), which includes entry to the fortress grounds, all the museums inside, and your funicular ride down—whether you want it or not. Within one hour of the museums' closing time, the entry price is reduced to €4.

Via Funicular: Most visitors enter the fortress by taking a one-minute trip on the funicular *(Festungsbahn)*. The lower station is on Festungsgasse, which is just off Kapitelplatz, behind Salzburg's cathedral. The top end of the funicular is inside the fortress complex. Your round-trip funicular ticket includes admission to the fortress grounds and all the museums inside—whether you want to see them or not (€11, €25.50 family ticket). If you board the funicular within one hour of the museums' closing time (i.e., May-Sept after 18:00 or Oct-April after 16:00), you pay only €7.80, or €6.40 if you don't want to take the funicular down; this is a good deal if you only want a glimpse  of the museums. After the museums have closed, the funicular continues to run until about 21:30 (later if there's a concert) and costs €3.80 round-trip, or €2.40 one-way.

Hours: The museums in the fortress are open daily May-Sept 9:00-19:00, Oct-April 9:30-17:00, tel. 0662/8424-3011. The grounds of the fortress stay open and the funicular continues to run even after the museums close—usually until about 21:30 or 22:00, especially when there's a concert (300 nights a year).

Concerts: The fortress serves as a venue for evening concerts (the Festungskonzerte), which are held in the old banquet rooms on the upper floor of the palace museum. A concert is a good way to see the fortress at its quietest. For details, see "Music in Salzburg" on page 307.

Eating: The cafés to either side of the upper funicular station are a great place to nibble on apple strudel while taking in the jaw-dropping view.

○ Self-Guided Tour: At the top of the funicular, most visitors turn left. Instead, head right and down the stairs to bask in the **view** to the south (away from town) toward the Alps, either from the café or the view terrace a little farther along. (You'll enjoy superb city views later on this tour.)

• *Once you're done snapping photos, walk through the arches into the fortress courtyard. Your ticket lets you into two exhibits: The first is a tour of the fortifications, while the second is a historical museum inside the "palace" in the fortress courtyard. The courtyards themselves offer a few other things to see, as well as great views in several directions. Go left (uphill). From here, you'll make a clockwise circuit around the courtyard. The first sight you'll come to, labeled #1, is the...*

Fortress Interior: Here you get to see a few rooms in the outer fortifications. Only 40 people are allowed in at a time, usually with an escort who gives a 30-minute commentary. While the interior furnishings are mostly gone—taken by Napoleon—the rooms themselves survived fairly well (no one wanted to live here after 1500, so the building was never modernized). Your tour includes a room dedicated to the art of "enhanced interrogation" (to use American military jargon)—filled with tools of that gruesome trade. The highlight is the commanding city view from the top of a tower. In summer, there can be a long wait to get in.

• *Continue uphill to sight #2—the fortress's "palace" (labeled Inneres Schloß). Immediately inside, visit the...*

Marionette Exhibit: Two fun rooms show off this local tradition. Three videos play continuously: two with peeks at Salzburg's ever-enchanting Marionette Theater performances of Mozart classics (described under "Music in Salzburg," later) and one with a behind-the-scenes look at the action. Give the hands-on marionette a whirl.

• *Head down the hall and up the stairs following Festungsmuseum signs to the...*

Fortress Museum (Festungsmuseum): The lower floor of this spacious museum has exhibits on the history of the fortress, from music to torture. One room explains how they got all this stuff up here, while another has copies of the pencil sketches for the Salzburg Panorama (described earlier). On the top floor are three pretty ceremonial rooms, including the one where the evening concerts are held. (Check out the colorfully painted tile stove in the far room.) The rest of the top floor is given over to the Rainer

Regiments Museum, dedicated to the Salzburg soldiers who fought mountain-to-mountain on the Italian front during World War I.

• *Exit the museum and continue on out into the...*

Fortress Courtyard: The courtyard was the main square for the medieval fortress's 1,000-some residents, who could be self-sufficient when necessary. The square was ringed by the shops of craftsmen, blacksmiths, bakers, and so on. The well dipped into a rain-fed cistern. As you enter, look to your left to see the well-described remains of a recently excavated Romanesque chapel. The current church is dedicated to St. George, the protector of horses (logical for an army church) and decorated by fine red marble reliefs (c. 1502). Behind the church is the top of the old lift (still in use) that helped supply the fortress. Under the archway next to it are the steps that lead back into the city, or to the paths across the Mönchsberg.

• *Near the chapel, turn left into the Kuenburg Bastion (once a garden) for fine city views.*

Kuenburg Bastion: Notice how the fortress has three parts: the original section inside the courtyard, the vast whitewashed walls (built when the fortress was a residence), and the lower, beefed-up fortifications (added for extra defense against the expected Ottoman invasion). Survey Salzburg from here and think about fortifying an impor-

tant city by using nature. The Mönchsberg (the cliffs to the left) and Festungsberg (the little mountain you're on) naturally cradle the old town, with just a small gate between the ridge and the river needed to bottle up the place. The new town across the river needed a bit of a wall arcing from the river to its hill. Back then, only one bridge crossed the Salzach into town, and it had a fortified gate.

• *Go back inside the fortress courtyard. Our tour is over. Either circle back to where you entered and ride the funicular down, or go through the archway and down the stairs if you prefer to hike back to town or along the top of the Mönchsberg (see "Mönchsberg Walk," later). If you take the funicular down, don't miss (at the bottom of the lift) the...*

Alm River Canal Exhibit: At the base of the funicular, below the fortress, is this fine little exhibit on how the river was broken into five smaller streams—powering the city until steam took up the energy-supply baton. Pretend it's the year 1200 and follow (by video) the flow of the water from the river through the canals, into the mills, and as it's finally dumped into the Salzach River. (The exhibit technically requires a funicular ticket—but you can see it by slipping through the exit at the back of the amber shop, just uphill from the funicular terminal.)

Mönchsberg Sights

▲**Mönchsberg Walk**—The paved, wooded walking path between the Mönchsberg elevator and the fortress is less than a mile long and makes for a great 30-minute hike. The mountain is small, and frequent signposts direct you between all the key points, so it's hard to get lost. The views of Salzburg are the main draw, but there's also a modern art museum, mansions to ogle, and a couple of places to eat or enjoy a scenic drink.

You can do this walk in either direction. (To save a few euros—and the climb—visit the fortress last: Take the Mönchsberg elevator, walk across to the fortress, pay the reduced entry price at the fortress gate, see the fortress, then take the funicular down—included in your fortress ticket.) The Mönchsberg **elevator** *(Aufzug)* starts from Gstättengasse/Griesgasse on the west side of the old town (€2 one-way, €3.20 round-trip, normally Mon 8:00-19:00, Tue-Sun 8:00-24:00).

You can also **climb** up and down under your own power; this saves a few more euros (no matter which direction you go). Paths or stairs lead up from the Augustiner beer hall (see page 325), Toscaninihof (near the Salzburg Festival concert halls), and Festungsgasse (at the base of the fortress).

Cafés: The elevator deposits you right at Mönchsberg 32, a sleek modern café/bar/restaurant adjacent to the modern art museum and a fine place for a drink or bite (they serve breakfast until 16:00). From there, it's a five-minute walk to the rustic Gasthaus Stadtalm café, with wooden picnic tables and a one-with-nature allure. Next to the Stadtalm is a surviving section of Salzburg's medieval wall; pass under the wall and walk left along it to a tableau showing how the wall once looked.

Museum of Modern Art on Mönchsberg—The modern-art museum, which features temporary exhibits, is right at the top of the Mönchsberg elevator.

Cost and Hours: €8, Tue-Sun 10:00-18:00, closed Mon.

In the New Town, North of the River

The following sights are across the river from the old town. I've connected them with walking instructions.

• *Begin at the Makartsteg pedestrian bridge, where you can survey the...*

Salzach River

Salzburg's river is called "salt river" not because it's salty, but because of the precious cargo it once carried—the salt mines of Hallein are just nine miles upstream. Salt could be transported from here all the way to the Danube, and on to the Mediterranean via the Black Sea. The riverbanks and roads were built when the river was regulated in the 1850s. Before that, the Salzach was much wider and slower moving. Houses opposite the old town fronted the river with docks and "garages" for boats. The grand buildings just past the bridge (with their elegant promenades and cafés) were built on reclaimed land in the late 19th century in the Historicist style of Vienna's Ringstrasse (see "Historicism" sidebar on page 139).

Scan the cityscape. Notice all the churches. Salzburg, nick-named the "Rome of the North," has 38 Catholic churches (plus two Protestant churches and a synagogue). Find the five streams gushing into the river. These date from the 13th century, when the river was split into five canals running through the town to power its mills. The Stein Hotel (upstream, just left of next bridge) has a popular roof-terrace café (see page 303). Downstream, notice the Museum of Modern Art atop the Mönchsberg, with a view restaurant and a faux castle (actually a water reservoir). The Romanesque bell tower with the green copper dome in the distance is the Augustine church, site of the best beer hall in town (the Augustiner Bräustübl).

• *Cross the bridge, pass the recommended Café Bazar (a fine place for a drink), walk two blocks inland, and take a left past the heroic statues into...*

▲Mirabell Gardens and Palace (Schloss)

The bubbly gardens laid out in 1730 for the prince archbishop have been open to the public since 1850 (thanks to Emperor Franz Josef, who was rattled by the popular revolutions of 1848). The gardens are free and open until dusk. The palace is open only as a concert venue (ex-plained later). The statues and the arbor (far left) were featured in *The Sound of Music*. Walk through the gardens to the palace. Look back, enjoy the garden/cathedral/castle view, and imagine how the prince archbishop must have reveled in a vista that re-minded him of all his secular and religious power. Then go around to the river-side of the palace and find the horse.

The rearing **Pegasus statue** (rare and very well-balanced) is the site of a famous *Sound of Music* scene where the kids all danced before lining up on the stairs with Maria (30 yards farther along). The steps lead to a small mound in the park (made of rubble from a former theater).

Nearest the horse, stairs lead between two lions to a pair of tough dwarfs (early volleyball players with spiked mittens) welcoming you to Salzburg's **Dwarf Park**. Cross the elevated walk (noticing the city's fortified walls) to meet statues of a dozen dwarfs who served the prince archbishop—modeled after real people with real fashions in about 1600. This was Mannerist art, from the hyperrealistic age that followed the Renaissance.

There's plenty of **music** here, both in the park and in the palace. A brass band plays free park concerts (May-Aug Sun at 10:30). To properly enjoy the lavish Mirabell Palace—once the prince archbishop's summer palace and now the seat of the mayor—get a ticket to a Schlosskonzerte (my favorite venue for a classical concert—see page 310).

• *Now go a long block southeast to Makartplatz, where, opposite the big and bright Hotel Bristol, you'll find...*

▲Mozart's Residence (Wohnhaus)

Mozart's second home (his family moved here when he was 17) is less interesting than the house where he was born, but it's also roomier, less crowded, and comes with an informative audioguide and a 30-minute narrated slideshow. The building, bombed in World War II, is a reconstruction.

Cost and Hours: €10, €17 combo-ticket includes Mozart's Birthplace in the old town—see page 294, daily 9:00-17:30, July-Aug until 20:00, allow at least one hour for visit, Makartplatz 8, tel. 0662/8742-2740, www.mozarteum.at. Behind the ticket desk is the free Ton und Filmsammlung, an archive of historic concerts on video (Mon-Tue and Fri 9:00-13:00, Wed-Thu 13:00-17:00, closed Sat-Sun).

Visiting Mozart's Residence: The exhibit—seven rooms on one floor—starts in the main hall, which was used by the Mozarts to entertain Salzburg's high society. Here, you can see the museum's prize possession, Mozart's very own piano. Notice the family portrait (c. 1780) on the wall, showing Mozart with his sister Nannerl, their father, and their mother—who'd died two years earlier in Paris. Mozart also had silly crude bull's-eyes made for the pop-gun game popular at the time (licking an "arse," Wolfgang showed his disdain for the mores of high society).

The rest of the seven rooms feature real artifacts that explore his loves, his intellectual pursuits, his travels, and his family life. At the end, the 30-minute slideshow runs twice an hour, with alternating German/English narration (confirm times when you enter, English usually starts around :40 after the hour).

This museum offers the same computer program as Mozart's Birthplace does, allowing you to see handwritten scores scroll along while actually listening to the same music.

• *From here, you can walk a few blocks back to the main bridge (Staats-brücke), where you'll find the Platzl, a square once used as a hay market. Pause to enjoy the kid-pleasing little fountain. Near the fountain (with your back to the river), Steingasse leads darkly to the right.*

▲Steingasse Stroll

This street, a block in from the river, is wonderfully tranquil and free of Salzburg's touristy crush. Inviting cocktail bars along here come alive at night (see "Steingasse Pub Crawl" on page 326).

The kid-pleasing fountain where Linzgasse meets Steingasse marks an important intersection: where the road to Vienna (Linzgasse) hit the road to Italy (Steingasse). From here traders and pilgrims would look across the river and see the impressive domed University Church (modeled after Vienna's Karlskirche) and know they were entering an important place. Heading up dank, narrow Steingasse, you get a rare glimpse of medieval Salzburg. It's not the church's Salzburg of grand squares and Baroque facades, but the people's Salzburg, of cramped quarters and humble cobbled lanes.

Stop at #9 and look across the river into the old town; this is where the city's original bridge once connected Salzburg's two halves. According to the plaque (of questionable veracity) at #9, this is where Joseph Mohr, who wrote the words to "Silent Night," was born—poor and illegitimate—in 1792. There is no doubt, however, that the popular Christmas carol was composed and first sung in the village of Oberndorf, just outside of Salzburg, in 1818. Stairs lead from near here up to a 17th-century Capuchin monastery.

On the next corner, the wall is gouged out. This scar was left even after the building was restored, to serve as a reminder of the American GI who tried to get a tank down this road during a visit to the town brothel—two blocks farther up Steingasse. Within steps of here is the art cinema (showing movies in their original language) and four recommended bars (described on page 326).

At #19, find the carvings on the old door. Some say these are notices from beggars to the begging community (more numerous after post-Reformation religious wars, which forced many people out of their homes and towns)—a kind of "hobo code" indicating whether the residents would give or not. Trace the wires of the old-fashioned doorbells to the highest floors.

Farther on, you step through the old fortified gate (at #20) and find a commanding Salzburg view across the river. Notice the red dome marking the oldest nunnery in the German-speaking world

SALZBURG

(established in 712) under the fortress and to the left. The real Maria, who inspired *The Sound of Music*, taught in this nunnery's school. In 1927, she and Captain von Trapp were married in the church you see here (not the church filmed in the movie). He was 47. She was 22. Hmmmm.

From here look back, above the arch you just passed through, and up at part of the town's medieval fortification. The coat of arms on the arch is of the prince archbishop who paid Bavaria a huge ransom to stay out of the Thirty Years' War (smart move). He then built this fortification (in 1634) in anticipation of rampaging armies from both sides.

Today, this street is for making love, not war. The Maison de Plaisir (a few doors down, at #24) has for centuries been a Salzburg brothel. But the climax of this walk is more touristic.

• *For a grand view, head back to the Platzl and the bridge, enter the Stein Hotel (left corner, overlooking the river), and ride the elevator to...*

Stein Terrasse

This café offers one of the best views in town. Hidden from the tourist crush, it's a trendy, professional, local scene. You can discreetly peek at the view, enjoy a drink or light meal, or come back later to gaze into the eyes of your travel partner as you sip a nightcap (small snacks, indoor/outdoor seating, daily 9:00-24:00).

• *Back at the Platzl and the bridge, you can head straight up Linzergasse (away from the river) into a neighborhood packed with recommended accommodations, as well as our final new town sight, the...*

▲St. Sebastian Cemetery

Wander through this quiet oasis. Mozart is buried in Vienna, his mom's in Paris, and his sister is in Salzburg's old town (St. Peter's)—but Wolfgang's wife Constanze ("Constantia") and his father Leopold are buried here (from the black iron gate entrance on Linzergasse, walk 17 paces and look left). When Prince Archbishop Wolf Dietrich had the cemetery moved from around the cathedral and put here, across the river, people didn't like it. To help popularize it, he had his own mausoleum built as its centerpiece. Continue straight past the Mozart tomb to this circular building (English description at door). In the corner to the left of the entrance is the tomb of the Renaissance scientist and physician Paracelsus, best known for developing laudanum as a pain-killer.

Cost and Hours: Free, daily April-Oct 9:00-18:30, Nov-March 9:00-16:00, entry at Linzergasse 43 in summer; in winter go around the corner to the right, through the arch at #37, and around the building to the doorway under the blue seal.

Near Salzburg

▲▲Hellbrunn Castle and Gardens—In about 1610, Prince Archbishop Sittikus decided he needed a lavish palace with a vast and ornate garden purely for pleasure (I imagine after meditating on stewardship and Christ-like values). He built this summer palace and hunting lodge, and just loved inviting his VIP guests from throughout Europe for fun with his trick fountains. Today, Hellbrunn is a popular sight for its palace, formal garden (one of the oldest in Europe, with a gazebo made  famous by *The Sound of Music*), amazing fountains, and the excuse it offers to simply get out of the city.

Cost and Hours: €9.50 ticket includes fountain tour and palace audioguide, daily May-Sept 9:00-17:30, July-Aug until 21:00—but tours from 18:00 on don't include the castle (which closes in the evening), April and Oct-Nov 9:00-16:30, these are last tour times, closed Dec-March, tel. 0662/820-3720, www.hellbrunn.at.

Getting There: Hellbrunn is nearly four miles south of Salzburg.

By Bus: Bus #25 leaves from the train station and from the Staatsbrücke bridge (2-3/hour, 20 minutes).

By Bike: In good weather, the trip out to Hellbrunn makes for a pleasant 30-minute bike excursion (see "Riverside or Meadow Bike Ride," later, and ask for a map when you rent your bike).

Visiting the Castle: Upon arrival, buy your **fountain tour** ticket and get a tour time. Tours generally go on the half-hour. The 40-minute English/German tours take you laughing and scrambling through a series of amazing 17th-century garden settings with lots of splashy fun and a guide who seems almost sadistic in the joy he has in soaking his group. (Hint: When you see a wet place, cover your camera.) If there's a wait until your tour, you can see the palace first.

With the help of the included audioguide, wander through the **palace** exhibit to the sounds of shrieking fountain-taunted

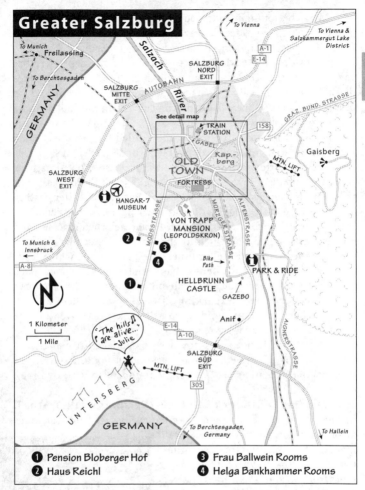

Greater Salzburg

To Vienna

To Vienna &
Salzkammergut Lake
District

To Munich · Freilassing

A-1
E-14

SALZBURG
NORD
EXIT

To Berchtesgaden

SALZBURG
MITTE
EXIT

AUTOBAHN

Salzach River

GRAZ. BUND. STRASSE

GERMANY

See detail map

TRAIN
STATION

158

GABEL

Gaisberg

SALZBURG
WEST
EXIT

OLD
TOWN

Kap-
berg

MTN. LIFT

FORTRESS

HANGAR-7
MUSEUM

MOOSSTRASSE

MORZGER STRASSE

ALPENSTRASSE

To Munich &
Innsbruck

A-8

2

VON TRAPP
MANSION
(LEOPOLDSKRON)

3

PARK & RIDE

4

Bike
Path

1

HELLBRUNN
CASTLE

GAZEBO

N

Anif

AIGNERSTRASSE

1 Kilometer

1 Mile

"The hills
are alive..."
~Julie

E-14
A-10

SALZBURG
SÜD
EXIT

MTN. LIFT

305

U N T E R S B E R G

GERMANY

To Berchtesgaden,
Germany

To Hallein

① Pension Bloberger Hof
② Haus Reichl
③ Frau Ballwein Rooms
④ Helga Bankhammer Rooms

tourists below. The palace was built in a style inspired by the Venetian architect Palladio, who was particularly popular around 1600, and it quickly became a cultural destination. This was the era when the aristocratic ritual was to go hunting in the morning (hence the decor's theme) and enjoy an opera in the evening. The first opera north of the Alps, imported from Italy, was performed here. The decor is Mannerist (between Renaissance and Baroque), with faux antiquities and lots of surprising moments—intentional irregularities were in vogue after the strict logic, balance, and Greek-inspired symmetry of the Renaissance. (For example, the main hall is not in the palace's center, but at the far end.) The palace exhibit also explains the impressive 17th-century hydraulic engineering that let gravity power the intricate fountains.

After the fountain tour you're free to wander the delightful **garden** and pop out to see the **gazebo** made famous by the "Sixteen Going On Seventeen" song from *The Sound of Music*.

▲▲**Riverside or Meadow Bike Ride**—The Salzach River has smooth, flat, and scenic bike lanes along each side (thanks to medieval tow paths—cargo boats would float downstream and be dragged back up by horses). On a sunny day, I can think of no more shout-worthy escape from the city.

Perhaps the most pristine, meadow-filled farm-country route is the nearly four-mile path along Hellbrunner Allee; it's an easy ride with a worthy destination (Hellbrunn Castle, listed earlier): From the middle of town, head along the river on Rudolfskai, with the river on your left and the fortress on your right. After passing the last bridge at the edge of the old town (Nonntaler Brücke), cut inland along Petersbrunnstrasse, until you reach the university and Akademiestrasse. Beyond it find the start of Freisaalweg, which becomes the delightful Hellbrunner Allee bike path...which leads directly to the palace (paralleling Morzgerstrasse; see map on page 305). For a nine-mile ride, continue on to Hallein (where you can tour a salt mine—see next listing; if heading to Hallein directly from Salzburg, head out from the north bank of the river, i.e. the new town side, which is more scenic).

Even a quickie ride across town is a great Salzburg experience. In the evening, the riverbanks are a world of floodlit spires. For bike rental information, see "Getting Around Salzburg—By Bike," earlier.

▲**Hallein Bad Dürrnberg Salt Mine (Salzbergwerke)**—You'll be pitched plenty of different salt-mine excursions from Salzburg, all of which cost substantial time and money. One's plenty. This salt-mine tour (above the town of Hallein, 9 miles from Salzburg) is a good choice. Wearing white overalls and sliding down the sleek wooden chutes, you'll cross underground from Austria into Germany while learning about the old-time salt-mining process. The tour entails lots of time on your feet  as you walk from cavern to cavern, learning the history of the mine by watching a series of video skits with an actor channeling Prince Archbishop Wolf Dietrich. The visit also includes a "Celtic Village" open-air museum.

Cost and Hours: €18, allow 2.5 hours for the visit, daily April-Oct 9:00-17:00, Nov-March 10:00-15:00—these are last tour times, English-speaking guides—but let your linguistic needs be known loud and clear, tel. 06132/200-8511, www.salzwelten.at.

Getting There: The convenient *Salz Erlebnis* ticket from Salzburg's train station covers your transport and admission in one money-saving round-trip ticket (€24, buy ticket at train station, no discount with railpass; covers train to Hallein, then 11-minute ride on bus #41 to salt mines in Bad Dürrnberg, runs hourly, check schedules when buying tickets).

Hangar-7—This purpose-built hangar at the Salzburg airport houses the car-and-aircraft collection of Dietrich Mateschitz, the flamboyant founder of the Red Bull energy-drink empire. Under the hangar's modern steel-and-glass dome are 20 or so glittering planes and racecars, plus several pretentious bars, cafés, and restaurants, all designed to brandish the Red Bull "culture." To learn about what's on display you can borrow an iPod Touch with English information, or get information on the iPads posted by each exhibit.

Mateschitz is Salzburg's big personality these days: He has a mysterious mansion at the edge of town, sponsors the local "Red Bull" soccer and hockey teams, owns several chic Salzburg eateries and cocktail bars, and employs 6,000 mostly good-looking people. He seems much like the energy drink that made him rich and powerful—a high-energy, anything's-possible cultural Terminator.

Cost and Hours: Free, daily 9:00-22:00, bus #8 from Hanuschplatz to the Salzburg airport, www.hangar-7.com.

Eating: At the hangar, the Mayday Bar serves experimental food, and Restaurant Ikarus features a different well-known chef each month. (Mateschitz's recommended Carpe Diem cocktail bar, in the old town, is also Red Bullish.)

Music in Salzburg

▲▲Salzburg Festival (Salzburger Festspiele)

Each summer, from late July to the end of August, Salzburg hosts its famous Salzburg Festival, founded in 1920 to employ Vienna's musicians in the summer. This fun and festive time is crowded—a total of 200,000 tickets are sold to festival events annually—but there are usually plenty of beds (except for a few August weekends). Events take place primarily in three big halls: the Opera and Orchestra venues in the Festival House, and the Landes Theater, where German-language plays are performed. Tickets for the big festival events are generally expensive (€50-600) and sell out well in advance (bookable from January). Most tourists think they're "going to the Salzburg Festival" by seeing smaller non-festival events that go on during the festival weeks. For these lesser events, same-day tickets are normally available (the ticket office on Mozartplatz, in the TI, prints a daily list of concerts and charges a

The Sound of Music Debunked

Rather than visit the real-life sights from the life of Maria von Trapp and family, most tourists want to see the places where Hollywood chose to film this fanciful story. Local guides are happy not to burst any *S.O.M.* pilgrim's bubble, but keep these points in mind:

- "Edelweiss" is not a cherished Austrian folk tune or national anthem. Like all the "Austrian" music in *The S.O.M.*, it was composed for Broadway by Rodgers and Hammerstein. It was the last composition that the famed team wrote together, as Hammerstein died in 1960—nine months after the musical opened.
- *The S.O.M.* implies that Maria was devoutly religious throughout her life, but Maria's foster parents raised her as a socialist and atheist. Maria discovered her religious calling while studying to be a teacher. After completing school, she joined the convent not as a nun, but as a novitiate (that is, she hadn't taken her vows yet).
- Maria's position was not as governess to all the children, as portrayed in the musical, but specifically as governess and teacher for the Captain's second-oldest daughter, also called Maria, who was bedridden with rheumatic fever.
- The Captain didn't run a tight domestic ship. In fact, his seven children were as unruly as most. But he did use a whistle to call them—each kid was trained to respond to a certain pitch.
- Though the Von Trapp family did have seven children, the show changed all their names and even their genders. As an adult, Rupert, the eldest child, responded to the often-asked question, "Which one are you?" with a simple, "I'm Liesl!"
- The family didn't escape by hiking to Switzerland (which is a five-hour drive away). Rather, they pretended to go on one of their frequent mountain hikes. With only the possessions in their backpacks, they "hiked" all the way to the train station (it was at the edge of their estate) and took a train

30 percent fee to book them). For specifics on this year's festival schedule and tickets, visit www.salzburgfestival.at.

Music lovers in town during the festival who don't have tickets (or money) can still enjoy **Festival Nights,** a free series showing videos of previous festival performances, projected on a big screen on Kapitelplatz (behind the cathedral). It's a fun scene, with plenty of folding chairs and a food circus of temporary eateries; schedules are posted next to the screen.

▲▲Musical Events Year-Round

Salzburg is busy throughout the year, with 2,000 classical performances in its palaces and churches annually. Pick up the events to Italy. The movie scene showing them climbing into Switzerland was actually filmed near Berchtesgaden, Germany... home to Hitler's Eagle's Nest, and certainly not a smart place to flee to.

- The actual Von Trapp family house exists...but it's not the one in the film. The mansion in the movie is actually two different buildings—one used for the front, the other for the back. The interiors were all filmed on Hollywood sets.

- For the film, Boris Levin designed a reproduction of the Nonnberg Abbey courtyard so faithful to the original (down to its cobblestones and stained-glass windows) that many still believe the cloister scenes were really shot at the abbey. And no matter what you hear in Salzburg, the graveyard scene (in which the Von Trapps hide from the Nazis) was also filmed on the Fox lot.

- In 1956, a German film producer offered Maria $10,000 for the rights to her book. She asked for royalties, too, and a share of the profits. The agent claimed that German law forbids film companies from paying royalties to foreigners (Maria had by then become a US citizen). She agreed to the contract and unknowingly signed away all film rights to her story. Only a few weeks later, he offered to pay immediately if she would accept $9,000 in cash. Because it was more money than the family had seen in all of their years of singing, she accepted the deal. Later, she discovered the agent had swindled them—no such law existed.

  Rodgers, Hammerstein, and other producers gave the Von Trapps a percentage of the royalties, even though they weren't required to—but it was a fraction of what they otherwise would have earned. But Maria wasn't bitter. She said, "The great good the film and the play are doing to individual lives is far beyond money."

calendar at the TI (free, bimonthly). I've never planned in advance, and I've enjoyed great concerts with every visit. Whenever you visit, you'll have a number of concerts (generally small chamber groups) to choose from. Here are some of the more accessible events:

Concerts at Hohensalzburg Fortress (Festungskonzerte)— Nearly nightly concerts—Mozart's greatest hits for beginners— are held atop Festungsberg, in the "prince's chamber" of the fortress, featuring small chamber groups (open seating after the first six more expensive rows, €31 or €38 plus €3.80 for the funicular; at 19:30, 20:00, or 20:30; doors open 30 minutes early, reserve at tel. 0662/825-858 or via www.salzburghighlights.at, pick up tickets at the door). The medieval-feeling chamber has windows overlooking the city, and the concert gives you a chance to enjoy the grand city view and a stroll through the castle courtyard. For €51, you can combine the concert with a four-course dinner (starts 2 hours before concert). The downside: Hearing Baroque music in an incongruously Gothic setting is not ideal.

Concerts at the Mirabell Palace (Schlosskonzerte)—The nearly nightly chamber music concerts at the Mirabell Palace are performed in a lavish Baroque setting. They come with more sophisticated programs and better musicians than the fortress concerts...and Baroque music flying around a Baroque hall is a happy bird in the right cage (open seating after the first five pricier rows, €29-35, usually at 20:00—but check flier for times, doors open one hour ahead, tel. 0662/848-586, www.salzburger-schlosskonzerte.at).

"Five O'Clock Concerts" (5-Uhr-Konzerte)—These concerts are cheaper, since they feature young artists. While the series is formally named after the brother of Joseph Haydn, it offers music from various masters. Performances are generally chamber music with a string trio playing original 18th-century instruments. On my last visit, the concerts were still being held next to St. Peter's Church in the old town—but they may relocate in 2014 (€12-15, mid-June-mid-Sept Tue and Thu at 17:00, no concerts in off-season, 45-60 minutes, tel. 0662/8445-7619, www.5-uhr-konzerte.com).

Mozart Piano Sonatas—St. Peter's Abbey hosts these concerts each weekend. This short (45-minute) and inexpensive concert is ideal for families (€18, €9 for children, €45 for a family of four, Fri and Sat at 19:00 year-round, in the abbey's Romanesque Hall—a.k.a. Romanischer Saal, mobile 0664-423-5645).

Marionette Theater—Salzburg's much-loved marionette theater offers operas with spellbinding marionettes and recorded music. A troupe of 10 puppeteers—actors themselves—brings the artfully created puppets at the end of their five-foot strings to life. The 180 performances a year alternate between *The Sound of Music* and various German-language operas (with handy superscripts in English). While the 300-plus-seat venue is forgettable, the art of the marionettes enchants adults and children alike (€24-35, May-Sept nearly nightly at 17:00 or 19:30, near Mozart's Residence at Schwarzstrasse 24, tel. 0662/872-406, www.marionetten.at). For a sneak preview, check out the videos playing at the marionette exhibit up in the fortress.

Mozart Dinner Concert—For those who'd like some classical music but would rather not sit through a concert, the recommended Stiftskeller St. Peter restaurant offers a traditional candlelit meal with Mozart's greatest hits performed by a string quartet and singers in historic costumes gavotting among the tables. In this elegant Baroque setting, tourists clap between movements and get three courses of food (from Mozart-era recipes) mixed with three 20-minute courses of crowd-pleasing music—structured much as such evenings were in Baroque-era times (€54, €9 discount for Mozart-lovers who book direct with this book, nightly at 20:00, dress is "smart casual," call to reserve at 0662/828-695, www.mozartdinnerconcert.com).

Music at Mass—Each Sunday morning, three great churches offer a Mass, generally with glorious music. The **Salzburg Cathedral** is likely your best bet for fine music to worship by, and many Masses are followed by a free organ concert (10:00 Mass, music program at www.kirchen.net/dommusik). Nearby (just outside Domplatz, with the pointy green spire), the **Franciscan church** is the locals' choice and is enthusiastic about its musical Masses (at 9:00, www.franziskanerkirche-salzburg.at—click on "Programm"). **St. Peter's Church** sometimes has music (at 10:15, www.stift-stpeter.at—click on "Kirchenmusik"). For more, see the Salzburg events guide (available at TIs) for details.

Free Brass Band Concert—A traditional brass band plays in the Mirabell Gardens (May-Aug Sun at 10:30).

Sleeping in Salzburg

Finding a room in Salzburg, even during its music festival (mid-July-Aug), is usually easy. Rates always rise significantly (20-30 percent) during the music festival, during Advent (four weeks leading up to Christmas, when street markets are at full blast) and usually around Easter. Unless otherwise noted, these higher "festival" prices do not appear in the ranges I've listed. Many places charge 10 percent extra for a one-night stay.

In the New Town, North of the River

These listings, clustering around Linzergasse, are in a pleasant neighborhood a 15-minute walk from the train station (for directions, see "Arrival in Salzburg," earlier) and a 10-minute walk to the old town. If you're coming from the old town, simply cross the main bridge (Staatsbrücke) to the mostly traffic-free Linzergasse. If driving, exit the highway at Salzburg-Nord, follow Vogelweiderstrasse straight to its end, and turn right. Parking is easy at the nearby Mirabell-Congress garage (€15/day, your hotel may be able to get you a €1-2 discount, Mirabellplatz).

$$$ Altstadthotel Wolf-Dietrich, around the corner from Linzergasse on pedestrians-only Wolf-Dietrich-Strasse, is well-located (half its rooms overlook St. Sebastian Cemetery). With 40 tastefully plush rooms—a third of them in an annex across the street—it projects a big-hotel feeling, but has small-hotel prices

SALZBURG

Sleep Code

(€1 = about $1.30, country code: 43, area code: 0662)
S = Single, **D** = Double/Twin, **T** = Triple, **Q** = Quad, **b** = bathroom, **s** = shower only. Unless otherwise noted, credit cards are accepted and breakfast is included. All of these places speak English.

To help you sort easily through these listings, I've divided the accommodations into three categories, based on the price for a standard double room with bath:

$$$ Higher Priced—Most rooms €120 or more.
$$ Moderately Priced—Most rooms between €60-120.
$ Lower Priced—Most rooms €60 or less.

Prices can change without notice; verify the hotel's current rates online or by email.

(roughly Sb-€80, Db-€120, rates vary with demand, family deals, readers of this book get a 10 percent discount on prevailing price—insist on this discount deducted from whatever price is offered that day, non-smoking, elevator, free Internet access and Wi-Fi, annex rooms have air-con, pool with loaner swimsuits, sauna, free DVD library, Wolf-Dietrich-Strasse 7, tel. 0662/871-275, fax 0662/871-2759, www.salzburg-hotel.at, office@salzburg-hotel.at).

$$ Hotel Trumer Stube, well-located three blocks from the river just off Linzergasse, has 20 clean rooms and is run by the Hirschbichler family (Sb-€65, Db-€105, Tb-€128, Qb-€147; for best prices, email and ask for the best Rick Steves cash-only rate; breakfast with a personal touch-€7.50 extra, non-smoking, elevator, free Wi-Fi, look for the flower boxes at Bergstrasse 6, tel. 0662/874-776, fax 0662/874-326, www.trumer-stube.at, info@trumer-stube.at; mom and daughter are both named Marianne).

$$ Hotel Goldene Krone, about five blocks from the river, plans to change its name to Hotel Krone1512. Back-facing rooms are quieter than the streetside ones. Stay a while in their pleasant cliffside garden (Sb-€69, Db-€119, Tb-€159, Qb-€189, claim your 15 percent discount off these prices with this book, elevator, free Wi-Fi in common areas, Linzergasse 48, tel. 0662/872-300, fax 0662/8723-0066, www.krone1512.at, hotel@krone1512.at, Günther Hausknost). Günther also offers tours (€10/person, 2 hours, 5 people minimum).

$$ Hotel Schwarzes Rössl is a university dorm that becomes a student-run hotel each July, August, and September. The location couldn't be handier. It looks like a normal hotel from the outside, and its 50 rooms, while a bit spartan, are as comfortable as a hotel on the inside (S-€46, Sb-€60, D-€76, Db-€92, Tb-€120, ask for Rick Steves discount, good breakfast, free Internet access and Wi-Fi in common areas, no rooms rented Oct-June, just off Linzergasse at Priesterhausgasse 6, tel. 0662/874-426, www.aca demiahotels.at, schwarzes.roessl@academiahotels.at).

$$ Institute St. Sebastian is in a somewhat sterile but very clean historic building next to St. Sebastian Cemetery. From October through June, the institute houses female students from various Salzburg colleges and also rents 40 beds for travelers (men and women). From July through September, the students are gone, and they rent all 100 beds (including 20 twin rooms) to travelers. The building has spacious public areas, a roof garden, a piano that guests are welcome to play, and some of the best rooms and dorm beds in town for the money. The immaculate doubles come with modern baths and head-to-toe twin beds (S-€37, Sb-€45, D-€58, Db-€72, Tb-€87, Qb-€98, includes simple breakfast, elevator, all bedrooms are non-smoking, free cable Internet in rooms, pay Wi-Fi in common areas, self-service laundry-€4/load, Oct-June reception closed 12:00-16:00—call to arrange key pickup if arriving after 21:00, Linzergasse 41, enter through arch at #37, tel. 0662/871-386, fax 0662/8713-8685, www.st-sebastian-salzburg. at, office@st-sebastian-salzburg.at). Students like the €21 bunks in 4- to 10-bed dorms (€1.50 less if you have sheets, no lockout, free lockers, free showers). You'll find self-service kitchens on each floor (fridge space is free; request a key). If you need parking, request it well in advance.

On Rupertgasse

These two similar hotels are about five blocks farther from the river on Rupertgasse—a breeze for drivers but with more street noise than the places on Linzergasse. They're both modern and well-run, with free on-site parking, making them good values if you don't mind being a 15-20-minute walk from the old town.

$$ Bergland Hotel is charming and classy, with 18 comfortable neo-rustic rooms. It's a modern building, spacious and solid (Sb-€65, Db-€105, Tb-€125, non-smoking, elevator, pay Internet access, free Wi-Fi, Rupertgasse 15, tel. 0662/872-318, fax 0662/872-3188, www.berglandhotel.at, office@berglandhotel.at, Kuhn family).

$$ Hotel Jedermann, a few doors down, is simpler and larger. It's tastefully done and comfortable, with an artsy painted-concrete ambience, a backyard garden, and 30 rooms (Sb-€65, Db-€95, Tb-€120, Qb-€160, non-smoking, elevator, cable Internet in rooms, Wi-Fi in common areas, free Internet access, Rupertgasse 25, tel. 0662/873-2410, fax 0662/873-2419, www.hotel-jedermann.com, office@hotel-jedermann.com, Herr und Frau Gmachl).

SALZBURG

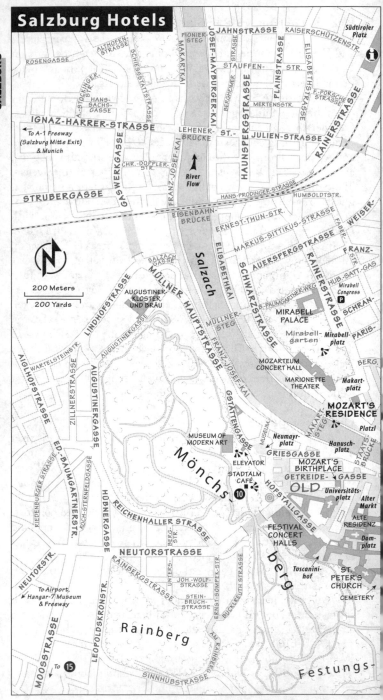

Salzburg Hotels

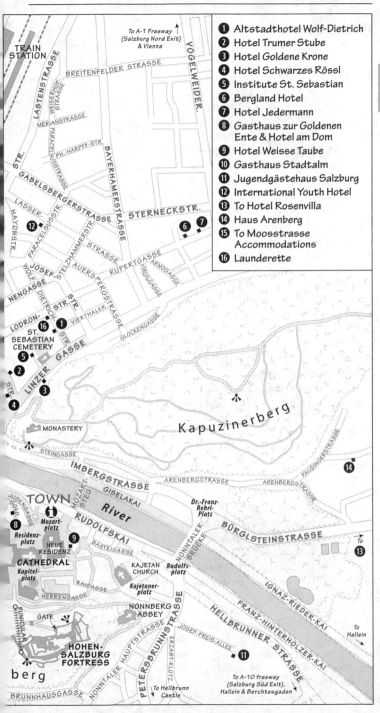

1 Altstadthotel Wolf-Dietrich
2 Hotel Trumer Stube
3 Hotel Goldene Krone
4 Hotel Schwarzes Rössl
5 Institute St. Sebastian
6 Bergland Hotel
7 Hotel Jedermann
8 Gasthaus zur Goldenen Ente & Hotel am Dom
9 Hotel Weisse Taube
10 Gasthaus Stadtalm
11 Jugendgästehaus Salzburg
12 International Youth Hotel
13 To Hotel Rosenvilla
14 Haus Arenberg
15 To Moosstrasse Accommodations
16 Launderette

In the Old Town

These three hotels are perfectly located near Residenzplatz. While this area is car-restricted, your hotel can give you a code that lets you drive in to unload, pick up a map and parking instructions, and head for the €14-per-day garage in the mountain (punch the code into the gate near Mozartplatz). You can't actually drive into the narrow Goldgasse, but you can park to unload at the end of the street.

$$$ Gasthaus zur Goldenen Ente is in a 600-year-old building with medieval stone arches and narrow stairs on a pedestrian street in old Salzburg. Located above a good restaurant, most of its 22 rooms are modern and newly renovated—ask for one when you book. Ulrike, Franziska, and Anita run a tight ship for the absentee owners (Sb-€100, Db-€125; festival rates Sb-€125, Db-€160; extra person-€40, non-smoking, elevator, free Internet access and Wi-Fi, Goldgasse 10, tel. 0662/845-622, fax 0662/845-6229, www.ente.at, hotel@ente.at).

$$$ Hotel am Dom, across from the Goldenen Ente, offers 15 chic, upscale rooms, some with their original wood-beam ceilings (Sb-€100-180, standard Db-€120-260, "superior" Db-€140-280, rates vary with demand, air-con, non-smoking, elevator, free Internet access, cable Internet and Wi-Fi available, Goldgasse 17, tel. 0662/842-765, fax 0662/8427-6555, www.hotelamdom.at, office@hotelamdom.at).

$$ Hotel Weisse Taube has 30 comfortable rooms in a quiet dark-wood 14th-century building, well-located about a block off Mozartplatz (Sb-€69-94, Db with shower-€104-139, bigger Db with bath-€119-185, higher prices are during festival, 10 percent discount with this book if you reserve direct and pay cash, elevator, pay Internet access and Wi-Fi, tel. 0662/842-404, fax 0662/841-783, Kaigasse 9, www.weissetaube.at, hotel@weissetaube.at).

Hostels

The Institute St. Sebastian, listed earlier, also has cheap dorm beds.

$ Gasthaus Stadtalm (a.k.a. the *Naturfreundehaus*) is a local version of a mountaineers' hut and a great budget alternative. Snuggled in a forest on the remains of a 15th-century castle wall atop the little mountain overlooking Salzburg, it has magnificent town and mountain views. While the 22 beds are designed-for-backpackers basic, the price and view are the best in town—with the right attitude, it's a fine experience (€19/person in 4- and 6-bed dorms, one double-bedded D-€43; includes breakfast, sheets, and shower; non-smoking, free Wi-Fi, recommended café, lockers, 2 minutes from top of Mönchsberg elevator, Mönchsberg 19C, tel. & fax 0662/841-729, www.stadtalm.at, info@diestadtalm.com, Peter). Once you've dropped your bags here, it's a five-minute walk down the cliffside stairs into Toscaninihof, in the middle of the old town (path always lit).

$ Jugendgästehaus Salzburg, just steps from the center of the old town, is nevertheless removed from the bustle. While its dorm rooms are the standard crammed-with-beds variety—and the hallways will bring back high-school memories—the doubles and family rooms are modern, roomy, and bright, and the public spaces are quite pleasant (bed in 8-person dorm-€24; Db-€80-120; includes breakfast and sheets, free Internet access and Wi-Fi, *The Sound of Music* plays daily, bike rental-€10/day or €6/half-day, parking-€5/day, just around the east side of the castle hill at Josef-Preis-Allee 18; from train station, take bus #5 or #25 to the Justizgebäude stop, then head left one block along the bushy wall, cross Petersbrunnstrasse, find shady Josef-Preis-Allee, and walk a few minutes to the end—the hostel is the big orange/green building on the right; tel. 05/708-3613, fax 05/708-3611, www.jufa.eu/salzburg, salzburg@jufa.eu).

$ International Youth Hotel, a.k.a. the "Yo-Ho," is the most lively, handy, and American of Salzburg's hostels. This backpacker haven is a youthful and easygoing place that speaks English first; has cheap meals, 186 beds, lockers, tour discounts, and no curfew; plays *The Sound of Music* free daily at 19:00; runs a lively bar; and welcomes anyone of any age. The noisy atmosphere and lack of a curfew can make it hard to sleep (€18-21/person in 4- to 8-bed dorms, €21-22 in dorms with bathrooms, D-€60, Ds-€75, T-€66, Q-€75, Qs-€87, includes sheets, breakfast-€3.50, pay Internet access, free Wi-Fi, laundry-€4 wash and dry, 6 blocks from station toward Linzergasse and 6 blocks from river at Paracelsusstrasse 9, tel. 0662/879-649, www.yoho.at, office@yoho.at).

Four-Star Hotels in Residential Neighborhoods away from the Center

If you want plush furnishings, spacious public spaces, generous balconies, gardens, and free parking, consider the following places. These two modern hotels in nondescript residential neighborhoods are a fine value if you don't mind the 15-minute walk from the old town. While not ideal for train travelers, drivers in need of no-stress comfort for a home base should consider these (see map on page 314).

$$$ Hotel Rosenvilla, close to the river, offers 15 rooms with bright furnishings, surrounded by a leafy garden (Sb-€79-108, Db-€135-165, bigger

Db-€145-199, Db suite-€168-255, higher prices are during festival, no elevator, free Wi-Fi, Höfelgasse 4, tel. 0662/621-765, fax 0662/625-2308, www.rosenvilla.com, hotel@rosenvilla.com).

$$$ Haus Arenberg, higher up opposite the old town, rents 17 big, breezy rooms—most with generous balconies—in a quiet garden setting (Sb-€85-104, Db-€135-159, Tb-€159-175, Qb-€165-185, higher prices are during festival, no elevator, free Wi-Fi, electric bikes-€12/day, Blumensteinstrasse 8, tel. 0662/640-097, fax 0662/640-0973, www.arenberg-salzburg.at, info@arenberg-salzburg.at, family Leobacher).

Pensions on Moosstrasse

These are generally roomy and comfortable, and come with a good breakfast, easy parking, and tourist information. Off-season, competition softens prices. While they are a bus ride from town, with a €4.20 transit day pass *(Tageskarte)* and the frequent service, this shouldn't keep you away (see map on page 314). In fact, many homeowners will happily pick you up at the train station if you simply telephone them and ask. Most will also do laundry for a small fee for those staying at least two nights. I've listed prices for two nights or more—if staying only one night, expect a 10 percent surcharge. Most push tours and concerts to make money on the side. As they are earning a commission, if you go through them, you'll probably lose the discount I've negotiated for my readers who go direct.

The busy street called Moosstrasse, which runs southwest of the Mönchsberg (behind the mountain and away from the center old town), is lined with farmhouses offering rooms. Handy bus #21 connects Moosstrasse to the center frequently (Mon-Fri 4/hour until 19:00, Sat 4/hour until 17:00, evenings and Sun 2/hour, 20 minutes). To get to these pensions from the train station, take any bus heading toward the center to Makartplatz, where you'll change to #21. If you're coming from the old town, catch bus #21 from Hanuschplatz, just downstream of the Staatsbrücke bridge near the *Tabak* kiosk. Buy a €1.90 *Einzelkarte-Kernzone* ticket (for one trip) or a €4.20 *Tageskarte* (day pass, good for 24 hours) from the streetside machine and punch it when you board the bus. The bus stop you use for each place is included in the following listings. If you're driving from the center, go through the tunnel, continue straight on Neutorstrasse, and take the fourth left onto Moosstrasse. Drivers exit the autobahn at *Süd* and then head in the direction of *Grödig*. Each place can recommend a favorite Moosstrasse eatery (Reiterhof, at #151, is particularly popular).

$$ Pension Bloberger Hof, while more a hotel than a pension, is comfortable and friendly, with a peaceful, rural location and 20 farmer-plush, good-value rooms. It's the farthest out, but reached by the same bus #21 from the center. Inge and her daughter Sylvia offer a 10 percent discount to those who have this book, reserve direct, and pay cash (Sb-€60-75, Db-€75, big new Db with balcony-€100-110, Db suite-€120-130, higher prices are during festival, extra bed-€20, 10 percent extra for one-night stays, family apartment with kitchen, non-smoking, free Internet access and Wi-Fi, restaurant for guests, free loaner bikes, free station pickup if staying 3 nights, Hammerauer Strasse 4, bus stop: Hammerauer Strasse, tel. 0662/830-227, fax 0662/827-061, www.blobergerhof. at, office@blobergerhof.at).

$$ Haus Reichl, with two good rooms at the end of a long lane, feels peaceful and remote (but may close in 2013). Franziska offers free loaner bikes for guests (20-minute pedal to the center) and bakes fresh cakes most days (Db-€60-64, Tb-€75-84, Qb-€92-104, higher prices are during festival, cash preferred, in-room tea/coffee, non-smoking, no Internet access, between Ballwein and Bankhammer B&Bs, 200 yards down Reiterweg to #52, bus stop: Gsengerweg, tel. & fax 0662/826-248, www.privatzimmer.at/haus-reichl, haus.reichl@telering.at).

$ Frau Ballwein offers eleven cozy, charming, and fresh rooms in a delightful, family-friendly farmhouse. Some rooms come with intoxicating-view balconies (Sb-€38-45, Db-€55-65, Tb-€75-85, Qb-€85-95, 2-bedroom apartment for up to 5 people-€95-110, higher prices are during festival, no surcharge for one-night stays, cash only, farm-fresh breakfasts amid her hanging teapot collection, non-smoking, free Wi-Fi, 2 free loaner bikes, free parking, Moosstrasse 69a, bus stop: Gsengerweg, tel. & fax 0662/824-029, www.haus-ballwein.at, haus.ballwein@gmx.net).

$ Helga Bankhammer rents four nondescript rooms in a farmhouse, with a real dairy farm out back (D-€48, Db-€52, no surcharge for one-night stays, family deals, non-smoking, no Internet access, laundry-about €7/load, Moosstrasse 77, bus stop: Marienbad, tel. & fax 0662/830-067, www.privatzimmer.at/helga. bankhammer, bankhammer@aon.at).

Eating in Salzburg

In the Old Town

Salzburg boasts many inexpensive, fun, and atmospheric eateries. Most of these restaurants are centrally located in the old town, famous with visitors but also enjoyed by locals.

Gasthaus zum Wilden Mann is *the* place if the weather's bad and you're in the mood for a hearty, cheap meal at a shared table in one well-antlered (and non-smoking) room. Notice the century-old flood photos on the wall. For a quick lunch, get the *Bauernschmaus*, a mountain of dumplings, kraut, and peasant's meats (€12). While

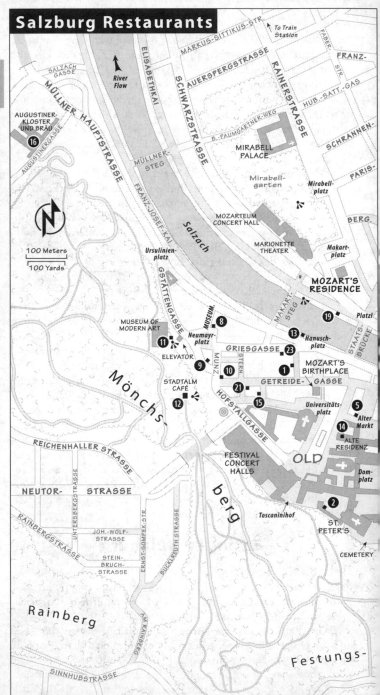

SALZBURG

Salzburg Restaurants

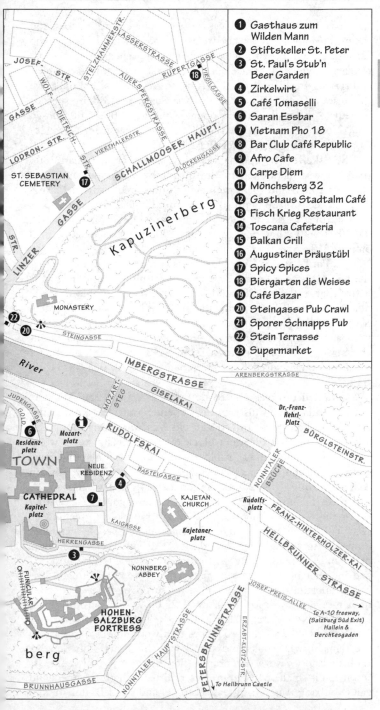

1 Gasthaus zum Wilden Mann
2 Stiftskeller St. Peter
3 St. Paul's Stub'n Beer Garden
4 Zirkelwirt
5 Café Tomaselli
6 Saran Essbar
7 Vietnam Pho 18
8 Bar Club Café Republic
9 Afro Cafe
10 Carpe Diem
11 Mönchsberg 32
12 Gasthaus Stadtalm Café
13 Fisch Krieg Restaurant
14 Toscana Cafeteria
15 Balkan Grill
16 Augustiner Bräustübl
17 Spicy Spices
18 Biergarten die Weisse
19 Café Bazar
20 Steingasse Pub Crawl
21 Sporer Schnapps Pub
22 Stein Terrasse
23 Supermarket

they have a few outdoor tables, the atmosphere is all indoors, and the menu is not great for hot-weather food. Owner Robert—who runs the restaurant with Schwarzenegger-like energy—enjoys fostering a convivial ambience, encouraging strangers to share tables, and serving fresh traditional cuisine at great prices. I simply love this place (€8.50 two-course lunch specials, €9-13 daily specials posted on the wall, kitchen open Mon-Sat 11:00-21:00, closed Sun, 2 minutes from Mozart's Birthplace, enter from Getreidegasse 22 or Griesgasse 17, tel. 0662/841-787).

Stiftskeller St. Peter has been in business for more than 1,000 years—it was mentioned in the biography of Charlemagne. It's classy and high-end touristy, serving uninspired traditional Austrian cuisine (€14-26 main courses, daily 11:30-22:30, indoor/outdoor seating, next to St. Peter's Church at foot of Mönchsberg, tel. 0662/841-268). They host the Mozart Dinner Concert described on page 310.

St. Paul's Stub'n Beer Garden is tucked secretly away under the fortress with a decidedly untouristy atmosphere. The food is better than at beer halls, and a young, bohemian-chic clientele fills its two troll-like rooms and its idyllic tree-shaded garden. *Kasnock'n* is a tasty mountaineers' pasta with cheese served in an iron pan with a side salad for €9—it's enough for two. Reservations are smart (€9-17 main courses, Mon-Sat 17:00-22:00, open later for drinks only, closed Sun, Herrengasse 16, tel. 0662/843-220, Bernard).

Zirkelwirt serves cheese dumplings and modern Mediterranean, Italian, and Austrian dishes, and always has a daily special (chalked on the board). It's an old *Gasthaus* dining room with a medieval tiki-hut terrace a block off Mozartplatz, yet a world away from the tourism of the old town. While the waitstaff, music, and vibe feel young, it attracts Salzburgers of all ages (€9-14 main courses, nightly 17:00-24:00, Pfeifergasse 14, tel. 0662/843-472).

Café Tomaselli (with its Kiosk annex and terrace seating across the way) has long been Salzburg's top place to see and be seen. While pricey, it is good for lingering and people-watching. Tomaselli serves light meals and lots of drinks, keeps long hours daily, and has fine seating on the square, a view terrace upstairs, and indoor tables. Despite its fancy inlaid wood paneling, 19th-century portraits, and chandeliers, it's surprisingly low-key (€3-7 light meals, daily 7:00-21:00, until 22:00 during music festival, until 20:00 Nov-March, Alter Markt 9, tel. 0662/844-488).

Saran Essbar is the product of hardworking Mr. Saran (from the Punjab), who cooks and serves with his heart. This delightful little eatery casts a rich orange glow under medieval vaults. Its fun menu is small (Mr. Saran is committed to both freshness and value), mixing Austrian (great schnitzel and strudel), Italian, and

Asian vegetarian, and always offering salads (€10-16 main courses, daily 11:00-15:00 & 17:00-22:00, often open later, a block off Mozartplatz at Judengasse 10, tel. 0662/846-628).

Vietnam Pho 18, fragrant with fresh cilantro, is where the Nguyen family dishes up Vietnamese noodle soups and other Asian standards in a six-table restaurant a long block from the cathedral (€8 main courses, eat in or take out, Sat-Thu 11:30-15:00 & 17:00-20:00, Fri 11:30-15:00, Kapitelgasse 11, mobile 0660-257-5588).

Youthful Cafés at the West End of the Old Town

Bar Club Café Republic, a hip hangout for local young people opposite the base of the Mönchsberg elevator, feels like a theater lobby during intermission. It serves good food both outdoors and in (with both smoking- and non-smoking rooms inside). It's ideal if you want something mod, untouristy, and un-wursty (Asian and international menu, €9-15 main courses, lots of hard drinks, open daily 8:00-late, trendy breakfasts served 8:00-18:00, Sun brunch with live music 10:00-14:00, music with a DJ Fri and Sat from 23:00, salsa dance club Tue night from 21:00—no cover, Anton-Neumayr-Platz 2, tel. 0662/841-613).

Afro Cafe, between Getreidegasse and the Mönchsberg elevator, is a hit with local students. Its agenda: to put a fun spin on African cuisine (adapted to European tastes). It serves tea, coffee, cocktails, and tasty food with a dose of '70s funk and a healthy sense of humor. The menu includes pan-African specialties—try the spicy chicken couscous—as well as standard salads (€7 weekday lunch specials, €10-15 main courses, Mon-Sat 9:00-24:00, closed Sun, between Getreidegasse and cliff face at Bürgerspitalplatz 5, tel. 0662/844-888).

Carpe Diem is a project by the local Donald Trump, Red Bull tycoon Dietrich Mateschitz. Salzburg's beautiful people, fueled by Red Bull, present themselves here in the chic ground-floor café and trendy "lifestyle bar," which serves quality cocktails and fine finger food in cones. Upstairs is a restaurant boasting a Michelin star (restaurant closed Sun, otherwise whole place open daily 8:30-late, Getreidegasse 50, tel. 0662/848-800).

On the Cliffs Above the Old Town

Riding the Mönchsberg elevator from the west end of the old town up to the clifftop deposits you near two very different eateries: the chic Mönchsberg 32 at the modern art museum, and the Gasthaus Stadtalm Café at the funky old mountaineers' hut—each with commanding city views.

Mönchsberg 32 is a sleek, modern café/bar/restaurant overlooking Salzburg from the top of the Mönchsberg elevator. Even if you're not hiking anywhere, this makes for a great place to enjoy a drink and the view (daily 9:00-24:00, closed Mon off-season, popular breakfast place daily 9:00-16:00, buy a one-way elevator ticket—they give customers a free pass to descend, tel. 0662/841-000).

Gasthaus Stadtalm Café, in Salzburg's mountaineers' hut, sits high above the old town on the edge of the cliff with cheap prices, good traditional food, and great views. If hiking across the Mönchsberg, make this a stop (€10-12 main dishes, €9-10 salads, cliff-side garden seating or cozy-mountain-hut indoor seating—one indoor view table is booked for a decade of New Year's celebrations, daily 10:00-18:00, June-Aug until 23:00, hours are weather-dependent, 5 minutes from top of Mönchsberg elevator, also reachable by stairs from Toscaninihof, Mönchsberg 19C, tel. 0662/841-729, Peter).

Eating Cheaply in the Old Town

Fisch Krieg Restaurant, on the river where the fishermen used to sell their catch, is a great value. They serve fast, fresh, and inexpensive fish in a casual dining room—where trees grow through the ceiling—as well as great riverside seating (€2.30 fishwiches to go, €7.50 self-serve main courses, salad bar, Mon-Fri 8:30-18:30, Sat 8:30-13:00, closed Sun, Hanuschplatz 4, tel. 0662/843-732).

Toscana Cafeteria Mensa is the students' lunch canteen, fast and cheap—with indoor seating and a great courtyard for sitting outside with students and teachers instead of tourists. Choose between two daily soup- and main-course specials, each around €5 (Mon-Thu 8:30-17:00, Fri 8:30-15:00, hot meals served 11:00-13:30 only, closed Sat-Sun, behind the Old Residenz, in the courtyard opposite Sigmund-Haffner-Gasse 16).

Sausage stands *(Würstelstände)* serve the town's favorite "fast food." The best stands (like those on Universitätsplatz) use the same boiling water all day, which gives the weenies more flavor. For a list of helpful terms, see page 26. The Salzburgers' favorite spicy sausage is sold at the 60-year-old **Balkan Grill,** run by chatty Frau Ebner (€3; survey the five spicy options—described in English—and choose a number; takeaway only, steady and sturdy local crowd, daily 11:00-19:00, hours vary with demand, hiding down the tunnel at Getreidegasse 33 across from Eisgrotte).

Picnics: Picnickers will appreciate the well-stocked **Billa supermarket** at Griesgasse 19a, just across the street from the recommended Fisch Krieg Restaurant (Mon-Fri 7:15-19:30, Sat 7:15-18:00, closed Sun). The bustling morning **produce market**

(Mon-Sat, closed Sun) on Universitätsplatz, behind Mozart's Birthplace, is fun, but expensive.

Away from the Center

Augustiner Bräustübl, a huge 1,000-seat beer garden within a monk-run brewery in the Kloster Mülln, is rustic and raw. On busy nights, it's like a Munich beer hall with no music but the volume turned up. When it's cool outside, you'll enjoy a historic setting

inside beer-sloshed and smoke-stained halls. On balmy evenings, it's like a Renoir painting—but with beer breath—under chestnut trees. Local students mix with tourists eating hearty slabs of schnitzel with their fingers or cold meals from the self-serve picnic counter, while children frolic on the playground kegs. For your beer: Pick up a half-liter or full-liter mug, pay the lady (*schank* means self-serve price, *bedienung* is the price with waiter service), wash your mug, give Mr. Keg your receipt and empty mug, and you will be made happy. Waiters only bring beer; they don't bring food—instead, go up the stairs, survey the hallway of deli counters, and assemble your own meal (or, as long as you buy a drink, you can bring in a picnic). Classic pretzels from the bakery and spiraled, salty radishes make great beer even better. For dessert—after a visit to the strudel kiosk—enjoy the incomparable floodlit view of old Salzburg from the nearby Müllnersteg pedestrian bridge and a riverside stroll home (open daily 15:00-23:00, Augustinergasse 4, tel. 0662/431-246).

Getting There: It's about a 15-minute walk along the river (with the river on your right) from the Staatsbrücke bridge. After passing the Müllnersteg pedestrian bridge, just after Café am Kai, follow the stairs up to a busy street, and cross it. From here, either continue up more stairs into the trees and around the small church (for a scenic approach to the monastery), or stick to the sidewalk as it curves around to Augustinergasse. Either way, your goal is the huge yellow building. Don't be fooled by second-rate gardens serving the same beer nearby.

North of the River, near Recommended Linzergasse Hotels

Spicy Spices is a trippy vegetarian-Indian restaurant where Suresh Syal (a.k.a. "Mr. Spicy") serves tasty curry and rice, samosas, organic salads, vegan soups, and fresh juices. It's a *namaste* kind of place, where everything's proudly organic (€6.50 specials served all day, €8 with soup or salad, Mon-Fri 10:30-21:30, Sat-Sun 12:00-21:30, takeout available, Wolf-Dietrich-Strasse 1, tel. 0662/870-712).

Biergarten die Weisse, close to the hotels on Rupertgasse and away from the tourists, is a longtime hit with the natives. If a beer hall can be happening, this one—modern yet with antlers—is it. Their famously good beer is made right there; favorites include their fizzy wheat beer *(Weisse)* and their seasonal beers (on request). Enjoy the beer with their good, cheap traditional food in the great garden seating, or in the wide variety of indoor rooms—sports bar, young and noisy, or older and more elegant (€10-13 main courses, Mon-Sat 10:00-24:00, closed Sun, Rupertgasse 10, east of Bayerhamerstrasse, tel. 0662/872-246).

Café Bazar, overlooking the river between the Mirabell Gardens and the Staatsbrücke bridge, is as close as you'll get to a Vienna coffee house in Salzburg. Their outdoor terrace is a venerable spot for a classy drink with an Old-Town-and-castle view (light meals, Mon-Sat 7:30-23:00, Sun 9:00-18:00, Schwarzstrasse 3, tel. 0662/874-278).

Steingasse Pub Crawl

For a fun post-concert activity, drop in on a couple of atmospheric bars along medieval Steingasse (described on page 302). This is a local and hip scene—yet is accessible to older tourists: dark bars filled with well-dressed Salzburgers lazily smoking cigarettes and talking philosophy to laid-back tunes (no hip-hop). These four places are all within about 100 yards of each other. Start at the Linzergasse end of Steingasse. As they are quite different, survey all before choosing your spot (all open until the wee hours).

Pepe Cocktail Bar, with Mexican decor and Latin music, serves Mexican snacks *con* cocktails (nightly 19:00-3:00 in the morning, live DJs Fri-Sat from 19:00, Steingasse 3, tel. 0662/873-662).

Saiten Sprung wins the "Best Atmosphere" award. After midnight, the door is kept closed to keep out the crude and rowdy. Just ring the bell and enter its hellish interior—lots of stone and red decor, with mountains of melted wax beneath age-old candlesticks and an ambience of classic '70s and '80s music. Stelios, who speaks English with Greek charm, serves cocktails and fine wine, though no food (nightly 21:00-4:00 in the morning, Steingasse 11, tel. 0662/881-377).

Fridrich, just next door, is an intimate little place under an 11th-century vault, with lots of mirrors and a silver ceiling fan. Bernd Fridrich is famous for his martinis and passionate about Austrian wines, and has a tattered collection of vinyl that seems hell-bent on keeping the 1970s alive. Their Yolanda cocktail (grapefruit and vodka) is a favorite. He and his partner Ferdinand serve little dishes designed to complement the focus on socializing and drinking, though their €12 "little of everything dish" can be a meal for two (€5-12 plates, Thu-Mon from 18:00 in summer, from 17:00 in winter, closed Wed, Steingasse 15, tel. 0662/876-218).

Selim's Bar, with cozy seating both inside and out, has a cool, conversation-friendly atmosphere with mellow music (Mon-Sat 17:00-late, also open Sun in summer and during festival, across street from cinema at Steingasse 10, mobile 0664-433-844).

Salzburg Connections

By Train

Salzburg's train station, located so close to the German border, is covered not just by Austrian railpasses, but German ones as well—including the Bayern-Ticket (see page 385).

From Salzburg by Train to: Berchtesgaden (roughly hourly, 1-1.5 hours, change in Freilassing, faster and prettier by bus—see below), **Reutte** (every two hours, 4.5-5.5 hours, quickest with changes in Garmisch and Munich), **Hallstatt** (hourly, 50 minutes to Attnang-Puchheim, 20-minute wait, then 1.5 hours to Hallstatt; also works well by bus—see below), **Innsbruck** (hourly, direct, 2 hours), **Vienna** (3/hour, 2.75-3 hours), **Munich,** Germany (2/hour, 1.5-2 hours), **Nürnberg,** Germany (hourly with change in Munich, 3 hours), **Ljubljana,** Slovenia (6/day, 4.25-5 hours, some with change in Villach), **Prague,** Czech Republic (8/day, 6.5-7.5 hours, 1-2 changes, no decent overnight connection), **Interlaken,** Switzerland (9/day, 7.5-8 hours, 2-3 changes), **Florence,** Italy (4/day, 8.5-9 hours, 2 changes, overnight options), **Venice,** Italy (7/day, 7-8 hours, 2-3 changes). Train info: Tel. 051-717 (to get an operator, dial 2, then 2), www. oebb.at.

By Bus

To reach **Berchtesgaden,** bus #840 is easier than the train (almost hourly Mon-Fri, 6/day Sat-Sun, 45 minutes, buses leave across from Salzburg train station and also stop in Mirabellplatz and near Mozartplatz).

The bus trip to **Hallstatt** via Bad Ischl is cheaper, more scenic (with views of the Wolfgangsee), and no slower than the train via Attnang-Puchheim—but the bus trip isn't covered by railpasses (bus #150 to Bad Ischl—Mon-Fri nearly hourly at :15 past the hour, fewer buses Sat-Sun, 1.5 hours, leaves from platform F outside Salzburg train station, also stops at

Mirabellplatz and Hofwirt, tel. 0810-222-333, www.postbus. at; at Bad Ischl station, change to the train—25-minute ride to Hallstatt, then ride the boat across the lake—or continue by bus to the Lahn section of Hallstatt with a change in Gos- aumühle).

Route Tips for Drivers

From Salzburg to Innsbruck: To leave town driving west, go through the Mönchsberg tunnel and follow blue A-1 signs for Mu- nich. It's 1.5 hours from Salzburg to Innsbruck.

From Salzburg to Hallstatt: Get on the Munich-Vienna autobahn (follow blue A-1 signs), head for Vienna, exit at Thal- gau (#274), and follow signs to Hof, Fuschl, and St. Gilgen. The Salzburg-Hallstatt road passes two luge rides (see Hallstatt chap- ter), St. Gilgen (pleasant but touristy), and Bad Ischl (the center of the Salzkammergut, with a spa, the emperor's villa if you need a Habsburg history fix, and a good TI, tel. 06132/277-570).

BERCHTESGADEN, GERMANY

This alpine ski town, just across the border from Salzburg in a finger of German territory that pokes south into Austria, is famous for its fjord-like lake and its mountaintop Nazi retreat. Long before its association with Hitler, Berchtesgaden (BERKH-tehs-gah-dehn) was one of the classic Romantic corners of Germany. In fact, Hitler's propagandists capitalized on the Führer's love of this region to establish the notion that the native Austrian was truly German at heart. Today visitors cruise up the romantic Königssee to get in touch with the soul of Bavarian Romanticism; ride a bus up to Hitler's mountain retreat (5,500 feet); see the remains of the Nazis' elaborate last-ditch bunkers; and ride an old miners' train into the mountain to learn all about salt mining in the region.

Getting There

Berchtesgaden is only 15 miles from Salzburg. The quickest way there **from Salzburg** is by bus #840 from the Salzburg train station (runs almost hourly Mon-Fri, 6/day Sat-Sun, usually at :15 past the hour, 45 minutes, buy tickets from driver, €9.80 *Tageskarte* day pass covers your round trip plus most local buses in Berchtesgaden—except bus #849 up to the Eagle's Nest, last bus back leaves Berchtesgaden Mon-Fri at 18:15, Sat-Sun at 19:15; check schedules at www.svv-info.at—click "Route Planner and Pricing," under "Find a timetable" select "Timetable book page," then enter "840"). On my last visit, bus #840 left from platform G across the street from the Salzburg train station (beyond the bike racks). You can also catch bus #840 from the middle of Salzburg—after leaving the station, it stops a few minutes later on Mirabellplatz, and then in Salzburg's old town (on Rudolfskai, near Mozartplatz).

Planning Your Time

The Nazi and Hitler-related sites outside Berchtesgaden are the town's main draw. Berchtesgaden also has salt mines (similar to the Hallein salt mine tour—see page 306) and a romantic, pristine lake called Königssee (extremely popular with less-adventurous Germans). Plan on a full day from Salzburg, including the drive or bus ride there and back. Drivers and those taking bus tours from Salzburg can do everything in one busy day trip; otherwise I'd skip the salt mines (which take about two hours to visit) and possibly the lake trip. If you're visiting Berchtesgaden on your way between Salzburg and points in Germany, you can leave luggage in lockers at the Berchtesgaden train station during your visit.

Remote little Berchtesgaden (pop. 7,500) can be inundated with Germans during peak season, when you may find yourself in a traffic jam of tourists desperately trying to turn their money into fun.

Orientation to Berchtesgaden

Buses from Salzburg to Berchtesgaden stop in front of the town's train station, which—though sorely dilapidated—is worth a stop for its luggage lockers (along the train platform), WC (free, also near platform), and history (specifically, its vintage 1937 Nazi architecture and the murals in the main hall). The oversized station was built to accommodate (and intimidate) the hordes of Hitler fans who flocked here in hopes of seeing the Führer. The building next to the station, just beyond the round tower, was Hitler's own V.I.P. reception area.

Tourist Information

The TI is across from the train station, in the yellow building with green shutters (mid-June-Sept Mon-Fri 8:30-18:00, Sat 9:00-17:00, Sun 9:00-15:00; Oct-mid-June Mon-Fri 8:30-17:00, Sat 9:00-12:00, closed Sun; German tel. 08652/9670, from Austria call 00-49-8652-9670, www.berchtesgadener-land.info). Pick up a local map, and consider the 30-page local-bus schedule *(Fahrplan)* if you'll be hopping more than one bus.

Getting Around Berchtesgaden

None of the sights I list are within easy walking distance from the station, but they're all connected by convenient local buses, which use the station as a hub (all these buses—except shuttle bus #849 between the Obersalzberg Documentation Center and the Eagle's Nest chalet—are free with the *Tageskarte* day pass from Salzburg; timetables at www.rvo-bus.de, or call 08652/94480). You'll want

BERCHTESGADEN

to note departure times and frequencies while still at the station, or pick up a schedule at the TI.

From the train station, buses #840 (the same line as the bus from Salzburg) and #837 go to the salt mines (a 20-minute walk otherwise). Bus #838 goes to the Obersalzberg Documentation Center, and bus #841 goes to the Königssee.

Tours in Berchtesgaden

Eagle's Nest Historical Tours—For 20 years, David and Christine Harper—who rightly consider this visit more an educational opportunity than simple sightseeing—have organized thoughtful tours of the Hitler-related sites near Berchtesgaden. Their bus tours, always led by native English speakers, depart from the TI, opposite the Berchtesgaden train station. Tours start by driving through the remains of the Nazis' Obersalzberg complex, then visit the bunkers underneath the Documentation Center, and end with a guided visit to the Eagle's Nest (€50/person, €1 discount with this book, English only, daily at 13:15 mid-May-late Oct, 4 hours, 30 people maximum, reservations strongly recommended, private tours available, German tel. 08652/64971, from Austria call 00-49-8652-64971, www.eagles-nest-tours.com). While the price is €50, your actual cost for the guiding is only about €23, as the tour takes care of your transport and admissions, not to mention relieving you of having to figure out the local buses up to Obersalzberg. Coming from Salzburg, you can take the 10:15 or 11:15 bus to Berchtesgaden, eat a picnic lunch, take the tour, then return on the 18:15 bus from Berchtesgaden (Sat-Sun at 19:15), which gets you back to Salzburg 45 minutes later. If you're visiting near the beginning or end of the season, be aware that tours will be cancelled if it's snowing at the Eagle's Nest (as that makes the twisty, precipitous mountain roads too dangerous to drive). David and Christine also arrange off-season tours, though the Eagle's Nest isn't open for visitors in winter (€100/up to 4 people; see website for details).

Bus Tours from Salzburg—**Bob's Special Tours,** based in Salzburg, bring you to (but not into) all the sights described here (Eagle's Nest, Obersalzberg Documentation Center, salt mines, Königssee) on one busy full-day trip in a minibus (€90, doesn't include €15.50 bus up to the Eagle's Nest, €10 discount with this book, half-day Eagle's Nest-only options available, tel. 0662/849-511, mobile 0664-541-7492, www.bobstours.com). **Panorama Tours,** which usually runs larger buses, also offers half-day excursions to the Eagle's Nest (€50, €5 discount with this book, tel. 0662/874-029 or 0662/883-2110, www.panoramatours.com). While these tours offer all-in-one convenience, the experience is more rushed than you would be on your own, and they don't visit the bunkers.

Sights in Berchtesgaden

▲▲▲Nazi Sites near Berchtesgaden

Early in his career as a wannabe tyrant, Adolf Hitler had a radical friend who liked to vacation in Berchtesgaden, and through him Hitler came to know and love this dramatic corner of Bavaria. Berchtesgaden's part-Bavarian, part-Austrian character held a special appeal to the Austrian-German Hitler. In the 1920s, just out of prison, he

checked into an alpine hotel in Obersalzberg, three miles uphill from Berchtesgaden, to finish work on his memoir and Nazi primer, *Mein Kampf.* Because it was here that he claimed to be inspired and laid out his vision, some call Obersalzberg the "cradle of the Third Reich."

In the 1930s, after becoming the German Chancellor, Hitler chose Obersalzberg to build his mountain retreat, a supersized alpine farmhouse called the Berghof. His handlers crafted Hitler's image here—surrounded by nature, gently receiving alpine flowers from adoring little children, lounging around with farmers in lederhosen...no modern arms industry, no big-time industrialists, no ugly extermination camps. In reality, Obersalzberg was home to much more than Hitler's alpine chalet. It was a huge compound of 80 buildings—built largely by forced labor and fenced off from the public after 1936—where the major decisions leading up to World War II were hatched. Hitler himself spent about a third of his time at the Berghof, hosted world leaders in the compound, and later had it prepared for his last stand.

Some mistakenly call the entire area "Hitler's Eagle's Nest." But that name actually belongs only to the Kehlsteinhaus, a small mountaintop chalet on a 6,000-foot peak that juts up two miles south of Obersalzberg. (A visiting diplomat humorously dubbed it the "Eagle's Nest," and the name stuck.) In 1939, it was given to the Führer for his 50th birthday. While a fortune was spent building this perch and the road up to it, Hitler, who was afraid of heights, visited only 14 times. Hitler's mistress, Eva Braun, though, liked to hike up to the Eagle's Nest to sunbathe.

In April of 1945, Britain's Royal Air Force bombed the Obersalzberg compound nearly flat, but missed the difficult-to-target Eagle's Nest entirely. In 1952, the Allies blew up almost all of what had survived the bombing at Obersalzberg; before turning the site over to the German government, they wanted to destroy anything that might attract future neo-Nazi pilgrims. The most extensive surviving remains are of the Nazis' bunker system, intended to serve as a last resort for the regime as the Allies closed in. In the 1990s, a museum, the Obersalzberg Documentation Center, was built on top of one of the bunkers. The museum and bunker, plus the never-destroyed Eagle's Nest, are the two Nazi sites worth seeing near Berchtesgaden.

Obersalzberg Documentation Center and Bunker—To reach the most interesting part of this site, walk through the museum and down the stairs into the vast and complex bunker system. Construction began in 1943, after the Battle of Stalingrad ended the Nazi aura of invincibility. This is a professionally engineered underground town, which held meeting rooms, offices, archives for the government, and lavish living quarters for Hitler—all connected by four miles of tunnels cut through solid rock by slave labor. You can't visit all of it, and what you can see was stripped and looted bare after the war. But enough is left that you can wander among the concrete and marvel at megalomania gone mad.

The museum above, which has almost no actual artifacts, is designed primarily for German students and others who want to learn and understand their still-recent history. There's little English, but you can rent the €2 English audioguide.

Cost and Hours: €3 covers both museum and bunker; April-Oct daily 9:00-17:00; Nov-March Tue-Sun 10:00-15:00, closed Mon; last entry one hour before closing, allow 1.5 hours for visit, German tel. 08652/947-960, from Austria tel. 00-49-8652-947-960, www.obersalzberg.de.

Getting There: Hop on bus #838 from Berchtesgaden's train station (Mon-Fri almost hourly, Sat-Sun 6/day, 12 minutes, 5-minute walk from Obersalzberg stop).

Eagle's Nest (Kehlsteinhaus)—Today, the chalet that Hitler ignored is basically a three-room, reasonably priced restaurant with a scenic terrace, 100 yards below the summit of a mountain. You could say it's like any alpine hiking hut, just more massively built. On a nice day, the views are magnificent. If it's fogged in (which it often is), most people won't find it worth coming up here (except on David and Christine Harper's tours—de-

scribed earlier—which can make the building come to life even without a view). Bring a jacket, and prepare for crowds in summer (less crowded if you go early or late in the day).

From the upper bus stop, a finely crafted tunnel (which will have you humming the *Get Smart* TV theme song) leads to the original polished brass elevator, which takes you the last 400 feet up to the Eagle's Nest. Wander into the fancy back dining room (the best-preserved from Hitler's time), where you can see the once-sleek marble fireplace chipped up by souvenir-seeking troops in 1945.

Cost and Hours: Free, generally open mid-May-late Oct, snowfall sometimes forces a later opening or earlier closing.

Getting There: The only way to reach the Eagle's Nest—even if you have your own car—is by specially equipped bus #849, which leaves from the Documentation Center and climbs steeply up the one-way, private road—Germany's highest (every 25 minutes, 15 minutes, €15.50 round-trip, *Tageskarte* day passes not valid, buy ticket from windows, last bus up 16:00, last bus down 16:50, free parking at Documentation Center).

▲Salt Mines (Salzbergwerk Berchtesgaden)

At the Berchtesgaden salt mines, you put on traditional miners' outfits, get on funny little trains, and zip deep into the mountain. For two hours (which includes time to get into and back out of your miner's gear), you'll cruise subterranean lakes; slide speedily down two long, slick, wooden banisters; and learn how they mined salt so long ago. Call ahead for crowd-avoidance advice; when the weather gets bad, this place is mobbed. You can buy a ticket early and browse through the town until your appointed tour time. Tours are in German, while English-speakers get audioguides.

Cost and Hours: €15.50, daily May-Oct 9:00-17:00, Nov-April 11:00-15:00—these are last-entry times, German tel. 08652/600-220, from Austria dial 00-49-8652-600-220, www. salzzeitreise.de.

Getting There: The mines are a 20-minute walk or quick bus ride (#837 or #840) from the Berchtesgaden station; ask the driver to let you off at the Salzbergwerk stop. (Since buses coming from Salzburg pass here on the way into Berchtesgaden, you can also simply hop off at the mines before getting into town, instead of backtracking from the station.)

▲Königssee

Three miles south of Berchtesgaden, the idyllic Königssee stretches like a fjord through pristine mountain scenery to the dramatically situated Church of St. Bartholomä and beyond. To get to the lake from Berchtesgaden, hop on bus #841 (about hourly from train station to boat dock), or take the scenically woodsy, reasonably flat 1.25-hour walk (well-signed). Drivers pay €3 to park.

Most visitors simply glide for 35 minutes on the silent, electronically propelled **boat** to the church, enjoy that peaceful setting, then glide back. Boats, going at a sedate Bavarian speed and filled with Germans chuckling at the captain's commentary, leave with demand—generally 2-4 per hour (late April-mid-Oct, no boats off-season, €13.30 round-trip, German tel. 08652/96360, from

Austria dial 00-49-8652-96360, www.seenschifffahrt.de). At a rock cliff midway through the journey, your captain stops, and the first mate pulls out a trumpet to demonstrate the fine echo.

The remote, red-onion-domed **Church of St. Bartholomä** (once home of a monastery, then a hunting lodge of the Bavarian royal family) is surrounded by a fine beer garden, rustic fishermen's pub, and inviting lakeside trails. The family next to St. Bartholomä's lives in the middle of this national park and has a license to fish—so very fresh trout is the lunchtime favorite.

HALLSTATT
and the
SALZKAMMERGUT

Commune with nature in the Salzkammergut, Austria's Lake District. "The hills are alive," and you're surrounded by the love-liness that has turned on everyone from Emperor Franz Josef to Julie Andrews. This is *Sound of Music* country. Idyllic and majestic, but not rugged, it's a gentle land of lakes, forested mountains, and storybook villages, rich in hiking opportunities and inexpensive lodging. Settle down in the postcard-pretty, lake-cuddling town of Hallstatt. While there are plenty of lakes and charming villages in the Salzkammergut, Hallstatt is really the only one that matters.

Planning Your Time

Hallstatt serves as a relaxing break between Vienna and Salzburg. One night and a few hours to browse are all you'll need to fall in love. To relax or take a hike in the surroundings, give it two nights and a day.

Orientation to Hallstatt

Lovable Hallstatt (HAHL-shtaht) is a tiny town bullied onto a ledge between a selfish mountain and a swan-ruled lake, with a waterfall ripping furiously through its middle. It can be toured on foot in about 15 minutes. Salt veins in the mountain rock drew people here centuries before Christ. The symbol of Hallstatt, which you'll see all over town, consists of two adjacent spirals—a design based on jewelry found in Bronze Age Celtic graves high in the nearby mountains.

Hallstatt has two parts: the tightly packed medieval town center (which locals call the Markt) and the newer, more car-friendly Lahn, a few minutes' walk to the south. A lakeside promenade connects the old center to the Lahn. The tiny "main" boat dock (a.k.a.

Market Dock), where boats from the train station arrive, is in the old center of town. Another boat dock is in the Lahn, next to Hallstatt's bus stop and grocery store.

The charms of Hallstatt are its village and its lakeside setting. Come here to relax, nibble, wander, and paddle. While tourist crowds can trample much of Hallstatt's charm in August, the place is almost dead in the off-season. The lake is famous for its good fishing and pure water.

Tourist Information

At the helpful TI, Teresa and the other staff can explain hikes and excursions, and find you a room (July-Aug Mon-Fri 9:00-18:00, Sat-Sun 9:00-15:00; Sept-June Mon-Fri 9:00-13:00 & 14:00-17:00, closed Sat-Sun; one block from Market Square, across from museum at Seestrasse 169, tel. 06134/8208, www.dachstein-salzkammergut.at).

In the summer, the TI offers 1.5-hour **walking tours** of the town in English and German (€4, mid-May-Sept Sat at 10:00). They can also arrange private tours (€95), or you can use an audioguide to explore (€5, €50 deposit).

Arrival in Hallstatt

By Train: If you're coming on the main train line that runs between Salzburg and Vienna, you'll change trains at Attnang-Puchheim to get to Hallstatt (you won't see Hallstatt on the schedules, but any train to Ebensee and Bad Ischl will stop at Hallstatt). Day-trippers can check their bags at the Attnang-Puchheim station (follow signs  for *Schliessfächer*, coin-op lockers are at the street, curbside near track 1, €2-3.50/24 hours). Note: Connections can be fast—check the TV monitor.

Hallstatt's train station is a wide spot on the tracks across the lake from town. *Stefanie* (a boat) meets you at the station and glides scenically across the lake to the old town center (€2.40, meets each train until 18:50—don't arrive after that, www.hallstattschifffahrt.at). The last departing boat-train connection leaves Hallstatt at 18:15, and the first boat goes in the morning at 6:50 (8:50 Sat-Sun).

Once in Hallstatt, walk left from the boat dock to reach the TI; you're steps away from the hotels in the old center and a 15-minute walk from accommodations in the Lahn.

By Bus: Hallstatt's bus stop is by the boat dock in the Lahn. It takes 15 minutes to walk from the bus stop into the old center along the lakeside path.

By Car: The main road skirts Hallstatt via a long tunnel above the town. Gates close off traffic to the old center during the daytime. As you approach town, electronic signs direct you to available spots in three parking areas. If you are staying at a hotel in the old town, drive to lot P1 (€9/day, reserved for hotel guests). Choose "Hotelticket" at the gate when you enter and hang onto your ticket—you'll need it when you leave. To reach your hotel, go to the Hotel-Shuttle Info-Point in the lot, tell the attendant (or the intercom) where you're staying, and hop on the free shuttle, which will drop you at or near your hotel. You can also use this shuttle when you depart; ask your hotelier for details. When you leave the lot, pay at the machine. (If you're staying at one of my recommended accommodations in the Lahn, you can park right at the hotel—all have free parking.)

If you're day-tripping, head to one of the other parking areas. P2 is a shorter walk to the old town center (€7/3-12 hours; www. hallstatt.net/parking-in-hallstatt/cars).

Helpful Hints

Internet Access: Try **Hallstatt Umbrella Bar** (€4/hour, summers only, weather permitting—since it's literally under a big umbrella, halfway between the old center and the Lahn along the lake at Seestrasse 145). For free Wi-Fi, drop by the café at the recommended **Heritage Hotel.**

Laundry: The staff of the **campground** in the Lahn will wash and dry (but not fold) your clothes for €8/load (drop off mid-April-mid-Oct daily 8:00-10:00 & 16:00-18:00, pick up in afternoon or next morning, closed off-season, tel. 06134/83224). In the center, the recommended **Hotel Grüner Baum** does laundry for non-guests (€13/load, on Market Square).

Boat Rental: Two places rent electric boats from two locations in high season. **Riedler** is next to the main boat dock and 75 yards past Bräugasthof (€13/hour, tel. 06134/20619). **Hemetsberger** is near Gasthof Simony and by the Lahn boat dock (€12/hour, tel. 06134/8228). Both are open daily until 19:00 in peak season and in good weather. Boats have two speeds: slow and stop. Spending an extra €3/hour gets you a faster, 500-watt boat. Both places also rent rowboats and paddleboats (slightly cheaper).

Dirndl Rental: If you feel compelled to re-enact the *Sound of Music,* **Dirndl to Go** rents authentic versions of these traditional dresses by the hour (€22/first hour, €6/hour after that, May-Oct Wed-Sun 13:00-18:00, closed Mon-Tue and

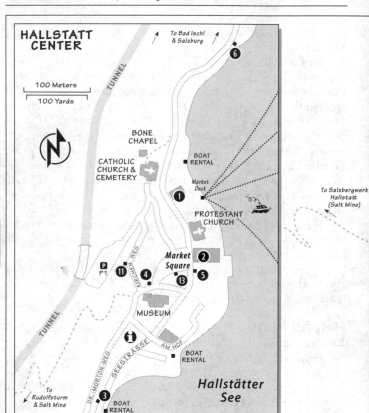

HALLSTATT CENTER

HALLSTATT

100 Meters
100 Yards

TUNNEL

To Bad Ischl
& Salzburg

6

BONE CHAPEL

CATHOLIC CHURCH & CEMETERY

BOAT RENTAL

Market Deck

1

PROTESTANT CHURCH

To Salzbergwerk
Hallstatt
(Salt Mine)

KIRCHEN WEG

P
P1

11

Market Square

4

13

2

5

MUSEUM

AM HOF

SEESTRASSE

DR. MORTON WEG

BOAT RENTAL

To
Rudolfsturm
& Salt Mine

3

BOAT RENTAL

Hallstätter See

ECHERNTAL

ECHERNTALWEG

1 Heritage Hotel
2 Hotel/Rest. Grüner Baum
3 Bräugasthof Hallstatt
4 Gasthof Zauner
5 Gasthof Simony
  & Rest. Am See
6 Pension Sarstein
7 Gasthof Pension
  Grüner Anger
8 Helga Lenz Rooms
9 Haus Trausner
10 Herta Höll Rooms
11 Gasthaus zur Mühle
   Hostel & Pizza
12 Pizzeria Bella Milano
13 Ruth Zimmerman Pub
14 Internet Access
15 Campground
   (Laundry Service)

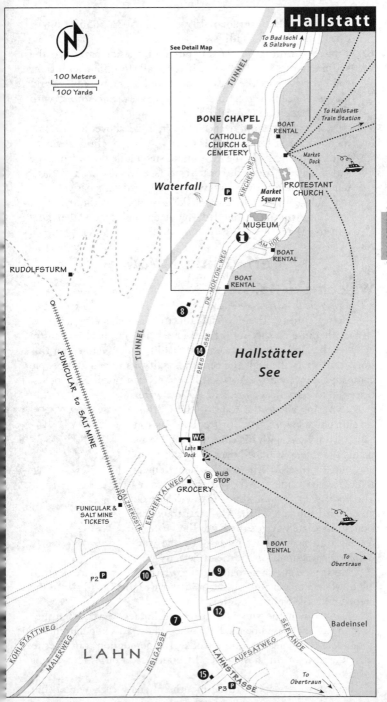

Hallstatt

Nov-April, Badergraben 189, tel. 06503/666503, www.
dirndl-to-go.at, Claudia).

Parks and Swimming: Green and peaceful lakeside parks line the
south end of Lake Hallstatt. If you walk 15 minutes south of
the old center to the Lahn, you'll find a grassy public park,
playground, mini-golf, and swimming area *(Badestrand)* with
the fun Badeinsel play-island.

Views: For a great view over Hallstatt, hike above the recommended Helga Lenz B&B as far as you like, or climb any path
leading up the hill. The 40-minute steep hike down from the
salt-mine tour gives the best views (see "Sights in Hallstatt,"
later). While most visitors stroll the lakeside drag between the
old and new parts of town, make a point to do the trip once
by taking the more higgledy-piggledy high lane called Dr.-
Morton-Weg.

Self-Guided Walk

Welcome to Hallstatt

• *This short walk starts at the dock.*

Boat Landing: There was a Hallstatt before there was a Rome.
In fact, because of the importance of salt mining here, an entire
epoch—the Hallstatt Era, from 800 to 400 B.C.—is named for this
important spot. Through the centuries, salt was traded and people
came and went by boat. You'll still see the traditional *Fuhr* boats,
designed to carry heavy loads in shallow water.

Towering above the town is the **Catholic church.** Its faded St. Christopher—patron
saint of travelers, with his cane and baby Jesus
on his shoulder—watched over those sailing in
and out. Until 1875, the town was extremely
remote...then came a real road and the train.
The good ship *Stefanie* shuttles travelers back
and forth from here to the Hallstatt train station, immediately across the lake. The *Bootver-
leih* sign advertises boat rentals. By the way,
Schmuck is not an insult...it means jewelry.

Notice the one-lane road out of town (below the church). Until
1966, when a bigger tunnel was built above Hallstatt, all the traffic
crept single-file right through the town.

Look down the shore at the huge homes. Several families
lived in each of these houses, back when Hallstatt's population was
about double its present 1,000. Today, the population continues to
shrink, and many of these generally underused houses rent rooms
to visitors.

Hallstatt gets about three months of snow each winter, but

the lake hasn't frozen over since 1981. See any swans? They've patrolled the lake like they own it since the 1860s, when Emperor Franz Josef and Empress Sisi—the Princess Diana of her day (see page 145)—made this region their annual holiday retreat. Sisi loved swans, so locals

made sure she'd see them here. During this period, the Romantics discovered Hallstatt, many top painters worked here, and the town got its first hotel (now the Heritage Hotel).

Tiny Hallstatt has two big churches: Protestant (bordering the square on the left, with a grassy lakeside playground) and Catholic (up above, with its fascinating bone chapel).

• *Walk over the town's stream, and pop into the...*

Protestant Church: The Catholic Counter-Reformation was very strong in Austria, but pockets of Protestantism survived, especially in mining towns like Hallstatt. In 1860, Emperor Franz Josef finally allowed non-Catholic Christians to build churches. Before that, they were allowed to worship only in low-key "houses of prayer." In 1863, Hallstatt's miners pooled their humble resources and built this fine church. Step inside (free and often open). It's very plain, emphasizing the pulpit and organ rather than fancy art and saints. Check out the portraits: Martin Luther (left of altar), the town in about 1865 with its new church (left wall), and a century of pastors.

• *Continue past the church to the...*

Market Square (Marktplatz): In 1750, a fire leveled this part of town. The buildings you see now are all late 18th-century structures built of stone rather than flammable wood. The three big buildings on the left are government-subsidized housing (mostly for seniors and people with health problems). Take a close look at the two-dimensional, up-against-the-wall pear tree (it likes the sun-warmed wall). The statue features the Holy Trinity.

• *Continue a block past Gasthof Simony. At*

the first corner, just before the Gemeindeamt *(City Hall), jog left across the little square and then right down the tiny lane marked* Am Hof, *which leads through an intimate bit of domestic town architecture, boat houses, lots of firewood, and maybe a couple of swans hanging out. The lane circles back to the main drag and the...*

Museum Square: Because 20th-century Hallstatt was of no industrial importance, it was untouched by World War II. But once upon a time, its salt was worth defending. High above, peeking out of the trees, is Rudolfsturm (Rudolf's Tower). Originally a 13th-century watchtower protecting the salt mines, and later the mansion of a salt-mine boss, it's now a restaurant with a great view. A zigzag trail connects the town with Rudolfsturm and the salt mines just beyond. The big, white houses by the waterfall were water-powered mills that once ground Hallstatt's grain. (If you hike up a few blocks, you'll see the river raging through town.)

Around you are the town's TI, post office, museum, City Hall, and Dachstein Sport Shop (described later). A statue recalls the mine manager who excavated prehistoric graves in about 1850. Much of the *Schmuck* sold locally is inspired by the jewelry found in the area's Bronze Age tombs.

The memorial wooden stairs in front of the museum are a copy of those found in Hallstatt's prehistoric mine—the original stairs are more than 2,500 years old. For thousands of years, people have been leaching salt out of this mountain. A brine spring sprung here, attracting Bronze Age people in about 1600 B.C. Later, they dug tunnels to mine the rock (which was 70 percent salt), dissolved it into a brine, and distilled out the salt—precious for preserving meat. For a look at early salt-mining implements and the town's story, visit the museum (described later).

Across from the TI, Pension Hallberg has a quirky hallway full of Nazi paraphernalia and other stuff found on the lake bed (€1). Only recently did local divers realize that, for centuries, the lake had been Hallstatt's garbage can. If something was *kaputt*, locals would just toss it into the lake. In 1945, Nazi medals decorating German and Austrian war heroes suddenly became dangerous to own. Throughout the former Third Reich, hard-earned medals floated down to lonely lake beds, including Hallstatt's.

Under the TI is the "Post Partner"—a government-funded attempt to turn inefficient post offices into something more viable (selling souvenirs, renting bikes, and employing people with disabilities who otherwise wouldn't work). The *Fischerei* provides the town with its cherished fresh lake fish. The county allows two commercial fishermen on the lake. They spread their nets each morning and sell their catch here to town restaurants, or to any locals cooking up a special dinner (Mon-Fri 9:00-12:00, closed Sat-Sun).

• *Nearby, still on Museum Square, find the...*

Dachstein Sport Shop: During a renovation project, the builders dug down and hit a Celtic and ancient Roman settlement. Peek through the glass pavement on the covered porch to see where the Roman street level was. If the shop is open, pop in and go downstairs (free). You'll walk on Roman flagstones and see the small gutter that channeled water to power an ancient hammer mill (used to pound iron into usable shapes). In prehistoric times, people lived near the mines. Romans were the first Hallstatt lakeside settlers. The store's owners are committed to sharing Hallstatt's fascinating history, and often display old town paintings and folk art.

• *From this square, the first right (after the bank) leads up a few stairs to...*

Dr.-Morton-Weg: House #26A dates from 1597. Follow the lane uphill to the left past more old houses. Until 1890, this was the town's main drag, and the lake lapped at the lower doors of these houses. Therefore, many main entrances were via the attic, from this level. Enjoy this back-street view of town. Just after the arch, near #133, check out the old tools hanging outside the workshop, and the piece of wooden piping. It's a section taken from the 25-mile wooden pipeline that carried salt brine from Hallstatt to Ebensee. This was in place from 1595 until the last generation, when the last stretch of wood was replaced by plastic piping. At the pipe, enjoy the lake view and climb down the stairs. From lake level, look back up at the striking traditional architecture (the fine woodwork on the left was recently rebuilt after a fire; parts of the old house on the right date to medieval times).

• *Your tour is finished. From here, you have boat rentals, the salt-mine tour, the town museum, and the Catholic church (with its bone chapel) all within a few minutes' walk.*

Sights in Hallstatt

▲▲**Catholic Church and Bone Chapel**—Hallstatt's Catholic church overlooks the town from above. The lovely church has twin altars. The one on the left was made by town artists in 1897. The one on the right is more historic—dedicated in 1515 to Mary, who's flanked by St. Barbara (on right, patron of miners) and St. Catherine (on left, patron of foresters—a lot of wood was needed to fortify the many miles of tunnels, and to boil the brine to distill the salt).

Behind the church, in the well-tended graveyard, is the 12th-century Chapel of St. Michael

(even older than the church). Its bone chapel—or charnel house *(Beinhaus)*—contains more than 600 painted skulls. Each skull has been lovingly named, dated, and decorated (skulls with dark, thick garlands are oldest—18th century; those with flowers are more recent—19th century). Space was so limited in this cemetery that bones had only 12 peaceful, buried years here before making way for the freshly dead. Many of the dug-up bones and skulls ended up in this chapel. They stopped this practice in the 1960s, about the same time the Catholic Church began permitting cremation. But one woman (who died in 1983) managed to sneak her skull in later (dated 1995, under the cross, with the gold tooth). The skulls on the books are those of priests.

Cost and Hours: €1.50, free English flier, daily May-Sept 10:00-18:00, Oct 10:00-16:00, closed Nov-April, tel. 06134/8279.

Getting There: From near the main boat dock, hike up the covered wooden stairway and follow the *Kath. Kirche* signs.

▲**Hallstatt Museum**—This pricey but high-quality museum tells the story of Hallstatt. It focuses on the Hallstatt Era (800-400 B.C.), when this village was the salt-mining hub of a culture that spread from France to the Balkans. Back then, Celtic tribes dug for precious salt, and Hallstatt was, as its name means, the "place of salt." The highlight of the museum is the countless number of artifacts excavated from prehistoric gravesites around the mine. The museum also offers a five-minute 3-D movie and 26 displays on everything from the region's flora and fauna to local artists and the surge in Hallstatt tourism during the Romantic Age. Everything is labeled in English, and the ring binders have translations of the longer texts.

Cost and Hours: €7.50, May-Sept daily 10:00-18:00, shorter hours off-season, closed Mon-Tue Nov-March, adjacent to TI at Seestrasse 56, tel. 06134/828-015, www.museum-hallstatt.at. On Thursdays in summer, when candlelit boats run, the museum stays open until 20:00 (see "Nightlife in Hallstatt," later).

▲**Lake Trip**—For a quick boat trip, you can ride the *Stefanie* across the lake and back for €4.80. It stops at the tiny Hallstatt train station for 30 minutes (note return time in the boat's window), giving you time to walk to a hanging bridge (ask the captain to point you to the *Hängebrücke*—HENG-eh-brick-eh—a 10-minute lakeside stroll to the left). Longer lake tours are also available (€9/50 minutes, €10/75 minutes, sporadic schedules—especially off-season—so check chalkboards by boat docks for today's times). Those into relaxation can rent a sleepy electric motorboat to enjoy town views from the water.

▲**Salt-Mine Tour**—If you have yet to tour a salt mine, consider visiting Hallstatt's, which claims to be the oldest in the world. The presentation is very low-tech, as the mining company owns all three mine tours in the area and sees little reason to invest in the experience when they can simply mine the tourists. Still, it gives an interesting look at mining through the centuries and culminates with a fun banister slide.

Cost and Hours: €24 combo-ticket includes mine and funicular round-trip, €18 for mine tour only, €2 audioguide (leave ID as deposit), buy all tickets at funicular station—note the time and tour number on your ticket, daily May-mid-Sept 9:00-16:00, mid-Sept-Oct 9:00-14:30, later funicular departures miss the last tour of the day, closed Nov-April, no children under age 4, arrive early or late to avoid summer crowds, tel. 06132/200-2400, www.salzwelten.at.

Funicular: You can also just take the funicular without going on the mine tour (€7 one-way, €12 round-trip, 4/hour, daily May-mid-Sept 9:00-18:00, mid-Sept-Oct 9:00-16:30, closed Nov-April). The funicular starts in the Lahn, close to the bus stop and Lahn boat dock.

Visiting the Mine: After riding the funicular above town, you'll hike 10 minutes to the mine (past excavation sites of many prehistoric tombs and a glass case with 2,500-year-old bones—but there's little to actually see). Report to the mine 10 minutes before the tour time on your ticket, check your bag, and put on old miners' clothes. Then hike 200 yards higher in your funny outfit to meet your guide, who escorts your group down a tunnel that was dug in 1719.

Inside the mountain, you'll watch a slide show, follow your guide through several caverns as you learn about mining techniques over the last 7,000 years, see a silly laser show on a glassy subterranean lake, peek at a few waxy cavemen with pickaxes, and ride the train out. The highlight for most is sliding down two banisters (the second one is longer and ends with a flash for an automatic souvenir photo that clocks your speed—see how you did compared to the rest of your group after the tour).

While the tour is mostly in German, the guide is required to speak English if you ask...so ask. Be sure to dress for the constant 47-degree temperature.

Returning to Hallstatt: If you skip the funicular down, the steep and scenic 40-minute hike back into town is (with strong knees) a joy. At the base of the funicular, notice the train tracks leading to the Erbstollen tunnel entrance. This lowest of the salt tunnels goes many miles into the mountain, where a shaft connects it to the tunnels you just explored. Today, the salty brine from these tunnels flows 25 miles through the world's oldest pipeline—made of wood until quite recently—to the huge modern salt works (next to the highway) at Ebensee.

▲**Local Hikes**—Mountain-lovers, hikers, and spelunkers who use Hallstatt as their home base keep busy for days (ask the TI for ideas). A good, short, and easy walk is the two-hour round-trip up the Echern Valley to the Waldbachstrub waterfall and back: From the parking lot, follow signs to the salt mines, then follow the little wooden signs marked *Echerntalweg*. With a car, consider hiking around nearby Altaussee (flat, 3-hour hike) or along Grundlsee to Toplitzsee. Regular buses connect Hallstatt with Gosausee for a pleasant hour-long walk around that lake. Or consider walking nine miles halfway around Lake Hallstatt via the town of Steeg (boat to train station, walk left along lake and past idyllic farmsteads, returning to Hallstatt along the old salt trail, *Soleleitungsweg*); for a shorter hike, walk to Steeg along either side of the lake, and catch the train from Steeg back to Hallstatt's station. The TI can also recommend a great two-day hike with an overnight in a nearby mountain hut.

Biking—The best two bike rides take nearly the same routes as the hikes listed previously: up the Echern Valley and around the lake (bikers do better going via Obertraun along the lakeside bike path—start with a ride on the *Stefanie*). There's no public bike rental in Hallstatt, but some hotels have loaner bikes for guests.

Near Hallstatt

▲▲Dachstein Mountain Cable Car and Caves

From Obertraun, three miles beyond Hallstatt on the main road (or directly across the lake as the crow flies), a cable car glides up to the Dachstein Plateau. Along the way, you can hop off to tour two different caves: the refreshingly chilly Giant Ice Caves and the less-impressive Mammoth Caves.

Getting to Obertraun: The cable car to Dachstein leaves from the outskirts of Obertraun. To reach the cable car from Hallstatt, the handiest and cheapest option is the bus (€1.70, 5-6/day, leaves from Lahn boat dock, drops you directly at cable-car station). Romantics can take the boat from Hallstatt's main boat dock to Obertraun (€5.50, 5/day July-Aug, 3/day in June and Sept, 30 minutes, www. hallstattschifffahrt.at)—but it's a 40-minute hike from there to the lift station. The impatient can consider hitching a ride—virtually all cars leaving Hallstatt to the south will pass through Obertraun in a few minutes.

Returning to Hallstatt: Plan to leave by mid-afternoon. The last bus from the cable-car station back to Hallstatt (at 17:05 in summer) inconveniently leaves before the last cable car down—if you miss the bus, try getting a ride from a fellow cable-car passenger. Otherwise, you can either call a taxi (€13, ask cable-car staff for help) or walk back along the lakefront (about one hour).

Dachstein Cable Car—From Obertraun, this mighty gondola goes in three stages high up the Dachstein Plateau—crowned by Dachstein, the highest mountain in the Salzkammergut (9,800 ft). The first segment stops at **Schönbergalm** (4,500 ft, runs May-late Oct), which has a mountain restaurant and two huge caves (described next). The second segment goes to the summit of **Krippenstein** (6,600 ft, runs mid-May-late Oct). The third segment descends to **Gjaidalm** (5,800 ft, runs mid-June-late Oct), where several hikes begin.

For a quick high-country experience, Krippenstein is better than Gjaidalm. Its "five-fingers" viewpoint features metal walkways that extend out from the mountain (not for the faint of heart). From Krippenstein, you get 360-degree views of the surrounding mountains and a good look at the scrubby, limestone, karstic landscape (which absorbs, through its many cracks, the rainfall that ultimately carves all those caves).

Cost and Hours: €26, last cable car back down usually at about 17:00, tel. 06131/50140, www.dachstein-salzkammergut. com.

Cable Car and Caves Combo-Tickets: Several combo-tickets are available for the cable car and caves. The round-trip cable-car ride to Schönbergalm, including entrance to one of the caves, is €27. The €33 combo-ticket includes the cable car and entry to both caves. If you're gung-ho enough to want to visit both caves and ride the cable car farther up the mountain, the €39 same-day, all-inclusive ticket makes sense (covers the cable car all the way to Gjaidalm and back, as well as entry to both caves). Cheaper family rates are available.

Giant Ice Caves (Riesen-Eishöhle)—Located near the Schönbergalm cable-car stop (4,500 ft), these caves were discovered in 1910. Today, guides lead tours in German and English on an hour-long, half-mile hike through an eerie, icy, subterranean world, passing limestone canyons the size of subway stations.

At the Schönbergalm lift station, report to the ticket window

HALLSTATT

Salzkammergut

See Near Berchtesgaden map

GERMANY

Freilassing

TRAIN
STATION

Salzburg

A-8

To
Munich

Untersberg

Hallein

305

Berchtesgaden

Kehlstein

HITLER'S
EAGLE'S
NEST

Königssee

Königssee

A-1

Mondsee

Fuschlsee

Mondsee

LUGE

Schafberg

St. Gilgen

St. Wolfgang

Wolfgangsee

AUSTRIA

158

A-10

162

166

Bischofshofen

To Innsbruck 311

To Italy

to get your cave appointment. Drop by the little free museum near the lift station—in a local-style wood cabin designed to support 200 tons of snow—to see the cave-system model, exhibits about its exploration, and info about life in the caves. Then hike 10 minutes from the station up to the cave entry. The temperature is just above freezing, and although the 700 steps help keep you warm, you'll want to bring a sweater. The limestone caverns, carved by rushing

HALLSTATT

water, are named for scenes from Wagner's operas—the favorite of the mountaineers who first came here. If you're nervous, note that the iron oxide covering the ceiling takes 5,000 years to form. Things are very stable. Allow 1.5 hours total from the station.

Cost and Hours: €27 includes cable car, various combo-tickets available (described earlier), open May-late Oct, hour-long tours start at 9:20, last tour at 15:30, stay in front and assert your-self to get English information, tel. 06131/50140.

Mammoth Caves (Mammuthöhle)—While huge and well-pro-moted, these are much less interesting than the ice caves and—for most—not worth the time. Of the 30-mile limestone labyrinth excavated so far, you'll walk a half-mile with a German-speaking guide.

Cost and Hours: €27 includes cable car, various combo-tickets available (described earlier), open May-late Oct, hour-long tours in English and German 10:15-14:30, entrance a 10-minute hike from lift station.

Summer Luge Rides (Sommerrodelbahnen) on the Hallstatt-Salzburg Road

If you're driving between Salzburg and Hall-statt, you'll pass two luge rides operated by the same company (www.rodelbahnen.at). Each is a ski lift that drags you backward up the hill as you sit on your go-cart. At the top, you ride the cart down the winding metal course. It's easy: Push to go, pull to stop, take your hands off your stick and you get hurt. For more details, see "Luge Lesson" on page 428.

Each course is just off the road with easy parking. The ride up and down takes about 15 minutes. The one in **Fuschl am See** (closest to Salzburg, look for *Sommerrodelbahn* sign) is half as long and cheaper (1,970 ft). The one in **Strobl** near Wolfgangsee (look for *Riesenschutzbahn* sign) is a dou-ble course, and more scenic with grand lake views (4,265 ft, each track is the same speed). These are fun, but the concrete courses near Reutte are better (see page 428).

Cost and Hours: Fuschl am See—4.30/ride, €30/10 rides, tel. 06226/8452; Strobl—€6.40/ride, €45/10 rides, tel. 06137/7085; courses open May-Oct 10:00-18:00 but generally closed in bad weather.

Nightlife in Hallstatt

Locals would laugh at the thought. But if you want some action after dinner, you do have a few options: **Gasthaus zur Mühle** is a youth hostel with a rustic sports-bar ambience in its restaurant when drinks replace the food (open late, closed Tue Sept-mid-May, run by Ferdinand). Or, for your late-night drink, savor the Mar-ket Square from the trendy little pub called **Ruth Zimmermann,** where locals congregate with soft music, a good selection of drinks, two small rooms, and tables on the square (daily May-Sept 10:00-2:00 in the morning, Oct-April 11:00-2:00, mobile 0664/501-5631). From late July to late August, **candlelit boat rides** leave at 20:30 on Thursday evenings (€13.50, €16 combo-ticket with Hallstatt Museum).

Sleeping in Hallstatt

Hallstatt's TI can almost always find you a room (either in town or at B&Bs and small hotels outside of town—which are more likely to have rooms available and come with easy parking). If you are arriving by car and have a reservation for a place in the old town, head directly to parking lot P1, where you'll catch a shuttle to your hotel (see page 339).

Mid-July and August can be tight. Early August is worst. Hallstatt is not the place to splurge—some of the best rooms are in *Gästezimmer*, just as nice and modern as rooms in bigger hotels, at half the cost. In summer, a double bed in a private home costs about €50 with breakfast. It's hard to get a one-night advance reservation (try calling the TI for help). But if you drop in and they have a spot, one-nighters are welcome. Prices include breakfast, lots of stairs, and a silent night. *"Zimmer mit Aussicht?"* (TSIM-mer mit OWS-zeekt) means "Room with view?"—worth asking for. Unlike many businesses in town, the cheaper places don't take credit cards.

As most rooms here are in old buildings with well-cared-for wooden interiors, dripping laundry is a no-no at Hallstatt pensions. Be especially considerate when hanging laundry over anything but tile—if you must wash larger clothing items here, ask your host about using their clothesline.

$$$ Heritage Hotel, next to the main boat dock, is the town's fanciest place to stay. It has 34 rooms with modern furnishings in a lakeside main building with an elevator; uphill are another 20 rooms in two separate buildings for those willing to climb stairs for better views (Sb-€150, Db-€209, free sauna, free cable Internet in rooms and Wi-Fi in lobby, laundry service-€13, Landungsplatz 120, tel. 06134/20036, fax 06134/20042, www.hotel-hallstatt.com, info@hotel-hallstatt.com).

$$$ Hotel Grüner Baum, on the other side of the church from the main boat dock, has a great location, fronting Market Square and overlooking the lake in back. The owner, Monika, moved here from Vienna and renovated this stately—but still a bit creaky—old hotel

HALLSTATT

Sleep Code

(€1 = about $1.30, country code: 43, area code: 06134)
S = Single, **D** = Double/Twin, **T** = Triple, **Q** = Quad, **b** = bathroom, **s** = shower only. Unless otherwise noted, credit cards are accepted, English is spoken, and breakfast is included.

To help you sort easily through these listings, I've divided the rooms into three categories, based on the price for a standard double room with bath:

$$$ **Higher Priced**—Most rooms €100 or more.
$$ **Moderately Priced**—Most rooms between €70-100.
$ **Lower Priced**—Most rooms €70 or less.

Prices can change without notice; verify the hotel's current rates online or by email.

with urban taste. Its 22 rooms are huge, each with a separate living area and ancient hardwood floors, but you may not need so much space and the high price that comes with it (suite-like Db-€140-210, price depends on view, 8 percent discount with this book, family rooms, Internet access in restaurant, laundry service-€13, closed in Nov, 20 yards from boat dock, tel. 06134/82630, fax 06134/826-344, www.gruenerbaum.cc, contact@gruenerbaum.cc).

$$$ Bräugasthof Hallstatt is like a museum filled with antique furniture and ancient family portraits. This former brewery, now a good restaurant, rents eight clean, cozy upstairs rooms. It's run by Virena and her daughter, Virena. Six of the rooms have gorgeous little lakeview balconies (Sb-€65, Db-€105, Tb-€155, just past TI along lake at Seestrasse 120, tel. 06134/8221, fax 06134/82214, www.brauhaus-lobisser.com, info@brauhaus-lobisser.com, Lobisser family).

$$$ Gasthof Zauner is run by a friendly mountaineer, Herr Zauner, whose family has owned it since 1893. The 13 pricey, pine-flavored rooms near the inland end of Market Square are decorated with sturdy alpine-inspired furniture (sealed not with lacquer but with beeswax, to let the wood breathe out its calming scent). Lederhosen-clad Herr Zauner recounts tales of local mountaineering lore, including his own impressive ascents (Sb-€63, Db-€108, lakeview Db-€116, cheaper mid-Oct-April, Internet access in office, closed Nov-early Dec, Marktplatz 51, tel. 06134/8246, fax 06134/82468, www.zauner.hallstatt.net, zauner@hallstatt.at).

$$$ Gasthof Simony is a well-worn, grandmotherly, 12-room place on the square, with a lake view, balconies, ancient beds, creaky wood floors, slippery rag rugs, antique furniture, and a lakefront garden for swimming. Reserve in advance, and call if arriving late (S-€45, D-€65, Ds-€70, Db-€105, third person-€20 extra, cash only, free Wi-Fi in lobby, kayaks for guests, Marktplatz 105, tel. & fax 06134/8231, www.gasthof-simony.at, info@gasthof-simony.at, Susanna Scheutz and family).

$$ Pension Sarstein is a big, flower-bedecked house right on the water on the edge of the old center. Its seven renovated rooms are bright, and all have lakeview balconies. You can swim from its plush and inviting lakeside garden (D-€55, Db-€70, Tb-€90; apartments with kitchen: Db-€65, Tb-€90, Qb-€100, apartment prices don't include breakfast; €3 extra per person for 1-night stay, cash only, free Wi-Fi in lobby, 200 yards to the right of the main boat dock at Gosaumühlstrasse 83, tel. 06134/8217, www.pension-sarstein.at.tf, pension.sarstein@aon.at, helpful Isabelle and Klaus Fischer).

$$ Gasthof Pension Grüner Anger, in the Lahn near the bus station and base of the funicular, is practical and modern. It's big and quiet, with 11 rooms and no creaks or squeaks. There are mountain views, but none of the lake (Sb-€43-48, Db-€76-90, third person-€20, price depends on season, non-smoking, free Internet access and Wi-Fi, free loaner bikes, free parking, Lahn 10, tel. 06134/8397, fax  06134/83974, www.anger.hallstatt.net, anger@aon.at, Sulzbacher family). If arriving by train, have the boat captain call Herr Sulzbacher, who will pick you up at the dock. They run a good-value restaurant, too, with discounts for guests.

$ Helga Lenz rents two fine *Zimmer* a steep five-minute climb above Dr.-Morton-Weg (look for the green *Zimmer* sign). This large, sprawling, woodsy house has a nifty garden perch, wins the "Best View" award, and is ideal for those who sleep well in tree houses and don't mind the steps up from town (Db-€52, Tb-€78, €2 more per person for one-night stay, cash only, family room, closed Nov-March, Hallberg 17, tel. 06134/8508, www.hallstatt.net/lenz, haus-lenz@aon.at).

$ Two *Gästezimmer* are a few minutes' stroll south of the center, just past the bus stop/parking lot and over the bridge. **Haus Trausner** has three clean, bright, new-feeling rooms adjacent to the Trausner family home (Ds/Db-€50, 2-night minimum for reservations, cash only, breakfast comes to your room, free parking, Lahnstrasse 27, tel. 06134/8710, trausner1@aon.at, charming Maria Trausner makes you want to settle right in). **Herta Höll** rents out three spacious, modern rooms on the ground floor of her riverside house crawling with kids (Db-€50, apartment for up to

HALLSTATT

five-€60-90, €2 more per person for one-night stay, cash only, free parking, free cable Internet, Salzbergstrasse 45, tel. 06134/8531, fax 06134/825-533, frank.hoell@aon.at).

$ *Hostel:* **Gasthaus zur Mühle Jugendherberge,** below the waterfall and along the gushing town stream, has 46 of the cheapest good beds in town (bed in 3- to 8-bed coed dorms-€16, twin D-€32, family quads, sheets-€4 extra, breakfast-€6, big lockers with a €15 deposit, free Wi-Fi, closed Nov, reception closed Tue Sept-mid-May—so arrange in advance if arriving on Tue, below P1 tunnel parking lot, Kirchenweg 36, tel. & fax 06134/8318, toeroe-f@hallstatturlaub.at, Ferdinand Törö). It's also popular for its great, inexpensive pizza (described later).

Eating in Hallstatt

In this town, when someone is happy to see you, they'll often say, "Can I cook you a fish?" While everyone cooks the typical Austrian fare, fish is your best bet here. *Reinanke* (whitefish) is caught wild out of Lake Hallstatt and served the same day. *Saibling* (lake trout) is also tasty and costs less. You can enjoy good food inexpensively, with delightful lakeside settings. Restaurants in Hallstatt tend to have unreliable hours and close early on slow nights, so don't wait too long to get dinner. Most of the eateries listed here are run by recommended hotels.

Restaurant Bräugasthof, on the edge of the old center, is a good value. The indoor dining room is cozy in cool weather. On a balmy evening, its great lakeside tables offer the best ambience in town— you can feed the swans while your trout is being cooked (€10-20 main courses, daily May-Oct 11:30-late, closed Nov-April, Seestrasse 120, tel. 06134/8221).

Hotel Grüner Baum is a more upscale option, with elegant (and often slow) service at tables overlooking the lake inside and out (€15-25 main courses, daily Dec-Oct 8:00-22:00, closed Nov, at bottom of Market Square, tel. 06134/8263).

Gasthof Simony's Restaurant am See serves Austrian cuisine on yet another gorgeous lakeside terrace, as well as indoors (€12-16 main courses, Thu-Tue 11:30-20:00, until 21:00 June-Sept and on winter weekends, closed Wed, tel. 06134/20646).

Gasthaus zur Mühle serves the best pizza in town. Chow down cheap and hearty here with fun-loving locals and the youth-hostel crowd. Note that smoking is allowed here (€8 pizza, lots of

Italian, some Austrian, Wed-Mon in summer 16:00-21:00, closed Tue, Kirchenweg 36, tel. 06134/8318, Ferdinand).

Pizzeria Bella Milano, in the Lahn area, is a local favorite and a good option after visiting the salt mines or going swimming. To-go meals are available if you want to eat by the lake. They serve mainly pizzas and Italian dishes, along with some Austrian options (€7-10 main courses, daily 11:00-22:00, Lahn 41, tel. 06134/20037).

Picnics and Cheap Eats: The **Zauner** bakery/butcher/grocer, great for picnickers, makes fresh sandwiches to go (Tue-Fri 7:00-12:00 & 15:00-18:00, Sat and Mon 7:00-12:00, closed Sun, uphill to the left from Market Square). The only **supermarket** is Konsum, in the Lahn at the bus stop (Mon-Fri 7:30-12:00 & 15:00-18:00, Sat 7:30-12:00, closed Sun, July-Aug no midday break and until 17:00 on Sat, Sept-April closed Wed). **Snack stands** near the main boat dock and the Lahn boat dock sell *Döner Kebab* and so on for €3 (tables and fine lakeside picnic options nearby).

Hallstatt Connections

By Public Transportation

From Hallstatt by Train: Most travelers leaving Hallstatt are going to Salzburg or Vienna. In either case, you need to catch the shuttle boat (€2.40, departs 15 minutes before every train) to the little Hallstatt train station across the lake, and then ride 1.5 hours to **Attnang-Puchheim** (hourly from about 7:00 to 18:00). Trains are synchronized, so after a short wait in Attnang-Puchheim, you'll  catch your onward connection to **Salzburg** (50 minutes) or **Vienna** (2.5 hours). The Hallstatt station has no staff or ticket machines, but you can buy tickets from the conductor without a penalty. In town, your hotel or the TI can help you find schedule information, or check www.oebb.at. Train info: tel. 051-717 (to get an operator, dial 2, then 2).

By Bus to Salzburg: The bus ride from Hallstatt to Salzburg is cheaper and more scenic than the train, and only slightly slower. You can still start off from Hallstatt by rail, taking the boat across the lake to the station and then the train toward Attnang-Puchheim—but get off after about 20 minutes in **Bad Ischl,** where you catch bus #150 to Salzburg (€8.80, Mon-Fri almost hourly, less Sat-Sun).

Alternatively, you can reach Bad Ischl by bus from the Hallstatt bus stop (€4.20, change in Gosaumühle) and then catch bus #150 to Salzburg. The Hallstatt TI has a schedule. In Salzburg, bus #150 stops at Hofwirt and Mirabellplatz (convenient to Linzergasse hotels) before ending at the Salzburg train station.

Route Tips for Drivers

Hallstatt to Vienna, via Mauthausen, Melk, and Wachau Valley (210 Miles): Leave Hallstatt early. Follow the scenic Route 145 through Gmunden to the autobahn and head east. After Linz, take exit #155 at Enns, and follow the signs for *Mauthausen* (five miles from the freeway). Go through Mauthausen town and follow the *Ehemaliges KZ-Gedenkstätte Lager* signs. When leaving Mauthausen for Melk, enjoy the riverside drive along scenic Route 3 (or take the autobahn if you're in a hurry or prone to carsickness). At Melk, signs to *Stift Melk* lead to the abbey. Other *Melk* signs lead into the town.

From Melk (get a Vienna map at the TI), cross the river again (signs to *Donaubrücke*) and stay on Route 3. After Krems, the riverside route (now the S-5) hits the autobahn (A-22), and you'll barrel right into Vienna's traffic. (See "By Car—Route Tips for Drivers" in the Vienna Connections chapter for details, page 218.)

Vice Versa: For tips on doing the above trip in reverse (Vienna to Wachau to Mauthausen to Hallstatt), see "Wachau Valley Connections" on page 358.

From Salzburg: For tips for drivers coming here from Salzburg, see the end of the Salzburg chapter.

TIROL

INNSBRUCK and HALL

Tirol—in Austria's panhandle, south of Bavaria—is a winter sports mecca known for its mountainous panoramas. In the region's capital, Innsbruck, the Golden Roof glitters—but drivers strike it rich by staying in neighboring Hall, which has twice the charm and none of the tourist crowds.

Innsbruck

Innsbruck is world-famous as a resort for skiers and a haven for hikers...but when compared to the music and architecture of Salzburg and Vienna, it's stale strudel. Still, a quick look is easy and interesting. Innsbruck was the capital of Tirol under the Habsburgs, and its medieval center—now a glitzy, tourist-filled pedestrian zone—still gives you the feel of a provincial medieval capital. The much-ogled Golden Roof is the centerpiece, and there's an alpine peak in every view.

Orientation to Innsbruck

Tourist Information

Innsbruck has two TIs: the main office **downtown** (daily 9:00-18:00, Burggraben 3, three blocks in front of Golden Roof, tel. 0512/5356, www.innsbruck.info) and a mini-office inside the **train station** bookstore (July-Aug daily 9:00-19:00; Sept-June Mon-Sat 10:00-18:00, closed Sun; tel. 0512/583-766). At either one, you can pick up a free city map (the €1 map, with more information on sights, isn't necessary). They can also help you find a room.

Innsbruck Card: The €31, 24-hour Innsbruck Card pays for

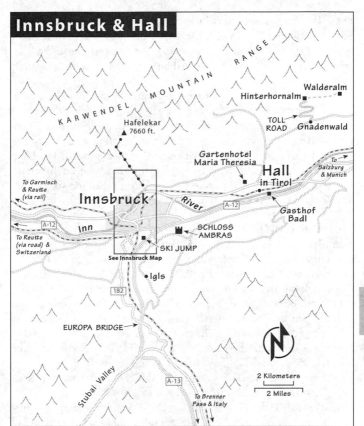

Innsbruck & Hall

KARWENDEL MOUNTAIN RANGE

Hafelekar
▲ 7660 ft.

Walderalm ▪

Hinterhornalm ▪

TOLL ROAD

Gnadenwald ▪

Gartenhotel
Maria Theresia ▪

To Garmisch
& Reutte
(via rail)

Innsbruck

River

Hall
in Tirol

A-12

To Salzburg
& Munich

A-12

To Reutte
(via road) &
Switzerland

Inn

Gasthof
Badl ▪

SCHLOSS
AMBRAS

▪ SKI JUMP

See Innsbruck Map

● Igls

182

EUROPA BRIDGE ◀

Stubai Valley

A-13

To Brenner
Pass & Italy

N

2 Kilometers

2 Miles

itself if you take in four major sights and connect them with the bus or Sightseer minibus (easy to do, since the card is valid 24 hours and covers public transportation, including local funiculars, cable cars, and other lifts). You could validate it in the early afternoon, visit two sights, climb the Stadtturm tower, and do two more the next day before your 24 hours expire. If you see only one sight and ride the lifts to the top of the Hafelekar and back, you'd still save money buying this pass. The Innsbruck Card is sold at the TI and most participating sights, and includes the Mint Museum in Hall (but not the Mint Tower).

Walking Tours: The TI offers a basic one-hour city walk of Innsbruck (€8, free with Innsbruck Card, daily at 14:00, July-Sept also daily at 11:00).

Arrival in Innsbruck

By Train: Some trains stop at Innsbruck's Westbahnhof, but stay on the train until you reach the main train station (Hauptbahnhof). The main station has lockers (€2-4.50), a post office (Mon-Fri 7:00-19:00, Sat 8:00-13:00, closed Sun), a supermarket (daily 6:00-21:00), a TI (inside the bookstore—see earlier), and a *Reisezentrum,* where you can get rail information and tickets (daily 6:30-20:45).

From the station, it's a 10-minute walk to the old town center. As you exit, walk to the right end of the square in front of the station (toward the building with the clock tower). Once there, turn left on Brixnerstrasse. Follow it past the fountain at Boznerplatz, where it turns into Meranerstrasse, and go straight until it dead-ends into Maria-Theresien-Strasse. Turn right and head 300 yards into the old town. You'll pass the TI on Burggraben (on your right), and then Hotel Weisses Kreuz and the Golden Roof.

Helpful Hints

Laundry and Internet Access: Bubblepoint is a handy self-service launderette (€4/load plus €1/10 minutes for dryer, Internet access-€2/hour, Mon-Fri 8:00-21:00, Sat-Sun 8:00-20:00, a block toward Golden Roof from train station at Brixnerstrasse 1, tel. 0512/5650-0750, www.bubblepoint.com). You can also get online (but not wash your skivvies) at **Call On Me,** in the center of town (€3/hour, daily 12:00-23:00, at the end of Herzog-Friedrich-Strasse—between Golden Roof and river, tel. 0512/574-952). To save a little money, walk a few minutes more to Call On Me's second café (€2/hour, between Maria-Theresien-Strasse and the river at Innrain 20).

Bike Rental: I-Bike, operated by Die Börse bike shop, is Innsbruck's best option for bike rentals. It has a good range of choices, from city cruisers (€18/day) to mountain bikes (€25/day). They'll drop off and pick up the bike at your city-center hotel (inquire about costs). Visit their shop, near the Triumphal Arch, to get fitted for the proper bike before your ride (Mon-Fri 9:00-18:30, Sat-Sun 9:00-17:00, closed Sun if bad weather; Leopoldstrasse 4, in the back courtyard, tel. 0512/581-742, www.i-bike.at). Die Börse is also a good contact for any adventure sports you might want to do (such as bungee jumping).

Getting Around Innsbruck

You won't need transportation if you're sticking to Innsbruck's compact medieval center. If you're headed beyond town (to the Bergisel ski jump, for example), the city's easy-to-use trams and buses are the cheapest way to go. A single ticket costs €1.90; a day ticket is €4.30. Buy tickets from the machine at the tram stop, train station, or the TI; single tickets can also be purchased from the driver (www.ivb.at).

A made-for-tourists minibus called the **Sightseer** follows two popular routes around town, connecting the key sights (€3 for any one-way trip, €6.30 for whole day, covered by Innsbruck Card, minimal headphone commentary in English, May-Oct 1-2/hour 9:00-17:30, Nov-April hourly 10:00-17:00, www.sightseer.at). If visiting several outlying sights, you can buy the Sightseer day ticket (*Tagesticket,* includes transportation on the city bus system) and use the Sightseer as a hop-on, hop-off bus. It's pricey—nearly twice the cost of a day pass on public transit—and runs less frequently, but some find it more convenient (for information and tickets, visit the TI, or buy directly from driver).

Sights in Innsbruck

In the Old Town

▲▲**The Golden Roof (Goldenes Dachl) and Herzog-Friedrich-Strasse**—The three-block pedestrian street (Herzog-Friedrich-Strasse) in front of the Golden Roof is Innsbruck's tourism central.

Stand in front of the Roof to get oriented. Emperor Maximilian I loved Innsbruck, and he built a palace here—including the balcony topped with 2,657 gilded copper tiles. The **Golden Roof** (1494) offered Maximilian an impressive spot from which to view his medieval spectacles.

Most buildings along this street are Gothic (notice the entry arches), but across the street from the Golden Roof (to the left as you face the Roof) is the frilly Baroque-style **Helblinghaus** facade. The arcades, common in Tirol, offer shelter from both sun and snow.

Above you is the bulbous **city tower** *(Stadtturm),* with 148 steps you can climb for a great view (€3, daily June-Sept 10:00-20:00, Oct-May 10:00-17:00, tel. 0512/561-500). This was the old town watchtower; a prison was on the second floor. Like many Austrian buildings (including the nearby Hofkirche), the tower originally had a pointy Gothic spire—replaced with this onion-shaped one when Baroque was in vogue.

A block in front of the Golden Roof—next to the McDonald's—is the historic **Hotel Weisses Kreuz.** It's built on Roman foundations, but has only been hosting guests for the last 500 years. The white cross *(weisses Kreuz)* is the symbol of the Order of Malta—knights who

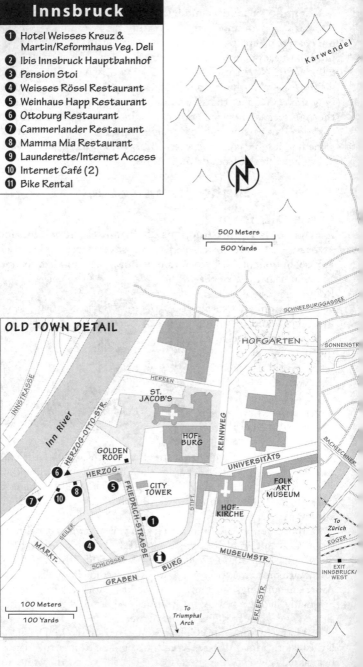

Innsbruck

1. Hotel Weisses Kreuz & Martin/Reformhaus Veg. Deli
2. Ibis Innsbruck Hauptbahnhof
3. Pension Stoi
4. Weisses Rössl Restaurant
5. Weinhaus Happ Restaurant
6. Ottoburg Restaurant
7. Cammerlander Restaurant
8. Mamma Mia Restaurant
9. Launderette/Internet Access
10. Internet Café (2)
11. Bike Rental

Karwendel

500 Meters
500 Yards

SCHNEEBURGGASSEE

OLD TOWN DETAIL

HOFGARTEN

SONNENSTR.

HERREN

ST. JACOB'S

INNSTRASSE

Inn River

HERZOG-OTTO-STR.

HOF-BURG

RENNWEG

BACHLECHNER

GOLDEN ROOF

HERZOG-

CITY TOWER

UNIVERSITÄTS

FOLK ART MUSEUM

FRIEDRICH-STRASSE

STIFT

HOF-KIRCHE

To Zürich

EGGER-

SEILER

MARKT-

SCHLOSSER

BÜRG

MUSEUMSTR.

EXIT INNSBRUCK/WEST

GRABEN

ERLERSTR.

100 Meters
100 Yards

To Triumphal Arch

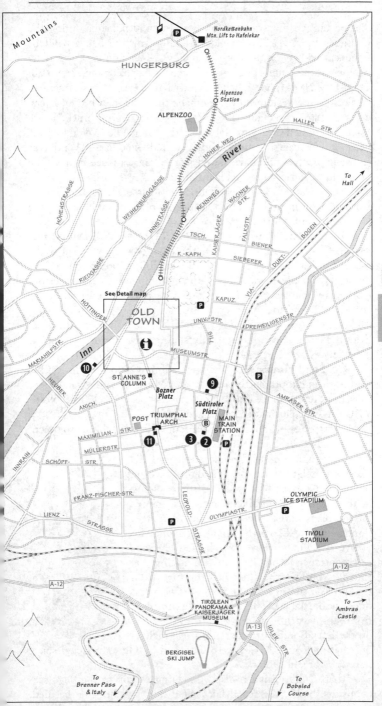

opened up guesthouses for Holy Land-bound pilgrims during the Crusades. In 1769, a 13-year-old Wolfgang Amadeus Mozart and his father stayed here on their way to Italy. A generation later, this hotel was one of the centers of resistance against Napoleon, and later still, against the Nazis (giving shelter to Jewish refugees). When American soldiers moved in from Italy, they made the hotel their headquarters. Today, it's still a functioning hotel (see "Sleeping in Innsbruck," later). It recently hosted Otto von Habsburg, the Man Who Would Be Emperor, if his great-great-uncle hadn't started—and lost—World War I. Though Otto could have stayed in the fanciest place in town, he chose this historic, comfortable inn instead.

If you walk down the shop-lined Hofgasse (facing the Golden Roof, go right), you'll reach the Museum of Tirolean Folk Art, the Hofkirche, and Hofburg palace.

▲▲**Museum of Tirolean Folk Art (Tiroler Volkskunstmuseum)**—This big museum offers the best look anywhere at traditional Tirolean lifestyles. Fascinating exhibits range from wedding dresses and gaily painted cribs and nativity scenes, to maternity clothes and babies' trousers. My favorite part is the carefully reconstructed interiors of several Tirolean homes through the ages. The free electronic text guide (leave ID as deposit) is worthwhile. Scan the barcode near most exhibits, and a description pops up on your device.

Cost and Hours: €10, includes admission to the Hofkirche, the Tirolean Panorama and Kaiserjäger Museum, and several lesser museums; daily 10:00-18:00, Universitätsstrasse 2, tel. 0512/5948-9510, www.tiroler-landesmuseum.at.

▲▲**Hofkirche**—Emperor Maximilian I liked Innsbruck so much, he wanted to be buried here, surrounded by 28 larger-than-life cast-bronze statues of his ancestors, relatives, in-laws...and his favorite heroes of the dying Middle Ages (such as King Arthur). They stand like giant chess pieces on the black-and-white-checkerboard marble floor. The good €1 English book tells you who everyone is, but you have to go back to the museum entrance to buy it. Don't miss King Arthur (as you face the altar, he's the fifth from the front on the right, next to the heavy-metal dude) and Mary of Burgundy, Maximilian's first—and favorite—wife (third from the front on the left). Some of these sculptures, including that of König Artur, were designed by German Renaissance painter Albrecht Dürer.

That's Maximilian himself, kneeling on top of the huge sarcophagus. Sadly, the real Max isn't inside. By the time he died,

Emperor Maximilian I
(1459-1519)

The big name in Innsbruck is Emperor Maximilian I, who made this city a regional capital and built the Golden Roof. This Habsburg emperor was a dynamic, larger-than-life Renaissance man—soldier, sculptor, and statesman (though not very good at any of those pursuits). At the same time, he clung to the last romantic fantasies of the Middle Ages; for example, he was the last Habsburg who personally led his troops into battle. (To see where he fits in among other Habsburgs, see the family tree on page 438.)

Most people associate the Habsburg Empire with Vienna, which was the capital of the empire's Eastern European holdings during its peak in the 17th and 18th centuries. But during Maximilian's time, two centuries earlier, the focus was on Italy—he took the "Roman" part of "Holy Roman Emperor" very seriously. This made Innsbruck very important, since it was the capital of Tirol (which then included much of today's northern Italy and was on the Italian frontier).

This visionary emperor hoped that once all of Italy was his, Innsbruck would become the permanent capital of his empire. In reality, he was unlucky at war and ran up huge debts. But his strategic marriage to Mary of Burgundy set the stage for the large-scale expansion of the empire. Though he wanted to be a war hero, as with most Habsburgs, his biggest victory came with a trip to the altar.

Maximilian had become notorious for running up debts, and his men weren't allowed to bring his body here.

Just inside the door to the church, you'll find the tomb of the popular Tirolean soldier Andreas Hofer, who fought against Napoleon.

Cost and Hours: €5, enter through Museum of Tirolean Folk Art—€10 combo-ticket, includes audioguide, Mon-Sat 10:00-18:00, Sun 12:30-18:00, Universitätsstrasse 2.

Hofburg—This 18th-century Baroque palace, built by Maria Theresa and full of her family portraits, is only worth a visit if you aren't going to the much bigger and better palaces in Vienna. The lone advantage is that, unlike the more famous Habsburg palaces, you'll have this one virtually to yourself. You get to see the empress' reception rooms, her private apartment, and a few rooms of exhibits.

Cost and Hours: €8, €10 combo-ticket includes Alpenverein-Museum, daily 9:00-17:00, Wed until 19:00, last entry 30 minutes before closing, tel. 0512/587-186, www.hofburg-innsbruck.at.

Alpenverein-Museum—Located on the lower floor of the palace, this museum is a somewhat peculiar but sincere exhibit put on by the Austrian Alpine Club. It explores humanity's fascination with mountains and evokes the sensations and emotions of mountaineering (English explanations).

Cost and Hours: €4, €10 combo-ticket includes Hofburg, same hours as palace, tel. 0512/59547, www.alpenverein.at/leidenschaft.

Nearby: Should you need a **Sacher-Torte** fix, opposite the Hofburg entrance you'll find the local outpost of the venerable Viennese institution, Café Sacher (daily 8:30-24:00).

St. James' Cathedral (Dom zu St. Jakob)—Innsbruck's own cathedral is your typical Baroque pastry: pink, frilly, and lots of gold. What makes it unique is that the high altar houses one of Lucas Cranach's best-known Madonna-and-Childs, the *Mariahilf.*

Cost and Hours: Free, Mon-Sat 10:30-18:30, Sun 12:30-18:30, Domplatz 6, tel. 0512/583-902.

Maria-Theresien-Strasse—The fine, Baroque Maria-Theresien-Strasse stretches south from the medieval center, dotted with interesting features.

St. Anne's Column (Annasäule) marks the middle of the old marketplace. This was erected in the 18th century by townspeople thankful that their army had defeated an invading Bavarian army and saved the town (it's the same idea as the plague columns throughout Central Europe).

At the far end of the street, the **Triumphal Arch** is a gate Maria Theresa built to commemorate a happy and a sad occasion. The happy: Her son Leopold II, archduke of Tuscany, met and married a Spanish princess here in Innsbruck—and Maria Theresa and her husband Franz came for the ceremony. But Franz partied a little too hard and died the day after the wedding. (Maria Theresa wore black for the rest of her life.) The south-facing side of the arch—what you see as you approach the center—shows the interlocked rings of the happy couple. But the flipside, visible as you leave town, features mournful statuary.

▲Slap-Dancing (Tyrolerabend)—For your Tirolean folk fun, Innsbruck hotels offer an entertaining evening of slap-dancing and yodeling nearly nightly at 20:30 from April through October (€29 includes a drink with 2-hour show, tickets and info at TI or your hotel). Every summer Thursday, the town puts on a free outdoor folk show under the Golden Roof (July-Sept, weather permitting).

Outer Innsbruck

These sights are within a tram ride of the old town.

▲**Ambras Castle (Schloss Ambras)**—Just southeast of town is the Renaissance palace Archduke Ferdinand II (1529-1595) renovated for his wife (it was originally a medieval castle). Its extensive grounds are replete with manicured gardens, a 17th-century fake waterfall, and resident peacocks. Visit the armory and the "curiosities" collection, containing the archduke's assortment of the beautiful and bizarre (*Kunst- und Wunderkammer*, ranging from stuffed sharks to ancient Portuguese frocks). The beautiful Spanish Hall (built 1569-1572) is clearly the prize of the whole complex. Its intricate wooden ceiling and 27 life-size portraits of Tirolean princes make this a popular venue for classical music concerts.

Cost and Hours: €10, daily 10:00-17:00, Aug until 18:00, closed Nov, audioguide-€3, Schlossstrasse 20; take tram #3 to last stop and then walk 15 minutes, or go direct on the Sightseer; tel. 01/525-244-802, www.khm.at/ambras.

▲**Ski Jump Stadium (Bergisel)**—A modern ski jump stands in the same location as the original one that was used for the 1964 and 1976 Olympics (de-

molished in 2000). With a car, it's an inviting side-trip with a superb view overlooking the city (it can also be worthwhile by public transportation, if you have the time). The jump is interesting, but for mountain thrills, you're better off riding up to the ridge on the other side of the valley (see "Nordkettenbahn up to Hafelekar," later).

For the best view of the jump itself, climb the steps to the Olympic rings under the dishes that held the Olympic flame, where Dorothy Hamill and a host of others who brought home the gold

are honored. Note the thoughtfully placed cemetery just below the jump. To get to the top of the ski jump, you can zip up in a funicular (2-minute ride), then an elevator—or walk up the 455 steps—for a great view and a panoramic café. As you ride the funicular down alongside the jump, imagine yourself speeding down the ramp, then flying into the air...gulp.

Cost and Hours: €9 whether you take funicular or not, €11 combo-ticket with Tirolean Panorama and Kaiserjäger Museum, daily June-Oct 9:00-18:00, Nov-May 10:00-17:00, last entrance 30 minutes before closing, funicular back down runs until 15 minutes after closing, tel. 0512/589-259, www.bergisel.info.

Getting There: Drivers find it just off the Brenner Pass road on the south side of town (follow signs to *Bergisel*). Using **public transportation,** it's an easy tram ride from the center (tram #1, 6/hour) and then a 10-minute uphill walk; near the top of the woodsy path, take the right fork for the ski jump, or the left fork for the Tirolean Panorama and Kaiserjäger Museum (described next). Or you can avoid the walk altogether by taking the pricier Sightseer bus, which drops you near the parking lot for both sights.

▲▲**Tirolean Panorama and Kaiserjäger Museum**—Right by the ski jump is a worthwhile complex of historical exhibits, including the *Cyclorama*, a huge 360-degree painting of Tirol's 1809 victory over Napoleon's forces at Bergisel. Much like Salzburg's similar panorama painting, this one also toured Europe more than a century ago, giving the wider world a sense of Tirolean identity. Make sure to pick up the free audioguide since it will explain the mostly German-captioned exhibits and will also describe important people, history, and artistic licenses within the painting.

Connected underground is the recently renovated Kaiserjäger Museum (admission is part of the same ticket), featuring the region's natural, religious, and political history, with a special focus on its military past (it's dedicated to the Habsburg emperor's 19th-century infantry division). Military-history buffs can groove on paintings of important battles and officers, maps, battle plans, flags, uniforms, weapons, and two rooms honoring Andreas Hofer, the Tirolean hero of the Napoleonic battles.

Cost and Hours: €7, €10 combo-ticket with Museum of Tirolean Folk Art, €11 combo-ticket with Bergisel ski jump, daily 9:00-17:00, mandatory bag check with €1 deposit, Bergisel 1-2 (for directions, see ski jump listing, earlier), tel. 0512/594-312, www.tiroler-landesmuseum.at.

Into the Mountains

A popular mountain-sports center and home of the 1964 and 1976 Winter Olympics, Innsbruck is surrounded by 150 mountain lifts, 1,250 miles of trails, and 250 hikers' huts. Ask your hotel or hostel for a free Club Innsbruck card (different from the Innsbruck Card sold by the TI), which offers overnight guests various discounts, bike tours, and free guided hikes in summer. Hikers meet in front of Congress Innsbruck daily at 8:45; each day, it's a different hike in the surrounding mountains and valleys (bring only lunch and water; boots, rucksack, and transport are provided; confirm with TI).

▲▲▲**Nordkettenbahn up to Hafelekar**—Right from the center of town, a series of three lifts—collectively called the Nordkettenbahn—whisk you above the tree line to the ridge

perched thousands of feet directly above the Golden Roof. This is the fastest and easiest way to get your Tirolean mountain high. It's not cheap, but on a clear day, the trip is worth every euro. If you're going to the top (€27 round-trip), it makes sense to get the Innsbruck Card for €31, which covers your trip, the Alpenzoo (described next), and much more; see page 360.

The first stage, the Hungerburgbahn **funicular,** leaves from the *Star Trek*-esque station outside Congress Innsbruck, right behind the Hofburg, and stops at the Alpenzoo station before reaching the Hungerburg hillside viewpoint (€6.80 round-trip, €11 combo-ticket with Alpenzoo, prices slightly higher in winter, Mon-Fri 7:00-19:30, Sat-Sun 8:00-19:30, every 15 minutes).

From the Hungerburg viewpoint, you'll catch the first of two **cable cars** that lead up into the mountains. The first one gets you to the Seegrube perch (with a reasonably priced self-serve cafeteria—no picnicking allowed); you'll change there for the highest station, Hafelekar, which has a café (round-trip: €27 from Innsbruck, €23 from Hungerburg, zoo not included; last lift down from Hafelekar at 17:00, from Seegrube at 17:30; both run every 15 minutes, cable-car tickets cover parking in Innsbruck's Congress garage).

If you've lucked out on weather, you'll see Innsbruck stretching across the valley to the Bergisel ski jump and, just to its right, the graceful Europa Bridge that leads up the Brenner Pass to Italy, beyond the peaks. Looking down the valley to the left, see if you can spot the town of Hall and its Mint Tower. Hike the 10-minute trail up to the Hafelekar peak (7,657 feet, no hiking boots needed), or choose from a range of longer hiking/walking options (well-explained in lift brochures). Serious mountain bikers will thrill at the steep trails—some of Europe's toughest (see page 362 for bike-rental information). At a minimum, walk the short path behind the lift station to peer over the ridge into the Karwendel Alps, jutting up between you and the German border. Take time to relax and soak in the view before returning to earth.

▲**Alpenzoo**—This zoo is one of Innsbruck's most popular attractions (not hard when the competition is the Golden Roof). You'll see all of the animals that hide out in the Alps, including bears, wolves, chamois, elk, marmots, and at least one gigantic vulture.

Cost and Hours: €8, €11 combo-ticket with Hungerburg-bahn funicular, daily April-Oct 9:00-18:00, Nov-March 9:00-17:00, Weiherburggasse 37, tel. 0512/292-323, www.alpenzoo. at.

Getting There: The easiest way up is with the funicular (described earlier). It's OK to stop off on a round-trip ticket to Hungerburg and continue up or down (follow signs 5 minutes from Alpenzoo station to the zoo itself). Or you could take the local #W bus, or just walk (following *Fussweg Alpenzoo* signs from the river).

Olympic Bobsled—For those who envy Olympic bobsled teams whooshing down curvy chutes (who doesn't?), Innsbruck offers the chance to ride an actual Olympic course. In the summer, you'll ride with a pilot and three others down the 4,000-foot-long course in a sled-on-wheels; in the winter it's the real thing on ice.

Cost and Hours: Summer—€25, July-Aug only, Wed-Fri 16:00-18:00; winter—€30, Jan-March only, Tue at 10:00 and 19:00, Thu at 19:00; in both seasons call ahead, no kids under 12, tel. 05275/5386, mobile 0664-357-8607, www.knauseder-event. at—select "Events," then "Gästebob" or "Sommerbob."

Getting There: From the city center, take bus #J from Markt-graben (near Maria-Theresien-Strasse and the TI) to the Olympia express stop (2/hour, 25 minutes)—it's a short walk along Römer-strasse to the building with the silver *Zielhaus* sign. Drivers coming from the A-12 autobahn should take the Innsbruck Mitte exit, and follow signs to *Igls* and then to *Olympia Bobbahn*.

Near Innsbruck

▲▲Alpine Side-Trip by Car to Hinterhornalm—In Gnaden-wald, a village sandwiched between Hall and its Alps, pay a €4.50 toll, pick up a brochure, then corkscrew your way up the mountain. Marveling at the crazy amount of energy put into such a remote road project, you'll finally end up at the rustic Hinterhornalm Berg restaurant (generally daily mid-May-Oct 10:00-18:00, open later in summer—but entirely weather-dependent and often closed, closed Nov-mid-May, mobile 0664-211-2745). Hinterhornalm is a hang-gliding springboard. On good days, it's a butterfly nest. From there, it's a level 20-minute walk to Walderalm, a cluster of three dairy farms with 70 cows that share their meadow with the clouds. The cows ramble along ridge-top lanes surrounded by cut-glass peaks. The ladies of the farms serve soup, sandwiches, and drinks

INNSBRUCK & HALL

Sleep Code

(€1 = about $1.30, country code: 43, area code: 0512)
S = Single, **D** = Double/Twin, **T** = Triple, **Q** = Quad, **b** = bathroom, **s** = shower only. Unless otherwise noted, credit cards
are accepted, English is spoken, and breakfast is included.

   To help you sort easily through these listings, I've divided
the rooms into two categories, based on the price for a standard double room with bath:

   $$ **Higher Priced**—Most rooms €85 or more.
   $ **Lower Priced**—Most rooms less than €85.

   Prices can change without notice; verify the hotel's cur-
rent rates online or by email

(very fresh milk in the afternoon) on rough plank tables. Below
you spreads the Inn River Valley and, in the distance, tourist-filled
Innsbruck.

Sleeping in Innsbruck

$$ Hotel Weisses Kreuz, near the Golden Roof, has been housing visitors for 500 years (see page 363). While its common spaces
still have an old-inn feel—with an airy atrium stairway, antique
Tirolean furniture, and big wood beams—its 40 rooms are recently renovated and comfortable, and a good value for the location (S-€45, Sb-€78, D-€79, small Db-€118, big Db at €134-142
is a better value, prices slightly lower Jan-May and Oct-Nov, extra
bed-€17-25, non-smoking rooms, elevator, pay Internet access, free
Wi-Fi in lobby, parking €12/day—reserve ahead, 50 yards in front
of Golden Roof, as central as can be in the old town at Herzog-
Friedrich-Strasse 31, tel. 0512/594-790, fax 0512/594-7990, www.
weisseskreuz.at, hotel@weisseskreuz.at).

   $$ Ibis Innsbruck Hauptbahnhof lacks character but has 75
predictable, acceptably priced rooms right next to the train station.
Reach the hotel through the underground passageway (by the lug-
gage lockers), or exit the station's main doors and then go up the
escalator of the black modern building that's at the left end of the
square as you emerge (Sb-€72, Db-€90, higher during infrequent
events, breakfast-€11, parking-€12, elevator, free cable Internet in
rooms, free Internet access and Wi-Fi in lobby, Sterzinger Strasse
1, tel. 0512/570-3000, fax 0512/570-300-555, www.ibishotel.com,
h5174@accor.com).

   $ Pension Stoi rents 17 pleasant, inexpensive, basic rooms

200 yards from the train station and a 10-minute walk from the old town center (S-€44, Sb-€49, D-€62, Db-€71, T-€85, Tb-€95, Q-€104, Qb-€113, cash only, no breakfast, free Wi-Fi, free parking but space limited, reception open daily 8:00-21:00; walk left as you leave the station to Salurnerstrasse, take first left on Adamgasse, then watch for signs in the courtyard on the right, Salurnerstrasse 7; tel. & fax 0512/585-434, www.pensionstoi.at, pensionstoi@aon. at, Stoi family).

Eating in Innsbruck

You'll find plenty of expensive places in the pedestrian zone around the Golden Roof. **Weisses Rössl** is a little off the tourist track and, for culinary adventurers, features traditional Tirolean treats such as oven-roasted liver and calf's head. Fear not: Schnitzels and steaks abound, as do the tasty *Grillteller* (an assortment of grilled meats) and *Hauspfandl*—meat, potatoes, and veggies served up in a cast-iron skillet (€9-16 main dishes, Mon-Sat 9:00-15:00 & 17:00-23:00, closed Sun; facing the Roof, go one block left to Kiebachgasse and turn left to #8; tel. 0512/583-057).

Locals also like **Weinhaus Happ,** offering standards like Wiener schnitzel, but also game, fish, and salads, all consumed in a labyrinth of cozy, traditional *Stuben* (€9-23 main dishes, daily 11:00-22:00, on the left as you face the Roof at Herzog-Friedrich-Strasse 14, tel. 0512/582-980). For a more elegant splurge, try **Ottoburg** (€16-26 main dishes, cheaper lunch menu, Tue-Sun 11:30-14:00 & 18:00-22:00, closed Mon, jog left down street in front of Roof to Herzog-Friedrich-Strasse 1—it's the gray mini-castle with the red and white shutters, tel. 0512/584-338).

Cammerlander is *the* place if you need a steak, and has a varied menu full of reliably tasty international and Austrian dishes. Sit in their sleek, candlelit dining room, on the glassed-in veranda, or riverside with a mountain view (€5 salad bar, €11-15 main dishes, €21-25 steaks, lots of good vegetarian options, daily 11:30-23:30, Innrain 2, tel. 0512/586-398).

Mamma Mia, a cheaper escape from traditional fare, dishes up hearty portions of pizza and pasta with indoor and outdoor seating (€7.50 pasta dishes, pizza also available by the slice-€3, daily 10:30-24:00, Kiebachgasse 2, tel. 0512/562-902).

Martin/Reformhaus is a health-food store with an eat-in or take-out deli where vegetarians can feast on tasty organic meals (daily soups and salads, €7 weekday lunch specials; open Mon-Fri 8:30-18:30, Sat 8:30-18:00, closed Sun; Herzog-Friedrich-Strasse 29).

Innsbruck Connections

From Innsbruck by Train to: Hall (4/hour, 9 minutes, Hall is usually the second stop; also 2 buses/hour, 25 minutes, take bus #4—leaves from area A, right in front of train station), **Salzburg** (almost hourly, 2 hours), **Vienna** (almost hourly, 5 hours), **Reutte** (every 2 hours, 2.5 hours, change in Garmisch; also bus connections with a change in Nassereith), **Füssen,** Germany (about every two hours, 3.5 hours, fastest via train to Reutte and then bus #74 to Füssen, last easy connection leaves Innsbruck around 14:30), **Zürich** (3/day direct, 3.5 hours; 2/day with 1 change, 4.25 hours), **Munich** (every 2 hours, 2 hours), **Milan** (6/day, 5.5 hours, most with change in Verona, fastest connections require seat reservation), **Venice** (fastest connection via Verona, 4/day, 5.5 hours; 1 direct night train). There are also night trains to **Vienna** (it's a short night, though), **Venice,** and **Rome.** Train info: tel. 051-717 (to get an operator, dial 2, then 2), www.oebb.at.

For driving directions to Reutte, Switzerland, and Italy, see page 381.

For driving directions to Reutte, Switzerland, and Italy, see page 381.

Hall

For drivers, Hall is a convenient overnight stop on the long drive from Vienna to Switzerland, or from Germany to Italy. Because Hall was a rich salt-mining center when Innsbruck was just a humble bridge *(Brücke)* town on the Inn River, it has a larger and more attractive old town than does its sprawling neighbor. Hall hosts a colorful morning scene before the daily tour buses arrive, closes down tight for its afternoon siesta, and sleeps on Sunday. Its main square is the scene of a brisk farmers market on Saturday mornings. Innsbruck's sights are a short drive, bus trip, or bike ride away.

Orientation to Hall

Tourist Information

Hall's helpful TI offers lots of town information and brochures on a wide range of topics. If it's not too busy, they can also help you find a room (Mon-Fri 9:00-18:00, Sat 9:00-13:00, closed Sun, just off main square at Wallpachgasse 5, tel. 05223/455-440, www.hall-wattens.at).

Hall

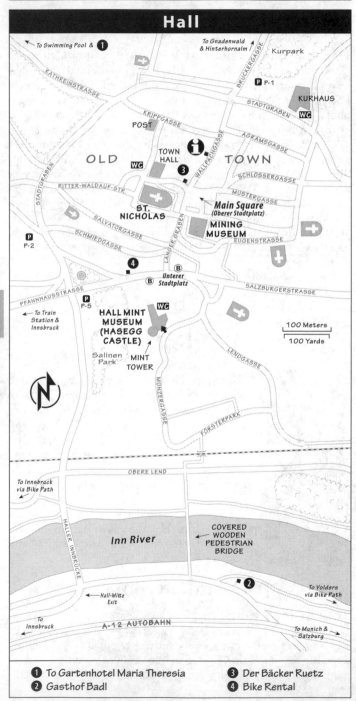

INNSBRUCK & HALL

To Swimming Pool & ❶

To Gnadenwald & Hinterhornalm

Kurpark

KATHREINSTRASSE

DRUCKERGASSE

P-1

STADTGRABEN

KURHAUS

WC

KRIPPGASSE

POST

OLD

TOWN HALL

❸

TOWN

WALLPACHGASSE

AGRAMSGASSE

WC

SCHLÖSSERGASSE

RITTER-WALDAUF-STR.

STADTGRABEN

ST. NICHOLAS

MUSTERGASSE

Main Square
(Oberer Stadtplatz)

SALVATORGASSE

SCHMIEDGASSE

P-2

LANSER-GRABEN

MINING MUSEUM

EUGENSTRASSE

❹

Ⓑ

SALZBURGERSTRASSE

PFANNHAUSSTRASSE

Ⓑ Unterer Stadtplatz

To Train Station & Innsbruck

P-5

HALL MINT MUSEUM (HASEGG CASTLE)

WC

Salinen Park

MINT TOWER

MÜNZERGASSE

LENDGASSE

FÖRSTERPARK

100 Meters
100 Yards

N

OBERE LEND

To Innsbruck via Bike Path

HALLER INNBRÜCKE

Inn River

COVERED WOODEN PEDESTRIAN BRIDGE

❷

To Volders via Bike Path

Hall-Mitte Exit

To Innsbruck

A-12 AUTOBAHN

To Munich & Salzburg

❶ To Gartenhotel Maria Theresia
❷ Gasthof Badl

❸ Der Bäcker Ruetz
❹ Bike Rental

The TI organizes one-hour town **walking tours** in English (€6, includes admissions, €8 also includes tour of Mining Museum; Mon and Thu at 10:00, Sat at 12:00).

Arrival in Hall

For directions to my two recommended hotels in Hall, see page 379.

By Bus: Coming from Innsbruck, get off at the Unterer Stadtplatz stop, just below downtown Hall. This bus stop is near the Mint Museum; it's a five-minute uphill walk to the town square and TI.

By Train: Hall's train station is a 10-minute walk from the town center (exit straight ahead up Bahnhofstrasse, turn right at the busy road, and you'll soon reach the fountain that marks the bottom of town).

By Car: Drivers approaching on the autobahn take the Hall-Mitte exit. You'll cross a big bridge, then look for signs to the P2 parking garage (5-minute walk from old town center, first hour free, €1.40/hour after that, free after 18:30). Soon after the bridge, the small P5 lot has a three-hour maximum (€1/hour, Mon-Fri 8:30-18:00 except free 12:00-14:00, Sat 8:30-12:00, free at other times and all day Sun).

On Foot or by Bike: Hall and Innsbruck are connected by a pleasant bike path along the Inn River and through some parks. From Innsbruck, cross the Inn River, then simply follow the river downstream along the *Inntal Radweg*, minding signs to *Hall*. A comfortable 30-minute pedal will get you there.

Sights in Hall

Main Square (Oberer Stadtplatz)—
Hall's quaint main square is worth a visit (TI just up the street). In the next square over (Pfarrplatz) is the Town Hall (Rathaus) and St. Nicholas Parish Church (Pfarrkirche St. Nikolaus). This much-appended Gothic church is decorated Baroque, with fine altars, a twisted apse, and a north wall lined with bony relics.

Hall Mint Museum and Mint Tower (Münze Hall und Münzerturm)—
Beginning in the 15th century, Hall began minting coins—most notably the *Taler* (which eventually became "dollar" in English). The former town mint, housed in Hasegg Castle, is next to the Unterer Stadtplatz bus stop, just below the old town. Inside, the

INNSBRUCK & HALL

Hall Mint Museum shows off the town's proud minting heritage. The centerpiece is a huge, fully functioning replica of a 16th-century minting press—powered by water and made almost entirely of wood. The renovated **Mint Tower** provides a workout (185 steps, or 202 if you go medieval and take the narrow original stairs) and a great view. Your tower ticket lets you check out the world's largest silver coin, worth roughly $40,000 (and weighing 44 pounds—suddenly the change in my pocket doesn't feel so heavy). It was made in 2008 to commemorate the 500th anniversary of Maximilian I's coronation and another event, apparently equally momentous: Austria's co-hosting of the 2008 European soccer championships.

Cost and Hours: Museum—€6, includes excellent audioguide, tower—€4, €8 combo-ticket for both; April-Oct Tue-Sun 10:00-17:00, closed Mon; Nov-mid-Jan Tue-Sat 10:00-17:00, closed Sun-Mon; closed mid-Jan-March; last entry one hour before closing, tel. 05223/585-5165, www.muenze-hall.at.

Getting There: The bus from Innsbruck drops you off right by the castle (stop: Unterer Stadtplatz, go through door marked *#17* and *Burg Hasegg*); from Gasthof Badl, it's the first big building you'll see after crossing the old wooden pedestrian bridge.

Mining Museum (Bergbaumuseum)—Back when salt was money, Hall was loaded. Try catching a tour at this museum, where the town has reconstructed one of its original salt mines, complete with pits, shafts, drills, tools, and a tiny-but-slippery wooden slide.

Cost and Hours: €3.50, €8 town walk includes museum; English tours May-Sept Mon, Thu, and Sat at 11:30; no need to reserve—but punctuality is crucial; one block south of main square, at corner of Fürstengasse and Eugenstrasse; tel. 05223/455-440.

Biking—If you're here for a few days, consider enjoying the valley on two wheels. The riverside bike path (7 miles from Hall to Volders) is a treat. Rent bikes at **Die Bike-Box** (€14/half-day, €18/day, electric bikes-€22/day, Mon-Fri 9:00-14:00 & 15:00-19:00, Sat 9:00-13:00, closed Sun, across street and 75 yards down from Unterer Stadtplatz bus stop at Unterer Stadtplatz 10, 05223/55944).

Swimming—To really make a splash, check out Hall's magnificent *Freischwimmbad*, a huge outdoor pool complex with four diving boards, giant lap pool, big slide, and kiddies' pool, all surrounded by a lush garden, sauna, mini-golf, and lounging locals.

Cost and Hours: €4, €2.30 after 16:00, mid-May-mid-Sept daily 9:00-19:00, closed off-season, at campground northwest of Hall near Gartenhotel Maria Theresia, follow *Schwimmbad* signs from downtown to Scheidensteinstrasse 24, tel. 05223/45464.

Sleeping in Hall

(€1 = about $1.30, country code: 43, area code: 05223)

Lovable towns that specialize in lowering the pulse of local vacationers line the Inn River Valley. I like Hall best, but up the hill on either side of the river are more towns strewn with fine farmhouse hotels and pensions. Most *Zimmer* in private homes cost about €25 per person. Rooms are cheaper here than in Innsbruck, and drivers appreciate the free parking.

$$ Gartenhotel Maria Theresia is just a 15-minute walk from Hall's center, next to a village church and across from a farm. This place makes you feel a little bit like landed Tirolean gentry, at prices that would get you only a commoner's lodgings in Innsbruck. This spacious, elegantly comfortable, 27-room family-run place is a good-value splurge and makes a great hub from which to explore the Inn Valley (Sb-€72-77, Db-€124-134, Tb-€186, price depends on room size, family deals, elevator, free Wi-Fi, beautiful garden patio, restaurant, fine-dining room in wine cellar, free parking, bike rentals-€18/day, playground, petting zoo, parrots and macaques, ask about mountain-bike tours, Reimmichlstrasse 25—see map on page 361, tel. 05223/56313, fax 05223/563-1366, www.gartenhotel.at, info@gartenhotel.at).

Getting to Gartenhotel Maria Theresia: If you arrive by **car** from Innsbruck, take the Hall-Mitte exit, and go over the bridge and through the light. At the roundabout, veer left (you'll already see signs) onto Speckbacherstrasse. Go left on Scheidensteinstrasse, right on Badgasse, and left on Reimmichelstrasse. If you arrive by **bus** or **train,** it's a long walk (especially from the train station)—take a taxi instead (about €10 from station or main bus stop). To shorten the walk, ride the bus three stops past the Unterer Stadtplatz stop to the Kurhaus stop, then follow Stadtgraben (with the town on your left) until it turns downhill, and go right onto Kathreinstrasse, which feeds into Scheidensteinstrasse (20-minute walk from Kurhaus stop to hotel).

$ Gasthof Badl is a big, comfortable, friendly, riverside place with 26 rooms run by Sonja and her family, with help from Leo, their enormous, easygoing dog. I like its convenience (right off the expressway but a short and scenic walk from the old town), peace, big breakfast, and warm welcome (Sb-€43-55, Db-€69-84, Tb-€83-112, Qb-€104-132, family rates, elevator, free Wi-Fi, laundry-€7, recommended restaurant; bike rentals-€5/12 hours, €7/24 hours, electric bikes-€12/24 hours; Innbrücke 4, tel. 05223/56784, fax 05223/567-843, www.badl.at, info@badl.at).

Getting to Gasthof Badl: It's easy for **drivers** to find—from the east, it's immediately off the Hall-Mitte freeway exit; you'll see the orange-lit *Bed* sign. From Innsbruck, take the Hall-Mitte exit, and rather than turning left over the big bridge into town, go straight. To reach Gasthof Badl from the Unterer Stadtplatz **bus stop,** go through the door next to the bus stop (marked *#17* and *Burg Hasegg*), cut through a couple of courtyards until you're under the castle tower, then follow Münzergasse (marked by red-and-blue no-parking signs) across the creek. Go straight until you hit the train tracks, then turn left to use the railroad underpass, which is about 10 yards away. Coming out of the underpass, go right up the ramp and, from there, cross the old wooden bridge to the hotel. From the **train station,** leave the station to the right, follow the tracks straight ahead, and as the street curves left, veer right on the footpath that follows the tracks to access the railroad underpass, then head straight across the old wooden bridge.

Eating in Hall

Hall's kitchens close early, but the restaurant at **Gasthof Badl,** one of my recommended hotels, serves excellent dinners until 21:30 (€9-12 entrées, closed Sun).

Der Bäcker Ruetz, located right off the main square just behind the fountain, is a solid place for a quick lunch. It offers good and filling sandwiches for €3-5—along with pretzels, rolls, and pastries. They have outdoor seating, so you can enjoy a coffee and *Erdbeerstrudel* (strawberry strudel) while people-watching in the sun, or get your food to go for a picnic (Mon-Fri 7:00-20:30, Sat-Sun 7:00-17:00, Sparkassengasse 1, tel. 05223/54828).

Hall Connections

From Hall, Innsbruck is the nearest major train station. Hall and Innsbruck are connected by train and bus. Trains do the trip faster (4/hour, 9 minutes); bus #4 takes a bit longer (25 minutes), leaves twice an hour, and drops you right in the center (see "Arrival in Hall," earlier). Buses go to and from the Innsbruck train station, a 10-minute walk from the old town center. Drivers staying in freeway-handy Hall can side-trip into Innsbruck on the bus.

Route Tips for Drivers

From Hall into Innsbruck: For old Innsbruck, take the autobahn from Hall to the Innsbruck Ost exit and follow the signs to *Zentrum,* then *Kongresshaus,* and park as close as you can to the old center on the river *(Hofgarten).* If you'll be riding up the cable-car section of the Nordkettenbahn (see page 371), you can park for free at the Congress garage (8:00-18:00).

Just south of Innsbruck is the ski jump (see page 369; from the autobahn take the Innsbruck Süd exit and follow signs to *Bergisel).*

Park at the end of the road near the Andreas Hofer Memorial, and climb to the empty, grassy stands for a picnic.

From Hall or Innsbruck to Reutte: Head west (direction Bregenz/Switzerland) and leave the freeway at Telfs, where signs direct you to Reutte (a 1.5-hour drive).

From Innsbruck to Switzerland: Head west on the autobahn, as above. (If you're coming directly from Innsbruck's ski jump, go down into town along the huge cemetery and follow blue *A-12/Garmisch/Arlberg* signs). The eight-mile-long Arlberg tunnel saves you 30 minutes on your way to Switzerland, but costs you lots of scenery and €8.50 (Swiss francs and credit cards accepted). For a joyride and to save a few bucks, skip the tunnel, exit at St. Anton, and go via Stuben.

After the speedy Arlberg tunnel, you're 30 minutes from Switzerland. Bludenz, with its characteristic medieval quarter, makes a good rest stop. Pass Feldkirch (and another long tunnel) and exit the autobahn at Rankweil/Feldkirch Nord, following signs for *Altstätten* and *Meiningen (CH)*. Crossing the baby Rhine River, you've left Austria.

Side-Trip over Brenner Pass into Italy: A short swing into Italy is fast and easy from Innsbruck or Hall (45-minute drive, easy border crossing). To get to Italy, take the A-13/E-45 expressway, which heads across the great Europa Bridge over Brenner Pass. It costs €8, but in 30 minutes you'll be at the border. (Note: Traffic can be heavy on summer weekends.)

In Italy, drive to the colorful market town of Vipiteno/Sterzing. **Reifenstein Castle** gives one of Europe's most intimate looks at medieval castle life. Let the friendly lady of Reifenstein (Frau Steiner) show you around her wonderfully preserved castle. She leads tours in German and Italian, squeezing in whatever English she can (€7, open May-Oct; tours Sun-Fri at 10:30, 14:00, and 15:00; mid-July-mid-Sept also at 16:00; always closed Sat, best to call ahead to reserve tour, minimum of 4 people needed for tour to run, picnic spot at drawbridge, from Austria tel. 00-39-339-264-3752, from Italy tel. 339-264-3752 or TI tel. 0472-765-325, www.sterzing.com).

BAVARIA and WESTERN TIROL

Germany: Füssen • King's Castles • Wieskirche • Oberammergau • Linderhof Castle • Ettal Monastery • Zugspitze • **Austria:** Reutte

In Germany's Bavaria and Austria's Tirol (2.5 hours west of Innsbruck), you'll find a timeless land of fairy-tale castles, painted buildings shared by cows and farmers, and locals who still yodel when they're happy.

In Germany's southern Bavaria, tour "Mad" King Ludwig II's ornate Neuschwanstein Castle, Europe's most spectacular. Stop by the Wieskirche, a textbook example of Bavarian Rococo bursting with curlicues, and browse through Oberammergau, Germany's woodcarving capital and home of the famous Passion Play (next performed in 2020). Then, just over the border in Austria's western Tirol, explore the ruined Ehrenberg Castle and scream down the mountain on an oversized skateboard.

This region—which has long spanned two nations—is best seen from one of two home-base towns, on either side of the border. Choose between Füssen, Germany (bigger, touristy-but-charming, handy to Munich, closer to the castles, and better if you're relying on public transportation) and Reutte, Austria (sleepy, handy to Innsbruck, ideal for drivers, and oh-so-Austrian). In this chapter, I'll cover Bavaria first (because it has more sights), then the area around Reutte in Tirol.

Planning Your Time and Getting Around Bavaria

While Austrians and Germans vacation here for a week or two at a time, the typical speedy American traveler will find two days' worth of sightseeing. With a car and more time, you could enjoy

Füssen & Reutte Area

three or four days, but the basic visit ranges anywhere from a long day trip from Innsbruck or Munich to a three-night, two-day stay. If the weather's good and you're not going to Switzerland on your trip, be sure to ride a lift to an alpine peak.

By Car

This region is best by car, and all the sights are within an easy 60-mile loop from Reutte or Füssen. Even if you're doing the rest of your trip by train, consider renting a car for your time here.

Here's a good one-day circular drive from Reutte (or from Füssen, starting half an hour later):

7:00	Breakfast
7:30	Depart hotel
8:00	Arrive at Neuschwanstein to pick up tickets for the two castles (Neuschwanstein and Hohenschwangau)
9:00	Tour Hohenschwangau
11:00	Tour Neuschwanstein
13:00	Drive to Oberammergau, and spend an hour there browsing the carving shops

15:00	Drive to Ettal Monastery for a half-hour stop (if you're not otherwise seeing the Wieskirche), then on to Linderhof Castle
16:00	Tour Linderhof
18:00	Drive along scenic Plansee Lake back into Austria (or return to Füssen)
19:00	Back at hotel
20:00	Dinner at hotel

Off-season (Oct-March), start your day an hour later, since Neuschwanstein and Hohenschwangau tours don't depart until 10:00; and skip Linderhof, which closes at 16:00.

The next morning, you could stroll through Reutte, hike to the Ehrenberg ruins, and ride the luge on your way to Innsbruck, Vienna, Munich, Switzerland, Venice, or wherever.

By Public Transportation

Where you stay determines which sights you can see most easily. Train travelers from Munich (or Salzburg) can use **Füssen** as a base, and bus or bike the three miles to Neuschwanstein and the Tegelberg luge or gondola. Staying in **Oberammergau** gives you easy access to Linderhof and Ettal Monastery, and you can day-trip to the top of the Zugspitze via Garmisch. Although **Reutte** is the least convenient base if you're carless, travelers staying there can easily bike or hike to the Ehrenberg ruins, and can reach Neuschwanstein by bus (via Füssen), bike (1.5 hours), or taxi (€35 one-way); if you stay at the recommended Gutshof zum Schluxen hotel (between Reutte and Füssen, in Pinswang, Austria) it's a 1- to 1.5-hour hike through the woods to Neuschwanstein.

Visiting sights farther from your home base is not impossible by local bus, but requires planning. The Deutsche Bahn (German Railway) website at www.bahn.com does a great job of finding bus connections that work, on both sides of the border. (Schedules for each route are available at www.rvo-bus.de, but only in German.) Those staying in **Füssen** can day-trip by bus to Reutte and the Ehrenberg ruins, to the Wieskirche, or, with some effort, to Linderhof via Oberammergau. From **Oberammergau,** you can reach Neuschwanstein and Füssen by bus. From **Reutte,** you can take the train to Ehrwald to reach the Zugspitze from the Austrian side, but side-trips from Reutte to Oberammergau and Linderhof are impractical. More transport details are provided later, under each individual destination.

Hitchhiking, though always risky, is a slow-but-doable way to connect the public-transportation gaps. For example, even reluctant hitchhikers can catch a ride from Linderhof back to Oberammergau, as virtually everyone leaving there is a tourist like you and heading that way.

Bavarian Craftsmanship

The scenes you'll see painted on the sides of houses in Bavaria are called *Lüftlmalerei*. The term came from the name of the house ("Zum Lüftl") owned by a man from Oberammergau who pioneered the practice in the 18th century. As the paintings became popular during the Counter-Reformation Baroque age, themes tended to involve Christian symbols, saints, and stories (such as scenes from the life of Jesus), to reinforce the Catholic Church's authority in the region. Some scenes also depicted an important historical event that took place in that house or town.

Especially in the northern part of this region, you'll see *Fachwerkhäuser*—half-timbered houses. *Fachwerk* means "craftsmanship," as this type of home required a highly skilled master craftsman to create. They are most often found inside fortified cities (such as Rothenberg, Nürnberg, and Dinkelsbühl) that were once strong and semi-independent.

If you'll be taking a lot of trains in Bavaria (for example, day-tripping to Munich), consider the **Bayern-Ticket**: It covers buses and slower regional trains throughout Bavaria for up to five people at a very low price (€22/day for the first person plus €4 for each additional person).

By Bike

This is great biking country. Many hotels loan bikes to guests, and shops in Reutte and at the Füssen train station rent bikes for €8-15 per day. The ride from Reutte to Neuschwanstein and the Tegelberg luge (1.5 hours) is a natural.

Helpful Hints

Welcome to Germany: Most of the destinations in this chapter (except for the Reutte area and the Austrian side of the Zugspitze) are in a different country. While Germans use the same euro currency as Austrians, postage stamps and phone cards only work in the country where you buy them. To call from Austria to Germany, dial 00-49 and then the number listed in this section (omitting the initial zero). To telephone from Germany to Austria, dial 00-43 and then the number (again, omitting the initial zero).

Sightseeing Pass: The **Bavarian Castles Pass** covers admission to Neuschwanstein (but not Hohenschwangau) and Linderhof, as well as many other castles not described in this book (including ones in Munich, Nürnberg, and Würzburg). If your travels will take you deeper into Germany, this might be worth considering (one-person pass-€24, family/partner version for up to two adults plus children-€40, valid 14 days, www.schloesser.bayern.de).

Local Guest Tax: Hotels and B&Bs in the region are usually required to collect a local tax (called a *Kurtax*) of about €1.50 per person per night, which is not included in the rates listed here and will be added to your bill.

Visiting Churches: At any type of church, if you'd like to attend a service, look for the *Gottesdienst* schedule. In every small German town in the very Catholic south, when you pass the big town church, look for a sign that says *Heilige Messe*. This is the schedule for holy Mass, usually on Saturday *(Sa.)* or Sunday *(So.)*.

Füssen

Dramatically situated under a renovated castle on the lively Lech River, Füssen (FEW-sehn) is a handy home base for exploring the region. This town has been a strategic stop since ancient times. Its main street sits on the Via Claudia Augusta, which crossed the Alps (over the Brenner Pass) in Roman times. Going north, early traders could follow the Lech River downstream to the Danube, and then cross over to the Main and Rhine valleys—a route now known to modern travelers as the "Romantic Road." Today, while Füssen is overrun by tourists in the summer, few venture to the back streets...which is where you'll find the real charm. Apart from my self-guided walk and the Füssen Heritage Museum, there's little to do here. It's just a pleasant small town with a big history and lots of hardworking people in the tourist business.

Halfway between Füssen and the Austrian border (as you drive, or a woodsy walk from the town) is the **Lechfall,** a thunderous waterfall (with a handy WC).

Orientation to Füssen

Füssen's train station is a few blocks from the TI, the town center (a cobbled shopping mall), and all my hotel listings.

BAVARIA

Tourist Information

The TI is in the center of town (July-mid-Sept Mon-Fri 9:00-18:00, Sat 10:00-14:00, Sun 10:00-12:00; mid-Sept-June Mon-Fri 9:00-17:00, Sat 10:00-14:00, closed Sun; one free Internet terminal, 3 blocks down Bahnhofstrasse from station at Kaiser-Maximilian-Platz 1, tel. 08362/93850, www.fuessen.de). If necessary, the TI can help you find a room. After hours, the little self-service info pavilion near the front of the TI features an automated room-finding service with a phone to call hotels.

Arrival in Füssen

From the train station (lockers available, €2-3), exit to the left and walk a few blocks to reach the center of town and the TI. Buses to Neuschwanstein, Reutte, and elsewhere leave from a parking lot next to the station.

Helpful Hints

Internet Access: CSI Internet Café has four computers and decent prices (€1.50/hour, daily 9:00-late, Luitpoldstrasse 8, tel. 08362/883-7073).

Bike Rental: Bike Station, sitting right where the train tracks end, outfits sightseers with good bikes and tips on two-wheeled fun in the area (€9-12/24 hours, March-Oct Mon-Fri 9:00-12:00 & 14:00-18:00, Sat 9:00-13:00, Sun 10:00-12:00, closed Nov-Feb, tel. 08362/983-651, mobile 0176-2205-3080, www.ski-sport-luggi.de). For a strenuous but enjoyable 20-mile loop trip, see page 406.

Car Rental: Peter Schlichtling, in the town center, rents cars for reasonable prices (€62/day, includes insurance, Mon-Fri 8:00-18:00, Sat 9:00-12:00, closed Sun, Kemptener Strasse 26, tel. 08362/922-122, www.schlichtling.de). **Auto Osterried/Europcar** rents at similar prices, but is an €8 taxi ride away from the train station. Their cheapest car goes for about €59 per day (daily 8:00-19:00, past waterfall on road to Austria, Tiroler Strasse 65, tel. 08362/6381).

Local Guide: Silvia Beyer speaks English, knows the region very well, and can even drive you to sights that are hard to reach by train (€30/hour, mobile 0160-901-13431, silliby@web.de).

Self-Guided Walk

Welcome to Füssen

For most, Füssen is just a home base for visiting Ludwig's famous castles. But the town has a rich history and hides some evocative corners, as you'll see when you follow this short orientation walk.

SELF-GUIDED WALK

Ⓐ Kaiser-Maximilian-Platz
Ⓑ Medieval Towers (2)
Ⓒ Historic Cemetery of St. Sebastian
Ⓓ Town View
Ⓔ Lech Riverbank

Ⓕ Church of the Holy Spirit, Bread Market & Lute-Makers
Ⓖ Benedictine Monastery
Ⓗ Füssen Heritage Museum
Ⓘ St. Magnus Basilica
Ⓙ High Castle

❶ Hotel Schlosskrone & Himmelsstube
❷ Hotel Hirsch
❸ Hotel Sonne
❹ Altstadthotel zum Hechten; Restaurant Ritterstub'n; Schenke & Wirtshaus
❺ Gästehaus Schöberl
❻ Mein Lieber Schwan Apartments
❼ House LA (2)
❽ Youth Hostel
❾ Restaurant Aquila
❿ Ristorante La Perla
⓫ Markthalle Food Court
⓬ Hohes Schloss Italian Ice Cream
⓭ Asian Eateries
⓮ Supermarket
⓯ Bike Rental
⓰ Car Rentals (2)
⓱ Internet Café

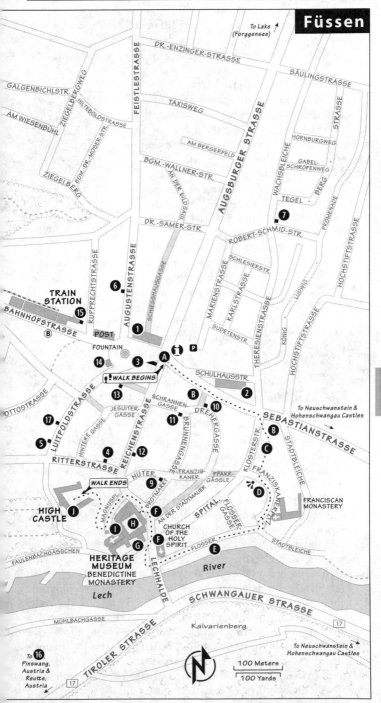

Füssen

To Lake (Forggensee)

DR.-ENZINGER-STRASSE

SÄULINGSTRASSE

FEISTLESTRASSE

GALGENBICHLSTR.

ZIEGELBERGWEG

HILTEBOLDSTRASSE

AM WIESENBÜHL

BGM.-DR.-MOSER-STR.

TAXISWEG

AM BERGERFELD

AUGSBURGER STRASSE

STRASSE

HORNBURGWEG

ZIEGELBERG

BGM.-WALLNER-STR.

GABEL-SCHROFENWEG

AN DER BILDSÄUL

WACHSBLEICHE

BERG

DR.-SAMER-STR.

ROBERT-SCHMID-STR.

TEGEL-

PROMENADE

7

LUDWIG

HOCHSTIFTSTRASSE

MARIENSTRASSE

SCHLESIERSTR.

KARLSTRASSE

THERESIENSTRASSE

KÖNIG

SCHIESSHAUSGASSE

RUPPRECHTSTRASSE

AUGUSTENSTRASSE

6

TRAIN STATION

BAHNHOFSTRASSE

15

B

POST

FOUNTAIN

14

1

SUDETENSTR.

3 A i P

OTTOSTRASSE

WALK BEGINS

SCHULHAUSSTR.

13

B

2

SEBASTIANSTRASSE

To Neuschwanstein & Hohenschwangau Castles

JESUITER-GASSE

SCHRANNEN-GASSE

DREHERGASSE

10

B

LUITPOLDSTRASSE

HINTERE GASSE

REICHENSTRASSE

11

BRUNNENGASSE

KLOSTERSTR.

STADTBLEICHE

C

17

4

12

FRANZISKANER-GASSE

FRANZISKANERPLATZ

5

RITTERSTRASSE

HUTER-

FRANZIS-KANER.

PFARR-GASSE

D

FRANCISCAN MONASTERY

WALK ENDS

9

BROTMARKT

AN DER STADTMAUER

SPITAL

FLOSSER-GASSE

HIGH CASTLE

J

MAGNUSPL.

A

CHURCH OF THE HOLY SPIRIT

STADTBLEICHE

I

H

F

FLOSSER-

E

FAULENBACHGÄSSCHEN

G

River

HERITAGE MUSEUM BENEDICTINE MONASTERY

LECHHALDE

Lech

MÜHLBACHGASSE

SCHWANGAUER STRASSE

Kalvarienberg

17

To **16**, Pinswang, Austria & Reutte, Austria

TIROLER STRASSE

17

N

To Neuschwanstein & Hohenschwangau Castles

100 Meters

100 Yards

BAVARIA

Throughout the town, "City Tour" information plaques explain points of interest in English (in more detail than I've provided).

• *Begin at the square in front of the TI, three blocks from the train station.*

❶ Kaiser-Maximilian-Platz: The entertaining "Seven Stones" fountain on this square, by sculptor Christian Tobin, was built in 1995 to celebrate Füssen's 700th birthday. The stones symbolize community, groups of people gathering, conviviality...each is different, with "heads" nodding and talking. It's granite on granite. The moving heads are not connected, and nod only with waterpower. While frozen in winter, it's a popular and splashy play zone for kids on hot summer days.

• *Just half a block down the busy street stands...*

❷ Hotel Hirsch and Medieval Towers: Recent renovations have restored some of the original Art Nouveau flavor to Hotel Hirsch, which opened in 1904. In those days, aristocratic tourists came here to appreciate the castles and natural wonders of the Alps. Across the busy street stands one of two surviving towers from Füssen's medieval town wall (c. 1515), and next to it is a passageway into the old town.

• *Walk 50 yards farther down the street to another tower. Just before it, you'll see an information plaque and an archway where a small street called Klosterstrasse emerges through a surviving piece of the old town wall. Step through the smaller pedestrian archway, walk along Klosterstrasse for a few yards, and turn left through the gate into the...*

❸ Historic Cemetery of St. Sebastian (Alter Friedhof): This peaceful oasis of Füssen history, established in the 16th century, fills a corner between the town wall and the Franciscan monastery. It's technically full, and only members of great and venerable Füssen families (who already own plots here) can join those who are buried (free, daily April-Sept 7:30-19:00, Oct-March 8:00-17:00).

Just inside the gate (on the right) is the tomb of Dominic Quaglio, who painted the Romantic scenes decorating the walls of Hohenschwangau Castle in 1835. Over on the old city wall is the World War I memorial, listing all the names of men from this small town killed in that devastating conflict (along with each one's rank and place of death). A bit to the right, also along the old wall, is a statue of the hand of God holding a fetus—a place to remember babies who died before being born. And in the corner, farther to the right, are the simple wooden crosses of Franciscans who lived just over the wall in the monastery. Note the fine tomb art from many ages collected here, and the loving care this community gives its cemetery.

• *Exit on the far side, just past the dead Franciscans, and continue toward the big church.*

❹ Town View from Franciscan Monastery (Franziskaner-kloster): From the Franciscan Monastery (which still has big responsibilities, but only a handful of monks in residence), there's a fine view over the medieval town. The Church of St. Magnus and the High Castle (the summer residence of the Bishops of Augsburg) break the horizon. The chimney (c. 1886) and workers' housing on the left are reminders that when Ludwig built Neuschwanstein, the textile industry (linen and flax) was very big here. Walk all the way to the far end of the monastery chapel and peek around the corner, where you'll see a gate that proclaims the *Ende der romantischen Strasse* (end of the Romantic Road).

• *Now go down the stairway and turn left, through the medieval "Bleachers' Gate," to the riverbank.*

❺ Lech Riverbank: This low end of town, the flood zone, was the home of those whose work depended on the river—bleachers, rafters, and fishermen. In its heyday, the Lech River was an expressway to Augsburg (about 70 miles to the north). Around the year 1500, the rafters established the first professional guild in Füssen. As Füssen was on the Via Claudia, cargo from Italy passed here en route to big German cities farther north. Rafters would assemble rafts and pile them high with goods—or with people needing a lift. If the water was high, they could float all the way to Augsburg in as little as one day. There they'd disassemble their raft and sell off the lumber along with the goods they'd carried, then make their way home to raft again. Today you'll see no modern-day rafters here, as there's a hydroelectric plant just downstream.

• *Walk upstream a bit, and head inland immediately after crossing under the bridge.*

❻ Church of the Holy Spirit, Bread Market, and Lute-Makers: Climbing uphill, you pass the colorful Church of the Holy Spirit (Heilig-Geist-Spitalkirche) on the right. As this was the church of the rafters, their patron, St. Christopher, is prominent on the facade. Today it's the church of Füssen's old folks' home (it's adjacent—notice the easy-access skyway).

Farther up the hill on the right (almost opposite an archway into a big courtyard) is Bread Market Square (Brotmarkt), with a fountain honoring the famous 16th-century lute-making family, the Tiefenbruckers. In its day, Füssen was a huge center of violin- and lute-making, with about 200 workshops. Today only two survive.

• *Backtrack and go through the archway into the courtyard of the former...*

❻ Benedictine Monastery (Kloster St. Mang): From 1717 until secularization in 1802, this was the powerful center of town. Today the courtyard is popular for concerts, and the building houses the City Hall and Füssen Heritage Museum (and a public WC).

❼ Füssen Heritage Museum: This is Füssen's one must-see sight (€6, €7 combo-ticket includes painting gallery and castle tower; April-Oct Tue-Sun 11:00-17:00, closed Mon; Nov-March Fri-Sun 13:00-16:00, closed Mon-Thu; tel. 08362/903-146, www.fuessen.de). Pick up the loaner English translations and follow the one-way route. In the St. Anna Chapel, you'll see the famous *Dance of Death*. This was painted shortly after a plague devastated the community in 1590. It shows 20 social classes, each dancing with the Grim Reaper—starting with the pope and the emperor. The words above say, essentially, "You can say yes or you can say no, but you must ultimately dance with death."

Leaving the chapel, you walk over the metal lid of the crypt. Upstairs, exhibits illustrate the rafting trade and violin- and lute-making (with a complete workshop). The museum also includes an exquisite *Festsaal* (main festival hall), an old library, an exhibition on textile production, and a King Ludwig-style "castle dream room."

• *Leaving the courtyard, hook left around the old monastery and go uphill. The square tower marks...*

❽ St. Magnus Basilica (Basilika St. Mang): St. Mang (or Magnus) is Füssen's favorite saint. In the eighth century, he worked miracles all over the area with his holy rod. For centuries, pilgrims came from far and wide to enjoy art depicting the great works of St. Magnus. Above the altar dangles a glass cross containing his relics (including that holy stick). Just inside the door is a chapel remembering a much more modern saint—Franz Seelos (1819-1867), the local boy who went to America (Pittsburgh and New Orleans) and lived such a righteous life that in 2000 he was beatified by Pope John Paul II. If you're in need of a miracle, fill out a request card next to the candles.

• *From the church, a lane leads high above, into the courtyard of the...*

❾ High Castle (Hohes Schloss): This castle, long the summer residence of the Bishop of Augsburg, houses a painting gallery (the upper floor is labeled in English) and a tower with a view over the town and lake (included in the €7 Füssen Heritage Museum combo-ticket, otherwise €6, same hours as museum). Its courtyard is interesting for the strik-ing perspective tricks painted onto its flat walls. From below the castle, the city's main drag (once the Roman Via Claudia, and now Reichenstrasse) leads from a grand statue of St. Magnus past lots of shops, cafés, and strolling people to Kaiser-Maximilian-Platz and the TI...where you began.

Sleeping in Füssen

(Germany country code: 49, area code: 08362)
Though I prefer sleeping in Reutte, convenient Füssen is just three miles from Ludwig's castles and offers a cobbled, riverside retreat. It's fairly touristy, but it has plenty of rooms, and is the region's best base for those traveling by train. All recommended accommodations are within a few handy blocks of the train station and the town center. Parking is easy at the station, and some hotels also have their own lot or garage. Prices listed are for one-night stays; most hotels give about 5-10 percent off for two-night stays—always request this discount. Competition is fierce, and off-season prices are soft. High season is mid-June-September. Rooms are generally 10-15 percent less in shoulder season and much cheaper in off-season. Remember, to call Füssen from Austria, dial 00-49 and then the number (minus the initial zero).

Big, Fancy Hotels in the Center
$$$ Hotel Schlosskrone, with 62 rooms and all the amenities, is just a block from the station. It also runs two restaurants and a fine pastry shop—you'll notice at breakfast (Sb-€99-109, standard Db-€119-139, bigger Db-€129-165, Tb-€145-165, Qb-€159-179, 4-person suite-€240-279, lower prices are for Oct-April, you'll likely save money by booking via their website, great breakfast, air-con in some rooms, elevator, free Wi-Fi and cable Internet, free sauna and fitness center, parking-€9/day, Prinzregentenplatz 2-4, tel. 08362/930-180, fax 08362/930-1850, www.schlosskrone.com, info@schlosskrone.com, Norbert Schöll and family).

$$$ Hotel Hirsch is a romantic, well-maintained, 53-room,

Sleep Code

(€1 = about $1.30, Germany country code: 49, Austria country code: 43)

S = Single, **D** = Double/Twin, **T** = Triple, **Q** = Quad, **b** = bathroom, **s** = shower only. Unless otherwise noted, credit cards are accepted, English is spoken, and breakfast is included.

To help you sort easily through these listings, I've divided the accommodations into three categories, based on the price for a standard double room with bath:

$$$ **Higher Priced**—Most rooms €100 or more.
  $$ **Moderately Priced**—Most rooms between €60-100.
    $ **Lower Priced**—Most rooms €60 or less.

Prices can change without notice; verify the hotel's current rates online or by email.

old-style hotel on the main street two blocks from the station. Their standard rooms are fine, and their rooms with historical and landscape themes are a fun splurge (Sb-€90, standard Db-€123-133, theme Db-€150-180, lower prices are for Nov-March and during slow times, family rooms, elevator, expensive Internet access, free Wi-Fi, free parking, Kaiser-Maximilian-Platz 7, tel. 08362/93980, fax 08362/939-877, www.hotelfuessen.de, info@hotelhirsch.de).

$$$ Hotel Sonne, in the heart of town, has a modern lobby and takes pride in decorating (some would say over-decorating) its 50 stylish rooms (Sb-€89-121, Db-€111-135, bigger Db-€155-185, Tb-€149, bigger Tb-€169-183, Qb-€189-219, lower prices are for Nov-March, 5 percent discount if you book on their website, elevator, free Internet access and Wi-Fi, free sauna and fitness center, parking-€5-7/day, kitty-corner from TI at Prinzregentenplatz 1, tel. 08362/9080, fax 08362/908-100, www.hotel-sonne.de, info@hotel-sonne.de).

Smaller, Mid-Priced Hotels and Pensions

$$ Altstadthotel zum Hechten offers 35 modern and newly renovated rooms in a friendly, traditional building right under Füssen Castle in the old-town pedestrian zone (Sb-€59-69, Db-€94-108, Tb-€130, Qb-€160, ask when you reserve for 5 percent off these prices with this book, also mention if you're very tall as most beds can be short, non-smoking, lots of stairs, free Internet access in lounge, free Wi-Fi, and parking-€3/day, laundry-€10-20/load, travel resource room with maps and books, fun miniature bowling alley in basement, recommended restaurant, electric-bike rental-€20/day; from TI, walk down pedestrian street and take second right to Ritterstrasse 6; tel. 08362/91600, fax 08362/916-099, www.hotel-hechten.com, info@hotel-hechten.com, Pfeiffer and Tramp families).

$$ Gästehaus Schöberl, run by the head cook at Altstadt-hotel zum Hechten, rents six attentively furnished, modern rooms a five-minute walk from the train station. One room is in the owners' house, and the rest are in the building next door (Sb-€40-50, Db-€70-75, Tb-€85-95, Qb-€100-120, lower prices are for Jan-Feb and Nov or for longer stays, cash only, free Wi-Fi, free parking, Luitpoldstrasse 14-16, tel. 08362/922-411, www.schoeberl-fuessen.de, info@schoeberl-fuessen.de, Pia and Georg Schöberl).

$$ Mein Lieber Schwan, a block from the train station, is a former private house with four superbly outfitted apartments, each with a double bed, sofa bed, and kitchen. The catch is the three-night minimum stay (Sb-€68-79, Db-€78-89, Tb-€88-99, Qb-€98-109, price depends on apartment size, slightly cheaper off-season, cash or PayPal only, no breakfast, free Wi-Fi, free parking, laundry facilities, garden, from station turn left at traffic circle to Augustenstrasse 3, tel. 08362/509-980, fax 08362/509-914, www.meinlieberschwan.de, fewo@meinlieberschwan.de, Herr Bletsch-acher).

Budget Beds

$ House LA, run by energetic mason Lahdo Algül and hardwork-ing Agata, has two branches. The backpacker house has 11 basic, clean four-bed dorm rooms at rock-bottom prices about a 10-min-ute walk from the station (€18/bed, D-€42, breakfast-€2.50, free Internet access and Wi-Fi, free parking, Wachsbleiche 2). A sec-ond building has five family apartments with kitchen and bath, each sleeping 4-6 people (apartment-€60-90, breakfast-€2.50, free Wi-Fi, free parking, 6-minute walk back along tracks from station to von Freybergstrasse 26; contact info for both: tel. 08362/607-366, mobile 0170-624-8610, fax 08362/925-1909, www.housela.de, info@housela.de). Both branches rent bikes (€8/day) and have laundry facilities (€9/load).

$ Füssen Youth Hostel occupies a pleasant modern building in a grassy setting an easy walk from the center. There are ping-pong tables and a basketball net out front (bed in 2- to 6-bed dorm rooms-€22, D-€50, €3 more for nonmembers, includes breakfast and sheets, laundry-€4/load, dinner-€5, office open 8:00-12:00 & 17:00-22:00, free Wi-Fi, free parking, from station backtrack 10 minutes along tracks, Mariahilfer Strasse 5, tel. 08362/7754, fax 08362/2770, www.fuessen.jugendherberge.de, jhfuessen@djh-bayern.de).

Eating in Füssen

Restaurant Aquila serves modern international dishes in a simple, traditional *Gasthaus* setting with great seating outside on the delightful little Brotmarkt square (€10-16 main courses, serious €9-10 salads, Wed-Mon 11:30-14:30 & 17:30-22:00, closed Tue, Brotmarkt 9, tel. 08362/6253).

Restaurant Ritterstub'n offers delicious, reasonably priced fish, salads, veggie plates, gluten-free options, and a fun kids' menu. They have three eating zones: modern decor in front, traditional Bavarian in back, and a courtyard. Demure Gabi serves while her husband cooks standard Bavarian fare (€8-15 main courses, €5.50 lunch specials, €19 three-course fixed-price dinners, Tue-Sun 11:30-14:30 & 17:30-23:00, closed Mon, Ritterstrasse 4, tel. 08362/7759).

Schenke & Wirtshaus (inside the recommended Altstadthotel zum Hechten) dishes up hearty, traditional Bavarian fare. They specialize in pike *(Hecht)* pulled from the Lech River, served with a tasty fresh-herb sauce (€8-14 main courses, salad bar, cafeteria ambience, daily 10:00-22:00, Ritterstrasse 6, tel. 0836/91600).

The **Himmelsstube** ("heaven's lounge," inside Hotel Schlosskrone, right on Füssen's main traffic circle) boasts good weekly specials and live Bavarian zither music most Fridays and Saturdays during dinner. Choose between a traditional dining room and a pastel winter garden. If your pension doesn't offer breakfast, consider their €13 "American-style" breakfast or huge €15 Sunday spread (open daily 7:30-10:30 & 11:30-14:30 & 18:00-22:00, Prinzregentenplatz 2-4, tel. 08362/930-180). The hotel's second restaurant, **Chili,** serves Mediterranean dishes.

Ristorante La Perla is the place to sate your Italian-food cravings, with friendly staff and fair prices. Sit either in the classic interior, or in one of two delightful outside areas: streetside seating, or the more peaceful back courtyard (€5-12 pizzas and pastas, €10-23 meat and fish dishes, daily 11:00-22:00, in winter closed 14:30-17:30 and all day Mon, Drehergasse 44, tel. 08362/7155).

The **Markthalle** is a fun food court offering a wide selection of reasonably priced, wurst-free food. Located in an old warehouse from 1483, it's now home to a fishmonger, deli counters, a fruit stand, a bakery, and a wine bar. Buy your food from one of the vendors, park yourself at any one of the tables, then look up and admire the Renaissance ceiling (Mon-Fri 7:30-18:30, Sat 7:30-14:30, closed Sun, corner of Schrannengasse and Brunnengasse).

Gelato: **Hohes Schloss Italian Ice Cream** is a good *gelateria* on the main drag and has an inviting people-watching perch for coffee or dessert (Reichenstrasse 14).

Asian Food: You'll find inexpensive Thai, Indian, and Chinese restaurants in the Luitpold-Passage at Reichenstrasse 33.

Picnic Supplies: Bakeries and *Metzger*s (butcher shops) abound and frequently have ready-made sandwiches. For groceries, try the underground **Netto** supermarket at Prinzregentenplatz, the round-about on your way into town from the train station (Mon-Sat 7:00-20:00, closed Sun).

Füssen Connections

From Füssen to: Neuschwanstein (bus #73 or #78, departs from train station, most continue to Tegelberg lift station after castles, 1-2/hour, 10 minutes, €2 one-way, €4 round-trip; taxis cost €10 one-way); **Oberammergau** (bus #73 to Echelsbacher Brücke, change there to bus #9622—often marked *Garmisch,* confirm with driver that bus will stop in Oberammergau; in summer 4-6/day Mon-Sat, 2/day Sun, 1.5 hours total, bus continues to **Garmisch/Zugspitze**)—from Oberammergau, you can connect to **Linderhof Castle** or **Ettal Monastery; Reutte** (bus #74; Mon-Fri almost hourly, last bus 19:00; Sat-Sun every 3 hours, last bus 19:00; 45 minutes, €4.10 one-way; taxis cost €35 one-way); **Wieskirche** (4-5 buses/day, 40-50 minutes each way, more frequently with a transfer in Steingaden); **Munich** (hourly trains, 2 hours, some change in Buchloe); **Innsbruck** (take bus #74 to Reutte, then train from Reutte to Innsbruck via Garmisch, about every 2 hours, 3.5 hours); **Salzburg** (hourly by train via Munich, 4 hours, 1-2 changes); **Rothenburg ob der Tauber** (hourly by train, 5 hours, look for connections with only 2-3 changes—often in Augsburg, Treuchtlingen, and Steinach); **Frankfurt** (hourly by train, 5-6 hours, 1-2 changes). Train info: tel. 0180-599-6633, www.bahn.com.

BAVARIA

The Best of Bavaria

Within a short drive of Füssen and Reutte, you'll find some of the most enjoyable—and most tourist-filled—sights in Germany. The otherworldly "King's Castles" of Neuschwanstein and Hohenschwangau capture romantics' imaginations, the ornately decorated Wieskirche puts the faithful in a heavenly mood, and the little town of Oberammergau overwhelms visitors with cuteness. Yet another impressive castle (Linderhof), another fancy church (Ettal), and a sky-high viewpoint (the Zugspitze) round out southern Bavaria's top attractions.

The King's Castles: Neuschwanstein and Hohenschwangau

The most popular tourist destinations in southern Bavaria are the two "King's Castles" (Königsschlösser) near Füssen. The older Hohenschwangau, King Ludwig's boyhood home, is less touristy but more historic. The more dramatic Neuschwanstein, which inspired Walt Disney, is the one everyone visits. I'd recommend visiting both, and planning some time to hike above Neuschwanstein to Mary's Bridge—and, if you enjoy romantic hikes, down through the gorge below. Reservations are a magic wand to smooth out your visit. With fairy-tale turrets in a fairy-tale alpine setting built by a fairy-tale king, these castles are understandably a huge hit.

Getting There

If arriving by **car,** note that road signs in the region refer to the sight as *Königsschlösser,* not Neuschwanstein. There's plenty of parking (all lots-€5). The first lots require more walking. Drive right through Touristville and past the ticket center, and park in lot #4 by the lake for the same price.

From **Füssen,** those without cars can catch **bus** #73 or #78 (1-2/hour, €2 each way, 10 minutes, catch bus at train station, extra buses often run when crowded), take a **taxi** (€10 one-way), or ride a rental **bike** (two level miles). The bus drops you at the tourist office; it's a one-minute walk from there to the ticket office.

From **Reutte,** take bus #74 to the Füssen train station, then hop on bus #73 or #78 to the castles. Or pay €35 for a taxi right to the castles.

The King's Castles Area

Forggensee

BIKE PATH

KREUZWEG

ROYAL CRYSTAL BATHS ❸

Schwangau

MÜNCHENER STR.

ST. COLOMAN'S

MITTELDORF

17

TEGELBERG

DEICHELWEG

Pöllat River

To Wieskirche, Munich & Rothenburg

AM EMBERG

SCHELLE-STRASSE

FÜSSENER STR.

WEG

SCHLOSS STR.

GIPSMÜHLWEG

STRASSE

N

400 Meters

400 Yards

To ❹

To ❷

BULLACHBERGWEG

SCHWANGAUER STR.

COLOMAN-

TEGELBERG BASE STN.

LUGE

Tegelbergbahn

TEGELBERG PEAK

To Füssen & Reutte (Austria)

See detail map

PARKSTR.

❶

#75 & #78 from Füssen

P

NEUSCHWANSTEIN CASTLE

Pöllat Gorge

Schwansee

HOHENSCHWANGAU CASTLE

P

ⓘ B

Hohen-schwangau Village

NEUSCHWANSTEINSTR.

MARY'S BRIDGE (MARIENBRÜCKE)

To Pinswang (Austria)

MUSEUM OF BAVARIAN KINGS

JUGENDSTR.

Alpsee

BOAT RENTAL

❶ Alpenhotel Allgäu
❷ Beim "Landhannes" Rooms

❸ Royal Crystal Baths
❹ To Festspielhaus & Bike Path Start

Orientation to the King's Castles

Cost: Neuschwanstein and Hohenschwangau cost €12 apiece. A "Königsticket" combo-ticket for both castles costs €23, and a "Schwanenticket," which also covers the Museum of the Bavarian Kings—described on page 404—costs €28.50. Children under 18 (accompanied by an adult) are admitted free.

Hours: The ticket center, located at street level between the two castles, is open daily April-Sept 8:00-17:00, Oct-March 9:00-15:00. The first and last castle tours of the day depart an hour after the ticket office opens and closes: April-Sept at 9:00 and 18:00, Oct-March at 10:00 and 16:00.

Getting Tickets for the Castles: Every tour bus in Bavaria converges on Neuschwanstein, and tourists flush in each morning from Munich. A handy reservation system sorts out the chaos for smart travelers. Tickets, whether reserved in advance or bought on the spot, come with admission times. If you miss your appointed tour time, you can't get in. To tour both castles, you must do Hohenschwangau first (logical, since this gives a better introduction to King Ludwig's short life). You'll get two tour times: Hohenschwangau and then, two hours later, Neuschwanstein.

Upon arrival, head to the **ticket center**. If you have a reservation, stand in the short line for picking up tickets. If you don't have a reservation...welcome to the very long line. Arrive by 8:00 in summer, and you'll likely be touring at 9:00. During August, the busiest month, tickets for English tours usually run out between 16:00 and 17:00.

Reservations: It's smart to reserve in peak season (June-early Oct—especially in July-Aug, when slots can book up several days in advance). Reservations cost €1.80 per person per castle, and must be made no later than 17:00 on the previous day. It works best to book online (www.ticket-center-hohenschwangau.de); you can also reserve by phone (tel. 08362/930-830) or email (info@ticket-center-hohenschwangau.de). You must pick up reserved tickets an hour before the appointed entry time, as it takes a while to walk up to the castles. (It doesn't usually take an hour, though—so this might be a good time to pull out a sandwich or a snack.) Show up late and they may have given your slot to someone else (but then they'll likely help you make another reservation). If you know a couple of hours in advance that you're running late and can call the office, they'll likely rebook you at no charge.

Tips for Day-Tripping from Munich: If coming by train, make a castle tour reservation and take a train leaving at least four hours before your reserved castle entry. (The train to Füssen takes over two hours, getting from Füssen to the castle ticket office by bus takes another half-hour, and you must be there an hour before your tour.) Trains from Munich leave hourly at :51 past the hour. So, if you take the 9:51 train, you can make a 14:00 castle tour. If you reserve a castle tour for 11:00, you'll need to pack breakfast and take the 6:51 train.

Getting Up to the Castles: From the ticket booth, Hohenschwangau is an easy 10-minute climb, while Neuschwanstein is a steep 30-minute hike in the other direction. To minimize hiking to Neuschwanstein, you can take a shuttle bus (leaves every few minutes from in front of Hotel Lisl, just above ticket office and to the left) or a horse-drawn carriage (in front of Hotel Müller, just above ticket office and to the right), but neither gets you to the castle doorstep. The shuttle bus drops you off near Mary's Bridge (Marienbrücke), leaving you a steep, 10-minute downhill walk to the castle—so be sure to see the view from Mary's Bridge *before* hiking down (€1.80 one-way, the €2.60 round-trip is not worth it since you have to hike uphill to the bus stop for your return trip; expect a wait in line, especially if it's raining, of up to 45 minutes—plan accordingly). Carriages (€6 up, €3 down) are slower than walking and stop below Neuschwanstein, leaving you a five-minute uphill hike. Here's the most economic and least strenuous plan: Ride the bus to Mary's Bridge for the view, hike down to Neuschwanstein, and then catch the horse carriage from the castle back down to the parking lot. Carriages also run to Hohenschwangau (€4 up, €2 down).

Entry Procedure: For each castle, tourists jumble at the entry, waiting for their ticket number to light up on the board. When it does, power through the mob (most waiting there are holding higher numbers) and go to the turnstile. Warning: You must use your ticket while your number is still on the board. If you space out while waiting for a polite welcome, you'll miss your entry window and never get in.

Services: A helpful TI, bus stop, ATM, WC (€0.30), and telephones cluster around the main intersection a couple hundred yards before you get to the ticket office (TI open daily April-Sept 10:00-18:00, Oct-March 11:00-17:00, tel. 08362/81980, www.schwangau.de).

Eating: Bring a packed lunch. The park by the Alpsee (the nearby lake) is ideal for a picnic, although you're not allowed to sit on the grass—only on the benches (you could also eat out on the lake in one of the old-fashioned rowboats, rented by the hour in summer). There are no grocery shops by the castles, but you can buy sandwiches and hot dogs across from the TI and at the Hotel Alpenstuben. The restaurants in the "village" at the foot of Europe's Disney castle are mediocre, feeding off the endless droves of hungry, shop-happy tourists. The **Bräustüberl cafeteria** serves the cheapest grub, but isn't likely to be a highlight of your visit (€6-7 gut-bomb grill meals, often with live folk music, daily 10:00-18:00, close to end of road and lake).

Sights at the King's Castles

▲▲▲Hohenschwangau Castle

Standing quietly below Neuschwanstein, the big, yellow Hohenschwangau Castle was Ludwig's boyhood home. Originally built in the 12th century, it was ruined by Napoleon. Ludwig's father, King Maximilian II, rebuilt it in 1830. Hohenschwangau (hoh-en-SHVAHN-gow, loosely translated as "High Swanland") was used by the royal family as a summer hunting lodge until 1912.

The interior decor is harmonious, cohesive, and original—all done in 1835, with paintings inspired by Romantic themes. The Wittelsbach family (which ruled Bavaria for nearly seven centuries)

"Mad" King Ludwig
(1845-1886)

A tragic figure, Ludwig II (a.k.a. "Mad" King Ludwig) ruled Bavaria for 22 years until his death in 1886 at the age of 40. Bavaria was weak. Politically, Ludwig's reality was to "rule" either as a pawn of Prussia or a pawn of Austria. Rather than deal with politics in Bavaria's capital, Munich, Ludwig frittered away most of his time at his family's hunting palace, Hohenschwangau. He spent much of his adult life constructing his fanciful Neuschwanstein Castle—like a kid builds a tree house—on a neighboring hill upon the scant ruins of a medieval castle. Although Ludwig spent 17 years building Neuschwanstein, he lived in it only 172 days.

Ludwig was a true romantic living in a Romantic age. His best friends were artists, poets, and composers such as Richard Wagner. His palaces are wallpapered with misty medieval themes—especially those from Wagnerian operas. Eventually he was declared mentally unfit to rule Bavaria and taken away from Neuschwanstein. Two days after this eviction, Ludwig was found dead in a lake. To this day, people debate whether the king was murdered or committed suicide.

still owns the place (and lived in the annex—today's shop—until the 1970s). As you tour the castle, imagine how the paintings must have inspired young Ludwig. For 17 years, he lived here at his dad's place and followed the construction of his dream castle across the way—you'll see the telescope still set up and directed at Neuschwanstein.

The excellent 30-minute tours give a better glimpse of Ludwig's life than the more-visited and famous Neuschwanstein Castle tour. Tours here are smaller (35 people rather than 60) and more relaxed.

▲▲▲Neuschwanstein Castle

Imagine "Mad" King Ludwig as a boy, climbing the hills above his dad's castle, Hohenschwangau, dreaming up the ultimate fairy-tale castle. Inheriting the throne at the young age of 18, he had the power to make his dream concrete and stucco. Neuschwanstein (noy-SHVAHN-shtine, roughly "New Swanstone") was designed first by a theater-set designer...then by an architect. It looks medieval, but it's modern iron-and-brick construction with a sandstone

BAVARIA

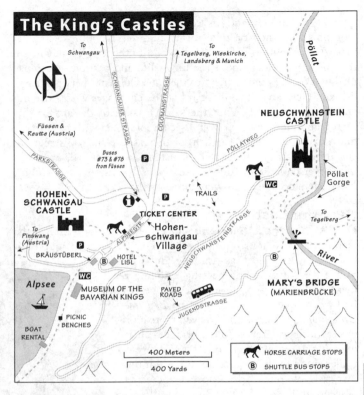

The King's Castles

veneer—only about as old as the Eiffel Tower. It feels like something you'd see at a home show for 19th-century royalty. Built from 1869 to 1886, it's the epitome of the Romanticism popular in 19th-century Europe. Construction stopped with Ludwig's death (only a third of the interior was finished), and within six weeks, tourists were paying to go through it.

During World War II, the castle took on a sinister role. The Nazis used Neuschwanstein as one of their primary secret storehouses for stolen art. After the war, Allied authorities spent a year sorting through and redistributing the art, which filled 49 rail cars from this one location alone. It was the only time the unfinished rooms were put to use.

Today, guides herd groups of 60 through the castle, giving an interesting—if rushed—30-minute tour. You'll go up and down more than 300 steps, through lavish rooms based on Wagnerian opera themes, the king's gilded-lily bedroom, and his extravagant throne room. You'll visit 15 rooms with their original furnishings and fanciful wall paintings. After the tour, before you descend to the king's kitchen, see the 20-minute video about the king's life and passions accompanied by Wagner's music (next to the café, alternates between English and German, schedule board at the entry says what's playing and what's on deck). After the kitchen (state of the art for this high-tech king in its day), you'll see a room lined with fascinating drawings (described in English) of the castle plans, construction, and drawings from 1883 of Falkenstein—a whimsical, over-the-top, never-built castle that makes Neuschwanstein look stubby. Falkenstein occupied Ludwig's fantasies the year he died.

Near the Castles

Mary's Bridge (Marienbrücke)—Before or after the Neuschwanstein tour, climb up to Mary's Bridge to marvel at Ludwig's castle, just as Ludwig did. This bridge was quite an engineering accomplishment 100 years ago. From the bridge, the frisky can hike even higher to the *Beware— Danger of Death* signs and an even more glorious castle view. (Access to the bridge is closed in bad winter weather, but many travelers walk around the barriers to get there—at their own risk, of course.) The most scenic way to descend from Neuschwanstein is to walk up to Mary's Bridge and then follow the signs down the Pöllat Gorge to the TI (*Pöllatschlucht*, 15  minutes longer than walking down the road but worth it, steel walkways and railings make this slippery area safer).

Museum of the Bavarian Kings (Museum der Bayerischen Könige)—About a five-minute walk from the castles' ticket center, in a former grand hotel on the shore of the Alpsee, this sparkling new exhibit documents the history of the Wittelsbachs, Bavaria's royal family. On display are a handful of paintings, pictures, and treasures, such as Ludwig II's monstrous royal robe and elaborately decorated fairy-tale sword, and the impressive dining set given as a golden-anniversary present to his cousin Ludwig III and his wife, the last reigning Wittelsbachs. A free audioguide lends some context to the family's history—but most of the artifacts and information here are similar to what's displayed inside the two castles. If you have time to kill between your castle reservations and a higher-than-average curiosity about arcane Teutonic dynasties, this might be worth a stop. For most visitors, however, the highlight is the view of the lake from the top floor—which you can enjoy for free outside the museum.

Cost and Hours: €28.50 "Schwanenticket" combo-ticket covers this museum as well as both castles, otherwise €8.50; no reservations required, includes audioguide, guided tour-€1.50 extra, daily April-Sept 9:00-19:00, Oct-March 10:00-18:00, mandatory lockers with refundable €1 deposit, Alpseestrasse 27, tel. 08362/926-4640, www.museumderbayerischenkoenige.de.

▲**Tegelberg Gondola**—Just north of Neuschwanstein is a fun play zone around the mighty Tegelberg Gondola, a scenic ride to the mountain's 5,500-foot summit. On a clear day, you get great views of the Alps and Bavaria and the vicarious thrill of watching hang gliders and paragliders leap into airborne ecstasy. Weather permitting, scores of adventurous Germans line up and leap from the launch ramp at

the top of the lift. With someone leaving every two or three minutes, it's great for spectators. Thrill-seekers with exceptional social skills may talk themselves into a tandem ride with a paraglider. From the top of Tegelberg, it's a steep and demanding 2.5-hour hike down to Ludwig's castle. (Avoid the treacherous trail directly below the gondola.) At the base of the gondola, you'll find a playground, a cheery eatery, the stubby remains of an ancient Roman villa, and a summer luge ride (described next).

Cost and Hours: €18 round-trip, €11.50 one-way, daily 9:00-17:00, closed Nov, 4/hour, last ride at 16:30, in bad weather call first to confirm, tel. 08362/98360, www.tegelbergbahn.de. Most buses #73 and #78 from Füssen continue from the castles to Tegelberg.

▲**Tegelberg Luge**—Next to the Tegelberg Gondola is a summer luge course. A summer luge is like a bobsled on wheels (for more details, see "Luge Lesson" on page 428). This course's stainless-steel track is heated, so it's often dry and open even when drizzly weather shuts down the concrete luges. A funky cable system pulls riders (in their sleds) to the top without a ski lift. It's not as long, fast, or scenic as Austria's Biberwier luge (described on page 428), but it's handy, harder to get hurt on, and half the price.

Cost and Hours: €3.30/ride, 6-ride shareable card-€11.50, July-Sept daily 10:00-18:00, otherwise same hours as gondola, in winter sometimes opens late if track is wet, in bad weather call first to confirm, waits can be long in good weather, no children under 3, ages 3-8 may ride with an adult, tel. 08362/98360, www.tegelberg-bahn.de.

▲**Royal Crystal Baths (Königliche Kristall-Therme)**—This pool/sauna complex just outside Füssen is the perfect way to relax on a rainy day, or to cool off on a hot one. The downstairs contains two heated indoor pools and a café; outside you'll find a shallow kiddie pool, a lap pool, a heated *Kristallbad* with massage jets and a whirlpool, and a salty mineral bath. The extensive saunas upstairs are well worth the few extra euros, as long as you're OK with nudity. (Swimsuits are required in the downstairs pools, but *verboten* in the upstairs saunas.) You'll see pool and sauna rules in German all over, but don't worry—just follow the locals' lead.

To enter the baths, first choose the length of your visit and your focus (big outdoor pool only, all ground-floor pools but not the saunas, or the whole enchilada—a flier explains all the prices in English). You'll get a wristband and a credit-card-sized ticket with a bar code. Insert that ticket into the entry gate, and keep it—you'll need it to get out. Enter through the yellow changing stalls—where you'll change into your bathing suit—then choose a storage locker (€1 coin deposit). When it's time to leave, reinsert your ticket in the gate—if you've gone over the time limit, feed extra euros into the machine.

Cost and Hours: €10.40/2 hours, €15.20/4 hours, €18.80/day, saunas-€5, towel rental-€2.50, bathing suit rental-€3, Sun-Thu 9:00-22:00, Fri-Sat until 23:00, nude swimming everywhere Tue and Fri after 19:00; from Füssen, drive, bike, or walk across the river, turn left toward Schwangau and then, about a mile later, turn left at signs for *Kristall-Therme,* Am Ehberg 16; tel. 08362/819-630, www.kristalltherme-schwangau.de.

Bike Ride Around the Forggensee—On a beautiful day, nothing beats a bike ride around the bright turquoise Forggensee, a nearby lake. This 20-mile ride is almost exclusively on bike paths, with just a few stretches on country roads. Locals swear that going clockwise is less work, but either way has a couple of strenuous uphill parts. Still, the amazing views of the surrounding Alps will distract you from your churning legs—so this is still a great way to spend the afternoon. Rent a bike, pack a picnic lunch, and figure about a three-hour round-trip. From Füssen, follow *Festspielhaus* signs; once you reach the theater, follow *Forggensee Rundweg* signs. From the theater, you can also take a **boat ride** on the Forggensee (€8/50-minute cruise, 6/day; €11/2-hour cruise, 3/day; or buy a one-way ticket and bike back, fewer departures Oct-May, tel. 08362/921-363, www.stadt-fuessen.de—click on "Forggensee - Schiffahrt").

Sleeping near the King's Castles

(€1 = about $1.30, Germany country code: 49, area code: 08362)
Inexpensive farmhouse B&Bs abound in the Bavarian countryside
around Neuschwanstein, offering drivers a decent value. Look for
Zimmer Frei signs ("room free"/vacancy). The going rate is about
€50-65 for a double, including breakfast. Though a bit inconve-
nient for those without a car, my listings here are a quick taxi ride
from the Füssen train station and also close to local bus stops.

$$ Alpenhotel Allgäu is a small, family-run hotel with 18
rooms in a bucolic setting. It's a 15-minute walk from the castle
ticket office, not far beyond the humongous parking lot (small
Sb without balcony-€48, Sb-€58, perfectly fine older Db-€80,
newer Db-€93, Tb-€120, these prices when you book direct,
ask about discount with cash and this book, all rooms except one
single have porches or balconies—some with castle views, family
rooms, free Wi-Fi, elevator, free parking, just before tennis courts
at Schwangauer Strasse 37 in the town of Schwangau—don't let
your GPS take you to Schwangauer Strasse 37 in Füssen, tel.
08362/81152, fax 08362/987-028, www.alpenhotel-allgaeu.de,
info@alpenhotel-allgaeu.de, Frau Reiss).

$ Beim "Landhannes," a 200-year-old working dairy farm
run by Conny Schön, rents three creaky but sunny rooms, and
keeps flowers on the balconies, big bells and antlers in the halls,
and cows in the yard (Sb-€30, Db-€60, €5 less per person for 3
or more nights, also rents apartments with kitchen with a 5-night
minimum, cash only, free Wi-Fi, nearby bike rental, poorly signed
in the village of Horn on the Füssen side of Schwangau, look for
the farm down a tiny lane through the grass 100 yards in front
of Hotel Kleiner König, Am Lechrain 22, tel. 08362/8349, www.
landhannes.de, info@landhannes.de).

Wieskirche

Germany's greatest Rococo-style
church, this recently restored
"Church in the Meadow"—worth
▲▲—looks as brilliant as the day
it floated down from heaven. Over-
ripe with decoration but bright and
bursting with beauty, this church
is a divine droplet, a curly curlicue,
the final flowering of the Baroque movement.

Cost and Hours: Donation requested, daily April-Oct 8:00-
19:00, Nov-March 8:00-17:00, tel. 08862/932-930, www.wi-
eskirche.de.

Getting There: The Wieskirche is a 30-minute drive north of Neuschwanstein. By car, head north from Füssen, turn right at Steingaden, and follow the signs. Take a commune-with-nature-and-smell-the-farm detour back through the meadow to the parking lot (€1/hour). You can take the bus from Füssen to the Wieskirche (see page 397), but return connections are infrequent, likely leaving you with more time at the church than you want.

➋ Self-Guided Tour: This pilgrimage church is built around the much-venerated statue of a scourged (or whipped) Christ, which supposedly wept in 1738. The carving—too graphic to be accepted by that generation's Church—was the focus of worship in a peasant's barn. Miraculously, it shed tears—empathizing with all those who suffer. Pilgrims came from all around. A tiny and humble chapel was built to house the statue in 1739. (You can see it where the lane to the church leaves the parking lot.) Bigger and bigger crowds came. Two of Bavaria's top Rococo architects, the Zimmermann brothers (Johann Baptist and Dominikus), were commissioned to build the Wieskirche that stands here today.

Follow the theological sweep from the altar to the ceiling: Jesus whipped, chained, and then killed (notice the pelican above the altar—recalling a pre-Christian story of a bird that opened its breast to feed its young with its own blood); the painting of a baby Jesus posed as if on the cross; the sacrificial lamb; and finally, high on the ceiling, the resurrected Christ before the Last Judgment. This is the most positive depiction of the Last Judgment around. Jesus, rather than sitting on the throne to judge, rides high on a rainbow—a symbol of forgiveness—giving any sinner the feeling that there is still time to repent, with plenty of mercy on hand. In the back, above the pipe organ, notice the empty throne—waiting for Judgment Day—and the closed door to paradise.

Above the entrances to both side aisles are murky glass cases with 18th-century handkerchiefs. People wept, came here, were healed, and no longer needed their hankies. Walk up either aisle flanking the high altar to see votives—requests and thanks to God (for happy, healthy babies, and so on). Notice how the kneelers are positioned so that worshippers can meditate on scenes of biblical miracles painted high on the ceiling and visible through the ornate tunnel frames. A priest here once told me that faith, architecture, light, and music all combine to create the harmony of the Wieskirche.

Two paintings flank the door at the rear of the church. One shows the ceremonial parade in 1749 when the white-clad monks of Steingaden carried the carved statue of Christ from the tiny church to its new big one. The second painting, from 1757, is a votive from one of the Zimmermann brothers, the artists and architects who built this church. He is giving thanks for the successful construction of the new church.

If you can't visit the Wieskirche, visit one of the other churches that came out of the same heavenly spray can: Oberammergau's church, the splendid Ettal Monastery (free and near Oberammergau), and, on a lesser scale, Füssen's basilica.

Route Tips for Drivers: If you're driving from Wieskirche to Oberammergau, you'll cross the **Echelsbacher Bridge,** which arches 230 feet over the Pöllat Gorge. Thoughtful drivers let their passengers walk across to enjoy the views, then meet them at the other side. Any kayakers? Notice the painting of the traditional village woodcarver (who used to walk from town to town with his art on his back) on the first big house on the Oberammergau side. It holds the Almdorf Ammertal shop, with a huge selection of overpriced carvings and commission-hungry tour guides.

Oberammergau

The Shirley Temple of Bavarian villages, and exploited to the hilt by the tourist trade, Oberammergau wears way too much make-

up. During its famous Passion Play (every 10 years, next in 2020), the crush is unbearable—and the prices at the hotels and restaurants can be as well. The village has about 1,200 beds for the 5,000 playgoers coming daily. If you're passing through, Oberammergau is a ▲ sight—worth a wander among the half-timbered *Lüftlmalerei* houses frescoed with biblical scenes and famous fairy-tale characters. It's also a relatively convenient home base for visiting Linderhof Castle, Ettal Monastery, and the Zugspitze (via Garmisch). A day trip to Neuschwanstein from Oberammergau is manageable if you have a car, but train travelers do better to stay in Füssen.

Tourist Information: The TI is at Eugen-Papst-Strasse 9A (Mon-Fri 9:00-18:00, Sat 10:00-13:00, closed Sun, tel. 08822/922-740, www.ammergauer-alpen.de).

Getting There

Trains run from Munich to Oberammergau (nearly hourly, 1.75 hours, change in Murnau). From Füssen to Oberammergau, **buses** run daily (in summer 4-6/day Mon-Sat, 2/day Sun, 1.5 hours, most

Oberammergau

1 Gasthof zur Rose &
    Gästehaus Magold
2 Hotel Fux
3 Pension Anton Zwink
4 Youth Hostel
5 Hotel Maximilian
    (Beer Garden)
6 To Sommerrodelbahn
    Steckenberg
    (Summer Luge)

change at Echelsbacher Brücke). **Drivers** entering the town from
the north should cross the bridge, take the second right, and park
in the free lot a block beyond the TI. Leaving town (to Linderhof
or Reutte), head out past the church and turn toward Ettal on Road
23. You're 20 miles from Reutte via the scenic Plansee. If heading
to Munich, Road 23 takes you to the autobahn, which gets you
there in less than an hour.

Sights in Oberammergau

Oberammergau Church—Visit the town church, which is typically Bavarian Baroque—but a poor cousin of the one at Wies.
Being in a woodcarving center, it's only logical that all the statues are made of wood, and then stuccoed and gilded to look like
marble or gold. Saints Peter and Paul flank the altar, where the
central painting can be raised to reveal a small stage decorated to
celebrate special times during the church calendar. In the central
dome, a touching painting shows Peter and Paul bidding each

Woodcarving in Oberammergau

The Ammergau region is relatively poor, with no appreciable industry and no agriculture, save for some dairy farming. What they *do* have is wood. Carving religious and secular themes became a lucrative way for the locals to make some money, especially when confined to the house during the long, cold winter. Carvers from Oberammergau peddled their wares across Europe, carrying them on their backs as far away as Rome. Today, the Oberammergau Carving School is a famous institution that takes only 20 students per year out of 450 applicants. Their graduates do important restoration work throughout Europe.

other farewell (with the city of Rome as a backdrop) on the day of their execution—the same day, in the year A.D. 67. On the left, Peter is crucified upside-down. On the right, Paul is beheaded with a sword. (A fine little €3 booklet explains it all.) Wander through the lovingly maintained graveyard. A stone WWI and WWII memorial at the gate reads, "We honor and remember the victims of the violence that our land gave the world."

Local Arts and Crafts—The town's best sights are its woodcarving shops. Browse through these small art galleries filled with very expensive whittled works. The beautifully frescoed **Pilatus House** at Ludwig-Thoma-Strasse 10 has an open workshop where you can watch woodcarvers and painters at work (free; mid-May-mid-Oct Tue-Sat 13:00-18:00, closed Sun-Mon; open two weeks after Christmas 11:00-17:00; closed rest of year, tel. 08822/949-511).

Oberammergau Museum—The museum's main branch at Dorfstrasse 8 showcases local woodcarving. A museum ticket also lets you into the lobby of the Passion Play theater, which houses a modest exhibition on the history of the performances, and into a small exhibit of "reverse glass" paintings in the **Pilatus House.** The museum also organizes guided tours of the theater (see next).

Cost and Hours: €6, €2 more for guided tour of the Passion Play theater—see next listing; museum and theater lobby open April-Oct and Dec-mid-Jan Tue-Sun 10:00-17:00; Pilatus House exhibit open same days 15:00-17:00; all three closed Mon, Nov, and mid-Jan-March; tel. 08822/94136, www.oberammergaumuseum.de.

Passion Play Theater—Back in 1633, in the midst of the bloody Thirty Years' War and with horrifying plagues devastating entire cities, the people of Oberammergau promised God that if they were spared from extinction, they'd "perform a play depicting the suffering, death, and resurrection of our Lord Jesus Christ" every decade thereafter. The town survived, and, heading into its 41st decade, the people of Oberammergau are still making good on the deal. For 100 days every 10 years (most recently in 2010), about half of the town's population (a cast of 2,000) are involved in the production of this extravagant five-hour Passion Play—telling the story of Jesus' entry into Jerusalem, Crucifixion, and Resurrection.

Until the next show in 2020, you'll have to settle for reading the book, seeing Nicodemus tool around town in his VW, or taking a quick look at the theater, a block from the center of town. The only way to see the theater hall itself is on a 45-minute guided tour organized by the Oberammergau Museum.

Cost and Hours: €8 theater tour ticket also covers Oberammergau Museum and Pilatus House exhibit; April-Oct Tue-Sun at 11:00 in English, at 10:00 and 14:00 in German; no tours off-season, tel. 08822/94136, www.oberammergaumuseum.de.

Sommerrodelbahn Steckenberg—This stainless-steel summer luge track (near Oberammergau) is faster than the Tegelberg luge, but not quite as wicked as the one in Biberwier.

Cost and Hours: €3/ride, €12/6 rides, May-Oct daily 8:30-17:00, closed when wet, Liftweg 1 in Unterammergau, clearly marked and easy 2.5-mile bike ride to Unterammergau along Bahnhofstrasse/Rottenbucherstrasse, take the first left when entering Unterammergau, tel. 08822/4027, www.steckenberg.de.

Sleeping in Oberammergau

(€1 = about $1.30, Germany country code: 49, area code: 08822)
$$ Gasthof zur Rose is a big, central, classic, family-run place with 21 straightforward rooms. At the reception desk, look at the several decades of photos showing the family performing in the Passion Play (Sb-€60, Db-€80, Tb-€90, Qb-€100, free Internet access and Wi-Fi, Dedlerstrasse 9, tel. 08822/4706, fax 08822/6753, www.rose-oberammergau.de, info@rose-oberammergau.de, Frank family).

$$ Hotel Fux, quiet and romantic and a little fancier than the Rose, rents eight large rooms and six apartments decorated in the Bavarian *Landhaus* style (Sb-€65, Db-€84; apartment prices without breakfast: Sb-€68, Db-€78, larger apartments-€89-120; cheaper Nov-April, free Internet access and Wi-Fi, Mannagasse 2a, tel. 08822/93093, www.hotel-in-oberammergau.de, info@firmafux.de).

$ Pension Anton Zwink offers 10 small, quiet, no-frills rooms in a neighborhood adjacent to the town center (Sb-€34, Db-€60, free Wi-Fi, behind Gasthof zur Rose at Daisenbergerstrasse 10, tel. 08822/923-753, www.pension-oberammergau.de, info@pension-oberammergau.de).

$ Gästehaus Magold is a homey, grandmotherly place with three bright and spacious rooms—twice as nice as the cheap hotel rooms in town, and for much less money (Db-€60, cash only, non-smoking, free cable Internet, also has two family apartments, immediately behind Gasthof zur Rose at Kleppergasse 1, tel. 08822/4340, www.gaestehaus-magold.de, info@gaestehaus-magold.de, Christine).

$ Oberammergau Youth Hostel, on the river, is a short walk from the center (€17/bed, includes breakfast and sheets, €3 extra for nonmembers, extra if over 26, closed mid-Nov-Dec, Malensteinweg 10, tel. 08822/4114, fax 08822/1695, www.oberammergau.jugendherberge.de, oberammergau@jugendherberge.de).

Eating in Oberammergau

Locals wouldn't be caught dead inside the chic, five-star **Hotel Maximilian.** But they fill its serene beer garden to enjoy the hotel's home-brewed beer while filling up on chicken, sausage, and spareribs (daily 11:00-22:00, right behind the church, Ettaler Strasse 5, tel. 08822/948-740).

Oberammergau Connections

From Oberammergau to: Linderhof Castle (bus #9622, 6/day Mon-Fri, 4/day Sat-Sun, 30 minutes; many of these also stop at **Ettal Monastery**), **Füssen** (in summer 4-6 buses/day Mon-Sat, 2/day Sun, most transfer at Echelsbacher Brücke and stop also at **Hohenschwangau** for Neuschwanstein, 1.5 hours total), **Garmisch** (nearly hourly buses, 40 minutes; also possible by train with a transfer in Murnau, 1.5 hours; from Garmisch, you can ascend the **Zugspitze**), **Munich** (nearly hourly trains, 1.75 hours, change in Murnau). Train info: tel. 0180-599-6633, www.bahn.com.

BAVARIA

Linderhof Castle

This homiest of "Mad" King Ludwig's castles is small and comfortably exquisite—good enough for a minor god, and worth ▲▲. Set in the woods 15 minutes from Oberammergau and surrounded by fountains and sculpted, Italian-style gardens, it's the only palace I've toured that actually had me feeling envious.

Ludwig was king for 22 of his 40 years. He lived much of his last 8 years here—the only one of his castles that was finished in his lifetime. Frustrated by the limits of being a "constitutional monarch," he retreated to Linderhof, inhabiting a private fantasy world where extravagant castles glorified his otherwise weakened kingship. He lived here as a royal hermit; his dinner table—pre-set with dishes and food—rose into his dining room from the kitchen below, so he could eat alone.

Beyond the palace is Ludwig's **grotto**. Inspired by Wagner's *Tannhäuser* opera, this performance space is 300 feet long and 70 feet tall. Its rocky walls are actually made of cement poured over an iron frame. The grotto provided a private theater for the reclusive king to enjoy his beloved Wagnerian operas—he was usually the sole member of the audience. The grotto features a waterfall, fake stalactites, and a swan boat floating on an artificial lake (which could be heated for swimming). The first electricity in Bavaria was generated here, to change the colors of the stage lights and to power Ludwig's fountain and wave machine.

Cost and Hours: €8.50, €3.50 for grotto only, daily April–mid-Oct 9:00-18:00, mid-Oct–March 10:00-16:00, last tour 30 minutes before closing, fountains often erupt on the half-hour, tel. 08822/92030, www.linderhof.de.

Getting There: Without a car, getting to (and back from) Linderhof is a royal headache, unless you're staying in Oberammergau. Buses from Oberammergau take 30 minutes (6/day Mon-Fri, 4/day Sat-Sun). If you're driving, park near the ticket office (obligatory €2.50). If driving from Reutte, take the scenic Plansee route.

Crowd-Beating Tips: July and August crowds can mean an hour's wait between when you buy your ticket and when you start your tour. During this period, you're wise to arrive after 15:00. Any other time of year, you should get your palace tour time shortly after you arrive. Unlike Neuschwanstein, Linderhof doesn't take advance reservations online.

Visiting the Castle: The complex sits isolated in natural splendor. Plan for lots of walking and a two-hour stop to fully enjoy this royal park. Bring raingear in iffy weather. Your ticket comes with an entry time to tour the palace, which is a five-minute hike from the ticket office. At the palace entrance, wait in line at the turnstile listed on your ticket (A through D) to take the required 30-minute English tour. Afterwards, hike 10 minutes uphill to the grotto (take the brief but interesting free tour in English, no reservations necessary). Then see the other royal buildings dotting the king's playground if you like. You can eat lunch at a café across from the ticket office.

Ettal Monastery and Pilgrimage Church

In 1328, the Holy Roman Emperor was returning from Rome with what was considered a miraculous statue of Mary and Jesus. He was in political and financial trouble, so to please God, he founded a monastery with this statue as its centerpiece. The monastery was located here because it was suitably off the beaten path, but today Ettal is on one of the most-traveled tourist routes in Bavaria. Stopping here (free and easy for drivers) offers a convenient peek at a splendid Baroque church. Restaurants across the road serve lunch.

Cost and Hours: Free, daily 8:00-19:45 in summer, until 18:00 off-season, tel. 08822/740, www.kloster-ettal.de. If you're moved to make a donation, you can use one of the self-serve credit-card machines (to the right as you enter).

Getting There: The Ettal Monastery is a few minutes' drive (or a delightful bike ride) from Oberammergau. Just park for free and wander in. Some Oberammergau-to-Linderhof buses stop here

(see "Oberammergau Connections," earlier).

❷ Self-Guided Tour: As you enter the more than 1,000-square-foot **courtyard,** imagine the 14th-century Benedictine abbey, an independent religious community. It produced everything it needed right here. In the late Middle Ages, abbeys

20 + C + M + B + 13

All over Germany (and much of Catholic Europe), you'll likely see written on doorways a mysterious message: "20 + C + M + B + 13." This is marked in chalk on Epiphany (Jan 6), the Christian holiday celebrating the arrival of the Magi to adore the newborn Baby Jesus. In addition to being the initials of the three wise men (Caspar, Melchior, and Balthazar), the letters also stand for the Latin phrase *Christus mansionem benedicat*—"May Christ bless the house." The little crosses

separating the letters remind all who enter that the house has been blessed in this year (20+13). Epiphany is a bigger deal in Catholic Europe than in the US. The holiday includes gift-giving, feasting, and caroling door to door—often collecting for a charity organization. Those who donate get their doors chalked up in thanks, and these marks are left on the door through the year.

like this had jurisdiction over the legal system, administration, and taxation of their district. Since then, the monastery has had its ups and downs. Secularized during the French Revolution and Napoleonic age, the Benedictines' property was confiscated by the state and sold. Religious life returned a century later. Today the abbey survives, with 50 or 60 monks. It remains a self-contained community, with living quarters for the monks, workshops, and guests' quarters. Along with their religious responsibilities, the brothers make their famous liqueur, brew beer, run a hotel, and educate 380 students in their private high school. The monks' wares are for sale at two shops (look for the *Klosterladen* by the courtyard or the *Kloster-Markt* across the street).

At the front of the church, you pass a **tympanum** over the door dating from 1350. It shows the founding couple, Emperor Louis the Bavarian and his wife Margaret, directing our attention to the crucified Lord and inviting us to enter the church contemplatively.

Stepping inside, the light draws our eyes to the **dome** (it's a double-shell design 230 feet high) rather than to the high altar. Illusions—with the dome opening right to the sky—merge heaven and earth. The dome fresco shows hundreds of Benedictines worshipping the Holy Trinity...the glory of the Benedictine Order. This is classic "south-German Baroque."

Statues of the **saints** on the altars are either engaged in a holy conversation with each other or singing the praises of God. Broken shell-style patterns seem to create constant movement, with cherubs adding to the energy. Side altars and confessionals seem to grow out of the architectural structure; its decorations and furnishings become part of an organic whole. Imagine how 18th-century farmers and woodcutters, who never traveled, would step in here on Sunday and be inspired to praise their God.

The origin of the monastery is shown over the **choir arch:** An angel wearing the robe of a Benedictine monk presents the emperor with a marble Madonna and commissions him to found this monastery. (In reality, the statue was made in Pisa, circa 1300, and given to the emperor in Italy.)

Dwarfed by all the magnificence and framed by a monumental tabernacle is that tiny, most precious statue of the abbey—the miraculous **statue of Mary and the Baby Jesus.**

Nearby: The fragrant demonstration dairy *(Schaukäserei)* about a five-minute walk behind the monastery is worth a quick look. The farmhouse displays all the steps in the production line, starting with the cows themselves (next to the house), to the factory staff hard at work, and through to the end products, which you can sample in the shop (try the beer cheese). Better yet, enjoy a snack on the deck while listening to the sweet music/incessant clanging of cowbells (free, daily 10:00-17:00, Mandlweg 1, tel. 08822/923-926, www.schaukaeserei-ettal.de). To walk there from the monastery's exit, take a left and go through the passageway; take another left when you get to the road, then yet another left at the first street (you'll see it up the road, directly behind the abbey).

Zugspitze

The tallest point in Germany, worth ▲▲ in clear weather, is also a border crossing. Lifts from both Austria and Germany meet at the 9,700-foot summit of the Zugspitze (TSOOG-shpit-seh). You can straddle the border between two great nations while enjoying an incredible view. Restaurants, shops, and telescopes await you at the summit.

German Approach: First, head to Garmisch (for details on getting there from Füssen, see page 397; from Oberammergau, see page 413). From Garmisch, there are two ways to ascend the Zugspitze: the whole way by cogwheel train (1.25 hours one-way), or a faster cogwheel train-plus-cable car option (about 45 minutes one-way). Both cost the same (€50 round-trip). Although the train ride takes longer, many travelers enjoy the more involved cog-railway experience. The train departs from Garmisch, stops at Eibsee for the cable-car connection, and then continues up—and through—the mountain (hourly departures daily 8:15-14:15). The cable car simply zips you to the top in five minutes from the Eibsee station. Cable cars go up daily 8:00-14:15. The last cable car down departs at about 16:15 (tel. 08821/7970, www.zugspitze.de). Allow plenty of time for afternoon descents: If bad weather hits in the late afternoon, cable cars can be delayed at the summit, causing tourists to miss their train connection from Eibsee back to Garmisch.

Drivers can park for €3 at the cable-car station at Eibsee. Hikers can enjoy the easy six-mile walk around the lovely Eibsee (start 5 minutes downhill from cable-car station).

Austrian Approach: The Tiroler Zugspitzbahn ascent is less crowded and cheaper than the Bavarian one. Departing from above the village of Ehrwald (a 30-minute train trip from Reutte, runs almost hourly), the lift zips you to the top in 10 minutes (€36.50 round-trip, departures in each direction at :00, :20, and :40 past the hour, daily 8:40-16:40 except closed late April-mid-May and most of Nov, last ascent at 16:00, drivers follow signs for *Tiroler Zugspitzbahn*, free parking, Austrian tel.

05673/2309, www.zugspitze.at). While those without a car will find the German ascent from Garmisch easier, the Austrian ascent is also doable: Either hop the bus from the Ehrwald train station to the Austrian lift (departures nearly hourly), or pay €8 for the five-minute taxi ride from Ehrwald train station.

❖ Self-Guided Tour: Whether you've ascended from the Austrian or German side, you're high enough now to enjoy a little tour of the summit. The two terraces—Bavarian and Tirolean—are connected by a narrow walkway, which was the border station before Germany and Austria opened their borders. The Austrian (Tirolean) side was higher until the Germans blew its top off in World War II to make a flak tower, so let's start there.

Tirolean Terrace: Before you stretches the Zugspitzplatt glacier. Each summer, a 65,000-square-foot reflector is spread over the ice to try to slow the shrinking. Since metal ski-lift towers collect heat, they, too, are wrapped to try to save the glacier. Many ski lifts fan out here, as if reaching for a ridge that defines the border between Germany and Austria. The circular metal building is the top of the cog-railway line that the Germans cut through the mountains in 1931. Just above that, find a small square building—the wedding chapel (Hochzeitskapelle) consecrated in 1981 by Cardinal Joseph Ratzinger (now Pope Benedict XVI).

Both Germany and Austria use this rocky pinnacle for communication purposes. The square box on the Tirolean Terrace provides the Innsbruck airport with air-traffic control, and a tower nearby is for the German *Kathastrophenfunk* (civil defense network).

This highest point in Germany (there are many higher points in Austria) was first climbed in 1820. The Austrians built a cable car that nearly reached the summit in 1926. (You can see it just over the ridge on the Austrian side—look for the ghostly, abandoned concrete station.) In 1964, the final leg, a new lift was built connecting that 1926 station to the actual summit, where you stand now. Before then, people needed to hike the last 650 feet to the top. Today's lift dates from 1980, but was renovated after a 2003 fire. The Austrian station, which is much nicer than the German station, has a fine little museum—free with Austrian ticket, €2.50 if you came up from Germany—that shows three interesting videos (6-minute 3-D mountain show, 30-minute making-of-the-lift documentary, and 45-minute look at the nature, sport, and culture of the region).

Looking up the valley from the Tirolean Terrace, you can see the towns of Ehrwald and Lermoos in the distance, and the valley that leads to Reutte. Looking farther clockwise, you'll see the Eibsee lake below. Hell's Valley, stretching to the right of Eibsee, seems to merit its name.

Bavarian Terrace: The narrow passage connecting the two terraces used to be a big deal—you'd show your passport here at the little blue house and shift from Austrian shillings to German marks. Notice the regional pride here: no German or Austrian national banners, but regional ones instead—*Freistaat Bayern* (Bavaria) and *Land Tirol*.

The German side features a golden cross marking the summit...the highest point in Germany. A priest and his friends hauled it up in 1851. The historic original was shot up by American soldiers using it for target practice in the late 1940s, so what you see today is a modern replacement. In the summer, it's easy to "summit" the Zugspitze, as there are steps and handholds all the way to the top. Or you can just stay behind and feed the birds. The yellow-beaked ravens get chummy with those who share a little pretzel or bread.

The oldest building up here is the rustic tin-and-wood weather tower, erected in 1900 by the *Deutscher Wetterdienst* (German weather service). The first mountaineers' hut, built in 1897, didn't last. The existing one—entwined with mighty cables that cinch it down—dates from 1914. In 1985, observers clocked 200-mph winds up here—those cables were necessary. Step inside the restaurant to enjoy museum-like photos and paintings on the wall (including a look at the team who hiked up with the golden cross in 1851). Near the waiting area for the cable cars and cogwheel train is a little museum that's worth a look if you have some time to kill before heading back down.

Reutte, Austria

Reutte (ROY-teh, with a rolled *r*), a relaxed Austrian town of 5,700, is located 20 minutes across the  border from Füssen. While overlooked by the international tourist crowd, it's popular with Germans and Austrians for its climate. Doctors recommend its "grade 1" air. I like Reutte for the opportunity to simply be in a real community. As an example of how the town is committed to its character, real estate can be sold only to those using it as a primary residence. (Many formerly vibrant alpine towns made a pile of money but lost their sense of community by becoming resorts. They allowed wealthy foreigners—who just drop in for a week or two a year—to buy up all the land, and are now shuttered up and dead most of the time.)

Reutte has one claim to fame among Americans: As Nazi Germany was falling in 1945, Hitler's top rocket scientist, Werner von Braun, joined the Americans (rather than the Russians) in Reutte. You could say that the American space program began here.

Orientation to Reutte

Reutte isn't featured in any other American guidebook. While its generous sidewalks are filled with smart boutiques and lazy coffeehouses, its charms are subtle. It was never rich or important. Its castle is ruined, its buildings have painted-on "carvings," its churches are full, its men yodel for each other on birthdays, and its energy is spent soaking its Austrian and German guests in *Gemütlichkeit*. Most guests stay for a week, so the town's attractions are more time-consuming than thrilling.

BAVARIA

Tourist Information

Reutte's TI is a block in front of the train station (Mon-Fri 8:00-12:00 & 14:00-17:00, no midday break July-Aug, Sat 8:30-12:00, closed Sun, Untermarkt 34, tel. 05672/62336, www.reutte.com). Go over your sightseeing plans, ask about a folk evening, pick up city and biking maps, bus schedules, and the *Sommerprogramm* events schedule (in German only), and ask about discounts with the hotel guest cards. Their free informational booklet has a good self-guided town walk.

Ask your hotel to give you an **Aktiv-Card,** which gives free travel on local buses (including the Reutte-Füssen route) as well as small discounts on sights and activities.

Arrival in Reutte

If you're coming by **car** from Innsbruck, take the south *(Süd)* exit into town. If you're coming from Germany, skip the north *(Nord)* exit and take the south *(Süd)* exit. For parking in town, blue lines denote pay-and-display spots. There is a free lot (P-1) near the train station on Muhlerstrasse.

Reutte's little **train** station is an easy, flat walk from my recommended hotels in central Reutte and Breitenwang (head left out of the station to reach the center of town). To reach hotels in Ehenbichl, take the bus from the station (get specifics from hotel), or consider asking your hosts to pick you up.

Helpful Hints

Internet Access: Café Alte Post has one expensive terminal in a back room (€7.20/hour, Mon-Fri 7:00-19:00, Sat-Sun 9:00-18:00, Untermarkt 15).

Laundry: There isn't an actual launderette in town, but the recommended Hotel Maximilian lets non-guests use its laundry service (wash, dry, and fold-€16/load).

Bike Rental: Try **Intersport** (€15/day, Mon-Fri 9:00-18:00, Sat 9:00-17:00, closed Sun, Lindenstrasse 25, tel. 05672/62352), or check at the recommended Hotel Maximilian.

Taxi: STM Shuttle Service promises 24-hour service (mobile 0664-113-3277). The car-rental agency listed below also operates taxis.

Car Rental: Reisebüro Köck rents cars at Mühlerstrasse 12 (tel. 05672/62233, www.koeck-tours.com, koeck@koeck-tours.com).

"Nightlife": Reutte is pretty quiet. For any action at all, there's a strip of bars, dance clubs, and Italian restaurants on Lindenstrasse.

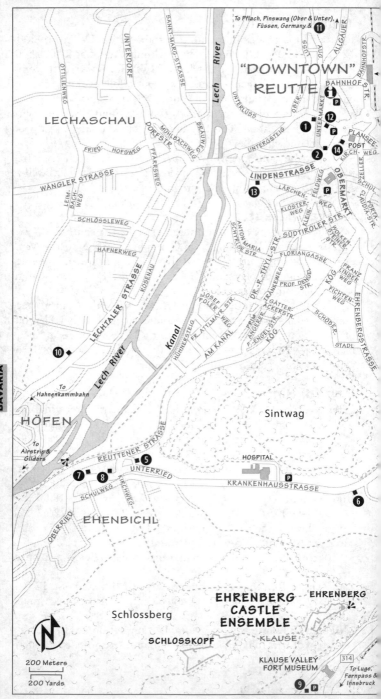

BAVARIA

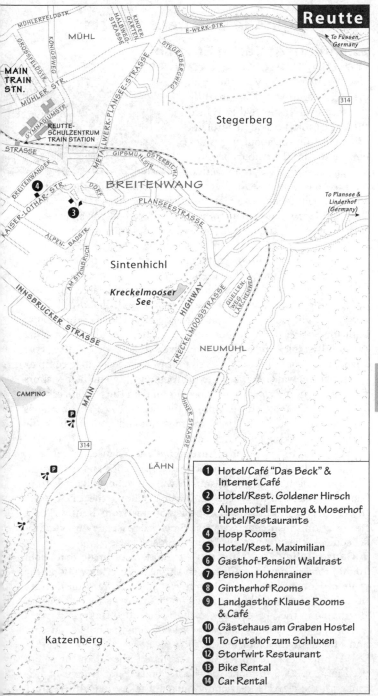

Reutte

To Füssen, Germany

314

Stegerberg

To Plansee & Linderhof (Germany)

MÜHLERFELDSTR.

MÜHL

MAIN TRAIN STN.

MÜHLER STR.

REUTTE-SCHULZENTRUM TRAIN STATION

STRASSE

BREITENWANGER

KAISER-LOTHAR-STR.

BREITENWANG

PLANSEESTRASSE

DORF

ALPEN-BADSTR.

Sintenhichl

Kreckelmooser See

INNSBRUCKER STRASSE

AM STEINBRUCH

HIGHWAY

KRECKELMOOSSTRASSE

QUELLENWEG

LÄRCHENWEG

NEUMÜHL

CAMPING

MAIN

314

LÄHN

LAHNER STRASSE

Katzenberg

BAVARIA

1 Hotel/Café "Das Beck" & Internet Café
2 Hotel/Rest. Goldener Hirsch
3 Alpenhotel Ernberg & Moserhof Hotel/Restaurants
4 Hosp Rooms
5 Hotel/Rest. Maximilian
6 Gasthof-Pension Waldrast
7 Pension Hohenrainer
8 Gintherhof Rooms
9 Landgasthof Klause Rooms & Café
10 Gästehaus am Graben Hostel
11 To Gutshof zum Schluxen
12 Storfwirt Restaurant
13 Bike Rental
14 Car Rental

Sights in and near Reutte

▲▲Ehrenberg Castle Ensemble (Festungsensemble Ehrenberg)

If Neuschwanstein was the medieval castle dream, Ehrenburg is the medieval castle reality. Once the largest fortification in Tirol, its brooding ruins lie about two miles outside Reutte. Ehrenburg is actually an "ensemble" of four castles, built to defend against the Bavarians and to bottle up the strategic Via Claudia trade route, which cut through the Alps as it connected Italy and Germany. Today, these castles have become a European "castle museum," showing off 500 years of military architecture in one swoop. The European Union is helping fund the project (paying a third of its €9 million cost) because it promotes the heritage of a multinational region—Tirol—rather than a country.

The four parts of the complex are the fortified Klause toll booth on the valley floor, the oldest castle on the first hill above (Ehrenberg), a mighty and more modern castle high above (Schlosskopf, built in the age when cannon positioned there made the original castle vulnerable), and a smaller fourth castle across the valley (Fort Claudia, an hour's hike away). All four were once a single complex connected by walls. Signs posted throughout the site help visitors find their way and explain some background on the region's history, geology, geography, culture, flora, and fauna. (While the castles are free and open all the time, the museum and multimedia show at the fort's parking lot charge admission.)

Getting to the Castle Ensemble: The Klause, Ehrenberg, and Schlosskopf castles are on the road to Lermoos and Innsbruck. These are a pleasant 30- to 45-minute walk or a short bike ride from Reutte; bikers can use the *Radwanderweg* along the Lech River (the TI has a good map). Local bus #5 runs from Reutte's main train station to Ehrenberg several times a day (see www.vvt.at for schedules—the stop name is "Ehrenberger Klause").

▲**Klause Valley Fort Museum**—Historians estimate that about 10,000 tons of precious salt passed through this valley (along the route of Rome's Via Claudia) each year in medieval times, so it's no wonder the locals built this complex of fortresses and castles. Beginning in the 14th century, the fort controlled traffic and levied tolls on all who passed. Today, these scant remains hold a museum and a theater with a multimedia show.

While there are no real artifacts here (other than the sword used in A.D. 2008 to make me the honorary First Knight of Ehrenberg), the clever, kid-friendly **museum** takes one 14th-century decade (1360-1370) and attempts to bring it to life. It's a hands-on experience, well-described in English. You can try on a set of armor (and then weigh yourself), see the limited vision knights had to put up with when wearing their helmet, empathize with victims of the plague, and join a Crusade.

The **multimedia show** takes you on a 30-minute spin through the 2,000-year history of this valley's fortresses, with images projected on the old stone walls and modern screens (50-minute English version runs Mon-Fri at 13:00 with a minimum of 5 people, or sometimes by request).

Cost and Hours: €7.50, €3 more to include multimedia show, €17.80 family pass (€20.80 with multimedia show) for 2 adults and any number of kids, daily 10:00-17:00, closed Nov-mid-Dec, tel. 05672/62007, www.ehrenberg.at.

Eating: Next to the museum, the **Landgasthof Klause** serves typical Tirolean meals (€9-15 main courses, officially Tue-Sun 10:00-20:00 but likely longer hours in summer, closed Mon, closed Nov and Jan-Feb, tel. 05672/62213). They also rent a few rooms if you'd like to stay right at Ehrenberg (see page 432).

▲▲**Ehrenberg Ruins**—Ehrenberg, a 13th-century rock pile, provides a super opportunity to let your imagination off its leash.

Hike up 30 minutes from the parking lot of the Klause Valley Fort Museum for a great view from your own private ruins. Ehrenberg (which means "Mountain of Honor") was the first castle here, built in 1296. Thirteenth-century castles were designed to stand boastfully tall. With the advent of gunpowder, castles dug in. (Notice the 18th-century **ramparts** around you.)

Approaching Ehrenberg Castle, look for the small **door** to the left. It's the night entrance (tight and awkward, and therefore safer against a surprise attack). Entering this castle, you go through two doors. Castles allowed step-by-step retreat, giving defenders time to regroup and fight back against invading forces.

Before climbing to the top of the castle, follow the path around to the right to a big, grassy courtyard with commanding views and a fat, restored **turret.** This stored gunpowder and held a big cannon that enjoyed a clear view of the valley below. In medieval times, all the trees approaching the castle were cleared to keep an unobstructed view.

Look out over the valley. The pointy spire marks **Breitenwang,** which was a stop on the ancient Via Claudia. In A.D. 46, there was a Roman camp there. In 1489, after the Reutte bridge crossed the Lech River, Reutte (marked by the onion-domed church) was made a market town and eclipsed Breitenwang in importance. Any gliders circling? They launch from just over the river in Höfen.

For centuries, this castle was the seat of government—ruling an area called the "judgment of Ehrenberg" (roughly the same as today's "district of Reutte"). When the emperor came by, he stayed here. In 1604, the ruler moved downtown into more comfortable quarters, and the castle was no longer a palace.

Now climb to the top of Ehrenberg Castle. Take the high ground. There was no water supply here—just kegs of wine, beer, and a cistern to collect rain.

Ehrenberg repelled 16,000 Swedish soldiers in the defense of Catholicism in 1632. Ehrenberg saw three or four other battles, but its end was not glorious. In the 1780s, a local businessman bought the castle in order to sell off its parts. Later, in the late 19th century, when vagabonds moved in, the roof was removed to make squatting miserable. With the roof gone, deterioration quickened, leaving only this evocative shell and a whiff of history.

▲**Schlosskopf**—From Ehrenberg, you can hike up another 30 minutes to the mighty Schlosskopf ("Castle Head"). When the Bavarians captured Ehrenberg in 1703, the Tiroleans climbed up to the bluff above it to rain cannonballs down on their former fortress. In 1740, a mighty new castle—designed to defend against modern artillery—was built on this sky-high strategic location. By the end of the 20th century, the castle was completely overgrown with trees—you literally couldn't see it from Reutte. But today the trees have been shaved away, and the castle has been excavated. In 2008, the Castle Ensemble project, led by local architect Armin Walch, opened the site with English descriptions and view platforms. One spot gives spectacular views of the strategic valley. The other looks down on the older Ehrenberg Castle ruins, illustrating the strategic problems presented with the advent of the cannon.

In the Town
Reutte Museum (Museum Grünes Haus)—Reutte's cute city museum offers a quick look at the local folk culture and the story of the castles. There are exhibits on Ehrenberg and the Via Claudia, local painters, and more—ask to borrow the English translations.

Cost and Hours: €3; May-Oct Tue-Sat 13:00-17:00, closed Sun-Mon; early Dec-Easter Wed-Sat 14:00-17:00, closed Sun-Tue; closed Easter-end of April and Nov-early Dec; in the bright-green building at Untermarkt 25, around corner from Hotel Goldener Hirsch, tel. 05672/72304, www.museum-reutte.at.

▲▲**Tirolean Folk Evening**—Ask the TI or your hotel if there's a Tirolean folk evening scheduled. During the summer (July-Aug), nearby towns (such as Höfen, on Tuesdays) occasionally put on an evening of yodeling, slap dancing, and Tirolean frolic. These are generally free and worth the short drive. Off-season, you'll have to do your own yodeling. There are also weekly folk concerts featuring the local choir or brass band in Reutte's Zeiller Platz (free, July-Aug only, ask at TI). For listings of these and other local events, pick up a copy of the German-only *Sommerprogramm* schedule at the TI.

▲**Flying**—For a major thrill on a sunny day, drop by the tiny airport in Höfen (across the river from downtown) and fly. You have two options: prop planes and gliders. Small single-prop planes, which take three passengers, can buzz the Zugspitze and Ludwig's castles and give you a bird's-eye peek at Reutte's Ehrenberg ruins.

Cost and Hours: €110/30 minutes, €220/1 hour, ask at Fliegerklause café, tel. 05672/63207, www.flugsportverein-reutte.at. The phone is rarely answered (and then not in English), so your best bet is to show up at the Höfen airport on good-weather afternoons.

▲**Gliding**—To try something more angelic, how about gliding *(Segelfliegen)*? For a relatively modest price, you and a pilot get 30 minutes in a two-seat glider. Just watching the towrope launch the graceful glider like a giant slow-motion rubber-band gun is exhilarating.

Cost and Hours: €40/30 minutes, €65/1 hour, May-mid-Sept 12:00-19:00 in good but breezy weather only, find someone in the know at the airport's "Thermik Ranch" café, English not always spoken, tel. 05672/64010, mobile 0676-945-1288, www.segelflugverein-ausserfern.at.

Hahnenkammbahn—This mountain lift swoops you high above the tree line to an attractive restaurant and starting point for several hikes. In the alpine flower park, special paths lead you past countless varieties of local flora. Unique to this lift is a barefoot hiking trail *(Barfusswanderweg)*, designed to be walked without shoes—no joke.

Cost and Hours: €11 one-way, €15.50 round-trip, flowers best in late July, runs mid-June-Sept daily 9:00-16:30, also in good weather late May-mid-June and through late Oct, base station across the river in Höfen, tel. 05672/62420, www.reuttener-seilbahnen.at.

Near Reutte

Bird Lookout Tower—Between Reutte and Füssen is a pristine (once you get past the small local industrial park) nature preserve, the Tiroler Lech Nature Park, with an impressive wooden tower from which to appreciate the vibrant bird life in the wetlands along the Lech River. Look for *Vogelerlebnispfad* signs as you're driving through the village of Pflach (on the road between Reutte and Füssen). The EU gave half the money needed to preserve this natural

Luge Lesson

Taking a wild ride on a summer luge (pronounced "loozh") is a quintessential alpine experience. In German, it's called a *Sommerrodelbahn* ("summer toboggan run"). To try one of Europe's great accessible thrills (€3-8), take the lift up to the top of a mountain, grab a wheeled sled-like go-cart, and scream back down the mountainside on a banked course. Then take the lift back up and start all over again.

Luge courses are highly weather-dependent, and can close at the slightest hint of rain. If the weather's questionable, call ahead to confirm that your preferred luge is open. Stainless-steel courses are more likely than concrete ones to stay open in drizzly weather.

Operating the sled is simple: Push the stick forward to go faster, pull back to apply brakes. Even a novice can go very, very fast. Most are cautious on their first run, speed demons on their second...and bruised and bloody on their third. A woman once showed me her travel journal illustrated with her husband's dried five-inch-long luge scab. He had disobeyed the only essential rule of luging: Keep both hands on your stick. To avoid getting into a bumper-to-bumper traffic jam, let the person in front of you get way ahead before you start. You'll emerge from the course with a windblown hairdo and a smile-creased face.

Here are a few key luge terms:

Lenkstange	lever
drücken / schneller fahren	push / go faster
ziehen / bremsen	pull / brake
Schürfwunde	scrape
Schorf	scab

area—home to 110 different species of birds that nest here. The best action is early in the day. Be quiet, as eggs are being laid.

▲▲**Biberwier Luge Course**—Near Lermoos, on the road toward Innsbruck, you'll find the Biberwier *Sommerrodelbahn*. At 4,250 feet, it's the longest summer luge in Tirol. The only drawbacks are its brief season, short hours, and a proclivity for shutting down sporadically—even at the slightest bit of rain. But if you don't have a car, this is not worth the trouble; consider the luge near Neuschwanstein instead (see "Tegelberg Luge" on page 405). The ugly cube-shaped building marring the countryside near the luge course is a hotel for outdoor adventure enthusiasts. You can ride your mountain bike right into your room, or skip the elevator by using its indoor climbing wall.

Cost and Hours: €7.30/ride, less for 3-, 5-, and 10-ride tickets, June-early Oct daily 9:00-16:30, closed early Oct-May, tel. 05673/2323, www.bergbahnen-langes.at. It's 20 minutes from Reutte on the main road toward Innsbruck; Biberwier is the first exit after a long tunnel.

▲**Fallerschein**—Easy for drivers and a special treat for those who may have been Kit Carson in a previous life, this extremely remote log-cabin village is a 4,000-foot-high flower-speckled world of serene slopes and cowbells. Thunderstorms roll down the valley like it's God's bowling alley, but the pint-size church on the high ground, blissfully simple in a land of Baroque, seems to promise that this huddle of houses will survive, and the river and breeze will just keep flowing. The couples sitting on benches are mostly Austrian vacationers who've rented cabins here. Some of them, appreciating the remoteness of Fallerschein, are having affairs.

Getting to Fallerschein: From Reutte, it's a 45-minute drive. Take road 198 to Stanzach (passing Weisenbach am Loch, then Forchach), then turn left toward Namlos. Follow the L-21 Berwang road for about five miles to a parking lot. From there, it's a two-mile walk down a drivable but technically closed one-lane road. Those driving in do so at their own risk.

Sleeping in Fallerschein: **$ Michl's Fallerscheiner Stube** is a family-friendly mountain-hut restaurant with a low-ceilinged attic space that has basic beds for up to 17 sleepy hikers. The accommodations aren't fancy, but if you're looking for remote, this is it (dorm bed-€19, cheaper without breakfast, dinner-€11, sheets-€4, open May-Oct only, wildlife viewing deck, mobile 0676-727-9681, www.alpe-fallerschein.at, michaelknitel@mountainmichl.at, Knitel family).

Sleeping in and near Reutte

(€1 = about $1.30, Austria country code: 43, area code: 05672)
Reutte is a mellow Füssen with fewer crowds and easygoing locals with a contagious love of life. Come here for a good dose of Austrian ambience and lower prices. While it's not impossible by public transport, staying here makes most sense for those with a car. Reutte is popular with Austrians and Germans, who come here year after year for one- or two-week vacations. The hotels are big, elegant, and full of comfy carved furnishings and creative ways to spend lots of time in one spot. They take great pride in their restaurants, and the owners send their children away to hotel-management schools. All include a great breakfast, but few accept credit cards. Most hotels give a small discount for stays of two nights or longer.

The Reutte TI has a list of 50 private homes that rent out

generally good rooms *(Zimmer)* with facilities down the hall, pleasant communal living rooms, and breakfast. Most charge €20 per person per night, and the owners speak little or no English. As these are family-run places, it is especially important to cancel in advance if your plans change. I've listed a few favorites in this section, but the TI can always find you a room when you arrive.

Reutte is surrounded by several distinct "villages" that basically feel like suburbs—many of them, such as Breitenwang, within easy walking distance of the Reutte town center. If you want to hike through the woods to Neuschwanstein Castle, stay at Gutshof zum Schluxen. To locate these accommodations, see the Reutte map.

In Central Reutte

These two hotels are the most practical if you're traveling by train or bus.

$$ Hotel "Das Beck" offers 17 clean, sunny rooms (many with balconies) filling a modern building in the heart of town close to the train station. It's a great value, and guests are personally taken care of by Hans, Inge, Tamara, and Birgit. Their small café offers tasty snacks and specializes in Austrian and Italian wines. Expect good conversation overseen by Hans (Sb-€48, Db-€72, Tb suite-€100, Qb suite-€115, these prices with this book in 2013 if you book direct, non-smoking, free Internet access and Wi-Fi for Rick Steves readers, free parking, Untermarkt 11, tel. 05672/62522, fax 05672/625-2235, www.hotel-das-beck.at, info@hotel-das-beck.at).

$$ Hotel Goldener Hirsch, also in the center of Reutte just two blocks from the station, is a grand old hotel with 56 rooms and one lonely set of antlers (Sb-€60-64, Db-€90-100, Tb-€135, Qb-€150, less for 2 nights, elevator, free Wi-Fi, restaurant, Mühlerstrasse 1, tel. 05672/62508, fax 05672/625-087, www.goldener-hirsch.at, info@goldener-hirsch.at; Monika, Helmut, and daughters Vanessa and Nina).

In Breitenwang

Now basically a part of Reutte, the older and quieter village of Breitenwang has good *Zimmer* and a fine bakery. It's a 20-minute walk from the Reutte train station: From the post office, follow Planseestrasse past the onion-dome church to the pointy straight-dome church near the two hotels. The Hosps—as well as other B&Bs—are along Kaiser-Lothar-Strasse, the first right past this church. If your train stops at the tiny Reutte-Schulzentrum station, hop out here—you're just a five-minute walk from Breitenwang.

$$ Alpenhotel Ernberg's 26 fresh rooms are run with great care by friendly Hermann, who combines Old World elegance with modern touches. Nestle in for some serious coziness among the carved-wood eating nooks, tiled stoves, and family-friendly backyard (Sb-€55, Db-€90, less for 2 nights, free Wi-Fi, popular restaurant, swimming complex nearby, Planseestrasse 50, tel. 05672/71912, fax 05672/719-1240, www.ernberg.at, info@ernberg.at).

$$ Moserhof Hotel has 40 new-feeling rooms plus an elegant dining room (Sb-€58, Db-€96, larger Db-€106, these special rates promised in 2013 if you ask for the Rick Steves discount when you reserve and pay cash, extra bed-€35, most rooms have balconies, elevator, free Wi-Fi, restaurant, sauna and whirlpool, free parking, Planseestrasse 44, tel. 05672/62020, fax 05672/620-2040, www.hotel-moserhof.at, info@hotel-moserhof.at, Hosp family).

$ Walter and Emilie Hosp rent three rooms in a comfortable, quiet, and modern house two blocks from the Breitenwang church steeple. You'll feel like you're staying at Grandma's (S-€26, D-€42, T-€60, Q-€80, cash only, Kaiser-Lothar-Strasse 29, tel. 05672/65377).

In Ehenbichl, near the Ehrenberg Ruins

The next listings are a bit farther from central Reutte, a couple of miles upriver in the village of Ehenbichl (under the Ehrenberg ruins). From central Reutte, go south on Obermarkt and turn right on Kög, which becomes Reuttener Strasse, following signs to Ehenbichl. These listings are best for car travelers—if you arrive by train you'll need to take a taxi (or brave the infrequent local buses; see www.vvt.at for schedules).

$$ Hotel Maximilian offers 30 rooms at a great value. It includes table tennis, play areas for children (indoors and out), a pool table, and the friendly service of Gabi, Monika, and the rest of the Koch family. They host many special events, and their hotel has lots of wonderful extras such as a sauna and a piano (Sb-€60, Db-€80-90, ask for these special Rick Steves prices when you book direct, family deals, elevator, free Internet access and Wi-Fi in common areas, pay Wi-Fi in rooms, laundry service-€12/load, good restaurant, Reuttener Strasse 1, tel. 05672/62585, fax 05672/625-8554, www.maxihotel.com, info@hotelmaximilian.at). They rent cars to guests only (€0.72/km, book in advance) and bikes to anyone (€6/half-day, €10/day, more if you're not a guest).

$$ Gasthof-Pension Waldrast, separating a forest and a meadow, is run by the farming Huter family and their dog, Picasso. The place feels hauntingly quiet and has no restaurant, but it's inexpensive and offers 10 nice rooms with generous sitting areas and castle-view balconies (Sb-€39, Db-€66, Tb-€82, Qb-€99; discounts with this book in 2013: 5 percent off second night, 10 percent off third night; cash only, non-smoking, free Wi-Fi, free parking; about a mile from Reutte, just off main drag toward Innsbruck, past campground and under castle ruins on Ehrenbergstrasse; tel.

& fax 05672/62443, www.waldrasttirol.com, info@waldrasttirol.com, Gerd).

$$ Pension Hohenrainer, a big, quiet, no-frills place, is a good value with 12 modern rooms and some castle-view balconies (Sb-€30-32, Db-€60-64, €1.50/person less for 2 nights, €3/person less for 3 nights, lower prices are for April-June and Sept-Oct, cash only, family rooms, non-smoking rooms, free Internet access and Wi-Fi, swimming pool, restaurant and reception in Gasthof Schlosswirt across the street, follow signs up the road behind Hotel Maximilian into village of Ehenbichl, Unterried 3, tel. 05672/62544 or 05672/63262, fax 05672/62052, www.hohenrainer.at, hohenrainer@aon.at).

$$ Gintherhof is a working farm that provides its guests with fresh milk, butter, and bacon. Annelies Paulweber offers geranium-covered balconies, six nice rooms with carved-wood ceilings, and a Madonna in every corner (Db-€70, Db suite-€75, €3/person less for third night, cash only, free Wi-Fi, Unterried 7, just up the road behind Hotel Maximilian, tel. 05672/67697, www.gintherhof.com, gintherhof@aon.at).

At the Ehrenberg Ruins

$$ Landgasthof Klause café, just below the Ehrenberg ruins and next to the castle museum, rents six non-smoking rooms with balconies on its upper floor. The downside is that the café closes a little early (at 20:00), and you'll need a car to get anywhere besides Ehrenberg (Sb-€40, Db-€80, Tb-€111, ask for Rick Steves discount when you book, discount for 2 or more nights, free Wi-Fi, apartments available, closed Nov and Jan, tel. 05672/62213, www.gasthof-klause.com, gasthof-klause@gmx.at).

A Hostel Across the River

The homey **$ Gästehaus am Graben hostel** has 4-6 beds per room and includes breakfast and sheets. It's lovingly run by the Reyman family—Frau Reyman, Rudi, and Gabi keep the 50-bed place traditional, clean, and friendly. This is a super value less than two miles from Reutte, and the castle views are fantastic. If you've never hosteled and are curious (and have a car or don't mind a bus ride), try it. If traveling with kids, this is a great choice. The double rooms are hotel-grade, and they accept nonmembers of any age (dorm bed-€26, hotel-style Db-€70, cash only, non-smoking, expensive Internet access and Wi-Fi, laundry service-€9, no curfew, closed April and Nov-mid-Dec; from downtown Reutte, cross bridge and follow main road left along river, or take the bus—hourly until 19:30, ask for Graben stop; Graben 1, tel. 05672/626-440, fax 05672/626-444, www.hoefen.at, info@hoefen.at).

In Pinswang

The village of Pinswang is closer to Füssen (and Ludwig's castles), but still in Austria.

$$ Gutshof zum Schluxen gets the "Remote Old Hotel in an Idyllic Setting" award. This family-friendly farm offers rustic elegance draped in goose down and pastels. Its picturesque meadow setting will turn you into a dandelion-picker, and its proximity to Neuschwanstein will turn you into a hiker—the castle is just an hour's walk away (Sb-€52, Db-€90-98, extra person-€29, these prices with this book in 2013, about 5-10 percent cheaper Nov-March, 5 percent discount for stays of three or more nights, free Wi-Fi in common areas, laundry-€9, mountain-bike rental-€10/day or €5/half-day, restaurant, fun bar, between Reutte and Füssen in village of Pinswang, tel. 05677/89030, fax 05677/890-323, www.schluxen.com, info@schluxen.at). While this hotel works best for drivers, it is reachable by bus from the Füssen train station (every 2 hours, 14 minutes, get off at Pinswang Gemeindeamt stop, verify details with hotel).

To reach Neuschwanstein from this hotel by foot or bike, follow the dirt road up the hill behind the hotel. When the road forks at the top of the hill, go right (downhill), cross the Austria-Germany border (marked by a sign and deserted hut), and follow the narrow paved road to the castles. It's a 1- to 1.5-hour hike or a great circular bike trip (allow 30 minutes; cyclists can return to Schluxen from the castles on a different 30-minute bike route via Füssen).

Eating in Reutte

The hotels here take great pride in serving local cuisine at reasonable prices to their guests and the public. Rather than go to a cheap restaurant, eat at one of the Reutte hotels recommended earlier (**Alpenhotel Ernberg, Moserhof Hotel, Hotel Maximilian,** and **Hotel Goldener Hirsch**). Hotels typically serve €10-15 dinners from 18:00 to 21:00 and are closed one night a week.

Storfwirt is *the* place for a quick and cheap weekday lunch. You can get the usual sausages here, as well as baked potatoes and salads (€5.50-9 daily specials, salad bar, always something for vegetarians, Mon-Fri 9:00-14:30, closed Sat-Sun, Schrettergasse 15, tel. 05672/62640).

Across the street from the Hotel Goldener Hirsch on Mühlerstrasse is a *Bauernladen* (farmer's shop) with rustic sandwiches and meals prepared from local ingredients (Wed-Fri 9:00-18:00, Sat 9:00-12:00, closed Sun-Tue, mobile 0676-575-4588).

Picnic Supplies: **Billa** supermarket has everything you'll need (across from TI, Mon-Fri 7:15-19:30, Sat 7:15-18:00, closed Sun).

BAVARIA

Reutte Connections

From Reutte by Train to: Ehrwald (at base of Zugspitze lift, every 2 hours, 30 minutes), **Garmisch** (every 2 hours, 1 hour), **Innsbruck** (every 2 hours, 2.5 hours, change in Garmisch), **Munich** (every 2 hours, 2.5 hours, change in Garmisch), **Salzburg** (every 2 hours, 4.5-5.5 hours, quickest with changes in Garmisch and Munich). Train info: tel. 0180-599-6633, www.bahn.com.

By Bus to: Füssen (Mon-Fri almost hourly, Sat-Sun every 3 hours, 45 minutes, €4.10 one-way, buses depart from train station, pay driver).

Taxis cost about €35 one-way to Füssen or the King's Castles.

BAVARIA

VIENNA: PAST and PRESENT

Timeline

c. A.D. 1 The Romans occupy and defend the "crossroads of Europe," where the west-east Danube River crosses the north-south Brenner Pass through the Alps. Their settlement in Vienna, called Vindobona, was centered on the site of today's cathedral.

c. 500 Lombard "barbarians"—following on the heels of the Vandals and Huns—drive the last Romans out, claiming this prime location as their own.

c. 800 Charlemagne designates Austria as one boundary of his European empire—the "Eastern Empire," or *Österreich*. Charlemagne is crowned Holy Roman Emperor, a title Austria's rulers would later claim for themselves. Vienna (now called Wenia) develops further as a thriving trade city.

1147 St. Stephen's Cathedral is begun in the Romanesque style (still seen today in the facade). The church would take more than 300 years to complete.

1200 Vienna's city wall is completed, financed with ransom money paid to liberate the kidnapped King Richard the Lionheart of England.

1273 An Austrian noble from the Habsburg family (Rudolf I) is elected Holy Roman Emperor, ruling Austria, Germany, and northern Italy. From 1438 until 1806, every emperor but one is a Habsburg. The Habsburgs arrange strategic marriages for their children with other prominent royalty around

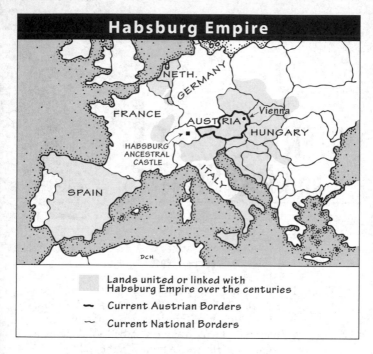

Habsburg Empire

Lands united or linked with
Habsburg Empire over the centuries

— Current Austrian Borders

~ Current National Borders

Europe, gaining power through international connections.

c. 1450 Vienna flourishes under Holy Roman Emperor Frederick III, considered the "father" of Vienna for turning the small village into a royal town with a cosmopolitan feel. Frederick makes the city his capital, and the Hofburg his home. St. Stephen's soaring 450-foot spire is completed (1433), the north tower is begun (1450), and the church is given a bishopric (1469), becoming a cathedral. Frederick's impressive tomb stands in the cathedral today.

1493 Maximilian I is crowned emperor, donning the stunning, jeweled Imperial Crown (c. 960) now displayed in the Hofburg Treasury. His marriage to Mary of Burgundy weds two kingdoms together, and their grandson, Charles V, inherits a vast empire. The combined lands instantly make the Habsburg Empire a major player in European politics. In 1498, Maximilian establishes the Vienna Boys' Choir to sing for him at Mass.

c. 1500 The elaborately-carved pulpit is erected in the nave at St. Stephen's Cathedral.

1519   Charles V (r. 1519-1556) is the most powerful man in Europe, ruling Austria, Germany, the Low Countries, parts of Italy, and Spain (with its New World possessions). Charles is responsible for trying to solve the problems of all those lands, including battling Ottomans in Vienna and Lutherans in Germany. While many lands north of the Danube turn Protestant, Austria remains Catholic.

1522   Charles V gives Austria (and the Ottoman problem) to his little brother, Ferdinand, who, four years later, marries into the Bohemian and Hungarian crowns.

1529   Ottoman invaders from today's Turkey besiege Vienna, beginning almost two centuries of battles between Austria and the Ottoman Empire. In the course of the wars, Austria gains possession of Hungary and much of Eastern Europe.

1533   Vienna—with 50,000 inhabitants and a long history as the major city of the region—becomes the official capital of the Habsburg Empire.

1556   Charles V retires from the throne to enter a monastery, leaving his kingdom to his son (King Philip II of Spain), and the crown of Holy Roman Emperor to his brother, Ferdinand I of Austria. From now on, Austria's rulers would concentrate on ruling their eastern empire, which includes part or all of present-day Austria, Hungary, the Czech Republic, Slovakia, Romania, Slovenia, Croatia, Bosnia-Herzegovina, Serbia, northern Italy (Venice), and, later, parts of Poland and Ukraine.

1648   The Thirty Years' War—a bitter struggle between Catholic and Protestant forces—finally comes to an end, leaving the Holy Roman Empire an empire in name only. Its figurehead emperor oversees a scattered group of German-speaking people, mainly in Austria and (what is now) Germany.

1679   A disastrous bubonic plague kills 75,000 Viennese (remembered today by the plague monument on the Graben).

1683   Almost 200,000 Muslims from Ottoman Turkey surround the city of Vienna once again. The Ottomans are driven off, leaving behind bags of coffee that help fuel a beverage craze around Europe. Vienna's first coffeehouse opens.

Habsburg Family Tree

RUDOLF IV
(1339–1365)

Founded Habsburg dynasty—for the next six centuries, descendants ruled Austria; many were elected Holy Roman Emperors as well.

Two ↓ *Generations*

MAXIMILIAN I
(1459–1519)

By war and marriage, extended realm in all directions—making the Habsburgs a major European power.

One ↓ *Generation*

CHARLES V
(1500–1558)

Ruled as the most powerful man in Europe, when Habsburg Empire reached its pinnacle, stretching from Bohemia to Bolivia.

Five ↓ *Generations*

**MARIA THERESA
(& FRANZ I)**
(1717–1780)

Defended Austria against France. Had 16 children, most of whom she married off to Europe's royalty, including Marie-Antoinette, who became Mrs. Louis XVI, the (last) Queen of France.

↓ *Son*

JOSEF II
(1741–1790)

Enlightened rule abolished serfdom and brought about other democratic reforms. Patron of Mozart.

↓ *Nephew*

FRANZ II
(1768–1835)

Demoted from HRE to Emperor of Austria after being defeated by (future son-in-law) Napoleon.

One ↓ *Generation*

**FRANZ JOSEF
(& SISI)**
(1830–1916)

The last Habsburg with any real power, his long reign saw the decline of his out-of-date empire.

Great- ↓ *Nephew*   *Nephew*

KARL I (& ZITA)
(1887–1922)

At the tail end of his ancestors' dynasty, ruled for two wartime years before renouncing political power.

FRANZ FERDINAND
(1863–1914)

Heir to the throne—until his assassination in 1914, which sparked World War I and the end of Habsburgs' rule...and Europe as they knew it.

1672-1714 Three wars with Louis XIV of France (including the War of the Spanish Succession) drain Austria.

1703-1711 The Habsburgs put down the Hungarian War of Independence, led by Transylvanian prince Ferenc Rákóczi.

1735 The Spanish Riding School is built at the Hofburg.

1740 Maria Theresa (r. 1740-1780) ascends to the throne. She eventually has 16 children and still finds time to fight two wars in 25 years, defending her right to rule. Adored by her subjects for her down-to-earth personality, she brings Austria international prestige by marrying her daughters to Europe's royalty. Under Maria Theresa, Schönbrunn Palace reaches its peak of luxury.

1781 Maria Theresa's son Josef II, who frees the serfs and takes piano lessons from Mozart, rules Austria as an "enlightened despot."

1791 Mozart's comic opera *The Magic Flute* debuts. Vienna is the world capital of classical music, home to Haydn (1732-1809), Mozart (1756-1791), and Beethoven (1770-1827). Mozart was married in St. Stephen's Cathedral, and, after his death, his Requiem Mass is played there.

1792 When the French queen, the Habsburg's Marie-Antoinette, is imprisoned and (later) beheaded by revolutionaries in Paris, her nephew, Austria's Emperor Franz II, seeks revenge, beginning two decades of wars between revolutionary France and monarchist Austria.

1805 Napoleon defeats Austria at Austerlitz, his greatest triumph over the forces of monarchy. Napoleon occupies Vienna, moves into Schönbrunn Palace, and forces Holy Roman Emperor Franz II to hand over the imperial crown (1806), ending a thousand years of empire. Napoleon even marries Franz II's daughter, Marie-Louise.

1814-1815 After Napoleon is defeated once and for all, an Austrian, Chancellor Metternich, heads the Congress of Vienna—reinstalling kings and nobles recently deposed by Napoleon. Metternich's politics sets the tone for Vienna's conservative, bourgeois-dominated society.

Early 1800s Throughout the Habsburgs' Central and Eastern European holdings, a gradual cultural revival takes place. Natives of Habsburg lands such as Hungary, the Czech Republic, Slovakia, and Slovenia enjoy a renewed appreciation for their unique, traditional, non-Austrian culture and language—setting the stage for a rocky century that will culminate in the fall of the empire.

1832 Franz Sacher invents Vienna's signature dessert, the Sacher-Torte.

1848 Emperor Franz Josef (emperor of Austria, but not the "Holy Roman Emperor") rules for the next 68 years, maintaining white-gloved tradition while overseeing great change—Austria's decline as an empire and entrance into the modern industrial world. During his first year on the throne, a wave of revolution sweeps Europe, endangering many of his holdings.

1849 Almost 100,000 Viennese attend the funeral of violinist Johann Strauss, responsible for the dance craze called the waltz. His son, Johann Strauss II (1825-1899), takes the baton of the Strauss Orchestra and waltzes on.

c. 1850 Vienna's Golden Age occupies the latter half of the 19th century. The city is the epicenter of European culture: fine music, exquisite art, coffee and chocolates, dress-up balls, enlightened city planning, and cutting-edge science.

1854 Franz Josef marries the beautiful/neurotic Elisabeth ("Sisi"), and they settle into their lavish home in the Hofburg's Imperial Apartments.

1857 Vienna—population 450,000—is bursting at the seams. The city embarks on a massive urban renewal project. The old city wall is torn down and turned into a wide, circular boulevard called the Ringstrasse, lined with grand buildings including the Opera, City Hall, and Kunsthistorisches Museum. The buildings are state-of-the-art, but decorated in styles that echo the past: Neoclassical, Neo-Gothic, and so on. Vienna's incredible transformation is overseen by Emperor Franz Josef, Mayor Karl Ludwig, and chief architect Otto Wagner.

1866 Prussia provokes war and defeats Austria, effectively freezing Austria out of any involvement in a modern German nation.

1867 *The Blue Danube*, a waltz by Johann Strauss II, debuts. But Austria—while at its cultural peak—is beginning its slow political decline. To better suppress the huge Slavic population in its sprawling empire, and facing a low-morale moment after the war with Prussia, Austria gives partial control over its territories to Hungary. This creates the "Dual Monarchy" of the Austro-Hungarian Empire. In a symbolic compromise, Franz Josef, "emperor" of Austria, is crowned "king" of Hungary (the origin of the royal boast "K+K"—*kaiserlich und königlich,* imperial and royal).

1869 The Vienna Opera House opens. Vienna in the late 19th century is home to composers Johannes Brahms, Richard Strauss, and Gustav Mahler.

1897 The Secession building opens, displaying works by Vienna's exciting young generation of artists who vow to "secede" from academic tradition.

1898 The Ringstrasse's horse-drawn trams give way to electric-powered streetcars.

1899 Viennese psychiatrist Sigmund Freud publishes *The Interpretation of Dreams,* launching psychoanalysis and the 20th-century obsession with repressed sexual desires, the unconscious mind, and couches.

c. 1900 As the century turns, Vienna is the globe's fifth-largest city (population 2.2 million)—bigger than it is today. It's balanced on the cusp between traditional Old World elegance and subversive modern trends. Stalin and Trotsky are rattling around Vienna. Women are smoking, riding bikes, and demanding the right to vote. In 1900, Adolf Loos builds his controversial, minimalist Loos House across from the old-school Hofburg.

1907 Gustav Klimt's painting *The Kiss*—sensual, daring, semi-abstract, and slightly decadent—epitomizes the Viennese *Jugendstil* (Art Nouveau) movement.

1908 A young aspiring artist named Adolf Hitler is rejected by Vienna's Academy of Fine Arts for the second time—one of many rejections and frustrations that will lead him to embrace his violent, anti-Semitic worldview.

1914 Austria fires the opening shots of World War I to avenge the assassination of its heir to the throne, Archduke Franz Ferdinand.

1919 After its defeat in World War I, the Austro-Hungarian Empire is divided into separate democratic nations, with Austria assigned the small, landlocked borders that it has today.

1927 Riots in the streets of Vienna between liberals and fascists leave dozens dead and hundreds wounded;

they show the deep rift in Austrian society. By the time the global Depression reaches Austria, the country is a powder keg of extreme ideologies.

1932 Mirroring events in Germany, a totalitarian government (headed by Engelbert Dollfuss) replaces a weak democracy floundering in economic depression.

1938 Led by Austrian-born Chancellor Adolf Hitler, Nazi Germany—using the threat of force and riding a surge of Germanic nationalism—annexes Austria in the *Anschluss*, and leads it into World War II. Hitler returns to Vienna in triumph, stands on the New Palace balcony at the Hofburg, and addresses his adoring throngs.

1939-45 During World War II, Austria is part of Nazi Germany and suffers the consequences. Of Vienna's 200,000 Jews, about a third die in death camps. Nearly 100,000 Jews, criminals, and political dissidents die at Mauthausen Concentration Camp, just up the Danube from Vienna.

1943 The first Allied bombs strike Vienna. Over the next two years, half of the historic center is destroyed in Allied air raids. St. Stephen's Cathedral catches fire, collapsing the wooden roof. Many of the city's top art treasures are stowed safely in cellars and salt mines.

1945 As the war ends, Vienna is liberated by Soviet troops. The city is in ruins. Like Germany, a defeated Austria is divided by the victors into occupied zones, but the country's occupation is short-lived.

1949 The movie *The Third Man* premieres, showing Vienna as a shady, espionage-laced city caught between Cold War superpowers.

1952 A new cathedral roof, rebuilt with local donations, is dedicated.

1955 Modern Austria (with Vienna as its capital) is born as a neutral nation, with the blessing of the international community. The treaty is signed at Belvedere Palace.

1961 Kennedy meets Khrushchev in Vienna for peace talks. As neutral territory between East and West, Vienna is a natural choice for summits between the Cold War superpowers. It also becomes home to several UN organizations. The OPEC nations make Vienna its seat in 1965.

PAST & PRESENT

1974 The Graben is pedestrianized, signaling the city's determination to modernize while preserving its historic core.

1978 The subway system (U-Bahn) opens its first line (U-1).

1990s Vienna absorbs tens of thousands of war refugees during the breakup of Yugoslavia.

1995 Austria joins the European Union.

2000 The European Union places sanctions on Austria (lifted a few months later) when the far-right Freedom Party—campaigning under the slogan *Überfremdung* ("Too many foreigners")—gains seats in Austria's parliament.

2002 The Freedom Party does badly in elections.

2003 Vienna's first Starbucks boldly opens—directly across from one of Vienna's oldest, best-loved coffee shops. *Gott in Himmel!*

2004 Heinz Fischer, a center-left career politician, is elected president. He is re-elected in 2010.

2008 In September, the revived far-right parties win 29 percent of the popular vote. But a month later, their leader Jörg Haider is killed in a car crash.

2013 Just after midnight on January 1, 50 million people around the world welcome the New Year by watching a broadcast of the Vienna Philharmonic playing a waltz by Strauss.

Today You arrive in Vienna and make your own history.

Notable Austrians

Charles V (1500-1558)

Through a series of marriages and unexpected deaths, Charles V inherited not only the Habsburg properties in Austria, but also the Netherlands and the Spanish Empire, including its colonies in the Americas. He said that he ruled an empire "upon which the sun never sets" (a phrase the British stole for their own dominions in the 19th century). But even the most powerful ruler on earth couldn't stop the spread of Protestantism. Charles' vision of a unified, Catholic, European empire was thwarted by Martin Luther, German Protestant princes, and their allies, the French.

Maria Theresa (1717-1780)

The first and only female head of the Habsburg dynasty, Maria Theresa consolidated the power of the throne but also reformed Austria by banning torture, funding schools and universities, and allowing some religious freedom for Protestants. Her changes, and those of her son, Josef II, allowed Austria to withstand the upheavals of the French Revolution. Her apartments at Vienna's Schönbrunn Palace are tourable today (see page 141; for more on the empress, see page 67).

Marie-Antoinette (1755-1793)

The youngest daughter of Maria Theresa, Marie-Antoinette's marriage to the heir to the French throne was supposed to cement the alliance between France and Austria. But she was not popular; even before the revolution, pamphleteers called her hopelessly stupid, accusing her of adultery, sexual deviance, and treason. During the Reign of Terror, she lost her head to the guillotine, inspiring countless romantic novels and two Hollywood movies.

Wolfgang Amadeus Mozart (1756-1791)

The ultimate child prodigy, Mozart started composing when he was five and performed for Empress Maria Theresa when he was eight. A giant of classical music, he wrote masterpieces in every genre he touched—operas, symphonies, chamber music, piano sonatas, and string quartets. Fans flock to visit his childhood homes in Salzburg (see pages 281 and 291).

Johann Strauss II (1825-1899)

Vienna was the hometown of many great composers, such as Josef Haydn and Franz Schubert, but Johann Strauss II (the Younger) best captured its spirit. "The Waltz King" helped popularize this musical genre in the 19th century and wrote the most famous waltz of all, *The Blue Danube,* as well as the operetta *Die Fledermaus.* These musical achievements came despite the objections of his father—also a famous composer—who wanted his son to be a banker.

Franz Josef (1831-1916)

At the age of 18, Franz Josef became emperor—beginning a 68-year reign surpassed in European history only by France's Louis XIV and a Lichtenstein prince. Franz Josef, a staunch conservative but a terrible general, presided over—and likely contributed to—the decline of the Austro-Hungarian Empire. His family life was similarly troubled; his estranged wife, "Sisi," was assassinated by an Italian anarchist, and his only son, Crown Prince Rudolf, committed suicide (or did he?) in the arms of a mistress. The end of the Habsburg dynasty came two years after Franz Josef's death. His Hofburg Imperial Apartments in Vienna are open to the public (see page 141; for more on the emperor, see page 150).

Sigmund Freud (1856-1939)

The Austrian physician and psychoanalyst revolutionized the study of human behavior. According to Freud, repressed desires—sexual desires in particular—explained why humans behave the way we do. Although he was a world figure of immense influence, the Nazis despised his Jewish roots and burned his books. After they took over Austria in 1938, Freud left for London, where he died a year later. His office in Vienna has been turned into the Sigmund Freud Museum (see page 90).

Gustav Klimt (1862-1918)

Erotic, symbolic, Byzantine, radical—the turn-of-the-century paintings of Gustav Klimt shook Viennese society. A leader of the Vienna Secession movement, Klimt was criticized at one point for "pornographic" art—years before the gold-wrapped lovers of *The Kiss* became an art school icon. His portrait *The Golden Adele* set a record when American billionaire Ronald Lauder bought it in 2006 for $135 million—at that time the most expensive painting ever sold. Klimt's art is displayed in museums throughout Vienna; *The Kiss,* for example, is in Belvedere Palace (for more on the artist, see page 85).

Franz Ferdinand (1863-1914)

No one expected Archduke Franz Ferdinand to be the heir to the Habsburg dynasty. But when Crown Prince Rudolf killed himself in 1889 and Franz Ferdinand's father died in 1896, the young archduke suddenly became the hope of the Habsburgs. As inspector general of the army, he was invited to Sarajevo to review Austrian troops. On June 28, 1914, after his chauffeur took a wrong turn on the city's streets, Franz Ferdinand and his wife were assassinated by a Serbian nationalist, triggering World War I and the eventual end of the dynasty.

Adolf Loos (1870-1933)

The man who said "decoration is a crime" was one of the most influential architects of the modern era. Born in what is now the Czech Republic, he trained in Germany and even spent three years tramping around America as a dishwasher and a mason. But it was in Vienna where he made his name. Excessive ornamentation was criminal, he declared, because it wasted labor and materials; the modern era deserved stripped-down facades. Examples of Loos' architecture—a bookstore, bar, and even WCs—are in downtown Vienna (see page 108).

Ferdinand Porsche (1875-1951)

This Austrian automotive engineer is best known as the father of the Volkswagen Beetle. Hitler demanded that Germany build a cheap "people's car," so Porsche began working on his world-famous design in 1934. Three years later, Hitler gave him one of Germany's highest awards. This automotive genius is also known for launching (with the help of his son) the Porsche sports car. But he was a century too soon with another one of his inventions: the world's first electric/gasoline hybrid car, the Mixte, created in 1901 in Vienna.

Adolf Hitler (1889-1945)

The future dictator—directly responsible for the deaths of more than 43 million people during World War II—was born in Braunau am Inn, north of Salzburg. After dropping out of high school at age 16, he spent eight years in prewar Vienna trying to make his way as an artist. (He was rejected twice by Vienna's Academy of Fine Arts.) Although Hitler served in the German army during World War I, he didn't become a German citizen until 1932, just one year before becoming the nation's chancellor and *der Führer*.

Maria von Trapp (1905-1987)

An orphan by age seven, Maria Augusta Kitschier was raised in Tirol by an anti-Catholic socialist. When she mistakenly attended a religious lecture (she had thought it would be a Bach concert), she was so moved that she became a staunch Catholic. Her memoir of life as a novitiate at a Salzburg convent and later as governess for the von Trapp family was the basis for *The Sound of Music* (see page 308). Salzburg remains the epicenter for *S.O.M.* sights and tours.

Billy Wilder (1906-2002)

Born in Austria, Hollywood legend Billy Wilder won Oscars for directing *The Lost Weekend* and *The Apartment*. He also wrote and/or directed such Hollywood classics as *Some Like It Hot*, *The Seven Year Itch*, *Ball of Fire*, *Sunset Boulevard*, *Stalag 17*, *Sabrina*, and the dark and brooding *Double Indemnity*. He lost his mother in the Holocaust and was often bitter about his native country. "The Austrians are brilliant people," he once said. "They made the world believe that Hitler was a German and Beethoven an Austrian."

Otto Preminger (1906-1986)

Like Wilder, Otto Preminger grew up in Vienna's Jewish community. His success in Viennese theater eventually led to Hollywood, where Preminger hit the big time directing the 1944 mystery *Laura*. Twice nominated for a best-director Oscar (for *Laura* and *The Cardinal*), Preminger made films that challenged Hollywood taboos of the time, such as rape *(Anatomy of a Murder)*, drug addiction *(The Man with the Golden Arm)*, and homosexuality *(Advise and Consent)*.

Arnold Schwarzenegger (b. 1947)

Born in a village near Graz, Arnold Schwarzenegger was obsessed with bodybuilding even as a teenager. After winning international bodybuilding contests, Schwarzenegger got his big break as *Conan the Barbarian*, a role that spawned a string of blockbuster action movies, including the *Terminator* series. In 2003, Ah-nold switched careers and was elected the Republican governor of California; the "Governator" was re-elected to a second term in 2006. After leaving office in 2011, news broke that Schwarzenegger had fathered a son more than 14 years earlier with the family housekeeper—prompting his wife, Maria Shriver, to file for divorce.

Felix Baumgartner (b. 1969)

After learning to parachute in the Austrian military, daredevil skydiver Felix Baumgartner, who was born in Salzburg, has made a career of high-profile, wildly dangerous jumps off buildings, bridges, and mountains. All of Austria (and millions around the world) watched on October 14, 2012, when he plummeted 24 miles to earth in a heart-stopping supersonic jump from a helium-balloon capsule. Baumgartner simultaneously set three world records: highest-altitude manned balloon flight (24 miles up), highest-altitude parachute jump (128,100 feet), and greatest free-fall velocity (834 mph).

APPENDIX

Contents

Tourist Information

Austria's national tourist office **in the US** can be a wealth of information. They have maps and information on festivals, hiking, the wine country, and more. Call 212/944-6880 or visit www.austria. info.

In Austria: The local tourist information office (abbreviated **TI** in this book) is your best first stop in any new town or city. Try to arrive, or at least telephone, before it closes. Throughout Austria, you'll find TIs are usually well-organized and have English-speaking staff. Many TIs have information on the entire country or at least the region, so try to pick up maps for destinations you'll be visiting later in your trip. If you're arriving in town after the TI closes, call ahead or pick up a map in a neighboring town.

As national budgets tighten, many TIs have been privatized. This means they have become sales agents for big tours and hotels, and their "information" becomes unavoidably colored. While TIs are eager to book you a room, you should use their room-finding service as a last resort. Even if there's no "fee," you'll save yourself and your host money by going direct with the listings in this book.

Communicating

Hurdling the Language Barrier

Austrians speak German (though with a distinctly Austrian flair that differs a bit across regional dialects). Most young and/or well-educated Austrians—especially those in larger towns and the tourist trade—speak at least some English. Still, you'll get more smiles by using the German pleasantries (see the "German Survival Phrases for Austria" on page 481). In smaller, non-touristy towns, the language barrier is higher.

German—like English, Dutch, Swedish, and Norwegian—is a Germanic language, making it easier on most American ears than Romance languages (such as Italian and French). These tips will help you pronounce German words: The letter *w* is always pronounced as *v* (e.g., the word for "wonderful" is *wunderbar*, pronounced VOON-der-bar). The letter *j* is always pronounced as *y* (so *Joghurt* is pronounced the same as English "yogurt"), and the letter *v* is pronounced as *f* (so the number *vier*—four—sounds just like "fear"). There are no silent letters. The rule for pronouncing *ie* and *ei* never changes: Always say the name of the second letter. So *ie* sounds like the letter "e" (as in *hier* and *Bier*, the German words for "here" and "beer"), while *ei* sounds like the letter "i" (as in *nein* and *Wein*, the German words for "no" and "wine"). The vowel combination *au* is pronounced "ow" (as in *Frau*). The vowel combinations *eu* and *äu* are pronounced "oy" (as in *neu*, *Deutsch*, and *Bräu*, the German words for "new," "German," and "brew"). To pronounce *ö* and *ü*, purse your lips when you say the vowel; the other vowel with an umlaut, *ä*, is pronounced the same as "e" in "men." (In typewritten German, these can be depicted as the vowel followed by an *e*—*oe*, *ue*, and *ae*, respectively.) The letter *Eszett (ß)* represents "ss." Written German always capitalizes all nouns.

Regional dialects aside, the language spoken by Austrians isn't all that different from the *Deutsch* spoken by Germans—but those small differences are a big deal to Austrians. The most important one is how you say "hello": Austrians will greet you (and each other) with a *Grüss Gott*, or perhaps *Servus*—but never with the German *Guten Tag*, a phrase that sounds oddly uptight to Austrians (and as foreign as being wished a "G'day" in the US). Instead, stick to *Grüss Gott* ("May God greet you"), or a simple *Grüss*, for "hello." You'll get the correct pronunciation after the first volley—listen and copy.

You're likely to run into a few other un-German German

words on your trip, such as *Jänner* and *Feber* for January and February (rather than the German *Januar* and *Februar*). A lot of food names are different: In Austria, potatoes are *Erdäpfel* (not *Kartoffeln*), tomatoes are *Paradeiser* (not *Tomaten*), a bread roll is a *Semmel* (not *Brötchen*), corn is *Kukuruz* (not *Mais*), green beans are *Fisolen* (not *grüne Bohnen*), cauliflower is *Karfiol* (not *Blumenkohl*), whipped cream is *Obers* (not *Schlagsahne*), and apricot jam and ice cream will be labeled as *Marille* (not *Aprikose*). Tacking an *-l* or *-erl* on the end of a word makes it a diminutive form—like adding "-ette" or "-ie" to an English word (or *-chen* in German German).

Austrians appreciate any effort on your part to speak German—even if it's just *ein Bissl* (a little bit)—and if you already speak some German German, they'll understand you just fine. Give it your best shot.

Telephones

Smart travelers use the telephone to reserve or reconfirm rooms, get tourist information, reserve restaurants, confirm tour times, or phone home. This section covers dialing instructions, phone cards, and types of phones (for more in-depth information, see www.ricksteves.com/phoning).

How to Dial

Calling from the US to Europe, or vice versa, is simple—once you break the code. The European calling chart in this chapter will walk you through it.

Dialing Domestically Within Austria

Austria, like much of the US, uses an area-code dialing system. If you're dialing within an area code, you just dial the local number to be connected; but if you're calling outside your area code, you have to dial both the area code (which starts with 0) and the local number. If you're calling a mobile phone within Austria, you must always dial the complete number (which starts with 06). You'll find area codes listed throughout this book, or you can get them from directory assistance (tel. 16).

For example, Vienna's area code is 01 and the number of one of my recommended Vienna hotels is 534-050. To call the hotel within Vienna, you'd dial 534-050. To call it from Salzburg, you'd dial 01/534-050.

These instructions apply to dialing from a landline (such as a pay phone or your hotel-room phone) or an Austrian mobile phone.

If you're dialing within Austria using your US mobile phone, you may need to dial as if it's a domestic call, or you may need to dial as if you're calling from the US (see "Dialing Internationally," next). Try it one way, and if it doesn't work, try it the other way.

APPENDIX

Don't be surprised if local phone numbers in Austria have different numbers of digits within the same city or even the same hotel (for example, a hotel can have a 6-digit phone number and an 8-digit fax number).

Dialing Internationally to or from Austria

If you want to make an international call, follow these steps:

• Dial the international access code (00 if you're calling from Europe, 011 from the US or Canada). If you're dialing from a mobile phone, you can replace the international access code with +, which works regardless of where you're calling from. (On many mobile phones, you can insert a + by pressing and holding the 0 key.)

• Dial the country code of the country you're calling (43 for Austria, or 1 for the US or Canada).

• Dial the area code (without its initial 0) and the local number. (If you're calling a mobile-phone number internationally, you also drop the 0.)

Calling from the US to Austria: To call the recommended Vienna hotel from the US, dial 011 (the US international access code), 43 (Austria's country code), 1 (Vienna's area code without the initial 0), and 534-050.

Calling from any European Country to the US: To call my office in Edmonds, Washington, from anywhere in Europe, I dial 00 (Europe's international access code), 1 (the US country code), 425 (Edmonds' area code), and 771-8303.

Mobile Phones

Traveling with a mobile phone is handy and practical. Whether you're using a smartphone or a conventional cell phone, the basics for how to make calls and send texts are the same. For specifics on using your smartphone to get online, see the sidebar.

Roaming with Your Mobile Phone: Your US mobile phone works in Europe if it's GSM-enabled, tri-band or quad-band, and on a calling plan that includes international calls. Phones from T-Mobile and AT&T, which use the same GSM technology that Europe does, are more likely to work overseas than Verizon or Sprint phones (if you're not sure, ask your service provider). Most US providers will charge you $1.29-1.99 per minute to make or receive calls while roaming internationally, and 20–50 cents to send or receive text messages. If you bother to sign up for an international calling plan with your provider, you'll save a few dimes per minute. Though pricey, roaming on your own phone is easy and can be a cost-effective way to keep in touch—especially on a short trip or if you won't be making many calls.

Buying and Using SIM Cards in Europe: You'll pay much

cheaper rates if you put a European SIM card in your mobile phone; to do this, your phone must be electronically "unlocked" (ask your provider about this, buy an unlocked phone before you leave, or get one in Europe—see "Other Mobile-Phone Options," next). Then, in Europe, you can buy a fingernail-size **SIM card,** which gives you an Austrian phone number. SIM cards are available at mobile-phone stores and some newsstand kiosks for $5-10, and often include at least that much prepaid domestic calling time (making the card itself almost free). When you buy a SIM card, you may need to show ID, such as your passport.

Insert the SIM card in your phone (usually in a slot behind the battery or on the side), and it'll work like a European mobile phone. Before purchasing a SIM card, always ask about fees for domestic and international calls, roaming charges, and how to check your credit balance and buy more time. When you're in the SIM card's home country, domestic calls average 10-20 cents per minute, and incoming calls are free. Rates are higher if you're roaming in another country, and you may pay more to call a toll number than you would dialing from a fixed line.

Other Mobile-Phone Options: Many travelers like to carry two phones: both their own US mobile phone (allowing them to stay reachable on their own phone number) and a second, unlocked European phone (which lets them do all their local calling at far cheaper rates). You could either bring two phones from home, or get one in Europe. If you have an old mobile phone sitting around, ask your provider for the "unlock code" so it can be used with European SIM cards. Or buy a cheap, basic phone before you go (search your favorite online shopping site for "unlocked quad-band GSM phone").

In Europe, basic phones are sold at hole-in-the-wall vendors at many airports and train stations, and at phone desks within larger department stores. Phones that are "locked" to work with a single provider start around $40; "unlocked" phones (which work with any SIM card) start around $60. Regardless of how you get your phone, remember that you'll need a SIM card to make it work.

Car-rental companies and mobile-phone companies offer the option to rent a mobile phone with a European number. While this seems convenient, hidden fees (such as high per-minute charges or expensive shipping costs) can really add up—which usually makes it a bad value. One exception is Verizon's Global Travel Program, available only to Verizon customers.

Calling over the Internet

Some things that seem too good to be true...actually are true. If you're traveling with a laptop, tablet, or smartphone, you can make free calls over the Internet to another wireless device, anywhere in

European Calling Chart

Just smile and dial, using this key:
AC = Area Code, LN = Local Number.

European Country	Calling long distance within ...	Calling from the US or Canada to ...	Calling from a European country to ...
Austria	AC + LN	011 + 43 + AC (without the initial zero) + LN	00 + 43 + AC (without the initial zero) + LN
Belgium	LN	011 + 32 + LN (without initial zero)	00 + 32 + LN (without initial zero)
Bosnia-Herzegovina	AC + LN	011 + 387 + AC (without initial zero) + LN	00 + 387 + AC (without initial zero) + LN
Britain	AC + LN	011 + 44 + AC (without initial zero) + LN	00 + 44 + AC (without initial zero) + LN
Croatia	AC + LN	011 + 385 + AC (without initial zero) + LN	00 + 385 + AC (without initial zero) + LN
Czech Republic	LN	011 + 420 + LN	00 + 420 + LN
Denmark	LN	011 + 45 + LN	00 + 45 + LN
Estonia	LN	011 + 372 + LN	00 + 372 + LN
Finland	AC + LN	011 + 358 + AC (without initial zero) + LN	999 (or other 900 number) + 358 + AC (without initial zero) + LN
France	LN	011 + 33 + LN (without initial zero)	00 + 33 + LN (without initial zero)
Germany	AC + LN	011 + 49 + AC (without initial zero) + LN	00 + 49 + AC (without initial zero) + LN
Gibraltar	LN	011 + 350 + LN	00 + 350 + LN
Greece	LN	011 + 30 + LN	00 + 30 + LN
Hungary	06 + AC + LN	011 + 36 + AC + LN	00 + 36 + AC + LN
Ireland	AC + LN	011 + 353 + AC (without initial zero) + LN	00 + 353 + AC (without initial zero) + LN

European Country	Calling long distance within ...	Calling from the US or Canada to ...	Calling from a European country to ...
Italy	LN	011 + 39 + LN	00 + 39 + LN
Montenegro	AC + LN	011 + 382 + AC (without initial zero) + LN	00 + 382 + AC (without initial zero) + LN
Morocco	LN	011 + 212 + LN (without initial zero)	00 + 212 + LN (without initial zero)
Netherlands	AC + LN	011 + 31 + AC (without initial zero) + LN	00 + 31 + AC (without initial zero) + LN
Norway	LN	011 + 47 + LN	00 + 47 + LN
Poland	LN	011 + 48 + LN	00 + 48 + LN
Portugal	LN	011 + 351 + LN	00 + 351 + LN
Slovakia	AC + LN	011 + 421 + AC (without initial zero) + LN	00 + 421 + AC (without initial zero) + LN
Slovenia	AC + LN	011 + 386 + AC (without initial zero) + LN	00 + 386 + AC (without initial zero) + LN
Spain	LN	011 + 34 + LN	00 + 34 + LN
Sweden	AC + LN	011 + 46 + AC (without initial zero) + LN	00 + 46 + AC (without initial zero) + LN
Switzerland	LN	011 + 41 + LN (without initial zero)	00 + 41 + LN (without initial zero)
Turkey	AC (if there's no initial zero, add one) + LN	011 + 90 + AC (without initial zero) + LN	00 + 90 + AC (without initial zero) + LN

- The instructions above apply whether you're calling to or from a European landline or mobile phone.

- If calling from any mobile phone, you can replace the international access code with "+" (press and hold 0 to insert it).

- The international access code is 011 if you're calling from the US or Canada.

- To call the US or Canada from Europe, dial 00, then 1 (country code for US and Canada), then the area code and number. In short, 00 + 1 + AC + LN = Hi, Mom!

Smartphones and Data Roaming

I take my smartphone to Europe, using it to make phone calls (sparingly) and send texts, but also to check email, listen to audio tours, and browse the Internet. If you're clever, you can do all this without incurring huge data-roaming fees. Here's how.

Many smartphones, such as the iPhone, Android, and BlackBerry, work in Europe (though some older Verizon iPhones don't). For voice calls and text messaging, smartphones work like any mobile phone (as described under "Roaming with Your Mobile Phone," earlier) —unless you're connected to free Wi-Fi, in which case you can use Skype, Google Talk, or FaceTime to call for free (or at least very cheaply; see "Calling over the Internet," earlier).

The (potentially) *really* expensive aspect of using smartphones in Europe is not voice calls or text messages, but sky-high rates for using data: checking email, browsing the Internet, streaming videos, using certain apps, and so on. If you don't proactively adjust your settings, these charges can mount up even if you're not actually using your phone—because the phone is constantly "roaming" to update your email and such. (One tip is to switch your email settings from "push" to "fetch," so you can choose when to download your emails rather than having them automatically "pushed" over the Internet to your device.)

The best solution: Disable data roaming entirely, and use your device to access the Internet only when you find free Wi-Fi (at your hotel, for example). Then you can surf the net to your heart's content, or make free (or extremely cheap) phone calls via Skype. You can manually turn off data roaming on your phone's menu (check under the "Network" settings). For added security, you can call and ask your service provider to temporarily suspend your data account entirely for the length of your trip.

Some travelers enjoy the flexibility of getting online even when they're not on free Wi-Fi. But be careful. If you simply switch on data roaming, you'll pay exorbitant rates of about $20 per megabyte (figure around 40 cents per email downloaded, or about $3 to view a typical web page)—much more expensive than it is back home. If you know you'll be doing some data roaming, it's far more affordable to sign up for a limited international data-roaming plan through your carrier (but be very clear on your megabyte limit to avoid inflated overage charges). In general, ask your provider in advance how to avoid unwittingly roaming your way to a huge bill.

APPENDIX

the world, for free. (Or you can pay a few cents to call from your computer to a telephone.) The major providers are Skype, Google Talk, and (on Apple devices) FaceTime. You can get online at a Wi-Fi hotspot and use these apps to make calls without ringing up expensive roaming charges (though call quality can be spotty on slow connections). You can make Internet calls even if you're traveling without your own mobile device: Many European Internet cafés have Skype, as well as microphones and webcams, on their terminals—just log on and chat away.

Landline Telephones

As in the US, these days most Austrians do the majority of their phoning on mobile phones. But you'll still encounter landlines in hotel rooms and at pay phones.

Hotel-Room Phones: Calling from the phone in your room can be great for local calls and for international calls if you have an international phone card (described later). Otherwise, hotel-room phones can be an almost criminal rip-off for long-distance or international calls. Many hotels charge a fee for local and sometimes even "toll-free" numbers—always ask for the rates before you dial. Incoming calls are free, making this a cheap way for friends and family to stay in touch (provided they have a long-distance plan with good international rates—and a list of your hotels' phone numbers).

Public Pay Phones: Coin-op phones are virtually extinct in Europe. To make calls from public phones, you'll need a prepaid phone card, described next.

Types of Telephone Cards

There are two types of phone cards: insertable (for pay phones) and international (cheap for overseas calls and usable from any type of phone). Both types of phone card work only in Austria. If you have a live card at the end of your trip, give it to another traveler to use— most cards expire 3-6 months after the first use.

Insertable Phone Cards: This type of card can be used only at pay phones, and they are sold in denominations starting at about €5 at TIs, tobacco shops, post offices, and train stations. To use the card, physically insert it into a slot in the pay phone. While you can use these cards to call anywhere in the world, they're only a good deal for making quick local calls from a phone booth.

International Phone Cards: With these cards, phone calls from Austria to the US can cost less than a nickel a minute. The cards can also be used to make local calls, and they work from any type of phone, including your hotel-room phone or a mobile phone with a European SIM card. To use a card, dial a toll-free access number, then enter your scratch-to-reveal PIN code. If the prompts are in German, wait to see if the announcement also follows in English. If not, experiment: Dial your code, followed by the pound sign (#), then the number, then the pound sign again, and so on, until it works. When you're using an international phone card to make a local call in Austria, you must dial the area code even if you're calling across the street.

You can buy the cards at small newsstand kiosks and hole-in-the-wall long-distance shops. There are many different brands of cards, so ask the clerk which one has the best rates for calls to America. Some cards are rechargeable; you can call the number on the card, give your credit-card number, and buy more time. Before buying a card, make sure the access number you'll dial is toll-free, not a local number (or else you'll be paying for a local call *and* deducting time from your calling card).

Buy a lower denomination in case the card is a dud. Some shops also sell cardless codes, printed right on the receipt. Since you don't need the actual card or receipt to use the account, you can write down the access number and code and share it with friends.

US Calling Cards: These cards, such as the ones offered by AT&T, Verizon, and Sprint, are a rotten value, and are being phased out. Try any of the options outlined earlier.

Useful Phone Numbers
Emergency and Directory Assistance
Emergency (police and ambulance): Tel. 112
Directory Assistance Within Austria: Tel. 16
International Directory Assistance: Tel. 08

Embassies
US Embassy in Vienna: Boltzmanngasse 16, tel. 01/313-390, embassy@usembassy.at; consular services at Parkring 12, daily 8:00-11:30, tel. 01/313-397-535, www.usembassy.at, consulatevienna@state.gov
Canadian Embassy in Vienna: Laurenzerberg 2, 3rd floor, Mon-Fri 8:00-12:30 & 13:30-15:30, tel. 01/531-383-000, after-hours emergencies call collect Canadian tel. 613/996-8885, www.austria.gc.ca, vienn@international.gc.ca

Travel Advisories
US Department of State: Tel. 888-407-4747, from outside US tel. 1-202-501-4444, www.travel.state.gov
Canadian Department of Foreign Affairs: Canadian tel. 800-267-8376, from outside Canada tel. 1-613-996-8885, www.voyage.gc.ca
US Centers for Disease Control and Prevention: Tel. 800-CDC-INFO (tel. 800-232-4636), www.cdc.gov/travel

Internet Access

It's useful to get online periodically as you travel—to confirm trip plans, check train or bus schedules, get weather forecasts, catch up on email, blog or post photos from your trip, or call folks back home (explained earlier, under "Calling over the Internet").

Your Mobile Device: The majority of accommodations in Austria offer Wi-Fi, as do many cafés, making it easy for you to get online with your laptop, tablet, or smartphone. Access is often free, but sometimes there's a fee.

Some hotel rooms and Internet cafés have high-speed Internet jacks that you can plug into with an Ethernet cable. A cellular modem—which lets your device access the Internet over a mobile phone network—provides more extensive coverage, but is much more expensive than Wi-Fi.

Public Internet Terminals: Many accommodations offer a computer in the lobby with Internet access for guests. If you ask politely, smaller places may let you sit at their desk for a few minutes just to check your email. If your hotelier doesn't have access, ask to be directed to the nearest place to get online.

Security: Whether you're accessing the Internet with your own device or at a public terminal, using a shared network or computer comes with the potential for increased security risks. Be careful about storing personal information online, such as passport and credit-card numbers. If you're not convinced a connection is secure, avoid accessing any sites that could be vulnerable to fraud (e.g., online banking).

Mail

You can mail one package per day to yourself worth up to $200 duty-free from Europe to the US (mark it "personal purchases"). If you're sending a gift to someone, mark it "unsolicited gift." For details, visit www.cbp.gov and search for "Know Before You Go."

The Austrian postal service works fine, but for quick transatlantic delivery (in either direction), consider services such as DHL (www.dhl.com).

Transportation

By Car or Train?

If you're debating between public transportation and car rental, consider these factors: Cars are best for three or more traveling together (especially families with small kids), those packing heavy, and those scouring the countryside. Trains and buses are best for solo travelers, blitz tourists, city-to-city travelers, and those who don't want to drive in Europe. While a car gives you more freedom—enabling you to search for hotels more easily and carrying

Public Transportation in Austria

- - - Rail
- - - Bus
- - - Boat

your bags for you—trains and buses zip you effortlessly and sceni-cally from city to city, usually dropping you in the center, often near a TI. A car is an expensive headache in cities such as Vienna and Salzburg.

Trains

Austrian trains are generally slick, speedy, and fairly punctual, with synchronized connections. They cover cities well, but some frustrating schedules make a few out-of-the-way recommendations (such as the Mauthausen concentration camp memorial, and—over the border—Bavaria's Wieskirche) not worth the time and trouble for the less determined. Note that it's illegal to smoke on Austria's trains and most of its buses.

Types of Trains

The Austrian Railways (a.k.a. Österreichische Bundesbahn, or ÖBB) operates several classes of trains, which differ substantially in speed and comfort.

Austria's newest, fastest, and reddest train, the Railjet, streaks between Budapest, Vienna, Munich (or Innsbruck), and Zürich. German ICE trains (white with red trim and streamlined noses) also cover those same main routes in air-conditioned comfort.

Red regional trains (labeled R and REX on schedules) are the slowest—the milk-run R trains stop at every small station—but cost much less. Mid-level IC and EC trains are air-conditioned, but look older than the Railjets and ICEs (and don't always have electrical outlets for your laptop).

In general, take the fastest train available—there's no supplement for the fast ICE and Railjet trains (but using a ritzy business compartment on the fast trains requires a paid seat reservation fee). Note that companions sharing an Einfach-Raus-Ticket need to take slower trains (see "Tickets," later).

Schedules

Schedules change by season and vary between weekdays and weekends. To verify train times shown in this book, visit www.oebb.

at (Austrian Railways) or www.bahn.com (Germany's excellent Europe-wide timetable). At staffed train stations, attendants will print out a step-by-step itinerary for you, free of charge. Schedules are also posted at stations. The computerized trackside machines marked *Fahrkarten* do not, unfortunately, give schedule information.

If you're changing trains en route and have a tight connection, note the numbers of the platforms (*Bahnsteig* or *Gleis*) where you will arrive and depart (listed on printed and online itineraries). This will save you precious time hunting for your connecting train.

You can call Austria's train information number from anywhere in the country: toll tel. 051-717 (to get an operator, dial 2, then 2). Ask for an English speaker.

Railpasses

The easy-to-use Austria Pass can be a good value for rail travel within the country if you are taking several longer trips. If you're traveling in a neighboring country as well, consider a two-country Eurail Pass, which allows you to pair Austria with Germany, Switzerland, the Czech Republic, or Hungary. The Austria-Croatia-Slovenia Pass covers travel in those three countries, and the European East Pass covers Austria and the Czech Republic, Slovakia, Hungary, and Poland. Another option is the Select Pass, which gives you up to 15 travel days (within a two-month period) in three, four, or five adjacent countries—you could choose Austria, Germany, and another bordering country. If you're planning a whirlwind tour of Europe, another possibility is the 23-country Global Pass. These passes are available in a saverpass version, which gives a 15 percent discount on railpasses for two or more companions traveling together. For specifics, check the railpass chart in this chapter and visit www.ricksteves.com/rail.

Railpass travelers should know what extras are covered by their pass, such as discounts on Danube boats. Flexipass holders should note that discounted trips don't use up a flexi-day, but fully covered ("free") trips do. The "used" flexipass day can also cover your train travel on that day (but if you're not planning to travel more that day, it makes sense to pay for, say, a short boat ride rather than use up a day of your pass for it).

Railpasses

Prices listed are for 2012 and are subject to change. For the latest prices, details, train schedules, and easy online ordering, see my comprehensive *Guide to Eurail Passes* at www.ricksteves.com/rail.

"Saver" prices are per person for two or more people traveling together. "Youth" means under age 26. The fare for children 4–11 is half the adult individual fare or Saver fare. Kids under age 4 travel free.

AUSTRIA PASS

	Indiv. 1st Cl.	Indiv. 2nd Cl.	Saver 1st Cl.	Saver 2nd Cl.	Youth 2nd Cl.
3 days in 1 month	$226	$159	$193	$136	$105
Extra rail days (max. 5)	26	19	22	15	12

AUSTRIA–GERMANY PASS

	Indiv. 1st Cl.	Indiv. 2nd Cl.	Saver 1st Cl.	Saver 2nd Cl.	Youth 2nd Cl.
5 days in 2 months	$406	$350	$350	$298	$300
6 days in 2 months	447	382	382	328	328
8 days in 2 months	532	454	454	391	392
10 days in 2 months	620	527	527	454	454

AUSTRIA–SWITZERLAND PASS

	Individual 1st Class	Saver 1st Class	Youth 2nd Class
4 days in 2 months	$386	$329	$271
Extra rail days (max. 6)	43	36	30

AUSTRIA–CZECH or AUSTRIA–HUNGARY PASS

	Individual 1st Class	Saver 1st Class	Youth 2nd Class
4 days in 2 months	$253	$215	$166
Extra rail days (max. 6)	34	30	22

AUSTRIA–CROATIA–SLOVENIA PASS

	Individual 1st Class	Saver 1st Class	Youth 2nd Class
4 days in 2 months	$268	$234	$194
Extra rail days (max. 6)	38	33	27

EUROPEAN EAST PASS

	1st Class	2nd Class
5 days in 1 month	$300	$206
Extra rail days (max. 5)	34	29

Covers Austria, Czech Republic, Slovakia, Hungary and Poland.

Map key:

Approximate point-to-point one-way second-class rail fares in US dollars. First class costs 50 percent more. Add up the approximate ticket costs for your trip to see if a railpass will save you money.

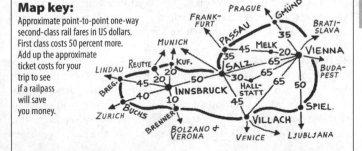

Tickets

When buying individual tickets, remember that traveling in second class instead of first class provides the same transportation for 33 percent less. Bikes cost €5-12 extra on EC and IC trains—must reserve in advance—and €5 extra for a day of travel on local trains. Ticket fares are shown on the railpass chart in this chapter and at www.oebb.at.

Deals: If you're not using a railpass, it's worth knowing about ticket specials in Austria.

Austrian Railways' **Einfach-Raus-Ticket** ("Just Get Outta Here" ticket) is a cheap way for couples and small groups to travel. It's valid only on slower regional trains: R, REX, S-Bahn, RSB, ER, and EZ (€32, €39 with bikes, covers 2-5 people for a whole day of travel, not valid Mon-Fri before 9:00, cannot be used by solo travelers).

The **Vorteils** card, which knocks 50 percent off all rail fares, isn't worth the expense for most visitors (€99, valid one year, requires photo). But the youth version (under 26 only, €20) and senior version (age 60 and above, €27) pay for themselves with just one trip from Vienna to Innsbruck. Bring a photo to any station to get a Vorteils card.

Austrian Railways offers €29-69 advance-purchase **"Spar-Schiene"** deals to major cities within Austria and around Europe (limited availability, locks you into a date and time).

For a whole day of travel on local trains within Bavaria, consider the Bayern-Ticket (€22/day for the first person plus €4 for each additional person).

Buying Tickets: Buying point-to-point tickets in Austria is a straightforward process, with no advance-purchase discounts or reservation requirement. Major Austrian stations have a handy *Reisezentrum* (Travel Center) where you can ask questions and buy tickets. Many smaller stations, though, are unstaffed, with tickets sold only from machines (marked *Fahrkarten,* which means "tickets"). You can pay with bills, coins, or credit cards (if your credit card isn't accepted, just use cash). You can buy tickets on board ICE, EN, and EC trains for a €3 fee. Boarding a local train without a ticket, however, can earn you a hefty fine if you could have bought a ticket at the station where you boarded.

Renting a Car

If you're renting a car in Austria, bring your driver's license. You're also technically required to have an International Driving Permit—an official translation of your driver's license (sold at your local AAA office for $15 plus the cost of two passport-type photos; see www.aaa.com). While that's the letter of the law, I've often rented cars in Austria without having—or being asked to show—this permit.

Most Austrian car-rental companies will not rent to someone under 19, and restrictions and "underage fees" can apply if you're under 24. There's generally not a maximum age limit, but if you are 70 or older, it's smart to ask. If you're considered too young or old, look into leasing (covered later), which has less-stringent age restrictions.

Research car rentals before you go. It's cheaper to arrange most car rentals from the US. Call several companies and look on-line to compare rates, or arrange a rental through your hometown travel agent.

Most of the major US rental agencies (including National, Avis, Budget, Hertz, and Thrifty) have offices throughout Europe. Also consider the two major Europe-based agencies, Europcar and Sixt. It can be cheaper to use a consolidator, such as Auto Europe (www.autoeurope.com) and Europe by Car (www.ebctravel.com), which compares rates at several companies to get you the best deal. However, my readers have reported problems with consolidators, ranging from misinformation to unexpected fees; because you're going through a middleman, it can be more challenging to resolve disputes that arise with the rental agency.

Regardless of the car-rental company you choose, always read the contract carefully. The fine print can conceal a host of common add-on charges—such as one-way drop-off fees, airport surcharges, or mandatory insurance policies—that aren't included in the "total price," but can be tacked on when you pick up your car. You may need to query rental agents pointedly to find out your actual cost.

For the best deal, rent by the week with unlimited mileage. To save money on fuel, ask for a diesel car. I normally rent the smallest, least-expensive model with a stick shift (cheaper than an automatic). An automatic transmission adds about 50 percent to the car-rental cost over a manual transmission. Almost all rentals are manual by default, so if you need an automatic, you must request one in advance; be aware that these cars are usually larger models (not as maneuverable on narrow, winding roads).

For a two-week rental, allow roughly $500 per person including parking, tolls, gas, and insurance. For trips of three weeks or more, look into leasing; you'll save money on insurance and taxes. Be warned that international trips—say, picking up in Vienna and dropping in Budapest—can be expensive (it depends partly on distance).

As a rule, always tell your car-rental company up front exactly which countries you'll be entering. Some companies levy extra insurance fees for trips taken in certain countries with certain types

Driving in Austria: Distance & Time

Note: Your times may vary based on traffic, construction, and road conditions.

20 Kilometers
20 Miles

m = miles
h = hours

GERMANY

To Prague

To Rothenburg

150m • 2h

240m • 4h

Munich

80m • 1.25h

Salzburg

80m • 1.25h

70m • 1.5h

100m • 1.5h

Füssen

12m • .25h

Reutte

60m • 1.25h

Hall

Innsbruck

110m • 2h

Berchtesgaden

15m • .5h

Lake Constance

140m • 3.5h

180m • 3.5h

25m • .5h

Brenner Pass

220m • 3.5h

To Zürich

150m • 2.5h

SWITZERLAND

ITALY

To Verona

of cars (such as BMWs, Mercedes, and convertibles). Double-check with your rental agent that you have all the documentation you need before you drive off (especially if you're crossing borders into non-Schengen countries, such as Croatia, where you might need to present proof of insurance).

You can sometimes get a GPS unit with your rental car or leased vehicle for an additional fee (around $15/day); be sure it's set to English and has all the maps you need before you drive off. Or, if you own a portable GPS device, consider taking it to Europe (buy and upload European maps before your trip). GPS apps are also available for smartphones, but downloading maps on one of these apps in Europe could lead to an exorbitant data-roaming bill (for more details, see the sidebar on page 456).

Big companies have offices in most cities; ask whether they can pick you up at your hotel. Small local rental companies can be cheaper but aren't as flexible.

Compare pickup costs (downtown can be less expensive than the airport) and explore drop-off options. When selecting a loca-

tion, don't trust the agency's description of "downtown" or "city center." In some cases, a "downtown" branch can be on the outskirts of the city—a long, costly taxi ride from the center. Before choosing, plug the addresses into a mapping website. You may find that the "train station" location is handier. Returning a car at a big-city train station or downtown agency can be tricky; get precise details on the car drop-off location and hours, and allow ample time to find it. Note that rental offices usually close from midday Saturday until Monday morning.

When you pick up the car, check it thoroughly and make sure any damage is noted on your rental agreement. Find out how your car's lights, turn signals, wipers, and fuel cap function, and know what kind of fuel the car takes. When you return the car, make sure the agent verifies its condition with you.

Car Insurance Options

When you rent a car, you are liable for a very high deductible, sometimes equal to the entire value of the car. Limit your financial risk by choosing one of these three options: Buy Collision Damage Waiver (CDW) coverage from the car-rental company, get coverage through your credit card (free, if your card automatically includes zero-deductible coverage), or buy coverage through Travel Guard.

CDW includes a very high deductible (typically $1,000-1,500). Though each rental company has its own variation, basic CDW costs $15-35 a day (figure roughly 30 percent extra) and reduces your liability, but does not eliminate it. When you pick up the car, you'll be offered the chance to "buy down" the basic deductible to zero (for an additional $10-30/day; this is often called "super CDW").

If you opt instead for **credit-card coverage,** there's a catch. You'll technically have to decline all coverage offered by the car-rental company, which means they can place a hold on your card (it can be up to the full value of the car). In case of damage, it can be time-consuming to resolve the charges with your credit-card company. Before you decide on this option, quiz your credit-card company about how it works and ask them to explain the worst-case scenario.

Finally, you can buy collision insurance from **Travel Guard** ($9/day plus a one-time $3 service fee covers you up to $35,000, $250 deductible, tel. 800-826-4919, www.travelguard.com). It's valid nearly everywhere in Europe, except the Republic of Ireland, and some Italian car-rental companies refuse to honor it. Note that various states differ on which products and policies are available to their residents.

For more on car-rental insurance, see www.ricksteves.com/cdw.

Leasing

For trips of three weeks or more, consider leasing (which automatically includes zero-deductible collision and theft insurance). By technically buying and then selling back the car, you save lots of money on tax and insurance. Leasing provides you a brand-new car with unlimited mileage and a 24-hour emergency assistance program. You can lease for as little as 21 days to as long as six months. Car leases must be arranged from the US. One of many companies offering affordable lease packages is Europe by Car (US tel. 800-223-1516, www.ebctravel.com).

Driving

Learn the universal road signs (explained in charts in most road atlases and at service stations). Seat belts are required, and two beers under those belts are enough to land you in jail.

Road Rules: Be aware of typical European road rules. For ex-

AND LEARN THESE ROAD SIGNS

peed Limit (km/hr)

Yield

No Passing

End of No Passing Zone

One Way

Intersection

Main Road

Freeway

Danger

No Entry

No Entry for Cars

All Vehicles Prohibited

Parking

No Parking

Customs

Peace

ample, many countries require headlights to be turned on at all times; in Austria, you're required to use low-beam headlights when driving in urban areas. It's generally illegal to drive while using your mobile phone without a hands-free headset. In Europe, you're not allowed to turn right on a red light, unless there is a sign or signal specifically authorizing it. Ask your car-rental company about these rules, or check the US State Department website (www.travel.state.gov, click on "International Travel," then specify your country of choice and click "Traffic Safety and Road Conditions").

Tolls: Austria charges drivers who use their major roads. You'll need to have a *Vignette* sticker stuck to the inside of your rental car's windshield (buy at the border crossing, big gas stations near borders, or a rental-car agency). The cost is €8 for 10 days, or €23 for two months. Not having one earns you a stiff fine. Place it on your windshield exactly as shown on the back of the sticker, and keep the peel-off paper—it's your receipt.

Fuel: Unleaded gasoline comes in regular (91 octane) and "Euro-Super" (95 octane). If you are also driving in Germany, pumps marked "E10" or "Super E10" mean the gas contains 10 percent ethanol—make sure your rental can run on this mix. You don't have to worry about learning the German word for diesel. Your US credit and debit cards may not work at self-service gas pumps. Pay the attendant or be sure to carry sufficient cash in euros.

Navigation: Use good local maps and study them before each drive. Learn which exits you need to look out for, which major cities you'll travel toward, where the ruined castles lurk, and so on. Ring roads go around a city. To get to the center of a city, follow signs for *Zentrum* or *Stadtmitte*. When navigating, you'll see *nord, süd, ost,* and *west.*

Autobahn: Every long drive between my recommended destinations is via the autobahn (super-freeway) and *Schnellstrassen* (expressway) system, and nearly every scenic backcountry drive is paved and comfortable.

The shortest distance between any two points is the autobahn. Blue signs direct you to the autobahn, and in Austria, unlike in

Germany, the autobahn has a speed limit (130 km/hour, unless otherwise signed). Learn the signs: *Dreieck* ("three corners") means a Y in the road; *Autobahnkreuz* is an interchange. While all roads seem to lead to the little town of Ausfahrt, that's the German word for exit. Exits are spaced about every 20 miles and often have a gas station, a restaurant, a mini-market, and sometimes a tourist information desk. Exits and intersections refer to the next major city or the nearest small town. Peruse the map and anticipate which town names to look out for. Know what you're looking for—miss it, and you're long autobahn-gone.

Parking: For parking on the street, you can pick up a cardboard clock (*Parkscheibe*, available free at gas stations, police stations, and *Tabak* shops). Display your arrival time on the clock and put it on the dashboard, so parking attendants can see you've been there less than the posted maximum stay (blue lines indicate 90-minute zones on Austrian streets). Your US credit and debit cards may not work at automated parking garages; be sure to carry sufficient cash in euros.

Theft: Keep your valuables in your hotel room or, if you're between destinations, covered in your trunk. Leave nothing worth stealing in the car, especially overnight. If your car's a hatchback, take the trunk cover off at night so thieves can look in without breaking in. Try to make your car look locally owned by hiding the "tourist-owned" rental-company decals and putting a local newspaper in your front or back window. While you should avoid parking lots with twinkly asphalt, thieves break car windows anywhere, even at stoplights.

Cheap Flights

If you're considering a train ride that's more than five hours long, a flight may save you both time and money. When comparing your options, factor in the time it takes to get to the airport and how early you'll need to arrive to check in.

The best comparison search engine for both international and intra-European flights is www.kayak.com. For inexpensive flights within Europe, try www.skyscanner.com or www.hipmunk.com. If you're not sure who flies to your destination, check its airport's website for a list of carriers.

Well-known cheapo airlines in Europe include easyJet (www.easyjet.com), Ryanair (www.ryanair.com), and Austria's own Niki (www.flyniki.com).

Be aware of the potential drawbacks of flying on the cheap: nonrefundable and nonchangeable tickets, minimal or nonexistent customer service, treks to airports far outside town, and stingy baggage allowances with steep overage fees. If you're traveling with lots of luggage, a cheap flight can quickly become a bad deal. To avoid unpleasant surprises, read the small print before you book.

Resources

Resources from Rick Steves

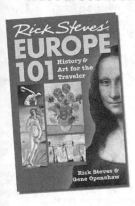

Rick Steves' Vienna, Salzburg & Tirol is one of many books in my series on European travel, which includes country guidebooks, city guidebooks (Rome, Florence, Paris, London, etc.), Snapshot guides (excerpted chapters from my country guides), Pocket Guides (full-color little books on big cities), and my budget-travel skills handbook, *Rick Steves' Europe Through the Back Door*. Most of my titles are available as ebooks. My phrase books—for German, French, Italian, Spanish, and Portuguese—are practical and budget-oriented. My other books include *Europe 101* (a crash course on art and history), *Mediterranean Cruise Ports* (how to make the most of your time in port), and *Travel as a Political Act* (a travelogue sprinkled with tips for bringing home a global perspective). A more complete list of my titles appears near the end of this book.

Video: My TV series, *Rick Steves' Europe,* covers European destinations in 100 shows, with three episodes on Austria. To watch episodes online, visit www.hulu.com; for scripts and local airtimes, see www.ricksteves.com/tv.

Audio: My weekly public radio show, *Travel with Rick Steves,* features interviews with travel experts from around the world. I've also produced free, self-guided audio tours of some of the top sights in Vienna and Salzburg. All of this audio content is available for free at Rick Steves Audio Europe, an extensive online library organized by desti-

nation. Choose whatever interests you, and download it for free via the Rick Steves Audio Europe smartphone app, www.ricksteves.com/audioeurope, iTunes, or Google Play.

Maps

The black-and-white maps in this book are concise and simple, designed to help you locate recommended places and get to local TIs, where you can pick up a more in-depth map (usually free). Better

Begin Your Trip at www.ricksteves.com

At ricksteves.com, you'll discover a wealth of free information on European destinations, including fresh monthly news and helpful tips from thousands of fellow travelers. You'll find my latest guidebook updates (www.ricksteves.com/update), a monthly travel e-newsletter (easy and free to sign up), my personal travel blog, and my free Rick Steves Audio Europe smartphone app (if you don't have a smartphone, you can access the same content via podcasts). You can even follow me on Facebook and Twitter.

Our **online Travel Store** offers travel bags and accessories that I've designed specifically to help you travel smarter and lighter. These include my popular carry-on bags (rolling carry-on and backpack versions), money belts, totes, toiletries kits, adapters, other accessories, and a wide selection of guidebooks, planning maps, and DVDs.

Choosing the right **railpass** for your trip—amid hundreds of options—can drive you nutty. We'll help you choose the best pass for your needs and ship it to you for free.

Want to travel with greater efficiency and less stress? We organize **tours** with more than three dozen itineraries and more than 500 departures reaching the best destinations in this book...and beyond. We offer a 14-day tour of Germany, Austria, and Switzerland; a 12-day "unguided" tour (covering hotel and transportation) of those countries; and a 12-day tour of Berlin, Prague, and Vienna. You'll enjoy great guides, a fun bunch of travel partners (with small groups of generally around 24-28), and plenty of room to spread out in a big, comfy bus. You'll find European adventures to fit every vacation length. For all the details, and to get our Tour Catalog and a free Rick Steves Tour Experience DVD (filmed on location during an actual tour), visit www.ricksteves.com or call us at 425/608-4217.

maps are sold at newsstands—take a look before you buy to be sure the map has the level of detail you want.

European bookstores, especially in touristy areas, have good selections of maps. For drivers, I'd recommend a 1:200,000- or 1:300,000-scale map for each country. Train travelers usually manage fine with the freebies they get with the train pass and from the local tourist offices.

Other Guidebooks

For most travelers, this book is all you need. But if you're traveling beyond my recommended destinations, $40 for extra maps and books is money well-spent.

The following books are worthwhile, though not updated annually; check the publication date before you buy. Lonely Planet's guides to Vienna and Austria are thorough, well-researched, and packed with good maps and hotel recommendations for low- to moderate-budget travelers. The similar Rough Guides are written by insightful British researchers. The skinny, green Michelin Guides are excellent, especially if you're driving. Michelin Guides are known for their city and sightseeing maps, dry but concise and helpful information on all major sights, and good cultural and historical background. English editions are sold in Europe at gas stations and tourist shops.

Recommended Books and Movies

To learn more about Austria past and present, check out a few of these books and films.

Nonfiction

For an overview of Austrian history, try *The Austrians: A Thousand-Year Odyssey* (Brook-Shepherd), though most of its focus is on the 19th and 20th centuries. Frederic Morton's *A Nervous Splendor* and *Thunder at Twilight* tell the story of the Austro-Hungarian Empire's last years in a light, lively way. *Fin-de-Siècle Vienna: Politics and Culture* (Schorske) is a dense but comprehensive analysis of the birth of modernism through Klimt, Freud, and other Viennese luminaries. *The Spell of the Vienna Woods: Inspiration and Influence from Beethoven to Kafka* (Hofmann) blends personal anecdotes, history, tourist information, and stories about artists who found inspiration in the 540-square-mile area that serves as Vienna's playground. *Beethoven: The Music and the Life* (Lockwood) includes details about the musician's life in Vienna and his contributions to its culture.

Memoirs: *The Story of the Trapp Family Singers,* written by Maria von Trapp, tells the true story behind the musical phenomenon. Stefan Zweig's *World of Yesterday* looks at how he became a successful writer in the "lost world" of prewar Vienna. In *The Hare* *with the Amber Eyes,* Edmund de Waal insightfully recounts the rise and fall of his storied family, whose Vienna home, the Palais Ephrussi on the Ringstrasse, was confiscated by the Nazis in the *Anschluss.*

Fiction

Much fiction set in Vienna concerns the imagined lives of famous artists. *The Painted Kiss* (Hickey) reflects the lush elegance of fin-de-siècle Vienna and the relationship between painter Gustav Klimt and his pupil Emilie Flöge, who posed for Klimt's masterpiece *The Kiss.* The rediscovered masterpiece *Embers* (Márai) also paints a rich picture of cobblestoned, gaslit Vienna just before the empire's glory began to fade. In *The Seven-Per-Cent Solution* (Meyer), Sherlock Holmes travels to Vienna to meet with Sigmund Freud and gets involved in a case. *Henry James' Midnight Song* (Hill) is another literary mystery with a cast of famous historical characters. Mystery fans could also consider *Airs Above the Ground* (Stewart), with Lipizzaner stallions and the Austrian Alps as a backdrop, as well as *A Death in Vienna* (Tallis), which involves a cover-up by the Catholic Church.

Austrian feminist Elfriede Jelinek, known for exploring dark themes, won the 2004 Nobel Prize in Literature. Her most famous novel, *Die Klavierspielerin* (*The Piano Player,* made into a movie) is about a troubled piano teacher who messes up the lives of her students. Robert Schneider's *Brother of Sleep,* set in an Austrian mountain village in the early 19th century, tells the story of a musical prodigy who goes unappreciated by the locals. Viennese writer Joseph Roth's classic novel *Radetzky March* follows four generations of a family during the decline and fall of the Habsburgs.

Films

The Great Waltz (1938) portrays the life of composer Johann Strauss. Orson Welles infuses *The Third Man* (1949, actually shot in bombed-out Vienna) with noir foreboding. In *Miracle of the White Stallions* (1963), the Lipizzaner stallions are the stars in this true story of how the horses were liberated by General Patton after World War II. The beloved musical *The Sound of Music* (1965), also partially set in World War II, helped turn Julie Andrews into a star. *Mayerling* (1968) is about the suicide of Habsburg heir Archduke Rudolf (played by Omar Sharif), which played a pivotal role in Austrian history.

Mahler (1974) describes the man behind the music, and *Amadeus* (1984) made Mozart into a flesh-and-blood man (who giggles), as did *Immortal Beloved* (1994) for Beethoven. To familiarize yourself with Sisi (a.k.a. Austria's Empress Elisabeth, a 19th-century

Princess Diana), look for the series of 1950s films starring Romy Schneider.

In *Before Sunrise* (1995), Ethan Hawke sightsees, talks, romances, and talks some more with Julie Delpy in Vienna. *The Illusionist* (2006) set in circa-1900 Vienna, is about a magician who uses his abilities to gain the love of a woman engaged to the crown prince.

Holidays and Festivals

This list includes selected festivals in major cities, plus national holidays observed throughout Austria. Vienna and Salzburg have music festivals nearly every month. Before planning a trip around a festival, make sure you verify its dates by checking the festival's website or contacting the Austrian national tourist office in the US (tel. 212/944-6880, www.austria.info); www.whatsonwhen.com also lists many festival dates.

Jan	Perchtenlaufen (winter festival, parades), Salzburg
Jan–mid-Feb	Vienna Ball Season (2,000 hours of dancing, www.wien.info, click on "Dance" tab)
Jan–Feb	Fasnacht (carnival season, balls, parades), western Austria
Good Friday	Karfreitag, March 29 in 2013, April 18 in 2014
Easter	Ostern, March 31 in 2013, April 20 in 2014; Easter Festival, Salzburg
May–June	Vienna Festival of Arts and Music (www.festwochen.or.at)
May 1	May Day with maypole dances, throughout Austria
Pentecost Monday	Pfingstmontag, May 20 in 2013, June 9 in 2014
Corpus Christi	Fronleichnam, May 30 in 2013, June 19 in 2014
Late June	Midsummer Eve Celebrations, throughout Austria
Late July–Aug	Salzburg Summer Festival (www.salzburgfestival.at)
Aug 15	Assumption (Mariä Himmelfahrt), parts of Austria
Late Sept	Ruperti-Kirtag (St. Rupert's Day), Salzburg
Mid-Sept–early Oct	Fall beer festivals, throughout Bavaria
Oct 26	Austrian National Day (Nationalfeiertag)

Nov 1	All Saints' Day (Allerheiligen)
Nov 11	St. Martin's Day Celebrations (feasts), Austria and Bavaria
Dec 6	St. Nicholas Day (Nikolaustag, parades), throughout Austria
Dec 24	Christmas Eve (Heilige Abend), when Austrians celebrate Christmas
Dec 25	Christmas
Dec 31	New Year's Eve (Silvester, a.k.a. Altjahrstag; fireworks), throughout Austria, particularly Vienna

Conversions and Climate

Numbers and Stumblers

- Europeans write a few of their numbers differently than we do. 1 = 1, 4 = 4, 7 = 7.
- In Europe, dates appear as day/month/year, so Christmas is 25/12/13.
- Commas are decimal points and decimals commas. A dollar and a half is 1,50, one thousand is 1.000, and there are 5.280 feet in a mile.
- When counting with fingers, start with your thumb. If you hold up your first finger to request one item, you'll probably get two.
- What Americans call the second floor of a building is the first floor in Europe.
- On escalators and moving sidewalks, Europeans keep the left "lane" open for passing. Keep to the right.

Metric Conversions (Approximate)

A kilogram is 2.2 pounds, and 1 liter is about a quart, or almost four to a gallon. A kilometer is six-tenths of a mile. I figure kilometers to miles by cutting them in half and adding back 10 percent of the original (120 km: 60 + 12 = 72 miles, 300 km: 150 + 30 = 180 miles).

1 foot = 0.3 meter	1 square yard = 0.8 square meter
1 yard = 0.9 meter	1 square mile = 2.6 square kilometers
1 mile = 1.6 kilometers	1 ounce = 28 grams
1 centimeter = 0.4 inch	1 quart = 0.95 liter
1 meter = 39.4 inches	1 kilogram = 2.2 pounds
1 kilometer = 0.62 mile	32°F = 0°C

Clothing Sizes

When shopping for clothing, use these US-to-European comparisons as general guidelines (but note that no conversion is perfect).

- Women's dresses and blouses: Add 30
  (US size 10 = European size 40)
- Men's suits and jackets: Add 10
  (US size 40 regular = European size 50)
- Men's shirts: Multiply by 2 and add about 8
  (US size 15 collar = European size 38)
- Women's shoes: Add about 30
  (US size 8 = European size 38-39)
- Men's shoes: Add 32-34
  (US size 9 = European size 41; US size 11 = European size 45)

Vienna's Climate

The first line is the average daily temperature; the second line, the average daily low. The third line shows the average number of days without rain. For more detailed weather statistics for destinations throughout Austria (as well as the rest of the world), check www.worldclimate.com.

J	F	M	A	M	J	J	A	S	O	N	D
Vienna											
34°	38°	47°	58°	67°	73°	76°	75°	68°	56°	45°	37°
25°	28°	30°	42°	50°	56°	60°	59°	53°	44°	37°	30°
16	17	18	17	18	16	18	18	20	18	16	16

Temperature Conversion: Fahrenheit and Celsius

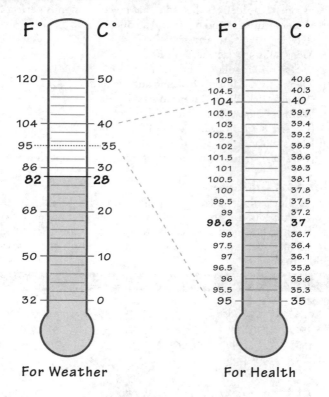

For Weather   For Health

Europe takes its temperature using the Celsius scale, while we opt for Fahrenheit. For a rough conversion from Celsius to Fahrenheit, double the number and add 30. For weather, remember that 28°C is 82°F—perfect. For health, 37°C is just right.

Packing Checklist

Whether you're traveling for five days or five weeks, here's what you'll need to bring. Pack light to enjoy the sweet freedom of true mobility. Happy travels!

- ❑ 5 shirts: long- and short-sleeve
- ❑ 1 sweater or lightweight fleece
- ❑ 2 pairs pants
- ❑ 1 pair shorts
- ❑ 1 swimsuit
- ❑ 5 pairs underwear and socks
- ❑ 1 pair shoes
- ❑ 1 rainproof jacket with hood
- ❑ Tie or scarf
- ❑ Money belt
- ❑ Money—your mix of:
  - ❑ Debit card (for ATM withdrawals)
  - ❑ Credit card
  - ❑ Hard cash (in easy-to-exchange $20 bills)
- ❑ Documents plus photocopies:
  - ❑ Passport
  - ❑ Printout of airline eticket
  - ❑ Driver's license
  - ❑ Student ID and hostel card
  - ❑ Railpass/car rental voucher
  - ❑ Insurance details
- ❑ Daypack
- ❑ Electronics—your choice of:
  - ❑ Camera (and related gear)
  - ❑ Computer/mobile devices (phone, MP3 player, ereader, etc.)
  - ❑ Chargers for each of the above
  - ❑ Plug adapter
- ❑ Empty water bottle

- ❑ Wristwatch and alarm clock
- ❑ Earplugs
- ❑ Toiletries kit
  - ❑ Toiletries
  - ❑ Medicines and vitamins
  - ❑ First-aid kit
  - ❑ Glasses/contacts/sunglasses (with prescriptions)
- ❑ Sealable plastic baggies
- ❑ Laundry soap
- ❑ Clothesline
- ❑ Small towel
- ❑ Sewing kit
- ❑ Travel information (guidebooks and maps)
- ❑ Address list (for sending postcards)
- ❑ Postcards and photos from home
- ❑ Notepad and pen
- ❑ Journal

If you plan to carry on your luggage, note that all liquids must be in 3.4-ounce or smaller containers and fit within a single quart-size sealable baggie. For details, see www.tsa.gov/travelers.

Hotel Reservation

To: _____   _____
              hotel   *email or fax*

From: _____   _____
              name   *email or fax*

Today's date: _____ /_____ /_____
                        day   *month*   *year*

Dear Hotel _____ ,
Please make this reservation for me:

Name: _____

Total # of people: _____   # of rooms: _____   # of nights: _____

Arriving: _____ /_____ /_____   My time of arrival (24-hr clock): _____
                  day *month* *year*   (I will telephone if I will be late)

Departing: ____ /____ /____
                  day *month* *year*

Room(s): Single____   Double ____   Twin____   Triple ____   Quad____

With: Toilet ____   Shower____   Bath ____   Sink only ____

Special needs: View____   Quiet____   Cheapest ____   Ground Floor____

Please email or fax confirmation of my reservation, along with the type of room reserved and the price. Please also inform me of your cancellation policy. After I hear from you, I will quickly send my credit-card information as a deposit to hold the room. Thank you.

_____
Name

_____
Address

_____
City   *State*   *Zip Code*   *Country*

Before hoteliers can make your reservation, they want to know the information listed above. You can use this form as the basis for your email, or you can photocopy this page, fill in the information, and send it as a fax (also available online at www.ricksteves.com/reservation).

German Survival Phrases for Austria

When using the phonetics, pronounce ī as the long I sound in "light."

Good day.	Grüss Gott.	**grews** gote
Do you speak English?	Sprechen Sie Englisch?	**shprehkh**-ehn zee **ehng**-lish
Yes. / No.	Ja. / Nein.	yah / nīn
I (don't) understand.	Ich verstehe (nicht).	ikh fehr-**shtay**-heh (nikht)
Please.	Bitte.	**bit**-teh
Thank you.	Danke.	**dahng**-keh
I'm sorry.	Es tut mir leid.	ehs toot meer līt
Excuse me.	Entschuldigung.	ehnt-**shool**-dig-oong
(No) problem.	(Kein) Problem.	(kīn) proh-**blaym**
(Very) good.	(Sehr) gut.	(zehr) goot
Goodbye.	Auf Wiedersehen.	owf **vee**-der-zayn
one / two	eins / zwei	īns / tsvī
three / four	drei / vier	drī / feer
five / six	fünf / sechs	fewnf / zehkhs
seven / eight	sieben / acht	**zee**-behn / ahkht
nine / ten	neun / zehn	noyn / tsayn
How much is it?	Wieviel kostet das?	**vee**-feel **kohs**-teht dahs
Write it?	Schreiben?	**shrī**-behn
Is it free?	Ist es umsonst?	ist ehs oom-**zohnst**
Included?	Inklusive?	in-kloo-**zee**-veh
Where can I buy / find...?	Wo kann ich kaufen / finden...?	voh kahn ikh **kow**-fehn / **fin**-dehn
I'd like / We'd like...	Ich hätte gern / Wir hätten gern...	ikh **heh**-teh gehrn / veer **heh**-tehn gehrn
...a room.	...ein Zimmer.	īn **tsim**-mer
...a ticket to ___.	...eine Fahrkarte nach ___.	ī-neh **far**-kar-teh nahkh
Is it possible?	Ist es möglich?	ist ehs **mur**-glikh
Where is...?	Wo ist...?	voh ist
...the train station	...der Bahnhof	dehr **bahn**-hohf
...the bus station	...der Busbahnhof	dehr **boos**-bahn-hohf
...tourist information	...das Touristen-informationsbüro	dahs too-**ris**-tehn-in-for-maht-see-**ohns**-bew-roh
...toilet	...die Toilette	dee toh-**leh**-teh
men	Herren	**hehr**-rehn
women	Damen	**dah**-mehn
left / right	links / rechts	links / rehkhts
straight	geradeaus	geh-**rah**-deh-**ows**
When is this open / closed?	Um wieviel Uhr ist hier geöffnet / geschlossen?	oom **vee**-feel oor ist heer geh-**urf**-neht / geh-**shloh**-sehn
At what time?	Um wieviel Uhr?	oom **vee**-feel oor
Just a moment.	Moment.	moh-**mehnt**
now / soon / later	jetzt / bald / später	yehtst / bahld / **shpay**-ter
today / tomorrow	heute / morgen	**hoy**-teh / **mor**-gehn

In the Restaurant

I'd like / We'd like...	Ich hätte gern / Wir hätten gern...	ikh **heh**-teh gehrn / veer **heh**-tehn gehrn
...a reservation for...	...eine Reservierung für...	ī-neh reh-zer-**feer**-oong fewr
...a table for one / two.	...einen Tisch für ein / zwei.	ī-nehn tish fewr īn / tsvī
Non-smoking.	Nichtraucher.	**nikht**-rowkh-er
Is this seat free?	Ist hier frei?	ist heer frī
Menu (in English), please.	Speisekarte (auf Englisch), bitte.	**shpī**-zeh-kar-teh (owf **ehng**-lish) **bit**-teh
service (not) included	Trinkgeld (nicht) inklusive	**trink**-gehlt (nikht) in-kloo-**zee**-veh
cover charge	Eintritt	**īn**-trit
to go	zum Mitnehmen	tsoom **mit**-nay-mehn
with / without	mit / ohne	mit / **oh**-neh
and / or	und / oder	oont / **oh**-der
menu (of the day)	(Tages-) Karte	(**tah**-gehs-) **kar**-teh
set meal for tourists	Touristenmenü	too-**ris**-tehn-meh-**new**
specialty of the house	Spezialität des Hauses	shpayt-see-ah-lee-**tayt** dehs **how**-zehs
appetizers	Vorspeise	**for**-shpī-zeh
bread	Brot	broht
cheese	Käse	**kay**-zeh
sandwich	Sandwich	**zahnd**-vich
soup	Suppe	**zup**-peh
salad	Salat	zah-**laht**
meat	Fleisch	flīsh
poultry	Geflügel	geh-**flew**-gehl
fish	Fisch	fish
seafood	Meeresfrüchte	**meh**-rehs-**frewkh**-teh
fruit	Obst	ohpst
vegetables	Gemüse	geh-**mew**-zeh
dessert	Nachspeise	**nahkh**-shpī-zeh
mineral water	Mineralwasser	min-eh-**rahl**-vah-ser
tap water	Leitungswasser	**lī**-toongs-vah-ser
milk	Milch	milkh
(orange) juice	(Orangen-) Saft	(oh-**rahn**-zhehn-) zahft
coffee	Kaffee	kah-**fay**
tea	Tee	tay
wine	Wein	vīn
red / white	rot / weiß	roht / vīs
glass / bottle	Glas / Flasche	glahs / **flah**-sheh
beer	Bier	beer
Cheers!	Prost!	prohst
More. / Another.	Mehr. / Noch ein.	mehr / nohkh īn
The same.	Das gleiche.	dahs **glīkh**-eh
Bill, please.	Rechnung, bitte.	**rehkh**-noong **bit**-teh
tip	Trinkgeld	**trink**-gehlt
Delicious!	Lecker!	**lehk**-er

For more user-friendly German phrases, check out *Rick Steves'*
German Phrase Book and Dictionary or *Rick Steves' French, Italian*
& German Phrase Book.

INDEX

MAP INDEX

Audio Europe™

Rick's Free Travel App

Get your FREE **Rick Steves Audio Europe**™ app to enjoy…

- Dozens of self-guided tours of Europe's top museums, sights and historic walks

- Hundreds of tracks filled with cultural insights and sightseeing tips from Rick's radio interviews

- All organized into handy geographic playlists

- For iPhone, iPad, iPod Touch, Android

With Rick whispering in your ear, Europe gets even better.

Find out more at ricksteves.com

Join a Rick Steves tour

Enjoy Europe's warmest welcome... with the flexibility and friendship of a small group getting to know Rick's favorite places and people. It all starts with our free tour catalog and DVD.

Great guides, small groups, no grumps.

▶ Explore Europe

Browse thousands of articles, video clips, photos and radio interviews, plus find a wealth of money-saving tips for planning your dream trip. You'll find up-to-date information on Europe's best destinations, packing smart, getting around, finding rooms, staying healthy, avoiding scams and more.

▶ Travel News

Subscribe to our free Travel News e-newsletter, and get monthly updates from Rick on what's happening in Europe!

▶ Travel Forums

Learn, ask, share—our online community of savvy travelers is a great resource for first-time travelers to Europe, as well as seasoned pros.

ricksteves.com

turn your travel dreams into affordable reality

▶ Rick's Free Audio Europe™ App

The Rick Steves Audio Europe™ app brings history and art to life. Enjoy Rick's audio tours of Europe's top museums, sights and neighborhood walks—plus hundreds of tracks including travel tips and cultural insights from Rick's radio show—all organized into geographic playlists. Learn more at ricksteves.com.

▶ Great Gear from Rick's Travel Store

Pack light and right—on a budget—with Rick's custom-designed carry-on bags, wheeled bags, day packs, travel accessories, guidebooks, journals, maps and Blu-ray/DVDs of his TV shows.

Rick Steves®

www.ricksteves.com

Rick Steves guidebooks are published by Avalon Travel,
a member of the Perseus Books Group.

NOW AVAILABLE:
eBOOKS, DVD & BLU-RAY

Credits

Researchers
To help update this book, Rick relied on...

Ian Watson
Ian has worked with Rick's guidebooks since 1993, after starting out with Let's Go and Frommer's guides. Originally from upstate New York, Ian speaks several European languages, including German, and makes his home in Reykjavík, Iceland.

Kevin Williams
Mozart, palaces, castles, mountain hikes, and crystal-clear lakes are just a few of the things Kevin enjoys in Austria. When he isn't indulging in hearty Austrian meals or a refreshing swim in Hallstatt, he can be found assisting a Rick Steves tour or answering travel questions at Rick's Travel Center in Edmonds, WA.

Cameron Hewitt
Cameron writes and edits guidebooks for Rick Steves, specializing in Eastern Europe. For this book, Cameron explored Bratislava. When he's not traveling, Cameron lives in Seattle with his wife Shawna.

Contributors

Gene Openshaw
Gene is the co-author of 10 Rick Steves books. For this book, he wrote material on art, history, and contemporary culture. When he's not traveling, Gene enjoys composing music, recovering from his 1973 trip to Europe with Rick, and living everyday life with his daughter.

Acknowledgments
Rick and his staff extend sincere thanks to tour guides Ursula Klaus, Wolfgang Höfler, Lisa Zeiler, and Martin Sloboda for their help with this book.